ALSO BY PATRICIA ALBERS

Shadows, Fire, Snow: The Life of Tina Modotti

Joan Mitchell

LADY PAINTER

Joan Mitchell

LADY PAINTER

A LIFE

PATRICIA ALBERS

ALFRED A. KNOPF · NEW YORK · 2011

THIS IS A BORZOI BOOK
PUBLISHED BY ALFRED A. KNOPF

Library of Congress Cataloging-in-Publication Data
Albers, Patricia.
    Joan Mitchell : lady painter / by Patricia Albers.—1st ed.
        p.   cm.
    "A Borzoi book."
    Includes bibliographical references and index.
    ISBN 978-0-375-41437-4
    1. Mitchell, Joan, 1926–1992.   2. Painters—United
States—Biography.   3. Abstract expressionism—United
States.   I. Title.
    ND237.M58A85 2011
    759.13—dc22
    [B]
2011000457

Front-of-jacket image: *Untitled* (detail) by Joan Mitchell,
1953–54. Courtesy of the Joan Mitchell Foundation;
Photograph of Joan Mitchell courtesy of the Joan Mitchell
Foundation and Cheim & Read Gallery, New York.

Jacket design by Carol Devine Carson

Manufactured in the United States of America
First Edition

To my parents,
Marjorie and Henry H. Albers,
and France Bequette

Contents

PARIS

VÉTHEUIL

Illustrations

COLOR INSERT

Joan Mitchell, *George Went Swimming at Barnes Hole, but It Got Too Cold*, oil on canvas, 1957. 85¼ × 78¼ in. (216.5 × 198.8 cm). Collection of the Albright-Knox Art Gallery. Gift of Seymour H. Knox, Jr., 1958. Courtesy of the Joan Mitchell Foundation and Albright-Knox Art Gallery, Buffalo, New York. © Estate of Joan Mitchell.

Joan Mitchell, *Ladybug*, oil on canvas, 1957. 77⅞ inches x 108 in. (197.8 × 274.3 cm). Collection The Museum of Modern Art, New York. Purchase. Licensed by SCALA/Art Resource, NY/Artists Rights Society. © Estate of Joan Mitchell.

Joan Mitchell, *Grandes Carrières*, oil on canvas, 1961–62. 78¾ × 118¼ in. (200 × 300.5 cm). Collection The Museum of Modern Art, New York. Gift of the Estate of Joan Mitchell. Licensed by SCALA/Art Resource, NY/ Artists Rights Society. © Estate of Joan Mitchell.

Joan Mitchell, *Untitled (Cheim Some Bells)*, oil on canvas, 1964. 84 × 78¼ in. (213.4 × 198.8 cm). Collection John Cheim. Courtesy of Cheim & Read Gallery, New York. © Estate of Joan Mitchell.

Joan Mitchell, *Sans Pierre*, oil on canvas, 1969. 103⅛ × 79⅞ in. (263.2 × 202.9 cm). Collection Mr. and Mrs. Robert Lehrman, Washington, D.C. Courtesy of Cheim & Read Gallery, New York. © Estate of Joan Mitchell.

Joan Mitchell, *La Grande Vallée XVIII (Luc)*, oil on canvas, 1983–84. 110 × 102 in. (280 × 260 cm). Courtesy of Cheim & Read Gallery, New York. © Estate of Joan Mitchell.

Joan Mitchell, *Lille V*, oil on canvas (diptych), 1986. 76¾ × 102⅛ in. (195 × 260 cm). Private Collection. Courtesy of Cheim & Read Gallery, New York. © Estate of Joan Mitchell.

Joan Mitchell, *No Birds*, oil on canvas (diptych), 1987–88. 87½ × 156 in. (222.3 × 396.2 cm). Courtesy of Cheim & Read Gallery, New York. © Estate of Joan Mitchell.

Joan Mitchell, *Rain*, oil on canvas (diptych), 1989. 94½ × 157½ in. (240 × 400 cm). Courtesy of Cheim & Read Gallery, New York. © Estate of Joan Mitchell.

Joan Mitchell, *Sunflowers*, oil on canvas (diptych), 1990–91. 110 × 157 in. (280 × 400.1 cm). Courtesy of Cheim & Read Gallery, New York. © Estate of Joan Mitchell.

Joan Mitchell, *Merci*, oil on canvas (diptych), 1992. 110¼ × 141½ in. (280 × 360 cm). Courtesy of the Joan Mitchell Foundation and Cheim & Read Gallery, New York. © Estate of Joan Mitchell.

Joan Mitchell, *Blue Territory*, oil on canvas, 1972. 103 × 71 in. (261.6 × 180.3 cm). Collection of the Albright-Knox Art Gallery. Gift of Seymour H. Knox, Jr., 1972. Courtesy of the Joan Mitchell Foundation and Albright-Knox Art Gallery, Buffalo, New York. © Estate of Joan Mitchell.

Acknowledgments

MY DECADE with Joan Mitchell has left me deeply indebted. At the top of the list of those who helped me take Joan's measure are her former husband, Barney Rosset, and his companion Astrid Myers, whose unflagging support and generosity of spirit and deed have been vital to this book. Joan's niece, Sally Perry; Susan Sloan; Carolyn Somers and her staff at the Joan Mitchell Foundation, especially Jen Dohne and Kira Osti; and John Cheim and his staff at Cheim & Read Gallery were equally wonderful and indispensable to my efforts.

I thank too Joan's friends for their insightfulness, helpfulness, patience, and good humor: Jill Weinberg Adams, Robert McCormick Adams, Jean-Max Albert, David Amram, David Anderson, Sally Apfelbaum, John Ashbery, Paul Auster, Deirdre Bair, Gisèle Barreau, Lynda Benglis, John Bennett, Bill Berkson, Marc Berlet, Martha Bertolette, Guy Bloch-Champfort, Franck Bordas, Peggy Bowman, Richard Bowman, Paul Brach, Carol Braider, Michael Brenson, Marion Cajori, Christopher Campbell, Jerry Carlin, Nic Carone, Hervé Chandès, Champlain Charest, Réjeanne Charest, Robert Chiarito, Ed Clark, Marabeth Cohen-Tyler, Ornette Coleman, Alicia Creus, Katy Crowe, Eldon Danhausen, Lydia Davis, Jacques Dupin, Victor Elmaleh, Louise Fishman, Catherine Flohic, Jean Fournier, Edi Franceschini, Jane Freilicher, Jaqueline Fried, Monique Frydman, Georgia Funsten, Michael Goldberg, Leon Goldin, Robert Gottlieb, Roseline Granet, John Gruen, Yvonne Hagen, Anne Hailey, John Hailey, James Harithas, Robert Harms, Robert Hasterlik, Elga Heinzen, Evans Herman, John Holabird, Sara Holt, Jacqueline Hyde, Ernst Jaffe, Shirley Jaffe, Hollis Jeffcoat, Paul Jenkins, Consuelo Joerns, Betsy Jolas, Howard Kanovitz, Stanley Karnow, Herbert Katzman, Nathan Kernan, Elisabeth Kley, Ellen Lanyon, Jeanne Le Bozec, Caroline Lee, Connie Lembark, Alfred Leslie,

Teru Osato Lundsten, Jean Lyons Keely, Robert Miller, Sarah Miller, Zuka Mitelberg, Malcolm Morley, Christine Mouillère, Jean Mouillère, Cynthia Navaretta, Alvin Novak, Sono Osato, Patricia Passlof, Philip Pavia, Joyce Pensato, Raymonde Perthuis, Shirley Petry, Carl Plansky, Paul Richard, Yseult Riopelle, Christiane Rousseaux-Mosettig, Irving Sandler, Miriam Schapiro, Michaële-Andréa Schatt, Pierre Schneider, Bill Scott, Margaret Shook, Manny Silverman, Rose Slivka, Marilyn Stark, Eugene V. Thaw, Yvonne Thomas, Sally Turton, Ken Tyler, Lynn Umlauf, Huguette Vachon, Kate Van Houten, Joanne and Philip Von Blon, Elizabeth von Klemperer, Mitch Waters, June Wayne, Lise Weil, Jane Wilson, Eleanor Wright, Rufus Zogbaum, Larry Zox, and Anonymous.

Christopher Campbell, Celia Stahr, Carol Steen, and Ramsay Breslin and the Psychobiography Group generously read drafts of my manuscript.

I thank Gisèle Barreau for permission to include an excerpt from "La Grande Vallée"; the Joan Mitchell Foundation for permission to use quotations by Joan Mitchell and from documents in the Joan Mitchell Archival Collection; Barney Rosset for permission to reproduce excerpts from his letters; Irving Sandler and the Getty Research Institute, Los Angeles (2000.M.43), for permission to use excerpts from documents in the Irving Sandler Papers, Getty Research Institute, Research Library Special Collections & Visual Resources, Los Angeles; the George Dillon Papers, Special Collections Research Center, Syracuse University Library, Syracuse, New York; and Joan's niece Sally Perry for permission to use Marion Strobel's poem "Bon Voyage"; and the Collection of Frank O'Hara Letters, Archives and Special Collections at the Thomas J. Dodd Research Center, University of Connecticut Libraries, for providing the transcript of a 26 August 1957 letter from Frank O'Hara to Michael Goldberg.

For love, friendship, advice, and support, I am also grateful to Kate Adams, Elliott and Max Albers, Kit and Rick Bennett, Amanda Carver, Sean Day and the Synesthesia List, Natalie Edgar, Pamela Glintenkamp, Sarah and Andrew Gross, Jack Herbert, Suzanne Jenkins, Klaus Kertess, Betty Klausner, Elizabeth and Todd Koelmel, Sonja Marck, David McKendall, Kristin McKendall, Kyle McKendall, Maysha Mohamedi, Honor Moore, Francis M. Naumann, Norman J. Pahls, Nick Parsons, Nancy Robb, Sandy Schimmel, Chris Sekaer, Bill Smith, Ellen Smith, Steve Van Buren, and Jeanie Hunt Van Nice.

My deep appreciation also goes to numerous librarians and archivists, unsung heroes all: Wendy Hurlock Baker, Archives of American Art; Bart Ryckbosch and Deborah S. Webb, Archives of the Art Institute of Chicago; Arts Club of Chicago; Timothy Young, Beinecke Rare Book and Manuscript Library, Yale University; Joanne Lauzon, Bibliothèque et Archives nationales du Québec; Holly Sherratt and Frank Hettig, Bonhams & Butterfields; Chicago Historical Society; Nancy Iona Glick, Havana Public Library District; Rebecca Sandler, Jewish Theological Seminary Library; Lake Forest–Lake Bluff Historical Society; J. Pierpont Morgan Library; New York Public Library; Charlotte Priddle, New York Studio School; Newberry Library; Andy Kaplan, Francis W. Parker School; Getty Research Institute; Aimee Brown, Smith College Archives; Special Collections Research Center, University of Chicago Library; Melissa Watterworth, Thomas J. Dodd Research Center, University of Connecticut; Video Data Bank, School of the Art Institute of Chicago; and Whitney Museum Library. Warm thanks also go to Sandra Olsen and Mary Moran, UB Anderson Gallery, University at Buffalo; Susan Shockley, The Parthenon; Galerie Jean Fournier; Lennon, Weinberg Gallery; Edward Tyler Nahem; and Robert Miller Gallery.

Money for Women/Barbara Deming Memorial Fund and the California Lottery Fund provided vital financial and morale-boosting support.

I owe special thanks to Laurie Fox, my agent extraordinaire, and, at Knopf, to the wonderful Carmen Johnson and my unparalleled editor, Vicky Wilson.

Finally, my love and gratitude go to my son, Sam Spiewak, and husband, Benjamin McKendall, for their love and unswerving support of this book.

My sister is always putting the past behind
her—Well I use the past to make my pics
and I want all of it and even you and me in
candlelight on the train and every "lover" I've
ever had—every friend—nothing closed out—
and dogs alive and dead and people
and landscapes and feeling even if it is
desperate—anguished—tragic—it's all part
of me and I want to confront it and sleep
with it—the dreams—and paint it.

JOAN MITCHELL

Prologue

60 ST. MARK'S PLACE, NEW YORK CITY, FALL 1957.

THIRTY-TWO-YEAR-OLD Joan Mitchell could nearly taste her love of oil paint. Working most afternoons and many nights, she abstained only when she felt too self-conscious, fell prey to depression, or wanted to intensify the feeling by resisting the urge to paint until it overwhelmed her. That her kitchen table and bed stood only steps away from her studio, the front half of an austere, turpentine-fragrant one-room apartment, attested to the centrality of painting in her life. Even when she wasn't working, she might be envisioning a wedge of space or mulling over an idea like "that dark idea with the white."

By early afternoon, this late riser would be padding around amid the gallon tins of turpentine, Medaglia D'Oro cans jammed with brushes, sheets of newspaper, smudged rags, battered tubes of oils, and half-filled ashtrays that littered her studio floor. From time to time she would pause to eyeball the charcoal and turpentine sketch on the primed linen, about eight by seven feet, stapled to her painting wall: the rudiments of her next picture.

Having dropped the needle on an LP and squeezed out her colors onto a sheet of plywood, Joan took her time mixing and thinning them in pie tins. Brushes too merited finicky consideration. Preferring them narrow, she rarely selected anything wider than her favorite beautifully worn one-inch flat hog-bristle. But she switched brushes often. (Work that evinced its maker's cluelessness about the subtleties of brushes earned a sneering "Ugghrrr, there's your typical one-brush painting!")

All the while, Charlie Parker's "Lover Man," Bach's Goldberg Variations, or Mozart's Symphony no. 40 in G Minor filled the room, making her "more available" to herself: conjuring colors and shapes, dissolving the hard edges of selfhood, and heightening her feelings about a certain grove, bridge, or waft of cloud from which she hoped to begin wresting a picture. Not that painting demanded only the amplification of memory and desire. It also required a delicate balance of surrender and will. She had to be scrupulously aware of what she was doing each time she let the paint fly. Line had to be discriminating, structure rigorous. Still, when she was really cranking, painting overleapt her conscious attention, and she skimmed along "no hands" like riding a bicycle. Or, better, she no longer existed.

Ready at last to address the canvas, Joan slid her brush into, say, a gleaming blue gray, and, all concentration, attacked with the precision of a fencer. Here her physical prowess came into play. She delivered slashing arm-long strokes, shot to her tiptoes, or wound up a sweep of her brush with a snap of the wrist and tiny explosion of paint. The rag in her left hand flew up to complete what the brush in her right had begun. She might effect a wisp of line by dry-brushing the canvas. Or plunge brush to canvas, the juiciest of pigments spitting from her bristles. Or (notwithstanding her misgivings about the drip, a cliché of Abstract Expressionism) allow thinned color to escape into dangling strings and jagged-tooth-comb shapes.

The brief skirmish ended after four or five strokes, Joan would retreat to the opposite end of her studio, twenty-three feet away, where she hunkered down, squinted, lit up a cigarette, sighted with her brush, and scrutinized what her marks were doing to each other. (Farsightedness accounted, in part, for her predilection for working big and looking from afar, but so did the challenge of heroic size set by male painters.) Minutes passed. Light from the trio of windows to her right raked the room. The record ended. A distant siren wailed. Footsteps sounded in the stairwell. Yet nothing hurried the peering and pondering essential to the self-demanding struggle painting required: "I 'stop, look, and listen' at railroad tracks. I really want to be accurate."

For, as much as she reveled in the physicality of the attack, as vigorously as she plowed wet into wet, as eagerly as she seized upon the genuine accident, Joan was never a true action painter, never a subscriber to the notion that one finds a picture intuitively. Aiming to define a feeling, she proceeded from a mental image or images, adjusted, and readjusted, as her picture caught fire. Her method was additive; rarely did she scrape or redo. If a picture was working, she pushed ahead, more slowly as it evolved. If she became self-conscious about it, she knew she was bored and put down her brushes. If it took a serious turn for the worse, she junked it. Ah, but "how to come down from the clouds"?

"The painting has to work," Joan believed, "but it has to say something more than that the painting works"—something exultant, tragic, raw. Something with the restraint and fire of Beethoven's *Appassionata* op. 57. Or the bittersweet yearning of Billie Holiday's "Autumn in New York," with its "shimmering clouds in canyons of steel." Something all the more transcendent for the artist's hard-shell unsentimentality. "All vanitas," a writer friend sums up Joan's paintings, "and monstrous in their beauty."

Joan Mitchell
LADY PAINTER

Introduction

ONE RAIN-SPITTING FEBRUARY MORNING several years ago, I stood in a hallway at the Bibliothèque Nationale François Mitterrand in Paris, frustrated in my efforts to locate a certain document. The hallway had marble-smooth concrete walls, dim natural light, and a high ceiling. For some reason, I glanced up: above me hung a large, squarish oil painting tingling with a marvelous blue lavender, a blue lavender that washed over me as if, having never before seen—no, *felt*—blue lavender, I'd plunged into a bracing pool of it. I sensed in the painting mingled sun and shade, meadow tangle, lurking dusk, yearning, and the touch of a human hand. But most of all I was caught up in that tonic hydrangea color. Breached by a loamy green black, it drifted upward, urged along by a burst of vivid yellow. No color was block-solid: each felt airy, each sputtered with others. And, like a river viewed through binoculars, the image was both tangible and otherworldly, stirring and still. I felt as if I'd been whisked from the Bibliothèque Nationale to a secular Sainte-Chapelle. The radiant flicker of ecstasy hanging above me was Joan Mitchell's *La Grande Vallée V,* and its ambush that day sealed my decision to write this book.

I insist upon my encounter with *Grande Vallée V* in part because, although this book includes illustrations, Joan Mitchell's art survives reproduction almost as poorly as it does verbal translation. Not to experience it in the flesh is not to experience it at all. The real thing never lets you get too comfortable: it jams your sensorial circuits, it lures you in even as it keeps kicking you back to the surface. And whether thinned and smudged or thick and glistening, hesitating or razoring along an edge, the pigment itself—Joan could do virtually anything with the stuff—packs a powerful punch. The right Mitchell at the right time can lift a film from your blasé adult eyes and get you drunk on being alive.

That was Joan, too. Tough, vulnerable, loving, bawdy, bullying, embattled, generous, and enraged, she was as singular as her art.

Her bluntness staggered people. The first time you met her, she might insult you, even make you cry, but later she might be so understanding and nurturing that she felt like a soulmate. Then insults again. Moreover, Joan at times made strange comments, which people tended to chalk up to drunkenness (she was a prodigious drinker), metaphor, or the mark of the artistic personality. She spoke of her painting, for instance, as "a sort of scaffolding made of painting stretchers around a lot of colored chaos."

How does a biographer cast a coherent account of such a character? In his preface to *Eminent Victorians,* Lytton Strachey affirms that a certain amount of ignorance can be a good thing for a biographer, since it prevents him from loading up on information about his subject, then foundering under the burden. The wise biographer, Strachey continues, "will attack his subject in unexpected places; he will fall upon the flank or the rear; he will shoot a sudden searchlight into obscure recesses, hitherto undivined. He will row out over that great ocean of material, and lower down into it, here and there, a little bucket, which will bring up to the light of day some characteristic specimen, from those far depths, to be examined with a careful curiosity."

I didn't lower a bucket so much as grab one thrust into my hands by Joan's niece, Sally Perry, in the form of a *Wall Street Journal* clipping dated June 28, 2002: "Why George Gershwin May Have Called It 'Rhapsody in Blue,'" by Sharon Begley. "That's what Joan had," Sally told me. Begley's article described synesthesia, an innate condition in which the stimulation of one sense (like hearing) triggers another (like seeing) as well. "Everyone is born with extra connections [among the senses], or synapses," Begley had written. "Most get pruned away in childhood. In synesthetes, the extra synapses seem to remain, producing a rich web of circuitry that connects the cortex's color processor to the numeral area next door, or links touch regions to vision regions." Some synesthetes taste shapes, others hear smells, still others experience pain as color. Reportedly Gershwin saw music, hence *Rhapsody in Blue*. The creator of the legendary album *Kind of Blue*, jazzman Miles Davis, may have been an emotion-color synesthete: if so, he literally got the blues—or maybe the oranges or greens. The painter of *Blue Territory* (among scores of her own glorious rhapsodies in blue), Joan Mitchell had musical sound-color, personality-color, emotion-color, and grapheme-color synesthesia (meaning that she saw the letters of the alphabet in color), plus eidetic memory, which she described as mentally carrying around a suitcase filled with pictures.

I set about trying to understand the role of Joan's neurology in the unfolding of her artistic and personal lives. We pay lip service to the idea that each of us sees the world differently, yet we operate as if ours were the only true way of seeing the world. Here was a highly trained, highly practiced artist who experienced the world in ways most of us do not: how did that matter? (The only other internationally renowned contemporary artist known to have synesthesia is David Hockney, but, except in his opera sets, Hockney has not intentionally used his synesthesia in making art. Among earlier artists, suspicion of synesthesia falls upon Vincent van Gogh, Wassily Kandinsky, Paul Klee, and Charles Burchfield, to name a few.)

Joan's synesthesia and eidetic memory, I came to realize, left their tracks all over her art. I don't mean to suggest that she was a primitive who simply mapped her neurological experience onto canvas. On the contrary: the consummate painter, Joan used all of her craft plus every scrap of experience at her disposal, including the perceptual "otherness" that helped her to swing open a window beyond the narrow crack of everyday awareness and create art of a rare incandescence.

Having come of age as an artist on New York's Tenth Street in the 1950s and reveled in its marvelous "community of feeling," Joan Mitchell has been written into the mythology of Abstract Expressionism. She knocked back beers with the boys at the Cedar Tavern, caroused in the Hamptons, hung out with hip cats at the Five Spot, and felt the pain and the thrill of belonging, or nearly, to the little band of rebels operating below Fourteenth Street. Art historians have labeled her a Second Generation Abstract Expressionist. (The term itself is problematic.) Yet, despite her personal and artistic self-identification with Abstract Expressionism, Joan's art confounds textbook classification. It has to do, she said, with memories of her feelings—feelings about "love and death and all that crap"—ensnared in lakes, trees, rivers, clouds, sunflowers, bridges, and so on. What other Abstract Expressionist would toss into a discussion of her painting process, as Joan did in 1957, the remark, "I feel like a little child coming up out of the basement and saying: who put the sidewalk there, who put the tree there?"

Given that the intellectual framework of modernism situated artists' work in a logical progression of stylistic development and prized above all the invention of new formal languages, the label Second Generation Abstract Expressionist appeared to doom Mitchell to the status of follower. It's true that she did not invent a new ism. But not only was her art formally idiosyncratic—above all, she was a supreme colorist—it also evinced what essayist and philosopher Ralph Waldo Emerson terms "an original relation to the universe."

Joan's is also a story of her struggle to cope with the gender bias of her time. Raised largely by her father, who never let her forget that he needed a son, not a daughter, and who made his love for her conditional upon her athletic, intellectual, and artistic achievements, she came of age in an era when even the brightest "co-eds" were expected to marry, then happily melt away into the kitchen and nursery, and when a woman, by definition, had no shot at winning recognition as a great artist. Yet at age twelve, the gutsy Miss Mitchell decided to be just that. Her vaulting ambition was for painting itself. About her career she felt more ambivalent: "Of course, then there was no question of succeeding, because I was a girl. I just did it, do you understand?"

After she hit upon the ironic, defiant, aggrieved-but-not-whiny phrase "lady painter," Joan trotted it out on every possible occasion. An incident that occurred during the installation of her 1988 traveling retrospective at the San Francisco Museum of Modern Art conveys the affect. Wearing her nerves on the outside, as usual, the sixty-three-year-old artist roamed the exhibition-in-process, eyeballing her paintings through unfashionable yellowish magnifying-lens glasses. Always her own toughest critic, she started apologizing for the works' shortcomings to the curators, critics, and installers milling around. With an imperious sweep of her arm, her tone abruptly shifted to sarcastic: "Not bad for a lady painter." A brisk toss of her hair. "I think everything is magnificent." Then, as a mock aside: "I'm trying to act like a male painter. You know, where you say that everything you do is wonderful."

Behind her hung many of the great Mitchells: *Cross Section of a Bridge, Hudson River Day Line, George Went Swimming at Barnes Hole but It Got Too Cold, Couscous, Calvi, Sunflower, Blue Territory, Salut Tom, La Grande Vallée,* and *Faded Air I.* Not bad indeed for a lady painter.

CHICAGO

Beams arch high, and girders—
The Z-bar, the truss—
That we may cross laughing,
Oblivious

That there is a river
Blackened by the night,
Where a mighty shadow
Glistens white.

MARION STROBEL, "Bridges"

CHAPTER ONE   Jimmie and Marion

A raw wind was weaving and reweaving Lake Michigan that bright
early spring afternoon. Trembling ropes of spume inched up
the slippery paved beach toward a strip of grass fluttering like a
feather boa along Lake Shore Drive. The slap of water and the rumble of
passing automobiles drowned out the sullen complaint of Depression-era
Chicago sprawling its smoky confusion on the March-hard Midwest
plain.

But inside the Mitchells' apartment, two blocks from the lake, the
mistress of the house, a poet, tolerated no dinginess or disorder. In the
library, sunshine moving in oblique shapes lightly varnished the hardwood floors, and a showy bromeliad rooster-tailed from its cachepot
against a window blooming with curtains of the heaviest, most brilliant
yellow satin, curtains that quickened the senses and transformed the
room into a vessel for joy.

A slender, saucy eight-year-old, Marion's daughter Joan had waded through a low tide of sunlight to a spot between the windows where her father, an enthusiastic shutterbug, was taking her picture. Masquerading as a grown-up, trying on womanliness, even seduction, she wore her costume for a children's play: oversized high heels, lace-edged gloves, and a John Singer Sargent–ish muslin garden-party outfit circa 1905. A hat bushy with ostrich feathers shaded the top half of her face, obscuring enormous eyes whose nut brown irises dwarfed the whites. A keenly observant child, Joan froze whenever she spotted something out of the ordinary. Like the library curtains: buttery slices of sunshine whose sight and touch, as Oscar Wilde once wrote of yellow satin, "could console one for all the miseries of life." So magical were these curtains that, even after the maid took them down each June and folded them into a trunk in preparation for the family's annual trek to Lake Forest, the little girl still pictured them "glowing, all summer long."

Eighteen years later, New York painter Joan Mitchell told her psychoanalyst how, as a child, she used to dissolve into the liquid light of her mother's library curtains, how caressing them had felt like "touching my own self." A second indelible childhood memory came on the heels of the first: once, while taking a bath, Joan had lost connection with the knobby limbs stretched out before her. "How strange these legs are," she had marveled. "Are they really mine or are they something outside? Maybe when they will be bigger I will not recognize them any more as mine."

Now in her late twenties, Mitchell had earned a reputation for steely toughness and unrelenting competitiveness, survival tactics in a macho art world. Too often, however, she lost control. When her fragile self-concept wobbled, she was apt to panic and fly into a rage, to which others would react by getting angry themselves or otherwise throwing up walls, thereby—analyst and patient theorized—salvaging Joan's self-identity. "I feel too much a part of you," the artist once confessed to a lover after yet another moment of intimacy had seized up into fury. "I'm surprised often that you're not looking at the trees with me—and even feel sometimes I am you painting. They call this fusion and say it's disastrous. . . . It's not much fun being nuts—or living among so many amorphous green trees and ideas." According to Joan's analyst, this pattern of meltdown and hostility, the major issue she and Joan were addressing, resulted from ego damage during childhood and had to be changed.

Joan, age eight, and the yellow satin curtains, c. 1933

Three decades passed. At age fifty-four, Joan Mitchell painted the splendid, spangled, twenty-six-foot-wide oil *Salut Tom*, packing in glassy blues, watery greens, brilliant blacks, and dazzling yellows that break into shards as if from their urgent delivery to the canvas. *Salut Tom* traffics in the artist's memories of feelings stirred by sunflowers, colza, September sunlight on the Seine, and, perhaps, yellow satin curtains. Believing that to speak of one's work is to destroy it, Joan was usually mute about what role particular mind-pictures played in this or that painting, part of her refusal to allow deeply felt experiences to fall into oblivion, her struggle to escape rote living and gain purchase this side of darkness. Yet she brooked no sentimentality. "It comes out of the tube, baby," she once rasped when an admirer fluttered over her color. Often she put it more bluntly: Cut the crap and *look*!

Alone in her studio (save for her dogs), Joan would size up a painting-in-progress, load her brush, look again, longer and harder. Then, she'd attack her canvas with astounding precision and energy: a brushful of ultramarine would strike with the fury of water droplets flung onto a hot skillet, a filament of green thread into white, an orange kick the legs out from under pink, a wad of blue squat on a cellophane stroke of alizarin crimson, a cadmium yellow dark skid into a swelling cumulus of black greens.

By now Joan had long understood the importance of using the vulnerability she had once struggled to overcome. "No one can paint— write—feel whatever without being vulnerable . . . Also one has to be very strong to be vulnerable. Think about it," she commanded her sister. Her own vulnerability rode the music that filled her studio as she settled in for all-night painting sessions: Bach's cantatas, Purcell's opera *Dido and Aeneas,* the arias of Maria Callas. Music and painting were both vital "means of feeling 'living.'" And: "If I can't paint," she growled, "I can't breathe."

As the aging artist spoke, five decades, an ocean and half a continent, and—how many?—studios, dogs, drinks, cigarettes, sunrises, operas, poems, painters, and lovers stood between her and the long-vanished yellow satin curtains in an old-fashioned library in Chicago. "And it is not yet enough to have memories," writes Rainer Maria Rilke, an essential author for Joan Mitchell, of the origin of the poem, the art form she perennially likened to her own.

> You must be able to forget them when they are many, and you must have the immense patience to wait until they return. For the memories themselves are not important. Only when they have changed into our very blood, into glance and gesture, and are nameless, no longer to be distinguished from ourselves—only then can it happen that in some very rare hour the first word of a poem arises in their midst and goes forth from them.

Like all family photographs, James Herbert Mitchell's snapshot of Joan in the library conceals as much as it reveals. Quite literally: the wide brim of the girl's hat hides her expression as she faces the lens that represented her father's judgmental scrutiny. Scoutmaster-ish and stern, he was (in the words of his niece Sally Turton) "the total influence in [Joan's] life."

A highly respected dermatologist and national player in medical politics, James Herbert Mitchell nonetheless never shed the mentality of a self-made man, nor did he ever put aside his strict regimen of self-improvement. ("To do a Jimmie," in family lingo, meant to work like a dog to surpass oneself and everyone else.) Strive as he did, however, he could never measure up to his wife in the ways that, for them, truly counted. She commanded the money, the social connections, and the artistic glory. The more she subtly patronized him, the more he pushed their daughters, setting high standards for them and basking in their many accomplishments but also competing with them and undermining their self-confidence when it threatened his own. Their strengths were his strengths; their weaknesses, his strengths too. His elder daughter, Sally, never quite met his standards. Joan came closer, purchasing evidence of her father's love with top grades, silver trophy cups, and blue-ribboned artwork, yet she too did not fully succeed because she was "only a girl." Once, for instance, determined that Joan should rank at the top of her high school French class, her father hired a tutor for her with a cutting remark she later remembered as: "You'll never speak French as well as I. You can't draw as well as I. You can't do anything as well as I because you are a woman."

When she reached her twenties, Joan realized that abstract painting was "completely out of the competition" because "he couldn't even criticize what it was, you know?" and thus it might deliver her at last from that judgmental eye. The figure disappeared from her work. "And then," she explained forty years later, "I felt protected. That I remember so clearly. Whew!"

Yet, as it turned out, this move didn't exactly "free [her] from him forever." The old man would not so easily tumble: Joan still identified with her father, still secretly craved his approval. At thirty-two, she had a vivid dream in which she reassured him, "Oh, I'll never leave you." Their relationship, as the aging artist once dryly summed it up for an interviewer sitting under her sad saurian eye, had proved "a very mixed bag."

Two hundred miles southwest of Chicago, James Herbert Mitchell's native Havana hugs a stretch of the Illinois River that unravels into finger lakes and curls around the Cuba-shaped island from which the town takes its name. His grandparents on his mother's side, George and Waity Vaughan, had moved to Havana from Vermont in 1839, a time when settlements were springing up across the Illinois prairie, a new Land of Milk and Honey. Barges groaned into Havana to disgorge plows, coal, and rye whiskey and groaned out loaded with grain. Stray cattle wandered its unclayed main street shaggy with weeds, yet its inhabitants valued order, commerce, education, and the law. A school went up, followed by the three-story Walker House Hotel (Abraham Lincoln, of nearby Salem, slept here), then the simple brick courthouse where Lincoln argued cases.

Descendants of British colonists and former tannery operators, George and Waity now began life anew as farmers. Joan claimed a paternal great-grandfather who fought in the American Revolution, but neither George's dates nor those of her other paternal great-grandfather bear out her statement. More important than the particulars is her Mitchell kin's self-image as players (albeit minor) in America's history, stout-hearted soldiers, frontiersmen, and homesteaders—self-reliant "pioneer stock"—a self-concept Joan shared.

With a land grant signed by President James Polk for 177 acres of sandy brushland six miles from town, George and Waity cleared trees, built a white-fenced farmhouse, sowed Indian corn and winter wheat, and raised horses, sheep, and milch cows. Waity bore two sons and a daughter. Meanwhile, George sank their life savings into forty acres of timberland from which he planned to harvest building planks, but, the ink barely dry on the bill of sale, realized he'd been swindled into investing in trees too small to cut. They would have lost everything had Waity not bootstrapped them out of the crisis, running the farm after George fell ill with pulmonary pneumonia and their elder son with another disease. The boy died just short of his seventeenth birthday. The effort chewed Waity up. When she breathed her last at age fifty-one, she looked eighty.

Six months after Waity's death, illness claimed the Vaughans' second son. Old George limped through two painful, insomniac years as a widower. After he too died, one Sunday morning in 1874, his elegist delicately reminded mourners that his "wife and children are all gone to the 'undiscovered country,' but one daughter who was married last fall to Mr. James Mitchell."

A photograph of the survivor, Sarah Felicia Vaughan, reveals a sturdy, sloe-eyed brunette with a judicious air and elegant arch of the eyebrows. Able to keep a bandbox home in manure-splashed surroundings and a level head in the midst of crisis, Sarah would go down in family history as the central figure in a line of determined and tough-minded women. Besides character, she brought a valuable homestead to her marriage with James Mitchell. In economic terms, their union was a modest out-of-town tryout for that of Joan's parents: a middle-aged man moves up in the world by marrying a comfortably fixed younger woman.

Sarah's husband was a thirty-seven-year-old widower with the fine Virginia name of James Hickman Herndon Mitchell. Of Scottish and English descent, his parents, Isaac Mitchell and Frances Stribling Mitchell, had quit the Old Dominion to homestead first in Kentucky, then on the east bank of the Illinois River. Frances gave birth to eleven children before she died. The youngest, Jim, as he was called, grew into a strapping pompadoured youth whose happiest hours were devoted to adventuring after wolves and wild turkeys.

Twenty-four years old when the Confederate bombardment of Fort Sumter triggered President Abraham Lincoln's appeal for 75,000 volunteers, Jim Mitchell had enlisted in the 17th Infantry Regiment of the Grand Army of the Republic. He saw early action at Fort Girardeau, Missouri, where he lost a half brother, Henry Harrison Mitchell, the county's first Civil War casualty. Jim's regiment then helped reverse what appeared a sure Confederate victory at the savage Battle of Shiloh in the Vicksburg campaign. By the time he was mustered out after three years, he had earned promotion to first lieutenant and received from admiring friends a sword (still handed down from one generation of Mitchells to the next) as an emblem of their respect and a tool for his deeds of valor. The war, however, had sapped Jim's strength and left him with chronic eye disease and a heart condition due, he claimed, to a horrific march across southern Kentucky. Pummeled for days by hard, cold rain, the men of Company K had caught what little sleep they could by curling up in the mud.

Yet Jim had proved his manliness, moral fiber, and iron will. During this central exploit of his life and crucible of his character, he had set the Mitchell standard for bravery and devotion to duty. He would raise his children on his own Civil War epic, which also became the measure of the "Spartan courage" that his youngest, James Herbert Mitchell (a lifelong Civil War buff), demanded of himself and of his daughters Sally and Joan.

Not until Jim married Sarah Vaughan in 1873 (his first wife and their child had both died) did his life again yield a modicum of sweetness, including the luxury of indulging his passion for horses. So deep was his love of horses that when his wife gave birth to one of their children, the local paper marveled that "Jim Mitchell hasn't talked horse for a week.

Blaze face sorrels, Mambrinos, Blackwoods, Hambletonians, and even Billy Wilkes have lost all charms for him." For succeeding generations of Mitchells, even city Mitchells, money meant, among other things, horses. Family scrapbooks abound in pictures of Sally and Joan at Chicago's Lincoln Park paddock, riding, jumping, wielding whips, and looking smart in their English-style show jackets, breeches, and tall, stiff boots. Although their grandfather had died more than two decades before their births, both girls inherited his animal-worshipping ways, which also took the form of soulful connections with dogs. Anyone who ever nervously negotiated the zone of barking German shepherds with whom the adult Joan surrounded herself, dogs she coddled, respected, and adored, will see in her what Havanans saw in her grandfather: a "genuine lover of [animals], an enthusiast, or crank, if you will."

By 1881, Jim and Sarah Mitchell had two children, seven-year-old Gertrude and five-year-old William. That August, Sarah gave birth to their third, a ten-pound boy they named James Herbert Mitchell but called Herbert.

Little Herbert was raised in a narrow and prosaic world. He might have befriended the German neighbor children but was told to keep his distance from these "foreigners" who worshipped a Lutheran god. A loner, he liked to go horseback riding down by the river, where he watched the comings and goings of snorting steamboats and Chicago industrial barons who, their citified sons in tow, holidayed in luxurious lodges and hunted the same Havana duck served on silver platters at Chicago's Palmer House. Such sights deeply marked the downstate farmboy pressing his nose to the glass.

Herbert was only seven or eight when the Mitchells became aware that death's truce with them was nearing its end: Sarah was slowly succumbing to the same chronic pulmonary pneumonia that had killed her father. They sold the farm and moved into town, where help was closer at hand. Astonishingly, as Sarah weakened, she gave birth to a six-pound boy she named Clare, though no one else had known she was pregnant. "He is quite small and was a perfect surprise to everyone," she gleefully wrote her friend Eva, "for they said they never suspicioned it for a moment and of course I did not publish it and they all thought I was down with . . . the consumption." As Sarah's condition worsened, she lay awake most nights wracked with pain and drenched in sweat. Nonetheless, as firm-minded and meticulous about dying as about living, she dictated how she should be dressed for burial, which hymns should be sung at her funeral, and which minister should preach.

Sarah Vaughan Mitchell's death, a few days before Herbert's ninth birthday, thrust her sixteen-year-old daughter Gertrude into the roles of housekeeper and surrogate mother to two boys and a sickly infant. The girl was overwhelmed, yet when Jim asked relatives to help with baby Clare, gossipmongers painted him out as a neglectful father who "had given his babe away." He issued a vehement denial in the local newspaper, but not before Clare had died of meningitis.

This character-shaping series of events fed in Herbert an us-against-them bitterness of spirit that never quite left him. In the weeks following Clare's death, he too fell seriously ill. Perhaps it was during his long recuperation that he honed the fluid, well-observed caricatures he later dismissed (belying his considerable pride) as "parlor tricks I developed as a child."

A family photo from this time shows young Herbert all spit and polish with a rube haircut, jumbo bow tie, and utterly blank expression. A mediocre student, he now turned surly and provoking at school. When he mouthed off one too many times to a certain teacher, the man hurled a book at him, then punched him in the face, an incident that made the front page of the *Mason County Democrat*. Not long thereafter, at Mrs. William L. Krebaum's boardinghouse, where Herbert, his father, and his brother had gone to live after Gertrude's marriage deprived them of a housekeeper, another fight or mishap toppled a massive display counter onto his foot, leaving him briefly hobbled. He dropped out of high school a year short of graduation and took a job as a manual laborer in Peoria. Here one is tempted to draw the curtain upon James Herbert Mitchell as he drifted downward, the West's promise to his settler grandparents unfulfilled.

His family life too was disintegrating: his father had fallen prey to cholera, neurasthenia, and senility. Big sister Gertrude still mothered and encouraged him, but she had a growing family of her own to care for. As for his brother Will—odd, taciturn, and lean as a rake—he impregnated a girlfriend who died in childbirth, then struggled along as a single father lurching from one job to another. Once he disappeared for a couple of years. Three times he married, and three times he was widowed. During Joan's childhood, Uncle Will would manifest himself occasionally in the form of a letter postmarked in some one-gas-station Iowa or Missouri town. Will's apparent aimlessness gave Herbert all the more reason to whip himself and his daughters into achievement, validating his favorite copybook maxim: "Jack of all trades, master of none!"

For, unlike his brother, Herbert had inexplicably roused himself, folding up prairie life at age twenty-two when he boarded a Chicago-bound train that sliced up the fields of rural Illinois and sent them into his past. By the time its clatter slowed and the light had reversed itself so that he stared at his own reflection against the glare of the steaming Chicago and Northwestern Depot, this aging Horatio Alger was on his way up in the world.

He enrolled in the University of Chicago (possible then without a high school diploma), dropped out, gained readmission, then plugged away at a degree in science. Four years later, he entered a graduate program in chemistry. A tightly wound figure toiling round the clock, Herbert eked out a living as a pharmacist's assistant. His academic achievements remained modest: he never earned above a D in anatomy, though he finally managed a B- average. After graduation, he toyed with the idea of becoming an artist but lacked the nerve. Family lore has it that, hoisting a few whiskies with a friend one day, Herbert declared that "you can be anything you want to be in the world, and I can prove it. I'm going to be a doctor." Admitted to Rush Medical College, he became the protégé of Dr. Oliver Ormsby, a national figure in dermatology, a field in which young MDs then specialized by apprenticing themselves to older practitioners.

Self-improvement figured heavily in Herbert's regimen. This young Arrowsmith kept an Ingersoll calculator in one pocket and a volume of Kipling in the other, for (he confessed to Gertie) he fell short as a mixer and tried to compensate by "attending to the mental worth." Not only did he read diligently but also he seized every opportunity to practice the German and French he had studied as an undergraduate and refined by boarding with a language professor. He polished his equestrian skills and took up tennis, watercoloring, and photography. Near the top of Herbert's steep climb came several switchbacks: only days before the end of World War I, he joined the Army Medical Corps (where he treated many cases of syphilis, which became one of his specialties), and twice he visited Europe. In one typically overachieving campaign, he presented France's most famous dermatologists with letters of introduction from their Chicago colleagues and made competent sketches of each, later presented as lantern slides accompanying a lecture at the Academy of Dermatology and Syphilology: "Some French Dermatologists I Have Known."

Then came internship, private practice, and a flurry of job offers, including a tempting professorship at the new Harvard Medical School in China. He turned it down, however, for a staff position at Chicago's Presbyterian Hospital, where he would enjoy a distinguished forty-year career as a dermatologist and syphilologist, including a term as president of the American Dermatological Association.

With a high, broad forehead, nearly lashless puppy-dog eyes, a little nose, and sensual lips, this MD in his very correct three-piece suit cut a boyishly attractive figure. As he reached middle age, however, the light in his face dimmed, his expression hardened, and his hair grayed. Slicked back on that domed head, it oddly called to mind a wet otter. At dinner parties, Dr. Mitchell was a courteous, buttoned-down bachelor trailing a "faint voluptuous smell of pomade and whiskey."

Deep inside this paragon of determination hibernated a romantic who viewed his sister Gertie, the only woman whose company he unreservedly enjoyed, as Motherhood and her son William Herbert Sloan, also called Herbert, as his own boyhood self. Indeed, he doted upon his favorite nephew, marveling at the youngster's inquiring mind, sterling character, Spartan courage, and childishly astute observations ("It takes a man to understand a man") yet endlessly preaching to him about duty and self-improvement. Little Herbert was his uncle's model child. Still, the doctor firmly rejected any notion of a family of his own: marriage would knock him off the narrow path he had set for himself and entail unnecessary expense.

Around 1918, thirty-seven-year-old Dr. James Herbert Mitchell met twenty-three-year-old poet, editor, and heiress Marion Strobel. Until now in no hurry to marry, Miss Strobel abruptly set her cap for this unpedigreed son of a downstate farmer, all the more attractive perhaps because he was so out of place in her own blue-blooded crowd.

She, not he, took the lead in their courtship. At first genuinely unwilling to be caught, Herbert had to be coached even into writing love letters. "Please, please, please consult what Edna Ferber is 'pleased to call' your heart," the adroit Miss Strobel once penned, "and if it has a syncopated diastole, put it on paper in what I would consider extravagant language.

(I know you won't do this, you careful old person whom I love entirely too much)." Gradually she pried open his heart like a miser's coin purse.

After their engagement, Marion exacted one major change. The ridiculous "Herbert" was out of the question for her husband's name, so she prevailed upon him to switch to his first name, James, from which she derived the smart "Jimmie." (At a soiree many years later, in the presence of *Chicago Herald-American* drama critic Ashton Stevens, Jimmie Mitchell responded to a colleague's inquiry about why old-timers called him "Herb": "Marion Jimmied out the Herbert.")

On December 6, 1922, James Herbert Mitchell wed Marion Strobel in an intimate ceremony at her parents' fashionable North Michigan Avenue apartment. Their monthlong honeymoon at a dazzlingly white Bermuda guesthouse overlooking a harbor framed with dark cedars brought Jimmie face-to-face with the charming reality of commanding the best life had to offer. As if half hoping, half fearing that the genie would return to its bottle, he wrote Gertie, "We are happy together at present and I am firmly convinced that it will go although I would be prepared for anything."

Whether measuring out words for a sonnet (her first volume of verse was a Chicago best seller), playing tennis (she ranked fifth among female amateurs in the western United States), or gossiping over "a dish of tea" with poet Archibald MacLeish (whose books she reviewed for the *Chicago Daily Tribune*), Marion Strobel Mitchell was competence personified. She now met with aplomb her every obligation as a doctor's wife, dashing off witty bread-and-butter notes, presiding over a table where flutes of champagne and spinach soufflés materialized on cue, and orchestrating storybook Christmases, down to perfect gifts for the domestics' children.

Yet, Marion was as strong-minded and impertinent—"Mitchelly," in family shorthand—as she was solicitous and sensitive. "Will you go to a concert with me next Sunday at the Blackstone Theatre?" this literary Tracy Lord once inquired of her then fiancé. "My teacher is singing, and if you don't like her I will at once not like you." At the more fatuous gatherings of the smart set, this dreary luncheon or that interminable club meeting, a look of grim patience would steal into her eyes and a tightness of the jaw betray her boredom.

In fact, for all of her social graces, Marion seemed happiest in solitary pursuits. At the Mitchells' Lake Forest summer retreat, always a tonic for her soul, "leaves, and crawling things and the best sunsets in the world" prompted riffs to city-bound friends: "If I had a dandelion I'd mash it in this letter just to show you how pretty a mashed dandelion is and that I'm in the country hurrah!" There she read voraciously, plunging into (as one summer's fare) Kay Boyle, Viola Meynell, Cervantes, Stefan Zweig, and stacks of volumes of poetry.

In these early days of their marriage, Jimmie's snapshots of Marion capture a slender, spirited young woman with newly bobbed hair, high cheekbones, a polished complexion, strong eyebrows, and, her most striking feature, brown velvet eyes that seemed to read straight into your soul. Commanding a regiment of seamstresses, Marshall Field's clerks, milliners, and laundresses, she easily turned herself out with the pared-down elegance inherited from her mother, a belle of the 1880s.

In 1857, Marion's maternal grandparents, Sarah Moore and Daniel Franklin Baxter, both from well-established families of Quincy, Massachusetts, had come west with their Chicago-sized ambitions. In their home on Ohio Street, Sarah bore and raised five children, while Daniel built a grain commission business that, by the time of the Great Fire, had reaped a $100,000 fortune. Later he outflanked all rivals in the rye futures market, earning the nickname "Rye Baxter." Then, one Friday in 1892, after a mild bout of illness, he knocked out his usual day at the Board of Trade, dined at seven, retired at nine, and, at ten, lay dead from pleurisy.

Of the life of the couple's eldest child, Joan's maternal grandmother Henrietta Baxter, time has spared only a few clippings, a will, and a handful of tattered pictures. Henrietta's big beautiful eyes give the impression of a compassionate soul; the determined set of her head and slight pointiness of her chin suggest she was stubborn. In formal portraits, she flaunts her wasp waist in décolleté silk and velvet gowns stiffened with petticoats or nestles her nutmeg curls into luxurious fur collars and hats. Diamond pendants flicker at her ears, an oversized locket gleams from her bosom. Never one to loll on her horsehair sofa, Henrietta chummed around with literary patroness and pioneer golfer Rose Chatfield-Taylor and yeoman hostess Anna Coleman, later the dowager queen of the smart set. Together they cut a swath as the Three Musketeers of Chicago Society, "a dashing and popular trio."

In 1890, Henrietta married Charles Louis Strobel, a native of Cincin-

Joan's grandfather, Charles Louis Strobel,
as a young engineer, c. 1890

nati who had grown up in Lutheran sternness and lace-doily ease. Descended from Bavarian porcelain merchants, Charles Louis's immigrant father, Karl Strobel, owned a lucrative pocketbook factory; his mother, née Ida Merker, reigned over a complex German American household including five children, two sisters-in-law, three cousins, and a staff of servants. After graduating from high school (where he was singled out for his excellent moral character), Charles Louis attended the renowned Royal Institute of Technology in Stuttgart, Germany, where he trained in civil engineering and from which he returned with notebooks brimming with small, spidery drawings of staircases, pulley arrangements, parquetry, chimneys, keystoned arches, piers, quoins, and bearing and nonbearing walls, many of them abstract to the non-engineer, all of them beautiful and later important to Joan as an artist.

Mr. and Mrs. Charles Louis Strobel soon became fixtures at Chicago Orchestra concerts, Passavant Hospital benefits, and Art Institute receptions. The couple weekended at their "cottage" in Wheaton, where they donned flannels to play at the Chicago Golf Club, and entertained brilliantly at their North Side Richardson Romanesque home. Henrietta gave birth to two children whom she raised among heavy antiques and volumes bound in morocco leather and taught to love the waltzes and *Lieder* she played on the piano. Accompanied by their children's nanny, the Strobels sailed to Europe, where they vacationed in ornate palace hotels. Theirs was a highly coded, Jamesian world upholstered in privilege.

Shortly after launching his career in 1874 with a job at the Cincinnati Southern Railway Company, Charles Strobel had been wooed by Andrew Carnegie to the team of crackerjack engineers at the Scotsman's Keystone Bridge Company. He would devote his next twenty-seven years to the Carnegie empire, all the while scrupulously recording in his diaries the ethical improprieties of Carnegie and his associate, coke baron Henry Clay Frick.

With postwar expansion back on track after the 1873 panic, Strobel's timing was impeccable. The nation's political reunification after the Civil War had laid the groundwork for a railroad-based transcontinental economy sanctioned by Manifest Destiny and stitched together with Bessemer steel rails. The system's major flaw was its bridges, either nonexistent or haphazardly engineered and thus prone to collapse under the sudden vibrations of hundreds of tons of hurtling train. Strobel eased this problem by inventing a method of calculating stresses based on both loads and locomotive-wheel

Joan's grandmother, Henrietta Moore Baxter Strobel, with her young daughter Marion Strobel (Joan's mother), c. 1898

concentrations. But the young engineer's outstanding contributions to his field were codifying the principles of bridge building in his brilliant rewrite of the *Carnegie Handbook*, the pocket bible of wrought iron and steel engineering, and inventing the Z-bar, a structural steel beam whose cross-section forms a right-angled Z (as the cross-section of an I-beam forms an I). Four Z-bars riveted to a central plate constitute a Z-bar column, "a structural signature" of the Keystone Bridge Company.

More glamorously and usefully to his painter granddaughter, Charles Louis Strobel also designed and built bridges: Kansas City's Chouteau Bridge, which opened the way for the first Chicago–Kansas City rail line, and the Ohio Connecting Railway Bridge below Pittsburgh, among many others. For the latter, he audaciously shouldered nine hundred tons of bridge on nine hundred tons of falsework set on coal barges, then floated into place. In Chicago, Strobel constructed the rolling bascule bridge at the Van Buren Street crossing of the south branch of the Chicago River, a modern drawbridge that straddled the water like a monumental cat's cradle, capable of nimble transfigurations to accommodate both road and river traffic.

Such achievements earned Strobel wealth and acclaim as an engineer hero who subdued the irrational with sheer brainpower and nerves. To his granddaughters, however, he would be "Grampie." With his clotted-cream complexion, expression locked in neutral, tidy walrus mustache, and penchant for top hats, morning coats, and spats, he cut a formal and remote figure.

In the adult Joan's telling, Grampie's Sunday-morning visits during her childhood (when he was nearly blind) were tableaux vivants in which a timid girl casts her gaze upon a sphinx:

"He never spoke. He liked me; I didn't speak either . . . he was very shy, I guess. Oh, no. He sat and I sat."

"You didn't talk?" inquired her interviewer.

"No, I mean, children were seen and not heard."

"In your family it was like that . . ."

"Well, around him."

Yet this grandfather who had designed bridges (and mother who lyricized about them) inspired young Joan's love of the monumentality, compressed energy, and spatial dynamics of steel spans. The girl reveled in the furious wrangling of water with piers and shivered with delight as shadows jumped at each other and metal cages rattled when motorcars sped across. Bridges naturally found their way into her adolescent paintings of typical Chicago scenes. Later she would live next to the Brooklyn Bridge, on the Brooklyn side, where, as ecstatic about that great vault as a young Hart Crane, she painted it over and over again. Even as a more sophisticated artist in her mid-twenties, Joan did not put bridges aside. Her artistic genealogy must list as progenitors not only Kandinsky, Mondrian, Gorky, van Gogh, Cézanne, Matisse, and de Kooning, but also her grandfather Charles Louis Strobel for his "beautiful, fabulous" engineering drawings.

The title of Mitchell's major canvas of 1951, *Cross Section of a Bridge*, for instance, flags the engineer's right-angled traverse section (as opposed to the plan or the elevation) as a way of engaging with space. Locked into the center of the canvas, a mangled post-Cubist fretwork ripples with quasi cords, arches, and wedges, partially open (using the *passage* technique favored by Cézanne) so that they half merge with those adjoining. Nearly ten feet wide, *Cross Section of a Bridge* is wrought with compressed tensions, congested with shallow planes, and jammed with brackish greens and slithery grays, relieved by flashes of red, yellow, and blue. It evokes the sulky yet swift-moving world beneath a bridge's water-knocking abutments and the dance of bottle-glass reflections on its underbelly. A list—almost a poem—that Joan jotted down on the back of a notebook as she worked on *Cross Section* evokes its feeling: "Toward Blue / Of Red / Glass / Landscape / Edge / Up / Outlet / March / Approach to Water / Bridge."

Later in that decade, Joan cleated her paintings with brushstrokes and continued to tap into the tensions and energies of bridges. Memories of bridges often kindled the feelings she needed to begin a work; bridge forms served as syntactical touchstones. *Hemlock,* for instance, acknowledges the cantilever, a beam that projects beyond its vertical support and that, set arm to arm with another cantilever, can span a wide river, while *Ladybug* suggests the marvelous variety of the truss, a trellis of girders, bars, struts, and beams based in the stability of the triangle. Such works also set up a dialectic between the part and the whole, a concept as vital to bridge engineers like Charles Louis Strobel, inventor of the Z-bar, as to painters like Cézanne and Pollock.

Of Joan's 1957 painting *Bridge,* then art critic Irving Sandler wrote that a "recollected landscape provided the initial impulse, but the representational image was transformed in the artist's imagination by feelings inspired by bridge and beach . . . sensations of girders and height and the varied meanings implicit in 'spanning a void.'" A few months earlier, Sandler had reviewed a major Mitchell exhibition, reporting that although "a visual image such as a landscape, water or a bridge is utilized to kick off these works, the object disappears in the exultation of the act of painting, and Miss Mitchell ends up with almost pure emotion." He added, "This show should be seen in the morning, for it can animate the entire day."

Joan's adoration of his bridges notwithstanding, bridge building did not mark the apogee of her grandfather's career. During the business boom of the mid-1880s, cities saw unparalleled demands for downtown office space, none more so than Chicago, still refitting after the Great Fire. There, as elsewhere, cast and wrought iron stood in good stead as structural materials, yet steel was mounting a challenge. Endowed with enormous tensile strength and suitable for riveting into rigid skeletons, steel would make possible the revolutionary structural system that launched the modern office tower. Upend the steel sleeve that is a bridge, architect William LeBaron Jenney once observed, and you have the rudiments of a skyscraper. That idea made Charles Louis Strobel—bridge builder, standards expert, inventor, and Chicago representative for Carnegie's steelworks (which was heavily invested in the manufacture of construction beams)—a man of the hour.

In 1885, after erecting Gustave Eiffel's innovative steel load-bearing structure for the Statue of Liberty (as tall as the skyscraper of its day), Strobel hurried out to Chicago, where Jenney had contracted with Carnegie to use Bessemer steel beams on the top three floors of the Home Insurance Building, debatably the first skyscraper. Carnegie had just posted Strobel to Chicago, where he quickly became a trusted colleague of architects Jenney, John Wellborn Root, and Louis Sullivan, to all of whom he so effectively touted the advantages of steel that he signed contracts to supply Carnegie steel columns and beams for seventeen classic buildings that figure in every detailed history of the Chicago School.

One of these—more closely tied to a city's identity than perhaps any other in modern times—made Charles Louis Strobel a Chicagoan. Underwritten by a *Who's Who* of tycoons, the Chicago Auditorium Building—a showplace intended to make the city as celebrated for its opera and its symphony as for its stockyards—was rising at the corner of Congress Street and Michigan Avenue. Inaugurated in 1889, the Auditorium Building answered a roll call of superlatives: the highest point in Chicago, the largest private structure in the United States, the heaviest structure in the world, the most expensive building ever built. Its centerpiece was the world's largest assembly hall, spangled with carbon-filament lights and adorned with intertwining vegetal arabesques in oak, plaster, leaded glass, and stenciled gold leaf. The hall's aesthetic allure, near-perfect acoustics, and inspired engineering helped earn lasting fame for the building's architects, Dankmar Adler and Louis Sullivan, assisted by the novice Frank Lloyd Wright. His Keystone Bridge Company an important subcontractor for the project, Charles Louis Strobel supervised the design of the hall's mammoth elliptical vaults, which are essentially truss-framed railroad bridges.

Fourteen months after the hall opened, Strobel anchored his position in Chicago society by marrying Henrietta Baxter at a splendid Episcopalian ceremony. Their fourteen-year union produced a son, Charles Louis, and a daughter, Marion. Life was rich. Then, one wine-dark January evening in 1905 at a charity ball at the Chicago Auditorium, Charles and Henrietta drank their stirrup cup.

Fragrant with the scents of Florida water, French perfume, and evergreen, the auditorium's ballroom had been transformed into a luxuriant bower of pines, orange trees, clematis, and chrysanthemums. Its usual light bulbs (whose greenish gold cast marred Madame's complexion) had vanished: instead, calcium fixtures cast a pink luster upon three thousand members of *le tout Chicago*. Below an enormous chandelier-hung wreath dripping with colored ribbons, storms of conversation rose and racked the hall. On its edges, half screened by potted palms and backlit as if by Degas, the First Regiment Band and Johnny Hand's Orchestra sat at the ready. When they finally struck up a flourish to announce the March of the Nations, the gala's signature for which a soldiery of clubwomen had endured "the ordeal of costumes, wigs, jewels, and all that went to make up [its] gorgeousness," the din abated and necks craned.

Represented by the distaff Palmers, Farwells, McCormicks, Ryersons, Blairs, Armours, Fields, and other mainstays of Chicago society, the "nations" included Alsatians in black velvet bodices over white guimpe and pink and yellow brocaded skirts; geishas played by Chicago's tiniest socialites wearing coral and lime kimonos; hoopskirted Civil War–era belles twirling parasols; Russian noblewomen, all embroidery, fur, tassels, and braids; and, at the first notes of the *Marseillaise*, Henrietta Baxter Strobel stepping a minuet across the polished floor, followed by ten French court dames. In her diamonds, her white-powdered topiary hairdo dotted with rosebuds, and her lacy pale blue panne velvet gown copied from that of the Princess Lamballe, Joan's grandmother was no less than splendid.

At thirty-eight, Henrietta Baxter Strobel surely had title to more than her share of the good things of this world. Was she happy? A poem written by her daughter Marion fifteen years later suggests that she was not:

> *Tapering fingers of nerves, weighted with glittering ware;*
> *Tired hands, where veins throbbed in the hope they might keep still;*
> *Beautiful, yet too white, wavering wearily on,*
> *Playing the song of life when the dirge of death had begun.*

In the days following the gala, Chicago's weather remained clay-cold, and the high spirits surrounding the event must have seemed as evanescent as the ladies' nosegays of Parma violets. With society in the doldrums, columnists wrote up only a smattering of events, among them a luncheon organized by Mrs. Charles Louis Strobel. But Henrietta had little time to entertain, for nine-year-old Marion had developed a painful abscess of the ear that turned out to be mastoiditis, in that era potentially life-threatening. The child underwent surgery and sustained substantial hearing loss. Throughout the ordeal, Henrietta remained at her daughter's side until she herself (it seems) took ill with pleurisy. Two weeks later, after Sunday breakfast, Henrietta unexpectedly died.

In a prominent obituary, Tuesday's *Tribune* reported that Mrs. Charles L. Strobel had succumbed to a pulmonary embolism, even though she had appeared to be recovering from the pleurisy: "In the morning Mrs. Strobel seemed much stronger and more cheerful. Shortly after her breakfast, however, complications developed and she sank rapidly. Dr. Robert B. Preble, the family physician, was summoned, but Mrs. Strobel was beyond medical aid. Death came at 9:30."

The *Tribune*'s account is inaccurate, however. No physician attended Henrietta as she lay dying. In truth, Marion had walked into a bathroom that morning to discover her mother lifeless in the tub: Henrietta had slashed her wrists. Marion would have seen a red fog filter through the bathwater, her mother's hair sway like wild black seaweed, her eyes stare from that white-mask face.

Was the tale of pleurisy, then, a clever fabrication, matching Henrietta's death to her father's in order to suggest a congenital predisposition? Pleurisy can be a complication of tuberculosis, lung cancer, pneumonia, viral infection, or congestive heart failure, so, lacking further information, it's impossible to assess the likelihood of an inherited susceptibility. Searches of Cook County death records, indexes to probate files, and coroner's inquest files yield nothing about Henrietta Strobel's not-inconspicuous death, as if Charles Louis Strobel (who would have deemed shielding the family's honor a plus on his moral report card) had pulled wires to forestall any mention of suicide.

But how could a loving mother take her own life just as her daughter was recovering from major surgery and adjusting to a serious physical handicap? On a Sunday, moreover, when servants have the day off and children freely roam the house? The answer may lie in the depression from which Henrietta (like her granddaughter Joan) suffered, including perhaps (again, as with Joan) seasonal affective disorder, which can turn dark winter months to bitter ashes.

Little Marion's wretchedness would have fused with guilty anxiety that she and her illness were to blame. She turned to her father, but, impassive as the facade of their gray stone Division Street home, the unbending autocrat never rallied to his children's emotional aid. In fact, he quit Carnegie that year and devoted longer than usual hours to establishing the Strobel Steel Construction Company, which helps explain why, as she raised her own children a quarter century later, Marion still struggled to put Henrietta to rest. According to Joan's sister Sally, the two girls were "more or less brought up on the horror that . . . [Marion] felt when she found her mother dead in the bathtub," a key moment in family history that seeded Joan's fascination with and abhorrence of suicide and her terror of abandonment and death.

At age fourteen, Marion faced a second abomination when Charles Louis Strobel married a spinster named Mary Wilkins ("Grammie" to Joan and Sally), the sister of Henrietta's close friend Anna Coleman. How *could* he, Marion raged, when surely she was more than enough for any father? The day after the ceremony, Charles Louis Strobel whisked his bride off to Europe for a six-week honeymoon, again leaving his children emotionally bereft.

But strength of character ran in the blood. At St. Timothy's School in Catonsville, Maryland, where she began boarding that fall, Marion put the world back together as a charm bracelet of privileged moments. In snapshots carefully arranged in her scrapbook, she captions the basketball team; angles for trout; water skis; poses with her lacrosse team; celebrates victory in a golf tournament; feeds the pigeons in the Piazza San Marco; climbs a mountain with her schoolmates and their chaperone, a Miss Bailey; and shows off a five-foot swordfish landed aboard the *Vencedor* in the Sea of Cortez. Her brother attended Yale, but Marion finished at Miss Wickham's School in New York and, in 1916, made her formal debut to Chicago society.

In fact, the sensitive and fundamentally lonely Marion had struggled mightily since her mother's death. It was thanks to poetry that she had cleared the emotional wilderness. Now re-ensconced in her father's luxurious and circumspect household, where a Luxembourgeois chambermaid, a Swedish laundress, and a Scottish cook danced attendance upon her, she poured her energies into writing, sports, social life, and volunteer work, including, during World War I, chairing the local publicity department of the women's division of the Council for National Defense. All very proper. However independently minded, the daughter of Charles Louis Strobel did not rebel by running away to Greenwich Village. Still, she indulged in at least one glorious indiscretion.

In April 1919, New Jersey poet and physician William Carlos Williams came to Chicago to give a Press Club lecture attended by Marion in the company of her friends the artist Manierre Dawson and the writers Ben Hecht and Carl Sandburg. They heard Williams, in command of his art if not yet widely known outside avant-garde circles, define the poet's mission as "To tear down, to destroy life's lies, to keep the senses bare, to attack" even one's own craft, for formal perfection leads to the threshold of self-parody. Taking to heart Williams's validation of risky emotional engagement, Marion immediately put it into practice: the two plunged into an affair, all the more cathartic, it seems, because the Great War had ended and Williams's father had recently died. During their weeklong romance, ferocious storms were spelled by watercolor-fresh clearings and Marion felt wild beauty fly at her from all sides.

Williams wrote for Marion the splendid "A Goodnight," which wraps visions of chilling insidiousness inside a lullabying wrangle of odors and noises and movements. Williams's poem batters the ear with the tonic vitality of Lake Michigan, which had raged all that week against the retaining wall outside his hotel. Indeed, Lake Michigan spills through Williams's lines with a vigor and variousness that parallel those of a Mitchell painting. "Poetry is a language of the emotions," he had observed in his lecture, which would have made perfect sense to Joan. "A poem is good when it hasn't a comma in it that doesn't contribute to the specific emotion of the poem. Nothing else is necessary. A bad poem is full of English literature."

"A Goodnight" begins:

> Go to sleep–though of course you will not—
> to tideless waves thundering slantwise against
> strong embankments, rattle and swish of spray
> dashed thirty feet high, caught by the lake wind,
> scattered and strewn broadcast in over the steady
> car rails! Sleep, sleep! Gulls' cries in a wind-gust
> broken by the wind; calculating wings set above
> the field of waves breaking.

Then, as abruptly as he had materialized, Williams disappeared back into his life in New Jersey as husband and father. In the weeks that followed, however, he seemed less able than his lover to put their liaison on the shelf. When he wrote, apparently laying out his duty to his family, Marion bristled at the suggestion that she had designs upon his marriage and informed him—her reaction uncannily Joan-like—that she was one to tough out heavy weather: "But in the future could you please do me the favour of leaving the subject alone—Good God, Bill, have a little mercy . . . You can trust me never to bring up personal subjects. It may be a little hard for me at first but I rather like hard things—. No sympathy please."

Among the emotional resources Marion brought to bear was a growing confidence in the poetry she had begun to urge into the world. "My dear Miss Monroe," opened her query to *Poetry* magazine, "I hope you may find some of the enclosed poems—'Paradox,' 'Hands,' 'Illusion,' 'Justice' and 'The Last Ritual'—useable for 'Poetry.'" Miss Monroe did not, but the two women, from the same milieu and the same Near North Side neighborhood, renewed their acquaintance.

Seven years earlier, in 1912, fifty-one-year-old poet and art critic Harriet Monroe had founded the monthly *Poetry: A Magazine of Verse,* then the only U.S. magazine devoted solely to poetry. Energetically seeking the great poet, Monroe had laid out her quest in an editorial refusing to preconceive of genius or to ally the magazine with any literary clique. She risked publishing free verse, haiku, children's rhymes, and cowboy ballads, and assailed the parochialism of American taste by engaging the cranky and brilliant London-based Ezra Pound as foreign correspondent. Monroe championed the work of Rabindranath Tagore, led one issue with Carl Sandburg's vernacular "Chicago," and published, for the first time anywhere, Wallace Stevens's "Sunday Morning," T. S. Eliot's "The Love Song of J. Alfred Prufrock," and Joyce Kilmer's "Trees." She also showcased the efforts of a babble of third-rate poets and, even as she brought recognition to the avant-garde, drifted toward her own conservative aesthetic.

Despite her grandmotherly demeanor ("Aunt Harriet's" wobbly false teeth always made young Joan nervous), Monroe defied expectations by lashing out at poets and colleagues. Her deputy, poet Alice Corbin Henderson, gave as good as she got, parrying Monroe's critical judgments with shrewd counterjudgments. After poor health forced Henderson to resign and her successor also departed, Monroe found another feisty assistant in Marion Strobel, who took the unpaid position of associate editor in April 1920. By then *Poetry* had achieved national and international stature, although the critical consensus is that it had already left its early brilliance behind, due in part to Monroe's espousal of too much easy-listening rhyme from the Corn Belt.

Moreover, Monroe's highhanded trimming, changes in capitalization, and rearranging of submissions had alienated several major poets including William Carlos Williams, who also objected to the magazine's paltry payments. After Marion joined *Poetry* this arrived from Ruther-ford, New Jersey: "Provided you will allow me to use small letters at the beginning of my lines, I submit the following excellent American poem to you for publication in your paying magazine:

> SPIRIT OF '76
> *Her father*
> *built a bridge*
> *over*
> *the Chicago River*
> *but she*
> *built a bridge*
> *over the moon.*"

For the next five and a half years, Marion Strobel (as she was known professionally) penned reviews, did first readings of some three thousand poems a month, kept order at *Poetry*'s Cass Street Victorian, and orga-nized luncheons at the trattoria around the corner. There, production schedule forgotten, talk and Chianti would transport the magazine's tiny staff and its visitors—the likes of Louis Untermeyer, Jean Starr Unter-meyer, Robert Frost, Vachel Lindsay, Carl Sandburg, Edward Steichen, and Marsden Hartley—into "that timeless unlocalized element called poetry." Marion proved herself charming, hardworking, astute, and prickly. In lively reviews, she sounded the praises of T. S. Eliot, Charlotte Mew, and May Sarton; argued that Marianne Moore's work amounted to tedious pedantry; and ripped into her ex-lover Williams's latest as the stuff of a swaggering middle-aged adolescent.

As fiercely devoted to Monroe personally as to *Poetry,* Marion Stro-bel was to enjoy two stints (twenty years apart) as a staffer. In addition, for forty-six years she entwined the roles of contributing poet, editorial committee member, hostess, fundraiser, and financial backer. A major player in the magazine's byzantine politics, she sought funding so zeal-ously that she may deserve credit for saving *Poetry* when, its chances of survival approximately nil during the Depression, Charles Louis Strobel's former employer, the Carnegie Corporation, materialized as fairy godmother, bestowing three major grants. Yet, as Joan later noted, Marion's contributions to this originally proto-feminist adventure went underrecognized, including in the Modern Poetry Association's official history, which fails to mention how, when the magazine's chief, George

Dillon, was drafted in World War II, Strobel stepped in as coeditor, a literary Rosie the Riveter.

An ambitious "lady poet"—as she was called—Marion published regularly in *Poetry* and less frequently in *The Bookman, Saturday Review, Good Housekeeping, The New Republic,* and *The New Yorker.* Her work is sensitive, lyrical, self-involved (though never confessional), and sometimes brittle. The stakes are often low; paradox and exclamation, annoying tics. But, at its finest, her pure and expertly molten language pours into lines as perfect as ingots of Bessemer steel.

a momentary vacuum into which rushes
all that I love. A sense of oneness with sun and
stone.

VLADIMIR NABOKOV, *Speak, Memory*

CHAPTER TWO Satin Curtains Redux

A month after her marriage to Jimmie Mitchell, Marion was pregnant. The birth of Sarah Vaughan, called Sally, in October 1923, inspired a flurry of radiant, tender, and popular poems later published as "Songs for Sally."

But Jimmie longed for a son, so the couple decided to have a second child, a boy named "John" (Marion's pet name for her fiancé after she nixed "Herbert"). Thus they were shocked when, on February 12, 1925, Marion gave birth to another girl. In a new "Sally poem," she expressed her surprise: "I kissed and kissed . . . and kissed and kissed her. / I never dreamed she'd have a sister." As for Jimmie, he acted out his frustration by writing "John" on the application for the birth certificate. Then: "Joan." No middle name, as if he couldn't be bothered with that too.

Substituting an *a* for the *h* proved easier for Jimmie than getting beyond his desire for a son. At first he took little interest in his second-born. When he did involve himself in her upbringing, he treated her as a boy manqué whose wrong sex had all the significance of some drama of succession to the crown. "My father wanted a boy," Joan would introduce an oft-repeated line: "That's why I'm Joan, just girl." Among the many who heard about the consequences of her father's blasted expectations was the art writer Cindy Nemser, who interviewed the painter in 1972. "It seemed that her father had expected her to have been a boy," wrote Nemser, "and was evidently disappointed in her sex."

> As time went on, he didn't seem to be able to reconcile himself to Mitchell's gender since, according to the artist, he was always telling her that she acted like a boy, moved like a boy and so on . . . It was clear that she had a defensiveness about being woman and a terrible ambiguity about her identity. She told me that she had been to several psychiatrists over the years as a result of this insecurity.

Painting, Joan believed, was neither male nor female. It existed beyond all that.

Joan's earliest memories were of a German nanny who carried her haphazardly and at least once left her alone and panic-stricken, thus stirring fears of falling and of abandonment. In family snapshots, this glum uniformed Fräulein dandles the Kewpie-doll Joan, all plump legs, clenched fists, and looming tantrum. Did the nanny really kill her pet bunny, as Joan claimed? Mutter about *Schrecklichkeit* and dark cellars and the horrid ends of bad children? Joan waffled on the particulars of these incidents, which escaped the shadows of early childhood and flared into scenes of biblical proportions. Freud argues, as she was later well aware, that anything that survives the forgetting of childhood is exceptionally meaningful, either at the time or as a consequence of subsequent experiences. In fact, Joan did harbor lifelong fears of abandonment, so ingrained that she refused to say routine good-byes and might explode at the mention of the word. ("How do you decide if you're going to abandon a painting?" a young admirer once innocently inquired. "And, oh my God!" he reports. "At the use of that actual word, she went ballistic! 'Don't you talk to me about abandonment!' ") As a child, however,

Joan concealed her feelings. Any mention of fear was strictly taboo in the Mitchell household. "Spartan courage!" From age seven, she was rigorously trained in diving.

Nannies loomed large in Joan's early years. Not unusual in their circles, the Mitchells' hands-off approach to childrearing had gained currency in the 1920s thanks to the practices of the British royal family, emulated by the parents of Gold Coast princesses and princelings, and to the theories of behaviorist John B. Watson, who chastised parents for over-devotion to their children and warned against the impulse to coddle:

> Dress them, bathe them with care and circumspection. Let your behavior always be objective and kindly firm. Never hug and kiss them, never let them sit in your lap. If you must, kiss them once on the forehead when they say good night. Shake hands with them in the morning. Give them a pat on the head if they have made an extraordinarily good job of a difficult task.

So essentially did Joan's father raise her.

Marion operated along different lines. "Forced to admit [my children's] claim to my time," she resigned her position at *Poetry* and became a stay-at-home mother. Calling her babes "the most vital thing in my life" and claiming an acute maternal instinct ("and if I don't know about *that*, I'd better be put out to pasture"), she certainly felt no compunction about hugging and kissing them. Yet, torn between her dual identities as Marion Strobel, poet, and Mrs. James Herbert Mitchell, wife and mother, she passed along routine child care to the servants, trusting her intuition about when to push back from her Hermes and go cozy up to her little ones. (Meanwhile, motherhood helped sanction her freedom as a poet to operate from a modern subjectivity and rummage around in untraditional subjects such as child discipline and thus take a hand in reinvigorating the medium.)

Shortly after Joan's birth, Marion fell ill for several months, so critically, she told friends, that she was "flapping around the pearly gates," and this long ailment put up another barrier to the crucial early attachment between mother and child. Marion's health problems were to continue. A few years later, she had a thyroid operation and, later still, a mastoidectomy, a hysterectomy, and surgery to remove a cervical tumor. Between times she entertained with panache, triumphed in tennis tournaments, and pounded out poems, short stories, book reviews, novels, and plays.

Joan she found exceptionally "strenuous." In "A Cloak for Joan," published when the girl was three, Marion evokes color, sound, movement, and mother-love laced with frustration. The cloak in question, a gift from mother to daughter, speaks of the twin impulses of parenthood, protecting and letting go:

> *Child, here is a cherry-gay*
> *Cloak to sway*
> *From your shoulders.*
> *If you will—throw it away.*
>
> *On it there are birds that sing,*
> *And a lifted crimson wing—*
> *These are all*
> *And everything.*
>
> *See there are no words to scold you.*
> *I have told you*
> *Not with words will I hold you.*
>
> *Hug it closer—there and there.*
> *(Turn it under where it's bare)*
> *It looks pretty with your hair.*

Little Joan, for her part, found her mother inaccessible: if Marion wasn't out, she was closeted with adults or undisturbable at her typewriter, and, in any case, her hearing loss made her remote. Yearning for a mother who demonstrated unconditional love by dropping everything to take her to the playground or tell one of the marvelous Polly and Betty stories she made up as she went along, Joan got instead long stretches of absence or aloofness punctuated by loving attention. Surely it's no coincidence that the yellow satin curtains in which Joan delighted in losing her sense of separateness were identified with Marion. "Fuck shit," fifty-seven-year-old Joan once cranked up a letter to her dying sister Sally (by then Joan had found deep appreciation for their mother, who had died sixteen years earlier), "just talked to you [by phone]—wish I could get back into my total recall 'when we were little girls bit'—wish I could tell you a Polly and Betty story—wish I could be a Maw for you—any kind of a nice one." (As teenagers, Sally and Joan had dubbed their parents "Maw" and "Paw.") "We loved and

I loved our Maw—wish I could be that mythical Maw that would make it all come out all right."

The adult Joan's more typical allusions to early family dynamics—she was by no means immune to hyperbole—bring to mind horror stories of Romanian orphans. Not only did her parents deprive their children of attention except at dinnertime, Joan claimed, but also Jimmie hired nannies for their cold sternness. Lacking opportunities to establish her own boundaries using the two-year-old "no!" and rarely allowed to practice fending for herself while knowing her parents to be safe havens, Joan found establishing her self-identity to be scary business indeed.

Around the time of Joan's birth, the Mitchells had moved from East Delaware Place to East Chestnut Street, on the lake side of Michigan Avenue in the same Streeterville district. A doorman attended the elegant checkerboard-tiled lobby of their recently constructed Tudor brick building, home too to the A. Badger Shreves, the Calhoun Lyfords, the R. Boynton Rogerses, and the J. Beach Clows. The Mitchells' spacious apartment comprised living and dining rooms, a library, four bedrooms, a dressing room for the master suite, and a kitchen with pantry, along with servants' quarters and a private jewel and silver vault.

An inveterate redecorator, Marion quickly cast a spell of pearly glamour over their new home, using antique mirrors, ivory Fortuny drapes, Chinese lacquered cabinets, ruffled chiffoniers, satinwood tables, and bamboo blinds that scored the sunlight soaking into an Aubusson rug. "I remember . . . your place in the elevator and mine (at the angle)," Joan once reminisced to Sally,

> Helen Belnap's curtains ("modern") in my room—one half blue and white checked—the other half orange filet—horror . . . I remember when Maw decided to paint your room in something she called—phonetic—"wah de rose," which was French and to this day I can't figure it out. However I can easily mix you that palish shit color on your walls—"wah de rose."

By this time their childhood home was four decades behind, yet, possessed of a gimlet memory, Joan could zoom-lens back to reexperience its colors, sounds, and feelings in their sensual fullness. She added that it's "nice to have [childhood memories] in my imaginary valise because I can go back to 190 [East Chestnut Street] or wherever when I want to. It can be depressing too but still—even some big pieces of music I can play in my head—pics—poems etc—and whole conversations (I could be in prison or a hospital and still have something)."

Like all autobiographic memories, Joan's were subjective and incomplete, an archipelago of remembering in a vast dark sea of forgetting. Yet hers took the unusual form of translucent images in her mind's eye or, as she put it, inside a mental suitcase or album. She spoke too of images that "roosted inside me—it's frightful." Such images were not only razor-sharp but also multisensory: Joan relived emotional states, sounds, even bodily movements. In other words, she was eidetic.

"Most of the studies of eideticism are German," writes neuroscientist Richard E. Cytowic of this type of memory, in which one reexperiences the sensory and emotional particulars of stimuli that have passed from sight.

> The German-born American neurologist Heinrich Klüver has been the principal reviewer of this work and [Erich] Jaensch systematized its study. Few papers are cited after 1937 until the subject was revived by the Habers [Drs. Ralph Norman Haber and Lyn Haber] who concluded that "no serious doubts were raised about the validity of eidetic imagery as a phenomenon, even though the methodology of assessment has been both poorly described and poorly executed. Eidetic imagery just ceased to excite scientists."

So the situation remains. Today virtually no one, it seems, is conducting serious research about eidetic memory.

Most earlier investigators agreed that eidetic memory is common among young children but typically disappears as they learn to read. From then on, they pay less attention to "unimportant" things: instead, experience is encoded, sorted, compressed, and ranked using language, and thus memory becomes "an apparatus for shaping reminiscences into words." Rare individuals, however, Joan among them, continue to think and remember in richly affective and highly detailed visuals. Neither daydreams nor afterimages nor metaphors nor hallucinations nor figments of the imagination, eidetic memories spontaneously revive past situations. Some eidetikers describe bodily involvement in memories, which are thus "felt" in both senses of the word; some distinguish between every-day memories and eidetic memories. Most attest that eideticism makes the past as fresh as the present.

A visual but not conceptual thinker, Joan scoffed at the "learned clichés" of those for whom " 'apple' means A.P.P.L.E., round R.E.D. things. They are always in the word stuff." For her, "apple" brought intensely felt images: a certain fruit tree, a Cézanne still life, a bowl of scarlet winesaps on her mother's table, a particular greengrocer's bins, and so on. Even though she was a highly developed reader, Joan did not code information primarily in words, nor did she normally reason from the general to the specific. Thus, for her, one plus one did not make two—they made one plus one—and a concept was something "very frightening: a vast land without trees or anything. Not even barren: nothing." Because she did not automatically translate her experiences into language, Joan resorted less frequently than most to predetermined categories and had greater access than most to what cannot be pigeonholed with words. Ill at ease with casual word formulas, Joan long considered herself troublingly inarticulate; indeed others did not necessarily catch the drift of what she was saying. "She is a girl in love," Marion would write of her adolescent daughter, "it is easier for her to act than to talk."

And impossible for her not to relive the past. In his biography of poet Edna St. Vincent Millay, who shared Joan's gift, Daniel Mark Epstein writes that Millay's childhood diary

> describes the rare phenomenon of eidetic memory, soon to become a major strength in her life as a writer, but for the present only a painful burden. "I can remember every thing I ever did, every place I was ever in, every face I ever saw. My mind is a labyrinthian picture gallery in which every painting is a scene from my life . . ." The faintest sound or scent can evoke scenes. A little yellow flower growing in clusters on a bush, called clove or flowering currant—the smell of it always "took her back" into a playhouse she made once under such a bush, against the church-yard fence.

Joan lived *now*, emphatically in the present. Yet eidetic memory, "that robust reality" (in the words of another fellow eidetiker, Russian-born novelist Vladimir Nabokov) had a way of making "a ghost of the present." Put differently, she was capable of simultaneously experiencing the

Six-year-old Joan (right) and seven-year-old Sally play tea party for a Chicago Daily Tribune *photographer, 1931.*

visual world of the present and the virtual world of the past. Past feelings did not necessarily stay put. That proved both a blessing and a curse.

From wealthy Chicago families whose connections with the Strobels often stretched back a generation or more, the Mitchell girls' playmates included the children of writer Dorothy Aldis and real estate mogul Graham Aldis; those of Janet and Robert McCormick Adams (he, the prominent attorney and politician); those of John and Dorothy Holabird, from the clan of famous architects (his Palmolive Building was going up on Michigan Avenue); and those of corporate lawyer Clay Judson and sculptor Sylvia Shaw Judson, the daughter of renowned architect Howard Van Doren Shaw.

One July afternoon in the late 1920s, five of these sons and daughters of privilege—John Holabird Jr., his sister Jean, Alice Clay Judson (whose curls, Marion had famously written, were "as wild / As a morning-glory vine"), Sally, and Joan—paused during Alice's birthday party in the Judsons' backyard to pose for a picture brimming with old-fashioned charm.

Their hands are clasped, their faces shyly tilted, their feet sturdily planted in the grass. As usual, Sally and Joan wear matching frocks and look eager to please. Another early picture of Joan, a solo portrait, reveals a prim, too-serious girl dabbed with lipstick and rouge and lopsidedly coiffed with a Christmas-ribbon curl. Her eyes, like big dark moons, illuminate a sweetly compliant face.

Yet this same youngster could not help but pop buttons, lose mittens, get dirty, and shove all the candies into her mouth at the same time. In "The Snow," a poem Joan wrote at age seven, she (who all her life would identify with water) conjures up, as if a self-image, a "wild little brook." No doubt her nannies thought less metaphorically and more along the lines of a hefty shot or two of Castoria.

At four, Joan was sent to a neighborhood kindergarten; the following year, she joined Sally at Francis W. Parker School in North Chicago.

Designed by architect James Gamble Rogers, Parker's rambling two-and-a-half-story half-timbered building resembled a fairy-tale mansion somehow transported to Webster Avenue. Classrooms boasted homey accoutrements like fireplaces and gabled windows, playing fields stretched out on either side, and the Lincoln Park Zoo, a stone's throw away, was more or less part of the campus.

It's difficult to overestimate the importance of Joan's Parker education. Her twelve years at this progressive school where learning was not (in the words of one classmate) "a catechism of fixed Truths but an endless voyage of exploration across an uncertain and dangerous ocean," instilled in her a freethinking attitude and a sense of herself as a full-blooded creative, political, and intellectual being.

The school dates to 1901, when Anita McCormick Blaine, an heiress to the great reaper fortune, persuaded Colonel (his Civil War rank) Francis W. Parker to establish a private institution based on the philosophy he had developed as a superintendent of public schools in Massachusetts and Chicago. Parker tied all other disciplines to the arts, for, according to his theory of the unity of knowledge (meaning that knowing is inextricable from doing), textbook-based lessons offer less vital motivation for learning than do hands-on activities like planting a vegetable garden, running a grocery store, or building a wigwam. Each lower grade was organized around a theme: life at home in the first, human progress in the second, Chicago in the third, and so on. In the fourth grade, the year of ancient Greece, each child assumed the persona of a god or goddess, traipsed around in a handmade toga, mapped the ancient world, made black figure vases, and listened to Miss Davis (who, for many, personified Parker's specialness) read unabridged passages from *The Odyssey.*

Parker also strove to make students aware of the realities of a working society. Notebooks in hand, Parkerites trooped through bakeries, rode the El, toured the locks on the Chicago River, and sewed clothes for the dolls they donated to charity. Three times a week, classes opened with Morning Exercise, essentially run by the students, where they might sing Negro spirituals or question guest speakers including (in Joan's day) Carl Sandburg, Chief Oshkosh, and Alexandra Tolstoy, the novelist's daughter. The goal was articulate citizens who took the measure of their social responsibilities and did not separate school from earnest and principled living. Still today the colonel's words hang in Parker's front hall: "A school should be a model home, a complete community, an embryonic democracy."

Why did the conservative Mitchells enroll their children in the unconventional Parker when the logical choice would have been Marion's alma mater, the traditional, prestigious, and more conveniently located Chicago Latin? In fact, Sally was switched to Chicago Latin after the eighth grade, and their parents no doubt intended the same for Joan, who probably objected and got her way in the end. In any event, Marion approved of Parker's emphasis on the arts and of the fact that, along with Chicago Latin, it was the school of choice for her social circle. And Joan adored Parker.

In first grade she made a best friend in lively Joan Van Buren (Joan V. to her Joan M.), the daughter of prominent lawyers. (The two girls would remain a close, if quarrelsome, duo through high school.) Though ill at ease with ordinary playground give-and-take, Joan gradually found other friends too. Often she invited two or three over on a Saturday morning for hot fudge sundaes (the Mitchells' cook had the knack of hot fudge as thick as a board) and sneak peeks at pictures of diseased penises in her father's medical tomes.

Quickly Joan won a reputation for belligerence: like an insecure boy eager to land a first blow on the younger and weaker, she would let rip so as not to cower. When Connie Joerns's first-grade class was herded past Joan's second-grade class in the stairwell, for instance, the older girl never lost an opportunity to chant, "Baby first graders! Baby first graders!"

.   .   .

At home, Joan and Sally played tea party, made believe at tiny desks like their mother's, put their stuffed animals to bed in boxes lined in cotton batting, arranged their collections of ceramic elephants and bunnies, and talked to Joan's goldfish, Dubonnet (later a tragic figure: in tidying up one day, Marion emptied the fishbowl into the toilet without noticing Joan's pet. My goldfish drowned!, Joan wailed—another devastating loss).

The two girls bickered fiercely but also shared fears of their father and other confidences in the "peanut butter and jelly conversations" that came to symbolize their sisterhood. Though Sally was a year and a half older than her "creepy little sister," Joan's assertiveness and achievements gave her an edge and made her seem their parents' favorite, to Sally's lasting bitterness and hurt. Sally was the social one, the pretty one, the normal one; Joan, the smart one, the oddball, the prodigy who learned to read at age three and demonstrated a flair for art at age four.

That spring Marion had reported to Harriet Monroe, "Joan has a talent for drawing. Of course it's too early to tell much, but she gets all flushed and absorbed and snappy if she's interrupted, and she draws chickens, a sun, a lake, a dancing girl, flowers, trees, smoke, and houses all in one grand conglomerate group—and it looks like something! (something a bit drunk, but most deliciously tipsily colorful)." Uninspired by her art teacher at Parker, whose pet project was ceramic ashtrays and whose favorite line was "Art means having fun" (a concept Joan had trouble grasping), the girl had been enrolled in Saturday-morning children's classes at the Art Institute, where she quickly became the star pupil.

Sundays too were often slotted for the Art Institute. On bone-piercingly cold winter mornings, Jimmie and his daughters would climb past the lions and thread their way through the crowds at the great Michigan Avenue museum to stand before the unearthly stillness of another Sunday, put to canvas half a century earlier: Seurat's *A Sunday on the Island of La Grande Jatte.* Nearby hung Monet's haystacks and views of the Seine, Renoir's plump girls and acrobats, the ballerinas of Degas, the still lifes and landscapes of Cézanne, and *The Poet's Garden* and *The Bedroom* by van Gogh, Joan's favorite artist from the time she was six. (Intuiting that the Dutch painter's work was not intellectual enough to meet with her parents' approval, however, she kept silent about her love of van Gogh.)

Thanks to a handful of status-seeking millionaires minted in the nineteenth century, notably the Potter Palmers of the dry-goods and real estate fortune, French painting held place of honor at the Art Institute. Bertha and Potter Palmer had loaded up on Impressionist and Post-Impressionist canvases for their behemoth Lake Shore Drive castle, paintings the widowed Bertha later willed to the museum. When Joan was eight, the Annie Swan Coburn and Martin Ryerson bequests—rich in Manets, Monets, Renoirs, Morisots, and Pissarros—swelled the Art Institute's late-nineteenth-century French holdings. To be sure, one could sample Egyptian bas-reliefs, Greek nudes, Roman busts, and masterworks by El Greco and Rembrandt (along with temporary exhibitions that ran to Venetian etchings or Chinese jade), yet the museum's narrative of art history lingered along the Seine. According to Katharine Kuh, then the city's only modern art dealer, French Impressionism was "considered *very*, very advanced" in Chicago. And very wonderful. Everybody *got* Monet: like State Street or the Cubs, he was a Chicago thing.

Jimmie's preference had settled upon another late-nineteenth-century French artist, Henri de Toulouse-Lautrec, whose lithographs, oils, and drawings depict the denizens of Parisian theaters, brothels, circuses, dance halls, and *cafés-concerts*. At meetings, lectures, and concerts, Dr. Mitchell filled the margins of an agenda or the back of program notes with fluid head-and-shoulders sketches of "types" (usually male professionals, tradesmen, or musicians) in the style of the alienated figures in Lautrec's *At the Moulin de la Galette*. Small (as befit his public stance of self-deprecating amateur) and carefully observed, with a jot of satire, Jimmie's sketches amused friends and colleagues when he informally yet self-importantly exhibited them at medical conferences.

Like Toulouse-Lautrec, Jimmie also adored watercolor. On warmer Sundays when he and his daughters had tired of the Art Institute (and of their other favorite, the Field Museum), they would drive up to the Lincoln Park Zoo or out to the country, where they planted easels and did plein air painting. Joan took wild delight in the landscape, filling her mental suitcase with images of the vast loom of the American Midwest— "the cornfields that go right out to Saskatchewan and the Great Lakes"— and of Jimmie's skillful yet conventional red barns, green fields, and blue skies. Considered by the family to be shining examples of artistic accomplishment, his pictures were the model to which she aspired. Joan's own most admired painting was a Lincoln Park Zoo scene in which a cop watches over a mosaic of folks in their Sunday best who, in turn, gawk at an elephant, a lion, and two monkeys, one brazenly swinging free of its cage. Instructed perhaps to do something suitable for framing, she had ruled off a border and sketched simplified shapes before applying her colors in varying degrees of transparency and opacity, wetness and dryness, respect and disregard for the lines. For years, this painting, which is essentially about looking, hung in the Mitchells' dining room where visitors were expected to notice and admire it.

Wonderful as it was to spend Sundays making art with her father, reassuring as it was to be taught the rules at an age when one strives to paint pictures "correctly," it was also tough to have a judgmental, even arbitrary, parent who made her fear messing up. Half of Joan craved the paternal attention; the other half wanted to scream and hurl her watercolors at him. In the evenings, she fled her father's critical eye by retreating to her bedroom closet, where she painted and drew unobserved. (All her life, Joan would prefer to work at night and would consider her studio deeply private territory.) Her future colleague, artist Philip Guston, had made art in his childhood closet too, only young Guston copied comic strips, while in the Mitchell household, funny papers were strictly verboten.

The original overscheduled children, Sally and Joan Mitchell also regularly attended the symphony and the ballet and took piano, swimming, diving, and skating lessons. From Marion, they learned to play golf; from Jimmie, to shoot, ride, and jump. Instruction from their father was serious business indeed. For instance, dropping one of the rolled-up newspapers he made them wedge under their arms when they rode would earn a sharp rebuke. (Another Jimmie favorite at the Art Institute, *Equestrienne*, comes to mind. Set at Montmartre's Circus Fernando, this Toulouse-Lautrec oil sketch depicts a young female trick rider poised to stand up on her horse and leap through a paper hoop under the stern yet sexually charged eye and whip of the ringmaster.)

The riding lessons took place at Lincoln Park's fashionable Saddle and Cycle Club, the same club where Joan's schoolmate John Holabird one day observed Jimmie drumming into Joan the principles of diving: "Dr. Mitchell . . . was very pushy. And he'd just sit there watching her dive, and it wasn't recreational, as far as I could see. *At all.*" One miscalculated plunge earned Joan a long scar on her thigh, yet, as Marion reported to friends, this eight-year-old, all animal vitality, was doing marvelous handstands at the tip of the diving board and "really beautiful front and back dives and swimming like a water bug."

Thus could the Mitchells subtly lord it over the other parents when they all gathered each July at Lake Forest's Winter Club (a children's club) for Big Splash Day. Competitors to be reckoned with, Joan and

Joan, age eleven, training at the Saddle and Cycle Club pool, c. 1936

Sally would rocket from the diving board, plow through the water, then emerge from the pool, their lithe bodies lustrous and streaming, to pad over to the mothers, all crisp white linen and spectator pumps. But for Joan only the approving or disapproving look in her father's eyes truly counted. "I was . . . in my mind a list of medals or whatever for *him*": First in the Ten-Yard Dash, Winter Club Girls' Diving Champion, Girls' Racing Champion, Girls' Swimming Champion, Onwentsia Club High Point Trophy in Diving, Girls' Tennis Champion, Girls' Junior High Point Trophy, and (later) Girls' Senior High Point Trophy, and Lake Forest Girls' Tennis Champion.

Marion had started Joan at tennis when she was eight. Jimmie's snapshot that summer of his coltish younger daughter about to serve a basket of balls reveals a child looking so spent she might well wobble on those pipe stem legs, yet she accurately placed each ball or knew why not. After all, her father's love seemed to come at the price of her disciplined accomplishment. Work is more fun than play once you get started, he pontificated, needlessly in the case of his fiercely competitive trophy child, who huffed at her mother's prodding to "Just have a good time, Joanie!" "Joan didn't play," her cousin Sally Turton remembers. "Joan was on a mission."

*Jimmie Mitchell and his adoring daughters,
Joan (left) and Sally (right), ages eight and
nine, summering in Lake Forest, 1933*

Yet bravado chased fear, and fear chased bravado. Diving, in particular, scared Joan out of her wits. Every gracefully swooping lady atop a trophy gleaming in the Mitchell home had been wrenched from the cold fingers of dread. One couldn't feel courage, she reasoned, unless one was afraid, so she tried to use fear to fuel herself. Coping with challenges by attacking rather than cowering earned Joan the family nickname "Bullethead," but the word belies the emotional dishevelment of a child who was simultaneously dutiful and frightened, privileged and neglected. No one bothered with the nervous, insomniac, depression-prone "fraidy cat" behind the outta-my-way achiever.

The setting for Joan's athletic triumphs was usually Lake Forest, the Newport of the Middle West, forty minutes by rail up the coast from Chicago, where the very rich escaped the city's sweltering heat (in those days before air conditioning) by retreating to their leafy "cottages" and "farms." Although Lake Forest's Old Guard, overwhelmingly Anglo-Saxon, Republican, and Episcopalian or Presbyterian, distinguished itself less by wallowing in luxury goods than by assuming class privilege as its due, snobbery was endemic. At cocktail and garden parties, as around the pool, tennis courts, and golf course at the swanky Onwentsia Club, one clinched deals and rubbed shoulders with people whose names bespoke Chicago's vast industrial fortunes. Lake Foresters raised their daughters for finishing schools and marriage and their sons for the University of Chicago or the Ivy League, followed by successful careers in business.

In the early thirties, when they were living primarily on Jimmie's income and thus not particularly rich by Lake Forest standards, the Mitchells summered in the president's home at Lake Forest College, whose brick faculty residences were popular with the younger Gold Coast set. Jimmie's snapshots record seemingly endless sun-spangled Julys, Augusts, and early Septembers: Joan and Sally strike poses at the Winter Club pool, pedal their bikes down unpaved roads like airy leaf tunnels, or sprawl in their bathrobes on screened-in porches to devour poetry and Nancy Drew books before bed.

A proud member of both the Onwentsia Club and Highland Park's exclusive Exmoor Country Club, Jimmie, like F. Scott Fitzgerald (who, as a young man, fell in love with a Lake Forest debutante, his model for Daisy Buchanan), thought Lake Forest "the most glamorous place in the world," and, because he did, so did Joan. Born to privilege and thus careless about this midwestern grand monde, Marion, on the other hand, charmed every Lake Forester who mattered yet privately indulged in wicked commentary about the local fauna. As time went on, Joan too grew uncertain, then frankly conflicted—split right down the middle—about Lake Forest and the values it represented, antithetical in many ways to those that prevailed at Parker.

As for brawling, industrial-strength Chicago, which fried up pedestrians on its dirty summer sidewalks, froze them with Arctic blasts in winter, and deafened them under the rattling iron roof of the El, it sometimes overwhelmed Joan. Synonymous with corruption, bootlegging, rackets, and violence, the Chicago of her childhood abounded in alarming tales. Two days after her fourth birthday, for instance, hit men for crime czar Al Capone had gunned down seven members of a rival gang at a North Clark Street garage near Parker School in the St. Valentine's Day massacre. Around that same time, according to Mitchell family lore, Capone had sought treatment for his syphilis by dispatching his henchmen to the office of Dr. James Herbert Mitchell, where they slipped a black hood over the head of the moralizing physician and spirited him away to care for Public Enemy Number One.

A few months later, the stock market panic on Black Thursday, October 24, 1929, set off a chain reaction of factory shutdowns, bank failures, mortgage foreclosures, bankruptcies, and suicides. By 1933, the year Roosevelt launched the New Deal and Joan turned eight, Chicago's industrial employment had been cut in half, one in four Americans was jobless, and hundreds of thousands had gone on relief. Folks slept under bridges, stood in long breadlines, or idled on street corners in grimy, shapeless coats. From the backseat of the Mitchells' chauffeured automobile, the little girl saw and felt deeply upset.

Her own well-heeled Streeterville district stirred other apprehensions. Sometimes Joan accompanied a favorite maid named Oxie to Rush Street, where Oxie bought buttons. On the way home, from the Fourth Presbyterian Church on Michigan Avenue all the way to 190 East Chestnut, Joan would put a damper on her fear of getting lost by compulsively stepping on every crack—or no cracks at all. While Oxie's presence brought a measure of security, the child still felt she had to muster the inner resources of an explorer: "I needed [total recall] to survive . . . and I was always afraid so I learned North—South—East—West etc.—very early and didn't feel I could count on Mother."

Another cause of anxiety was the rash of kidnappings spawned by the Depression. With brazen gangs lining their purses with ransom payments, Illinois saw over four hundred abductions in 1930 and 1931, more than any other state in the nation. Wealthy parents hired Pinkertons to escort their children to school. Some, like Joan, glimpsed bogeymen everywhere.

Then, on the evening of March 1, 1932, the twenty-month-old son of aviator hero Charles Lindbergh and writer Anne Morrow Lindbergh vanished from his second-floor nursery in their Hopewell, New Jersey, home. Muddy footprints led from the baby's crib to the window, where a note demanding a $50,000 ransom was found. Sixty feet from the house lay a crude ladder. In the weeks that followed, the most intensive manhunt in U.S. history dominated the life of the nation, knocking the Japanese invasion of China from the headlines, thundering from the newsreels, and thrusting itself into even the most casual conversations.

Following this story intensely in the *Chicago Daily Tribune,* Joan flew into a panic. Located on the second floor (like that of little Charles Lindbergh Jr.), her room overlooked a back alley. Bad guys, she calculated, could easily throw up a ladder to the window, only heartbeats from her bed, and snatch her away. The knowledge that adults hovered nearby brought little reassurance: little Charlie's parents and nurse had been close at hand when he was kidnapped. Nor would the Mitchells' money do any good. The Lindberghs paid the full $50,000 the extortionists demanded, yet somebody had bashed in the child's skull and dumped his body in a woods where, seventy-three days after the disappearance, a truck driver chanced upon it, badly decomposed and half covered with debris.

The idea that she too might be abducted had acquired large and dreadful proportions in Joan's mind. Still obsessed two years after the Lindbergh tragedy, she read every news account of the grotesquely sensationalized New York custody battle over ten-year-old Gloria Vanderbilt, the beneficiary of her deceased father's $4 million trust fund. Although the Vanderbilt case was really a struggle for money and power, pitting the child's mother, socialite Gloria Morgan Vanderbilt, against her paternal aunt, sculptor Gertrude Vanderbilt Whitney, each side accused the other of kidnapping little Gloria, and at least one actual threat materialized. Joan understood the affair in terms of threat of abduction and secretly died of worry.

Fleeing her own room each night after she was put to bed and crawling in next to Sally, Joan tried to distract herself with conversation. Only too soon, however, her sister would slide away into sleep, leaving Joan sentry-boxed into the night. To quell her terrors, she imagined a book of the happiest events of her life spun into dreams, but usually that didn't work either. In her favorite real dreams, always vividly colored, birds nested in her hair; in her many nightmares, crocodiles crept toward her, she got lost in black stairwells, and the waters of Lake Michigan raged.

Joan's fear of the lake—like all fears, forbidden—had no doubt sprung in part from an incident that profoundly marked her at age three. One day as Jimmie pulled her in a sled along the ice-clogged shore, enormous inky swells ominously raising their heads and waves crashing and thundering, she had somehow pitched off and ended up in the frigid water. Her father kept on walking—he had forgotten her!—as she flailed and cried and panicked in the tumultuous icy swirl. An eternity later, he spotted her red beret and dragged her out, chattering with terror and cold but uttering not a word of complaint.

There was yet another cause for worry. One day Joan's kindergarten teacher had mentioned that the letter A on their alphabet chart was red. Joan jumped up to object: "It's not true." Every pair of eyes flew at her as if to ask, "Are you crazy?" Timorously, she sat down and clammed up. Earlier the color of A had been at issue when Joan burbled to Sally, "Don't you love the green of A?" and Sally snapped back, "I don't know what you're talking about." Thus Joan had realized that her perceptions of the world were wrong. "Because I was timid," she told a friend sixty years later, "I never again said anything [about my colored letters]."

What she was talking about was the unvarying brilliant young-fern green of the letter *A*, the only intense color in her otherwise dull name. *J*, in contrast, resembled tarnished silver. Pale metallic *O* was like the mouth of a ghostly cannon, and *N* had the dirty, brown gold prickliness of late-autumn underbrush. In other letters, certain blues—oh, what blues!—took center stage. There was blue black velvet *I*; billowing, deep-space *X*; soft blue *B*; and *D*, tinny and cerulean. Endowed with red amber translucence, *S* was the most likeable of the warm hues. *Z* approximated a grape juice stain. Joan's yellows—*C, E, M*—were mostly subdued (*E* as pale and loose as runny scrambled eggs), but *Y* leapt to the eye with the splendor of a wheat field in August. *R* was a furry pellucid black, while *H* limped along like a slow windshield wiper on an overcast Monday. All of Joan's letters had a stained-glass quality, but some held firm while others ran together, almost in puddles. Some dominated the words in which they appeared. "*S* is always red and sea has red but also a bit of green at the end, and that changes the entire word," she once tried to explain. Indeed, one can put words to Joan's letters, but to do so is to ignore the gap between her perceptions and their verbal descriptions and to disregard the fact that she not only saw but also felt color.

Moreover, musical sounds conjured multicolored, kaleidoscoping, abstract shapes, which appeared in a mental space Joan could "go to." Shiny or dull, metallic or opalescent, deep-dyed or pale, they floated, faded, squiggled, quivered, and vanished, sometimes edging off a background, itself in motion. Piano notes might stir a slow-drifting fog of burgundy and silver, a clarinet melody trigger an assault by needle-like greenish orange flares, the pounding of drums flash like blue black patent leather.

Joan did not sift such perceptions from the sum of her lived experiences. How would she know to do so? Aware at an early age that she was out of step with the rest of the world, she nonetheless at first took for granted the colored hearing she had known from birth as one takes for granted smell or taste or left-handedness. When Joan was in her mid-sixties, an interviewer asked, "Do you associate words with color?"

"No," the artist shot back, "they're made up of color. The alphabet is colored."

"What is *A*?"

"Green. Obviously."

"Why?"

"Because it is."

Apparently she remained unaware that her visual candy store was called synesthesia.

Commonly described as sensory cross-wiring in the brain, synesthesia is an involuntary neurological condition in which a stimulus to one of the senses triggers perceptions through another sense, or along another dimension. Some synesthetes see smells; others smell sights, taste shapes, or experience pain as color. The most common form of synesthesia is colored letters. Almost equally common is colored hearing, in which sounds manifest themselves as a macédoine of colors, shapes, and textures, which are not distinct from sound but rather part of what sound *is*. Fantastic though it may seem from the outside (albeit mundane from the inside), synesthesia is an unlearned, hardwired-from-birth, lifelong perceptual condition. (It is also anecdotally linked to eideticism, although hard scientific data about this connection is lacking.)

First scientifically described by George Sachs in 1812, synesthesia notably captured the imaginations of late-nineteenth-century Symbolist poets, whose holy grail was sensory unity and whose urtext was Baudelaire's "Correspondances": "Like prolonged echoes mingling far away / in a unity tenebrous and profound, / vast as the night and as the limpid day, / perfumes, sounds, and colors correspond." Not only poets but also fin-de-siècle musicians and painters explored intersensory metaphor. Seduced by the concept of synesthesia, composer Alexander Scriabin wrote *Prometheus: The Poem of Fire* for an organ that correlated colors with musical keys, and artist Wassily Kandinsky created the cross-sensory opera *Der gelbe Klang (The Yellow Sound)*. Meanwhile, in a wave of investigation that crested in the early twentieth century, psychologists studied synesthesia as a real-life mode of perception.

Then this neuro-curiosity went out of intellectual fashion, and relatively little was heard about synesthesia until the early 1990s, when neuroscientist Richard E. Cytowic published an account of the phenomenon in his book *The Man Who Tasted Shapes*. Today scientists are probing synesthesia using fMRI (functional magnetic resonance imaging) as they debate various conceptual models for its origin and function. Some investigations suggest that we are all born into a dizzying scramble of the senses that disappears around four months of age as the brain begins to differentiate among visual, auditory, gustatory, olfactory, and tactile stimuli. Current studies of synesthesia promise not only a better understanding of the phenomenon itself but also of brain development, the interaction of the senses, links between emotion and reason, and perhaps the very nature of consciousness.

Many synesthetes experience multiple forms of this condition. Given the sketchiness of Joan's testimony, it's impossible to map precisely her modes of perceptual experience. It is clear, however, that, besides colored letters and colored hearing, she had personality-color synesthesia, a phenomenon deriving entirely from the brain of the beholder in which other people induce colors that appear to synesthetes on the surface of their skin and/or clothing. "Every time I see you," Joan once told a friend, "I see gold. You're gold. But not an aura, not a halo, not a new age-y thing." (This conversation occurred when Joan was in her fifties, still struggling to understand her odd perceptions, yet having achieved self-acceptance after decades of paying a psychological price for being "crazy.") At times a person's color felt right to her; other times it seemed disconcertingly at odds with that person's name. Someone might be—literally *be*—shiny orange yet have a sooty, wind-scattered gray name.

In addition, Joan had relatively rare emotion-color synesthesia (also called emotionally mediated synesthesia), in which mental states take on, or rather *are,* certain hues. Thus color and emotion were one and the same. Hope was sun-drenched, satin-curtainy yellow. Ecstasy was blue. Loneliness was "dark green and clinging." Despair and depression showed up as silvery white, "that white metallic color, that horrible color which is not at all a color," that hoary hood slipped over her head by an invisible hand. When young Joan read in *Moby-Dick* of the "vague nameless horror" of "the whiteness of the whale that above all things appalled me," she felt a terrible jolt of recognition. Joan didn't get the blues, she got the silvery whites. (Synesthesia is thought to be the cognitive basis of metaphor, given that our rag-rug language abounds in synesthetic idioms: a cool color, a loud tie, black humor, a sharp look, a salty tongue, purple prose, a bittersweet memory, and on and on.)

Like many synesthetes, Joan struggled with both mathematics and direction. Or, rather, she avoided mathematics and struggled with direction: "I need to know where I am, to look at maps. I want to know where the north is, . . . and New York, and what street I am on." Finding her way around a new city was inevitably a challenge.

When her occasional incautious remarks (along the lines of "I hate that gray smell!") provoked ridicule from other children and puzzled concern from teachers, little Joan felt freakish and scared. Like many synesthetes, she learned at a young age not to talk about her green *A*s or her silvery white dejection. When writer Patricia Duffy realized, at six-teen, that most people did not see the world as she did, she "suddenly felt marooned on my own private island of navy blue C's, dark brown D's, sparkling green 7's, and wine-colored V's. What else did I see differently from the rest of the world? I wondered. What did the rest of the world see that I didn't?" Private islands can be lonely, uncomfortable places. Not only did Joan suffer from feelings of solitude, but also she experi-enced living as "chaos perhaps and occasionally going berserk and feeling myself alive in a terrible way." She half joked that she was a nutcase.

Thus two intertwined forms of perceptual otherness, the eidetiker's vintages of memory and the synesthete's perceptual mélange, accrued to Joan, and both operated powerfully upon her. The feeling of an *A* printed in blue rather than in the "correct" green might provoke intense irritability, the sensory glut of a full load of moving colors might tip her into a kind of seasickness. On the other hand, a person's voice or the right music could swim her to ecstasy. Her life experience abounded in unconventional associations, intense pleasures, equally intense displea-sures, and sudden insights.

Moreover, her consciousness proved exceedingly porous, which meant that dreams easily impinged upon her waking reality and that objects sometimes merged with her physical being, as if the door to her-self hung ajar and the world had come rushing in. "The divide between conscious and unconscious experience is merely a curtain," suggests one eidetic synesthete, "not a bearing wall."

Joan's psychoanalyst, Edrita Fried, framed her analysand's experi-ences in terms of defective ego boundaries. Psychiatrist Ernest Hart-mann, on the other hand, normalizes modes of perception such as Joan's by classifying personalities according to boundary width. People with thin boundaries perceive the self as vulnerable, sensitive, and fluid, he writes, and may overreact to stimuli or be at a loss to determine the limits between themselves and their surroundings. Working from yet another point of view, psychologist Akhter Ahsen argues that eideticism "involves the whole physiological system" and can bring "a strong, at times unbearable, somatic impact." A description of such boundary-lessness appears in "Torpid Smoke," a short story by eidetic synesthete Vladimir Nabokov, set in Berlin in the 1930s. One evening, as Nabokov's protagonist Grisha lay on a couch in an unlit room, he visualized now the sidewalk's surface right under his eyes (with the exhaustive accuracy of a dog's sight), now the design of bare branches against a sky still retaining some color, or else the alteration of shop windows. . . .

To move was . . . incredibly difficult; difficult, because the very form of his being had now lost all distinctive marks, all fixed boundaries. For example, the lane on the other side of the house might be his own arm, while the long skeletal cloud that stretched across the whole sky with a chill of stars in the east might be his backbone.

So young Joan sat in the bathtub feeling that her alien legs "had now lost all distinctive marks, all fixed boundaries."

Notwithstanding the extent of Joan's neurological "differences," it would be a mistake to reduce them to mental anarchy or romanticize them as an artist's mode of escape from the tyranny of rationality. They belonged to the fabric of everyday living, and she could as easily ignore them as be less than fully aware of them (as one easily filters out extraneous conversations in a noisy room). Eventually they cut close to the bone of her art. Yet, no more than other modes of cognition did they determine her art, which was also very much a matter of training, practicing, thinking, interacting with other artists, and looking at the world and at art.

Like Joan, the French synesthete Jacques Lusseyran frequently attended the symphony as a child:

At concerts for me [Lusseyran writes], the orchestra was like a painter. It flooded me with all the colors of the rainbow. If the violin came by itself, I was suddenly filled with gold and fire, and with red so bright that I could not remember having seen it on any object. When it was the oboe's turn, a clear green ran all through me, so cool that I seemed to feel the breath of night. I visited the land of music.

Sitting in Chicago's Orchestra Hall, Joan experienced intense, joyful, scintillating intersensory opulence. Maybe she assumed the lights were dimmed so that the audience could better see the swirling aurora borealis.

Music often takes me like a sea!

CHARLES BAUDELAIRE, "La Musique"

CHAPTER THREE The Lake

A stunningly handsome poet had set Mitchell family life on edge. The story is long and complex, and it must have been hazy to Joan. In that era, what was private was private, and adults did not confide in their children. But having witnessed certain scenes and half understood certain phrases, she was at least aware that her mother too had a secret life.

Marion Strobel Mitchell had met George Dillon in 1925, a few months after Joan's birth, when the University of Chicago junior took a summer job at *Poetry* and so impressed Harriet Monroe that she published his work, awarded him the Young Poet's Prize, assigned him the review of Marion's first book (which he praised), and coaxed him into the associate editorship when Marion resigned. Mentoring her inexperienced successor was reason enough for Marion's frequent lunch meetings with George, whose Persian lamb hair, silent film star eyes, full lips, soft jaw, and lean

Poet George Dillon a few years after he met Marion Strobel, 1930

swimmer's body—not to mention his sensitivity, nervousness, and impeccable southern gentleman's manners—roused her every girlish and maternal instinct. (George was twelve years her junior, and she fourteen years younger than her own grayed husband.) For giggles, as Marion put it, the two poets collaborated on a play, but George poured his real writing energies into the lyric poetry published by Viking in 1927 as *Boy in the Wind*, widely acclaimed by critics as the year's best first book of verse.

In the fall of 1928, Dillon was tapped to introduce legendary poet Edna St. Vincent Millay at a University of Chicago reading that he had helped to arrange. A tiny, incandescent figure in lustrous black silk, which dramatized her milky skin and burnished copper hair, Millay sent chills up and down listeners' spines with her melodious voice and lyrical verse. At a party afterward, she and George (fourteen years younger than Millay) felt the first stirrings of the deep passion to which they fell prey. Believing that routine and convention gnawed away at his wife's genius, her husband, Eugen Boissevain—a charmer, a fixer, her rock—indulged Edna's secret affair and understood when to make himself scarce. Marion, of course, knew all.

The Boissevains were soon reensconced at their farm in upstate New York, and the lovers saw each other infrequently, though passionate letters and sonnets flew between them. Then in 1932, the same year Marion and Jimmie celebrated their tenth wedding anniversary, George won the Guggenheim that would buy him an interlude with Vincent in Paris. No sooner had he departed Chicago than word shot over the wires that his second book, *The Flowering Stone,* had won the Pulitzer Prize for Poetry. He was the youngest person ever to receive it. A card postmarked Le Havre landed on Harriet Monroe's desk: "I'm having the time of my life!"

Glamorous author Marion Strobel Mitchell, c. 1931

For Marion, in contrast, the early 1930s were painful, both personally and professionally. Slotted as a Chicago poet, she struggled for wider recognition, yet her career had stalled. Editors and anthologizers were passing on her verse, producers rejecting her plays, and reviewers knocking her novels (rightly so: peopled with socialites, sycophants, and cads, Marion's fiction is airless and unconvincing). Moreover, a new round of health problems arrived on the heels of the publication of her third novel. One summer day she was rushed to a Lake Forest hospital for surgery to remove infected mastoid air cells behind the ears, a condition today treated with antibiotics. She lost most of her hearing, already so impaired by childhood mastoiditis that she had tried lip-reading lessons. Up and about but "feeble as a rag," she crawled back to the hospital only a week later when Joan needed an emergency tonsillectomy. (Barely out of surgery, the obstreperous child kicked up a fuss over the coarseness of the hospital sheets and the odd taste of the junket served for dessert.) Grappling with near deafness, Marion nonetheless threw on her pearls, tested an ear trumpet and a hearing aid, and, with a brisk "I don't like mentioning my no-good ears ... the darn things," returned to an active life. Joan, on the other hand, experienced panic-button alarm over her mother's hearing loss and couldn't stop brooding about "what kind of silence must be inside a deaf person." Characteristically, she pictured that silence as landscape: cold and vast January fields, icy blue shadowed crystalline drifts, twisting tourniquets of white.

A similar stillness pervades the second stanza of "Autumn," a lyric poem Joan wrote when she was ten and whose ending she would remember (more or less accurately) all her life: "Bleakness, through the trees and bushes, / Comes without sound." And "that eerie line, its mood of grieving silence—that shivering of landscape," wrote *Washington Post* art critic Paul Richard in his 1988 review of her traveling retrospective, "still haunts her abstract art."

Growing up in a home where famous poets read in the living room and volumes of Dickinson, Donne, MacLeish, Frost, Millay, Thomas, Yeats, and Eliot abounded, Joan not only wrote poetry—"a perfectly normal way to express oneself," she felt, "perfectly clear"—but read it nonstop. Like her mother, she had settled upon T. S. Eliot as her favorite poet. Marion once compared reading Eliot's *Poems* to ascending a mountain with much "perilous leaping from crag to crag" and pointed out that Eliot required "a dictionary, an encyclopedia, an imagination, and a martyr's spirit." While she did not discount the difficulties of the great poet's work, her daughter, in contrast, saw little need to wrestle meaning out of a "Prufrock" or "Hippopotamus."

Indeed, for Joan, poetry had to do with treasuring sounds (or rather sound-colors), interlacing nature and self, and experiencing language as resonant, vital, and pure. She had learned from her mother that in a good poem each word is "weighed and balanced and each phrase suggestive of so much more than appears on the surface."

Thus, when Joan wrote in "Autumn" of fields "matted with sun-tanned stalks," she would have been acutely aware of "stalks," with its ruddy *s* throwing light upon its yellow-greenish *t*, dry and angled like *l* and *k* (whose glottal crunch seized up the throat). The word would also have conjured up pictures: a spent October cornfield perhaps, half-broken shafts, a haughty hunter in pursuit of his prey. And her poem's last line—"Comes without sound"—may have brought a frisson of fear for its "sound" as well as its silence. In one Strobel novel, a character asks, "Have you ever thought of the words that frightened you as a child?" Yes, comes the reply—surely Joan's—the word "sound," for its *ow,* a cry of pain.

Joan had written,

> The rusty leaves crunch and crackle,
> Blue haze hangs from the dimmed sky,
> The fields are matted with sun-tanned stalks—
> Wind rushes by.
>
> The last red berries hang from the thorn-tree,
> The last red leaves fall to the ground.
> Bleakness, through the trees and bushes,
> Comes without sound.

The next morning Marion fired off a note to Harriet Monroe:

Dear H.M.—My infant Joan (aged ten) wrote this last night and I—with five years' experience as associate editor of THE magazine of verse—thought it good, in fact I still do! WHAT the hell—it IS good—and if you don't think so, Lady, lady, I'll be ready to cut you into small quarters and feed you to the Bandy-Bandy.

With tentative love—ST.

Incidentally the infant does not know I'm sending this to you so the murder is to be between us if there is one.

The publication of "Autumn" in the December 1935 issue of *Poetry* earned Joan a modest place in the magazine's annals as the second-youngest writer ever published and brought a generous fan letter from Dillon, who was now freelancing as an advertising copywriter in New York. Joan replied,

Dear Mr. Dillon,

I got your letter and I liked it very much. I am glad you liked my poem. I have read some of your poems too. I loved "Fall of Stars" in "A Boy in the Wind." The line . . . "The air like a great glittering tree, bloomed noiselessly with light" was one of my favorites. "Toe Ballet" reminds me of the Ballet Russe that I saw just a little while ago. Thank you for writing to me.

Love, Joan Mitchell

For Marion, the publication of her daughter's poem that December raised the curtain on a singularly eventful year. In April 1936, Charles Louis Strobel died, leaving her heiress to two-thirds of his $500,000 fortune. Days later, she won the coveted Chicago Foundation for Literature Award for Poetry. September saw the devastating loss of her mother figure, too, when Harriet Monroe, traveling in South America, succumbed to a cerebral hemorrhage. Before departing Chicago, Monroe had judged submissions to the prestigious new Oscar Blumenthal Prize and selected as its winner a group of nine lyrics by Marion Strobel—"splendid" work, raved one of her colleagues, "by far the best she has ever done ... as though she had started in all over again on a larger scale." From this pinnacle of distinction, Marion established the Harriet Monroe Prize for Poetry, naming George Dillon the sole permanent member of its panel of judges.

The "bridge money" brought a flurry of partying to 190 East Chestnut Street, where the Mitchells served up dry martinis, thick steaks, juicy gossip, and readings by poets like Robert Frost, Edna St. Vincent Millay, Carl Sandburg, Louise Bogan, May Sarton, and George Dillon. The *Poetry* crowd, the Gold Coast culturati, Jimmie's colleagues, and a handful of University of Chicago people counted among their well-heeled guests. Regulars included writer Dorothy Aldis and her husband Graham; poet and teacher Gladys Campbell; *Chicago Daily Tribune* literary critic Fanny Butcher Bokum; writer and philanthropist Inez Cunningham Stark (the angel of the Renaissance Society); novelist and dandy Arthur Meeker; poet and editor Morton Zabel; socialite "Bobsy" Goodspeed (the president of the Arts Club) and her husband Charles, a Republican stalwart; Alice Roullier (another Arts Club powerhouse and friend to artists like Alexander Calder and Fernand Léger); future Arts Club president Rue Winterbotham Shaw; and Janet and Robert McCormick Adams, who was running for Congress that year on the Republican ticket.

One of their visitors—an avuncular type with a big forehead, owlish glasses, and a lively expression—took particular notice of Sally and Joan. An adviser to *Poetry* and a visiting professor at the University of Chicago (hence, he joked, the bottles of Teacher's Highland Cream he brought as hostess gifts), Thornton Wilder, the author of *The Bridge of San Luis Rey*, would amble down the hall to read them bedtime stories.

When there were no guests, Jimmie liked to quip, "Now we are having dinner in the best society."

That June, the Mitchells decamped as usual to Lake Forest, but now they rented a tree-canopied Italianate villa with eight bedrooms, a playroom, a darkroom, a bar, a lush garden, and the oleomargarine king for a next-door neighbor. From that same home the following summer, Marion prepared for the family's three-week August vacation at the Hot Foot Dude Ranch in Wyoming as she launched the next phase of her one-woman crusade to lure George back to Chicago. His affair with Millay having nearly exhausted itself, Dillon had inexplicably shrunk back from full-blooded, self-assertive living. "Let loneliness be mute. Accuse / Only the wind for what you lose," he wrote, sounding old before he turned thirty. Millay's brother-in-law, painter Charles Ellis, was not alone in finding George "weak, queer as a three-dollar bill. . . . He was a handsome boy, a very good-looking boy. But weak all the way through." Suffering from acute writer's block, George speculated that returning to Chicago might jolt him into working again.

In a drumbeat of letters, Marion now urged him to make use of their apartment during an upcoming visit to evaluate his prospects. He demurred, but she insisted:

NOTHING is pleasanter than being of use without having to go to any trouble, *so* I most certainly shall *not* reconsider my offer. I'm delighted. I'll be perfectly honest about the whole matter—it's the only way to be after all—and tell you exactly when I wish you to leave, which will be about Sept 1st (possibly August 27th) when the decorators come in and would calcimine you if you didn't. Till then the place is yours. I won't even unshroud it. Take either Jimmie's bed or mine (Mine's best, *I* think). Oh, really, it's all so simple and so nice and I can't wait to see you.

Love, Marion

The Ford can rest under an elm outside the door. I do appreciate your offer but *please* don't make it with Joanie around or she'd probably try to drive your Ford at once and I should worry more than I do already.

George's sojourn at 190 East Chestnut that summer brought leisurely lunches tête-à-tête with Marion during her weekly excursions to the city.

Working from another angle, she had also set her fine hand to easing Morton Zabel out of the editorship of *Poetry,* which he had assumed after Monroe's death, and persuading the trustees to replace him with her young protégé. After Zabel resigned that fall to pursue a teaching career, Marion jubilantly dashed off to Adah Dillon in Richmond, Virginia, the news that her son had sewed up the job that would bring him to "his full stature." As a witty rejoinder to Adah's observation that she was George's lamp, Marion quipped—alluding to Edna St. Vincent Millay's famous line, "My candle burns at both ends"—"if I find I'm unequal to a lamp I'll try to be a candle (burning only at one end however)."

With his wife fawning over Dillon and running the show financially and certain people whispering that he owed his professional success to her social status, Jimmie was feeling jealous and emasculated. Moreover, though publicly deferential, Marion was often privately disparaging. And the two fought over sex, Jimmie demanding it, Marion refusing. In the language of the day, she was frigid. (A self-appointed authority on the male sex drive, Jimmie had once entered into discussions with publisher John Farrar about writing a sex guide for men. The book never materialized, however.)

So Jimmie held on to family authority by riding herd on his daughters. The two were expected to not only compete like boys but also, confusingly, behave like little ladies. Sally, to her credit, dressed immaculately. Joan did not, though she sometimes changed outfits several times a day in order to please her father. As time went on, rules multiplied. Elbows had to be covered. Mosquito bites were not to be scratched: a lady never touches her own body. And discipline was stern. Once Jimmie punished Joan by tying her to her bed, yet she worshipped him all the more. In fact, the Oedipal moment played itself out with such force that when Parker's psychology teacher, Alfred Adler, came for dinner he noted that Marion was "practically jealous—as if Joan had been in a, um, love affair with her father." Erasing Sally's presence during their many excursions with Paw, the ever-competitive Joan would rattle on about "my father and I . . . ," "my father and I . . . ," "my father and I . . ."

In thinking back to this era decades later, Joan identified primarily with her mother, caught in a mesh of conflicting feelings. But for now Marion took second place to Jimmie, whom Joan tried to protect when her mother made lofty remarks, even as the girl secretly wondered how much respect her father deserved. At the same time she learned to disdain men's weaknesses, to play off one against the other, and to lapse, now and again, into bitter and exaggerated submissiveness. "You do what the man wants, don't you, sweets?" the sixty-six-year-old veteran of more battles with male partners than she could remember once mordantly minced to an interviewer.

A late-life letter from Joan to Sally suggests how early family dynamics had fueled her rage:

> Do you remember . . . that Paw made us afraid (we were not supposed to be like females) candy was for women and children—elbows— oh horror—moitié cachée moitié pardonnée (half hidden-half pardoned)—meaning us—poor slobs. Well *I* realize you idealized him but really I was supposed "to run like a boy"—"had no hips"— beautiful etc. and [later] liked to fuck unlike our Mother. I wish he had been *stronger.* Well who wants to be rammed when one is sick? One can jerk off—no?

Relentlessly faultfinding—Sally was too heavy, Joan too scrawny ("no hips")—Jimmie photographed his daughters primping at the bathroom mirror or modeling their gowns before a club dance. His sometimes devastatingly negative comments about Joan's efforts to make herself attractive sealed her conviction that she was ugly. When he turned around and called her beautiful, she felt condescended to, hence her overreaction, years later, to a casual comment by writer and photographer John Gruen at a Thanksgiving party in New York: "And then [after dinner]," remembers Gruen,

> as was the custom among the young New York painters [of the early 1950s], there would be a lot of dancing, and we would put on recordings of Frank Sinatra and Ella Fitzgerald and we would dance. And I recall being mellowed probably by drink and being, what?, twenty-four years old, asking Joan to dance with me. And she did. She was a good dancer. We danced quietly. I was the more sophisticated dancer, so I would glide . . . and she was in my arms. And we glided. And she was pleasantly high, I guess. The only really poignant thing I remember about her is that during our dancing she had her

eyes sort of half closed, and we were dancing to a slow beat. A slow piece of music. And her eyes were half closed, and her head was very back. And at this moment she looked wonderful . . . and I said, "Joan, you look beautiful!" I said that to her. I remember that vividly. And she suddenly opened her eyes wide, stopped, stopped dancing, left my arms, and walked into the next room. "Oh, my God! What have I done? Now what?" Because she was so unpredictable. So, in fact, I followed her into the bedroom. And she sat down where all the coats were. On a mountain of coats. And she sat there at the edge of the bed looking down. And I said, "*What* is your problem?" She said, "First of all, I'm not beautiful." And I said, "Well, you seemed beautiful at that moment." She said, "Well, that was your imagination. I am not and don't say that to me ever again." And I said, "OK." And then she said, "And fuck you too."

Tears spilled from Joan's eyes. She refused to speak to Gruen for the rest of the night.

As for George Dillon, he edited *Poetry* until his induction into the armed forces in 1942, the same year the Mitchells celebrated their twentieth wedding anniversary. As he was wrapping up his affairs in Chicago, Marion penned for him the poignant "Bon Voyage," its long floating lines powerfully stopped short at each stanza's end:

> *That you take yourself overseas, who have taken*
> *Love from my heart, who were never my lover—*
> *The cry of love to which I awaken,*
> *The dream of love which my eyelids cover—*
> *That you take yourself overseas shouldn't grieve me:*
> *What can I lose who have nothing to lose?*
> *I knew, for me, you were gone: that you leave me*
> *Isn't news.*
>
> *I knew long ago though at many a meeting,*
> *In the place where the yellow awning obscures*
> *A table at which one loiters at eating*
> *The vivid face in the shadows was yours.*

That your boat blurs out from a widening harbour
Shouldn't alter the sky from the blue that it was,
Shouldn't strip the green from an April arbor,
As it does.

After the war, George and Marion coedited *Poetry* until 1949, when George quit Chicago for his native South. Once among the most promising voices of his generation, he had never published another book of verse, nor had he married. For the next seventeen years, letters packed literary gossip between the grand apartment in Chicago and the modest bungalow in Charleston, even as the two soulmates grew old and stodgy and sad. Both literary reputations had tumbled (as had that of Edna St. Vincent Millay, albeit from much greater heights), passions on all sides had flamed out (Millay died in 1950), and the Mitchells' marriage had survived. For their wedding anniversary in 1947, Marion had written "To James," a wry poetic self-congratulation at the "long and lovely thought of five-and-twenty years all lit by flames / Five-and-twenty years in one four-poster, *Here's to James.*" Jimmie treasured her gift as he did his 1933 award naming him Chicago's "best progressive father of the year."

Besides writing poetry, twelve-year-old Joan had begun drawing upon her prodigious powers of observation and recollection in prose vignettes with an American Scene flavor. "The Inn" was among those published in Parker's literary annual:

The day was hot and sultry and the smell of fish hung heavily around a small inn with a meandering river beyond . . . The sound of a motor disturbed the stillness, followed by the grating of wheels stopping on the gravel road. A hard looking woman stepped upon the well worn doorstep. She had a great deal of make up on and had her hair slicked back from her forehead with Brilliantine. Her eyebrows were plucked and she wore French heels. A very cheap fancy dress adorned her slim figure and a small hat was perched on the back of her head. Her heels clicked over the unpolished floor and her gleaming ruby nails clicked impatiently on the counter . . . [This provincial Mae West then bought some soda-pop and gum from a testy old clerk.] When she had finished the Coca-Cola, she tore open the package of gum and popped a piece into her mouth and chewed on it savagely. She clambered into her car and drove quickly onto the road.

Never a good storyteller, Joan nonetheless excelled at the kind of visual language that also enlivens her "Street Scene," in which Chicago businessmen with "beet red noses"—literary versions of the characters in Jimmie's sketches—stride through the Loop in snow-dusted coats and "tall apartment houses were leaning forward and almost touching the others across the street, there was such a narrow ribbon of sky between."

Marion beamed at her daughter's most recent accomplishments, while, curiously, Jimmie expressed concern. Though he was a Renaissance man himself, he again wielded the old saw "Jack of all trades, master of none," warning his wunderkind that one did not "diddle with things" and instructing her to choose between writing and painting. Behaviorist John B. Watson saw "no reason why a boy shouldn't pick out his career at the age of 12 or earlier," and so should Joan.

Hit with this paternal fiat to decide upon her life's work, Joan felt "pressure to become, quote, a professional." "I've got to be something," she fretted. "What is it? It's going to be either painting or writing, and it can't be both. I mean, Jack of all trades, master of none." So it was painting. But Jimmie retorted, "You can't draw! How can you be an artist? You can't draw!"

Such peremptoriness would turn many twelve-year-olds into self-pitiers or rebels, but not Joan; nor did she later drift from painting into something else but lived the rest of her life by the decision her father demanded. He was talking career, however, and, to Joan, painting as a career would sometimes seem a bust: "a solitary arrangement and without the chicken in the pot at the end of the day—queer kind of life." On the other hand, painting as a way of being would prove indispensable. It beguiled her, solaced her, and literally kept her alive.

Joan had made her decision against the backdrop of Chicago art of the Depression era, an undigested mix of towering ambition, complacent sentimentalism, Francophilia, provincialism, North Side salons, South Side saloons, eccentric individualism, and WPA politics. At the School of the Art Institute, the Regionalism of Grant Wood, John Steuart Curry, and Thomas Hart Benton—a vigorous rendition of rural life larded with nostalgia for a simpler past—served as the house style. Egalitarian in both its subject matter and its easy appeal, Regionalism proved immensely popular too with Chicago audiences. Meanwhile, the city's most powerful critic, Eleanor Jewett of the *Chicago Daily Tribune,* an acquaintance of Marion's since their Chicago Latin days, was dismissing not only Regionalist painting and other vital work emerging from local studios but also European modernism. An agriculture major in college who owed her job to the fact that she was the cousin of the *Tribune*'s publisher, Jewett waxed poetic over the beauty of academic art while labeling van Gogh, Gauguin, and Cézanne "brutal, primitive, and childish." On the day they hung her in effigy, School of the Art Institute students brandished signs reading "Nervous Hysteria Is Not Art Criticism."

More than its artists and critics, its great art was the major advantage of growing up in Chicago rather than, say, Bismarck or Peoria. In 1933, the Art Institute had presented the Century of Progress Exhibition, a seven-century chronology that filled forty-one galleries and, for the first time, admitted the School of Paris to its narrative of art history. Picasso and Duchamp in the Grand Staircase, no less! Even more consequential to Joan was the first major U.S. exhibition of the work of Vincent van Gogh, which opened at the Art Institute in August 1936. As intoxicated by van Gogh's colors as he had been by the colors of the South of France, she lit into her first serious oil paintings — "violent" pictures. "All those reds and yellows!"

If the Art Institute was cautiously moving in the direction of European modernism, the Renaissance Society and the Arts Club regularly presented dazzling and controversial vanguard art. Founded in 1915, the University of Chicago's Renaissance Society had remained true to its mission of encouraging and promoting understanding of the avant-garde. As for the Arts Club, it had transcended its original swank tea-party style to focus on literature, drama, dance, painting, film, and sculpture unavailable elsewhere in Chicago. Buckminster Fuller lectured on Dymaxion design, Léger presented his *Ballet mécanique,* Martha Graham danced, and the work of Braque, Calder, Hartley, Chagall, Noguchi, Dalí, Picasso, and Gorky made its debut in the Midwest or, in some cases, the United States.

Joan was no stranger to either venue. At the Arts Club she would be powerfully impressed by Picasso's *Guernica,* which was touring the United States to raise funds for Spanish Civil War refugees. (Two years before viewing this impassioned response to the Fascist bombing of a Basque village, Joan had written a compassionate short story about the final hours of a Chinese orphan killed in the savage Japanese bombing of Shanghai.) She was no less overwhelmed by the abstract sculpture of Constantin Brancusi, shown at the University of Chicago's Goodspeed Hall.

Occasionally Joan and Marion walked up Michigan Avenue from the Arts Club's Wrigley Building quarters to Chicago's third venue for modern art, the Katharine Kuh Gallery, electric with the work of Klee, Kandinsky, Léger, Nolde, Tamayo, Le Corbusier, Noguchi, Albers, Picasso, and Miró (whom the *Tribune*'s Eleanor Jewett once accused of framing and exhibiting a used desk blotter). A one-woman outpost of advanced art, the Kuh Gallery fought at the front lines of Chicago's battle over modernism: philistines smashed its windows, and the Society for Sanity in Art (founded by clubwoman Josephine Logan, with Jewett's endorsement, to combat "the menace" of abstraction) kept the gallery in its crosshairs. From a distance, Joan worshipped Kuh, a polio survivor, recent divorcée, and fiercely independent intelligence.

The child was better acquainted with another target of the art vigilantes, painter Hubert C. Ropp. The Mitchells' close friendship with Ropp's patrons, the Aldis family, gave Joan entrée to the private, supposedly adults-only classes at the Ropp School, held each summer at the Aldises' lively Lake Forest compound. Ropp encouraged his students not to copy but rather to interpret their subjects in a semiabstract or surrealistic style. Struggling at her easel planted under the Aldises' venerable oaks during the summer after seventh grade, Joan experimented with new visual ideas while gaining an "in" at the School of the Art Institute, where Ropp was about to assume the powerful deanship.

Parker too figured prominently in Joan's early art education. In 1938, a group of juniors launched the Mezzanine Gallery to showcase contemporary Chicago art, and, though she was only a freshman, Joan got herself into the act. In one snapshot, this skinny bobbysoxer in her regulation Marshall Field sweater and skirt and her saddle shoes from A. G. Spalding hangs a show with a trio of schoolmates, looking as if she might break into a little jitterbug of happiness.

The Mezzanine Gallery had opened that spring with a dozen paintings and drawings by Chicago artist Aaron Bohrod, richly anecdotal, slightly screwball depictions of ordinary street corners, tenement blocks, and derelict farms. Bohrod had studied at New York's Art Students League with Ashcan School artist John Sloan, who sought freedom from European conventions by painting what was real in everyday life. Then

Bohrod returned to his native city resolved to "do for Chicago what Sloan had done for New York." Identified with the Regionalists, Bohrod approached art as neither a vehicle for self-expression nor a means of formal experimentation but rather a site of shared human experience. In a talk at Parker, the artist focused on his methods, explaining how he inlaid his fuzzy gouache washes with precisely rendered figures and dabbed his oils with fire-engine reds and neon magentas to make them sing.

Joan's encounter with Bohrod's art offered her yet another point of entry into painting. Her own exhibition at Parker shortly thereafter, of works on paper using casein (a fast-drying medium similar to gouache), depicted, Bohrod style, the Midwest-plain Main Streets and Elm Streets of Chicago's blue-collar suburbs. Her paintings, like his, emphasized her subjects' small-town qualities, yet, filled with the gnarled trees and curdled skies of adolescent expressionism, lacked the older artist's tongue-in-cheek humor. Setting for herself the daunting task of representing staircases, railroad tracks, awnings, fences, jalopies, and buildings at various angles, Joan painted awkwardly and got the perspective wrong

Bobbysoxer Joan Mitchell (right) at Parker's Mezzanine Gallery, c. 1938

yet pulled off complex compositions that allowed no dead space. For the show, her paintings were expensively matted and framed in pale varnished wood, another token of her parents' and her own vaulting ambition. When one sold, she swelled with pride.

Her earnest striving notwithstanding, Joanie was no grind. In the eighth grade, this blur of lithe limbs distinguished herself by either falling or jumping down a manhole. Boys wanted to hang out with her. "I loved the way she looked," remembers John Holabird of the plucky tomboy three years behind him at Parker. "She was just fun to be with and fun to see." With her big brown eyes and tawny pageboy blending into flawless milk-with-coffee skin, Joan was, in truth, attractive. And coyly flirtatious: "Seventh and eighth grade girls like to tease high school boys, so she was teased back," continues Holabird. But, speaking for other classmates, Connie Joerns characterizes Joan's wry humor as camouflage for an "aggressive, masculine quality. She could be charming, but even if she was putting on the charm, you were always on your guard."

That Joan, the one you wanted to pick up with tweezers, dominates a color picture splashed across the society page of one Sunday's *Herald and Examiner.* "Five little sub-debs all in a row," begins its caption in jump rope cadence, "taking their ease and a sun bath at the same time, after a swim in the pool up at Saddle and Cycle Club." From their deck chairs lined up on the left, Sally Mitchell and three Chicago Latin pals, young matrons in their flowered sundresses and heavy saddle shoes, uneasily half turn toward the slouching little glamour-puss, all attitude in her striped frock and poppy-red lips, all scornful insolence behind the baby starlet sunglasses.

Yet this same twelve-year-old charmed all who read Marion's 1937 poem "Joan":

> *Joan, in a dream, has said, "I think"—*
> *Lifted her cup and forgotten to drink.*
>
> *Joan, in a dream, is sliding up*
> *The silver side of her cocoa cup.*
> *What does she see from over the dim*
> *Curve of her lips and a silver rim?*
> *Where does she go? . . . If I do not stir,*
> *I, who am old, may follow her.*

"I think," she says, and her parted lips
Open a door, and her breathing dips
Over a hill and into a glade
Against the moss where flower and blade
Are clipped apart by sun and shade.

"I think," she says, and her lowered hand
Has opened wide the hidden door
Into the lost and silver land—

"I like this cocoa. I want more."

More cocoa, yes. But also *more*—more of what matters and cannot be named.

In Marion's poem, Joan slips, like lyric poetry itself, from mundane living to "the lost and silver land," and back again. That interiority also set her apart. Schoolmates knew her, said one, only "as well as you could know Joan. I'm not sure that anyone could know her. I think she was very introverted." Another, typically, wasn't "close enough to Joan to [gain an] . . . understanding of what made her tick." Whether joking around, speaking seriously, or dismissing others with barbed-wire brusqueness, she remained chary and guarded.

Moreover, one wrong turn and that "lost and silver land" became a bewildering swamp. Unable to take for granted, get rid of, or comprehend her perceptual differences, despairing at her inarticulateness, and frequently overwhelmed by adolescent angst, Joan cast about for who she really was. What was hers was *hers* in a fiercely territorial way. (No wonder she was wild about Gershwin's "They Can't Take That Away from Me.") But what was hers? She liked to stick it to snobs yet acted like a snob; she fiercely valued honesty yet felt fraudulent, especially with her parents, who loved her—or not—but wouldn't if they really knew her. She would sum up her youth in terms of discontinuities: "I was very competitive, very afraid, very isolated, very bright."

In September 1938, Joan entered the upper division at Francis W. Parker School. Her intelligence, competitiveness, and conscientious study habits (she was a meticulous note taker) made her a first-rate student, though

"Five little sub-debs all in a row" at the Saddle and Cycle Club: Carol Blossom, Barbara McNulty, Sally Mitchell, Mary Cornelia Aldis, and (far right) Joan (aka Bullethead), c. 1938

she could never shake the feeling that she wasn't working hard enough. Jimmie kept pushing. In that era, Parker issued written evaluations rather than letter grades, a practice so frustrating to Joan's father that he hounded teachers and administrators until finally they placated him by sending home grades for her alone.

On the sports field, as in the classroom and the art studio, Joan spared no effort. A crack softball player who made merciless "irritated-at-the-uncoordinated-slob" faces when a teammate flubbed the ball, she was also skilled enough at field hockey (she played center and wing) to win berths on the All-Chicago Girls' Team in her junior and senior years. These brought regular afterschool practices in Jackson Park, on the South Side, and an important Thanksgiving Day championship match at Northwestern's Dyche Stadium. But, more than team sports, individual competition, with its requisite self-reliance, appealed to Joan, and, in the 1930s, no athletic endeavor appeared more deserving of a young woman's attention than figure skating.

Skating's rise in popularity had begun at the 1924 Olympics, where the Norwegian Sonja Henie shortened the traditional ankle-length dress, substituted white skates for black, and replaced simple acrobatics, then standard fare in a free-skating program, with a rousing sequence of jumps, twirls, spins, rockers, and counters choreographed like ballet.

Having reinvented her sport, Henie went on to win three Olympic gold medals and a decade's worth of world championships. After she skated the "Dance of the Dying Swan" before a 1934 Chicago audience of eighteen thousand, no doubt including the Mitchells, the ranks of midwestern skaters swelled with little misses yearning to be ice princesses. While girls' athletics remained controversial (mainly on grounds of potential harm to the reproductive organs), smart Chicago looked favorably upon this half sport/half art that demanded grace, spotlighted beautiful bodies, and inspired glamorous attire. In 1936, a Streeterville riding academy was transformed into the Chicago Arena, a state-of-the-art indoor rink for the Figure Skating Club of Chicago, which thereby gained the wherewithal to train champions.

Having first put blades to ice as tots at their Lake Shore Drive playground, Joan and Sally were already longtime members of the Figure Skating Club. With the opening of the arena, the family went gangbusters: the girls drilled their school figures and passed one after another USFSA proficiency test; Marion joined the ranks of skating mothers (a subset of stage mothers); and Jimmie underwrote the club's trophies and documented its every event using 8 mm film, lantern slides, and black-and-white photographs. He worked the edge of the rink at the jubilee ice show in which Joan and Sally came whizzing out of the gates of Old Fort Dearborn and into a marvelous pair; at the winter carnival where Joan soloed, then linked up with Sally for a pair; and at the next winter carnival, in which an elaborate Snow White and the Seven Dwarfs routine featured one hundred tykes on skates and Joan in the unlikely role of Snow White. One Jimmie Mitchell shot of his spinning daughters, stony-faced and stagy in heavy lipstick, Dietrich brows, and bellhop outfits, made the pages of a big Chicago daily, whose readers learned that the "little girls have such fun in the Chicago Arena."

Participation in benefits and ice follies was expected of the club's best, but Joan had not gone into skating for the powder puff numbers. Fiercely determined to become a great skater, she rolled out of bed at five o'clock each weekday morning, drove with her father through the predawn streets, and opened up the arena, flicking its switch to floodlight the vast milk-blue rink. (How many skaters were entrusted with the key to the Chicago Arena? The Mitchells had pull.) She would put on and lace up her skates, her eyes, in Marion's words, going "remote like a musician's tuning a stringed instrument," then, with a snap of her skate guards and flash of her blades, launch herself onto the ice and begin warming up. She arrived earlier and trained harder (both with Jimmie and a series of top coaches) than did any of her rivals and made damn sure she got perfect ice.

Surprisingly, Joan lacked balance and coordination. Muscular yet slightly pigeon-toed and occasionally clumsy (she was capable of tripping on her way across an empty room), Joan was "a marvelous athlete, but not the skating kind of athlete," thought one schoolmate. "That takes balance. A great ballerina could become a great skater if she had the strength. But not Joan. She could have been a great hockey player. Skating was against every rule of her body." Quitting, however, was against every rule of her mind. What she lacked in natural ability, Joan made up for in hard work, self-discipline, and nerve, the same tools she would use to offset her lack of native talent in drawing. At times, her synesthetic experience of sensory overload—the simultaneous movement, music, rumble of the crowd, and glare at center ice—added to her problems; other times, the sensory-motor-aural dynamism of skating brought surrender to a feeling of absolute rightness.

Watching Joan perform, one family friend had an epiphany: skating could be something more than he had ever imagined. He was not alone. Many saw in her muscular elegance on ice a specialness that meant she was on her way to something important. Wrote one *Chicago Daily Tribune* reporter, "Chicagoans often [watch Joan] floating over the ice of the Arena like a butterfly over a poppy field—making incredibly beautiful swoops."

In the first championships ever held at the Chicago Arena, thirteen-year-old Joan made short work of skaters with twice her experience to take home the Senior Ladies' trophy. But she was only warming up: the following January she pulled down second place in the junior division of the Midwest Regionals in Cleveland, and, two weeks later, fifth among novices at the U.S. championships in St. Paul, Minnesota.

For the finest coaching, Joan and Marion traveled that summer to the famous figure skating school at Lake Placid, New York. Staying at the tony Lake Placid Club, they plunged into ten weeks of training (Marion gamely skated too) in the Olympic Arena, where Joan worked with the legendary Gustave Lussi. A Swiss ex–ski jumper who was arguably the world's foremost skating coach, Lussi conceived of skating as physics, taking moves apart to improve them and singling out spinning as the essence of the skater's art. What's a jump, after all, but a spin in the air? His method focused on leading with the core of the body rather than with an extremity. Moreover, Lussi insisted that every move be deliberate—nothing hit-or-miss. Deliberate and gutsy and beautiful. "Do the best that you can every time," he would urge. Like Henie, he transformed the sport itself: in 1948, Lussi student Dick Button would successfully execute a double axel for the first time in competition, thereby ushering in the era of technically advanced skating in which Dorothy Hamill and many other Lussi-trained champions would shine.

Opening its doors at dawn, the Olympic Arena was quickly aswirl in skaters punishing the ice with spins and jumps or dancing to jazz piped in over loudspeakers. Serious skaters like Joan put in five patch sessions a day, worked with Lussi in the "bull pen," squeezed in a demonstration or lecture, and occasionally relaxed at Little Alps, Gus's camp in the Adirondacks. Always they hit the sack early, "courting their nine hours of sleep with the tender regularity of counting a rosary."

Besides skating, Marion took advantage of her long weeks in Lake Placid to dream up murder mysteries set in the skating world. Two were eventually published. Marion's signature character is natty detective A. Lincoln Lacy, but the real protagonist of *Ice Before Killing* is Chicago skater Liz Soames, "who had had tough luck in the Nationals," and of *Kiss and Kill,* Nina Alexander, a sportswoman vacationing at the Adirondack Club, both based on Joan. Well aware that her opinionated daughter would find fault with the way in which she was portrayed, Marion preempted their arguments by making Joan promise, in advance of publication, never to read the two books, a promise Joan characteristically kept, even after her mother's death.

Back in Chicago to start tenth grade, Joan ramped up her commitment to her sport, adding pair skating with Bobby Specht, the friendly, dimpled Nordic-looking son of a Wisconsin dentist. In his first major competition, the men's novices at the 1938 Nationals, Bobby had won third place with the most difficult free-skating program in anyone's memory. The following year he took the novice gold, and, shortly after linking up with Joan, captured the U.S. men's junior crown. That the rising star of American men's figure skating would choose Joan as his partner is one measure of her excellence.

Not only is pair skating one of the rare sports in which men and women compete together, but it is also arguably the most demanding and dangerous of the figure skating disciplines. Whipping around at hazardously close range, partners draw upon stores of power, speed, grace, balance, timing, and trust as they mix mirror skating, shadow skating, and individual maneuvers, among them the crowd-pleasing death spiral in which the arching woman orbits the man at breakneck speed.

Despite their intense training, new partners Mitchell and Specht did not place at the 1940 U.S. Championships. Worse, Joan fared no better than tenth in the junior division. She would have ranked much higher, however, had not one judge knocked her out of contention for a top spot: her scores were 10, 8, 10, 10, and 5 — "tough luck in the Nationals." (On the other hand, she was featured in *Skating* magazine's fashion column for the severely cut pale blue crepe dress she wore in the singles and the red-lined white satin number with matching tiny red cap with which she turned eyes in the pairs.) Training in Canada that July and August, Joan redoubled her efforts.

They paid off. She performed brilliantly at the 1941 Midwesterns in Cleveland, missing the women's crown by a razor's edge. In the pairs, she and Bobby trounced a local couple with a gutsy routine that captured the lyricism of the music and achieved a beautiful line. "To Bobby Specht and Joan Mitchell, goes acclaim for their superb Senior Pair number," raved the head of the Cleveland club. "It was a beaut!"

At the Nationals in Boston two weeks later, however, they faltered. Joan failed to place, Bobby fell short of a grand slam (novice-junior-senior in three years) because of an infected ankle, and two Angelenos skimmed to first in the pairs. The contest for second then shifted into a battle between Mitchell-Specht and Vaeth-Might. The Chicagoans hit the ice like a wildfire and, with Bobby skating through the pain and the crowd roaring, put in a performance blazing with daring and fight — yet slightly off. They left town bearing third-place trophies.

The previous summer, the Mitchells had moved from their East Chestnut Street apartment to a co-op on North State Parkway, a short, leafy avenue more tranquil than its name suggests. Lined by Richardson Romanesque mansions like portly old gentlemen cheek by jowl, North State Parkway was anchored at its Lincoln Park end by the splendid Queen Anne residence of the Roman Catholic cardinal of Chicago. Diagonally across the street stood the fifteen-story Beaux-Arts building at 1530, a world of stability, order, and politesse where the distinguished architect David Adler occupied the sixth floor and the Mitchells had purchased the tenth.

Before decorating, Marion had the spacious public rooms coffered in dark wood, adding to the apartment's rarefied, old-money atmosphere. In the living room, artfully placed silver bowls caught the late-afternoon light; in the library, expensively bound volumes stood at attention in floor-to-ceiling bookshelves. Most impressive to visiting classmates and Jimmie's relatives from the suburbs, the front elevator opened directly into the foyer, where the Mitchells' Irish American maid, Nellie, or her husband, their butler and chauffeur, stood at the ready—"just like in the movies!", as some guests put it.

Cousin Sally Turton still remembers herself as a girl stepping saucer-eyed out of that elevator for a luncheon visit one day with her mother, grandmother, and aunt. Intimidated by the sight of the dining-room

Pairs champions Joan Mitchell and Bobby Specht on the ice, c. 1940

table gleaming with fine china, crystal, and silver, she had finally relaxed to the point of feeling sophisticated as she sipped ice water from a long-stemmed goblet when Joan flew through the room, ignoring her parents' guests in a mad dash for the elevator. Startled, Sally missed her mouth, and the water plopped into her lap. No one noticed, yet she was mortified. Would they think she had wet her pants? Surreptitiously she channeled the liquid onto the Persian carpet.

Neither Persian carpet nor any other superfluity adorned Joan's bedroom, however, so Spartan and unorganized that it looked like a storeroom for odd pieces of furniture. Yet it possessed a luxury rare in the metropolis: its own small balcony. From this aerie, Joan spent long hours contemplating the city and sky, marvels of spatial complexity and fugacious color and light.

Decades later, a conversation among three painter friends turned to the topic of their first deeply felt art experiences. Hard-edge abstractionist Shirley Jaffe spoke of the stenciled wallpaper in her childhood home in Brooklyn, while Zuka Mitelberg, whose paintings frequently enlist history and myth, remembered an icon of St. Michael and the Dragon at the Russian Orthodox church she had attended as a girl. Joan said: the Chicago sky from my balcony. In a sense, she would spend the rest of her life painting that panorama.

Lake Michigan was visible too, just barely, but she could feel it in the quality of the light. The windows and terrace at the front of the apartment, on the other hand, commanded magnificent views of the lake, interrupted near its shore by a breakwater, a flattened backwards C. Lincoln Park stretched far to the north, the jumble of downtown Chicago filled the view to the south. "Damn beautiful city all below"—as Joan once put it—"and clouds running against the birds." As for the lake, it "looked vast. No, infinite. Bleak. In winter it was icy, broken ice. Sometimes it's very blue. It has a lot of quality to it. It's changing, alive. Not just a dull body of water. Even summers, it's very dangerous." Often she set up an easel on the front terrace and painted the lake.

Lake Michigan had been present at East Chestnut Street too: to walk east on Chestnut and across Lake Shore Drive (not yet the thunderous highway that swallowed up half the beach) had been to wriggle out of Chicago and into a primal place of blasting winds and furious whippings of spray. Now, from her perch on the tenth floor at North State Parkway, Joan became an eye in the sky. She watched rain clobber the lake, ice lock it up, thunderheads billow above it, storms as fast moving as freight trains speed across it. It shimmered, turquoise and sapphire like a tropical lagoon, or pulsed with dark ochre along its edges, or withdrew behind enormous curtains of gray. At night, the lake might fold itself up like a length of black velvet upon which was laid out a twinkling string of far-distant Indiana towns. It both delighted and scared her.

With so many pictures of Lake Michigan stamped on her brain, Joan would never be without it. "The Lake is with me today," she would assert, years after leaving Chicago. "The memory of a feeling. And when I feel that thing, I want to paint it." Indeed, every painting she ever did began with Lake Michigan.

I remember the yellow cornfields ... Saugatuck
in summer ... oaks ... dark birches ... wild
pines ... Those things cohere.

JOAN MITCHELL

CHAPTER FOUR   War and Peace

On Saturday mornings when she wasn't competing, Joan would
meet a group of girlfriends downtown for lunch, followed by an
early matinee. On Saturday nights, she and Sally double-dated
brothers Milton and Malcolm Hughes. And at Parker, she was forever
charging across Clark Street to the Belden drugstore for gossip, chocolate Cokes, and cigarettes, so loving her weeds that the school newspaper's waggish "Rumor Humor" columnist assigned her the theme song
(a variant on the popular show tune) "Smoke Gets in My Eyes." All
the same, Joan kept slightly apart. Wanting to give skating and painting her all, she passed on the plays, school newspaper activities, and
political clubs that dominated extracurricular life. Because of skating,
she missed so much school in her junior and senior years that Parker
considered expelling her. Her contemptuous attitude toward teachers she judged ineffectual also came up in faculty discussions of Joan's

case—"contemptuous or frightened," clarifies a schoolmate—but she had her defenders, and, in the end, she was permitted to stay. Her fellow students perceived Joan as "bright, poignant, witty, subtle" and "marching to her own drummer."

Less subtly, she was gleefully shocking her parents and their friends by flinging around words like "fuck," "piss," "damn," "penis," and her favorite, "balls," this last earning Sally's nickname for her, "J. Balls." In that era such longshoreman's language from the mouths of sub-debutantes was nothing short of scandalous. (Consider that after Lillian Smith's 1944 best seller about interracial marriage, *Strange Fruit,* was banned for obscenity in Massachusetts—one character uses the word "fucking"—its publishers' legal challenge collapsed when their attorney could not bring himself to put the offending word in a brief or pronounce it in court.)

More serious disagreements had also begun to roil Mitchell family life. Her staunchly conservative father infuriated Joan by fulminating against Roosevelt and all liberals, clipping editorials from the then right-wing *Chicago Daily Tribune* and leaving them on her pillow. A Jew-hater too, he fumed over the fact that Parker had become a magnet for Jewish students. Moreover, he forbade his daughters to ride the bus to school since that would mean mixing with Negroes. Even by the unenlightened standards of 1940s Chicago, Jimmie Mitchell had a reputation as a fierce bigot. Marion was more discreetly racist and anti-Semitic. In one of her novels, however, a character muses that all intelligent Jews have the makings of psychoanalysts, versed as they are in "the unusual, the devious, the elusive." In another, her murder victim is an aging rink rat with "eyes with an oriental slant," "a wolf's nose," "dark-skinned hands," and a stocky frame emitting an "animal odor."

Her father's rancor over her beloved Parker was particularly hurtful to Joan. Waspy and solvent in the 1920s, the school had hit hard times when its founder scaled back her support and enrollment plummeted during the Depression. Doubly motivated by pragmatism and principle, Parker began recruiting more widely, and, by the mid-1930s, half the student body was Jewish. Joan's schoolmate, thirteen-year-old John Holabird, encountered Dr. Mitchell's indignation about Jews at Parker when he consulted the physician for boils. In the midst of issuing instructions about hot compresses and poultices of gentian violet, the doctor abruptly leaned over the young man and peevishly asked, "Isn't it hard to be at Parker with all those Jews?" Unnerved at the time, John could not bring himself to mention the incident to Joan until many years later. Her clipped response: "That's impossible." All her life, Joan would repudiate racism and anti-Semitism (though some mistook her blunt political incorrectness for just that) and delight in raking racists and anti-Semites over the coals. But by the time her former schoolmate opened up to her, she preferred, all things considered, not to rock the pedestal upon which she had placed her father. A gracious man, Holabird tells this story with a bemused wince, as if the memory of Jimmie and Joan Mitchell still provokes mild heartburn, a reaction not unlike that of Joan's later best friend Zuka Mitelberg, who perceived "a flaw in that family. There was really something wrong in that family. It was like a gene in them. Of hatred. And they were all wonderful charmers."

Not only had Parker recruited Jewish students, but also it had hired Jewish teachers, some of them refugees from Nazi Europe, like Joan's new French teacher, Helen Richard.

Having fled their native Austria, Helen and her husband, Edgar, a science teacher, had landed in Massachusetts, from where they were recruited to Parker. The minute they arrived, they knew they belonged, the institution's ethos of intellectual rigor and strong-minded individualism a perfect match for theirs.

A tiny (five-foot-two) actress manquée, Helen Richard, affectionately known as Madamie, leavened her demand for excellence with a bubbly *joie de vivre*. If the vocabulary word was "*balayer*," she swung an imaginary broom; if the lesson was the Moulin Rouge, she picked up her skirts and cancanned across the classroom, even though she had just given birth to twins. Parkerites adored her, not least Joan.

Speaking French was part of her Francophile father's agenda for Joan, but she too gravitated to the language of Verlaine and Proust, even though she had to wrestle with languages (she was also taking Latin), in part because the color cues that worked for her in English lapsed in other tongues. Her French "*bleu*," for instance, was less intensely blue, less alive, than her English "blue." Blueness inhered not only in the sound of the first letter (Joan's *b* was the color of a gas flame) but also in the concept, and thus the Frenchness of "*bleu*" turned the English word's energized hue into something moody and hermetic. The entire French language, in fact, proved slightly amiss, as if, expecting something sweet, Joan had chomped down on something salty instead and had to turn it over on her tongue in order to detect its true flavor.

Such difficulties aside, Joan delighted in Madamie's enthusiasm for all things French, literary, and avant-garde. Thus writer André Gide, the subject of Richard's doctoral dissertation at the Sorbonne, came to Joan's attention. Gide makes a strong case for seeking the authentic self, mistrusting received ideas, and staying open to life's possibilities; he lays out the concept of the gratuitous act, the act, if such exists, unfettered by rationality and self-interest. How could such ideas, utterly foreign to the way in which she was raised, fail to impress the adolescent?

As much as Gide, Freud was an intellectual hero to Joan's Viennese émigré teacher. Unfamiliar to the Chicagoan on the street (the idea of a talking cure, so patently un-midwestern), psychoanalysis had nonetheless secured a place in psychiatric practice and attracted the attention of the intelligentsia. A star student in Alfred Adler's advanced psychology class, Joan was familiar with Freud's theories, yet Helen Richard may have been the first to bring them to bear on the adolescent's own inner turmoil. Joan realized that her demons could be disempowered and hidden meanings wrested from life. Psychoanalysis was not self-indulgence but rather a form of authenticity, even heroism.

Madamie's empathy and understanding also proved a godsend. This first of her surrogate mothers spoke with her unpuritanically about boys, moods, sex, and parents. At home, Marion accused Joan of having B.O. and of lying about her hygiene; Madamie had a European matter-of-factness about the body. Marion instructed Joan to inquire politely about people's ailments, whether she cared or not; Madamie made no bones about her horror of falseness.

Nor did Joan, who refused to tell the little lies that serve as social glue. She also regularly knocked her teachers when they tried to tell her what to think or when she simply wanted to "get their goats." Many still felt she should be expelled.

Not Madamie. "Joanie was magnificent—and arrogant," Helen Richard recalled half a century later. "We had a wonderful relationship. I loved her very much." Richard was speaking to her son, *Washington Post* art critic Paul Richard, who had recently met sixty-three-year-old Mitchell at a reception for her exhibition at the Corcoran Gallery of Art. When he told the artist who he was, she burst into tears—in the midst of the crowd—gasping, "Your mother saved my life! She taught me passion—I really mean that."

Another new addition to Parker's faculty, artist Malcolm Hackett, also taught passion. The kind of man adults tag as ersatz but adolescents worship, Hackett "held court" in the art room, where he opened "vast visions to the few of us who listened," according to Joan, who had a huge crush on her teacher. She was not alone. "Oh, Christ! Malcolm Hackett!" offers painter Herbert Katzman, who studied with Hackett from age eleven. "I would have traded forty of my fathers for one Malcolm Hackett!"

The Hackett mystique began with his tales of dropping out of the University of Wisconsin and knocking around South America for seven years, an adventure capped with a pilgrimage to Gauguin's Tahiti, where the locals had supposedly offered him their virgin daughters. Back in Illinois, he had earned a degree from the School of the Art Institute, then taught here and there while daubing buttery nudes and earnest landscapes for the WPA easel project. At Parker, he played the role of perennial malcontent, scorning all but a few of the "mollycoddled" students and boycotting faculty meetings on grounds they were nothing but hot air.

A big man with a shock of slate-gray hair, wiry brows, a rugged face, and an oversized mustache of the type that requires crumbing after lunch, Hackett affected plaid lumbermen's shirts, baggy trousers, and painters' smocks. Reacting to the American stereotype of the artist as clubwoman's lapdog, he anticipated a new stereotype: the artist as manly beer-drinking joe. Paul Richard remembers Hackett as "a cartoon Abstract Expressionist," a Cedar Tavern–type *avant la lettre*, "hanging out and getting into fistfights."

Hackett's teaching methods too were prone to caricature. He did assign drawing from the skeleton and encourage those so inspired to paint the setup: a jug, a plant, a wineglass, and a lemon or two artfully arranged on a cloth-draped table. But he also allowed his acolytes simply to hang around the art room, inhaling its perfume of linseed oil and talking Art. Students did not complete a semester with Malcolm Hackett having learned to paint. Yet in one voice they credit Hackett with putting them on the road to artistic maturity thanks, in part, to the rules he laid down in an easy, authoritative manner.

Rule number one: In order to develop taste and avoid compromising your talent, allow yourself to be influenced by only the greatest artists. Joan had been painting still lifes beholden to Cézanne (whose work she knew from the Art Institute) for their radically upturned tabletops and attention to structure. Pushing her to expand her horizons and move beyond her careful little-girl manner, Hackett taught her to admire the work of Titian, Goya, Manet, and Soutine and insisted she see the Arts

Club's exhibition of Austrian Expressionist Oskar Kokoschka's agitated, high-keyed panoramic cityscapes and psychologically complex portraits.

Second, dictated Hackett, art is not a career but an identity. You must present yourself—and dress—like an artist. Here Joan was of two minds. She adored beautiful clothes, like the perfectly pressed skirts she wheedled from Sally (her own typically amounting to wrinkled messes) and the stylish junior evening gowns and print dresses she purchased using her generous charge account at Marshall Field. But she also loved knockaround shirts and dungarees, which in those years still had the power to upset status-conscious midwesterners like Jimmie who had been raised on the farm—from dungarees to dungarees in only two generations. Wont to emerge from primping sessions at the bathroom mirror flaunting scarlet lips, she would growl with principled indignation at an artist girlfriend who indulged in the same: "Wipe that lipstick off your mouth!"

Finally, Hackett decreed that you must endure poverty and pain for your art. His concept of artists as a race of van Goghs hewed to the Romantic tenet that great art requires great suffering, a fate preordained for those who open themselves up to the mysteries of love and inspiration in this philistine world. Joan seized upon her teacher's words, pointing as they did to a way of sublimating her aloneness and difference: artists were supposed to be alienated. Measuring Hackett's vision of art against her father's hobbyism, she found Jimmie diminished.

In her junior and senior years, Joan ran around with the art clique: Lucia Hathaway (her rival for teacher's pet), Connie Joerns, and Connie's sort-of boyfriend, tall, jolly, topaz-eyed Edward St. John Gorey. For Ted Gorey too, Malcolm Hackett served as a compass. Under the older man's tutelage, the "fact that I couldn't paint for beans" seemed curiously irrelevant to his future as an artist. Though a newcomer to Joan's Class of '42, Ted had claimed a central position in that class, owing to a jaunty individualism that took the form of odd stunts like painting his toenails green, then strolling barefoot down Michigan Avenue. Already he was obsessively drawing little men in raccoon coats, a signature of the long career as an artist and writer that would bring macabre cult classics like The Gashlycrumb Tinies (an abecedary of ill-starred children, one of whom toddles over the brink of life with each passing letter) and the introductory sequence of the PBS series Mystery!

Two exceptional intelligences and strong personalities, Joan and Ted frequently "did stuff" together. After graduation, each would blow into

Chicago around the holidays, and they would get together for an evening or two, crabbing about life as they killed a bottle of Scotch. At one Parker class reunion, they sauntered into the old gym, noses stuck in the air, then sauntered back out again without saying hello to anyone, as if they didn't want to risk infection by the bourgeois element. But there was also a mutually undercutting edge to their friendship. According to Connie Joerns, who remained close to Gorey all his life, "Ted was intrigued by Joan" yet "thought her paintings were absolute garbage, and he continued to think that." On the other hand, Gorey is on record as labeling everybody after Cézanne "a lot of hogwash."

Joan also remained close to best friend Joan Van Buren. But perhaps her most vital high school relationship was with dreamy, bitter, brilliant, and wild Timmy Osato, the son of Japanese photographer Shoji Osato and rebellious Irish Quebecois blue blood Francis Fitzpatrick, and the brat brother of Ballets Russes dancer Sono Osato and feisty beauty Teru Osato, Bennington Class of '43. Timmy had no problem holding up his end of this extraordinary family. With dark-pearl eyes, delicate features, smooth skin, and raven hair, he was as stunning as he was brainy. A top history student, Timmy performed on the radio every Wednesday evening as one of the popular WTTW "child genius" *Quiz Kids*. Smitten with Parker's star "figure (ah!) skater," he played the daredevil around "the Mighty Mitchell" at every opportunity. When Joan threw a party, Timmy and another classmate, future real estate magnate Jerry Wexler, hung off her tenth-floor balcony "just to show they could."

Then, in the middle of their senior year, Japan unleashed its devastating attack on Pearl Harbor, killing 2,300 Americans and stripping Timmy Osato of his peace of mind. His father was interned, and Timmy burned with self-hatred because of his Japanese blood. He left Parker, where rumors flew about his fate. Eighteen months later, Joan received a letter ("Dear Enigma . . .") from Camp Shelby, Mississippi, and the two began corresponding. Tim had joined the segregated 442nd Nisei Regiment, the most decorated U.S. combat unit, with which he would serve in Europe, where he won the Bronze Star. After the war, he entered Yale and wrote again, from New Haven: "I suppose it's senseless trying to preserve images of saddleshoes and middy blouses, leopard-skin coats and the fragility of an inexplicable tenderness—but then I have never been sensible, and I shall probably be quite blue if you decide to ignore me." Joan did not. The two became sporadic lovers. Of Osato, Joan's later husband, Barney Rosset, once said, "He was the real love of Joan's

Tim Osato, 1940s

life." That he is all but absent from her official biography attests to both the fitfulness of their encounters and her deeply private nature.

On January 16, 1942, the battle for the Midwest women's senior figure skating championship got underway in Chicago. Having again laid her shoulder to intense summer training with Gus Lussi at Lake Placid, Joan was in top form. And Bobby was favored to win both the Midwest and U.S. men's titles. The two skipped pairs competition in order to focus on singles.

The women's event opened with the compulsory school figures, which counted for 60 percent. At day's end, Mitchell led by less than a point, with four rivals, notably the 1940 U.S. champion, Mary Louise Premer of St. Paul, in hot pursuit. Politely attentive that Friday, the crowd warmed up on Saturday as, one by one, the competitors cut loose with their free-skating routines. For most of the day first place was a coin toss between Mitchell and Premer, but Joan delivered her finest and eventually bested her opponent. With reporters' flashbulbs popping, she claimed the trophy of 1942 figure skating queen of the Midwest. The pictures catch her capable shoulders, thighs like Lincoln Logs, heavily scuffed skates, and flush of exertion and joy.

This victory working to her psychological advantage, Joan was poised to place in the fast-approaching Nationals, moved at the last minute from California to Chicago because of wartime restrictions on travel to the West Coast. Among her opponents, however, loomed two of the great American skaters, defending senior champion Jane Vaughn Sullivan and future six-time national titleholder Gretchen Merrill, both of whom are today enshrined in the U.S. Figure Skating Hall of Fame.

Normally a paragon of steel-meets-ice mental toughness—picture her arching into a powerful warm-up stretch while fixing her rivals with a withering stare—Joan shrank back. Wisely perhaps, but atypically, she ducked the full challenge by registering for the junior rather than the senior competition, thus enhancing her chances at a national singles prize. In that era, categories were based solely on skill level as determined by USFSA tests; dropping back one category was legal and not uncommon.

The championship opened with the school figures, in which Joan placed fifth. Performing under intense pressure during the free-skating segment that followed, she fell and seriously damaged her kneecap. But even before this accident she had hit heavy weather. One Dorothy Goos, the thirteen-year-old daughter of a Bronx electrician, had sailed through a performance that "verged on the sensational"—double flip, double loop, double salchow, lutz, split, and on and on—earning her close to perfect scores and making her the sweetheart of the day. Everyone knows that ice is pitiless and crowds are fickle, yet Joan's fourth-place finish behind a kid in the juniors at her own Chicago Arena would have felt raw and humiliating. So quickly knocked off her pedestal! Her fans' attention was now glued to Bobby and Jane Vaughn Sullivan, the new national champs, and to the adorable Dorothy Goos. This had been Joan's best shot at the national prize for which she had worked hard for years. Within hours, it was over. She kept her feelings to herself, but eventually the episode reinforced her hardheaded, self-coaching realism. You don't indulge what-ifs. You confront the facts. You go on.

Officially, Joan gave up skating because of the knee injury, but her real reasons were more complex. On the practical side, college would complicate her access to a suitable trainer and rink. The bigger picture also took in the war. Boys she knew from school were rushing head-long into combat, which was *real*, she felt, in a way that skating was not. And what did she want? She wasn't going to turn pro and run around the country in anything as corny as the Ice Capades. Skating wasn't her future. It was only hedging her bets. Joan was going to do what she was going to do—and that was painting, and the hell with it.

Five years of competitive skating would have brought to Joan's atten-tion what historian Susan Cahn terms the "underlying tension in Ameri-can women's sport, the contradictory relationship between athleticism and womanhood." Raised in many ways like a boy and educated at that rarest of American schools where something like gender equality pre-vailed, Joan owed to skating the full realization that, as her father always said, girl equals second class. She lived in a man's world where even a "feminine" sport was contrived to ensure that a woman could never truly excel. For one thing, male skating was considered inherently more conse-quential than female skating. When both Bobby and Joan won midwest-ern senior titles, the *Tribune* had headlined, "BOBBY SPECHT TAKES FIGURE SKATING CROWN; Joan Mitchell wins Senior Women's Title." For another, different standards of value applied. A male skater "took a commanding lead," proved himself "the boss," or otherwise invaded and conquered; a female skater, in contrast, delivered an "intri-cate and beautiful" performance, as if the rink were an embroidery hoop, or proved "graceful," as if it were a ballroom. Joan, not Bobby, appeared in the papers in the throes of a dance-like arabesque, the glittery spectacle of skating projected upon her body, not his. Joan loved looking but hated being looked *at*.

Men—her father, Gus, Bobby—had advanced Joan's skating career, and men's opinions counted, so it was men's opinions Joan courted, a practice that would also mark her life as a painter. Artist Ellen Lanyon remembers how in the 1940s "women were subservient to men in the art world, and Joan made it her life's business to show that she was not going to give in to this idea, that she was going to run with the pack, and she did!" Like the sports world, the art world assumed a contradiction between subjectivity and womanhood. Yet Joan lived in a place where gender did not operate: "on the inside" (in the words of French writer Nathalie Sarraute), where she was, "sex does not exist."

After achieving success as a painter, Joan would keep publicly quiet about her skating past. Not that she wasn't proud of it—has any other major American artist competed in sports at the national level?—but she considered the inevitable comparisons between skating and abstract painting irrelevant and trivializing. Noting the whiplash linearity of her work and the whispery gray, tallow, and pale blue palette she then favored, a few commentators in the early 1950s hit upon the skating conceit. Artist/critic Robert Goodnough, for one, asserted in an *ArtNews* review that Mitchell canvases "whirl in abstract activity," resulting in "something like a sheet of ice into which linear movements are worked, like a skater performing acrobatic stunts"—thereby infuriating Joan.

From the perspective of late middle age, she did concede a commonality: "If you use your body [in painting] as you do in any sport, that's all part of your coordination." One could also draw parallels between skating and painting in terms of discipline and psychological release. The rare and exalted place of simultaneous concentration and self-forgetting that athletes call "the zone" bears a distinct resemblance to the painting nirvana that Joan sought: "Painting is a way of forgetting oneself. Sometimes I am totally involved. It's like riding a bicycle with no hands. I call that state 'no hands.' I am in it. I am not there any more. It is a state of non-self-consciousness. It does not happen often. I am always hoping it might happen again. It is lovely."

Arguably, too, though she never said so, the Lussi method seeded Joan's process. At each stage of a painting, she looked hard, then approached the canvas with a clean plan of attack. "I don't close my eyes and hope for the best," she harrumphed. (Use mental rehearsal, Gus commanded.) Moreover, she was scrupulous about "accuracy," a way of saying that every element had to be "meaningful and sensitive." (Nothing hit or miss, said Gus.)

A few weeks after her seventeenth birthday, Joan hung up her skates with the thought, "I've won my last medal for you, Daddy." It was like saying no to God.

A bright but distracted freshman at Sarah Lawrence, in Bronxville, New York, the flawlessly put-together Miss Sally Mitchell made her debut that summer on the right weekend at the right club with the right guests, among them the junior Wrigleys, Ryersons, Armours, Swifts, and Wackers. Sally knew exactly what she wanted from Chicago society;

Joan, on the other hand, agonized. She poured at teas, dated preppy types, attended sub-debutante dances, stood in receiving lines, was written up in the society columns, and took pleasure in her privileged life, yet she often felt bored or appalled by a way of living exemplified by Lake Forest and its "*S.R.* [*Social Register*] phoniness." What position should an artist take toward the world of fashion? Her mother's friends included highly accomplished people of means committed to advancing modernism, people Hackett nonetheless held in contempt. Joan's erratic friendship with the dynamic, funny, and popular Joan Van Buren (later a society columnist for the *Chicago Daily Tribune*) betokens her confusion; the two adored each other, hated each other and weren't speaking, then adored each other again.

Impatient to get on with her painting, Joan was turning up her nose at the idea of attending the "right" college (although she would not be caught dead at the "wrong" college) and arguing for art school instead. But, believing her too young, Jimmie turned thumbs down. Of the three colleges to which Joan had been accepted, she chose Bennington. Again Jimmie refused: too arty. Having recently grabbed a few hours from skating in Philadelphia to tour the Bryn Mawr campus, she had pronounced it "death warmed over." That left Smith.

In those days, a journey from Chicago to Northampton, Massachusetts, meant the New York Central sleeper through Gary (where factories belched smoke day and night because of the war), then on to Cleveland, Albany, and Springfield, the link with a commuter train for the short push to Northampton. A midwesterner's first impressions of Smith's hometown were typically of the quaint shops along Main Street, the stately houses on Elm, and the campus itself, serene and Emersonian. Hung each fall in splendid autumnal hues, Smith distilled eastern-ness like the parlor of a great house.

In 1942, however, Smith lacked some of its usual tranquility. Among the first colleges to host the Navy's WAVES program to train women for support positions and thus free men for combat overseas, it swarmed with two thousand crisply uniformed female sailors pounding the sidewalks in a *hup*-two-three-four beat. The school's staff of white-aproned maids had vanished, and Smithies now made their own beds, wielded their own mops, and slung their own creamed chipped beef on toast and broiled tomatoes with bread crumbs (aka "train wreck"). Student heat cops patrolled the residential houses each night before dawn, shutting windows to conserve fuel (sleeping in fresh air was at that time considered a requisite of healthy living), and volunteers dug potatoes at local farms, thus giving shape to the war effort in a way the college president's assurance that the "study of liberal arts was a promise to the world that peace would return" did not.

Assigned to Park House, a rambling old mansion where forty-five young women lived under the eagle eye of one Miss Atossa Herring, Joan quickly formed two fast friendships. With Martha Burke (now Martha Bertolette), from Plainfield, New Jersey, she indulged in talkfests lasting into the small hours, when they would drift into the john so their roommates could sleep while they rattled on. An intent listener, Joan put questions to Mopse—as Joan dubbed her—like nobody else's: "What does your father *really* think of your mother?" "How do your brothers feel about sex?" Joan's other best friend was Joanne Witmer (today Joanne Von Blon), called Wit, a Minneapolis native from a privileged background. They too talked incessantly, taking long "wallowing walks" in the course of which Joanne discovered "a wonderful friend, the kind of friend you dream of, very emotionally available, very open."

Others at Park House found Joan inconsiderate, hard-nosed, or unkind. They disapproved of her cruel dig at a certain southern student with large rubbery lips—"Can you imagine kissing her? It would be like kissing a wet toilet seat!"—and her careless rich girl's acts like taking other people's bicycles without asking and bumming cigarettes but never repaying. Her language ("Well, did you *fuck* him?") shocked some; her intellectual snobbery rankled others. Once two housemates turned the tables on Joan by talking up imaginary books, then calling her bluff when she claimed to have read them. Mopse observed that her friend was less self-confident than she pretended to be.

An English major (Smith did not then offer a major in art), Joan was bright and defiant enough to use her grades as evaluations of her professors, as much as the other way around, turning in stellar performances for only those she respected. She pulled a C in psychology because she took a dim view of the instructor's approach and later earned another C, from a geology teacher for whom she had little but scorn.

The exception was an assignment in the figure-drawing class she took freshman year from artist and art historian Priscilla Van der Poel. Joan plugged away at her drawing, yet (according to Martha Bertolette, who was in the same class) "didn't really know what a line was." "I hit it just right," Martha remembers of her own drawing, which earned an A– while Joan's came back with a B+. Joan long obsessed on those two grades. "Joan!" Martha insisted. "You know it was just a mistake!" In 1986 art historian Linda Nochlin conducted an oral history interview of Joan for the Archives of American Art. "Is there anything particularly important about Smith?" inquired Nochlin. "I mean, anything important that you think took place that might be relevant to your later career?" "Well, I got a B+ in art," the painter deadpanned.

At Smith, Joan lived by her own code of embattled idealism, sly defiance of authority, and loyalty to friends. In the words of Joanne Van Blon, Joan's "sense of justice and her sense of integrity and her sense of truth were monumental." So too was her generosity. After Wit spoke of her love of Milton, a leather-bound, gold-leaf-trimmed edition of *The Poetical Works of John Milton* appeared on her bed, thoughtfully shoplifted by Joan at the Hampshire Bookshop. Joan could easily have afforded the book, but not only was pilfering daring and fun, it was also gratifying to the resentful daughter in her, who was not at all sure she wanted to be at Smith. With this, as with other acts, she said: My parents made me be here, they asked for it. As for the college, acting in loco parentis, Joan did as she pleased but made sure they never got anything on her. When she royally violated curfew one weeknight, straggling in from a date at two thirty a.m., she contested the demerit with the cleverly fabricated story that she had been visiting a poet friend of her mother's who was teaching at Amherst and she could not possibly have slighted the distinguished bard by leaving in time to meet the ten p.m. curfew. Moreover, she demanded that Mopse back her up with a lie.

A date was something of an event during those war years, when Saturday nights found many Smithies catching a movie together or tossing back a few beers at Rahar's, the local joint, and bemoaning the chronic shortage of "man-power." The issue went beyond dateless weekends, for even at a top academic institution like Smith, many women were fundamentally in the business of finding Mr. Right. Preparing for a career was less a matter of making one's mark in the world than of establishing a holding pattern: the real future began with a wedding to the guy whose name one took, whose children one bore, whose household one managed, and whose way of life one assumed.

Though Joan did not rule out marriage, she already knew that traditional domesticity wasn't for her because it could derail a female artist's career. She might marry, but she would never be a wife. When Joanne,

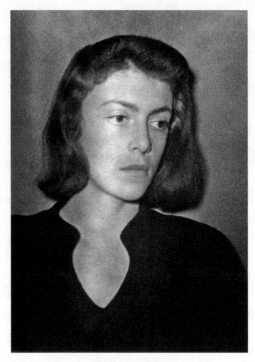

Joan, age twenty-one, insisted she was not
beautiful, c. 1946.

an aspiring writer, got a diamond solitaire engagement ring from her
Amherst boyfriend, Phil, Joan appeared in her friend's room wielding
scissors, grabbed a clump of her hair, and hacked it off. This gesture
oddly recalls French townspeople's later head shaving of women who
consorted with the Nazis, an act of public humiliation inflicted upon the
tresses that represent their seductive powers. Ah, you don't subscribe to
my view after all, Joan seemed to say. You've betrayed me. You're really
one of *them.*

Not that Joan didn't adore men. With her splendid 124-pound body,
full breasts, caramel coloring, Lauren-Bacall-as-Slim-Browning hairdo,
little nose, and intriguing half smile, she exuded a young, smoky, tough-
cookie glamour. Her uniform in those days was a double-breasted trench
coat over a plaid flannel shirt and dungarees rolled to the knees, but on
special occasions she donned a boxy, well-tailored suit and her one precious pair of silk stockings, a gift from Sally, and looked "sexy as hell."

Letters between the two sisters (Sally remained at Sarah Lawrence)
dished "dirt with a capital D": gossip and tales of the pleasures and ter-

rors of marginal virginity. A certain Dick had drugged Sally with four bourbons, then drove her to a lover's lane, and "before I knew what was happening, he had my bra undone and my panties off . . . BE SURE TO TEAR THIS UP." (Joan did not.) "M.L." (the sisters coded men's names in case their letters fell into parental hands) was a "complete wreck" over Joan. Sally meanwhile was "plodding forth" with "a sex-starved veteran of the Sicilian campaign—cousin of a Marine who tried to lay me about four weeks ago." Joan had finally let Dickie Moore kiss her: "not bad but I'm afraid he's undersexed." And one of the Hughes boys, their perennial double dates in Chicago, still had "chronic hot-pants" for Sally. After some incident during one of Joan's breaks, Mr. Hughes Senior had vigorously complained to Marion that Joan was a bad influence on his sons. Sally got mad that "Mr. H." would "dare say you are leading those dumb sots of sons astray," while Joan reacted by writing "Mr. H." a wickedly sarcastic letter that had Sally both scolding her for bad breeding and admiring her "super duper job."

Both sisters played the man game enthusiastically, but unlike Sally—who wanted a husband, children, a big house, the works—Joan was not playing for keeps. She wisely chided Sally for running her love life like a factory:

> What's your hurry—you drop one man and expect another to move up on the assembly line—one's love life is hardly a modern mechanized thing—and hell—having a man is an artificial stimulus—a little like taking dope—perhaps to appreciate the dope you should go without it—I know I'm no example—but you can find what you like in one man in many people—men and women . . . A man is nice to lean upon—good for the vanity but most of what's going to make you happy is inside you . . . You've got to be strong, S.—let things come to you—you've got to decide what to you is valuable—what will make you happy (and not kid yourself into thinking another person will do it) and when you alone have more self-confidence, only then is it safe to lean on someone else . . . There's a lot to be enthusiastic about, S.—if you look for it—qualities in people (not the whole person)— qualities in things—that you can discriminate—like walking through a garden—just picking certain flowers.

Back in Chicago that June, Joan began dating the older brother of her ex-classmate Lucia Hathaway. A student leader and enthusiastic actor at

Parker (his famous line: "It's this *beastly* neuralgia"), Bullock Hathaway loved to hold forth on subjects ranging from the Oedipus complex to Hamlet to democracy. A recent cum laude graduate of Harvard in the accelerated program and one of those outstanding young people who incarnate the best hopes of a generation, Bullock was destined for a career in politics and law. He was dark, handsome, charming, and, according to Mopse (who visited her friend in Chicago that June), "crazy about Joan." But, by early July, Bullock had departed for basic training on Parris Island, and Joan for the Ox-Bow Summer School of Painting near Saugatuck, Michigan.

Founded as an artists' haven in 1910, Ox-Bow lay at the end of a dirt trail through a fragrant dark birch and pine forest on Lake Michigan's eastern shore. Named for a bygone loop of the Kalamazoo River, the school occupied an assortment of rustic, sun-bleached, unelectrified cabins, plus the old Ox-Bow Inn, haunted by memories of lumber barons and captains of the Great Lake steamers. Burr oaks, some encircling an ancient Pottawattamie mound, dotted its sand dunes where people played volleyball and, after dark, built bonfires and gazed up at a million stars. Ox-Bow was sweet-smelling and drowsy and Hopperesque and wild.

Joan took three classes that summer. The first, a morning class in figure painting, was taught by Robert von Neumann, a German émigré via Milwaukee who had lost a leg in World War I. A loosely expressionistic artist, von Neumann pushed no particular agenda but rather took student work-in-progress for what it was, critiquing it in a humane, encouraging way. Their easels set up in a field of blond grasses skirted with resinous blue green woods, von Neumann's students painted nude models perched on old kitchen chairs. Joan loved doing outdoor nudes, so odd and exciting, especially when the model was Cleo, with her marvelous soft, round body as if from a Renoir—"really Frenchy." In the afternoon, Joan took landscape painting from the perennial Malcolm Hackett, and, in the evening, she learned lithography by kerosene lamp.

She found von Neumann particularly genial and inspirational. He spoke to his students about decisions. A faraway look in her globular eyes, Joan listened intently, distractedly flicking her cigarette in the direction of the little bucket she carried around as an ashtray. During the war years, you improvised your life. If the world is sliding out from under you, Joan felt, it's time to quicken your steps. Bracing for a storm at home, she resolved to transfer to Chicago's School of the Art Institute, where von Neumann taught—a scary but necessary decision, she felt. "My decision to leave college was the decision that time is short," she later explained. "Time to become a painter. I felt one doesn't paint by being an English major. One paints by painting. Full time."

Back at Smith nonetheless for her sophomore year while she negotiated with her parents, Joan watched Mexican artist Rufino Tamayo create a forty-foot fresco for the art library and took drawing and painting from George H. Cohen, who, to her amusement, stole a kiss at their first meeting. Finding Cohen a mediocre artist and teacher, however, she preferred to work on her own. "J-child," purred Sally, "you are painting so well."

That Thanksgiving, newly commissioned Marine Corps Second Lieutenant Bullock Hathaway visited her in Northampton. Then Christmas came and went. She had a small show at Parker. Spring brought watercoloring under Smith's apple trees and sketching along the grassy banks of Paradise Pond and Mill River. Said Joan, "I'd always go further than Paradise Pond ... I always wanted *more*." Yet, stopped dead in her tracks for several weeks that spring by one of the deep depressions that would plague her adult life, she wanted nothing at all for a time.

During her final semester at Smith, Joan studied English literature with Dr. Helen Randall, the last of the trio of teachers who profoundly affected her. Randall specialized in Romantic poetry—Wordsworth, Shelley, Keats, Byron, and Browning—writing that touched her soul even as she applied the highest standards of scholarship to its analysis. Her student and later colleague Margaret Shook describes Randall as "the first teacher I had ever encountered whose intense love of poetry was equaled by her intellectual power. She had an intricate mind, awake to contradictions, paradox, and irony. She seemed to speak in paragraphs rather than sentences, and often these paragraphs took the form of a contradiction: 'on the one hand ...; on the other hand.'"

Thus, in her lectures on Wordsworth, with whose poetry Joan promptly fell in love, Randall would have distinguished between, on the one hand, the vigorous rebel of the *Lyrical Ballads,* a poet of ordinary but specific and intensely felt moments, and, on the other, the (in the words of writer Margaret Drabble) "lover of Nature, friend to butterflies, bees and little daisies, in fact a sentimental tedious old bore." (Joan too detested shopworn pastoralism: "I hate the word 'nature' as it is used in the bird-watching sense.")

Joan with fellow student Dan Sparling at Ox-Bow, 1943 or 1944

Seeking to communicate her approach to painting, Joan would later use an analogy with lyric poetry, famously defined by Wordsworth as "the spontaneous overflow of powerful feelings." Such feelings, he writes in *The Prelude*, leap from the sky, hills, caves, and trees that make "The surface of the universal earth, / With triumph and delight, and hope and fear, / Work like a sea." For Joan, too, landscape was vital: her Lake Michigan was not "a dull body of water," but rather "changing, alive," as Wordsworth's earth was "not a dead cinder turning aimlessly in time, but a living, moving, feeling thing." A Mitchell painting—the 1991 *L'Arbre de Phyllis*, for instance, which involves feelings inseparable from a certain November-yellow gingko tree standing in a certain village in France, a tree once loved by a certain Phyllis—is as firmly rooted in time and place as is Wordsworth's "The Daffodils," with its wind-combed blossoms discovered by the poet and his sister on a March walk in Townend, Grasmere. At their best, both painter and poet—herein lies an important ingredient in their greatness—retain not conventionalized memories neatly fitting the preset schematics of adult experience but rather something closer to the unwieldy and unnamable raw material of life. Psychoanalyst Ernest G. Schachtel writes of how "adult memory reflects life as a road with occasional signposts and milestones rather than as the landscape through which this road has led," meaning that adults recollect the events the world deems important and then not so much the events themselves as the fact that the events took place. Wordsworth and Mitchell, on the other hand, body forth what Schachtel calls "a vision given only to the most sensitive and differentiated mind as the rare grace of a fortunate moment."

Moreover, a Mitchell canvas takes as its subject not nature, but rather the artist's felt memories of nature, an approach which (as several critics have pointed out) parallels Wordsworth's use of "emotion recollected in tranquillity." The poet draws from remembered sensations in "Tintern Abbey," for instance, and, most memorably, in "The Daffodils":

> *For oft, when on my couch I lie*
> *In vacant or in pensive mood,*
> *They flash upon that inward eye*
> *Which is the bliss of solitude;*
> *And then my heart with pleasure fills,*
> *And dances with the daffodils.*

"They flash upon that inward eye / Which is the bliss of solitude"—as if Wordsworth, like Mitchell, treasured up moments of visual splendor to be pulled out when life brought scant pleasure and anxieties crowded the mind.

As that semester continued, "Randall's Romantics" yielded to Victorian poets, and they to essayists and novelists including, incongruously, Tolstoy, whose *War and Peace* had been patched into the syllabus of every English II class in recognition of the times. In her term paper for Dr. Randall, Joan examined Tolstoy's epic through the lens of his 1896 essay *What Is Art?* The result—a tight, even, four-thousand-word braid of handwriting (like boys in those days, Joan never bothered to learn typing, smug in the knowledge she would never need to be a secretary)—is remarkable. Though ill at ease with abstract reasoning and conceptual language, she conceived of such assignments as compulsory "mental gymnastics" and badgered herself into excellence. Her attitude: Why do it if you're not going to do it well? Any dope can write a C paper. It doesn't stand for anything. Besides, she deeply respected Helen Randall and thus gave her all.

Joan begins her paper by recapitulating Tolstoy's attacks on formalism on grounds that art for pleasure's sake, as favored by the upper class, subverts art's rightful purpose, which is to transmit feelings. The better (i.e., the more morally uplifting) the feelings, Tolstoy continues, the more readily they are conveyed to the viewer, and thus the better the work of art. The pure and infectious feelings of songs sung by peasant women, for instance, make them superior to Beethoven's Piano Sonata in A Major, op. 101. No art at all is preferable to art that fails to advance the brotherhood of man through shared feelings. Bad art should rightfully be destroyed.

Joan counters that, because art builds upon what has come before, Tolstoy's assumption of the existence of an ultimate criterion for art is flawed. She accuses the Russian of a narrow, dogmatic response to a complex set of circumstances: if Tolstoy pins his faith on morally uplifting art, so be it, but others should not be compelled to follow suit as he, a firm believer in freedom, should recognize. Furthermore, argues Joan, Tolstoy essentializes the classes, demonizing the aristocracy and idealizing the peasantry. She concludes by lauding *War and Peace* (which antedates *What Is Art?* by nearly thirty years) for conjuring rather than preaching about the human condition, recognizing that human actions (if not human nature) can improve, and balancing moral considerations with the complexities of life.

With her Tolstoy paper, Joan mapped out her lifelong position that an artist must command the freedom to set the terms of her art: "There is no one way to paint. There can't be. There is no one answer." Nor, she believed, is there any morality in making a picture: either it works, or it doesn't. Prodded by one interviewer, years later, to pronounce on whether artists should take a political stance in their work, she responded, "I don't think there's any shoulds." The interviewer kept fishing: "You don't like work that tells you what to think as opposed to work—." Joan finished: "that allows you to feel." Mitchell and Tolstoy's shared preoccupation with feelings appears to establish a mutuality between the artist and the writer; for the Russian, however, the feelings in a work of art need not be powerful but must be infectious. Joan, on the other hand, took for granted that only the very few who really care about painting will engage with her work at a deep level. In that sense, she was an elitist.

"This is a superb analysis," Dr. Randall comments at the bottom of Joan's essay, "... for straight and vigorous critical thinking in a college paper ... one could hardly ask for anything better. A."

Having made a point of getting to know her teacher, Joan received a rare invitation to tea at the farmhouse where this shy but intrepid Vermonter, a poodle her sole companion, competently met the challenges of rural New England life. Little did the young painter know that she was glimpsing her own future years in the country, off the power grid of the art world.

Back at Ox-Bow that summer, Joan one morning found herself painting next to Zuka Omalev, née Booyakovitch, the daughter of escapees from the Russian Revolution, a fine arts major at the University of Southern California, and the young wife of All-American basketball player Alex Omalev. Joan sized up Zuka's dark mane, Modigliani look, and likeable manner and, after class, inquired, "Do you want to go for a swim?" The two slipped into their bathing suits, Joan's a beige tank suit and Zuka's a two-piece powder blue number with a little skirt. (Her hometown was Hollywood, California.) But Joan forgave her. When they got to the beach, Zuka remembers, "Joan went psssst! She dived in, swam I don't know how many yards out, turned around, swam back. She was a terrific swimmer. And she was out! That was it." Zuka, meanwhile, splashed around, swam a bit, and splashed around some more, and Joan forgave that too.

Still feeling the spell of *War and Peace* and assuming that "Russian" was shorthand for "soulful," Joan latched onto Zuka's Russianness. As an antidote to her own family's cold, stoic midwesternness, she played with a pseudo-Russianness of her own that led her (and two or three others that summer) to throw paint at their canvases and sound off about how only the *act* of painting counted.

Along the same lines, New York artist Jane Wilson recalls hearing in the early 1950s about a certain

> little dinner with painters and friends and so on. And there was a great deal of drinking, and it got exceedingly nasty. And there was yelling and there was screaming and there was carrying on. Between Joan and almost everybody. And finally people got tired and went home. And the person at whose house this took place thought that this was a disaster. Never again! This is the worst thing that has ever happened. I can't imagine how this came about, but I'll never do it again. Then Joan called her up and said, "What a *wonderful* Russian evening!"

In contrast with the Joan of 1951, the Joan of 1944 demonstrated a classy reserve—"very Anglo-Saxon and keep a stiff upper lip and you don't complain and that kind of thing"—that Zuka, in turn, romanticized. The forceful personality that led Joan to insist, for instance, upon teaching Zuka how to make a bed properly, a skill she herself had acquired only recently at Smith, also fed Zuka's fascination with her new friend. However, the Californian soon tasted Joan's arrogance and ruthless competitiveness. One night mischief-makers crept into their painting studio and mixed up the easels, normally kept at the very same spots over the several days of a pose. Arriving early, as usual, the next morning and seeing what had happened, Joan grabbed an easel, scribbled her name on it, positioned it, and started painting. Later a middle-aged classmate entered and said, "That's my easel." Joan replied, "My name is on it. This is my easel." When the man protested, she stonewalled him. Zuka mentally gasped, "Oh, my God! This is terrible!" But Joan had the easel. So what if it was his? Fuck him. She was working. She showed no inclination to negotiate, no twinge of understanding, no feeling of remorse.

That summer was notable too for Joan's bloodless decision that it was time to have sex. Scouting around for a partner, she chose twenty-six-year-old painter and assistant teacher Richard Bowman. The son of a courthouse employee and a housewife from Rockford, Illinois, Dick had graduated from the School of the Art Institute in 1942 having won one of four coveted traveling fellowships the school awarded in the belief that a first-rate art education must be crowned by a sojourn abroad. Bowman had spent his in Mexico, where he stayed for a time in Michoacán with painter Gordon Onslow Ford and his writer wife, Jacqueline Johnson. There primal volcanic landscapes and pellucid skies had unveiled to him "a vision of nature as energy." Pierced by the realization that, their apparent stability notwithstanding, rock formations pulsate with movement and light, Dick had made beautiful drawings, then swung into a long series of paintings in which skies throb with color, and matter and energy interpenetrate. Intuiting kinetic theory, he titled the pictures *Rock in Motion* or *Tense Form* or *Dynamic Tension* and, collectively, the Rock and Sun series.

A husky outdoorsman squarish of shoulders and face, Dick hid his shyness under cocksure masculinity. His nickname, Rocky, alluded to the Mexican work but also suited his vaguely pugilistic manner. At first glance, Bowman seems an odd, too-provincial choice for Joan, yet his marvelous canvases, up-and-coming career (he was a protégé of Art Institute director Daniel Catton Rich), and eagerness to help Joan with her work (he advised that she "get good and clean color" and "penetrate reality but abstract it") met her needs. As for Dick, Joan's big-shot family and assertive manner impressed him. Like a smitten schoolboy, he carried her paint box. And the physical attraction between the two was palpable.

Come Labor Day, Ox-Bow closed its doors, and silence once again settled over the rustic cottages soaking in Indian summer sun. On one wall of the so-called White House had appeared a scrawled message that was to survive for years to come: "Joan, will you marry me?"

Dick Bowman, Joan's first lover, painting in Mexico, 1942 or 1943

Four months after shipping out to join the 8th Marine Gun Battalion on Guadalcanal, Bullock Hathaway had taken part in the perilous invasion of Peleliu Island, where eight thousand Japanese occupiers met the Americans with punishing fire. Two weeks later, the young officer volunteered to accompany a detail of machine gunners supporting an artillery unit's attack on the island's heavily fortified caves. His men facing fierce resistance as they searched out enemy targets, Bullock courageously laid himself open to danger as he directed counterfire until he was killed by a sharpshooter's bullet.

Bullock Hathaway's death on September 30, 1944, on that remote strip of hot coral sand threw many into profound grief. Some of his professors wept at the news. Joan was devastated. She phoned Martha, "really broken up, just hating the fact that he wasn't coming back," and carried away by her razor-sharp pain: "But I was engaged to him! But I was going to marry him!" Bullock's was her first important death.

In describing Joan, her friends often bring up her primal terror of death and dying, her anguish at the thought of light extinguished. For her, forgetting the horrid finality of not being alive was ultimately what painting was all about.

I am learning to see. I don't know why it is, but
everything enters me more deeply and doesn't
stop where it once used to. I have an interior
that I never knew of. Everything passes into it
now. I don't know what happens there . . .

I am learning to see. Yes, I am beginning.
It's still going badly. But I intend to make the
most of my time.

RAINER MARIA RILKE, *The Notebooks of
Malte Laurids Brigge*

CHAPTER FIVE Taking from Everybody

Only days before Bullock Hathaway's death, Joan had started
classes at the School of the Art Institute.
Founded in 1866 as the Chicago Academy of Design and
rooted in neoclassical tradition, the School of the Art Institute had originally shaped its curriculum around the idealized representation of the
human body, the application of Old Master techniques, and the idea of
art as moral uplift. Eighty years later, humanist values still underpinned
its training of painters. In first- and second-year classes, students concentrated on craft and anatomy, drawing from plaster casts in preparation
for working from the live model. Thus, unlike many artists identified
with Abstract Expressionism (Willem de Kooning is a notable exception), Joan had rigorous Beaux-Arts training, the kind that should belie
the skepticism of a certain public quick to label abstract artists as inept,
if not fraudulent.

At the School of the Art Institute, Robert von Neumann remained Joan's favorite teacher, though two others reigned like demigods: each student "belonged" to either Boris Anisfeld or Louis Ritman. Joan belonged to Ritman. Russian born and Chicago raised, Joan's mentor was nonetheless considered French, having spent eighteen summers at the artists' colony in Giverny, the home of Impressionist Claude Monet, where the American had shelved somber academicism in favor of a fluid intimism à la Renoir and indulged the shadowy blues and pale yellows of an Impressionist palette. By 1944, history had long since passed Louis Ritman by, and Joan secretly sided with history, yet she pulled out all the stops for her teacher. In her three years at the school, she took his class (three hours daily) every term, slaved over his assignments, and never earned less than an A.

Thanks to her credits from Smith, Joan's only academic requirement was two years of art history with Kathleen Blackshear, a protégée of Helen Gardner, the author of the enduring textbook *Art Through the Ages*. Emphasizing her own favorite periods, styles, and artists—Romanesque architecture, early Renaissance painting, Cézanne, Cubism, and what was then termed "primitive art"—Blackshear complemented her lectures with class trips to the Oriental Institute and the Field Museum. A painter herself, she emphasized the formal elements of art from many cultures and assigned as homework an Egyptian mural, a Japanese scroll, a Kuba mask, and a Cubist oil, projects Joan tackled with enthusiasm.

More important than any teacher, however, was the glamorous material presence of the great museum upstairs, which served as an injunction to think within history, look beyond Chicago, and take what one needed for one's art. Joan fell in love with—her ultimate competition—Giotto, Bellini, Chardin, Degas, and the Mexican modernists. Some works she copied; some she visited more or less daily. Among the latter was Édouard Manet's radiant kitchen still life *Fish (Still Life)*, which depicts a shimmery copper kettle behind a hefty stippled-white carp, an ugly little redfish, a gleaming eel, a rocky heap of oysters, and, off to one side, a lemon as candent as the sun, which Joan loved and mentally kept with her always.

Although she claimed to dislike ugly Darwinian behavior, Joan quickly earned a reputation as a head-butting competitor with no qualms about taking sly advantage of family connections or hustling into a painting studio early on the first day of a pose to stake out the best spot. Artist Leon Goldin, whose years at the school overlapped hers, once spent the

better part of a day fending off Joan's strident demands to see his paintings, which were rolled up and ready to load into the car for a trip to
California. "Well, unroll them." In the end, he relented, but, watching
her reaction as he unfurled the canvases, he realized she wasn't genuinely
interested in his work. She just wanted to see if he was competition.

Goldin was among the dozens of returning GIs who, in Joan's second September, set the school spinning with their unruly energies and
sheer numbers. Whether hanging out in the smoking lounge or tagging
along to the New Orleans jazz clubs around Rush Street, where they all
danced, sucked on Camels, traded wisecracks, and nursed boilermakers,
Joan, the youngest of the gang and often the only female, held her own
with these vets, and woe to any man who came across as wishy-washy
about his life or his art.

Sauntering around school with T. S. Eliot's *Four Quartets* under her
arm, Joan could also give the impression of aloneness and hard-shell
reserve. "Her manner set her apart," reflects painter Ellen Lanyon,
who was a year behind her. "She was fairly austere. I don't want to use
the word arrogant because that's too harsh. But she was a person unto
herself. She had an aura of sophistication." That aura of sophistication
doubled as self-protection: at times emotional closeness so frightened
her that she had to shut her eyes for relief, other times hostility spilled
out of nowhere. Once, as she negotiated a narrow corridor carrying a
paint-laden palette, Joan brushed up against a classmate walking in the
opposite direction and, accidentally or not, smeared the other's sleeve
with paint. According to the story that went around school, she immediately launched a preemptive strike: "You deserved that!"

As for her money, it set her apart, and it didn't. Some of Joan's less
privileged classmates were stuck in revolving doors of school and work.
Her friend Herby Katzman, for instance, arrived at six a.m., did his jani-
torial chores, attended classes, reverted to janitor at lunchtime, attended
more classes, finished cleaning, and then headed for night school. Joan,
on the other hand, not only commanded her own schedule but also purchased the finest oils and linen canvas and tooled around in a new Buick
coupe. On days when she left it at home and had the chauffeur drive her
to school, she insisted he drop her a few blocks away so she could appear
to have walked. Romanticizing poverty, she had little idea how bitter and
incapacitating it can be.

Considering a working-class style to be testimony to artistic authenticity, she tried for a proletarian look. Her cousin Sally Turton tells a

story about a former neighbor in Columbus, Ohio, who once mentioned having attended the School of the Art Institute, to which Sally responded that she had had a cousin there, Joan Mitchell. And the neighbor replied, "Oh, poor Joan! I felt so sorry for her. All her clothes had holes in them, and she didn't have any shoes to wear. We shared everything with her because she had nothing." But another classmate remembers Joan ambling down a hall dragging a fur coat behind her.

Joan's spending money came in the form of a monthly allowance from Jimmie and Marion. She griped to Sally, still at Sarah Lawrence:

> Both parents claim I use them—i.e., only live here—spend their money but don't give a damn about them—if they want it that way they'll get it—and then apologetically mother comes in to talk—haven't I any news—one minute they grovel—the next they're resentful—why can't they act like people—I guess my ignoring them gets them down and they act nice. Anyway I've been looking for part time jobs—doesn't look too hopeful—and there are a lot of things against moving out so I'm being rational and waiting at least until you come home—furthermore if I did leave I could never return and if I got syphilis in a back alley it would be slightly distressing—when I get my degree I'll be able to teach and that will be something else again . . . J. Herbert gives me about two packs of weeds per week—if you could do anything on that score it would be much appreciated.

Toward Jimmie, Joan had assumed an attitude of scornful amusement, telling friends he had a bloated opinion of himself and tagging him the "skin and siph" man, which sounds like a song-and-dance man from hell. Marion, too, was treated perfunctorily or angrily rebuffed when she gingerly broached the subject of Joan's relationship with Dick Bowman. When Joan joined her mother and father at their daily cocktail hour, battles would rage over Bowman or politics or the Jews. At school, she broadcast her hostility toward her uptight, conservative parents and congratulated herself for combating their anti-Semitism.

Joan did hold strong opinions about social justice. Her next big move (around 1945), joining the Communist Party, hewed to her values but also served to spite her parents and atone for their position and wealth. Deeply moved by a quote from Lenin ("Man's dearest possession is life, and since it is given to him but once to live he must so live as to fear no torturing regrets of years without purpose . . ."), she embraced Commu-

A portrait of Joan by boyfriend Dick Bowman, lithograph, 1945

nism in order to help liberate the mental power of the masses, even as she questioned the party's positivism and doctrinaire positions on art.

Packing a party membership card, which she once carelessly left on the El, Joan studied the classic Marxist texts and regularly attended meetings, where she learned a great deal about the dynamics of power. Yet she refused to follow party rules that made no sense to her. Once brought up on charges of sleeping with a Trotskyite (Dick Bowman, who was also trying his political wings) and of liking Picasso (having joined the party in 1944, Picasso had won acclaim in the French Communist newspaper *L'Humanité* as the greatest painter alive, but Chicago remained at antipodes to Paris), she was in and out of trouble with her comrades.

On North State Parkway, the shock value of Joan's relationship with Dick rivaled that of her politics. As often as not during this "terribly sick period" (as she later framed it), Joan spent the night at her boyfriend's slummy basement apartment at Forty-third and Ellis on the South Side near Cottage Grove. She had something to prove to herself by frequenting the dingy bedbug- and cockroach-infested flat: shortly before starting art school Joan had made her debut (low-key, like that of most on the

1943 list, because of the war), the traditional coming-out party replaced by a luncheon at the chichi Pump Room. More recently, she had modeled at the high-society Ravinia Festival Style Show. These were (and would remain) secrets from the art world. If Joan did not technically lie about being a debutante, a word she spit out dripping with scorn, she came close. (Another secret: until well into the 1970s, her name appeared annually in the *Chicago Blue Book,* the city's social register.)

From Dick's point of view, theirs was a committed and exclusive relationship, a prelude to marriage. From Joan's, it was almost a thing of the past, though Dick remained useful as both mentor teacher and irritant to her parents. In a reversal of the usual script of that era in which a young man itches for sex but a young woman rejects premarital experimentation as too risky of pregnancy and too damaging to her reputation, Joan had proved a willing sex partner to Dick but also cheated on her boyfriend (who was oblivious) at every opportunity. Sally dubbed her "D.G.," Damaged Goods. Joan did scruple to sleep with married men whose marriages were intact, yet when Sally got engaged to quarterback-handsome Yale dropout and bandleader I. Newton Perry III the following year, Joan reportedly attempted to seduce her sister's fiancé.

Though careful to get a diaphragm and contact information for a good abortionist, Joan operated from a resolve to live fully and radically, which was considered normal for a man but intolerable in a woman. But there was also an edge of desperation in Joan's sexual adventuring. Because eros is experienced as surging beyond one's psychic boundaries and merging with the other, sexual fusion left her feeling less frighteningly alone. Moreover, by making a raw connection with another human being, casual sex skips the awkwardness and discomfort of getting acquainted. Still, at times she experienced the sex act as attack and reacted with panicky rage.

Meanwhile, she had set her wits to learning everything she could from Dick Bowman. The two spoke endlessly about French artist Pierre Bonnard, whose intimate, luminous, and evasive canvases Dick considered kin to his own. And Joan sat for at least two portraits by her boyfriend, a lithograph that adopts her bold and direct manner and an oil that depicts her as a remote, psychologically divided, and vaguely troubled soul.

That March, Richard Bowman made his New York debut at Pinacotheca, a gallery on West Fifty-eighth Street, with a show that won raves from *ArtNews* for its "powerful abstractions" and "vision . . . of the strength and might in things elemental." In New York, he lunched with artists Max Ernst and Dorothea Tanning and visited the studio of painter Fernand Léger. Unimpressed with the young man's success, Jimmie buttonholed Dick upon his return to give cold notice that Joan should not marry an artist "unless he was of the reputation and stature of somebody like Picasso."

At the end of Joan's first year at the School of the Art Institute, she and Zuka, her friend from Ox-Bow, struck out for Mexico, triply alluring to foreign artists for its affordability, aura of bohemian radicalism, and rich modernist heritage. During the Depression, many U.S. painters had found inspiration in Mexican paintings that propounded revisionist histories or protested capitalist injustices. Others had renewed American Scene painting by enlarging their definitions of "American" to include colorful markets, colonial towns, and volcanic landscapes south of the border. Moreover, a number of School of the Art Institute teachers and traveling fellowship winners had worked in Mexico; their art, along with that of Mexican painters and printmakers, proliferated in local galleries and museums, spinning a complex web of artistic and personal connections between Chicago and Mexico. Spending a summer in Mexico was a smart move for an ambitious young painter.

Originally objecting to Joan's travel plans, Marion and Jimmie finally surrendered to their daughter's intransigence and proceeded pragmatically. Wise to Joan's ploys and half-truths, Marion promised her daughter her own copy of *Lady Chatterley's Lover* if she made it through the summer without getting pregnant or contracting syphilis, while Jimmie supplied a colossal duffle bag bulging with medicines, bandages, and cans of purified water, atop which Joan and Zuka piled paint boxes, Anderson portable easels, and tins of turpentine. Hoisted onto the Texas Eagle in Chicago, this behemoth was off-loaded in Laredo, where the travelers caught Rita Hayworth in *Gilda* and spent the night, then on-loaded the next morning for the long gritty haul to Mexico City.

Their final destination, some 250 miles from the capital, was Guanajuato, a self-contained and virtually unmappable colonial city crammed into a long, narrow ravine. Guanajuato's crooked streets, plunging staircases, ornate mansions, Churrigueresque churches, and ochre, turquoise, and rosy pink houses hewed to steep cliffs, propped each other up, and strove for order but lapsed into disorder, as if they were the product of some deranged Mexican Cézanne. There the two friends took rooms

Joan's self-portrait from her art school years, graphite on paper, c. 1944

in a faded palace-turned-hotel on a leafy plaza where noises and smells drifted in through tall, old-fashioned windows. Setting up her easel in their light, Joan quickly got down to energetic and sustained work, leaving no question about her iron will and unstoppable ambition.

For raw material, they roamed the streets, sketchbooks in hand, besieged by begging children and would-be Romeos. Joan's softly modeled pencil drawings typically depicted a figure or two sensitively placed on the page: a boy feeding pigeons, two miners conversing, an everyman with head bowed and arms defensively locked across his chest (the latter a leitmotif of her work in these early years). Clearly she was involved in both the physical feeling of gesture and its emotional impulse.

Excited by Guanajuato's abundance of "real" subject matter, Joan also used her sketchbook to work out ideas for paintings. These focus on the urban underclass, particularly melancholy waifs, nuns, beggars, weeping women, and nursing mothers. Fusing stylization (stem legs, a big-eyed mask/face) with meticulous rendering (an oversized hand, a gnarled foot), she isolated social types in an aestheticized vision of poverty, availing herself of stagy gestures and agitated drapery in a way that manages to suggest modern dance as much as capitalist injustice. Her use of chiaroscuro heightened the dramatic effect while simple horizon lines acted as framing devices and signaled barren landscapes and lives.

Typical of Joan's figure paintings that summer is her portrait of a sleeping young man whose head and arms hug a stark white table suggesting a halo, a favorite device of Mexican muralist Diego Rivera. Carefully structured, appealingly roughcast, chunky and restricted in palette (chiefly zinc white, bituminous blue black, raw sienna, and thalo green), Joan's canvas effectively mixes abstracting spatial ambiguities with expressionistic rendering. But her subject's tortured posture and shapeless clothing don't quite mask the shaky draftsmanship of an art student who fretted that she was, in her classmate Herby Katzman's overstatement, "a lousy figure painter."

In subject and style, Joan's Mexican painting reveals a confluence

Joan's Mexican oils exhibited at the University of Illinois gallery, 1947

of sources. Besides Cézanne, a constant presence in her early work, it invokes the Picasso of the Blue Period, particularly *The Tragedy* (this bleak depiction of an impoverished family belonged to the Chester Dale collection, then on extended loan to the Art Institute) and the woeful *Old Guitarist*, a fixture at the Chicago museum. Joan's art also points to her familiarity with that of José Clemente Orozco, relevant to her for its dynamic gesturalism, organic groupings of figures, and sociopolitical cast. Not least, she struggled to emulate the powerful and ennobling images of the poor by German printmaker Käthe Kollwitz, whom she venerated. Kollwitz, who had recently died, was a feminist, social democrat, and shining example of a wealthy woman who ran a household with servants while commanding respect as an artist of the people.

But all was not work in Guanajuato. Joan and Zuka (whose marriage had ended) soon acquired Mexican boyfriends, Zuka's a recent law school graduate named Eugenio Trueba Olivares, and Joan's his best friend, Manuel de Ezcurdia, a slender young man with cherubic dark blond curls, pale skin, and round brown eyes. An economics student, poet, and romantic hedonist, Manuel shared Joan's love of Mexican hot chocolate, Bacardi Special Reserve, Monte Carlo cigars, Chopin's preludes, and Bach's Third Brandenburg Concerto. The two danced (she was a marvelous dancer) to "You'll Never Know," "La Bamba," and the haunting theme song from the film *Laura*, which was everywhere that summer. Manuel read Neruda to Joan, and she read Eliot to him. With Zuka and Eugenio, they attended bullfights and spent many evenings at El Estudio, the informal salon of Guanajuatan intellectuals (both boyfriends would go on to distinguished academic careers) where Joan, who had taken Spanish lessons at Berlitz that spring, strained to follow the political and philosophical debates. From her hours with Manuel came "Juana," Joan's longtime pet name for herself at her happiest with men.

Enraptured by Guanajuato, Joan and Zuka laid plans to return in the summer of 1946. That second year, they visited the famous Mexico City murals by Orozco and Rivera. In an initiative worthy of her father, Joan had arrived in Mexico bearing letters of introduction from Art Institute Director Daniel Catton Rich to these two of the three (along with David Alfaro Siqueiros) Mexican *grandes*. Rivera was out of town, but the young women did finagle a visit to the studio of Orozco, a better painter than Rivera in the opinion of the typical art student of that time because Orozco was more expressionistic and Rivera more decorative. (Joan was a font of such judgments, another being that "Michelangelo had no sense of color." Zuka harbored doubts, but Joan wore an incontrovertible air of authority.) From the awkward encounter between the sexagenarian Mexican master and the young American students fumbling with their Spanish, Joan took Orozco's remark that Matisse was the world's greatest painter, which would prompt her to make a close study of the French artist's work.

The two friends had rented the upper rooms of a house clinging to a hillside on the outskirts of Guanajuato. Driven by Joan's powerful work ethic, they again put in long hours of painting, fueled by plates of tortillas and beans delivered by the black-braided *criada*. The rooftop terrace, theirs for the summer, commanded a splendid view of the mountain La Bufa, thus dictating plein air landscapes. La Bufa became Joan's Mont Sainte-Victoire—Cézanne's perennial late-career motif—as she attempted to marry Mexican subject matter with the methods of the Master of Aix.

In the lower half of Joan's painterly oil *La Bufa*, a concretion of houses wedges between a road zigzagging to the left and a staircase ascending on the right. These angular forms contrast with the curvy, writhing flanks of the mountain above, which converge in a V mirroring that of the buildings' edges. From Cézanne, Joan had learned to favor formal composition over verisimilitude and to break her subject into dynamic angled planes rotating around a central axis: thus the dramatically receding road, outsized staircase, and flayed and stretched houses. She also borrowed from Cézanne the technique of setting up linear continuities among objects at various distances. But *La Bufa* does more than recapitulate lessons from Cézanne. Its slit-like windows and doors, wrought-iron balconies, and other incidentals rhythmically hopscotch across the lower half of the canvas in a very Mitchell manner, and the artist audaciously bisects the image with a telephone pole, thus playing rupture off continuity and auguring her multi-panel paintings of the future.

One of Joan's two known early self-portraits, a Matisse-like pencil drawing, probably also dates from that summer in Mexico. Here the artist depicts herself as a visual person: her big eyes are overarched by heavy brows and encircled by the frames of the glasses she had had since age three but rarely wore except when she worked. (They corrected both farsightedness and an astigmatism that unevenly blurred her vision. Without them, she admitted to Zuka, she strained to see the details of what lay before her.) In this self-portrait, however, Joan's eyelids droop, and

Joan Mitchell, La Bufa, *oil on canvas, 1944*

her gaze is averted and interiorized, as if she were mentally roaming her canvas, listening to music, or wandering in "the lost and silver land." We see her but we don't.

In another picture of Joan in Mexico, a snapshot with Zuka, she wears a pretty pinecone-print sheath baring arms that, for once, are neither smeared with paint nor dotted with the gentian violet her father insisted she apply to cuts and bites. The Californian returns the photographer's gaze, but the Chicagoan again slips away. One wouldn't guess that Joan was the bolder and more flirtatious of the two, the one who played her men as enthusiastically as the little band whose Sunday concerts they attended at the Jardín de la Unión did their brass winds.

Dick Bowman visited Guanajuato that summer, even though, from Joan's point of view, their relationship had all but ended. He, on the other hand, fixes the time of their breakup as the following fall when he discovered she had been sleeping around. Meanwhile Manuel continued to lay siege to her. She briefly embraced, then rejected, a future of "bearing Catholic children in Mexico." That August, Barney Rosset, a Parker graduate she had been dating in Chicago, also drove down to Guanajuato. Suddenly it was the day before classes were to start at the

Bridesmaid Joan, groom I. Newton Perry III, and bride Sarah, 1946. Note one of Joan's still lifes hanging on the wall.

School of the Art Institute, so Barney sped Joan home nonstop except for the time he dozed at the wheel, the car drifted off the road, and they rattled into a ditch—"it was a marvelous trip!"

In her third and final year at the school, twenty-one-year-old Joan took life drawing five times, served as monitor for both Max Kahn's lithography class and Louis Ritman's painting class, and edged out all rivals for the faculty high mark. "Talented painter, very promising," glowed Ritman.

Yet she labored under the handicap of gender: the wisdom of the day held that women couldn't really paint. Supposedly men were by nature creators and women by nature followers, and thus even the most brilliant female artist was no match for a male. Influential New York teacher Hans Hofmann typified the attitude of the 1940s when he critiqued the work of his then student, painter Lee Krasner: "This is so good that you would not know it was done by a woman." And when at a dinner party thrown by another Hofmann student, sculptor Lila Katzen, he gave a toast to art that included the phrase "Only the men have the wings."

Female students lacked role models, endured what is now termed sexual harassment, and lived with the reasoning that men had to support families and thus, in all fairness, should take priority. If a woman was serious about her art, people said, she should remain single, even though, in those postwar years, a woman's whole happiness and success were equated with idealized marriage, child rearing, and domesticity. How were such attitudes internalized and self-negotiated, affecting the woman's sense of artistic personhood? In Joan's case, with denial, defiance, and a certain bewilderment. Over coffee at the Walgreens across from the Art Institute, she and Peggy Polivka, a poet who had become engaged to Dick Bowman, bemoaned the unfairness of it all and tossed around the question of whether a woman should take her husband's name after marriage. Arguing that she should have a life independent of the one she shared with a man, Joan vowed to keep her own.

Yet, abruptly jettisoning her ideas about parity for women and her disdain for high society, Joan took star billing in "Society Artists," a March picture story in the *Chicago Sunday Times* that led with the sentence "Idle hours of Chicago debutantes are converted into talent at the Art Institute." Logically, the piece should have galled her—probably it did—but, had the *Times* passed her over, she would have been no less galled. "No dilettantes," the story continued, "the debs are serious about studies." But simply raising the issue implies genteel dabbling and minor accomplishment. Moreover, by directing readers' attention to the physical charms of its five subjects, including the classy sexiness of Joan Mitchell, and treating their art as fashion props, the feature turned the female art students into objects to be visually consumed. Not one returned the viewer's gaze. They were not future professionals but rather their parents' daughters who had proven "artistic," a word, as art historian Anne Bermingham has written, that "inscribes art on to the body and into the personality of the subject who makes art. 'Artistic types' are works of art themselves, embodying art without necessarily mastering it."

"What's this? What's this? Is Joan Mitchell really married or is she turning to fiction like her famous authoress mother, Marion Strobel Mitchell?" teased gossip king Cholly Dearborn (actually, the collective nom de plume of local Hearst society tattlers) in the *Herald-American*'s May 28th "Smart Set." Tidbits about the Mitchell family showed up regularly in Dearborn's column, as they did in those of rivals Irv Kupcinet of the *Chicago Sun-Times* and Judith Cass of the *Tribune.* "The story as we heard it is that Joanie took herself a husband last summer while she painted in Mexico, and, what must have been a great strain on all of her feminine instincts, kept it a secret all this time . . . and for those who think she's kidding there's a wedding ring on her third finger, left hand." The secret marriage, Cholly rambled on, eliminated Richard Bowman as "the matchmaker's favorite man for Joan." (Dick, in fact, had just wed, his friends Gordon and Jacqueline Onslow Ford cheering him for choosing Peggy and dumping that "*bruja* [witch] Joan.") Milking the idea that his subject was "just the Bohemian to say pooh-pooh to the conventions" of Gold Coast society, Dearborn continued: "Has Joan Mitchell told papa and mama . . . that she has a husband?" The very next day, papa and mama's preferred chronicler, the *Tribune*'s Cass, published Joan's denial. The young socialite, Cass revealed, wore a wedding ring just for fun. ("If anyone in Chi kept a close watch on the papers," Sally once observed, "we sound like a very odd family.")

Neither reporter knew that, having fallen in love with Barney Rosset, Joan was jokingly threatening to make another wedding ring by twisting a swizzle stick because she wanted "like hell to get married."

Joan had first noticed Barney eight years earlier when she was a lowly eighth grader and he a tenth-grade BMOC at Parker. An actor, track and football star, participant in student government, and mover in the school's chapter of the American Student Union (a national organization of radical and progressive students), this cheerful hell-raiser and champion of social justice and freedom, his own very much included, was as prone to giggling hilariously as to waxing nostalgic over the great cause he had missed because of his age, the Spanish Civil War. Medium in stature, with wire-rimmed glasses, dark hair, and an endearingly Chaplinesque gait, he was less handsome than high-strung, excitable, shy, and contentious.

Not until two years later, during a break from college, had Barney asked Joan for a date. On that occasion, the two saw *Citizen Kane*, then zoomed around Lake Michigan in a motorboat, her frilly white dress tossing in the wind. She briefly had a crush on him, but he was in love with someone else and soon disappeared from her life.

That boat, along with flashy cars and other marvelous toys, came courtesy of Barnet L. Rosset Senior, the wealthy and powerful head of Chicago's Metropolitan Trust, business partner of Jimmy Roosevelt, and big-league investor. A self-made man of Russian Jewish descent, Rosset had married Mary Tansey, the Irish-Catholic beauty-queen daughter of a construction worker and a housewife from Marquette, Michigan. Barney was their only child.

After Parker, Barney had hopscotched from Swarthmore to UCLA to the University of Chicago (not to complete his BA until years later at the New School in New York), then, inspired by Edgar Snow's *Red Star Over China,* wangled a lieutenancy in the Army Signal Corps photographic service in China. Back in Chicago one evening after the war, he glimpsed Joan walking down the stairs from the ladies' room at the far end of a Rush Street bar called Tin Pan Alley. They chatted briefly. Later he phoned. They clicked. Then came Mexico.

Joan proved highly susceptible to Barney's antic charm. Once, during a snowstorm, he took her up for a high-bouncing ride in the Air Cougar he co-owned with his best friend, cinematographer and fellow Parker alumnus Haskell Wexler, a ride which ended in a deliciously dangerous skid off the runway. Another time, he dug up a pair of walkie-talkies and gave one to Joan. As luck had it, nothing but open space separated his bedroom in the Rossets' penthouse at 1540 Lake Shore Drive from Joan's on the tenth floor at 1530 North State Parkway. Below sat the august residence of the cardinal of Chicago. Their radiowaved messages flew back and forth over the head of His Eminence like very naughty putti.

Then in the first weeks of 1947, Barney (who had long since rejected the idea of following his father's career path) left for New York to gauge the possibility of producing a feature film based on a screenplay written by an Antioch College professor. Joan shot him one letter after another:

January 27: hell I miss you—the coffee—the pinching—the fucking— and now after some 20 hrs of sleep I feel like a vitamin pill in a bottle and I can't very well go wrestle with my father . . . I convinced von Neumann that marriage wasn't such a bad institution and he gave me wine and a copper plate to etch on and was nice to my ego.

January 29: God it was wonderful to talk to you—I love you madly and your letter rode down on the bus with me this morning—second best to you and the Oldsmobile.

January 30: Today it was so dark I could only paint for a little while and I felt it was darkness wasted—you must come soon because this missing you makes me miserable and I'm a spoiled child and want to be on the floor and scream I want Barney . . . But I did lots of good drawings today and read lots of Marx and wanted so to get in the Oldsmobile and pinch and bite and be generally irritating and go drink beer with potato chips and go fuck and then drink six cups of coffee and talk about China and whether Marshall will move the troops and tell you how God damn much I love you.

February 4: I went out to the water at North Ave, thinking I might paint water and something desolate looking . . . I loved your letter— Thank you muchly but now put a stamp on your rump and come special delivery . . . I'm thinking it was mean of God, not to let me draw like Kollwitz.

February 11: At this moment I feel almost drunk—maybe 8 shots are warming me insides—it all came out of a bottle and very quickly—for medicinal purposes of course but it's making me feel a little desperate like ringing my alarm and waking father up. [The bottle was likely Jimmie's: her father had begun hiding his gin in her underwear drawer, to which he made frequent visits.]

February 24: I think I've been mad at something or someone ever since you left. I don't know—something violent is eating me and painting has been like walking up an escalator when it's going down—it's so easy to hate. You told me to be happy but B.R. isn't around and so there isn't any me to be happy with.

During spring break, Joan flew to New York to join Barney at his apartment on Brooklyn's Old Fulton Street almost under the Brooklyn Bridge. In this romantic box seat on the spectacle of the East River, heaven for young lovers rebelling against their hidebound families, the two feasted upon each other.

Back in Chicago, Joan poured herself out on paper:

My darling empathy,

I don't know where to how to begin and so soon it's all squashed together—the little boat—the tremendous curve of the bridge and you—semi yellow against the blue walls making eggs—naked and with big slippers—the night noises—the bus—the fog horns and train whistles and always so damn warm against me in the little white

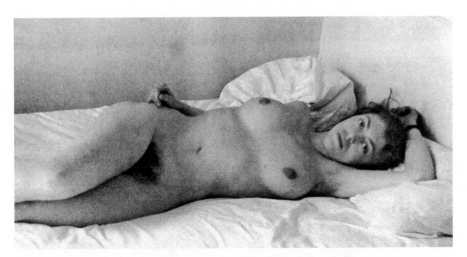

At the apartment she shared with Barney on Brooklyn's Old Fulton Street, c. 1948

room was Barney—the whole end of Fulton Street became human so quickly and the air wailed like a horse below glad we had found a bed at last—Rosset you were wonderful—I love you—I love you and I got in that plane and wanted to crawl under the seat and cry—it was all so much more than I knew existed.

That spring Joan intended to gather up as many trophies as possible and make a triumphal exit from the School of the Art Institute. In January her long-planned two-person show with Dick Bowman opened at Rockford's Burpee Art Gallery (where she scandalized locals by showing up barefoot) before traveling to the University of Illinois gallery in Champaign-Urbana. From that show she culled several pieces for the ten running feet of wall space allotted graduating students for their senior exhibitions. Among the pieces was *Still Life*, in which she emulates Matisse by handling paint in a supremely *felt* manner and including a painting-within-a-painting, namely the French master's 1939 portrait *France.*

On the basis of the senior exhibitions, the entire faculty voted for winners of the four coveted traveling fellowships, though the final decision rested in the hands of a committee headed by Dean Hubert Ropp. One afternoon around this time a handful of students observed Joan "taking Ropp [into one of the painting classrooms] and being outraged about something," recalls Ellen Lanyon. "And Joan ended up with a traveling

Talking things out with Barney on the East River under the Brooklyn Bridge, c. 1948

fellowship. Not to say that she conned him into it, but there was some contention." In fact, Joan picked up one of two top awards, the James Nelson Raymond Travel Fellowship, worth $2,000, yet, curiously, she would erroneously remember that she had received the Edward L. Ryerson Travel Fellowship, a second-tier prize amounting to $1,500. One plausible scenario is that, slated for the Ryerson, she had pressured Ropp into giving her the Raymond but later confused the two names. Joan always testily contended that she had succeeded in school on merit alone, but would a student who had not known the dean since childhood and whose parents were not the close friends of the man's longtime patrons have found the nerve to dress down the brass?

June brought the museum's *Chicago and Vicinity Annual,* a juried exhibition to which any artist living within one hundred miles of the city was eligible to submit work. Accepted in 1944 and 1945, Joan had been humiliatingly rejected in 1946. Thus she sweated and fussed over her 1947 entry, *Tired Children,* a lithograph depicting two urchins simplified to downcast heads and crisscrossed asparagus limbs. Not only did it earn a place in the show, but it also netted the Print Committee Prize of $150 from a jury that included painter Philip Guston. That meant a full-page reproduction in the catalog and a mention in *ArtNews.* Moreover, she basked in the prestige of having a "SOLD" sticker next to her print; the buyer, it turned out, was one James Herbert Mitchell.

Only days after graduation, Joan, still yammering about hating her parents, bolted from 1530 North State Parkway, sneaking out in the middle of the night and, with Francine Felsenthal, a girlfriend from school, burning up the highway to Brooklyn. Along the way, she felt awed by "the great and vast country we drove through—so beautiful with American Legion posts and signs advertising God . . . What paintings I could do in Pittsburgh—in Gary—ah that orange smoke—the bridges—the people."

Yet when it came time to put brush to canvas in Brooklyn, Joan was neither satisfied with the results nor able to move forward. What kind of painting should she do now that she had left school, where the figure had been all-important? Her native sensibilities inhered in the small, moody, loose (if occasionally belabored) landscapes she had never stopped painting in her free time. Often done en plein air in Lincoln Park, these watercolors and gouaches over pencil sketches depict—in sensuous greens and reds, blues and oranges, yellows and violets—an opalescent lagoon, a billowing grove, a turbulent sky. But this was no way to make important modern art.

Believing her sensibilities to be wholly different from those of Picasso, whose influence was omnipresent in the work of young artists "going modern," Joan strove to avoid the Spanish master "like the plague," yet the interlocking planes, open scaffolding, and cloisonné color of her increasingly abstract oils betray his powerful pull. At first she trotted out "Mexican" subject matter like beggars and nursing mothers, but soon she turned to the Brooklyn Bridge hulking outside her window. In the robust, congested, awkward post-Cubist canvases it inspired she sought "bridgeness" in a grammar of line, shape, color, texture, and pattern. The bridge lent itself beautifully to formal inventiveness but also embodied the city's energy, modernity, and power, and thus possessed the social meanings she still wanted for her art. Or did she? She wondered.

What these paintings missed, although she didn't understand this until years later, was the fact that the bridge so *moved* her.

Meanwhile she and Barney lived simply, doting on Gluten, their cat, and entertaining friends with dinners that sometimes ended with everyone sprawled on the floor, banging out accompaniment to jazz LPs on their pots and pans. Marriage had become less urgent, even vaguely frightening, to Joan, and in any case Barney's attention remained riveted to his work as producer of *Strange Victory,* a one-hour documentary directed by Leo Hurwitz that declared Hitler alive and well as long as bigotry persisted in the United States. Joan vowed to use her own time equally constructively. In order to come to grips with her self-concept as a "neurotic child" whose parents drove her nuts, she tried psychoanalysis, but her analyst turned out to have his own flair for driving her nuts. She also restlessly cruised Manhattan's East Fifty-seventh Street galleries. At Betty Parsons, she discovered Jackson Pollock's drip paintings, which she disliked; at Pierre Matisse, she gazed approvingly at Surrealist Roberto Matta's elastic humanoid forms in cosmic space; at Julien Levy, she fell in love with the tense and sensuous canvases of Arshile Gorky.

Hans Hofmann also exhibited that winter, at Samuel Kootz. Seeing this German-born artist's intensely colored abstractions may have finally decided Joan to try the Hofmann School on West Eighth Street, which she knew about from clippings Barney had mailed to Chicago. Integrating Matisse's Fauvist ideas about color with Cézanne's concepts of structure, Hofmann's systematic approach to picture making stressed the flatness of the canvas but also implied pictorial depth. Working from a model or still life, Hofmann students learned to activate the entire image, consider positive and negative space, regard a painting as a metaphorical field, and think in terms of complexes of colored planes (rather than perspective or modeling) in a dynamics of space he termed "push and pull."

Hofmann would seem to be precisely what Joan needed at this unsettled time. Besides offering substantially different and more purely aesthetic approaches to painting than she had previously known, the sixty-seven-year-old master teacher fostered in his students the same excitement about the vital importance of art that Joan took for granted, not to mention that enrolling in the Hofmann School would give her a community of peers. One afternoon she ventured over to Eighth Street. But Hofmann's nearly incomprehensible English put her off, as did his practice of correcting student drawings by erasing and redoing, or tearing off and moving, certain sections. Back in Chicago, Ritman had irked Joan by repainting the hands of her figures. (Each time he headed in her direction, she would hide the brush she knew he would want to use.) "They were only drawings," she reasoned of the student work Hofmann rectified, "but I wondered why and why and why?" After a single lesson, she scurried back to Brooklyn, vaguely frightened, not to set foot again for a long time in the Hofmann School. Still, Hofmann's ideas and methods crept into her work. She wasn't crazy about his art, but she believed he was right about painting.

Meanwhile, Joan had been posing for photographs Barney was taking in and around their classic brick-and-fire-escape building at One Old Fulton Street. Nude, tousled, silken, and bitchy, she lollygags on their unmade bed, about to claw up a pack of cigarettes, arching her brows as she shoots her lover that challenging look that kept people taut in her presence. Barney caught her too in the unvarnished wintry light outside the bar and grill downstairs. Her haunted eyes, the plainness and forties-ness of her cloth coat, and the straight-arm gesture with which she pulls open a door—that physical directness paralleling her verbal directness—make these black-and-whites surprisingly poignant. Other pictures focus on tugboats plying the East River or on the Whitmanesque Brooklyn Ferry landing across from their building. Once a friend captured Barney and Joan together lounging on the rotting, fishy-smelling piers in the shadow of the bridge. At sunset, guttural river noises blended with the dim racket of the city like the tremulous, shimmering sound of the voix céleste, the organ stop in which two pipes are tuned slightly off pitch.

The year of Arshile Gorky's *Agony,* Willem de Kooning's *Zurich,* Jackson Pollock's *Cathedral,* and Mark Rothko's *Untitled,* 1947 saw the awakening of New York painting, not that anyone besides a handful of fellow artists and a few others was paying attention. As unsure of herself as she was filled with yearning to become a great painter, Joan made no attempt to take Manhattan by storm or meet more sophisticated artists. Her next move? The traveling fellowship, intended by the School of the Art Institute to be used immediately after graduation, still hung fire. Back in Chicago she had announced her plans to travel to China in order to study prints and then, as she put it, to lose herself in the country's vastness in order to work day and night. But no one had doubted she would ultimately choose Paris. After thirteen months in Brooklyn, it was time.

On June 24, 1948, Joan sailed for France on the Liberty ship SS *Ernie Pyle.* Greeted in Le Havre ten days later by an apocalyptic scene of sunken warships lit by a low, red, swollen sun, she felt simultaneously horror-stricken and flooded with joy at the thought that she was about to set foot upon the continent of Mozart.

In Paris, Zuka and Nancy Borregaard met Joan's boat train bearing a big bouquet of blue and orange flowers. A lively painter buddy of Joan's from Chicago, Nancy had come to Paris on a 1945 School of the Art Institute fellowship, fallen in love with a Frenchman, and never gone home. As for Zuka, having been invited to travel around Europe with a wealthy Los Angeles collector and dealer, she had remained after her mentor's departure to study at the Académie de la Grande Chaumière and then married Polish-born leftist political cartoonist Louis Mitelberg. Joan was to stay with the Mitelbergs, who lived near Pigalle, until she found a place of her own.

Paris disappointed her. Thanks to the GI Bill, the French capital was once again swarming with Americans on the café circuit, but Joan found it shabby and sad. People trudged along heads down, loaves of brown bread (there was no white flour) tucked under their arms. Even the children looked listless and old. Though disoriented, she managed a pilgrimage on foot up to Picasso's old Bateau Lavoir studio in Montmartre and prowled the quays of the Seine, where she turned up her nose at the bridges, "squat like dachshunds" and sorely lacking the splendid grittiness of New York's. Seeing the old treasures of Paris only cemented her scorn: "charm all over the God damn place" but "no guts."

Self-pity spilled from her letters to Barney:

> Christ how I'm missing you—really—at times life at 1 Fulton St. seems like a dream—Gluten—you and the bridge—it doesn't seem real—like it happened—and anyway you make up your impression of a place starting with the person you love and building around it . . . when please will S.V. [*Strange Victory*] be finished—you must have seen the first print by this time—good?—of course—what I'm asking is when will you be here—I'm lonely—and writing you makes me think of it more and I don't want to think of it more because I don't know why I came in the first place and I haven't all this Promethean strength one is supposed to have and I don't know what to paint.

For four dollars a month, Joan had rented a one-room flat sans running water or electricity. Rats scurried through the hallway outside her door, and on the landing festered a stand-up toilet that flushed with a bucket of water. Situated on the ancient rue Galande in the Latin Quarter near the Seine, her building was drafty and damp. Yet just outside her two tall windows admitting the north light ideal for painting stood the Romanesque Saint-Julien-le-Pauvre, whose interior bathed in chilly white medieval stillness, and across the river was Notre Dame—"this view, I mean, God!"

Joan faced not only the great achievements of the past but also her own blank canvases. Having bet everything on painting, she found she knew neither what nor how to paint. Besides, she was thrown off by the paint itself, Lefebvre-Foinet oils she purchased directly from their artisanal manufacturer on the rue Bréa. (In later life, she would absurdly claim she had been so poor during these first months in Paris that, unable to afford art supplies, she had had to "fuck for canvas.") The actual colors of her French oils were rather different from those of American brands, but so too were the colors of their names: "*terre de Sienne brûlée*," for instance, was greener than the silverish (the color name, not the paint itself) "burnt sienna." Hunched over her palette, Joan muttered, "Why don't I quit this stuff, be strong enough to kick this?" But what else could she do? There was no other way. The eighteen paintings Joan eventually completed in Paris stayed turned to the wall whenever she wasn't working. Her upstairs neighbor, sculptor Eldon Danhausen, an ex-classmate and friend from Chicago, who was also in Paris on a traveling fellowship, found her annoyingly buttoned-up and uncollegial. He would ask to see her canvases, "and she'd reply, 'Oh, they're not ready yet.'" For once, she found herself incapable of competing.

Neither could she "eat enough or smoke enough or get warm or sleep or keep clean." A lump of anxiety, she would lie in bed at night choking on "so much nothing—strange and stupid choice I made—expensive choice—so white these walls and hollow noises in the street," then blearily get up at two or three a.m., light a kerosene lamp, and try to paint. Once, craving blueness and warmth, she laid her hands on a car in order to flee Paris for Avignon, in the south of France. Several days later she threw the episode on paper for Barney: "strange how I left at night after painting so hard telling nobody and not caring—I . . . drew the bridge—lonely—without you and beautiful in October and no people—I went to the sea and got brown and swam and talked to the fisherman—the fluid ran out of the brakes but they fixed them—Christ what am I."

Joan, Barney, and the Braque-like stove on the rue Galande, 1948 or 1949

Not long after her arrival, Joan had had a brief affair with an English writer, the first in a string of casual lovers who eased her self-consciousness and loneliness that summer and fall. A practiced deceiver whose usual ploy was to tell a fraction of the truth, she casually mentioned the Englishman in a letter to Barney, slyly adding that he was "married just so you won't think impossible thoughts." Yet she desperately missed Barney. In mid-August, *Strange Victory* finished at last, he had come to Paris; in mid-September he had left again to handle its distribution and promotion. A month later Joan wrote, "I wait Christ how long—to wake and find you and hold you and smell you, darling with all my heart I want you and the tears and salt are mixed."

His return that November brought Joan back from the brink of emotional collapse. Not only was he there for her in the night, but also he cooked for her (badly, the spaghetti once coming out in a single chunk) and improved her social life. Joan and Barney spent time with their upstairs neighbors, painter Herby Katzman and his bride Duny. They also saw a lot of young artists Warren Brandt and Herman Cherry, who introduced Joan to Philip Guston when the older painter stopped in Paris on his way home after a year in Italy. And Timmy Osato's sister, the famous ballerina Sono Osato, and her husband, Victor Elmaleh, in Paris that winter, got them together with visiting entertainer Gene Kelly and his wife, actress Betsy Blair, and the six of them went dancing at the famous Le Bal Nègre, hopping with African Legionnaires and American coeds.

All the same, life in the City of Light continued dismal. The fetchingly Braque-like stove in Joan's apartment stung their eyes with its acrid smoke but proved no match for the penetrating November chill. Coal, bread, eggs, butter, milk, and cheese were rationed. Thanks to the jeep station wagon Barney had flown over—his father's friend owned the airline—and a foreigner's relatively generous allotment of gas, the two did have the luxury of short getaways: excursions to see the Romanesque architecture Joan loved and, with Zuka, a quick and rather miserable trip to Franco's Spain, where they visited Guernica and the Prado and locals pelted with rocks their obviously American car. Reacting to bad memories of grand-touring with his parents, Barney refused to indulge in anything that smacked of tourism: they drove, ate, saw the town and the museum, and whipped back to Paris.

Two weeks later, Joan and Barney flew to Czechoslovakia, officially to present *Strange Victory* at the Karlovy Vary Film Festival, but also to get a feeling for a country that was Sovietizing after February's Communist coup. In those early days of the Cold War, the Communists enjoyed enormous prestige among French intellectuals and Joan had been attending party lectures in Paris, but in Prague she and Barney found the discourse stifling and the art leaden. Having long romanticized Communism, which they equated with personal freedom, they were appalled when authorities attempted to confiscate Barney's bottle of cognac, a small thing but telling. Nor could the two get visas for Hungary, where they had planned to join Dutch filmmaker Joris Ivens. They took pains to sort out and weigh their observations, but essentially they left Prague as apostates. Shortly before Christmas, the Communist chapter of Joan's life closed at Ruzyně Airport: "Let's be bourgeois pigs," joked Barney, "and go back to Paris!"

Nineteen forty-nine staggered in at a huge party at a friend's *hôtel particulier* with tattered red velour walls where everyone got sick on bad liquor. For weeks, icy rain had been slicing down. January days were only quick yawns of light. Joan fell into deep depression, then developed bronchitis. When she was briefly hospitalized at the American Hospital in Neuilly, her doctor advised that she finish out the winter in the south of France.

So, taking advantage of Sono Osato's connection to Sidney Simon and Joan Lewisohn Simon, a wealthy American couple who were leaving their rented villa in Le Lavandou, between Toulon and Saint-Tropez, Joan and Barney moved to Provence in late January. Designed by a Dutch architect and used in the 1920s by the writer André Gide, the lovely Villa Le Pin had eleven rooms, including a big living room with a wisteria-framed view of the Mediterranean that served as Joan's studio.

Joan felt as if she had been whisked from ditchwater murkiness into the magical color and light of the art she loved best. The boats on the beach might have been those van Gogh had painted at Saintes-Maries-de-la-Mer, and the Promenade des Anglais in Nice, a short drive east, came straight out of Matisse. It was an easy run to Cannes, where the couple liked to alight at a certain hotel bar for the brandy Alexanders they consumed for the cream as much as the liquor before rolling on to Italy (where there was no rationing) to stock up on olive oil, coffee beans, and other luxuries. At first Joan's spirits soared, but the Mistral unstrung her, and boredom lurked. She and Barney played bridge with their real estate agent and his wife, but, with few other artists or friends at hand, Le Lavandou felt more isolated than paradisiacal.

For subject matter in her painting, Joan turned to the picturesque Provence where fishermen untangle their nets, old men play billiards or boules, and solitary figures brood by the edge of the sea. All lent themselves to semiabstract treatment (the reticulation of the nets, the X of crossed cues, the scatter of rocks along the shore) and blessedly offered a provisional answer to the question: What constitutes meaningful subject matter? Not only did the new work alternate between dullish and vividly hued (Mediterranean blues, baize greens, velvety ochres), but also it straddled two paradigms. Trained to think in terms of fixing an optical relationship with a modeled figure using a plumb line, Joan had begun paying stricter attention to ways in which marks map relationships to each other and to the rectangle they occupy. (Hans Hofmann taught that the first lines of any composition are the four sides of the paper.) Yet Joan's attempts to combine the two strategies in paintings of reductive human forms in tumbling architectonic spaces yielded, at best, semi-satisfying results.

Her most abstract works were her most resolved: *Game of Boule,* for instance, with its interlocking geometric and curvilinear forms, attention to lights and darks, and clothespin-like human figures, including a recurring standing figure with arms crossed as if in a straitjacket. Another relatively successful work, the Cubo-Futuristic-looking *Bicycle Race, Tour de France,* painted after Joan and Barney watched the annual contest, then chased it in his jeep, centered around a dynamic streak of palmated circles. This canvas would win acceptance to the Art Institute's 1950 Society for Contemporary American Art exhibition. Later it was purchased by Marion's wealthy friends Julia and Augustine Bowe, who hung it above a marble bust of Dante in the living room of their lakefront apartment. There it became a familiar presence to the Bowe children and their close pal, a young art student named Claes Oldenburg.

Come August, Joan put down her brushes to travel with Barney, Zuka, and Zuka's husband Louis to Italy, where she was seduced by the Belliniesque landscapes, by Venice, and especially by Florence, so lucid, untouristed, and architectural—so *yellow!*—that it resembled a dream of Florence. In one snapshot from Florence, Barney idles on a sun-baked wall along the Arno as Joan—young and summery in her white shirt, full skirt, and strappy sandals—drapes an arm over his leg and relaxes into him. She stares at the camera as he throws her a look testifying to his tender and resilient devotion. "He cared so much about her," observes one friend. "It was really one of the great love stories."

But that trip too had its miseries, in part because Louis, a Jew, relished telling Jewish jokes to which Barney responded with humorless theories about how ethnic jokes seed prejudice. And when Louis capped their discussion of artist Käthe Kollwitz with the comment "Well, I wouldn't want to be married to her!" Barney interpreted the remark as anti-woman and exploded, and Joan seconded him. The two were adamant about speaking out against what they were quick to see as intolerance. (Ironically, Louis's fiercely satirical sculptures and drawings in the tradition of Daumier, works published in *L'Humanité, L'Express,* and *Le Monde* using the moniker "Tim," were to win him a reputation as a leading French champion of democratic values, free speech, and human rights.) The two couples split.

Still puzzling over his life's work, Barney had spent his first months in Le Lavandou writing and planning a film he hoped to make in China, but gradually lethargy and depression had slackened this coil of energy, leaving him staring at the horizon or creeping back to bed at noon. The sight of him sleepwalking through the day irritated Joan, yet she had not refused the marriage proposals with which he had been peppering her since his arrival in France.

Eventually, she wrote to ask advice from her mother (distance had brought the two closer), who replied that this choice must be fully her own. Having recognized that the "marriage deal" was too "solemn and non-elastic" for comfort, Joan knew she was unready for matrimony "in the deep sense." Yet in the end she decided to close her eyes and do it quickly. She was not immune to the charms of having a husband, and it was understood that the usual rules would not apply. It never crossed anyone's mind that Barney's career would automatically take priority or that Joan would iron his shirts and cook his pot roast. Was she still in love with him? Friends felt she took him for granted. The more cynical among them, aware of Joan's steely self-interest when it came to painting, suspected she was marrying a wealthy and supportive man in order to further her art. What were her other options?, she wondered. Return to Chicago? Hardly. Her allowance wasn't big enough to make it in New York on her own. The clincher: she had gone through her fellowship money, and Barney claimed he wouldn't take her home unless they wed.

The two erstwhile Communists made arrangements to depart Cannes, traveling first class on the SS *Atlantic,* for which Barney paid $960, nearly half the amount of Joan's fellowship. He also underwrote transport for her paintings, which were ferried by rowboat to the ship anchored offshore, without her having to unstretch them.

But first, on the morning of September 10, 1949, Joan and Barney married at the town hall of Le Lavandou. In a paroxysm of Gallic enthusiasm, the mayor put the icing on the ceremony with his cry "Vive Chi-ca-go!" But Chicago was history. They felt the gravitational pull of New York.

NEW YORK

It's so beautiful it breaks your heart.

Painter FRANZ KLINE
about a downtown New York loft
building with a storefront and an
enormous neon sign

CHAPTER SIX Tenth Street

In late March 1950 readers of *Life* magazine opened to a ten-page
cover story hailing Howard Warshaw, Aleta Cornelius, Franklin
Boggs, Honoré Sharrer, and fifteen other painters—Buffalo, Jersey
City, and Beloit were all represented—as the nation's best under age
thirty-six. These young artists' sentiment-laced scenes of candy stores,
carnivals, slums, Chinese swans, and automobile graveyards in retooled
versions of traditional modes had earned *Life*'s kudos for their felicitous sureness of style. Millions saw the work. In contrast, the handful of
New Yorkers who ventured into Talent 1950, curated by critic Clement Greenberg and art historian Meyer Schapiro for the Samuel Kootz
Gallery that same spring, found the slatherings of twenty-three young
artists who had rejected standard answers to the question "How should
one make a painting?" and had stripped their work of finesse. Grace
Hartigan, Esteban Vicente, Elaine de Kooning, Franz Kline, Alfred Les-

lie, and the others searchingly mixed it up with raw pigment. Shunned by galleries (the result of a cancelation, Talent 1950 was a first), collectors (nothing sold), and critics (more or less mute), these fiercely ambitious upstarts made art not for the indifferent or eye-rolling readers of middlebrow magazines but for each other and for History. Indeed, they derived a certain artistic freedom from knowing that nobody wanted it: "Well, we don't sell anyway, so why not?"

That same spring, the Metropolitan Museum presented an expanded version of *Life*'s "19 Young Americans." "Timid practitioners of various sorts of anecdotal romanticism," scoffed the devastatingly articulate Thomas B. Hess, managing editor of *ArtNews,* one of the young progressives' few allies. Moreover, the Met had recently announced a regional jurying system for its new competition for painters, thus guaranteeing conservative choices. At stake was prize money as well as inclusion in an important upcoming survey of American painting. Outraged, older progressive artists responded with a letter of protest in the *Times.* Fifteen of them were subsequently photographed by *Life,* which dubbed these stern-looking veterans—fourteen men and one woman—"the Irascibles."

The one in the middle, Jackson Pollock, had already earned notoriety for his wildly unorthodox drip paintings, thanks to an earlier *Life* feature ("Jackson Pollock: Is He the Greatest Living Painter in the United States?") which had simultaneously patronized him as a paint-drooler and celebrified him as a brooding jeans-wearing, cigarette-dangling-from-the-lips Brando. Pollock's next opening, at Betty Parsons's Fifty-seventh Street gallery on November 21, 1949, had brought a bolt out of the blue: besides the usual studio rats and smattering of critics, a well-heeled uptown crowd occupied Parsons's attractive white space. "What's going on here?" a startled Milton Resnick turned to his fellow painter, Willem de Kooning, after observing these strangers "going around shaking hands." "Look around," de Kooning famously replied. "These are the big shots. Jackson has broken the ice." Eighteen Pollocks sold.

Not long thereafter, the Museum of Modern Art's powerful director of collections, Alfred Barr, selected vanguard painters Pollock, de Kooning, and the late Arshile Gorky as three of the six artists for the contemporary section of the U.S. Pavilion at the 1950 Venice Biennale. Barely dry at the Biennale, de Kooning's *Excavation* would then travel to the

Art Institute of Chicago, where it was crowned with a $4,000 prize and purchased.

Was 1950 a fulcrum year after all? Sculptor Philip Pavia had prophesied as much at the downtown artists' New Year's Eve bash: "The first half of the century belonged to Paris. The next half century will be ours."

Nowhere else on earth was painting lived as intensely as below Fourteenth Street, where, after every night of beery camaraderie, painters still had to face the decrepit walk-ups and the scramble to make rent. Many lived along East Ninth Street, near Wanamaker's department store, or East Tenth, especially between Third and Fourth Avenues, a block dreary with a metal stamping factory, an employment agency for "bums," and a wino bar or two. Unheated except for gas or kerosene stoves, their naked-light-bulb apartments or illegal-for-habitation lofts went for only thirty or forty dollars a month, but even that was a stretch. Then there were the bills at Rosenthal, for canvas, brushes, jumbo tubes of Bocour oils, and whatever else they couldn't beg, borrow, steal, improvise, or get wholesale. An old incorruptible who had long since chosen art and poverty over compromise and solvency, Bill de Kooning once walked home forty blocks from a museum appointment rather than spend a nickel for the subway. Grace Hartigan, who was raising a young son alone, stocked her window-ledge larder with bruised fruit and day-old bread. Almost everyone took odd jobs.

Making a virtue of rough-edged living (as opposed to the self-conscious bohemianism of the Village or the middle-class lifestyles of advanced artists uptown), the downtown crowd survived on coffee, cigarettes, beer, and talk, venting the tension and solitude of painting by gathering on stoops, at bars, and in all-night cafeterias, chop suey joints, and cheap Italian places, where they washed down seventy-five-cent plates of spaghetti "with green sauce" with ten-cent glasses of Chianti.

Their mutuality—*the life*, good and bad—outweighed all else. "You couldn't be an artist in the middle of Ohio," as Pavia put it. "You'd isolate yourself too much. You really needed someone to *kick* you." As for the "toughness and pressure of neglect" by the art establishment, it had resulted, Tom Hess observed of the younger contingent, in "a group that seems as blithe and as debonair as were the bohemians of the Impressionists' Café Guerbois."

As time went on, the downtown artists talked about having a place of their own, so they could be among themselves to chew over their art-making as the old-timers among them had once chewed over Picasso's, a place more congenial than the Waldorf, where, for years, they had been staking out tables and nursing nickel cups of joe loaded with sugar and milk. Thus when a cheap vacant loft materialized at 39 East Eighth Street, around the corner from their favorite bar, the Cedar, a nucleus of artists met, decided, scared up the $250 deposit, and set about putting the space to rights. At the end of that year the Eighth Street Club opened to "no manifestoes, no exhibitions, no pictures on the walls," just keys for its charter members and informal gatherings arranged by jungle telephone. Not until Pavia started organizing Friday-evening lectures and panels, however, did the Club emerge as a vital meeting place for downtown artists and uptown intellectuals, a conduit for their prodigious social energies, a heady land's end.

The oldest among them could trace their attitude of collective struggle back to the 1930s, when the Federal Arts Project of the Works Progress Administration had lured them out of their studios. By decade's end, a number had organized against the antimodernist regionalism typified by Grant Wood as well as the social realism identified with artists like Reginald Marsh and the Soyer brothers. Painter Lee Krasner, for one, had begun working in an apolitical nonrepresentational style, as championed by the American Abstract Artists, while Adolph Gottlieb, Mark Rothko, and others had formed The Ten to search for ways to conjugate social consciousness with abstraction.

Then World War II had sent into history the best years of the School of Paris and brought to New York leading European modernists including Piet Mondrian, Marc Chagall, Salvador Dalí, Fernand Léger, Yves Tanguy, André Masson, Max Ernst, and Roberto Matta. Though distanced from the New Yorkers by language and attitudes, the Europeans had deeply impressed locals with their unfailing bohemian élan and native faith in the vital meaningfulness of art. And, while the American avant-garde had little use for the formally retardaire Surrealist style exemplified by Dalí, painters like Arshile Gorky and Jackson Pollock began taking cues from the abstract Surrealism of Matta, whose automatism seemed to unwrap the latent content of the individual psyche.

By war's end, the most self-confident American artists were dismissing the refinements of Continental painting, some even considering Cubism (once revolutionary for its overthrow of Renaissance space) to be a still-useful but concept-driven academicism that clipped one's risk-taking wings. Rothko and Barnett Newman—the former with luminescent fields of color, the latter with meticulous calibrations of scale, proportion, and hue—would soon dare the elimination of all that stood between the artist, the viewer, and the sublime. No longer would they paint experiences: their pictures would *be* experiences in the viewer's own space. Meanwhile, de Kooning and Pollock were engaging in what painter John Ferren termed "searching itself as a way of art," de Kooning shuttling back and forth between abstraction and representation as he laid out on canvas his struggle and self-doubt, Pollock transforming the act of painting into an experience of self-realization: the artist as hero in the badlands of modern life.

Such bold experimentation took shape against a backdrop of military victory and triumphant Americanism, shadowed, however, by knowledge of the moral failure of all absolutes during the war. The early 1950s brought the displacement of national purpose by shallow materialism as well as Cold War paranoia and threat of nuclear holocaust. With the world teetering on the brink of annihilation, politics as usual felt irrelevant. Anxiety worked itself deep into the American psyche, and, as many artists saw it, abstract painting became the paradigmatic vehicle for self-discovery and manifestation of the zeitgeist. Akin to psychoanalysis in its preoccupation with process, instinct, free association, and the unconscious, the new art proclaimed existentialist attitudes. Its younger practitioners, however, refugees from the "silent generation," would turn their backs on despair, the better to confront self-created freedom through the act.

Notwithstanding the heterogeneity of this new art, painters Robert Motherwell and Ad Reinhardt organized a three-day artists' symposium in April 1950 to address, in part, the issue of packaging its attitudes and practices. The only non-artist in attendance, MoMA's Alfred Barr (who believed that every work of art is assignable to its rightful place in a flowchart of historical progression) pressed the others to choose a name for their movement or direction. But they dragged their feet. Why falsely imply that an ethos of volatility and possibility, an attitude of adventurous searching, constituted a unified body of work? De Kooning responded, "It is disastrous to name ourselves." Yet Motherwell's term based in geography—"the New York School"—took hold, as would the process-oriented term "action painting" and the stylistically focused "Abstract Expressionism."

In the fall of 1949, Mr. and Mrs. Barnet Rosset Jr., only vaguely aware of recent developments in New York painting, debarked in Manhattan. Following a short stay at the Chelsea Hotel and a Christmas visit to Chicago, they rented a vintage artist's studio behind a brownstone at 267 West Eleventh Street. With its wide-planked floors, fireplace, skylight, and miniature garden, this charming dollhouse, no bigger than twenty by twenty (plus a semifinished basement), put Joan's painting literally at the center of their lives.

In early January 1950, two months before *Life*'s touting of "19 Young Americans," Joan made overtures to a few New York galleries, of which there were then about thirty, and was promptly rejected. Dealer Julius Carlebach, for one, told her, "Gee, Joan, if only you were French and male and dead." So she retreated, not unhappily, to her "ivory tower," where she continued to flog semiabstract scenes in a shallow pictorial space.

French subjects had quickly given way to New York–based fare: *Coney Island, Subway, The Bridge,* and *The City.* Jazzed with the urban energies of Gotham at dusk, yet stiffly controlled, *The City* is a paean to New York, Cubist city par excellence. Windows and assorted details identify its rigging of rectangles, triangles, circles, and arcs as buildings, bridges, streetlights, and signs, while the whorled beams of a Great White Way at its activated center entangle themselves in orthogonal form. The artist's concern with pictorial dynamics converges with her attention to light (solar, tungsten, neon), light depicted, rather than felt.

Two less successful oils from this very early New York period—which Joan later described as "horrible"—all but demand psychobiographical readings. One (all grays relieved by bits of white, ochre, and blue) represents a row of windows, their lower panes inlaid in a rote pattern that vaguely evokes Cubism as a tired, codified art-making practice. Presumably Joan intended a view of Manhattan's spatial jumble, yet one can't help but read up-against-the-wall frustration. The other, *Figure and the City,* is surely the weirdest painting of Mitchell's career. Here, against a backdrop of jittering jigsaw geometry, a faceless young woman turns from the breakaway shapes that descend upon her as if to swallow her up. Was the idea to capture on canvas her experience of boundaryless-

Joan, twenty-six, and Jimmie with Figure and the City, *around the time she turned to abstraction, thinking that her father "couldn't even criticize what it was, you know?" c. 1951*

ness? Encased in thick, dark lines, the figure's impossibly thin arms go on forever, while her head and shoulders meld with the geometric forms. On a pictorial level, stylized figuration and post-Cubism unhappily cohabit. As she pushed through this failed attempt at a more subjective kind of art, Joan knew that she would never again paint the human form. But what now?

One day later that January, Joan walked into the Annual of American Painting at the Whitney Museum (then on West Eighth Street) and, in the very first gallery, stopped dead in her tracks. Muscular, unruly, and ambiguous, Willem de Kooning's six-foot-nine-inch-wide *Attic* ramped up before her. Black lines knifed through its shallow whites, forming vaguely anatomical, vaguely cartoony fragments—heads, orifices, spiky limbs akimbo—that tightened into each other as they darted to oblivion and back. Smudged with red, these elusive forms bore ghost images of the newspaper with which the artist had covered the wet pigment between painting sessions, thus heightening the effect of random information and foregrounding the material facts of *Attic*'s making. Moreover, its snaggly lines, zonked energies, and refusal to hold form made *Attic* a quintessential painting for the age of anxiety. It also lived up to its title. Abstraction, by de Kooning's lights, was not a way of "taking things out or reducing painting" but rather a way of "putting more and more things in it: drama, anger, pain, love, a figure, a horse, my ideas about space."

Joan had never heard of Willem de Kooning, but, in the days that followed, she went looking for him. In fact, he lived only five minutes away, on Fourth Avenue across from Grace Church School. But she was somehow directed instead to the Ninth Street digs of painter Franz Kline. After climbing three flights of worn stairs one evening, she knocked on Kline's battered door. The sight that met her eyes when he opened it struck another tremendous blow. In the cluttered studio, separated from his living quarters by a half wall the painter had built, hung several large, bold, stark unstretched canvases, among them perhaps the artist's masterworks from that period: *Hoboken, Nijinsky, Cardinal,* and *Chief.* Built from black and white brushstrokes that braced, clobbered, sideswiped, clinched, and/or slammed into each other, Kline's abstractions manifested a powerful materiality, evoking, at times, steel bridges, railroad trestles, and urban scaffoldings.

The quintessential action painter, Kline would begin by sliding a wide housepainter's brush into a big can of glistening housepainter's enamel. Fixing his gaze on a spot at the far end of his five- or six-foot-wide canvas, he would then crouch, spring, land, and race on, dragging and twisting his paint-juicy brush across the gessoed linen field. Later he worked the edges of his strokes: white on black, black on white. As much drawing as painting, as much act as drawing, Kline's big oils immediately had Joan climbing the high ropes of art. And the gouache and ink sketches done on the pages of telephone books (he loved their gray sidewalk look) that littered his floor impressed her as "the most beautiful things I'd ever seen in my life."

Franz Kline in his studio, 1954

If the art wowed Joan, so did the man, the prototype, she felt, of the "seedy, exciting" New York painter up against the world. Not that Kline looked arty. No New York School painter did. His natty mustache, Ronald Colman face (an Anglophile, Kline adored Colman), and black snap-brim fedora could no doubt pass at the Rotary Club in his birthplace, Wilkes-Barre, Pennsylvania, but the doleful eyes and the widow's peak that made of his face a lumpy heart set him apart. So did the irresistibly ebullient, wisecracking loop-de-loop barfly talk that kept Joan at Kline's studio until seven thirty the next morning. Poet Frank O'Hara once made a valiant attempt at capturing the painter's cataract of words:

Which reminds me of Boston, for some reason. You know I studied there for a while and once I was up there for a show and met this Bostonian who thought I looked pretty Bohemian. His definition of a Bohemian artist was someone who could live where animals would die. He also talked a lot about the 8th Street Club and said that Hans Hofmann and Clem Greenberg run it, which is like Ruskin saying that Rowlandson and Daumier used up enough copper to clad the British Navy and it's too bad they didn't sink it.

Raised in a railroad town in the Lehigh Valley—coal country—Franz Kline had captained his high school varsity football team. After two years at Boston University and three at the Heatherley School of Fine Art in London, he had moved to New York and married his British sweetheart, dancer Elizabeth Parsons. Living in grim cold-water flats from which they were more than once evicted because they couldn't make the rent, the couple barely scraped by. In 1946, Elizabeth's mental illness reached the point where Franz could no longer care for her, and she was committed to a state hospital on Long Island. Nor had Kline earned the unqualified respect of his colleagues. Some considered him a loser for having traveled the route of illustration (he had started as a cartoonist and eked out a living peddling at street fairs and doing murals in bars) rather than that of Cubism and the WPA, and for painting sentimentalized pictures like rocking chairs and heads of his alter ego, the dancer Nijinsky in the role of Petrushka the clown. Around 1947, Kline had finally closed in on his signature style, which fully emerged (by one account) after the revelation of seeing his drawings enlarged with a Bell-Opticon projector. Thirty-nine years old when he met Joan, he had never had a solo show.

Wild as she was for Kline's bold abstractions, Joan took little from them save permission to throw out her academic ballast. One could not really mine Kline's work. Asked why it so captivated her, she would point to its "crudeness and accuracy." In fact, her feelings about the paintings were inextricable from her friendship with Franz, whose disarming warmth tinged with sadness truly moved her (and many others) and whose willingness to take her seriously as a painter she never forgot. Years later she would speak of how very generous Kline was

about other painters, which is very unlike many painters. He would say, "Gee, trying to do it, Joan, is great, I mean, it's not so bad. Look—look at that," about a young, unknown person, anybody. "It's great.

Come on, do it." This is really true. He was so honest and not snobby, not saying: "Why don't you forget it—get a job or something?" Always generous. No, he really never forgot and always helped other people . . . Absolutely marvelous.

Joan's account of Franz's encouragement in the midst of a difficult, doubting world finds echo today in tales of her generosity to young and struggling artists. For Franz and Joan, painting and painters were supremely important: Joan would pass on what the older artist had given her, what he called "the dream."

Not long after meeting Franz, Joan stood knocking at the door of the painter who had first sent her heart racing.

Though Bill de Kooning's debut one-man show, at Egan Gallery in 1948, had confirmed his reputation as a rising star, it had not lifted the forty-three-year-old out of dire poverty. Joan found him in a chilly, cavernous Fourth Avenue studio doing battle with the *Attic*-like *Excavation*, a painting today considered a masterwork of the twentieth century. (As she viewed *Excavation* in various stages during her several visits that early spring, Joan kept thinking: "Why doesn't he stop? It's finished!" But, famously unwilling to let go, de Kooning continued to lavish pigment upon his canvas, scraped, painted, and pushed on.)

Looking like a sturdy blue-eyed Dutch sailor, this product of an unstable Rotterdammer working-class family had apprenticed at a decorating firm, then studied at Rotterdam's Academy of Fine Arts and Techniques, where craftsmanship reigned. At twenty-two, he had stowed away on a U.S.-bound freighter; by the dawn of the 1930s, he was earning steady paychecks as a display artist in New York City. Around that time he befriended several deeply committed painters, notably Armenian émigré Arshile Gorky, whose dedication to art proved an irresistible magnet to the younger man. De Kooning dropped his day job and began painting moody, apparitional male figures. After falling in love with young artist Elaine Fried (they married in 1943), he turned to pictures like *Pink Angels*, a metamorphosis of rosy, taffy-pulled female flesh that stops short of resolving itself into human figures, thus transmitting his feeling for content as "a glimpse of something," as he put it, "an encounter, you know, like a flash." His next major works comprised black-and-white fields of flat forms. Rejecting the idea that abstraction was more advanced than figuration, de Kooning considered them two sides of a coin.

As for Joan, she reveled in the felt quality, raw facture, expressive shapes, whiplash lines, and assertion of flatness in the veteran artist's work. She studied the way he let paint fly yet built his pictures with Cézannesque rigor, the way he retained the battered remnants of the Cubist grid yet worked in figure-ground mode, setting up unstable relationships between figure (the thing depicted) and ground (the flat surface of the canvas seen as background). Time and again, de Kooning visually pulls the rug out from under his viewers, forcing them to see his admixtures of fragments as images, and then not. Her encounter with de Kooning's paintings immediately cracked open Joan's own. No one would mistake a Mitchell for a de Kooning, but when, years later, Joan's acolytes expressed a need to steer clear of her siren influence, she would reply, "Do you know how many de Koonings I've done?"

As much as Mitchell loved de Kooning's taut abstractions, she was less thrilled by his more expressionistic work, epitomized by the 1950–52 *Woman I*. In other respects, too, the artists diverged. De Kooning proceeded by trial and error while Mitchell painted additively, preferring to destroy a work in progress rather than scrape and redo. And, although both adored oil paint for its light and life, they brought different sensibilities to the medium. For de Kooning, who seldom lost touch with the erotics of the human body, "Flesh was the reason why oil painting was invented." For Mitchell, on the other hand, paint incarnated water in its every mood, "the flow of paint," as curator Klaus Kertess once wrote, becoming in her art "a metaphor for the flow of ocean or river, and vice versa."

Not only did Joan worship Bill for his painting intelligence, but also she deeply respected his long struggle, ascetic lifestyle, and willingness to help. Along with Kline and, to a degree, Hofmann, this "hell of a nice guy" was accessible and encouraging to young painters. He kidded around, showed up at the Cedar with various "girls" on his arm, and washed the cups at the Club. A tense workaholic who took nothing for granted in the studio, he also stood slightly apart. Overcome with an anxiety Joan understood all too well, Bill sometimes roamed the streets, insomniac, at two a.m.

For Joan the flux of gritty, steaming-manhole-cover, glaring-morning-light, dirty-brick, din-of-construction Manhattan was inseparable from de Kooning, the man and the painter. Bill's jumpy brushstrokes—he spoke of the "leap of space"—resonated with the dense and unpredictable play of shape and light in the city. Finding freedom in having to work "to get a view," Joan realized that a glimpse of Manhattan sky made

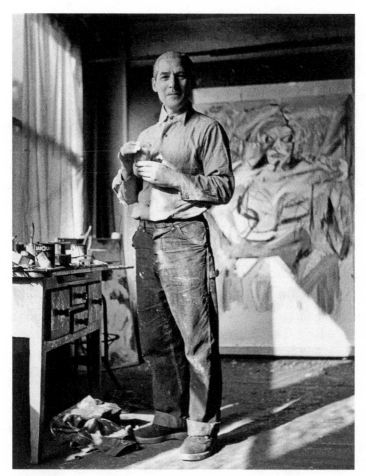

Bill de Kooning with Woman I, *1952*

her intensely aware of space in a way the sterile azure dome of southern France never had: "You don't feel courage unless you're afraid. You
don't feel space unless you're hemmed in."

Moreover, Bill might deliver her from Jimmie at last. Joan mentally
replaced Jimmie with de Kooning, whom she now considered (as she
once told sculptor Lynda Benglis) "my father."

Months after her arrival in New York, Joan was still acquainted with few
artists. Then one day she got a call from Miriam Schapiro and Paul Brach,
friends of Dick Bowman during their graduate school days at the Uni-

versity of Iowa, where Dick had then taught. Having sublet a place on MacDougal Alley, Mimi and Paul were making prints at Stanley William Hayter's Studio 17 that summer between Paul's two years of teaching at the University of Missouri. Not long afterward the couple dropped by West Eleventh Street with a lean-faced, dark-haired artist friend named Michael Goldberg. During their long afternoon together (under the strange *Figure and the City*), Joan hit it off famously with Paul, gregarious and opinionated, and Mimi, serious and rather shy. Barney too was present—and Mike. As the hours wore on, it became obvious that Joan and Mike had eyes for each other. An erotic tension filled the room, Barney looked daggers at Joan, and the two bickered fiercely.

The eruption of Mike Goldberg into their lives (as Barney surely suspected, he and Joan started secretly meeting) roiled the Rossets' already-troubled marriage. Paradoxically, a series of normal domestic crises then restored a semblance of harmony. Joan needed an emergency appendectomy, Barney developed hay fever, and together they apartment-hunted after learning that, for reasons now forgotten, they had to give up the little house. Having signed a lease on an expensive duplex in a brownstone at 59 West Ninth Street, where Joan could paint in an upstairs space, they flew to Havana, the first stop on what was for Barney a working vacation.

A lure for Chicago mobsters and Hollywood stars, the Cuban capital's stylish Hotel Nacional, co-owned by Barnet Rosset Sr., lavished attention upon the junior Rossets. However, a hurricane soon lashed the island, forcing guests to evacuate, clinging to ropes. After a stay in Haiti, at the romantic Hotel Oloffson, the so-called Greenwich Village of the Tropics, where Barney worked on a short documentary about the tropical disease yaws, the two flew to the Yucatán, where they rode a narrow-gauge railroad to the Mayan ruins at Chichén Itzá. Though Joan loved Mexico as much as ever, her longing to be with Mike triumphed over her desire to revisit Mexico City or vacation with her husband. Making some excuse to Barney, who was meeting with film people in the Mexican capital, she flew back to New York and straight into the arms of Mike Goldberg. He helped her move into the West Ninth Street apartment, setting up her white-walled, stripped floor studio with a rack of reflector lights, alternating tungsten and halogen, yellow and blue.

A few days later Barney too returned to New York, and life once again fell into a semblance of routine, including the small dinner parties the couple hosted, Joan cleaning, Barney cooking. Officially a painter friend of Joan's, Mike was sometimes invited, as were Kline and de Kooning. (Bill and Joan liked to tease Barney—who was "visually illiterate," Joan claimed—by insisting that the taped windows of new buildings were really small Klines.) But their dinner guest list was eclectic, ranging from Marion's friend the poet Ellen Borden Stevenson, who had recently divorced Illinois governor Adlai Stevenson, to cinematographer Leonard Stark and his artist wife Marilyn, who easily picked up that her hosts' marriage "was not very substantial." Indeed, the Rossets had turned to couples therapy. Joan, however, heaped scorn upon their therapist, who wanted her to draw pictures of how Barney made her feel. And the stubborn fact remained: she was wild for Mike Goldberg.

With feral joy, Joan had rushed blindly into the affair, never pausing to consider its consequences. She took what she needed. Sex, yes. But also the fact that Mike was a painter. Joan was drunk on painting, drunk on New York, drunk on Mike—all the same thing. Barney, in contrast, was merely a "civilian."

Demanding to see her lover's work, Joan had been walked over to Bond Street, where some of his paintings were stored at a friend's place. The friend wasn't home. So Mike hoisted himself onto the fire escape, broke into the apartment, and grabbed a rolled canvas, which he carried down and unfurled on the sidewalk. Gestural, impastoed, and de Kooningesque, it won Joan's enthusiastic approval. So too did Mike's newfound resolve to build his life around art. The two spent long hours walking, seeing museum and gallery shows, and talking, smoking, and making love on the roof of his building on Ninth Street near Broadway. In the evening, Mike's friends Cynthia and Emanuel Navaretta, an architect and writer respectively, would interrupt their strolls around the Village to drop by Joan and Barney's apartment and, on the sly, deliver messages from Mike to his lover. "I don't know if Barney knew what we were up to," says Cynthia. "But we did this for several months, so we played a terrible role."

A son of the Depression-era Bronx, Mike Goldberg had grown up in knickers with the knees worn through, a badge of parental neglect. Seldom had he felt loved by his parents, nor had he sensed much love between them. A tough kid, he ran away at fourteen (his parents never bothered to look for him), then discovered drugs and art more or less simultaneously. After taking classes at the Art Students League and Hans Hofmann's, he was drafted in 1943. He was sent to Fort Benning, Georgia, where, harassed by a self-proclaimed King of the Ozarks, he waited until his anti-Semitic tormenter was asleep, then smashed his kneecaps with bricks, and later popped up at the man's hospital bed to finish the job by administering a concussion. During his four years in the Army, Mike served in Burma and India but not (as he later boasted in his irresistibly breezy manner) in the fabled guerrilla unit, Merrill's Marauders. After the war came a stint as a roustabout in a remote Venezuelan oil town where he wed a visiting Martha Graham dancer (a marriage later annulled) before returning to New York and resuming at Hofmann's, thanks to the GI Bill.

There were other pieces to Mike's past, more than fit together, for the man was a Zelig, "a marvelous, marvelous, to put it baldly, a marvelous liar, but let's say marvelous embellisher," according to one friend; "a great and charming liar," confirms another; "quite crazy," adds a third. Born Sylvan Goldberg, he was (perhaps) a vaudevillian's son. In any case, a perverse sense of humor and love of the limelight once compelled him to take the floor before a large crowd at the Club, improvise a twisted epic having to do with some obscure art historical topic, and get the panelists very agitated. Mike also invented degrees from St. Paul's and Princeton and used the Waspy name "Michael Stuart," until Joan badgered him out of it. At the same time, he flaunted his street savvy, claiming, for instance, that he could get anyone a deal on anything. "Mike used to say 'I can get canvas for you at a great price,' " remembers Paul Brach. "And he'd pay the full price for a load of canvas and write bad checks for it, or something like that, just for the prestige." He owed everyone money. Still, many found this white hipster and finger-popping aficionado of bebop and blues—another Goldberg persona—frankly seductive. "Hey! Gimme a pig's foot and a bottle of beer," he and Joan would greet each other, with a nod to the Bessie Smith classic.

Joan, for her part, glossed over Mike's mix of casual dissimulation and brutal honesty. He was a painter, and she believed that good painting was necessarily honest. Never tallying up Mike's good and bad points, she loved him recklessly and unconditionally. Those vaguely troubled glass-blue eyes, those classy cheekbones, that voice fusing the resonance of a Shakespearean actor with the glibness of a deejay, that sexy belly, that grab for her ass when they met—God!

Years later Mike figured out that Joan had fallen for a bad-boy Jewish "Noo Yawk" artist because she was still rebelling against her parents. In any case, her sense of self became inextricably tangled up with Mike. Together the two lived and breathed the urgent and dangerous adventure of painting. "Painting could change the world then," said Mike. "And within that climate, Joan and I . . . existed." Feeling "omnipotent," she brushed off her demons: here was the *more* she had long wanted. Her "vision of what life could be," Mike discovered, "was a helluva lot broader than most of us had."

"Darling," Joan murmured, "I can't look at you enough or feel you enough . . . blue eyed one." The following summer she wrote,

> I know a man with blue black eyes and a blue shirt and a beautiful belly. He told me there was so much to believe in and I must memorize it so neither of us will forget. He showed me a fall, a winter and part of spring and in the summer there were orchids. He showed me a fear and a hope and a twitter in the park. I saw his painting through a glass by the ashtray. His name and his past I don't know—I see his eyes and I love him.

A half century later, when Joan was dead and Mike could find nothing good to say about her, some tender ghost nagged, and he quietly confessed, "I was very much in love with her."

That fall of 1950, one shatteringly beautiful exhibition after another left Joan "dizzy and silent": Anne Ryan's splendid small abstract collages at Betty Parsons, Franz Kline's powerful calligraphy at Egan, Hans Hofmann's exuberant painterly abstractions at Kootz. The following year would bring the Museum of Modern Art's important Matisse retrospective, but first came another bombshell: the Whitney's magnificent Arshile Gorky Memorial Exhibition. Some of these paintings Joan knew from Gorky's 1948 show at Julien Levy, but the Whitney retrospective (which she and Mike saw weekly for the six weeks of its duration) laid out an even more dazzling array of the great Gorkys, among them *The Liver Is the Cock's Comb, The Leaf of the Artichoke Is an Owl, Diary of a Seducer, The Betrothal II, Agony,* and *The Plow and the Song.*

Born Vosdanik Adoian in Turkish Armenia around 1904, young Gorky had deeply absorbed the complexion and culture of his native region. His childhood was devastated, however, by the Ottoman Turks' persecution of Armenians in a campaign of extermination culminating in a forced death march that took the lives of nearly one million people.

Fifteen-year-old Vosdanik watched his mother die of starvation. The following year, he arrived in the United States, where he re-baptized himself Arshile Gorky. Whether stalking along New York sidewalks in a black greatcoat or zoning out in solitary peasant dances at parties, Gorky cut a dramatic figure. With extraordinary discipline, he apprenticed himself to Uccello, Ingres, Cézanne, Miró, and Picasso by painting his way through their work. His encounter with the exiled Surrealists in the early 1940s precipitated virtuoso canvases at once intensely felt and radically new. A series of personal tragedies overtook him, however, and, in July 1948, at age forty-four, he committed suicide by hanging.

In the late work that took Joan's breath away, Gorky's brushstrokes of calligraphic precision and seaweed fluidity slip among undulating veils of smoky, translucent color as forms hovering around the threshold of legibility make bittersweet allusion to feathers, claws, insects, plows, waterfalls, and erotica, evoking the artist's childhood and adult domestic life. Thinning his paint with turpentine, Gorky unclasps line, color, and form and makes flawless wild gardens of figures and ground.

Joan's passion for the Armenian-born painter flowed in part from her recognition of a kindred lyrical temperament. As intimate, volatile, and emotionally precise as lyric poetry, Gorky's pictures make paint newly visible as poetry does language; like lyric poetry, it is "a highly concentrated and passionate form of communication between strangers." Portmanteau images of present and past, Gorky's oils also repossess his childhood. *How My Mother's Embroidered Apron Unfolds in My Life,* for instance, plaits then and now in a manner recalling the words of Vladimir Nabokov: "I confess I do not believe in time. I like to fold my magic carpet, after use, in such a way as to superimpose one part of the pattern upon another. Let visitors trip . . . This is ecstasy."

Around the same time Joan began diluting her pigments with turpentine, expanding her formal vocabulary, changing her paint handling, and freeing her forms as if untying the black outlines of *The City.* Two or three kinds of edges gave way to a profusion. Lines scrambled and skimmed the surface. Shapes pullulated. From the motifs she had painted repeatedly, especially the Brooklyn Bridge, she salvaged certain forms — a section of pier, rippling cables, bits of flotsam, a triangle of water glimpsed through trusses — which she used (a lesson learned from both de Kooning and Gorky) neither representationally nor symbolically but expressively. Yet by no means did everything change. Her new work retained the yellowish gray concrete-reflected light (more matter-of-fact than Gorky's), scruffy line (less fluent than his), and active center–inactive edges (versus his implied horizon) of the old.

By the time the Gorky show closed in February, Joan again had a new studio, at 51 West Tenth Street (which was to East Tenth, the legendary main vein of Abstract Expressionism, as Park Avenue South to Park Avenue). A romantically shabby pre–Civil War structure designed for painters and sculptors, the Studio Building had seen many vintages of artists, from Winslow Homer to William Merritt Chase to Kahlil Gibran to Philip Guston. Consisting of three stories of ateliers surrounding a skylit central gallery occupied by a fashion photographer, it had wide wooden stairs, long dim corridors, and wainscoted walls, which lent people's voices a rich resonance. Joan's second-floor studio, soon cluttered with rolls of canvas, half-finished paintings, tins of turpentine, pie plates caked with paint, and other detritus, boasted the single luxury of a coal stove, smack in the middle. The toilets were down the hall, but, mensch that she was, Joan peed in her cold-water sink and offered the same to visitors who asked for the john.

An escape from Barney and a hideaway with Mike, Joan's space in the Studio Building, where she was jokingly called "Jana Mitch" (the super's version of her name), brought new friendships. From time to time, tenants would phone people they knew, chip in for cheap booze, and fling open their doors. At one such party, Joan met painter Jane Wilson and her husband, writer and arts maven John Gruen. Soon the Gruens and the Rossets were inviting each other to dinner, as Gruen recounts in his chronicle of the 1950s scene. At first, he writes,

> our function was to bear witness to their endless fights. It was like a game in which a naïve audience was needed for "the performance." I vividly remember one dinner party Jane and I gave in our brand-new, freshly painted apartment on Bleecker Street. We had finally moved out of West Twelfth Street, and the first thing Jane insisted on was immaculately white walls. It was an intimate little dinner—just the four of us by candle light. Things started out smoothly enough, until Barney noticed that Joan was reaching for a second helping of food. "I wouldn't eat that, if I were you," interjected Barney, "you're getting fat around the middle." With that, Joan took a ripe tangerine out of our fruit bowl, stood up, and aimed it with enormous violence at Barney's head. Barney ducked, and the tangerine landed with splattering force on our virgin walls. Thus began one of the more memorable

of their many fights, with a barrage of four-letter words filling the air, mercifully replacing the tangerines.

That April all hell broke loose. One day Mike walked into Barney's Fifth Avenue bank, wrote a check to himself for $400 (using one of the blanks available on the counter), forged Barney's signature, and cashed it. To an impoverished artist, $400 seemed an immense sum, yet gossip on the streets put Barney's fortune at an unfathomable $55 million. As it happened, Barney had not been using that account, which was virtually empty. When he received an overdraft notice, he responded that he hadn't written any checks. The bank put two and two together and called the police. Mike was arrested and jailed in the Tombs pending a hearing.

Shocked into a state of "gray, gray emptiness," Joan barely functioned. By day, she sat on the floor of her studio, chain-smoking, shaking, and crying; by night, she mentally composed an endless letter to Mike, in which she accused herself of pressuring him and abetting his fantasies. Her omnipotence had been shattered, her rose-tinted glasses knocked to the ground. Days passed. She couldn't see Mike because visitors were barred from the Tombs. Finally she took pen in hand:

> I have no words even for what I feel—I wouldn't want to because you have it worse than all of us—but I have gone through the worst thing in my life—real reality as they say—and it's small compared to yours. I've learned to be honest I guess and that's it—and maybe adult—just maybe—I'll try very hard and for you too. It seems strange now to exist at all . . . We've both got to make some kind of inhuman effort to stand it all—to straighten you out. It will take time—a hell of a lot of courage and I do believe in you—no fantasy there anymore either but something very real.

With Mike awaiting his hearing, it came as a relief to Joan to help his parents close the apartment he could no longer afford to keep. She picked up his laundry, packed his winter clothes in mothballs, and parked his canvases in the hall at West Tenth Street. Operating on a loan from Martha, her friend from Smith (how could she take money from Barney?), she paid Mike's back rent, settled his bill for art supplies at Rosenthal, reimbursed Guston for the six yards of canvas Mike had borrowed, and forked over the forty bucks he owed Milton Resnick.

Ironically, her relationship with Barney improved. He refused to press charges—in fact, he was "extremely nice" about the whole mess—but now he insisted she choose between the two of them. She couldn't. Leaving Barney felt no less impossible than not leaving him. And if she did have to choose, she was determined "for once" to be an adult and make her own choice, not her parents' or Barney's. She asked him to wait. Resolved to act despite her depression, she then purchased a cot, had a hot-water heater installed in her studio so she could bathe in the sink, and moved the rest of her belongings to West Tenth Street (while continuing to spend time with Barney on West Ninth). She was certain of only two things. First, she had to be financially independent, which meant finishing her MFA and getting a teaching job. (In her last year at the School of the Art Institute, she had racked up all but the non-studio credits for a graduate degree.) So she arranged to enroll at Columbia that summer as a special student. Second, she needed to step up her sessions with her new analyst, Dr. Edrita Fried. Among their art friends, only the Navarettas knew what had really happened to Mike (others had been told he was traveling), and Joan ached for sympathetic understanding. Feeling closer than ever to her lover, she nonetheless wanted to crawl into "someplace without any light at all."

Viennese-born psychoanalyst Edrita Fried, named by her actor parents for a sylph in an obscure classic of the Germanic stage, had grown up in a household where Lutheran asceticism tempered bohemian emotivity. Deeply shaken during her adolescent years when her father deserted the family, then unexpectedly died, she had nonetheless weathered the crisis and gone on to earn a doctorate in English literature. Beautiful, shy, theatrical, and skilled at masking her plebeian origins, this young intellectual tripped lightly through the Vienna of Zweig and Berg. At a Beaux-Arts masquerade ball, she met her husband-to-be John Fried, a law student from a distinguished Jewish family. Hitler's annexation of Austria made their meeting an end as well as a beginning: after the two married, they fled Vienna, eventually landing in New York, where Edrita trained at the Postgraduate Center for Mental Health and earned a license as a non-MD psychoanalyst. Joan was one of her very first patients.

Though dismissive of mindless optimism, Dr. Fried worked from a core belief in humans' natural inclination toward healthy growth and development. In those early days of her practice, she adhered rather

strictly to Freud's theories, revisiting her patients' childhood memories, using free association, and regarding dreams as flares sent up by
the unconscious. At the same time she saw herself as one of a new breed
of analysts, giving practical advice and demystifying psychoanalysis by
teaching her patients its principles and methods and urging them to help
set the course of their treatments.

Ash-blond, perfumed, glamorous, and fond of décolleté necklines
and pearls, Fried (as Joan called her) was a queenly presence. Mitchell was not. Yet the young artist's intelligence, creative achievement,
and gutsiness in the face of the male art establishment quickly won her
analyst's respect. As for Joan, having chosen a father in de Kooning, she
now found a mother in Fried. This compassionate woman who disre-
garded Freud's recommendation of opacity and emotional neutral-
ity gave Joan the undistracted nurturing attention that the artist's own
mother had not.

The immediate task in their five sessions a week was to come to grips
with the havoc wreaked by that spring's disaster. Having conferred with
Mike's analyst, Fried issued to Joan a series of forceful instructions:
install a telephone in your studio; keep regular painting hours; drop X,
who is not good for you, but make friends with Y. Having vowed to run
her own life, Joan promptly handed over every major decision to Fried.

One of her analyst's directives probably accounts for the strange visit
Joan paid to painter Pat Passlof at her East Tenth Street apartment. After
Pat had brewed coffee and the two looked at Pat's recent work, Joan
announced, "I've decided to be your friend." An awkward silence. "But
there are conditions. I'm very vulnerable and sensitive, and you have to
be very careful how you talk to me." Pat replied, "Well then, Joan, I'm
very sorry, but I just, I can't be your friend. Especially with a friend, I'm
not likely to be that careful. It's when I really want to feel free. So thanks
for the offer but no thanks."

This derailment of Joan's friendship with Pat fit into a larger picture:
Joan had long ago registered that life went "along fine while I'm painting and then afterwards the bottom drops out of things." One day she
drunkenly opened up on this topic to young critic Irving Sandler, who
summarized: "Fucked up inside, she grabbed for life with an intensity
that often verged on fury and spilled over into insanity." But now her
hopes mounted: Fried was going to repair her "fucked-up" insides, quell
her monstrous anxiety, and make everything okay.

A case study Dr. Fried published nine years later, using the pseudonym "Barbara," describes Joan's behavior with Barney:

> When Barbara married she soon felt engulfed by the proximity of her
> husband. She reacted with panic and tried to salvage a sense of iden-
> tity through hostility outbursts. Her husband countered by violent
> reproaches, which, in turn, devastated her already feeble self-esteem.
> Moreover, she felt almost as anxious when quarrels detached her from
> him as when his proximity overwhelmed her. She tried to escape the
> threatening closeness through a love affair . . . She said, "I close my
> eyes often. Then things frighten me less, because there is no close-
> ness. . . . Then I go wild, I go on a mad binge of hostility. I recover, but
> I have broken up everything around me. I see Brad's [Barney's] face
> looking at me tortured, because I have been hostile."

Flushing out her demons, Joan told Fried about her "wrong" perceptions: colored letters, colored music, colored emotions, colored personalities, boundary deficits, too-insistent memories and dreams. Unfamiliar
with synesthesia as a named neurological condition (as were the vast
majority of mental health professionals of that day), Fried made little distinction between Joan's neurology and her psychology. She labeled Joan's
affliction "archaic fusion" or "symbiotic fusion." Coined by Fried, this
phrase refers to the normal mental state in which a baby feels no separateness between her own being and that of her primary love object, the
mother. The analyst theorized that Marion's too-frequent absences during Joan's infancy had prevented the child from taking for granted her
mother's accessibility, a vital step in the separation-individuation process. Thus, Fried continued, Joan had never developed a healthy ego or
established a real sense of selfhood. Stuck in a state of "symbiotic fusion,"
she was not always able to cope with ego regression—the normal slippage of ego boundaries during daydreaming, drinking, falling in love,
or having sex—hence her inappropriate use of hostility as psychological
protection.

Back from Missouri that June, Mimi and Paul dropped by West Ninth
Street one day to find Barney and Joan together. In the course of that
visit, Paul casually inquired after Mike. Joan tightened, Barney turned

ashen. Only after her husband had left the room did Joan reply: "Mike is in Rockland State nuthouse." Having avoided prison by agreeing to psychiatric evaluation and care, Mike had entered a six-month treatment program at Rockland State Hospital in Orangeburg. For the past two months, he and Joan had communicated by letter alone. She had written,

> Michael I miss you and it's such pain always—You are everything I guess to me and so far away.

> If I could be strong enough Udnie [her nickname for Mike]—I've never tried so hard. If I could give you something—only my love if it helps—if I could cry loud enough for you to hear. Hold me tight Michael—it's so dark.

> I'm kissing you—this I do all the time . . . I sat in the park this morning and you were with me and we talked about things that we had never mentioned and much we had and I held your hand . . . It's so quiet and stays light so long and what are you thinking—Oh Mike I wish I could help you.

> Someday we'll line a room with canvas and you'll have an enormous brush and lots of black and white and cad. red deep and you'll paint them all at once and I'll have my arms around you.

When at last Mike was allowed visitors, Paul drove Joan, clutching a bagful of her lover's favorite turkey sandwiches with Russian dressing, up to Rockland. "Darling Michael," she wrote the next day, "I still can't believe it—closed my eyes all the way home and we were riding together—you're alive and whole too and your eyes are still blue. Hey Udnie—we made it so far—and yesterday we were together—c'est formidable. Thought of so much I didn't say and my feelings are so mixed and I love you so much."

Yet Joan had been sleeping with other men, including painter Ray Parker and musician Gerry Mulligan. She and Mike had met Mulligan, probably at a jazz club, the previous September. At that seminal moment of cool jazz, the baritone saxophonist was playing and recording in Miles Davis's Birth of the Cool nonet. When he and Joan crossed paths again that spring, they ended up dining together at the Grand Ticino. Afterward she invited him up to her studio to play Mike's recorder, and they hopped into bed.

Not that Joan was emotionally involved with Gerry or the others. But she was irresistibly drawn to sex, to the quick, primitive, scary, and satisfying reenactment of the drama of losing one's self in, then separating from, the other, as symbolized by the proverbial postcoital cigarette. Like many men, she felt that casual sex meant little. It did mean, however, putting on a false face with Mike, to whom she coyly mentioned Mulligan in a way that implied that their encounter had amounted to nothing more than an impromptu dinner.

That same summer, Joan was raped by an attendant at Rockland after one of her visits to Mike in Ward Four. Surely she put up a fierce struggle, yet, revealing her strong masochistic streak, she abjectly accepted the rape. Somehow it represented (she told Paul Brach) "the dark side of being with Mike."

Joan having helped the Brachs get a place upstairs in the Studio Building, the three had grown closer. In early evening, they would often stroll over to the Cedar Tavern, the artists' watering hole on University Place near Eighth Street. Drab and proletarian, the Cedar had murky green walls, a long bar in the front where a pair of ex-Marines served up mostly beers, and, in the back, brass-studded leatherette booths and hanging fixtures, whose white light glared through a haze of nicotine-blue. There was no jukebox or TV, just the din of talky artists, mounting as the night went on.

Savoring the pleasures of belonging to a little band of renegades, Joan had met many artists at the Cedar and the Club and kept up her friendships with others. At least once she, Mimi, and Paul dined with Bill de Kooning, who then walked with them back to the Studio Building to look at their work. Joan pulled out Mike's too. "He seemed very enthusiastic," she reported to her lover. "He said he'd like to go see you—you were very talented etc. We talked about Stuart Davis and Gorky and Mondrian and color and I missed you horribly."

Since April Joan had barely touched a brush, but following Bill's visit she cleaned the studio, trundled Mike's painting cart into the middle of the room, stirred and thinned the globs of color stuck on his palette (using her lover's paint felt like having sex with him), and slowly got back into a big green and black thing that had been sitting around half finished. While she loved afternoon light, she preferred working at night and couldn't sleep anyway. At midnight she would tune in to gravelly voiced Symphony Sid's radio program *Live from Birdland* and, smoking and sucking on a bottle of beer, listen to Miles Davis, Dizzy Gillespie, Lester Young, and Charlie Parker as she sat scrutinizing her canvas. But she couldn't decide if she liked the radio on or off when she actually painted.

Leo Castelli too had been to her studio. In 1957 this wealthy Trieste-born cosmopolite would establish the Castelli Gallery, soon making stars of Robert Rauschenberg, Jasper Johns, and Andy Warhol, who supplanted the Abstract Expressionists as the leading artists of their day. But Castelli's launch of a powerful art world utterly unlike the little rebeldom that enchanted Joan lay in the future. In 1951 he was biding his time, dabbling in private dealing and occasionally doing exhibitions, beginning with the Ninth Street Show.

By one of several accounts, Bill de Kooning, Franz Kline, and Milton Resnick, all charter members of the Club, had conceived of the Ninth Street Show as a means of putting the new art in front of the public in other than piecemeal fashion. Most downtown artists had never had a solo show. Moreover, many remained irate over their exclusion from the Met's American Painting 1900–1950. Along the route between the Club and the Cedar, on one hand, and the Ninth Street studios of Kline, Conrad Marca-Relli, John Ferren, and Jean Steubing, on the other, an empty furniture store had caught their attention. After the building was scheduled for demolition, its ground floor and basement became available for two months for only seventy dollars. Suddenly serious about mounting their own salon-style show, one work per artist, they rented the space, cleaned it up, and whitewashed the walls.

The Club's ad hoc organizing committee, especially Marca-Relli and Kline, took the lead in inviting some five dozen artists to participate (seventy-two eventually did), many of them Club members, others artists like Joan who moved in its orbit, still others so-called uptown artists. Castelli was useful as a diplomat and proxy. (Usefully, too, he paid many of the bills.) The show was cooked up in two weeks.

Castelli had ended his visit to Joan's studio by helping carry her canvas and Mike's over to Ninth Street. So arresting was the sight of this pair negotiating the front doors of the Studio Building that passing artist Friedel Dzubas would remember it for years to come. In fact, Castelli had told Joan he was taking her work but would have to see if there was room. When they arrived, however (Castelli having complained along the way that Joan's painting, about six by six, was too big), de Kooning, Hofmann, and Kline (according to Joan) "all said, 'What a marvelous painting!' and hung it in the best part of the show." Though the organizers took pains not to imply an artistic agenda or endorse anyone's art over anyone else's, Kline saw to it that certain essential works, including Joan's, were clustered in what became the focal point of the exhibition.

The Ninth Street Show opened on a beautiful, warm, late-May Sunday evening to an unexpectedly large and keyed-up crowd, klieg lights blazing (a Kline touch), taxis on the fly. Joan loved the idea of a show organized by a brawl of renegade artists operating outside the system of galleries and museums, a version of the 1863 French Salon des Refusés (with the Metropolitan playing the role of the old-fogyish French Academy). Paradoxically, however, what was intended as a celebration of the artists' outsider status quickly attracted the attention of the art establishment, swayed opinions, and launched a scene.

Asked by an interviewer forty years later, "And you were part of the expressionist group?" Joan replied, "I wanted to be."

"*Were* you?"

"Well, I thought they were marvelous."

Bound by no rules, and for myself alone.

New York School collagist and painter
ANNE RYAN, on the fly leaf of a notebook

My great hope was to be, if I worked very hard,
an Anne Ryan. . . . Why? Look—she was a lady
painter I admired. How many are there?

JOAN MITCHELL

CHAPTER SEVEN   Savage Debut

The Ninth Street Show rang up the curtain on a new cast of characters in Joan's life, among them twenty-nine-year-old painter
Grace Hartigan. On the New York scene since 1945, Hartigan
had absorbed Pollock's alloverness and de Kooning's figurative abstraction into the woven, brushy, outwardly expanding canvases she signed
"George Hartigan" in romantic self-identification with novelists George
Eliot and George Sand. Born and raised in New Jersey, Hartigan had
worked as a draftsman during the war, twice married and divorced,
given birth to a son, and lived briefly in Mexico. Blunt and tough, with
big-boned Breck Girl good looks, she met life head-on. Leaving a party
and heading to the Cedar one night with friends, for instance, she got
annoyed because a certain runty painter with a too-neat ginger-colored
mustache was stringing along. Not only was the man stumbly and slurry
from liquor, but also he had never had a one-man show, ergo, he was a

loser. Abruptly Grace pivoted and punched him on the side of the head, so hard that he shot into the gutter. She strode on: "I can't stand a man who doesn't act like a man!" Little wonder that when then–art student, later-reporter Pete Hamill first spied Hartigan at the Cedar a few years hence, she struck him as "looking like fifty miles of trouble out of a film noir."

Grace's first impression of Joan was that she had never heard anyone swear like this new girl on the block. (Grace herself was no slouch in that department.) From the start, the two competed fiercely. More subtle than her rival, Joan often resorted to the sly put-down, and she knew enough not to reveal her hand. Grace, on the other hand, was perceived as "too blatant. She sort of advertised. 'I'm going to do this, I'm going to do that.'" Hartigan's first New York "one-man show" the previous January had given her major bragging rights. Her subsequent move from abstraction to expressive figuration inspired by Old Master paintings would meet with disapproval from many of her colleagues (Joan included), but Grace would again ride high and mighty in 1953 when the Museum of Modern Art purchased her *Persian Jacket*. (MoMA's curator of modern collections, Dorothy Miller, considered Hartigan the most important contemporary female artist in America.) And yet again in 1957 when *Life* crowned her the "most celebrated of the young American women painters." Along the way, her high-flown *"pronunciamentos"* irked the hell out of Joan, while Joan's feigned poverty had the same effect on Grace. The two were never girlfriends, but they understood and respected each other.

At the time she met Joan, Grace was living with painter Alfred Leslie in a ramshackle loft on Essex Street on the Lower East Side. A brash former Mr. Bronx who survived thanks to carpentry jobs, Alfred painted raw, let-it-all-hang-out, "make-it-tough-even-ugly" abstractions that flew in the face of middle-class sensibilities and pumped their rough-and-tumble energies straight from the streets. He liked Joan's aggressiveness and steely determination about painting yet felt she came from another planet: Smith College, high culture, always plenty of dough for dinner and booze.

And at first both Alfred and Grace found Joan's painting less remarkable than her personality. Side by side with a 1951 Leslie or a 1951 Hartigan, a 1951 Mitchell does look "tasty French," as the two put it. Too correct, too academic, too finished, too steeped in Cubism, Joan's work remained "in a corset" in terms of paint handling, objected Leslie, who had just rolled out the crudely beautiful *Painting on Four Pieces of Wrapping Paper*, included in the New Generation show at Tibor de Nagy Gallery.

Launched six months earlier in a prosaic railroad flat on East Fifty-third Street, this up-and-coming gallery bankrolled by Harry Dwight Dillon Ripley (scion of the prominent Dillon family) and business-managed by Hungarian-born banker Tibor de Nagy drew its energies from de Nagy's flamboyant partner, John Bernard Myers, devotee of Surrealism, confidant of poets, and avant-garde puppeteer. Myers was pulling together a stable of the most exciting progressive young artists: Hartigan, Leslie, Larry Rivers, Elaine de Kooning, Robert Goodnough, Jane Freilicher, and Helen Frankenthaler, next in line for a show.

Unlike Mitchell, twenty-two-year-old Frankenthaler rarely let a vulgarity escape her lips, yet the two had much else in common. Willful, hardworking, literary, and rich, this daughter of a late justice of the New York Supreme Court had grown up on Park Avenue and studied at the Dalton School, Bennington, and Hofmann's. In 1950, she saw Pollock's exhibition at Betty Parsons, an experience as jaw-dropping to her as discovering de Kooning's work at the Whitney that same year had been to Mitchell. Now Frankenthaler was feeling her way from Cubist-derived imagery to a lyrical biomorphism distinctly her own. In 1952, she would draw upon Pollock's method in the wheeling, watercolor-radiant *Mountains and Sea*. Pouring thinned paint onto raw canvas, she created an atmospheric picture that wed pigment to fabric and thus achieved the acknowledgment of flatness required of high modernist painting as defined by her forty-two-year-old lover, Clement Greenberg.

A powerful and pontifical art critic for the *Partisan Review* and early champion of Jackson Pollock, Greenberg dictated that painting should turn its back on the outside world, measuring itself only by criteria internal to the medium. In Greenberg's construction of painting's linear progression toward autonomous formal purity, Frankenthaler's soak-stain technique would later serve to link New York School painting to the Color Field work of Morris Louis and Kenneth Noland. Eventually a standard in art history textbooks, *Mountains and Sea* earned the painter the badge of formal innovator, modernism's sine qua non of greatness.

Joan claimed no particular commonality with Frankenthaler or Hartigan. In fact, she always insisted that male painters helped her more than did female painters. All the same, the three were fighting similar battles for respect on the macho New York scene, and at least once Joan called upon the others when she wanted them as strategic allies. On the eve of a Club panel on the topic of the woman artist, in which Joan and painter Jon Schueler were to participate, Schueler told her he believed that women's creativity resided in the womb—"and all hell broke loose," he later remembered. "Joan got Grace and Helen to join the panel, and they raked me over unmercifully."

As time went on, circumstances conspired to position Mitchell and Frankenthaler as a polar couple of art, but, already in the 1950s, their personal and artistic differences loomed large. Frankenthaler's well-bred haute bohemian style and infrequent appearances at the Cedar and the Club squared with her uptown allegiances, while Mitchell's rather sloppy self-presentation and take-no-prisoners attitude were the very image of the downtown artist. Moreover, Joan detested rich girls, a category from which she excluded herself. The tension between the two also hewed to the growing artistic split between the de Kooning camp, on one hand, and the smaller Pollock camp, on the other. Joan remained an unconditional de Kooningite; Helen, aligned with Pollock, "did not go for the de Kooning satellite group," as she once tartly put it to art historian Barbara Rose. She and Joan remained superficially congenial, yet Joan rarely let pass an opportunity to snipe at "that Kotex painter."

Joan also tangled with Philip Guston, although she genuinely liked the painter, twelve years her senior, who taught at NYU and lived upstairs in the Studio Building during the winter months when his house in Woodstock was more or less uninhabitable. Talky, testy, intellectual, and anxiety ridden, Guston was a veteran figurative-painter-turned-abstractionist whose delicate, tortured, impastoed pinks and grays clustered near the center of his canvases. Vociferous about her likes and dislikes, Joan discounted Guston's work, labeling it tonal painting and sniffing that it lacked vitality. A Guston, she felt, merely flaunted the artist's sensitivity—and "so what"? One night the two argued their way through a bottle of bourbon. Guston "doesn't like Gorky or de Kooning," Joan reported to Mike the next day, "likes Mondrian—and more intellectual or classic or whatever you call them things. I would like to paint a million black lines all crossing like [German expressionist Max] Beckmann—to hell with classicism—this is only momentum—beautiful—agony and not in a garden." (She was referring to Renaissance artist Andrea Mantegna's *Agony in the Garden,* a painting Guston deeply admired for its visionary intensity and rigorous architectural space.)

As for Mondrian, his work had preoccupied Joan too since February, when the Sidney Janis Gallery had shown nine paintings from the period of the Dutch artist's encounter with Analytic Cubism. In his lyrical, semiabstract 1908 *Red Tree*, 1909 *Blue Tree*, and 1912 *Gray Tree*, Mondrian depicts, as a spiritual as well as pictorial act, a certain venerable apple tree. While retaining its airy treeness, Mondrian's subject increasingly devolves into compressed and complex networks of lines, an architecture of space that eschews traditional perspective. The ways in which these early Mondrians move yet ensnare themselves in thickets of lines enchanted Joan. Obtaining permission from the Museum of Non-Objective Art (later the Guggenheim) to study its Mondrians not on public display, she steeped herself in the older artist's work.

Not only the paintings of Beckmann and Mondrian but also those of scores of others passed before Joan's eyes that summer of 1951 after she turned full-time graduate student at Columbia, taking three of the five art history classes required for her MFA: northern European painting of the early Renaissance, nineteenth-century painting and sculpture, and modern art. Sitting in the Fine Arts Library one brutally hot day, Joan mentally crabbed over this triple dose of academics as she rehearsed titles and dates for a test. Her gaze drifted out the window: "why did so many people have to paint and I couldn't care less about half of them and in the room the people come and go loathing Michelangelo." That half included Géricault, Gérard, Gros, and all those responsible for the "millions of horses' rumps and Napoleons" that crop up in early-nineteenth-century French painting, about which "these people"—art historians—"can think up more crap to say." She had written several papers, but, facing a major assignment for the early-Renaissance class, struck a bargain with Paul Brach, a critic as well as a painter: in exchange for six stretched canvases, Paul came up with "Fashion as a Formal Device in Piero's *Meeting of Solomon and the Queen of Sheba*," earning Joan an A– from Professor Smith.

Joan's unwillingness to write the paper stemmed in part from her visceral recoil at the intellectualizing that made art history a dry-as-dust landscape. As a painter, she looked hard at the art of the past, registering everything she cared about; unlike certain colleagues who aimed to remake painting from scratch, she "tried to take from everybody." But the arrangement of images in her mental suitcase bore little resemblance to an art historian's taxonomy. Joan's connections were visual and emotional; her shifts in attention—like light playing over foliage, illuminating this or that branch, picking out what was significant and alive at that moment—responded to the needs of her art. Ingres, for instance, briefly meant something because de Kooning had drawn upon the work of the nineteenth-century neoclassicist, and she upon that of de Kooning. But more vital were the paintings of Kandinsky, Matisse, Mondrian, Gorky, and de Kooning himself.

Though Joan had felt too depressed to paint much that late spring and now had to limit her studio time primarily to weekends, things were happening. She experimented with a buttery white that Mike too liked and that she felt gave their paintings a "Renaissance look," and she was equally smitten with black. Her most recent black painting had "turned out OK," she informed Mike, "with the help of Bach and you and [bluesman Snooky Pryor's] 'Come on Down to My House.'"

After only a year and a half in New York, Joan was developing an underground reputation: major players in the art establishment had begun to take note of her work. One was fellow Chicagoan Katharine Kuh, now an important curator at the Art Institute. Three years earlier (while Joan was in Paris), Kuh had dropped by 1530 North State Parkway, where Marion had shown her Joan's work and then sent word to her daughter that Kuh would help her get a solo show a year or two down the road. Accordingly, the curator visited the artist in New York that spring of 1951, scrutinizing her still-wet canvases as the "terrified" Joan hung back, feeling as if she were "in a coffin" and as if Kuh, whom she feared as much as she venerated, was "talking at a great distance." Kuh promised to write both the Whitney Museum and Alexandre Iolas, the owner of the Hugo Gallery, on Joan's behalf. Meanwhile Barney had arranged for the distinguished Swiss-born poet, Surrealist, and critic Nicolas Calas to make a studio visit. Impressed, Calas sent dealer Betty Parsons, who represented big boys Jackson Pollock, Mark Rothko, Clyfford Still, and Barnett Newman.

The prow of Abstract Expressionism, the Betty Parsons Gallery was also a place unusually open to the work of female artists. Of the twenty-one artists on the gallery's roster that year, eight were women; Parsons's stable included Lee Krasner, Anne Ryan, Sonia Sekula, Hedda Sterne, and Perle Fine. In contrast, not a single woman showed at the prominent Kootz or Janis galleries, a state of affairs that reflected prevailing attitudes glorifying men as leaders, marginalizing women, and assuming that male painters would build the future of progressive art, leaving female painters to follow and domesticate. (Clem Greenberg had advised Sam Kootz not to take any women because they'd just get pregnant.) Women artists were considered women first and artists second. As for married women artists, their status as wives trumped all else: when veteran painters Janice Biala and Hedda Sterne had solo shows in 1950, for instance, *ArtNews* had led its review of the former with "Janice Biala, wife of *The New Yorker*'s cartoonist Alain [Brustlein]," and the latter with "Hedda Sterne is the wife of the brilliant cartoonist Saul Steinberg." It was tough for anybody to get a gallery in those days but really tough for women. So women had to be really tough, Joan believed. Though keenly aware of this state of affairs, she was too proud to protest or complain. Those who did were crybabies and losers.

Still she was all nerves and conflicting desires as the art VIPs studied her work. Parsons waxed enthusiastic but said her gallery was full. She then volunteered to drop a note to MoMA curator Dorothy Miller. Miller, however, was never a big Mitchell fan, and, in the end, nothing came of this nascent old girls' network.

Logically, Joan should have joined Tibor de Nagy Gallery, but reportedly its director, Johnny Myers, advised by Clem Greenberg, disliked her work. According to Tibor de Nagy (Joan's lifelong friend), the artist herself decided not to join "because of those two bitches" Hartigan and Frankenthaler. Yet she keenly felt her exclusion.

Mike too would have issues with Myers. Offered a show at Tibor in 1953, when he was on probation for possession of drugs, Mike saw his paintings installed by Alfred Leslie. A few days later, however, he heard from his probation officer, who had taken the trouble to visit the show, that "this fat queer [Myers] came up [to the probation officer] and he said, 'You don't want to look at this. You want to look at the things I've got in the back," meaning work by Hartigan, Frankenthaler, Leslie, and others. Goldberg continues, "So I took my truck, and I got all the work off the wall, and I said to Myers, 'You know, if you cross my path again, I'll kill you.' He knew I meant it. I really meant it." Leslie, however, insists that when Greenberg got wind of Myers's offer to Goldberg, he quashed plans for a show, that not a single gallery artist defended Mike, and that Mike's paintings never made it to Tibor's walls. In any case, there was bad blood between Goldberg and Mitchell, on one hand, and the Tibor mafia, on the other.

Meanwhile, back in the summer of 1951, painter Conrad Marca-Relli, a prime mover of the Ninth Street Show, had brokered a connection between Joan and Eugene V. Thaw, a young Columbia art history graduate and partner in the fledgling New Book Shop and Gallery, where Marca-Relli had recently made his solo debut. Thaw had heard of this semi-socialite painter from Chicago. When he saw Joan's canvases, he immediately offered her a slot the following winter. She hesitated, then accepted. With plans for her first "one-man show"—first in New York, first that counted—bowling along, the consistently inconsistent artist turned ill at ease: it felt so "dirty," so "hollow," so sick with ambition.

At twenty-six, Joan was lissome and seductively androgynous, albeit full-breasted. Sternly disapproving of makeup and jewelry, frugal about purchases for herself (she wore holey underwear), and fond of jeans, khakis, Mike's old shirts, and loafers sans socks, she nonetheless had what her lover considered "Greta Garbo style." Young United Press reporter Roland Pease, introduced to Joan around this time by his neighbor, the ubiquitous Johnny Myers, also saw her as "stylish, girlish." For all of her pooh-poohing of fashion, she knew she looked good in her well-tailored trousers and her signature taupe leather trench coat.

Such a uniform made a strong statement in the early 1950s, when women wore perky dresses with cinched waists and flirty little hats, fashion magazines did not show pants, and many people had never set eyes upon a woman in jeans. Even New York School women, however carelessly thrown together in the studio, typically dressed smartly on the street. "When I go out, I'm all woman," announced Grace, who posed for photographer Cecil Beaton in drop pearl earrings.

When gorgeous painter Jane Wilson started moonlighting as a fashion model, most of her colleagues expressed disapproval. Insensitive to the realities of living without a parental allowance, Joan openly sneered. And when Mimi Schapiro took her to Lord & Taylor to purchase a dress for one rare occasion when she deigned to don anything other than pants, Joan turned their excursion into an exercise in frustration. Dress shopping was too icky, too prom queen, too uptown.

Evenings often found Joan, Mimi, and Paul together. But the Brachs were a couple, and Joan was making her way alone through the raucous, neurotic downtown scene, where, in Mimi's words, a woman "was rated on her looks; if she was young and pretty, it was automatically assumed that she was sleeping with the artist she came with. Then he was rated as to his ability to pick 'em and con 'em." Nonetheless, Joan adored this tribe of artists, this "community of feeling."

People weren't so sure about her. Cynthia Navaretta, for one, had observed that Joan was "a strange combination of quasi-shyness with toughness. She didn't come on very strong at first, and you didn't find out until later how tough she really was." At a party Joan would knock back a few drinks, then click on "like an energy machine" spewing sarcasm, loud laughter, insults, whatever it took to shake people up. Boisterous and fun one minute, she could be dreadfully hurtful the next. If she was bored, she would stir trouble, but the surest way to set her off was to venture an opinion at variance with hers. In return, remembers Jane Wilson, you'd get "a chop on the head, always public, always a karate chop on the head, so that you would be knocked on your rear." At that point, you could either go passive or "engage in the kind of battling that . . . was her favorite form of entertainment."

When she wasn't laying down a barrage of hostilities, Joan was picking her way through a list of grievances. The embattled defender of causes obscure to everyone but herself, she would imply that nobody was true enough or honest enough, that nobody properly understood her. Her vagaries could be disarming. John Gruen, for one, glimpsed "something really rather poignant" in this "*very* strange girl." But Alfred Leslie quickly tired of putting himself on guard, as one does with an unpredictable drunk. Coping with Joan required more energy than he was usually willing to expend. Sitting with friends in a booth at the Cedar one night, wearing a dungaree jacket and white thrift-shop dress shirt (painting garb, ten for a buck), Alfred was gesturing to make a point when Joan strode up and planted herself before him. Staring at the alizarin crimson and cadmium red smears on his cuffs, she started in: "Ah, no, no, no! You can't fool us with that, Alfred!" Everyone laughed, but no one really knew what she was banging on about. Only later did Alfred realize she had been upbraiding him for supposedly pretending he had slashed his wrists.

Yet Joan often proved an extraordinarily caring human being, lavishing attention on anyone in need, especially rookie artists, and wanting nothing in return. During a hard time for painter Marilyn Stark, for instance, Joan phoned virtually every day, introduced Marilyn to the right dentist, and set her up with Fried. "Joan was my big sister," says Marilyn. Joan told Marilyn too that she wanted to sleep with her husband, handsome cinematographer Leonard Stark (then in New Mexico filming the classic *Salt of the Earth*), but, out of respect for Marilyn, would not. Still, Marilyn felt privileged to know her. She wasn't alone. Twenty-two-year-old jazz-trombonist-turned-painter Howard Kanovitz, who had moved down from Woodstock shortly after the Ninth Street Show, also gratefully reaped the rewards of the older artist's solicitousness: she taught him about art materials, ordered that he buy his paint from Bocour, and explained "how to live, how to make it, what it was all about."

Marginalized by temperament, age, and gender, Joan herself was and was not an insider. She had not been invited to join the Club, center stage of advanced art. Few women had. In fact, until painters Mercedes Matter, Elaine de Kooning, and Perle Fine got the nod in 1952, every one of its charter and voting members (as opposed to regular members) was male. Finding the Club scene "very anti-woman," painter Pat Passlof once asked boyfriend Milton Resnick, a charter member, the reason for the rule "No homosexuals, no communists, no women." Each of those groups has "a tendency to take over," he replied.

It required guts for a woman to walk by herself into the Club or the Cedar. (The graffiti on the wall of the men's room convey the prevailing machismo: "I'm ten inches long and all man." And underneath: "Great! How long's your dick?") According to Mimi Schapiro, "Under no circumstances were you to consider yourself a human being who arrived there for the same purpose that men did, namely to establish human relations." But that's what Joan did.

Rising to the challenge of the "gladiatorial" (to use Jane Wilson's word) atmosphere of the Cedar and the Club, Joan would confront anyone. Once, as she arrived at the Club still paint-speckled from work, artist Walter Kamys tossed out an offer to take her to dinner after she cleaned up, and she flipped back: "Go fuck yourself, Walter!" Another time her old Chicago and Paris friend, figurative painter Herby Katzman, walked into the Cedar, "and there were Joan and Kline, leaning against the bar. And I said 'Hi' and looked at Franz, and he was a different man. [Kline had charmed Katzman when the two served together on an exhibition jury.] He was loaded. And he said, 'Anything I can do for you?' Fuck you, boy. And then Joan was there, and I said, 'Hi, sweetheart.' And she kind of, 'Hi.' Cause when they got in the bar, there was venom dripping from the walls." Joan had always had a knack for getting in with the right people, Herby noted, yet he liked her "a hell of a lot."

So did Jackson Pollock. When Pollock showed up at the Cedar after

the weekly appointments with his therapist that brought him into Manhattan from his home in Springs, Long Island, he repulsed most women
with his drunken groping and boorish greeting: "Wanna fuck?" But Joan
was unfazed by the Great Artist's cave-dweller behavior. She groped
back, and they got along fine.

Not only Pollock but any man was fair game for Joan's grab at his
crotch. One night when she was drinking at the bar, painter Landes
Lewitin approached her from behind. Thirty-three years older than Joan,
with a bulky belly and one glass eye, the Egyptian-born Lewitin was a
curmudgeonly, self-important man respected for his deep knowledge of
the craft of painting. He reached up and cupped one of Joan's breasts in
his hand. Without missing a beat, she swung her arm down and hooked
him between the legs. The place froze.

Though at first some of the older guys mistook Joan for a society
girl playing at artist, this ballsy, hero-worshipping little sister soon won
acceptance as few other women did. Painter Nic Carone found her "a
lovely girl. Wonderful girl!" Not only did he like her art but also he got
a kick out of that blend of moxie and brains that had her swearing like a
sailor in one breath and quoting Eliot in the next. Sculptor Philip Pavia
too adored this "very serious girl" to whom he lent Henry Miller's *Tropic
of Cancer* after they had a long talk about Miller, whom Pavia had met
in Paris in the thirties. Yet Joan lacked the easy wit and articulateness
that allowed the brilliant Elaine de Kooning to "get away with murder."
Yeah, Joan bragged, but *she* never once passed out from the booze like
Elaine.

In the 1950s one could hardly be a teetotaling artist, writer, or intellectual. Liquor honed one's creative edge, loosed one's conversational
talents, eased the tensions of existence. Franz Kline, Philip Guston, Jackson Pollock, and critic Harold Rosenberg, to name four Big Men, all
drank prodigiously. Big Men got drunk. On beer or—a few years later,
when they had more cash—on Scotch. By then, as Elaine de Kooning put
it, the whole downtown crowd was "on a decade-long bender."

Raised by martini-swilling parents and loving the way liquor diluted
her anxiety and lifted her out of the mundane, Joan had long since become
a heavy drinker. She would start in around five: beer, Scotch, gin, brandy,
bourbon, it didn't much matter. (A favorite customer at Astor Wines and
Spirits on Astor Place, she always had a big stash at the ready.) Never one
to slur or stumble around, Joan held her liquor well, but, even among
downtown artists, she consumed more than most. She was considered an

alcoholic under control—or maybe not. Edi Franceschini, a young musician she met around this time, found her a "wonderful person, friendly, laughing, very pleasant . . . *until* she drank" and turned into a time bomb. One night a trio of friends, including Edi and a very tanked-up Joan, took a cab home from a party. Annoyed with the driver for some reason, she abruptly laid into him with such white-hot rage that Edi, raised on the streets of New York, got scared.

Boozing, yelling, and swaggering like a man did not, however, bring male privileges. The older guys—especially Kline, de Kooning, and Hofmann—encouraged Joan, yet they had nothing to lose by helping a female painter, who, by definition, was not a real contender. Nor did it seem in the realm of possibility for women to make common cause. At parties they fixed the food and talked girl talk. "The men would get together in studios to talk about their work," recalls Miriam Schapiro. "The women really didn't respect each other deeply. I don't think that another woman, at that time, really cared about my opinion of her work. She wanted a man's opinion." For Joan, it was more important to be one of the boys than to think too hard about the implications of their macho attitudes for a "lady painter."

"I have a message from Michael that he's fine."

"Come in."

Joan's doorway framed a twenty-three-year-old stripling, lean-faced and clean-shaven, with the kind of dark good looks and soft-spoken seriousness that can melt women instantly. Evans Herman had stopped to deliver Mike's message on his way from Brooklyn uptown to search out a certain out-of-print volume of poetry, but Joan waylaid him with an offer to buy lunch. Afterward, the two took a long walk, dined with Mimi and Paul, then had drinks at Louis's Tavern, a half-basement hangout of writers and actors on Sheridan Square. He spoke of his past.

Raised in Brooklyn, Evans Herman had trained as a pianist at Juilliard before hitchhiking down to Key West, where he spent a year writing and night-clerking for a small hotel. Back in New York, he had sent President Truman a letter protesting the policy of peacetime military training. Drafted when the Korean War erupted, he replied to his induction notice with a scrawled "I would rather not"; a second notice rated a quote from George Bernard Shaw's *Pygmalion*: "Act 3—Eliza: Not bloody likely." Leaving his parents' home in Brooklyn one morning some months later for his job as an assistant English teacher at the Walden School, he was taken into custody by two FBI agents. Freed on $2,500 bail, he was assigned a lawyer who negotiated a deal that put him outside the purview of the courts by way of the Bellevue Mental Health Board. In Bellevue's reading room, he had struck up a friendship with Michael Goldberg that continued after both landed at Rockland State Hospital. Released after three months, Evans made it his first order of business to listen to his LPs of Beethoven's sublime late quartets: his life revolved around music. Then he set out to find Joan Mitchell.

That night, Evans declined Joan's invitation to join her in bed, opting instead for a blanket on the floor. As he rubbed sleep from his eyes the following morning, he was startled to find those big-lidded, slightly protruding eyes staring at him. Joan had been caught off guard by a non-predatory male who didn't see her as another notch on his belt. More precious than an affair, their friendship was nonetheless soon laced with glorious sex. Evans moved in while he searched for an apartment.

Joan introduced him to Jane Wilson, John Gruen, Ray Parker, Grace Hartigan, Walter Silver (Grace's new photographer boyfriend), and Alfred Leslie (who was now seeing a beautiful young student named Naomi Bosworth), yet Evans became Joan's private life, her friend away from what he called her "phony friends," her refuge from the chaos of the Club and the Cedar, where he refused to set foot on grounds that he couldn't stand to watch children squabbling. As sensitive and dependable as Mike was rash and unbalanced, Evans appealed to a different side of Joan. "They loved each other," testifies John Gruen. "That was the only time we ever saw Joan Mitchell soften up. She loved this boy so much. He was no Mike Goldberg, my God, no! He was a sensitive pianist . . . They were entranced with each other. Quietly entranced."

After Evans moved into a fourth-floor walk-up in Chelsea, unheated but graced with a superb view of that talisman of romantic modernism, the Empire State Building, and, more important, a good piano, he and Joan got into the habit of going out to dinner, then strolling back to West Twenty-sixth Street, where he played for her, brilliantly. They spoke incessantly of classical music, Evans using language that made perfect sense to a synesthete. He talked about seeking the right place for each sound, envisaged symphonies as rivers, and conceived of music as either vertical (Palestrina) or horizontal (Debussy).

With Joan's coaxing, he plunged again and again into the adagio from Beethoven's Appassionata op. 57, into Debussy's shimmering "Girl with

Evans Herman, 1955

the Flaxen Hair" and "Clair de Lune" from the *Suite Bergamasque* (she loved too the Verlaine poems that had inspired Debussy), and into certain Haydn piano sonatas, the sheet music for which (marked in a childish hand "Joan Mitchell, June 1936") she pulled out from somewhere. Her eyes dreamily closed, she would sit listening, enjoying her colors, and feeling the taps open to release her monstrous anxiety. Evans chalked up the cathartic effect of his playing to Joan's dearth of opportunities to be romantic. Her parents and Barney, he felt, had constantly harped at her: "She never had a chance to relax. She relaxed by coming up to my apartment without sex and listening to me play." Music, as he put it, created for the two of them "a pocket of civilization . . . something like Thoreau playing his flute in the woods to fortify himself against the 'enemy.' " In a sense, Joan felt, she wanted "only . . . the moonlight—the music and the fantasy—the rest of life is a bloody bore."

Three months after Evans's appearance, Mike too finally emerged from "the wigwam." On that day that climaxed so much longing and expectation, Joan drove with friends to Rockland to pick him up and take him to the apartment he had rented on Horatio Street. In recent weeks, she had been trying to keep her feelings for Mike on ice. If not, she felt she'd go crazy from desire: her rock-bottom self was as wild as ever for the Blue-Eyed One. Not only was their sex life fabulous (Joan's nick-name for Mike, Udnie, referred to Francis Picabia's 1914 oil *I See Again in Memory My Dear Udnie,* in the collection of the Museum of Modern Art, a painting that depicts a complex, abstracted, and erotic machine, all blades, gears, and phallic hoses), but also Joan deeply believed in Mike as an artist, and he in her. Grace Hartigan points out that Mike "had a big impact [on Joan's art]. Joan was smarter than Mike, but Mike was very instinctive." On the painting level, they completely understood each other. However, as they got out of the car that day, Mike accidentally but portentously slammed the door on Joan's finger. "And I think she took that as a sign," he once said. "Of lost love—or whatever the fuck it was." From that time forward, their relationship was forever circling the drain.

Or maybe the incident was portentous only in retrospect. In any case, strapped for cash, Mike briefly took a factory job upstate, then started working on the loading docks at the corner of Horatio and Washington streets and driving a truck between New York and Pittsburgh. During his absences, Joan was haunted by mental images of her lover's enigmatic eyes, classy cheekbones, and gorgeous belly, yet she continued to have sex with Evans and others. (Sleeping around was another way to be one of the boys. Like Elaine, Mercedes, and Grace, Joan made no secret of it. Why couldn't a woman, like a man, love one person yet satisfy her physical needs with others? Sexual conquest? Sure, we can do that too.) And no sooner was she with Mike than the two were battling ferociously. He too saw others, sometimes on the sly, thus stirring up the hornet in Joan. Did he really love her? Or was it all lies? She wanted in the worst way for them to make it as a couple: "My heart and my crotch [were] so fucking open to you, and then all [the] shit closed it up . . . and who in hell was that babe with the bubble gum?" she later wrote Mike. Paul tried to convince her that Mike loved her deeply. But she now had "the great disease—doubt—because of the 'lies'—and it invaded everything."

Typically, Mike would spend the night at the Studio Building, shove off early to paint in his studio, then go to work. At the end of the day, the two would dine with friends in Chinatown or the Village and later hang out at the Cedar or hit a party in somebody's loft, booze flowing copiously at every turn. Their happiest times together were their evening walks in Gramercy Park, followed by hamburgers and drinks tête-à-tête at the San Remo, the well-worn literary bar and restaurant at the corner of MacDougal and Bleecker.

One of Joan's favorite haunts, the smoke- and stale beer–perfumed

San Remo had black-and-white tiled floors, a pressed-tin ceiling, a dark-mirrored bar, and a clientele that included James Agee, Miles Davis, Judith Malina, Tennessee Williams, and young New York poets. There painter Jane Freilicher used to observe Joan and Mike across the room—she in jeans and the talismanic long leather coat—smoking, drinking, huddling conspiratorially over a little table, and looking "very French New Wave."

Besides painting, jazz held the two rapt. A connoisseur of early jazz—Louis Armstrong, Buck Clayton, Bessie Smith—Mike knew everything and everybody, while Joan dug, above all, Charlie Parker, Ella Fitzgerald, and that fabulous "B. Holiday woman." Jazz had seduced her with its urban cast, moody romanticism, blend of discipline and instinct, and aura of freedom and authenticity. Trombonist and painter Howard Kanovitz (to whom she introduced Beethoven's late quartets) saw distinctly, however, that Joan

wasn't really *there* as far as I was concerned. She was a square, and we were hip. A very clear distinction as far as I was concerned. Although Joan smoked some grass like everybody else, that didn't make her hip . . . Mike Goldberg was hip. And Miles Forst was hip. And Ray Parker was hip . . . [But] Joan didn't have rhythm in her soul.

She did have a near-mystical feeling for paint. Squeezed by the class she was taking at NYU (Painting of the Early Middle Ages), three weekly sessions with Fried, and a chockablock social life, Joan nonetheless painted hard all that fall. Loading her brushes with blacks, whites, ochres, blues, and reds, she was producing muscular, jostling canvases rife with ambiguities, complexities, and urban tensions, using Hofmannesque push and pull. By the first of the year, Joan had what she considered sixteen decent paintings, fifteen of them squarish and around six by seven feet, and one, *Cross Section of a Bridge*, six and a half by nearly ten feet. In early January these went to the New Gallery, where they were installed by consultant Leo Castelli.

Two flights above the Algonquin Hotel's Oak Room restaurant, the New Gallery occupied the top floor at 63 West Forty-fourth Street. Up on Fifty-seventh Street, Betty Parsons had invented the white-box gallery, but the New Gallery retained the staid gray walls and abbreviated neoclassical decor of an earlier day. A modest outpost of the art world in the theater district, it lacked the cachet of a Fifty-seventh Street venue, yet, with the *New Yorker* a block away and Times Square just to the west, it enjoyed a little scene of its own. The cast party of the popular Broadway play *I Am a Camera*, starring Julie Harris, took place at the New Gallery during Joan's show.

Her opening threw the artist into a panic but turned out okay. Marion and Jimmie flew in for the event, but, more important, her fellow downtown artists came out in force. Grace perceived "a fantastic display of youthful talent and virtuosity, without the real thing," but others who felt Joan had been slow to assimilate avant-garde thinking now lavished praise upon her. John Gruen found her a "remarkable artist, full of fire and sweeping gestures," and Mimi saw her as "full of talent and drive—articulate, as though [she] were ripe with intention to hold the sun in [her] orbit as long as possible." The older men also took notice. One day Pollock strode into the New Gallery, stared hard at her paintings, then turned heel without uttering a word. According to Tom Hess, writing in 1976, another (unnamed) Abstract Expressionist elder

> proclaimed ruefully that it had taken him eighteen years to get to where Joan Mitchell had arrived in as many months. He didn't intend it as a compliment. He felt that the situation had changed so drastically between 1947 and 1950 . . . that younger artists could make direct contact with new ideas almost as soon as they came off the easel. Looking back, however, it becomes clear that it was a compliment; Mitchell didn't jump on a bandwagon; she made tough decisions and she stuck to them. It took courage, skill, and a fierce delight in competition.

Most of Joan's paintings bore the names of places or place concepts: *East Side, Le Lavandou, Guanajuato, Coastline, Midwest 5 P.M.* These she bestowed after the work was completed. Her *34th St. and 7th Ave.*, for instance, got its title when Surrealist Max Ernst blurted out as he stood before it during the installation: "Oh! But this is Thirty-fourth Street, at the corner of Seventh Avenue!"

Hired by the ever-attentive Barney to write a thousand-word essay for Joan's announcement, Ernst's pal, literary man Nicolas Calas, saw the work's grounding in the material world as a relief after other avant-garde painters' suffocating insistence upon expressing their feelings. For Calas, a Mitchell painting derived its meaning as much from shrewd omission as from subtle observation: fragmented and heterogeneous, it was "endlessly interrupted" yet forever becoming. (Not only had Barney persuaded Calas to produce this first important essay on Joan's work, but also he paid for the announcement on which it appeared, and he personally documented the show using his old Rolleiflex.)

Joan also garnered three brief but generally positive critical notices. Betty Holliday of *ArtNews* praised her "savage debut" (what looked savage then looks lyrical today), while *New York Times* critic Stuart Preston looked favorably on the paintings' fast-paced shapes and serial explosiveness even as he detected a certain shrillness and monotony. And Paul Brach, writing for *Art Digest,* singled out *Cross Section of a Bridge,* Joan's first self-consciously important canvas, for its "tense tendons of perpetual energy" and "wide arc-shaped chain reaction of spasmodic energies." Reflecting New York School attitudes about putting oneself on canvas, he heralded the show as "the appearance of a new personality in abstract painting."

As usual in those days, nothing sold. Shortly after the show closed, however, the gallery's co-owner, Eugene Thaw, visited the small yet elegant apartment of twenty-four-year-old William Rubin, then a conductor in training but later chief curator of painting and sculpture at the New York Museum of Modern Art. There hung a Mitchell, Rubin's first serious art purchase, made directly from the artist, paid for in fifty- or seventy-dollar installments, and financed, in part, by the sale of two fine prewar clarinets.

On the heels of her show, Joan more or less cut Thaw dead: "She already knew she was a star." Indeed, she was quickly elected to membership in the Club, the mark of approval that mattered to her more than anything else. A month later she participated in a Club panel about Abstract Expressionism, alongside Grace Hartigan, Alfred Leslie, painter Larry Rivers, and poet Frank O'Hara—a bunch of kids (the oldest, Grace, turning thirty the following day) sharing their tremendous excitement about what was still to come.

In her third semester of graduate study that spring, Joan took late-medieval art and advanced French at NYU and audited Wallace Fowlie's course on Marcel Proust at the New School. Fowlie's class coincided with her slow plow through the final volume of the "absolutely marvelous" *In Search of Lost Time,* which she was reading in the original French.

There were many reasons for Joan to adore Proust's novel, including its sensuousness, luminosity, poetic language, psychological subtlety, intense opticality, and inward and outward focus. Beginning with the opening episode of the narrator's traumatic bedtime separation from his mother, she would have seen her own childhood self in the work's ultrasensitive protagonist. Moreover, reading Proust made her even more acutely aware of music's capacity for delicious magnification and confusion of desire. When the novelist's character Swann hears a stirring little musical phrase as he is falling in love, that ineffable phrase—"airy and perfumed"—unseals an otherwise inaccessible part of him and amplifies his being.

At novel's end, Proust's narrator discovers the secret of the bliss he first felt when, against his habit, he had tasted a madeleine soaked in linden tea that whisked him back to childhood Sunday mornings in the country. This slipping outside time explains, Proust writes, "why it was that my anxiety on the subject of my death had ceased at the moment when I had unconsciously recognised the taste of the little madeleine, since the being which at that moment I had been was an extra temporal being and therefore unalarmed by the vicissitudes of the future." The only way to grasp and make meaningful the past, which is all that truly belongs to us, he realizes, is through art made from one's resurrected past. Similarly, the memory of a feeling, transformed as she painted, would become the basis for Joan's work. She would think of painting—"not motion . . . not in time"—as a way of forgetting death: "I am alive, we are alive, we are not aware of what is coming next." Moreover, for Mitchell as for Proust, art had the power to transform pain into beauty and to make sense of the messes we call our lives.

Not infrequently the insomniac Joan read all night. Besides Proust, she devoured novels by Faulkner and Joyce as well as the brilliant six-volume autobiography of Irish playwright and socialist Sean O'Casey. She also kept up with newsmagazines and the *Times* (and always held strong opinions about current events). But, above all, poetry still held her rapt. She dipped into Valéry, reread Baudelaire, knew much of Verlaine by heart, and discovered what proved to be an abiding passion for Prague-born Rainer Maria Rilke.

Rilke's woundedness, yearning for transcendence, feeling that ordinary life is not real life, and love of trees and stars deeply moved her. So too did his vulnerability to the external world: witness the scene in Rilke's autobiographical novel *The Notebooks of Malte Laurids Brigge* (which she read many times) in which the narrator remembers dining in his family's banquet hall as a child:

> You sat there as if you had disintegrated—totally without will, without consciousness, without pleasure, without defense. You were like an empty space. I remember that at first this state of annihilation almost made me feel nauseated; it brought on a kind of seasickness, which I only overcame by stretching out my leg until my foot touched the knee of my father, who was sitting opposite me.

Moreover, Rilke looked to painting, especially Cézanne's, as a model for poetry. In late 1907, the writer visited the Paris Salon d'Automne nearly every day, seeking to memorize the work of the Post-Impressionist, whose discipline, nuance, precision, and chromatic emotion he emulated. Having visually devoured the blues that dominate Cézanne's late work, Rilke wrote, in *Letters on Cézanne* (another Joan favorite), of "an ancient Egyptian shadow blue" seen while crossing the Place de la Concorde, of the "wet dark blue" in a certain van Gogh, of the "hermetic blue" of a Rodin watercolor, of "the dense waxy blue of the Pompeiian wall paintings," and of "a kind of thunderstorm blue" in a work by the Master of Aix—fabulous stuff for the future painter of *Hudson River Day Line*, *Blue Territory*, and *La Grande Vallée*, among myriad triumphs of blueness.

Joan's no-credit course on Proust that spring took her far afield from the practical considerations that had led her to pursue an MFA. As her relationship with Mike frayed and married life with Barney retreated into the past, her determination to gain financial independence had waned. That June she wrapped up her coursework with straight As and received an MFA from the School of the Art Institute of Chicago. She never got a teaching job, however. Instead, she kept living on the monthly stipend from her parents, peevishly because she hated having to answer in any way to Jimmie and Marion, even though she begrudged Sally the larger checks she received because she had children. At the same time Joan tried to hide from her fellow artists how very privileged she was. Still, her claims to struggle along on one hundred dollars a month like everyone else met with raised eyebrows and mostly unspoken resentment. It did not escape notice that she could afford the Studio Building; that she never stinted on liquor, paint, or analysis; that her leather trench coat was beautifully tailored; that she didn't have to take day jobs and thus enjoyed the luxury of time. In fact, the only clock Joan was punching was Fried's: three sessions a week, plus a new seven-member "neurotics club" that caused her to feel "the most collective" she had ever felt—no exception made for the Artists' Club.

Joan relied on Fried more than ever. After two years, her psycho-analysis remained a central element in her life. Joan's dependence struck Evans one midday when he met her at Tenth Street after her regular ses-sion with Fried up on Riverside Drive. Having wiggled out of her dress slacks, Joan was pattering around in her underwear when she dropped the news that, Fried having decided that sleeping with Evans was unhealthy for her, they could no longer have sex.

"Well, I'm sorry because I—are we allowed to be friends?"

"Oh, yes, yes, yes."

More discussion, then: "I'll leave now, because you seem very confused."

In a sense, Evans was relieved by Joan's announcement. Their rela-tionship was going nowhere, and he needed to get his life together. He told himself he didn't care.

"Marisol would like to sleep with you."

A Paris-born artist of Venezuelan parentage studying at Hofmann's, Marisol Escobar would shoot to fame in the sixties for her witty assemblage portraits viewed as Pop Art. Famously elegant, silent, and beautiful—the "first girl artist with glamour," as Andy Warhol once put it—she would later have affairs with both Bill de Kooning and Mike Goldberg. (Joan's astringent comment regarding the latter: "I imagine with all the crotch sharing, N.Y. will soon be like one incestuous royal family.")

Evans responded to Joan's matchmaking attempt: "This is happening so fast, Joan. You lost a lover, and now you're playing my pimp." That went down badly.

The Village tom-toms lost no time in spreading the news. Two days later, Alfred Leslie's ex-lover Naomi Bosworth knocked at Evans's door, and thus began another drop-the-hanky love affair. One night Evans took Naomi for a ride on the Staten Island ferry and caught a bad cold. Afterward they returned to her place. When his cold worsened the fol-lowing evening, Naomi phoned her doctor uncle, who walked in, glow-ered at the young man in his niece's bed, applied a mustard plaster to his chest, and ordered rest. After he departed, Naomi too left for class. Then the phone rang: Joan.

"What are you doing over there?"

"Why are you interested?"

"I'm with Mike, and, if you don't get out of there, I'm going to go home with Mike."

"You've been going home with Mike a thousand times. When I get well, I'll see you, and we'll have a drink. Right now, I need a cup of tea."

Half an hour later, Joan let herself into Naomi's apartment, stripped, and forced Evans to make love, mustard plaster or no. Then they squabbled over whether or not she would have to lie to Fried. Evans too was in analysis, but he considered Joan's reliance on her analyst, not unlike the reliance of her younger self on her father, extremely unhealthy.

No doubt Edrita's method of issuing injunctions did inhibit Joan's progress, because it simultaneously replicated her father's directive manner and gave her the warm, intimate attention she craved. When Fried decided that she should stop having sex with Evans, Joan felt compelled to fulfill that prescription as a step on the path to mental health, yet, like a child testing her parent, also acted defiantly, rashly asserting her own will by dashing over to Naomi's apartment and forcing Evans to succumb to her lust. Still she remained deferential to Fried, her only hope, she felt, of overcoming her defective psychological birth. At stake was nothing less than a second chance at personality development.

At times, Joan caught herself making Mitchells. That summer wasn't one of them, however; she felt the ground sliding thrillingly, unpredictably, under her feet. Risk meant "believing in yourself enough to push it, to never feel that you are making a picture of a painting, copying yourself." If she wrecked a painting, she had Mike take it down with the trash; if it was working, she told Barney, "Just while I stand there putting paint on, life is maybe wonderful and beautiful after all."

During the year since Joan had walked out of Ninth Street, she and Barney had seen each other often. Together they had taken their first trip to the Hamptons, Sammy's Beach on Gardiner's Bay, where Joan's friend and former classmate, painter and designer Francine Felsenthal, and Francine's boyfriend, Ramón, had thrown a birthday party in their portable beach house from Gimbels. It was through Francine that Joan had learned of Grove Press, a tiny, nearly moribund publishing company

A half smile, cigarettes, beer . . . and a male companion later excised from the photograph? Very Joan. c. 1950

named for the Village street where it was founded. Grove was for sale, and Joan urged Barney to buy. He knew nothing about publishing, but why not? It sounded interesting. So for $3,000 he acquired three suitcases full of books, a negligible backlist, and the manuscript of one gothic novel. Joan then suggested he publish *The Golden Bowl,* Henry James's psychologically complex out-of-print classic, which she had stumbled upon three years earlier at an English-language bookshop in southern France, and adored. Accordingly, Barney purchased the rights from Scribner's, hired a Princeton professor to write an introduction, and brought out the novel. Over the years he would publish other neglected classics, along with New Left theory, world literature, Existentialist drama, poetry, erotica, Beat novels, and works of social science. Grove's publication of D. H. Lawrence's *Lady Chatterley's Lover* and Henry Miller's *Tropic of Cancer,* both banned in the United States on grounds of obscenity, and the legendary court battles that ensued, lay in the future. But already he had vowed to publish *Tropic of Cancer.* Barney had first read Miller's novel during his freshman year in college at a time when a girl with whom he was desperately in love was slipping away: "There was nothing to replace her. It was like Miller, when he really lost Mona [the nymphomaniac wife/muse in *Tropic of Cancer*], he's free. A catastrophe that sets him free to go out and be himself, whatever that is." Now, facing a new catastrophe—really losing Joan—he stored his inventory in her abandoned studio and threw himself into building Grove Press.

White dawns and dusks grow warm beneath my skull
Gripped in an iron ring like an old tomb
And sad I seek a vague and lovely dream
Through fields where sap begins to strut and swell

STÉPHANE MALLARMÉ, "Renewal"

CHAPTER EIGHT The Hurricane

The following April, Barney traveled to Chicago to divorce Joan. Illinois had liberal divorce laws, and friends there were willing to testify that he was a resident.

Joan, however, opposed his move. Not unhappy with the status quo, she wanted an open but mutually supportive marriage à la Elaine and Bill de Kooning, who lived apart and had many affairs yet remained committed in their own fashion. Don't get divorced, she'd been urging, I'll come back. But she hadn't.

The night before the hearing, Barney called Joan in a last-ditch attempt to shock her into returning. Again, she told him to drop the idea of divorce, but he felt he had to go through with it. On May 14, 1952, Superior Court Judge Julius Hoffman (later notorious for his handling of the trial of the Chicago Eight) granted Barnet L. Rosset Jr. a divorce from Joan M. Rosset on grounds of desertion. Through her attorney,

Joan had contested Barney's assertions that he was "a good, kind and dutiful husband" and that she had deserted him "without any reasonable cause or provocation." But she wanted no alimony or settlement, only payment of her attorney's fees and restoration of full legal rights to her original name.

This divorce that neither wanted did not radically alter their relationship. Married or not, they remained (dysfunctional) family. She still treated him proprietarily; he still loved her romantically. Nonetheless, Barney started dating, among others beautiful Eileen Ford model (and later Los Angeles gallery owner) Patricia Faure, who recalls that "he was actively looking for some replacement [for Joan] and [Joan] was actively looking to disparage any choice he'd make." When he invited anthropologist Margaret Mead to dinner but pointedly excluded Patricia, she dropped him. The next future Mrs. Rosset was German-born Loly Eckert, but, even after Loly moved in, Barney semi-surreptitiously pursued Joan, who didn't hesitate to take advantage of his feelings. Once Paul Brach watched her try to wheedle Barney into doing something he didn't want to do, then offer him sex if she got her way.

The divorce took place not long before Joan learned she was pregnant, reportedly by Evans Herman. In an incestuous twist, Evans had joined the tiny staff of Grove Press, where his quixotic employer put him to work packing books and managing a contest for writers from India. The young man's future in publishing dimmed, however, after he ordered the "wrong" champagne for a literary dinner Barney was hosting, and the two never really got along. How could they when Barney was arranging with Fried for Joan's abortion of Evans's child? (At that time, abortion could be had legally in New York State if two psychiatrists declared that the woman was not up to the strains of motherhood.) Evans, in fact, didn't learn of the pregnancy until after Joan came home from New York Presbyterian Hospital, exhausted, still cramping, and deeply depressed.

At twenty-seven, Joan longed for children yet knew that a baby was incompatible with the realities of an artist's life, and acknowledged, moreover, that she herself still needed mother-love. Besides, she had the radical idea that her partner should assume half the responsibility. That eliminated Mike. Later, when Joan found out she was pregnant again, this time by Mike, or so she claimed, the two went to his place on Horatio Street and had rough sex until they provoked a miscarriage.

Not until Barney sent word from Paris, where he was scouting books, that a Frenchman was arriving to replace him did Joan's depression ease.

Finding herself the owner of a pedigreed chocolate brown baby poodle from a fancy pet emporium on the Champs-Élysées, she named the dog after George Dillon, for his good temper, non-husbandness, and luxuriant dark, curly hair. "Very bouncy and unhousebroken and sweet," George (full names: Georges du Soleil and Georgeous George Sunbeam) took up "a great deal of time—I haven't even time to dislike people any more," she reported with dry humor to her old friend Joanne Von Blon. "In fact the poodle, male, is more interesting than anything else."

By the time George arrived, the finality of divorce had led Joan to undertake the tedious business of searching out more livable quarters. (Tenth Street lacked a kitchen, a bath, and central heat.) That August she found a 680-square-foot fourth-floor walk-up in a classic if worn brownstone with a "melting staircase" at 60 St. Mark's Place. Essentially one big room plus a cooking area and charmingly old-fashioned bath, her new place boasted fourteen-foot ceilings, steam heat, a parquet floor, and north light from three windows overlooking the street.

A neighborhood of synagogues, Ukrainian clubs, and Turkish baths, what is now called the East Village was home primarily to recently arrived Ukrainians, Poles, and Russians (and to poet W. H. Auden, who lived at 77 St. Mark's Place). Butchers festooned their shops with rabbits hanging in furs, pushcart vendors hawked pots and pans or dished up steaming kasha and kielbasa, and (as Joan wrote Joanne) "choice young men in zoot suits [made] crime waves." On summer evenings, sunglow lingered upon the dirty old brownstones of St. Mark's Place, and scraps of polkas floated here and there. Joan loved it. To her, that neighborhood, especially anything east of Avenue A, was "the real New York . . . a haven from the Philistines . . . an island within an island."

The legendary New York School studios of the 1950s are de Kooning's, Pollock's, and Kline's, but the publication, in the October 1957 issue of *ArtNews,* of photos of Joan working at St. Mark's, photos that epitomize the artist's lonely tangle with paint, inextricably linked her studio too to a romanticized idea of Abstract Expressionist New York. During the thirty years she kept St. Mark's, Joan lent it, traded it, sublet it, and hosted virtually everyone in the art world, yet found satisfaction above all in the autonomy and privacy it afforded—it was *hers!*

In another photo, by Walt Silver, the artist sits in her lair in front of a painting-in-progress, one hand on George, who stands sentinel. Her gaze rests upon her dog, and her right foot is behind him, so that he and she form a unit for Walt's camera. Art historian Linda Nochlin sees this picture in light of "one of the most famous youthful self-images of the artist as a young subversive, Gustave Courbet's *Self-Portrait with a Black Dog* of 1842." Here Joan possesses the essential, Nochlin continues: her dog, her studio, her work. "For a photographic instant, at least, Mitchell is one of the boys—indeed, a very big boy, Courbet."

By one or two o'clock most afternoons, Joan would be mentally and physically confronting her work: studying her canvas, churning up sticky globs of pigment, trying to get into the joyful, loving frame of mind—feeling a tree, perhaps, or a bridge—that would transport her to the place where painting as such would take over.

At the back of her mind lurked the art of Russian-born painter Wassily Kandinsky. Joan had first seen the early modernist's work at Chicago's Arts Club in 1945. During her winter in Brooklyn with Barney, she had frequented the Museum of Non-Objective Art, the idiosyncratic upper Fifth Avenue institution where recorded classical music played in the galleries in line with the ideas of Kandinsky, its patron saint. A recent exhibition at Knoedler had again brought her face-to-face with paintings like *Blue Mountain* (1908) and *Black Lines* (1913), dazzling dream landscapes in which the artist discards all but traces of the material world.

Joan was not alone among downtown artists in her enthusiasm for Kandinsky's early watercolors and oils. Hans Hofmann deeply admired both Kandinsky's spirituality and his pictorial structure, and Hofmann students like Helen Frankenthaler and Mike Goldberg had caught their teacher's excitement about the European painter's dynamic compositions, wondrous colors, and formal inventiveness. Moreover, Kandinsky's imperative of inner necessity had prefigured the New York School attitude of truth to one's own experience.

Taking inspiration from Symbolist reliance on suggestion and fascination with sensory minglings, Kandinsky had carried painting across the threshold of abstraction in search of the immateriality, universality, and emotional power of music, which he believed to be the highest art. His creative imagination may owe as much to the neurological as to the metaphorical and the theoretical: historians of neuroscience have long debated whether or not Kandinsky was a true perceptual synesthete. The evidence is inconclusive. Passionate for music and color in any case, he associated a musical sound and a smell with each hue, once vividly describing the euphoria of hearing Richard Wagner's *Lohengrin*: "The violins, the deep tones of the basses, and especially the wind instruments . . . embodied for me all the power of that pre-nocturnal hour. I saw all my colours in my mind; they stood before my eyes. Wild, almost crazy lines were sketched in front of me." Did Joan sense something akin to her own soulful colors and lightning-fast shapes in Kandinsky's chromatic fireworks?

Around the time she moved, she had purchased a record player and scads of LPs: Billie Holiday, Ella Fitzgerald, Charlie Parker, Beethoven, Bach, and Mozart, including everything she could get her hands on by Viennese pianist Paul Badura-Skoda. (So enamored was Joan of Badura-Skoda's performances that she once dreamed she was marrying him.) As she was preparing to paint, she would click on her machine and lower the needle on a carefully chosen record. Everyone in the building knew that when classical music, usually Mozart, was blaring from the top-floor front apartment, Joan Mitchell "was in her 'painting mode' and was not to be disturbed," one ex-neighbor reports. "The music was often very loud, but no one ever seemed to complain."

Music allowed Joan to shed the burdens of selfhood and luxuriate in colors, movements, textures, shapes, and feelings. It may have raised unsettling questions, however. If authentic art was "an extension of one's inner life at its highest intensity," as critic Harold Rosenberg put it, should not Joan, with her scathing insistence on truthfulness, open her art to her hearsight? But how does a painter admit the emotional assault of colored music? How does she elide the boundaries between eye, ear, body, and hand? Illustrating her volitant musical landscape was as unacceptable as it was impossible. (Colored music is layered, swift, translucent, and impossibly subtle; paint is flat, motionless, less translucent, and based in standard colors.) Nor was her response to music wholly visual: beyond the airy starbursts, zigzags, and tides that accompanied changes in timbre, pitch, loudness, and key, Joan felt music on her body. (T. S. Eliot writes of "music heard so deeply / That it is not heard at all, but you are the music / While the music lasts.") She may have begun fumbling toward what she had long mastered by the 1980s when she said bluntly of music: "I use it in my painting."

As the late-afternoon light waned, Joan would put her brushes aside, wash up, and reach for her pewter cocktail shaker, two highball glasses, whiskey, Triple Sec, sugar, and a lemon to fix her version of a sidecar for herself and her neighbor when the latter came home from work.

The woman found Joan "very tough and hard to get to know," never "girlsy-chummy," yet straight-arrow and decent.

Across the hall lived Robert and Muriel Gottlieb, recently back from England, where he had been in graduate school. Bob Gottlieb would later become editor in chief at Simon & Schuster, Knopf, and the *New Yorker,* but, at that time, he and Muriel, both a few years younger than Joan, were relatively poor and unsophisticated, so, matter-of-factly and without ulterior motive, Joan looked after them. When their electricity was turned off, for instance, she expertly snaked in a line from her apartment. No big deal. Bob thought her "a great guy."

Similarly, Joan continued to keep a solicitous older artist's eye on Howard Kanovitz. When she and Mike got their first look at the cramped painting space at Howie's new flat on Seventeenth Street, they insisted it had to be bigger. "Why don't you just break down this wall right over here that separates the kitchen from the living room?" "Yeah, I guess so." "Let's do it right now." They did. As Mimi Schapiro once archly noted, Joan "could raise walls with the best of them." Or raze them.

But not everyone liked her. She was denied insurance coverage after disapproving neighbors tsk-tsked to investigators that she was a wild partier and a drunk. "Shit," Joan crabbed, "a single girl in America is like a Negro in the South."

Thanks to an invitation from painter George Ortman, whom she had met at the Brachs', Joan showed that September at the Tanager Gallery, a new artists' co-op on Tenth Street. Four months later, she participated in the first artist-juried Stable Annual, a seventy-work "family affair" (including Pollock's 1952 masterwork *Blue Poles*) that short-circuited institutions to put artists' work before the eyes of their colleagues and rekindled the exuberant camaraderie of the Ninth Street Show to which it was heir. Then, in April, the Stable opened the first in a twelve-year string of Mitchell exhibitions.

Once home to Central Park's riding horses, the ample, three-story Stable, at the corner of Seventh Avenue and Fifty-eighth Street, still smelled faintly and not unpleasantly of manure, especially when it rained. Its brick walls were whitewashed; imprints of horseshoes punctuated its rough-hewn timber floors. Unusual for its day, such hip-chic decor reflected the flair for gallery as theater that had helped the Stable burst upon the scene. A mandatory stop on critics' and curators' circuits, it also served as uptown New Yorkers' box seat on the art of downtown's bohemian brush throwers.

Credit for the Stable's style goes to its enterprising owner, a twice-divorced (once from a Rockefeller) forty-one-year-old art novice and former aide to couturier Christian Dior named Eleanor Ward. Ward had laid the groundwork for her business with a Christmas crafts boutique that she skillfully parlayed into an art partnership with dealer Alexandre Iolas. After Ward and Iolas had a falling-out, Eleanor hired as the Stable's manager the voluble Italian American artist Nic Carone, from whose short course on contemporary art she emerged an energetic champion of the avant-garde.

Aligning herself with the up-and-coming Stable proved a shrewd career move for Joan. Not only did she figure prominently on the same roster as Elaine de Kooning, Biala, Conrad Marca-Relli, Joseph Cornell, John Graham, and Marisol (the first to actually sell), but also she acquired a dealer with absolute faith in her work. Ward could be cagey and "bitchy in the grand manner," and Joan, whether sober or drunk, regularly confronted, challenged, and intimidated her dealer, yet the two enjoyed an affectionate rapport. Eleanor recruited Joan for her artists' advisory committee, numbering "six people (but nobody knows who the other five are)," quipped Elaine de Kooning, also a member.

In its early days the Stable retained that hey-gang-let's-put-on-a-show spirit Joan so loved. When Carone picked up her work for the installation of this first exhibition, they tied a stack of paintings to the car's luggage rack, but on East River Drive the rope came loose, and three or four canvases went sailing. Nic swerved and hit the brakes, and the two painters chased after Mitchells.

Joan was nervously pleased with what she was showing: shimmering, cinereous abstractions, more personal and meaningful, she felt, than anything she had previously done. Thicketed at their centers with narrow stabs, smudges, and trickles of blacks and whites complicated with ochres, reds, and verdigris and spatially steadied with soft bruises of violet and blue, they dissolve at their edges into silver blues, misty grays, oyster whites, and bald gessoed ground.

One can parse the 1953 paintings for the influences of Kandinsky, Mondrian, Gorky, and de Kooning, and one can note that they marry the permission of New York painting with the rigor of Analytic Cubism, yet they were fully Mitchell's own. Freely admitting the subjectivity of consciousness to their negotiations between the materiality of paint and feelings of weather and landscape, these were not pictures of the world "out there" but rather pictures consonant with the world. In a comment that feels apropos of their effulgent grays and urban space-feelings (even as it misses their pulsing energies), Joan once wrote to Mike, "The rain so closed the landscape and makes a room of my house and truly makes me remember some so closed and soft rains on 10th St. and Horatio St." A later review by Frank O'Hara underscored the restraint and inscrutability of these same paintings, "strikingly vital and sad, urging black and white lights from the ambiguous and sustained neutral surface, reminding one of Marianne Moore's remark on obscurity: 'One must be only as clear as one's natural reticence permits.'"

Joan's exhibition was reviewed briefly but positively (in *ArtNews, Art Digest*, the *New York Times*, the *Herald Tribune*, and *Arts & Architecture*) within a context shaped by Harold Rosenberg and Thomas B. Hess, two heavyweights, friends of Joan, who passionately believed in New York School painting.

Indeed, Joan was a frequent guest at the well-lived-in Tenth Street apartment that lawyer, poet, and intellectual Harold shared with his writer wife, May Tabak Rosenberg, and their daughter Patia, a nest of "warmth and ideas" (as Joan once waxed nostalgic) where one might find Patia reading Shakespeare aloud, Harold listening, and May "steaming up something divine." Joan showed up regularly too at soirées at the posh Beekman Place apartment of starmaker *ArtNews* editor Tom Hess, a man of glamour and power, and his civic activist wife Audrey, an heiress to the Sears, Roebuck fortune. There one could observe the artist, all acerbic humor and billows of cigarette smoke, taking a verbal razor blade to someone's cocktail party inanity or curling up in an armchair, Scotch in hand, to dish dirt or talk Proust with the urbane Francophile Tom. For all of Joan's pooh-poohing of careerism, she had a knack for getting in with the "right" people.

The third member of downtown New York's critical triumvirate of the 1950s, painter, writer, and queen bee Elaine de Kooning, was also close to Joan. Known for her witty intelligence, scrappy indestructibility, innumerable connections, and trenchant articles for *ArtNews*, Elaine championed her separated husband, Bill de Kooning, as a creative genius and worked their unconventional marriage to both of their advantages. In fact, she had affairs with both Rosenberg and Hess, Bill's two major critical supporters. An artist and athlete from childhood, the Brooklyn-raised Elaine had much in common with Joan, who was not unmindful of Elaine's connection to Bill. After a rocky start, the two had cut a deal: they would get along, no matter what, and Joan, reportedly, would abstain from sleeping with her friend's husband.

De Kooning, Rosenberg, and Hess valued above all the creative act. Witness the concept of Hess's signature series (by various writers, often de Kooning) in *ArtNews*: So-and-So "Paints a Picture." Moreover, the previous fall, Rosenberg had published, also in *ArtNews*, his landmark polemic (and first major critical writing on art), "The American Action Painters." In this essay, he argued that the future of American art (the definition of which preoccupied critics in the 1950s) fell upon the shoulders of a handful of artists for whom the canvas had begun "to appear . . . as an arena in which to act—rather than as a space in which to reproduce, re-design, analyze or 'express' an object, actual or imagined." For such artists, continued Rosenberg, painting was a heroic act of self-revelation inseparable from their biographies, and a canvas no longer a "picture but an event." Rosenberg termed these artists "action painters." Lest Jackson Pollock, the painter championed by Rosenberg's chief rival, Clement Greenberg, appear to be the exemplar, Rosenberg hastened to establish as the test of the bona fide existential painting act that it be rife with dialectical tension engaging the artist's whole being. This statement, insiders knew, adverted to Willem de Kooning, famously unable to resolve a painting and famously unwilling to adopt a fixed style. (De Kooning had recently painted the raw, high-anxiety *Woman I*.) Rosenberg thus endorsed de Kooning as the quintessential action painter even as, many thought, he misconstrued the picture-making act. He then turned upon the painter who has remade himself "into a commodity with a trademark," a slap at Pollock, whose drip paintings, Rosenberg implied, copped out as "apocalyptic wallpaper."

Bristling with military metaphors and prophetic utterances, Rosenberg's article drew a battle line between Pollock/Greenberg, on one hand, and de Kooning/Rosenberg and Hess (whose recent "De Kooning Paints a Picture" also enshrined the Dutch-born painter as Existentialist hero), on the other. Moreover, it imposed a gendered conceptual framework upon a painting attitude supposedly based in absolute freedom: the Abstract Expressionist as hairy-chested, heroically individual he-man doing battle with his canvas. In contrast, there was no overarching critical language for the tough but lyrical canvases of a Joan Mitchell who played music to achieve egolessness as she worked. Her painting, like that of other younger and female artists, did not fit the mold of modern man's confrontation with absolute freedom and existential angst and thus was, in effect, sidelined by Rosenberg's rhetoric.

From the late 1800s, when artist Thomas Moran planted his easel on East Hampton's dunes and painted the sea, through the World War II era, when vacationing Surrealists substituted Amagansett for France's Deauville, the fashionable East End of Long Island had been a favorite artists' retreat. Then, in 1945, Jackson Pollock and Lee Krasner had purchased a run-down farmhouse on Fireplace Road in Springs, the town "below the bridge" from East Hampton, and this less stylish precinct began attracting a new breed of artists.

At that time most locals still earned a living from farming and fishing, but, as the lower fork of the island transformed itself into the Hamptons, blue-collar Springs supplied the carpenters, cleaning women, plumbers, and cooks who kept the richer area's showplaces humming. A scattering of modest bungalows, plus a church, community center, and handful of stores around Accabonac Harbor, Springs boasted stands of cedar and oak, grass-tufted marshland, sandy beaches, sweet air, and sea-washed light. Manhattan loft rats lucky enough to afford summer in the country found its irresistible beauty as appealing as its low rents, which made Pollock, as some locals saw it, the nutty, lazy, boozing advance man for a traveling bohemian circus.

With the help of a real estate agent recommended by Leo Castelli, who owned a home in East Hampton, Joan, Mimi, and Paul now leased for the 1953 season (for a total of $500 or $600) a house on Flaggy Hole Road near Maidstone Beach in Springs. The meager charm of this two-bedroom, called the Rose Cottage, derived wholly from its woodsy setting and its name. The house and its furnishings were nondescript. The windows were equipped with only shutters and screens, but its wide overhanging eaves gave each of its occupants an outdoor studio on one side of the house, and all three painted beautifully that summer.

Unable to afford a share and, in any case, employed at his uncle's box factory, Mike came out mainly on weekends. But Howie Kanovitz and composer Morty Feldman, both deeply involved in psychoanalysis, often hung out with Joan, analyzing each other's dreams and comparing notes on their shrinks. Howie was playing trombone to the baritone sax of the wiry, black-eyed painter Larry Rivers, at the local roadhouse, Jungle Pete's, where they all schmoozed, danced, and drank around the oak bar. And Grace Hartigan and Walt Silver frequently camped at Rose Cottage, including one night that ended with Grace sobbing in the bedroom after Paul expressed skepticism over her assertion that Larry was the Picasso of their day and she the Matisse. From the older generation, Austrian American stage designer Frederick Kiesler and artist Marcel Duchamp turned up occasionally. Around the corner lived Rose and David Slivka, a writer and painter, respectively. Though Rose felt she had to guard against Joan's efforts to seduce her husband, she found her neighbor adorable.

After day's light waned and work was put aside, they would all converge upon the beach. Someone might drag down an old bedspring while others collected wood for a bonfire (still legal then). Cases of beer would materialize, champagne corks pop. A fire soon crackled and soared, and an aroma of hamburgers or steaks wafted from the grill. As Joan's notoriously out-of-control dog George tore up the sand, people would gossip, horse around, or go skinny-dipping. When they went to Louse Point, on the ocean side, a place of spectacular sunsets, fireflies swarmed after dark, illuminating the beachgoers' bodies in pale phosphorescence. The attitude was easy and asexual, yet Joan disliked the idea of public nudity and usually sat out the swimming. On the other hand, once when they were lying in a row on their backs gazing up at the stars, she reached over and groped Paul, who had the normal male reaction. Turning her head in his direction, she murmured, "Oh! You're not so loyal to Mimi after all."

This was not exactly what Fried had in mind in urging Joan to adopt the strategy of seeking the least damaging forms of hostility. Yet psychoanalyst and patient agreed she was making progress. After two and a half years of analysis, Joan had a better grip on the old cycle of ego regression, tension, panic, and rage, a better ability "to look upon [objects in the external world] as things or persons existing according to their own laws and separate from her." Having been walked by Fried through numerous "reality situations," she now recognized many options for releasing antagonism and happily found herself able to experience quiet strength and to "feel affection, love, sex, and not have to tense up and get ready to attack."

That summer in the Hamptons and back in the city that fall, Joan chummed around with poet Frank O'Hara. Vital, intellectual, and talky, this slender man of twenty-seven, with a fighter's broken nose, periwinkle-blue eyes, a receding hairline, and a jaunty birdlike walk, pirouetted through life, a cocktail, half-smoked cigarette, and profusion of friends ever at the ready. His capacity for friendship was legendary.

Raised in Grafton, Massachusetts, O'Hara had served in the Navy before studying at Harvard (where he roomed for a time with Ted Gorey). After Cambridge had come a restless year in graduate school at the University of Michigan, followed by a move to New York City in 1951. Boggled by the city's sensory excitement and chaotic energies, O'Hara could not, he famously wrote, "even enjoy a blade of grass unless I know there's a subway handy, or a record store or some other sign that people do not totally *regret* life." From a job selling postcards and tickets at the Museum of Modern Art, he had worked his way up to front desk manager, a position he had recently resigned to join the staff of *ArtNews*, thus becoming poet–art critic to the Abstract Expressionists as his French role model Guillaume Apollinaire had been poet–art critic to the Cubists.

O'Hara wrote fast, revised little, and half joked that his poems, born in a staccato clamor of keys on his Royal, were unmade phone calls. Yet, steeped in a deep knowledge of literature, especially French modernism, his work was richly complex. Scholar Marjorie Perloff characterizes O'Hara's poetry in terms of its shifts between realism and surrealism, liberal use of proper nouns as nonsymbolic fragments of real life, anti-confessional "I," and syntactic breaks giving rise to contradictions that cannot be sorted out and thus (as in Cubism) force the reader "to accept the flat surface with all its tensions." Sometimes called "action poetry," O'Hara's work insists upon its own coming into being. In many ways, it is analogous to Mitchell's.

Frank was as devoted to painting, including Joan's, as Joan was to poetry, very much including that of "Genius Frank." His selfless generosity and marvelous outpourings of affection touched her. In some ways they were alike: both drank prodigiously, adored New York, relished playing the irritator, and shifted the energy of a room when they entered.

Frank had drawn Joan and Mike closer to the Tibor crowd, especially Alfred, Grace, Larry, and Jane Freilicher. O'Hara's witty, brainy, and sensitive muse, Jane found Joan "boisterous and good humored and haranguing." Joan's edginess, Jane perceived, did not preclude "unexpectedly generous winning qualities." Joan threw a party, for instance, to celebrate Jane's first solo show (a figurative painter, she was not direct competition), and, several years later, she would again fête Jane, on the eve of her wedding. ("I'm serving cognac and nothing else, and I don't want to hear any bitching," Joan warned anyone within earshot before that occasion.)

Jane was also close to poet John Ashbery, who had moved to Manhattan from Sodus, New York, via Harvard. Playful, low-key, and ironic, Ashbery had poems "going on all the time in my head, and I occasionally spin off a length." He too started palling around with Joan, who brought "a festive quality" to their evenings together, he thought, even as she turned simple conversations into something like "embracing a rose bush."

They all saw each other everywhere (May Rosenberg had dubbed the downtown scene a "flying circus"), from Nell Blaine's loft, where the Virginia-born painter led the drumming at wild parties, to the San Remo, where they sat around drinking and smoking Camels and the poets exchanged what they had written that very day.

Along with O'Hara and Ashbery, poets James Schuyler, Barbara Guest, and Kenneth Koch had blown off the dust that had settled upon American poetry, collaboratively reinventing it as a fresh, witty, anti-academic medium that drew as easily from bits of overheard conversation, self-invented games, and the tabloids as from the poet's imagination. In the same way as New York School paintings asserted themselves as pigment on canvas, New York School poems stacked up as words on a page. Abstract yet intensely in the world, confounding to the literal minded, poems and paintings shot forth in the same electric atmosphere. Poets and painters were each other's inspirers, collaborators, audiences, and critics, the poets, Schuyler once wrote, profoundly affected "by the floods of paint in whose crashing surf we all scramble." In a prophetic 1951 essay read at the Museum of Modern Art, poet Wallace Stevens had proclaimed that the "world about us would be desolate except for the world within us. There is the same interchange between these two worlds that there is between one art and another, migratory passings to and fro, quickenings, Promethean liberations and discoveries."

As it happened, Joan and Frank had a huge fight over Wallace Stevens, after which it took weeks for their friendship to right itself. Then came a hysterically funny and long-remembered incident involving the two drunkenly toppling all over each other. (Even years later, O'Hara closed a letter to Joan, "Kisses and falling-downs, Frank.") This moment of supreme silliness probably took place late at night: both Joan and Frank had a gift for twenty-four-hour living, and it was not unusual for them to end up a rowdy or mellow duo at three or four a.m., after everyone else had dragged off to bed. Elaine de Kooning recounts how one night she and Franz Kline

> were sitting alone at a table at the Cedar when the waiter came over and said, "Last call for drinks." "We'll have sixteen Scotches and soda," Franz said grandly. "Sixteen?" the waiter asked, looking around to see who would be joining us. "That's right," Franz said, "eight apiece." Frank O'Hara and Joan Mitchell came in from a party just as the waiter was filling up our table with glasses and gleefully joined us.

In the morning a bleary-eyed Joan would walk George in nearly deserted Washington Square, where she might cross paths with Hans Hofmann, who would doff his hat and inquire: "Micha, why aren't you working?" Or linger on a bench with painter Ad Reinhardt, indulging the theorizing of the curmudgeonly anti–Abstract Expressionist geometric abstractionist. Or sit alone, thinking of Mike.

Their relationship had staggered on. That spring Mike moved to Second Street between Second and Third Avenues, where his neighbor, composer and pianist Alvin Novak, was startled by the fearsome sounds of Joan and Mike trying to kill each other and amazed at how fiercely Joan held her own. When she turned up "really black and blue," with bruises and black eyes half-concealed by sunglasses, friends were at a loss for words.

That January or February, Frank had introduced Mike to a pudgy, full-lipped dark-blond poet from Boston, the same woman who, dressed "as a louche femme-fatale," had days earlier stolen the show at Larry Rivers's costume ball for which Joan and Alfred had painted enormous paper murals and other artists had created outlandish outfits for the poets. Mike had then embarked upon a "violent affair" with Violet Ranney Lang, aka Bunny.

The daughter of a Boston society woman and a King's Chapel organist, Bunny Lang lived with her widowed father in a deteriorating Bay State Road brownstone. Though raised in old-money circles, this stagy eccentric, later the subject of an irresistible posthumous memoir by her friend, novelist Alison Lurie, preferred dirty dishabille and ratty thrift shop gaudery to pearls and a hat. To pay off her debts (the family fortune had dwindled), she took a series of odd jobs that she treated as acting opportunities, most famously as a chorus girl at Boston's Old Howard

A lull in the storm: Joan, age twenty-nine, with longtime lover Michael Goldberg, c. 1954

burlesque theater. She also wrote, directed, produced, acted, and played the role of querulous ringleader at the avant-garde Poets' Theatre in Cambridge, a bid to revive poetic drama. Members included Harvard and ex-Harvard poets John Ciardi, Richard Eberhart, John Ashbery, Frank O'Hara, and Ted Gorey. Moreover, as V. R. Lang, she had published in *Poetry* and the *Chicago Review*. The production of her verse play, *Fire Exit*, at the Amato Opera Theatre had brought her to New York that winter.

Back in Boston in March, Bunny wrote Mike, "You are my love and you are a wonder and I want to live with you more than anything else in the world." They agreed he would come up to "ask her old man for her hand," after which they would marry and live in New York, where she would find a job and support him like any good long-suffering Abstract Expressionist's wife.

"On April 9, as announced," reports Lurie in her memoir, "Mike arrived in Boston, a city which he had never before visited. He proved to be a medium-sized young man with black hair, burning eyes, and a large pale bony face, dressed as an abstract painter. He said almost nothing at all and moved everywhere with a quiet, catlike walk in sneakers spotted with abstract paint," sometimes steering Bunny by the back of the neck, which was not done in Boston. Throughout Mike's visit, the crusty Mr.

Lang had kept his own counsel on the matter of his daughter's suitor, until finally he summoned Bunny for a private conversation in which he proved himself a vicious anti-Semite. Furious, Bunny and Mike swept off to New York. Friends awaited telegrams announcing their marriage.

But they never came. For months Bunny had been undergoing tests for flu-like symptoms, and, around this time, they confirmed a diagnosis of Hodgkin's disease, a type of lymphoma at that time incurable. Unable to handle this looming catastrophe, Mike put the brakes on the relationship. Moreover, he had continued to see Joan, as if nothing had changed, and a third woman too. After several weeks, Bunny returned to Boston alone.

Bunny's very existence gave Joan apoplexy, her rival's easy command of Mike's heart casting into relief her own failure at love and stirring up a demon's nest of fears of abandonment. Yet long before *l'affaire Bunny*, Joan had stopped allowing herself the vulnerability of blissing out in Mike's arms and Mike had wearied of Joan's excessive emotional demands. When she spoke, he listened, she felt, "at a great distance if at all," and this ambiguity and hostility were far worse than Sturm und Drang. "I would like to be loved or destroyed by you," Joan told him, "but not left crippled like an insect."

Yet she herself was leading a messy, reckless, and distracted life. Her many lovers included painter Jon Schueler, with whom she went home one night after a party at Guston's studio. Jon was stunned by the beauty of Joan's breasts. But when he tried to get intimate again a few days later, he was dismissed: *that* was over, now they would be just friends. Another former sex partner who crossed paths with Joan at the theater one night was heartily greeted, "Oh, boy! You were shitty in bed."

One affair mattered, however, more than the others. The grandson of famous *Harper's Weekly* illustrator Rufus F. Zogbaum and son of a Navy admiral, Yale graduate Wilfred Zogbaum had abandoned a successful career as an advertising photographer to become a sculptor and a painter of foamy-white abstract cloudscapes infused with the lights and colors of Springs. He and his wife Betsy lived with their six-year-old son in a renovated Coast Guard building on Fireplace Road. The marriage was disintegrating, however, and Betsy stood at the threshold of a long, vital relationship with Franz Kline.

That summer, Joan, Mimi, and Paul again rented together in Springs, this time Bossy Farm, also on Fireplace Road. The Brachs would take the house, and Joan the former duck shed out back, and they would share the kitchen and bath. By then Zog had moved to a fisherman's cabin just down the road.

Given the intelligence, charm, and enthusiasms of this artist, French speaker, and music intellectual with an impressive record library and an abiding passion for Bach, an enduring romance might have been born. Joan was telling everyone she had left Mike for Zog, but, in fact, the chemistry was lacking for anything but a deeply affectionate friendship.

One day early that summer, as Zog was attempting to start the cabin's defective space heater, he dropped a lighted match into the fuel tank, either by accident or out of frustration. The resulting explosion blew the building four inches off its foundation and sent him to the hospital with third-degree burns. Joan's summer would unfold no less disastrously.

On June 9, after a sleepless night, Joan hitched an early-morning ride out to Springs with Harold Rosenberg, who owned a house on Neck Path. Along the way, the two stopped at the red Victorian on the edge of Bridgehampton that Bill de Kooning, Ludwig Sander, Elaine de Kooning, and Franz Kline were sharing that summer. The late-carousing household barely stirred, except for Franz, "charming and unshaven," who fixed the visitors dry martinis and caught them up on the latest: Jackson Pollock's broken ankle.

A day or two earlier, Franz, Bill, and Lutz had driven over to East Hampton to collect furniture and books they were going to store for their friends Don and Carol Braider. Meanwhile, Jackson had pulled up to the Red House in his Ford. He was now painting little, drinking hard, and making himself unwelcome almost everywhere. Nervous to find herself alone with the liquored-up and glowering artist, Elaine had phoned Bill at the Braiders'. After he returned, the men started carrying books to the basement, all the while bantering and roughhousing. Then Jackson tripped, and Bill tumbled over him. Jackson's ankle snapped. Even as Carol was driving Pollock to the local clinic in her station wagon, stories of what seemed a symbolic bout began flying around the art world. "At least he'll be quiet for a few days until he can wield his cast through Hattie Rosenberg's glass," Joan dryly observed, referring to the pianist who lived on Louse Point in a spectacular home designed by her architect husband.

Thanks in part to a groundswell of confidence among artists, Springs was fast becoming East-Tenth-Street-by-the-Sea. Now that their work was beginning to sell, more painters could afford summer in the country. Dealers Sam Kootz and Sidney Janis were around, vacuuming up the biggest names and taking the line that, as Eleanor Ward paraphrased Kootz's pitch, "Now you're successful you need a knowledgeable man around. You've had that scene and now you need the real thing." But Eleanor too was shopping for artists, as was Martha Kellogg Jackson, heiress to a Buffalo chemical fortune, who was buying directly from painters for her new East Sixty-sixth Street gallery. Not from Joan, however. During a visit to the Rose Cottage the previous year, the dealer had, in Joan's opinion, asked stupid questions and made insulting comments. With her usual point-blank directness, the artist had chased Jackson away: "Why don't you leave?"

Gallery politics notwithstanding, summer in Springs brought a chance for artists to catch their collective breath in the midst of the long struggle to make it. Most were working—few as intensely as Joan—but they also indulged in beach walks, clambakes, cocktail parties, outdoor suppers, and softball games on the Zogbaums' lawn, where Joan played alongside Bill de Kooning, Elaine de Kooning, Charlotte Park, James Brooks, Saul Steinberg, John Little, Leo Castelli, Harold Rosenberg, Larry Rivers, Philip Pavia, Esteban Vicente, Howard Kanovitz, and Franz Kline. Pavia proved a star slugger, Rosenberg a fine pitcher (because of his bad leg, his daughter ran the bases), and Joan a third baseman who practically took the glove off someone's hand when she blasted a ball, thus terrifying the foreign born, like the Italian Castelli, the Romanian Steinberg, and the Dutch de Kooning. According to Tom Hess's version of an oft-told story, Franz, Bill, and Elaine once spent a long evening painstakingly painting a coconut and two grapefruits to resemble softballs. The following day a grapefruit was duly pitched by Harold to Philip:

> Pavia swung, and it exploded in a great ball of grapefruit juice. There was general laughter [so much so that outfielder Castelli fell over backward] and little shouts of, "Come on, let's get on with the game."
> Esteban Vicente came in from behind first base (where Ludwig Sander was stationed with a covered basket containing ammunition); he pitched the first ball over easily. Pavia swung. There was another ball of grapefruit juice in the air. More laughter. Finally they decided that fun was fun, but now to continue play, seriously. Rosenberg came back to the mound. He smacked the softball to assure everyone of

its Phenomenological Materiality. He pitched it over the plate. Pavia swung. It exploded into a wide, round cloud of coconut . . . then, from nowhere, a crowd of kids appeared around home plate and began to pick up the fragments of coconut and eat them. They had to call the game.

Life at Bossy Farm was proving less mirthful. For reasons she never spelled out, Joan had soured on erstwhile best friends Mimi and Paul. Once that summer she picked up Mimi's Egyptian-style necklace, draped it across her forehead, did a few bumps and grinds, then wrapped it around one breast, wiggled some more, and finally made of the pendant a surrogate penis. No doubt she was sloshed and going for laughs, but her performance came off as mocking and disturbed. Another time she and Mike tried to plant lice in the Brachs' bed, a prank they found hysterically funny. Never at a loss for sly barbed put-downs of Mimi and Paul, Joan treated the two, thought Paul, as if they were "a bourgeois couple playing itself, and she was the one going into uncharted waters."

Similarly, at a small dinner party at the Braiders', a very drunk Joan offended her hostess when she shot down some casual remark of Don's with a disdainful "What's so sacred about your asshole?" Moving in a haze of liquor and smoke, she awoke each morning dreading the moment when she would remember her horrid behavior the night before. But she never apologized.

She had started taking Dexedrine, a potentially habit-forming amphetamine used to treat depression (though rendered less effective by alcohol). It exacerbated her insomnia. So too did her fear of the deep blackness surrounding the lonely duck shed. After dark, the trees outside her window looked "Seuratish and colorless," and the wind moaned and rattled her shades. Night after night she lay in bed reading Dostoevsky until, light finally leaking into the sky, she drifted off, and the sons, fathers, elders, and prosecutors of *The Brothers Karamazov* trooped through her nightmares. Dostoevsky also fed her brief obsession with the gratuitous beating death that summer of a Brooklyn bum by four shy, bookish teenagers with whom she identified.

Joan's distress went hand in hand with a growing frustration with painting. "My hand doesn't always feel and my eye sees just clichés," she complained to Mike. Color eluded her. With a record spinning on the turntable she had lugged out to Springs and a tumbler of gin by her side, she escaped one afternoon's searing heat in the shade of her shack, staring critically at "one blue and one yellow pitcha—smallish and the kind one would say 'talent' about and not much more." She continued,

> I distrust my painting in color—I think it's because people said I ought to—and I distrust [my painting that relies less on color] . . . and I hate little paintings because they're "quickies" and big ones because they're pretentious—and when I start cataloguing all things in this manner the real meaning isn't there. I better get myself in order with some honesty and the ability to fail. I've always painted out of omnipotence I guess—pretty shaky method. Gimme a pigfoot and some dexedrine and don't disturb my fantasy.

Joan was seeking—and, she felt, failing miserably at—"a complete synthesis of accuracy and intensity." By accuracy, she meant rigorous structure and discriminating line that worked "in terms of describing forms, making forms work, and in terms of the lines themselves." For lessons in accuracy, she looked to Beethoven, whose music rarely left her machine; Cézanne, whose reproductions torn from art magazines she had tacked to a wall; and especially van Gogh, whose landscapes, she felt, supremely fused accuracy with intensity. Not only was a van Gogh scrupulously built but also its every brushstroke delivered authentic feeling. Obsessed with the Dutch artist's roiling, hallucinatory landscape *The Starry Night* (in the collection of the Museum of Modern Art) for its pulsing line, fabulous crudeness, violent lyricism, and painfully intense color, Joan stared at the luminous blues surrounding her that summer by the sea and ruminated about "that Van Gogh intensity idea."

Claiming that she experienced painting in a physical way, nothing more, she did allow to Mike that, well, "maybe mystically" too. And she fell into near rapture when Barney's fiancée Loly Eckert brought her a brilliant yellow sunflower, "an absolute headlight. I like what Van Gogh made of that starry night—to animate something—insanity and fanaticism. My painting natch is horrible." Filled with false starts, her work again and again fell short of her exalted aims, even short, she felt, of genuine failure. But she soldiered on, destroying as much as she kept.

Then there was the "fucking, emotional bankruptcy" of her relationship with Mike. Tortured by memories of the marvelous complicity of their early days, of their old San Remo suppers, Joan felt "on the edge of my life and I'd like to get back into it. I'd like to carry it with me as

Harold [Rosenberg] does in the briefcase." After a dash into the city to buy paint, see Mike, and talk to Fried (who had a great deal to say about her lover's continual threats to cut and run), Joan lamented in a letter to Mike,

It was sad driving back—all surrounded with the failure and so completely aware of all the reasons. The Russian Icon book [a gift from Mike] is beautiful. We do pay a high price for our sensitivity—or is this a rationalization. It's such crap to say I need to be alone to be able to see you again. And it's empty to say I'm sorry—but I am Mike—and guilty—and I miss you completely already and remember that strange hospital bed with gold ends and remember you're leaving. Te quiero tanto—tanto.

Yet Mike's visit to Springs the following weekend proved the usual disaster.

Mike was simultaneously living a long-distance drama with Bunny. "All through the summer of 1954 the affair dragged on," writes Alison Lurie. "Mostly by mail: Bunny would not go to New York, and Mike would not come to Boston. Sometimes they telephoned, and shouted insults at each other." Bunny suffered intensely. By fall, however, she was telling Lurie she was "getting very tired of the whole thing, at last. It is so feeble and psychopathic." She locked herself in her bedroom and brewed revenge, needling Mike by letter: "You stopped believing in me, how did I fail you? Go to Arabia and I'll go there too as a company typist. Go to China and the first coolie you'll see in a rice paddy will be me. Or I'll live in the Y at 12th and Hudson and come every day to sit in front of the Merit Company [where he worked]. A forbidding and reproachful figure." She considered mortifying him by writing a long rant against abstract painting, signing "Michael Goldberg," and mailing it to *ArtNews* or *Time*. Then she got a better idea.

In Joan's letters to Mike, line after line of elegant barbed wire prose as edgy, free-associative, articulate, and as paratactic as a Mitchell painting or O'Hara poem, the painter kept reverting, that summer of 1954, to her abhorrence of the art world's "knifing and competition." Grace, of course, was around and issuing *pronunciamentos,* the latest of which had to do with excess and restraint. Grace and Larry and Ingres and a few other "great painters" were "excessive." Jane Freilicher, unfortunately, was not. Joan had not been considered. "It's like looking at painting at a girl scout camp," retorted Grace's rival, "so many demerits for peeing in bed, etc, a gold star if you shit enough."

The whole season, Joan felt, had lapsed into one long, drunken-nauseous, ego-bloated party: at the Red House in Bridgehampton, at the Castellis' elegant digs, at Larry Rivers's place in Southampton, at painter Alfonso Ossorio's estate, at the modernist Quonset-hut-inspired home Barney had recently purchased from painter Robert Motherwell, where, with Loly, he was throwing "Gatsby-like parties" around the pool. Cars were constantly pulling up to Bossy Farm too, friends stopping by, friends of friends butting into Joan's life. She wanted to flee. The "pressure of the summer has been unbearable," she confided to Mike. "I feel in a goldfish bowl . . . I want to pull the shades down . . . I want to hide." Even the gregarious Elaine de Kooning was experiencing a "pleas-ant but nightmarish summer, parties every night, entertaining in the way a nightmare could be entertaining . . . too many friends, too much talk, too much booze, too much of a good thing."

Even too many pictures. At one cocktail party at Ossorio's, Joan and Alfonso had persuaded Don and Carol Braider to add a gallery to their House of Books and Music on East Hampton's Main Street. Thus the carport out back (consisting of a wall, a roof, and the wooden platform where a plumber used to park his truck) was transformed into an exhibi-tion space. Everybody participated in the Braiders' shows. Nothing was priced at more than $300. Nothing was guarded or insured. Never again would Abstract Expressionist work, today sold for millions, be shown that casually or offered that cheaply. The Braiders' openings should have felt to Joan like happy tribal moments, especially since she had helped to initiate them, yet she disliked these "crappy clothesline shows," another spin of the wheel in "the rat race."

To loosen her straitjacket of anxiety, Joan listened to classical music with Zog, took George to Barnes Hole beach, or simply commanded herself to breathe deeply. Often she felt incapable of positive action: "How very weak I am after all—and how very overwhelming any feel-ing is." She had trouble sorting out time, seemed to slide into water or trees, could not always mentally distinguish herself from Mike. Would her edgeless white gin-blurry fog of depression ever lift?

The predawn hours of August 9 brought a downpour that persisted all day, cutting a stifling heat wave. Having dashed her supplies inside the shed, Joan started a "cad yellow pale thing," then put it aside to work on a half-finished canvas. A third oil, small, with a problematic green square, awaited clear weather so she could take it outside and examine it in full light. Inside the shed, the air was pungent with turpentine and cigarette smoke. She felt acutely alone. She had given her adored George to the dog-loving Braiders because, she told Carol, he was getting too sexy and was always trying to mount her. As for her pictures, she had "put all my nickels in the slot machine" and, pull the lever as she might, nothing was paying off. She had just ripped apart four failed canvases. Why drag another brush across another piece of linen?

Four days later Joan wrote Mike a chatty letter, ending, however, on an ominous note: "Sweetie pie the ship is rocking at high noon. You paint for both of us for a while—and miss me." She would leave him on her terms, not his. Placing Mozart's *Don Giovanni* on the turntable, she lowered the needle, turned up the volume to cover the drumbeat of the rain, and started swallowing Dexedrine tablets, washed down with gin. (Her selection of *Don Giovanni* was meant to send a message to Mike, whom she sometimes called "il mio tesoro," the title of one of its arias: as Mozart's lyrical opera concludes, the unrepentant libertine Don Giovanni is consigned to hell.)

Joan and George on the beach in Springs, 1954

Joan slept off the overdose, which she experienced as "another kind of blue on a palette." To botch even her suicide, "a bastard affair," more absurd than dramatic, was further evidence, she felt, of a "real dull mind."

Nothing changed. A few days later she wrote Mike,

We have no new beginnings the way you had always hoped and never even clean endings—we just drag ourselves along and if we're lucky there's a nice blue line someplace—and I think we're lucky. I would like to write something very simple to you that would perhaps connect us . . . Still I'm always meeting you at the station—shit Mike—it's not much fun being nuts—or living among so many amorphous green trees and ideas—forgive me for being such a schmuck. I've loved you so much and it sticks us at two ends of a railroad station—and perhaps it should bore you by this time—my love, I mean—and yet it's meant much to me—and of course I would do the same thing all over again—miss your fucking enigmatic eyes—te quiero—all colors Juana.

That Saturday the two showed up together at the blowout end-of-the-summer party at the Red House. Cars lined both sides of Montauk Highway, and people thronged house and yard where Elaine had hung the trees with big papier-mâché flowers sprayed with perfume. Even the toilet seat of the outhouse was decorated. The party, Mike later remembered, "was very beautiful and people were very drunk and crawling off into the corners."

The next day, Joan flew to Chicago because Jimmie was severely ill. Though he seemed "old at last and like a wound," he turned out to be well enough to say something cruel. Retreating into her parents' dim, cool, silent apartment, Joan read Mallarmé and felt guilty and "sad about us," she told Mike, "and frightened."

On the eve of her departure a week later, she chronicled her summer in a letter to Evans Herman:

I painted so much and destroyed so much—kept thinking of something fantastic like Van Gogh's Starry Night and came out mostly with my own lack of belief all mirrored and distorted in a cocktail shaker—Christ I'm certainly not a Prince Hamlet but I can gather all the images around me here—heavy carpet, all bells chiming and late-afternoon sunlight on pewter—more realistic than gold but to hell with that . . . I'll go to Europe in the winter—I'll start out all over again without the knowledge of suicide and carry myself with me this time—I wonder if you'll come with me also—oh I wonder lots of things.

Back in New York City the following day, Joan received word that George was sick and rushed out to Springs. (In the midst of moving and coping with their own unruly boxer and Great Dane, the Braiders were returning Joan's dog.) The next morning, August 31, 1954, as she hastened to get George to a vet, the most destructive storm in sixteen years, Hurricane Carol, crashed into eastern Long Island. Winds reached one hundred miles an hour. Debris cartwheeled down the streets. Boats hurtled ashore. Roofs blew off houses. The electricity flickered off as power lines collapsed under the weight of falling trees. Paul Brach watched an old apple tree "levitate about six feet, turn on its side, and then exit stage left." Many artists gathered at the Pollocks' house, rushing out to help neighbors when they could. At high tide, the ocean raced across Montauk Highway and down Fireplace Road, its dark, dirty waters swirling around cars and flooding homes. Noon abruptly brought dazzling sunshine and sparkling colors. Then the hurricane briefly turned landward again.

At some point that day, Mike stood beside Joan watching Georgica Pond, and then, at the ocean, the two gaped at huge, beautiful, mysterious waves. That morning, according to someone who later heard it from Joan, "she [had] had to risk her life to save the dog . . . The harrowing experience stayed with her for a very long time." Joan would tell Irving Sandler, "It was a very devastating experience. Trees fell over. It seemed as if the wrath of God fell upon East Hampton. The hurricane is a ghastly symbol of a frightening period in my life." It lodged in her memory alongside terrifying Lake Michigan storms, becoming vital feeling material for at least four tumultuous and beautiful paintings based (as Mallarmé famously prescribed) on not the thing, but the effect it produces. As for her summer's work, Joan later claimed that the duck shed had been demolished and that she had lost many paintings, but Mike recalled that the little building stayed intact.

Before returning to the city, Joan gave George to a farmer. Soon thereafter he was killed by a car. She grieved long and hard.

And in the same way as the luminosity of the water
and its every throb pass through a medusa,
so everything traversed his inner being,
and that sense of fluidity became transfigured
into something like second sight.

VLADIMIR NABOKOV

CHAPTER NINE Hudson River Day Line

It's safe to say that Joan never saw *I Too Have Lived in Arcadia,* a
verse play à clef by V. R. Lang (after Sir Philip Sidney's pastoral
romance *The Countess of Pembroke's Arcadia*), staged that fall at
the Poets' Theatre of Cambridge. But she would have heard all about it
from the gossipy Ted Gorey, who designed the poster. As Lang's *Arcadia* opens, its protagonists, the anarchists Damon (Mike) and Chloris
(Bunny), are observing his December 24th birthday, which is also the
first anniversary of their move to the bucolic French-speaking island
of Miquelon, east of Canada, where they forage and breed goats. The
couple's idyll is troubled, however, by the approach of a sinister figure in a black trench coat and black rubber boots. Phoebe (Joan) has
come to steal her ex-lover away from the island and back to the City.
("I am the City.") She is accompanied by her hipster poodle Georges,
who apostrophizes in fake-beatnik French (*"Quelle femme carrée!"*).
(The cognoscenti identified Georges with Frank O'Hara, Bunny's tar-

get because he had not intervened with Mike on her behalf.) Alternately charming and irksome, rife with sly digs and cumbersome conceits, *Arcadia* ends on a vaguely feminist note: Phoebe wins back Damon, but he proves a weak, self-deceitful louse, unworthy of the two strong women fighting over him.

Joan *had*, in fact, bested her rival, but only by default. Claiming she still believed in the two of them, she pressed Mike to believe or not, to love her or leave her.

When Jimmie suffered a severe heart attack in early December, Joan again rushed out to Chicago. In the week that followed, she visited him in the hospital two or three times a day, wearing lipstick and a different outfit each time and bringing little diversions like pictures of Sally's three kids. He was "so collapsed and natch—sweet the way he isn't otherwise," she told Mike:

> Oh Mike—all day long I've been like Gibraltar and with all my problems about him—now later at night—it's hard—it's worse when you see it—and I've imagined that damn hospital scene for years and his saying—"You've never cared" and holding my hand. And yet I've never been here when he wasn't and I can play music and wander about—the mixture of feelings is almost impossible—n'importe—each letter to you has been a hideola and I'm sorry—got to turn my mind off—"Teach me to care and not to care"—à la Eliot [the line is from Eliot's poem "Ash Wednesday"].

> Oh Mike—may it all happen quickly.

Unexpectedly, Jimmie recovered, and old patterns reasserted themselves. Back home two weeks later, he gave Joan *A Guide to Drawing* as a Christmas gift. She *had* been mulling over the role that drawing should play in her work, but he meant the book as a rebuke for poor draftsmanship. "Pose for me," she teased Mike in her next letter, "and I'll send him detailed drawings of pretty pricks." When Ted Gorey came by, the two old friends polished off a bottle of Scotch but managed only to get "cross-eyed and dull." That same evening, Joan scrawled disturbing, self-pitying caricatures in a letter to Mike. In one, Jimmie ("no comment") sits stiffly in an armchair, eyes glued to the nude odalisque "J.M."

across the room; in another, Mike steps out with a buxom babe on each arm as George weeps and Joan squats and weeps too, into her ashtray and drink.

> I can see how living here would force anybody to paint [she had written Mike]. Through successive vacations I've covered all old nostalgia and now it's drained—fuck the lake—and fuck my reactions to it and the past—shit it's depressing—I so depress myself . . . give me a pig-foot and a marvelous poodle . . . my Father terrifies me—really—and tells me what to do every five minutes until I almost scream the way I used to "leave me alone"—and my Mother can't hear. It's so hard to keep breathing here I can barely visualize 2nd Ave. I'm damn miserable and it's worse without crying or anger—balls! . . . Please if you can meet me at the plane and we'll have coffee—Medaglia d'Oro type—and make me believe in painting again the way I once did only wrongly and now it may become rightly—il mio tesoro.

She didn't need Mike, however, to find the magic of painting again. Having made a last-minute decision to accept her mother's offer of a plane ticket to Santa Barbara, California, Joan flew out to visit sister Sally and her family, and the fantastic panoramas she saw from the air stirred up a wild desire to paint. So too, at one point, had the way "the city stretch[ed] out so mysteriously and crudely" below her parents' terrace in Chicago. The months that followed brought pictures one critic likened to "huge sprawling city-scapes seen from vast distances"—*City Landscape* and *The Lake,* to name two—their midsections knit together using vigorous strokes of newly robust color: reds, blues, yellows, blacks, pinks, and greens. That spring, Joan would paint intensely.

Interviewed in 1985, she indirectly flagged 1955 as a key year, noting that her work hadn't "changed much over the last 30 years—not in what I've wanted to do." In 1986, another interviewer elicited this from the artist:

> I "frame" everything that happens. I can see you now. This will be a photograph in my head: you against the sky, and that way I will remember you, but I won't see you moving around, dropping that recorder, or having lunch. You are living and I keep you in one still piece alive. It will be like a painting. It's not only a piece of life, it's an image, a real image. Of course, there is movement, what people

call movement, within the frame but it is certainly caught and if the painting works, the motion is made still, like a fish trapped in ice. It is trapped in the painting. My mind is like an album of photographs and paintings. I do not conceive.

In the translucent, raw-silk 1955 *Hudson River Day Line,* for instance, Joan catches a felt memory-image as if in slow motion half an hour before sunset. Its thinned "cloud"-girded blues swelling, plunging, dripping, dancing, flaring into bright ochre, and coalescing into a shape roughly that of a map of Spain, *Hudson River Day Line* mobilizes a lover's sensuality, a painter's passion for her medium, and an eidetic's insight. Following her crisis summer, 1954, she had, it seems, decanted her atypical modes of perception—that "secret magic that other people don't understand"—into her painting.

One day some thirty years later, Joan sat talking with Edrita Fried's adult daughter, Jaqui Fried. The artist's back was turned to a window outside which loomed an overcast sky. "I've never told you this," she began. "I see in colors. When I look at you, I see gold, even though it's a gray day. It has nothing to do with the light or with your gold hair." Jaqui ventured that this was part of Joan's gift. Had it always been this way? Joan spoke of the yellow satin curtains, then went on to assert that (in Jaqui's paraphrase) it had taken her "a long time to figure it out" and that her idiosyncratic mode of perception had "made her feel very crazy and odd and stupid in her early years . . . But it was paramount [in her art] and very, very present for her." Did she now see this perceptual idiosyncrasy as a positive thing? "Yes, oh yes. She loved it. She embraced it. She loved that part of herself."

Many artists work from memory, but, for most, memory takes the form of a mental image or of self-talk. Joan, on the other hand, made art in thrall to reexperiencing people and places in their affective plenitude. The difference is analogous to thinking about an old favorite song as opposed to hearing it again and thus falling prey to its raw flick of emotion. (One eidetic synesthete speaks of a "waking dream that doesn't interfere with consciousness.")

By using the same incomprehensible differences that sometimes made her feel a stranger to the world, Joan transformed a negative into a positive and regained control of her life. By sublimating her fears and refusing to succumb to passivity in the face of life's overwhelmingness, she also gave full dimension to her art.

One can speculate that *Hudson River Day Line,* coalescing as it does in the center of the canvas as if upon the artist's plane of consciousness, draws upon her mind's-eye view, her eidetic "album of photographs and paintings." Or that *Evenings on Seventy-third Street* (a 1956 painting), with its scaffolding of leaping, colliding, fusing, and darting strokes, takes inspiration from her colored hearing. But to attempt to figure out how Joan brought her full sensate world into this or that painting is a fool's errand. Focus instead upon the results: the flaring up of fluid, translucent strokes, the presence of color with soul at center stage. A celery ochre, an opulent burgundy, and a gamut of light-rinsed and storm-tossed blues now appeared on Joan's palette.

Color, however, is an exacting discipline: one cannot simply slap down one color after another and expect a painting to work. To say that Joan availed herself of her synesthesia and eideticism in painting is not to suggest that her neurology explains her work, nor is it to say that her art amounts to exploded views of her inner visions. To reduce her to a case is to disregard her painterly intelligence, her professionalism, her years of training and work. If *Hudson River Day Line*'s tumultuousness, lyricism, charged color, and loose and rhythmic strokes are those of an eidetic synesthete, they are also those of a practiced and passionate painter deep in conversation with van Gogh's *Starry Night.*

By the time Joan's second show at the Stable closed on March 12, summer was fast approaching, and she and Fried were debating how to avoid another psychological pileup in the Hamptons. Joan toyed with the idea of spending June and July in Alaska; Fried was urging her to ask Marion for a ticket to Paris. At first Joan turned up her nose. All the same, she started prodding Elaine to go to France with her, even offering to pay Elaine's way. In the end, however, de Kooning decided the timing was wrong, and Joan went alone. The idea, worked out with her analyst, was to play tourist, improve her French, and ventilate her relationship with Mike while she tried new behaviors, including moderating her drinking. In a letter to Mike years later, she framed her trip somewhat differently: "you do know Fried sent me [to Paris] because of you [in] 1955 (an unorthodox thing to do as she said) and you do know it had to do with your lies—and only that." Tagging her summer "the experiment," she gathered a list of phone numbers of friends of friends whom she was to call and to see as an exercise in healthy social behavior, and, after a "*grand dernier* fuck" with Mike, flew off to Paris for two months.

No sooner had Joan settled into the dull and expensive Left Bank Hôtel Montalembert (selected and paid for by her mother) than she found herself unexpectedly seduced by the French capital. She visited the Rodin Museum, caught several organ concerts at St.-Sulpice, ogled the poodles in the Tuileries Gardens, and went drawing along the Seine "where the barges squat with wonderful fat asses and names like Charmine and Adolphine." Losing weight was also on her agenda: with her usual exemplary self-discipline, she fasted every day until dinnertime, when she would find some unpretentious bistro and tuck into an omelet or her favorite steak *au beurre* topped with watercress. Out came a book: Rilke's *Notebooks of Malte Laurids Brigge*, de Beauvoir's *Les Mandarins,* or Orwell's *Keep the Aspidistra Flying.* (The British writer's satire about the impossibility of escaping almighty Mammon, in which the dowdy aspidistra plant symbolizes middle-class striving for security, so delighted Joan that she began bandying about the phrase "Keep the aspidistra flying!," and she was to title a 1958 painting *Aspidistra.*) Back at her hotel, she often read through the night, chain-smoking Gauloises Bleues and capping her waking hours with a stroll along the Seine, where the reflection of a neon "AIR FRANCE" sign shimmered in the silent blue dawn.

The boulevard Saint-Michel served as one pole of her mental geography: when a "hideous numbness" overtook her, she would drag up and down its sidewalks in soggy espadrilles and a sad raincoat missing most of its buttons (the weather had turned rainy and cold). In more upbeat moods, she gravitated to Saint-Germain-des-Prés, with its humming café scene. Within hours of her arrival, Joan had phoned Shirley Jaffe, a longtime American resident of Paris whom she had met two years earlier when Shirley briefly sublet New York studio space from Mike. And that very evening Shirley had coaxed her to the Royal, a boulevard Saint-Germain hangout of musicians and artists (later torn down to make way for the Drugstore Publicis).

With a confluence of vacationing New Yorkers—poet Kenneth Koch, composer and businessman Morris Golde, painters Mary Abbott and Jacqueline Lambda, and sculptors Marisol and David Hare, to name a few—Joan's social life picked up speed. She went to the opera with Golde, poked around the Saint-Ouen flea market with Jacqueline and David, accompanied David on a visit to Surrealist painter Roberto Matta, and sipped Pernod with Shirley and Marisol, whose "silent hostility" annoyed her. Ditto Koch's grin. The charming Hedda Sterne and Saul Steinberg also came into Joan's life. In New York, she had casually known the Romanian-born couple, she a painter and he a cartoonist famous for his work in the *New Yorker,* but that summer in Paris, where the Steinbergs were renting on the rue Jacob, they struck up a friendship. She particularly adored the witty Saul, with whom she sipped champagne and chewed over life.

Among those in Shirley's crowd, Joan already knew the lyrical abstractionist Kimber Smith, who had shown at the New Gallery until his wife Gabrielle's job as a correspondent for *Life* brought them to Paris. Now she met Norman Bluhm, an abstract painter and a Brando in cowboy boots, born in Chicago, raised in Italy, and unhappily married to a Frenchwoman. Norm — "Bubble," Joan dubbed him — promptly made "horizontal propositions" to his compatriot, who promptly refused — the start of a close and enduring friendship. She was also introduced to Bluhm's mentor, the Californian Sam Francis, as easygoing as Norm was tough. Sam quickly seduced her by whipping her around the city and out to his studio in Arcueil on the back of his motorcycle, and the two had a brief affair. But she found him less than wonderful in bed, and, for years thereafter, would clatter on to mutual friends about his sexual inadequacies. Nor was Joan wild at first about Sam's paintings, bright organic clusters drifting through airy white spaces, worlds without bottom or top. Notwithstanding his Americanness, they represented to her the French gestural abstraction she dismissed as "watered-down Pollock and Rothko." Not until a decade later would she fall in love with their transparent colors and irrational luminosity.

Along with French artist Georges Mathieu and the Canadian Jean-Paul Riopelle, Sam Francis was among the most highly regarded members of the Paris-based Tachiste movement (its name refers to the splatters resulting from spontaneous paint handling), alternately termed Art Informel (meaning "formless art," a phrase that emphasizes its supposed disregard for the French tradition of stylistic elegance). Soon Joan met the mandarins of this Continental avant-garde: painter, critic, theorist, and bass player Michel Tapié, who ran the important Galerie Rive Droite, and Georges Duthuit, a tweedy, pipe-smoking art historian and critic married to Marguerite Matisse, the eldest child of painter Henri Matisse. Both treated her as "de Kooning's emissary."

Painter Sam Francis's shot of his then lover Joan, Paris, 1955

Joan, for her part, considered Paris "a small town—half the Cedar running on half its fuel," its art less consequential, less driven, less appealingly brutal than that of New York, of which it was derivative. In the same way as the intellectual tonic of Existentialism had ceded to rive gauche mannerisms, French painting was drifting along on elegance of surface (talk to the contrary notwithstanding), Joan felt, the continuing verve of prewar masters Picasso, Miró, and Giacometti only confirming its has-been status. "Not much art here," she once groused to Harold Rosenberg, "except the kind sauces are poured over." So why the hell had she come?

For personal reasons, she reminded herself. Attempting to gain perspective on her relationship with Mike, she mentally relived ugly scenes like "puking in that delicatessen" last summer. She pondered his low tolerance for her emotional outpourings and chastised herself for using him "like a garbage pail for my sickest feelings." Though relieved to detoxify her life by putting over three thousand miles between them, she also daydreamed about showing him Paris, obsessed over who he was sleeping with, and became frantic any time several days went by without a letter, the "fuck you kind" a hundred times better than the terrible silence.

Joan's feelings were further complicated by her desire for "one small child" and a real home: "white walls, a kitchen like [her painter friend] Biala's, red tomatoes, and bright color . . . all preferably with a man who makes me feel like a woman." Her thirtieth birthday that February had hit her hard, especially coming as it did on the heels of her stay with Sally, Newt, and their three kids. By no means did she want her sister's bourgeois life, yet a note of desperation crept into certain discussions with friends. For weeks, she (untruthfully) told Mike, no one had touched her except in a perfunctory manner: "How did I get myself out so far on a limb with nobody—even a strange language?"

Fearing that Mike would act like a stranger when she went home, she wrote, "I wonder how glad you are that I'm gone. I wonder how you'll be when I return. Oh, Mike, where am I and why? Paint, paint, and make it different when I return. Or will you be around. I wonder. I love you very much." Meanwhile, she was bragging to Shirley that she had dumped him.

Taking stock of her relationship with Mike figured into a wider self-assessment. Feeling old, ugly, and inarticulate, Joan sorely missed her New York friends, "people who understand me as a spoiled child," yet she had to acknowledge that some of them missed her less because she "dished [so much] shit." "I want so much to love and not to hate," she wrote Mike, "and I suppose I mostly want someone to love me. I fear dying." Mulling over the quiet strength of really talented people, Joan decided she had a great deal of what they call courage (only sometimes I get afraid). Well, who doesn't." Enumerating her elemental desires—"I want so much to make it—I mean my life—I want not the nightmares . . . I want to smile"—she mustered what she thought of as midwestern Puritan resolve and vowed to do better with her hostility issues: "I must push myself further—take chances—not be omnipotent—i.e. scared—yes and I will . . . I want to be strong enough to be able to be unprotective — vulnerable." When all else failed, she mentally clung to Fried: "Well — fuck — I can't disappoint her."

A rather different picture of Joan emerges from the testimony of musician David Amram, whom she met one night when Norm took her to the Bar de l'Hôtel des Etats-Unis, the Birdland of Paris, on the boulevard Montparnasse.

Early the next morning, Joan went home with the handsome, hip, ebullient French horn player to his closet-sized room (into which he had shoehorned a rented piano) at the Hôtel de l'Université on the rue Mazarine. In this woman with wise eyes, which gave her an air of having "been living for hundreds of years," David discerned a primitive sensitivity, almost more than she herself could bear. He saw too that she had been wounded.

On their second day together, Joan spoke of her father's bitter disappointment that she wasn't a man and thus a world conqueror and her unhappiness over the fact that, in Jimmie's eyes, she would forever fall short. At breakfast she had grilled David about his future: "What are your career goals?" Discharged from the Army the previous August after serving two years, mostly with the Seventh Army Symphony near Stuttgart, he had cobbled together a quintet and toured Germany before hitting the jazz scene in Paris. He dreamed of composing classical music and writing a book. "How do you propose to be able to do that?" she fired back. In the discussion that followed, Joan left no doubt that, having accomplished the impossible, doing exactly what she wanted and still coming out ahead in a man's world, she intended to keep going. She was in it for the long haul. She advised David to do the same: remain grounded in the great work of the past while making art from the world of the present. He saw that she was brilliant, savvy, sophisticated, and way beyond him.

That summer Joan instructed David in "the machinations of the art world, international politics, and basic principles of adult behavior." Once, at a club, when he responded to a fan's praise with a litany of his weaknesses and mistakes, Joan castigated him for insulting the woman's taste and rejecting her gift. At art openings, she wowed him with her excellent French, keen radar for phoniness, and shrewdness about art politics. Already she had clued him in on the collecting practices of millionaire businessman and Museum of Modern Art board chair Nelson Rockefeller. According to Joan, Rockefeller would outflank a dealer with whom he was negotiating by phoning the artist directly to wheedle a discount, to which most, though cash strapped, consented, given the prestige of having a work in the Rockefeller Collection. Presumably her tale was true: if Joan suspected something was factually inaccurate, she would jump all over you. Yet, for all of her worldliness, she could never turn off her emotions, David noticed, and she operated straight from the heart.

Prey to "great romantic feelings," he wound up their conversation that second morning, "Joan, look, what can I possibly offer you?"

"You're fun."

Moreover, he blew a beautiful French horn, and he was serious about composing. Tickled by the twittering of birds each dawn as he left the Hôtel des Etats-Unis, he wrote the sweet, playful "The Birds of Montparnasse" and put it on the record he cut that summer in Paris, along with "Plays This Love with Me," a song he composed thinking of Joan—those beautiful eyes and that "soul connection to music."

Joan often popped up when David performed at the Club St. Germain, the Caméléon, the Mars Club, or the Salle Pleyel, but their music headquarters remained the freewheeling Bar de l'Hôtel des États-Unis, haunt of expats like clarinetist Albert Nicholas and tenor sax man Don Byas and magnet for touring jazzmen including Lionel Hampton, Clifford Brown, and Dizzy Gillespie. When the musicians weren't wailing, poets would stand up and read in an atmosphere so casual that they easily wandered offstage to flirt with girls in the audience. The *Paris Review* crowd hung out at the bar: between sets Joan would chat with George Plimpton, Terry Southern, Harold "Doc" Humes, Richard Wright, or (less party animal than the rest) William Styron. Or maybe some hipster from Nantes.

She and David had agreed that jazz was of a piece with classical music. Once he expressed a dim view of critics who loved Beethoven but dismissed jazz, while she compared jazz musicians' struggle to be taken seriously to that of painters, insisting that (in Amram's paraphrase) "People will never understand what we are doing if they can't *feel*." And that "All art is abstract. All music is abstract. But it's all *real*. When you improvise, I can see the seeds of a symphony you could write. When I first heard Charlie Parker in Chicago, I could see he *was* a symphony."

Joan had dutifully worked through her list of people to call until, around mid-June, her demons rose up again. Despite the Seconal she took for insomnia and anxiety, she started having terrifying nightmares, scenarios involving insecurity and parental disapproval. In one, the walls of her room sprouted plaster cast monsters; in another, Fried chided her for writing inarticulate letters. In a fuck-it-all mood, she "quit midstream" in her phone calls and introductions, sulking: "I don't want to meet any more people—I don't care—I don't care." She decided to spend a couple of weeks getting tan in the south of France, then fly home to New York.

Two events intervened. First, Kimber and Gaby Smith offered her their apartment and studio in Batignolles, the Bronx of Paris, during their monthlong vacation in Italy. She leapt at the offer, which not only got her out of the stuffy Montalembert but also meant she could paint. She lost no time in "[buying] out that bastard Lefebvre-Foinet," asking Mike to mail her staple gun, and setting up her studio space.

As always, painting saved her. It felt so damn good! Yet it proved particularly difficult that summer. For one thing, she again had to put enormous energy into adjusting to French oils—Lefebvre-Foinet's colors were not exact equivalents of Bocour's—and to French color names. Consider, for example, that the French word for "yellow"—"*jaune*"— must have been gray, since Joan's *J* was gray and the initial letter of a word usually dominated its color, while the English word "yellow" was ochre, since her *Y* was ochre. She had to will herself to "paint . . . with other color names—to try to control them—make them work—like a hindu and a snake." Joan's metaphor is perfect, conveying as it does the requisite skill, the secret methods, and the vital role of music. At first, however, she couldn't coax much meaning out of paint, which refused to be more than inert lumps of colored pigment: "I look at my palette and hope for magic."

Joan's problems in the studio no doubt derived too from her changed drinking habits. She was not trying to quit, but, aware that alcohol exacerbated her difficulties with people and offered false solutions to problems that had to be squarely addressed, she had vowed to stay in control. On Bastille Day she touched not a drop. She especially wanted to paint stone-cold sober. This was no easy matter since liquor, like music, melted away her self-consciousness and intensified the feeling essential to her art. Or did it? Had she been painting out of counterfeit emotion? Her letters to Mike reveal an awareness that drinking can foster a deluded belief in the authenticity of the feelings it brings out. An ocean away from the "fraught, drunken tensions and competitions" of New York, she curtailed her alcohol consumption to a degree that she was experiencing delirium tremens.

Evoking as it does the stereotype of Abstract Expressionists flinging paint as they stagger around in an alcoholic fog, the subject of drinking while painting was always a touchy one with Joan. Even when no one was accusing her, she would hotly defend herself against the charge that she merely slopped paint onto canvas, and at least once she made a younger artist swear never to tell anyone that she or her colleagues ever touched a bottle in the studio. Because (she continued) people think that de Kooning and Pollock and Kline just get tanked up and paint junk, it's important that you always say we paint in our sober moments and drink afterwards as a social thing. Never a secret drinker—indeed, a militant drinker—Joan was a secret quitter who, at intervals, discreetly struggled to cut down or stop altogether. The truth is that she typically had a lot of gin or Scotch or Ricard or Chablis inside her when she painted. Yet, in painting as in living, she was a high-functioning alcoholic with an astonishing capacity for mental and physical concentration.

The second event, which transformed not only that summer but also Joan's life, was meeting "the great Riopelle"—French Canadian painter Jean-Paul Riopelle—at a party thrown by Hedda and Saul. The encounter was momentous enough that she took the trouble to misrepresent it to Mike: "The party last night was frightful—French Canadians—I felt old and ugly—I think I'm seeing the wrong people." By every other account, sparks flew. Riopelle made his overture to her in a raucous Quebecois accent: "Tonight I will teach you how to fuck. Tomorrow I will teach you how to paint." Surely Joan wore her mischievous little cat grin thirty-seven years later when she bragged to his biographer, Hélène de Billy, "I impressed him because I was Wasp."

One hot summer evening, Riopelle roared up to Joan's building in Batignolles in one of his five Bugattis, and she hopped in. Weaving through traffic, ignoring stop signs, and riding the gas pedal, he raced her out to the country, where they went swimming in the Seine. On another occasion, he courted the painter as well as the woman, appearing at her doorstep bearing an enormous bouquet of exquisite and expensive rolled canvases from Lefebvre-Foinet. Joan mentally gasped as she took in the most beautiful present she had ever received. Even decades later, she was visibly moved when she invoked that mythic moment in their long, passionate love affair.

Behind the bouquet stood a thirty-one-year-old man of medium height and sturdy build, with olive skin, a thick neck, sensuous lips, an aquiline nose, dark eyes, and wavy black hair sprung from a high forehead. (Teased about its unruliness, he would respond with a boyish grin and droll doubletalk: "I go to the barber on Sunday and to the Louvre on Monday," the days when both are closed.) Part Anthony Quinn, part Chico Marx, Riopelle was a playful bullshitter, a natural-born surrealist, a kid in a candy shop, who lived with animal energy and invented everything on the spur of the moment. In one much-quoted essay, his mentor Georges Duthuit described a creature who "seems hardly to contain the flooding energies of youth at its full."

The son of a skilled carpenter and a housewife from East Montreal, Jean-Paul Riopelle had grown up an indifferent student but avid artist. At nineteen, he enrolled in the École du Meuble, a school of arts and crafts where, a disciple of Quebecois master Paul-Émile Borduas, he worked in the unpremeditated gestural manner known as automatism or abstract Surrealism. On a 1947 visit to Paris, he haunted museums and galleries and met Surrealist André Breton, who included the fledgling Canadian's luminous parrot-hued watercolors overlaid with inky black nets in that year's International Exhibition of Surrealism. The European romantic imagination could not resist the idea of the New World primitive: Breton's invocation, in his catalog essay, of "the art of a master trapper" lent wings to a mythic persona. What could be headier for an aspiring twenty-four-year-old than the blessing of the Pope of Surrealism in the great City of Art? Only, perhaps, rubbing shoulders with Breton's entourage, the likes of Marcel Duchamp and especially Antonin Artaud, whose visionary crankiness deeply impressed the young artist.

Back in Montreal the following year, Riopelle was among sixteen Quebecois artists, writers, and dancers who signed the Refus Global, a violent and joyful declaration of self-liberation that scandalized conservative Quebec and marked a turning point in the cultural life of the province. Then he and his wife Françoise, a dancer and cosigner of the Refus Global, moved to Paris.

The material difficulties of those early years rather quickly yielded to success: thanks to his "discoverer" Duthuit, the young abstractionist's work found favor with leading opinion makers. In 1954, Riopelle participated in Canada's group exhibition at the Venice Biennale and showed for the first time in New York, at the Pierre Matisse Gallery. (The second child of painter Henri Matisse, Pierre was Duthuit's brother-in-law.) By the time he met Joan the following year, Riopelle was flying on all cylinders. A second show had opened and closed at Matisse; others were in the works at Gimpel and Sons in London and Jacques Dubourg in Paris. The heir to the automobile fortune, Walter P. Chrysler Jr., was amassing Riopelles, and Rockefeller was showing serious interest. In Canada, where his name remains a household word, Riopelle was on his way to earning the status of founder of Canadian modernism. Among major players, only the American critics, most of whom positioned him as a second-rate Abstract Expressionist, remained aloof from the clamor of international acclaim. Chalking up their negativity to perverse nationalism, Pierre Matisse believed the French Canadian's conquest of the U.S. to be only a matter of time.

The artist's method was congruent with his personality. He often let weeks or months pass without touching a blank canvas until, his need to paint grown thunderhead sized, he sequestered himself in his studio. Though he bragged he could create an entire exhibition in one night, he typically painted nonstop for days, with little food, coffee, sleep, or contact with the outside world. Using slow-drying poppy-oil-based paints, he worked *alla prima* (completing his oils in one session as opposed to building them in layers), troweling up pigment from an enormous masonite palette and thrusting it onto the canvas. Or decapitating his tubes and stabbing out his colors. Brilliant horror vacui resulted: edge-to-edge tumults of reds, blues, whites, and yellows; forests of crisscrossing strings; expanses of writhing globs of pigment; effects of exploding stained glass.

Jean-Paul's personal life was no less complex. He and Françoise, the parents of seven-year-old Yseult and six-year-old Sylvie, entertained frequently at their apartment on the elegant rue Chardon-Lagache, the perfectionist Françoise assuming, in classic 1950s mode, the roles of gourmet cook, hostess extraordinaire, primary parent, dance teacher, housewife, and her husband's business manager. Even Jean-Paul's jeans were impeccably pressed. Though she surely guessed her husband's extraconjugal activities, she was disinclined to dwell upon them, and, reportedly, she too had lovers. However, she seemed unaware of his current mistress, a young literature student at the Sorbonne who, despite his pleadings, was about to go home to New York.

Joan saw in her new lover an art star (in a pre-Warholian and very French manner) who turned heads as he strode into a café or bar, flirted with women, kidded with everyone, and bear-hugged his pals, ranging from his mechanic to the bartender at the Dôme to sculptor Alberto Giacometti to the Paris chief of police, all the while burning up immense amounts of cash and consuming staggering quantities of Ricard and cigarettes. An irrepressible raconteur, Riopelle simultaneously relished and disliked the attention, typically peeling off from official occasions, including his own openings, which he often celebrated by holding court at the rear of the café across the street. Friends and strangers would throng his table, and he would set them all up with drinks. He loved making money so he could waste it.

Behind such bonhomie lurked a timidity the artist managed by turning everything into a joke. Rarely self-revealing, he could be moody and unpredictable, one day grabbing you by the neck and asking jovially if you wanted to take his Jag for a spin, the next day not even saying hello. Indeed, the tension of Riopelle's newfound success had translated into bouts of dark anger and brooding self-absorption. But it also brought sprees of self-indulgence at circuses (where he buddied around with the clowns), automobile racing circuits (where he hero-worshipped the drivers and talked himself into the pits), and body shops (where he carried on his love affair with Bugattis — "*les Bugs*").

Both Jean-Paul and Joan adored animals, sports, drinking, and art. Both loved to provoke, and both were instinctual, forthright, and reticent to discuss ideas, she talking feelings and he communicating essentially by zany anecdote. Soon other differences surfaced. Joan couldn't survive without music and poetry, but neither held any particular charms for Jean-Paul. (Her education was superior to his, but she could care less: she admired the fact that, like her father, he was a self-made man.) She had a visceral need to hang out with artists, while he thrived in the company of carpenters, mechanics, and other skilled blue-collar folks. She hid her family's wealth, but Jean-Paul didn't mind if people knew he had plenty of cash. Nor did he have any hang-ups about sorting out his good paintings from his bad. He left that to critics.

As much as her painting, Joan's past skating glories won the respect of Riopelle, an avid ice hockey fan. And he seemed truly to need her: this smart, sexy phenomenon brimming with piss, vinegar, and hard-edged New York glamour was, he proclaimed, the first woman ever to understand him. Suddenly his world revolved around Joan.

It is a testimony to the acuteness of Joan's longing to be loved and the force with which Jean-Paul swept into her life that she now considered the possibility, unthinkable even a month earlier, of giving up New York and all it meant to her. She sought advice. "Decisions are hideous," responded her mother, to whom she had confided by letter, "and this, of course, is an important time in your life and the decision, whatever it is, is all yours." Joan made it Fried's too, asking in a rambling letter to her analyst whether she should stay in Paris. Picking up her pen yet again, she added up the situation for Barney and Loly: "If I stayed I suppose I could get a show . . . I would stay because of the man and he won't live in America and to get him to go there would take time and then it probably wouldn't work and hell—why is it always shit?"

Then there was Mike.

Spotting a stack of letters from his rival next to the staple gun in Joan's apartment one day, Jean-Paul swept them up and impetuously tacked them, one by one, to the wooden floor, thereby seducing Joan all over again. But Mike too had fabulous style. Out of the blue, he sent her some records—including Billie Holiday's "What a Little Moonlight Can Do"—thus mentally whisking her back to New York and into his arms. That summer, various people had made sure Joan heard all the gossip about Mike, including details of his brief affair with Grace Hartigan. But Joan persisted in loving him. Or her idea of him. "Michael," she wrote, "what am I doing always writing you love letters since you left me a long time ago." And:

> I wanted a man in a blue shirt. I would do anything for that man—if he stayed in the blue shirt—if he didn't disappear—and perhaps it's too late—too long gone. I'm like a heroin addict . . . and that man in the blue shirt I would find if I took a plane to NY—all over again like from Mexico City.

After Kimber and Gaby returned, Joan house-sat for a friend in the suburbs but stayed on the café circuit thanks to her purchase of a cheap used Renault. Her studio situation was another matter. She needed a larger space and desperately missed the Smiths' record player. How to paint without it? "My memories are so rich at least," she reasoned. Straining over another "mess with a sky on top," as well as a medium-sized blue thing that she wanted as profluent as *Hudson River Day Line,* Joan found she couldn't "make the freedom," so it was "accuracy and scraping and nothing very pretty." She wished she had one of her New York paintings in order to compare, and she longed for Mike's always dead-on-target advice.

Her situation improved after she sublet a lovely rue Jacob studio, including a record player, which the Steinbergs had found for her before leaving Paris. Not only did a friend lend her some Mozart and Bach, but also she wore out her landlord's one Billie 78 rpm, Ellington's classic "In My Solitude." All night every night, or at least as long as she could honestly and unself-consciously hold a feeling, she painted. But, still seeking that "Van Gogh intensity," she fretted that her colors lacked freshness or *something.* Around four a.m. she would pause to smoke a few cigarettes and watch a gorgeous blueness percolate into the sky.

Except for Americans, Paris was its usual ghost town that August. (Jean-Paul had left for a family vacation.) Often Joan would amble over to the Flore, the Royal, or the Deux Magots, where she introduced David Amram to Alberto Giacometti, whom she had met through Jean-Paul. An internationally known and admired Italian Swiss artist who had worked in a Surrealist manner during the 1920s and 1930s, Giacometti created emaciated walking figures that evoked existentialist solitude and portraits that recorded his struggles with the mysteries of appearance. This "little spidery man" revealed to David that he too had once played the French horn, as an adolescent in his native village of Stampa.

Other times Joan took off for Montparnasse, hanging out at the Select, where Hemingway's ghost resided, with an always-shifting bevy of compatriots leading the alternately electric and dismal lives of young Americans in Paris: painters Shirley Jaffe, Sam Francis, Ruth Francken, and Shirley Goldfarb, and junior reporter for *Time* (and later Pulitzer Prize–winning author) Stanley Karnow. In the midst of divorcing Claude Sarraute, the daughter of novelist Nathalie Sarraute, Stanley befriended the boisterous, pleasant, intellectually curious, and occasionally shrewish newcomer. But the two were not lovers. In fact, practically the last words Joan ever spoke to Karnow (in a 1988 phone conversation) were to be, "We never fucked, did we?"

That summer of 1955, Stanley and Joan ran around Paris together, talked politics, traded paperbacks, and feasted on thick steaks and *vin ordinaire* at the family-run bistros around the wholesale wine market, the Halles aux Vins. In the midst of one such dinner, Joan blurted out, "Oh, my God! My visa's running out tonight! What should I do?" In order to renew a tourist visa, one had to leave the country and then return with a new entry stamp on one's passport. So, around eleven p.m., they jumped into Stanley's car and sped off to Belgium, enlivening the three-hour ride with scat singing. Both knew the words to lots of tunes.

In September, Joan borrowed Stanley's apartment (he was out of town) in Boulogne-sur-Seine, a pleasant leafy suburb. The top floor of a comfortable old house, it was lined with windows and graced with excellent books, a Columbia portable record player, stacks of records, and access to the garden below. Her stay was short, however, and she had to move three more times that fall. She considered her nomadic life a metaphor for unbelonging. The moves were difficult, each requiring that she and the various cleaning women she hired scrub and scrape away her painting messes. Then she had to roll up and lug off her heavy, still-wet canvases (given the damp weather, the white *never* dried), and set up and adjust to new working conditions. Once she was devastated to discover that all the manipulation had caused the paint on six good large paintings to crack. They were ruined, yet she couldn't yet bear to throw them away, so every once in awhile she unrolled one and half-heartedly tried to paint over the problem.

October found Joan in a working-class neighborhood on the avenue Émile Zola, which sometimes felt as far from Paris as from New York. There she experimented with a *siccatif* (dryer), which yielded "a charming patent leather effect," and conceived of her work in terms of color series: red paintings, green paintings, and so on. She rather successfully pulled off a six-and-a-half-by-eight-foot red piece, yet an ochre one maddeningly eluded her. She would wind up each night's work with a café crème and a few Gauloises at the corner café, elbow to elbow with cabdrivers breakfasting on white wine, then catch three or four hours' sleep until it was time to dress for her rendezvous with Jean-Paul at Le Dragon, off the boulevard Saint-Germain. Affecting dark glasses and wreathed in cigarette smoke, Joan would sip aperitifs and chat with friends as she waited for her lover to finish his appointments and appear at her side. Often they hung out with Jean-Paul's pals at the rue Didot body shop the Canadian had made his base of operations. Once he took her to the circus to see the Zavattas, the aristocrats of clowns. Most typically, the two café-crawled through the evening: the Royal, the Coupole, the Bar du Dôme, the Select, the Falstaff, and La Palette were all on their charts.

Thus had Joan's two months in Paris stretched to six. By early November, however, she was preparing to leave. Having garnered an invitation to participate in a group show at Tapié's Galerie Rive Droite the following March, she had an excuse to return. Depositing half a dozen paintings with the French dealer, she destroyed nine others, set aside four to roll

HUDSON RIVER
DAY LINE
oil on canvas
1955

GEORGE WENT
SWIMMING AT
BARNES HOLE, BUT
IT GOT TOO COLD
oil on canvas
1957

LADYBUG, *oil on canvas, 1957*

GRANDES CARRIÈRES, *oil on canvas, 1961-62*

UNTITLED (CHEIM SOME BELLS), *oil on canvas, 1964*

SANS PIERRE
oil on canvas
1969

LA GRANDE VALLÉE XVIII
(LUC)
oil on canvas (diptych)
1983-84

LILLE V, *oil on canvas (diptych), 1986*

NO BIRDS, *oil on canvas (diptych), 1987-88*

RAIN, *oil on canvas (diptych), 1989*

SUNFLOWERS, *oil on canvas (diptych), 1990-91*

MERCI, *oil on canvas (diptych), 1992*

BLUE TERRITORY, *oil on canvas, 1972*

up and carry with her on the plane, and shipped the rest, some still less than fully dry.

And "the experiment"? All those hard-fought psychological battles with herself? "Yes—I'm changed but not enough and maybe never will be," she conceded in a letter to Barney and Loly. To Mike she gave acerbic warning: "And look, baby doll, . . . I'm still the same old bitch only a bit worn down at the edges—nothing new or exciting—and I guess I'll see you after all . . . So keep the aspidistra flying—and save me a little moonlight—off nights." Succumbing to a feeling of being old and acutely childless, dreading her separation from Jean-Paul, her next round in the love ring with Mike, and the need to face the "knifing and competition" of New York, Joan seemed a lost soul during those last days in Paris. She slept little. Her anxieties pooled: "I think of time slipping by and wonder and wonder—age and death—God I've got that anxiety now, and I used to laugh at yours," she acknowledged to Barney. "It's like a lump in my throat, a hurt in my stomach. Those analysts bring everything to the surface like plumbing gone backwards and then there's no difference between day and night—dreaming and waking." Not even Jean-Paul's tonic refusal to take her angst seriously lifted her spirits.

Joan's first appointment with Fried after returning to New York on November 26 coincided with the arrival of the first of the letters from Paris that would rain upon her that winter. "I will write to you [again] tomorrow, sublime master [*maître*]," she read in Jean-Paul's schoolboy hand, "but I think it is better that I write you with 'sse' [*maîtresse*, i.e., mistress] since that's the feminine."

Thanks in part to her inclusion in two important group shows, Joan's New York reputation had been building. In December, Vanguard 1955, artist Kyle Morris's pick of contemporary paintings, traveled from the Walker Art Center in Minneapolis to the Stable, where it overlapped with U.S. Painting: Some Recent Directions, organized by Tom Hess. While both curators singled out younger artists, they refused to label or classify contemporary work beyond loose affiliations based on age and geography. Still, these shows figured among a spate of attempts to put a finger on the dynamics of New York School painting now that it was moving from marginal to mainstream and money was following. When Franz Kline joined Sidney Janis that spring, adding his name to a roster that included Rothko, de Kooning, Pollock, and Still, Joan helped him hang his first show at the prestigious Fifty-seventh Street gallery. Franz jocularly instructed her to "tell everybody I sold out," then whispered, "I only sold one painting." But sales picked up after Janis astutely cut Kline's prices from $3,000 to $1,500, then continued strong as he doubled and redoubled that figure. Meanwhile, strangers were turning up at openings that had once been "just us."

Art was popular in the mid-1950s. Thousands of veterans had studied painting or sculpture on the GI Bill, and Ike himself relaxed at the White House by daubing at portraits and landscapes. There were now 180 galleries in New York, a fivefold increase in a decade, and magazines like *Esquire* and *Life* were running features on collecting. Among those flush with Eisenhower-era prosperity, a number of businessmen—sanctioned by high-profile exhibitions like the Museum of Modern Art's 1956 Twelve Americans, featuring Guston, Hartigan, Rivers, and other avant-garde artists—had begun buying New York School work, more affordable and daring than French Impressionism or Old Masters and just as good for tax write-offs.

Thus artists who were perceived as potential "blue-chip" material started earning serious money while the others still faced penury and indifference, and this disparity strained family relations below Fourteenth Street. Was success compatible with their values? Once they had all been outcasts together. Now there was too much fawning, too much partying, too much Scotch. Arguments at the Cedar over, say, Masaccio's use of color, had made way for sniping, as those suspicious of money leveled charges of self-aggrandizement at those accused of selling out. As both leader of the rebeldom and increasingly successful artist, Bill de Kooning bore the brunt of the criticism. Old-timer Milton Resnick stepped up his resentful complaints that Bill was an operator; even Conrad Marca-Relli now viewed his longtime pal with a jaundiced eye.

The Club too was changing. That spring, Pavia had resigned as organizer. The old artists now showed up less often; the younger ones took leadership roles. Friday-night panels still drew a crowd as did Club parties, where Joan and Franz Kline would rock 'n' roll "till they rolled on the floor dancing horizontally," but the feeling wasn't the same. In another shift, the Five Spot had the edge on the Cedar, or, rather, artists went to the Cedar to talk and to the Five Spot to party after openings and get high on jazz. The owners of this once cracked-plaster drinking hole for derelicts on the Bowery, Iggy and Joe Termini, had taken advantage of the demolition of the Third Avenue El outside their door to spruce up a bit, install a piano, and hire two amateur performers, a short-order cook and a merchant marine. They then brought in the brilliantly improvisational pianist Cecil Taylor and his group, followed by the David Amram quartet, and the Five Spot transformed itself into a crossroads for modern jazzmen, avant-garde writers, and abstract artists. Bill de Kooning, Franz Kline, Herman Cherry, Philip Guston, David Smith, Grace Hartigan, Larry Rivers, Alfred Leslie, Elaine de Kooning, Mike Goldberg, and Joan were among the many who thronged the smoky joint, clustering around small tables and ordering one seventy-five-cent pitcher of beer after another. One night around three a.m. Amram's group swung into the wistful "Lover Man," a Billie Holiday standard. After they finished, the house went dreamily quiet. Until Joan boomed, "*Well*, David, I hope you're not selling out! You're playing as if you're trying to *épater la bourgeoisie* [stun the middle class]!"

Writer Jack Kerouac—still a year away from *On the Road*—also showed up at the Five Spot. Joan liked Jack and approved of the spirit and immediacy of his writing and of the fact that he ignored literary fashion and (despite a vast knowledge of literature) worked from the gut. But Frank O'Hara remained her closest writer friend. Once again on the staff of the Museum of Modern Art, Frank had just taken a leave to become playwright-in-residence at the Poets' Theatre in Cambridge. Meanwhile Joan had begun hanging out with his lover-turned-roommate, the gregarious Joe LeSueur. Raised in Utah and California in the Church of Jesus Christ of Latter-Day Saints, this decorated veteran and soon-to-be-ex-fourth-grade teacher with Tab Hunter looks had raved over Joan's paintings when the two met at a party the previous spring. Now Joan and "Mormon Joe" enjoyed a fast friendship, one of many she would form with gay men.

Joan had also befriended poets Barbara Guest and Jimmie Schuyler, both reviewers for *ArtNews,* and aficionados of her work, and she theirs. Guest's poetry is strikingly analogous to Mitchell's painting, embodying as it does (in the words of writer Charles Bernstein) "the transient, the ephemeral, the flickering in translucent surfaces that we call painterly for lack of a term to chart the refusal of a pseudo-depth of field." As for Schuyler, a charming but psychologically fragile man and lover of weather and light, he cherished words for their own sake, as Joan cherished paint, and lyrically asserted "things as they are."

That winter Joan also drew closer to Frank's ex-roommate in both

Cambridge and New York, Harold (Hal) Fondren, who worked as Eleanor Ward's assistant at the Stable. For one thing, she had acquired a serious taste for opera, and Hal was her main cohort in things operatic. For
another, this cordon bleu was hosting a string of high-spirited dinner
parties at his Seventy-third Street apartment at which Joan, Mike, Jane
Freilicher, painter and businessman Joe Hazan, and a pandemonium of
poets all made regular appearances. Those dinners live on in the title of
Joan's inspired *Evenings on Seventy-third Street,* among the mid-decade
Mitchells that critic Patricia Bailey has rightly characterized as "open,
lively, spreading, and full of youthful excitement."

Having sublet St. Mark's through December, Joan had at first stayed
with Mike, who was now living on East Tenth Street. As painters, the
two still enjoyed an exceptional complicity—edged with rivalry—and
Mike still generously stretched Joan's canvases before they went to the
Stable. Beyond that, their relationship defies easy characterization. On
the "bright white light-Michael mornings" Joan so loved, winter sunshine flooded his studio, and she felt extravagantly happy. Still wild
about his blue eyes and brute masculinity, she was unable to let go of
the idea that someday he would truly love her. David, for one, perceived
that Mike was "crazy about Joan." Yet Joan fiercely resented her lover's
duplicity, couplings with other women, and indifference to her feelings.
With a few slugs of Scotch stirring her awareness of "all [the old] shit"
between them, she would let the nasty cracks fly, and another drunken
melodrama would flare, leaving her bruised and infuriated. But a day or
two later the two would drift back together again.

Meanwhile, Joan had renewed her love affair with her old Parker
School sweetheart, Tim Osato, a moody, handsome artist-soldier and
professor of history at West Point with degrees from Yale, Harvard,
and Columbia and combat experience in Korea. Osato had married poet
Ruth Ludlow, who was pregnant with their second daughter. His newest
liaison with Joan would leave behind a damaged family and a painting
everyone else resented but Tim insisted on hanging over the fireplace in
every home they ever had.

Thus plunged again into nonstop living, Joan was back to heavy
drinking. Alfred Leslie once cracked that surely she "had a liver like a
shopping bag." Yet she was not a binge drinker like Bill de Kooning,
who occasionally stopped by St. Mark's Place that spring to listen to her
record of Mozart's *Requiem.* When Bill was drunk, she would sober him
up by walking him around Tompkins Square Park or feeding him ice

cream on the theory, no doubt tested on herself, that it cut one's cravings for liquor.

Happy to be back in the land of real painting, Joan nonetheless deeply missed Jean-Paul. If she lingered in New York that spring, it was because she, Mike, Paul Brach, and Robert Goodnough were scheduled to show in April and May at Sidney Janis, who hoped to broaden his gallery's appeal by exhibiting young painters. In Paris the previous summer, she and David had dined one evening with Janis, whose son Conrad, a trombone player, was a mutual friend. The dealer had wanted to line up Joan's work for a group show, but she had set as a condition that he also include Mike's. Even after Janis agreed, she hesitated: Goodnough was somewhat marginal, but, as far as she was concerned, Brach was the real clunker.

In fact, nothing about Four Americans was destined to be easy. The evening before her ten paintings were to go to the Stable, from where they would be transported to Janis, Joan dined with Mike at St. Mark's Place. (Although she was no cook, she occasionally scrambled some eggs or grilled a steak for Mike, who found her not bad in the kitchen.) He was seriously working on a bottle of bourbon, and she a bottle of Scotch. Her attention kept straying to one of the works for the Janis show, hanging nearby. Finally she lashed out: "I hate it! It's not finished! It's not finished!" Disappearing into the bathroom, she emerged wielding a double-edged razor blade and started slashing the canvas. Wild yelling erupted, Mike slamming into Joan and she shoving and kicking back, until Mike, who was extremely drunk, knocked her out cold. When she came to, sober, she felt a throbbing eye and an ice bag on her forehead. Then she dropped into a deep sleep. Mike spent the rest of the night reweaving her canvas with threads pulled from others and repainting the damaged spots in Joan's manner, doing "a damn good job, I must say."

On the day her paintings were moved, by open truck, from the Stable to Janis, gale-force winds nearly ripped that same (reportedly) ill-fated canvas from its stretcher. "Homely and hasty repairs were made," according to Hal Fondren, "and the painting duly delivered to the baleful eye of New York's premier dealer where it was refused." Another was substituted, and the "only loss was emotional and that was considerable." So too may have been the loss to Joan's dignity when the dark glasses Mike purchased for her on the morning of their opening failed to conceal her ugly mauled-purple globular eye.

Simultaneously moving and still, like a river seen through binoculars, Joan's pictures at Janis offered testimony to her glorious, all-consuming involvement with memory, landscape, and paint. Critic Eleanor Munro, for one, felt it would be "impossible to criticize the breathless, loaded, river-like progressions of paint in *Monongahela* [named for a river near Pittsburgh] by Mitchell, or the perfect, endlessly revolving spray-world of her *To Roger (white)*."

I wanted to be sure to reach you;
though my ship was on the way it got caught
in some moorings. I am always tying up
and then deciding to depart. In storms and
at sunset, with the metallic coils of the tide
around my fathomless arms, I am unable
to understand the forms of my vanity
or I am hard alee with my Polish rudder
in my hand and the sun sinking. To
you I offer my hull and the tattered cordage
of my will. The terrible channels where
the wind drives me against the brown lips
of the reeds are not all behind me. Yet
I trust the sanity of my vessel; and
if it sinks, it may well be in answer
to the reasoning of the eternal voices,
the waves which have kept me from reaching you.

FRANK O'HARA, "To the Harbormaster"

CHAPTER TEN To the Harbormaster

The Janis show over, Joan threw a big party, then flew to Paris, where she took a room at a Montparnasse hotel. Spreading a drop cloth over the carpet and tacking up sheets of paper to protect the walls, she quickly improvised a studio and set to work. By the time she moved into the rue Daguerre atelier of Austrian American sculptor Day Schnabel (her sublet for the summer) some two weeks later, she had completed six small oils.

Joan's implacable need to paint contrasts with Jean-Paul's evasion, all that past winter and for the better part of a year, of his vast new studio in the suburb of Vanves. After he resumed working that spring and when Joan too took up her brushes in France, their friends noted the beginnings of a dialogue in paint. Prompted to take greater risks, Jean-Paul tackled gouache, experimented with brushstrokes as form, and painted at least one uncharacteristically lyrical series. Joan, for her part, tried activating her typically "empty" bottoms and tops, and accommodated new colors like the raw, Riopellian red oranges that slash across and tighten into vivid blues and brackish green blacks in the "painty" *Harbor December*. Spewing as if from some dark engorgement, her strokes in *Harbor December* saw and surge past a patch of thick ice blue, then scatter, a few barreling along the top edge of her canvas, about to lose momentum like spring-driven pinballs.

Indebted, in part, to the work of Sam Francis (who was tight with Jean-Paul), both artists repeatedly reached for white, long vital in Joan's painting but now more color-like. Gritty brumal hues powerfully assert themselves amid *Harbor December*'s chromatic and spatial dynamics, while the chalky whites of *King of Spades* and the airy greenish whites of *October Island* lift and bite into the detritus riding their powerful currents. Jean-Paul, in turn, substituted ice-spangled whites for his usual opulent palette in *L'Autriche*, a work his lover, so dismissive of French *métier* (artfulness), might have written off under other circumstances but now viewed as freighted with realities other than those that prevailed in New York.

Shortly after Joan settled into Schnabel's studio, her discovery that she was pregnant distracted her from painting and forced the issue of the couple's mutual commitment. Consumed by her desire for a child and panicky about time passing, Joan agonized over whether or not to have the baby, finally making the wrenching decision to end her pregnancy. She had the abortion (illegal in France at that time) in a clandestine clinic as Jean-Paul waited at a café. In the course of this first crisis the pair weathered together, Joan may have broached the subject of his divorcing Françoise, but Jean-Paul saw no reason to change the status quo. And he would have made no promises regarding children: he had two already and didn't know what to do with them.

Only two or three weeks later, on Saturday, August 11 (Sunday, August 12, Paris time), Jackson Pollock died in an automobile crash in Springs, Long Island. Surly, desperate, and prone to uncontrolled weeping that summer, the brilliant painter of *Number One* and *Autumn Rhythm* had long been stymied in his work. On Saturday evening, he had set off in his Oldsmobile convertible with his lover, Ruth Kligman, and her friend Edith Metzger for a piano recital and party at Alfonso Ossorio's East Hampton estate. But too sodden with booze to get to Ossorio's, he eventually turned around and was barreling down Fireplace Road, flooring the accelerator, Metzger screaming in terror, when he lost control. The car flew off the pavement and smashed into a grove of trees. Thrown clear, Kligman survived, but Metzger was crushed and Pollock slammed into a tree and died instantly.

Four days later, a stunned New York art world halted its summering on Long Island and in Provincetown, to gather, sans Joan, at Springs Chapel and the Green River Cemetery for the painter's memorial service and burial. Given Pollock's towering achievement and galvanizing role in American art, his tragic disappearance not only meant a gaping absence but also assumed a mythic significance, sealing a vital destiny and shaking out everyone's artistic relationship to everyone else. While Joan knew how impossible Jackson had become, she also respected his inability to accommodate himself to a small-souled world—"Such joy, such desperate joy," Bill de Kooning had once said of Pollock—and she deeply admired his art. Raking out her memories of him in August-empty Paris, she began the tender *Sunday, August 12th*. She was probably still working on it two weeks later when *Life* published "Rebel Artist's Tragic Ending," which she tore out and kept. But she resisted people's attempts to get her to articulate "the greatness of Jackson Pollock and what he meant and continues to mean to me . . . enormous generosity and lyricism of feeling."

Pollock, of course, had brought the drip into the lexicon of New York painting, and Joan continued to feel her way around that iconic form of mark making. In the early 1950s, she would visibly flinch when paint accidentally dribbled from her brush, then usually let it go. Now when thinned colors coursed down her canvas or turpentine cut a path through a patch of pigment (a sort of negative drip) she might allow gravity and paint to assert themselves, or she might half obscure or ghost the festive fringes with a swipe of a loaded brush. Of such marriages of "hazard and decision," critic Leo Steinberg had recently written (in what became the most famous critic's line about Mitchell's work) that paint is "left to run and rake the field in wriggling perpendiculars; until the artist's stroke—like a cat's paw on a truant mouse—descends again to score triumphantly for the willed act as against chance effect." For a time Joan tried attaching her canvases to a plywood panel that stuck out slightly farther from the wall at its top than at its bottom (a method invented by Bill de Kooning) in order to avoid the issue altogether. She hated mannerism and fake accident: "I don't make drips purposely," she once testily told critic Irving Sandler. "This drip business is a pile of shit. If I see them, I take them out like cleaning the house." More significantly, she had begun exploring the idea of a nervous, dancing, loosely Pollockian calligraphic field.

A flurry of letters from Jean-Paul in Paris to Joan in New York places her near Fried that October, still paying the steep emotional price of the abortion. The city's crisp, exciting autumn light no doubt helped lift her spirits, as did the couple's rendezvous in Quebec that November. The two had arranged to meet in Saint-Hilaire, in the Monteregian Hills east of Montreal, where Jean-Paul's pal, art dealer Gilles Corbeil, had lent them his vacation home. Probably it was during this early-winter interlude on the edge of a dense beech, maple, and evergreen forest carpeted with ferns that Jean-Paul built a "little snow cave" that thrilled Joan "and we screwed in this cave."

She took several paintings done in Quebec back to New York, among them the dazzling *Hemlock*. With an agitation that belies its Cubist-derived discipline, her canvas's vertically coaxial lines—damp dark greens and chlorophyll greens threaded with orange reds and pavonine blues—weave through, rush headlong into, rise above, and skim across viscous gray whites. Although *Hemlock* emerged, in part, from Joan's intense tree feelings and proclivity to mentally lose herself in trees, its floating scaffolding refuses to be reified: the painter subverts the traditional relationship between figure (the thing depicted) and ground (the background), never allowing the image to come together as a tree. Taking little interest in composition as such, she exploited, as she would throughout her career, the tensions inherent in ambiguous figure-ground relationships: "You make it one way and then deny it."

In casting about for a title (Bill de Kooning jokingly suggested *Christmas Tree*), Joan lit upon the "dark and blue feeling" of the Wallace Stevens poem "Domination of Black," one line of which reads, "Yes: but the color of the heavy hemlocks." So she chose *Hemlock*, "but everyone thought I meant poison." What she really meant was something congruent with the feelings roused by the swirling hues of Stevens's reeling and repeating lines. Conflating inner and outer worlds in an atmosphere of isolation and cosmic fear, his poem begins,

Joan palling around with painter Paul Jenkins on East Tenth Street, c. 1958

At night, by the fire,
The colors of the bushes
And of the fallen leaves,
Repeating themselves,
Turned in the room,
Like the leaves themselves
Turning in the wind.
Yes: but the color of the heavy hemlocks
Came striding.
And I remembered the cry of the peacocks.

In an interview with Irving Sandler, Joan declared that she wanted for her painting "the feeling in a line of poetry which makes it different from a line of prose," meaning the feeling of a line that precludes paraphrase because (in the words of scholar Edward Hirsch) "what is being said is inseparable from the way it is being said." To verbalize her painting, Joan felt, was to objectify and thus destroy it. One tends to equate such indefinability with vagueness, yet both lyric poetry and Mitchell painting are, to extend a quote from Flaubert, subjects as precise as geometry.

Moreover, the artist cut a fine definition of "feeling," distinguishing between genuine object-based emotion, on one hand, and objectless, self-indulgent moodiness, on the other: "Sentimentality is self pity, your own swamp. Weeping in your own beer is not a feeling. It lacks dignity and hasn't an outside reference." She detested sniveling.

Joan's March 1957 show at the Stable, twelve light- and color-riotous canvases, proved a critical and financial success. "Joan Mitchell continues to be one of America's most brilliant Action-Painters," cheered Sandler in *ArtNews*. "At a time when many young artists are withdrawing introspectively from the bold experimentation of their elders, Miss Mitchell exuberantly and relentlessly presses forward in technique and expression; her art expands in the wake of her generous energy."

Over the past two years Eleanor Ward had tripled Joan's prices, which now topped out at $1,200 for the eighty-by-one-hundred-inch *October Island*. Her work was moving briskly: lawyer and museum trustee Gifford Phillips snapped up *14th of July*, millionaire publisher J. Patrick Lannan chose *Mont Saint-Hilaire* for his New York pied-à-terre, *Casino* went to Air France for its terminal at Idlewild. Asked by Chicago industrialist Arnold Maremont to select a Mitchell as that year's gift from the Society for Contemporary Art to the Art Institute of Chicago, Katharine Kuh, now art critic for the *Saturday Review*, decided on *Hemlock*. But the Whitney beat her to it and was planning to tour the painting nationally in its Nature in Abstraction show, so Kuh opted instead for *City Landscape*. London dealer Peter Cochrane, on the other hand, "flatly refused to look at your work," Eleanor informed Joan, "as he told me in no uncertain terms that he did not believe in women artists as they have proved to be so unreliable."

Notwithstanding the achievements of Joan Mitchell, Grace Hartigan, Jane Freilicher, Helen Frankenthaler, Hedda Sterne, Louise Nevelson,

Jane Wilson, Elaine de Kooning, Nell Blaine, Alice Neel, Lee Krasner, Louise Bourgeois, and others, female artists continued to struggle
for their share of American art's new place in the sun. Up at *Life*, their
would-be ally, art editor Dorothy Seiberling, was working on a feature
that acknowledged the five most critically acclaimed young female painters, Joan included. In late March, however, Joan dispatched a Western
Union to Seiberling: "I urgently request you withdraw my photograph
from your forthcoming story on five women painters." But her message either arrived too late or went unheeded. In the four-page color
spread that came out on May 13, "Women Artists in Ascendance," Grace
Hartigan took honors as the "most celebrated of the young American
women painters," the chic Jane and the winsome Helen rated full-page
photographs, and Joan ended up with a smaller picture plus a head shot
in the table of contents, next to the kicker "Laurels for lady artists." In
other words, everyone was upset. "YOU! Why is your picture bigger
than mine?" Joan barked at Jane the next time they met, even though
she hadn't wanted it there at all. Shot at Schnabel's in Paris, Joan's picture reveals a sober-looking artist with bags under her eyes, marooned in
the midst of unstretched edge-to-edge oils teeming with painterly markings, crashing, writhing, pitching, plunging, and making viewers slightly
seasick.

The "lady artist" had also received backhanded kudos from jazz-
historian-turned-chronicler-of-visual-art Rudi Blesh. "Best of all," wrote
Blesh of the current state of Abstract Expressionism in his high-profile
Modern Art U.S.A.: Men, Rebellion, Conquest, published in 1956, "hard
on the heels of the Pollocks and the De Koonings, the Klines and the
Rothkos" came young artists who had "found new leaders of their own.
One of these, remarkably enough, is a woman: Joan Mitchell. Rosa Bon-
heur and Mary Cassatt must surely be turning in their graves with joy."

Shortly before midnight on June 15, 1957, a pounding-hot Saturday, Joan
Mitchell, Mike Goldberg, Frank O'Hara, Norm Bluhm, and actress Irma
Hurley threaded their way through a sellout crowd of 2,500 to seats in
Loew's Sheridan movie theater at the corner of Seventh Avenue and Elev-
enth Street. Professionally, all five had hit their stride. Having moved to
New York the previous year, Norm was readying his first solo show at
Leo Castelli's new gallery. Irma had been appearing on Broadway. Frank
continued to live, on the wing, a prodigiously connected, amusing, and

The three "goddesses who [competed] for the golden apple": Joan, Helen Frankenthaler, and Grace Hartigan at Helen's 1957 opening at Tibor de Nagy

productive life that now included stepped-up responsibilities as a curator in the international program of the Museum of Modern Art as well as his first book, *Meditations in an Emergency,* due from Grove that September. As for Joan, she had been painting splendidly. So too had Mike, embarked upon his bold, bristling *House* series. Norm had introduced him to deep-pockets collector Walter P. Chrysler Jr., whose purchase of seventeen canvases, in addition to Martha Jackson's recent buying spree, put $20,000 in Mike's pockets. When the first installment of $2,500 came in from Chrysler, on a bitterly cold winter day, the long-straitened painter had rushed out to buy an electric blanket, then spent the weekend in bed with his blanket and his wad of cash. Later he indulged in a Jaguar, and now he and Norm were summering in Springs, where Mike was seeing writer Patsy Southgate, a high-spirited blond divorcée. But Joan too remained in the mix. Often she spent weekends at Mike and Norm's place. All night she would sip Scotch, listen to Beethoven, and air her grievances to Frank, Hal, Joe, whomever, finally heading off to the bedroom she shared with Mike. During one visit it popped into Mike's head that he might as well say it: "Hey, why don't we get married?" He'd never said it before. No, she replied, too little, too late. Yet when they

Life magazine's shot of Joan at the Paris studio she borrowed from sculptor Day Schnabel, *1957*

put Al Hibbler's "After the Lights Go Down" ("How does it feel when the lights go down low / And time moves so slow") or Billie Holiday's "Ooh, ooh, ooh / What a little moonlight can do" on the turntable, Joan surrendered to all her old feelings for Mike.

A rare Manhattan appearance by Lady Day brought the five to Loew's Sheridan that evening. Billie Holiday, they knew, had been deserted by her father as a child, raped at ten, addicted to heroin at twenty-five, subjected to all manner of racial discrimination, but had nonetheless triumphed, collaborating with saxophonist Lester Young and performing with Count Basie and Artie Shaw in the 1930s and recording for Decca in the 1940s. If liquor and dope had begun to ravage that throaty, rueful, knowing voice, the singer's regal public manner and salty good humor conceded nothing to the tawdriness and tragedy of her life. Arrested repeatedly on narcotics charges, Billie had lost her New York cabaret card and thus her right to perform in clubs. Except for her 1956 triumph before a packed house at Carnegie Hall and scattered performances at other alcohol-less venues, she had not caught the New York spotlight for years.

At midnight, the Charlie Mingus Quintet opened for a remarkable lineup. Billie's first gig that evening, at a Philadelphia nightclub, had ended after eleven, and, by the time she was chauffeured to New York, it was going on three a.m., the hour the city's entertainment curfew took effect. But palms had been greased, and, at three a.m. sharp, the singer emerged, looking slightly lost, onto the stage of the cavernous theater, acknowledged her boisterously adoring fans, cocked her head, and began nodding to the beat. A *New York Times* reviewer felt that Holiday "was not always in full control of her voice. But once she had worked away a tendency toward thickness and lumpiness, she sang with a quiet passion that was deeply moving." She stunned the audience with "God Bless the Child," "Don't Explain," and a plaintive "Billie's Blues."

Two years later, at 3:10 a.m. on July 17, 1959, Billie Holiday would lie dead in a charity ward from heart failure, congestion of the lungs, and cirrhosis. A packet of heroin had been found in her bed, so technically she was under arrest. She had seventy cents in the bank. That afternoon Frank O'Hara would dash off "The Day Lady Died" (its title a witty play on the singer's nickname), a stunning elegy that sets the stage for its own creation with an inventory of the poet's midtown Manhattan lunchtime rounds, including a stop at a tobacconist where the *New York Post* shocks him with banner news of her death. He is mentally whisked to the Five Spot, where (nearly a year after that night at Loew's Sheridan) he had once again heard Billie sing. Having dropped into the club to say hello to her accompanist Mal Waldron, Holiday had allowed herself to be coaxed into one impromptu and unauthorized number. O'Hara's poem ends,

> And I am sweating a lot by now and thinking of
> leaning on the john door in the 5 SPOT
> while she whispered a song along the keyboard
> to Mal Waldron and everyone and I stopped breathing

Joan, in contrast, lost no time in paying homage to Billie after the Loew's Sheridan performance that Saturday night. Imagine the transporting, heart-piercing "Billie's Blues" ("Lord, I love my man, tell the world I do") drifting through her studio, its windows thrown open to the summer night, the music tossing up colors and pulling Joan by the sleeve into a painting. She was always a girl in love when she listened to Lady Day, who no doubt supplied the feeling material for the splendid *Ladybug*.

Luscious garden hues — cadmium red, celadon, cobalt blue, ultramarine, slurry brown, carmine, ochre, acid raspberry — splash and streak through this luminous nine-foot-wide oil. Some colors optically blend. Others pop from the picture plane, thanks in part to the painter's astute use of red-green and blue-ochre polarities. (The latter, along with *Ladybug*'s architectural exactitude and play of colors against aerating whites, evoke the late work of Cézanne.) Mitchell's gloriously variegated brushstrokes push and tug and shimmer and float, like the edges of planes jostling in a shallow space or foliage lifted and twirled by a breeze, kissing the light, then heaving away. As in nature, they provoke a myriad of spatial sensations, here a to-and-froness, there a churning stillness like that of the sea, or, for that matter, that of a phrase hanging as if forever in the air ("and everyone and I stopped breathing").

Fitfully interiorized, *Ladybug* also exudes the landscape quality inherent in its emphatically horizontal format. Blues and neutrals skimming along its top suggest distance and depth through atmospheric perspective. These "hills" and "sky" should, of course, recede, yet the artist also insists upon the picture's flatness, pulling those same strokes forward using white and meshing them into a nearly edge-to-edge reticulation. Knowing that viewers instinctively seek a horizon line, she simultaneously supplies and denies one, a strategy worthy of that distiller of nature who loved to visually clasp surface to depth, Henri Matisse.

Seeking visual equivalents for his intense emotional engagement with his subjects, the French painter had, in Fauvist works such as the 1905 *Open Window,* used vibrant, unnatural colors for expressive and structural purposes, masterfully planting whites among them (à la Cézanne) in order to create, rather than depict, light. Matisse's achievement of luminosity through lights and whites thrilled Joan, as did his sensitive paint handling, joie de vivre, and linking of inner and outer worlds. In depicting a window, a favorite motif, Matisse forced the traditional rules of painting to bow to the experience of a human consciousness: the flicker of the out-of-doors bursts onto the picture plane like happiness itself. This *Ladybug* too achieves.

Though unsparingly self-critical, Joan must have derived a particular satisfaction from her virtuoso canvas, purchased in 1961 by the Museum of Modern Art. *Ladybug* not only conveys the scintillant excitement of painting but also impeccably carries out her ideas about conjoining accuracy and intensity: rigorously built, it achieves the ineffable. Joan's lofty ambition for her work was no less than transubstantiation: in her phrase implying both a physical and a metaphysical program, "painting as cathedral."

October 1957 brought the first major feature story about Joan: Irving Sandler's "Mitchell Paints a Picture" in *ArtNews,* the latest installment in the prestigious signature series of this "house organ" of New York School art. Though reluctant to discuss her work, the artist had agreed to sit down with the fledgling editorial assistant in what turned out to be six conversations, the first of which she disrupted by playing provoking verbal games until Frank O'Hara, also present, told her to cut the bullshit.

Back in February, Joan had moved crabwise into the first picture whose making Sandler describes. Seeking an emotional toehold, she remembered a certain child's drawing of the Brooklyn Bridge that conjured fresh sense-memories of that magnificent structure and the surrounding riverscape. Seizing upon her feelings for the bridge at specific remembered moments, Joan had tacked to the wall a ninety-by-eighty-inch canvas, made a sketch, mixed her colors, and painted for five hours. Her second work session, two days later, burned up an entire night. Applying her pigments with brushes, fingers, and rags, the artist saw the bridge

"Mitchell Paints a Picture" for ArtNews, *1957*

become remote, which was okay, she felt, as long as the picture retained the feeling of spanning a void. When Sandler viewed it, he felt "a wonderful airiness" and speculated that it might be finished, but Joan promptly disabused him of that notion. Not only were certain lines insensitive, even meaningless, she pointed out, but also the color was inaccurate and the painting didn't hold together. Later she phoned Irving to say she had "lost" *Bridge* to an irremediable lack of accuracy and intensity, and she supposed that was the end of the article too. No, he replied, do another, and I'll contrast the aborted picture with the finished one.

The ravishing painting that followed wrested from pigment a feeling of mercurial light, swirling air, and turbulent water. Joan's subject, Sandler later wrote, was

> her memory of a beloved dog she once owned who jumped into the water in East Hampton on a pleasant, sunny day. She laid down a large splash of yellow, which she whitened as she remembered a hurricane that swept over Long Island that summer in which several of her paintings had been destroyed. It ended up being titled *George Swimming at Barnes Hole But It Got Too Cold.* It turned out to be one of Joan's finest works.

Emphasizing the roles of landscape and memory in the work of the painter who declared to him, "I carry my landscapes around with me," Sandler explained to *ArtNews* readers.

> There are those fleeting moments, those "almost supernatural states of soul," as Baudelaire called them, during which "the profundity of life is entirely revealed in any scene, however ordinary, that presents itself before one. The scene becomes its symbol." Miss Mitchell attempts to paint this sign, to re-create both the recalled landscape and the frame of mind she was in originally. Memory, as a storehouse of indelible images, becomes her creative domain.
>
> However, a "state of soul" is indefinite, and cognition of the total "profundity of life," unattainable. Still, if sparks of these are experienced, a yearning so poignant arises, so superior to what is accessible, that it can only be called "joy," in C.S. Lewis' sense of the word. The most complete satisfaction is achieved, not in the realization of the possible, but in the most intense desire for the illimitable. The lack of yearning for any length of time causes an inquietude and despondency, a sedulous longing for the yearning. Miss Mitchell paints to reawaken this desire.

No less charged with desire, Frank O'Hara's poem "To the Harbormaster," published that fall in *Meditations in an Emergency,* haunted Joan. Using the extended metaphor of the lover as battered vessel, O'Hara evokes corporeality ("the metallic coils of the tide / around my fathomless arms"), sexuality ("I am hard alee with my Polish rudder / in my hand"), and volition ("I offer my hull and the tattered cordage / of my will") in seeking lover or muse. Hindered by winds, waves, and moorings—the very beliefs and habits that make one feel secure—he nonetheless submits with grace to the "reasoning of the eternal voices." Using assonance and irregular metrics and avoiding end stops and stanzas, the poet stirs a sense of order and drift, ego and egolessness.

Joan's buffeted and beautiful *To the Harbormaster,* also painted that year, shares the emotional texture of O'Hara's poem, its feeling of riffling currents and disorienting reflections inextricable from the viscous and chromatic pleasures of paint. A green-cast matrix of whites acts as foil to *Harbormaster*'s red oranges, blues, greens, and blacks, suggesting deeply seen filamentous tangles riding the water, with patches of sunlessness here, light slicing through vegetation there—not these things themselves, however, but the sensations, pulsations, susceptibilities, and transformations they excite.

Two years earlier, the Museum of Modern Art had acquired one of Impressionist Claude Monet's immense *Water Lilies* canvases, thus stirring controversies about the relationship between the late Monet and New York School painting. Five years before that, Elaine de Kooning had coined the term "Abstract Impressionism," meaning painting that retains "the Impressionist manner of looking at a scene but leave[s] out the scene." De Kooning had written, "As the Impressionists attempted to deal with the optical effects of nature, the followers are interested in the optical effects of spiritual states, thereby giving an old style a new subject."

To Joan's displeasure, certain critics and curators had begun labeling *To the Harbormaster* and other Mitchell works "Abstract Impressionist" and bundling them off to shows with that theme. Monet had rarely been among her inspirations, yet the luminosity, lyricism, wide pictorial field, liquefaction of boundaries between nature and self, and simultaneous allusion to three worlds—watery surface, underwater depths, reflection of sky—of *To the Harbormaster* and other Mitchell paintings brought to some lips a knowing "Impressionist."

Art, O'Hara's great poem suggests, can salvage heartache, failure, and loss. Capable of soaring above the tedious and complex dynamics of everyday living, painting continued to serve Joan as a means of controlling life, coping with crises, and compensating for worldly disappointments, among them the inadequacies of psychoanalysis. For seven years, she and Fried had soldiered on, Joan keeping regular appointments with her glamorous earth mother when the artist was in New York, in fact, spending long months in New York largely because of her analysis. Fried now pronounced the process complete, yet Joan demanded that it continue. Over the years, their relationship had evolved, Joan sometimes getting the upper hand when they saw each other socially but inevitably running to Edrita in a crisis and counting on her as much for mother-love, for reparenting, as for the mind cure. "I'm sure my love for her interfered with my shrinkery," she once observed, "but I couldn't care less—and I doubt if she did."

According to Fried, the goal of psychoanalysis was the evolution of the entire person, which was self-motivated once one's fears and resistances had been addressed. Yet, by all appearances, Joan's remained undiminished. Ruing the thought that, in the end, analysis added up to "only a method of learning to swallow a bitter pill that you'll never like anyway," she judged hers more failure than success.

Yet she commanded the language and method of psychoanalysis and relished playing "witch doctor" with anyone and everyone, ferreting out and pouncing upon people's weaknesses, secrets, and anxieties. Her quick mind and sharp tongue kept them alert. Those who felt strong might enjoy her, but most couldn't relax around Joan. She'd pin them down and probe them. "One great big long needle," winces Chicago-born Parisian sculptor Caroline Lee, "scared the hell out of me." Yet Lee acknowledged the rewards of Joan's incisiveness, once writing, "You know so much that I cannot imagine you not knowing how deeply, joltingly beneficial was your directness with me." Another Chicago native, printmaker June Wayne, observes that being with Joan was "like having sensitive teeth," yet adds, "I, for my part, admired her a great deal."

Joan's arrival in Paris that August may have been the occasion when Jean-Paul picked her up at Orly, zoomed off toward the city, then abruptly pulled over, dragged her out of the car, and made passionate love to her in a field—the kind of caveman stuff she adored.

Old patterns quickly reasserted themselves: Joan again sublet Day Schnabel's studio on the rue Daguerre, where she spent late-rising days alone with her cigarettes, books, booze, and painting, then hooked up with her lover in late afternoon. He might whisk her off to an automobile race or hockey match, or, more likely, they would make the rounds of Montparnasse, schmoozing, playing a little pinball (Joan was an ace), maybe stopping at Buttercup's Chicken Shack, owned by Buttercup Powell, the common-law wife of their new pal, the great jazz pianist Bud Powell, and drinking, drinking, drinking.

No one doubted the two were crazy about each other, yet Jean-Paul was under enormous work pressure that summer and fall, and, when he was not in a paroxysm of painting for an upcoming show, he was pulled right and left by dealers, curators, critics, and collectors. Ruminating that she was "shockingly the same wherever I am and tenuously complex," Joan fought off depression and, even before August had slipped by, hankered for a crisp New York autumn: "I'm beginning to imagine Fifth Avenue in fall light," she wrote Mike,

> clear—57th St. with you—a bourbon in front of your new pictures and a few other very beautiful thoughts—It's time to cut my hair again and wash my underwear and clean my brushes—I make always such a mess—and it seems meaningless—my cathedral is miles away—after all—and the damn workers still fix the roof and the town is all empty, empty.

Some of Joan's idle hours were absorbed by late-summer visitors, among them the funny and serious New York poet Kenneth Koch. But writer and painter quarreled over whether or not Joan had money and whether or not Kenneth had friends and ended up hating each other. Joan spilled the whole story to their mutual pal, John Ashbery, who was briefly back in Paris (where he had been living) after a stay in London and was about to depart for New York. John phoned Joan, who invited him to a party at the studio of painter Paul Jenkins, and, by the time the two "were finally en route," John later reported to Frank O'Hara of their evening together,

> Joan had collected three more uninvited guests: a French girl, a French Canadian named Yves something and an Arab. The host blanched when he saw us all but he let us in and I immediately began to drink large quantities of red wine, cognac and pernod and soon had to be helped down several flights of stairs for fresh air. Luckily Joan forced one of the other guests to drive us both to our respective homes, which I thought was very dear of her. She was very sweet and we talked about you for hours, as well as about Mike and Jane. I will be seeing her again on Tuesday at [painter] Fay Lansner's.

Barney too swung through Paris, on business for Grove Press, which was still losing money yet boasted an expanding staff, offices on Broadway, and a list of nearly three dozen books. (Joan received a share of Grove revenues, one of Barney's ways of sustaining their connection, not to mention a $325 monthly allowance from her mother and sporadic checks from the Stable. Koch was right about the money.) Her former husband had earned Joan's deep respect because, with Grove, he had put his money where his mouth was. His stellar achievement, she felt, was

Edrita Fried and her daughter
Jaqui sailing to Europe in 1960

publishing the Irish-born writer living in Paris, Samuel Beckett.

Four years earlier, Barney had stumbled across Beckett's tragicomic French-language play about absurdity, alienation, and despair, *Waiting for Godot*. After he and Loly met the author during their 1953 honeymoon in Paris, Grove had purchased the American rights, and, in 1954, published Beckett's own translation. Only 341 copies had sold that year. However, staged in London and New York, *Godot* soon won fame beyond intellectual circles, and eventually Grove's sales of Beckett's play would surpass two million. Now Beckett put the translation of *Endgame*, another work for the stage, directly into Rosset's hands, and Joan joined the two in a string of convivial rum-and-Coke-, Pernod-, and Irish whiskey–washed nights at the dark paneled bar of the Hôtel Pont Royal and other Left Bank drinking establishments.

Joan had met Beckett two summers earlier, when, thanks to Barney, the Irishman had figured on her list of people to call. Nineteen years her senior, Sam was gaunt and stern-looking with a deeply lined forehead, strong nose, long ears, and all-seeing blue eyes framed by steel-rimmed spectacles. Wary of the corruptions of language, he was alternately laconic, cordial, and inscrutable, sometimes sardonic and brilliant. He had taken an immediate liking to Joan, with whom he shared not only a first-rate mind and a feeling for the impossibility of contentment but also a deep love of music, literature, and painting. Sam also understood Joan's feeling for color. On one occasion, the two spent an entire day with Barney, during which, remembers Rosset, his companions rarely stopped discussing color: "Color, all they talked about was color. For hours. All day. Shades of blues and yellows. A lot about blue."

The Irish writer and the American artist also shared a predilection for billiards. Under Sam's tutelage, Joan became expert at this exacting game of concentration and angles. At times they played daily, often at Les Mousquetaires, a brasserie–billiard parlor on the avenue du Maine.

More fundamentally, the existentialist writer saw Joan as a version of his close friend, Dutch painter Bram van Velde, whom he associated with the famous final lines of *Waiting for Godot*: "I can't go on. I'll go on." Moreover, writes Beckett's biographer, Deirdre Bair, Mitchell's

large, sprawling canvases drew him in, and he would pore for hours over the intricacies of the paint and the patterns. He liked her refusal to explain or justify her art, since it reflected his own inability and unwillingness to discuss his writings. And, as an added attraction, Mitchell was a prodigious drinker, whose conversation became more rarefied and intriguing the more she drank. She and Beckett became companions at this time and it was to Mitchell that he turned when life in Paris became too hectic. She was the one person with whom he could drink, relax and talk, and her friendship became a crutch he leaned on heavily.

Joan had also formed a solid friendship with bearded Kansas City–born Paul Jenkins, a painter of alluvial streams of mystical color, who, as well as anyone, could prod her into good humor. But now, after four years in Paris, Paul was preparing to leave for New York. In fact, he and Joan had arranged to exchange her St. Mark's Place apartment for his sixth-floor atelier at 15, rue Decrès—*métro* Plaisance—south of Montparnasse.

Decrès proved a godsend. Even on glum, rainy days when Joan awoke whimpering, "oh God—Paris—Paris," light filtered through its ample windows and angled skylights. She could run her eyes over the rooftops of Paris as she lifted paint from her palette and could stretch out on the living-room floor and gaze up at clouds drifting past. From the mezzanine bedroom, where one long wall was lined with books, she could step out to a divine terrace where she sunbathed nude, watched sunsets, and devoured mystery novels, Isaac Babel short stories, and Isak Dinesen's *Out of Africa*. "Your descriptions of your new quarters are marvellous"—Frank offered her an epistolary posy—"especially walking around between Arabs and machine guns, does it make you feel sort of nervous and Joan of Lorraine-ish?"

O'Hara was referring to police barricades erected in response to the drive-by shootings and acts of sabotage that had accompanied the intensification of the Algerian War. Tensions ran high. One evening when two gendarmes approached Jean-Paul and Joan and demanded their papers, Jean-Paul, who could easily pass for Algerian, was unwilling or unable to produce his. "Who are you?" "Myself." The artist's goofy reply got him arrested, at which point Joan started screaming bloody murder, and she too was hauled in. Reportedly, the cops worked over Riopelle with a billy club that night. "Don't ever get into a French prison," Joan tersely advised friends.

Behind Riopelle's overwrought state lay the pressures of success as he struggled to meet the demands of his French, American, and British galleries. His prices shot up and up. *Maclean's* magazine dubbed him Canada's "Native Genius," while a French TV show crowned him heir to Leonardo, Rembrandt, Rubens, and Matisse: "Make no mistake, fifty years from now the work of this man will be classed as masterpieces, and we are fortunate indeed to be living in the same moment in history as one of the masters."

Drained and sunk into self-doubt after his feverish painting marathons, Riopelle drifted from bar to bar that fall, consuming forty or fifty Ricards a day. Observed writer Harry Mathews, a close friend,

> Visibly . . . he was very anguished. I remember that he told us really incredible stories about his father and the Catholic Church. To hear him talk, the priests were ruining his father. Riopelle, who was, moreover, remarkable, seemed to me at that time obsessed by a fear of hell, hounded by remorse, subject to a kind of divine condemnation. He was forever punishing himself. In that regard, Joan seemed to me less vulnerable than he. Still it was sometimes terrifying to be with them.

To Jean-Paul, Joan seemed a tyrannical if wondrous force: "I must be crazy because I cannot control myself. I am a prisoner of this obsession, you." To hear him talk, even his liaisons with other women figured into his passion for Joan because—femme fatale, maternal figure, soulmate, fellow lunatic, and overgrown kid—she understood his weaknesses better than he. And she could match him, drink for drink. "Don't become too rational," he cracked. "I like you the way you are."

Painting, they joked, was their mutual disease. Offering each other a fellow artist's understanding and support, they administered advice with dollops of irony. Sitting around with a bevy of friends one evening at a Montparnasse café, Jean-Paul blurted out, "When I paint, I never think about what I'm going to do." Joan's eyes popped. But she who felt that letting pigment fly without premeditation amounted to giving the ego free rein also believed there was no one right way to paint. Her eyes drilled into Jean-Paul's head as she mouthed a mordant, *"Oh."*

That November, after Françoise took the children to Canada, Jean-Paul and Joan vacationed with a quartet of friends on Belle-Île, an island off the coast of Brittany. It rained torrentially, and they partied so hard that their few fellow guests fled. But the innkeeper was not unhappy: Jean-Paul was deliriously throwing money around like confetti.

A few hours a day, plus longer escapes now and then, do not, however, add up to commitment. Joan had left her studio, her friends, her shrink—her life!—to be with Jean-Paul, and she desperately missed Tenth Street camaraderie. "There is nothing like loneliness when a head doctor has made you less detached," she lamented. "You know what has hit you." Paris effused the "ghostly decadence of mistresses and lovers and sadness . . . , less ghastly than the false glitter of East Hampton" but also less vital than the bars and boys of Gotham. Moreover, though she loved Jean-Paul, he continued to resist the idea of divorcing Françoise, marrying Joan, and having another child—and the mistress business wasn't all it was cracked up to be.

That fall John and Jenk left for New York, and Stanley Karnow won a fellowship at Harvard. Sam Francis was now living in Japan. Shirley and Kimber and Gaby, good friends all, remained in France, as did Zuka, but she had a family. Joan fell in with misfits, problem people, and injured birds, including Marcelle, a French Canadian woman estranged from her husband, and Guy, a nutty French doctor with whom Joan was having a desultory affair. She also hung out with Allen Ginsberg and Gregory Corso.

The two poets were living in a cheap, rat-infested rooming house with damp, greasy walls, later dubbed the Beat Hotel, on the ancient, narrow rue Gît-le-Coeur, behind the place Saint-Michel. But they may have first crossed paths with Joan under the wide awning of the Café Select, where Ginsberg sat weeping one day as he wrote the opening lines of "Kaddish," a powerful lament for his mother and a meditation on life and death. Some time later the disheveled poet in owlish glasses served Joan lousy lentil soup cooked on the two-burner gas stove in his hotel room while she raved about what a genius Frank O'Hara was. They spoke too of "Howl," Ginsberg's frenzied cry against the establishment, seized earlier that year by U.S. customs agents in San Francisco on grounds of obscenity. The subsequent trial of Ginsberg's publisher, poet Lawrence Ferlinghetti, which had just ended in acquittal, made Ginsberg internationally famous and brought the Beat movement into public consciousness. Because of Part III of "Howl," the Rockland section, in which Ginsberg iterates his solidarity with Carl Solomon, the poem's dedicatee whom he had met at a psychiatric hospital ("Carl Solomon! I'm with you in Rockland . . ."), Joan told Allen about Mike's experiences at that same Rockland State Hospital, but Ginsberg had never been there.

Ginsberg's cohort, the voluble and uninhibited Gregory Corso, a small man with a low forehead, was flapping around Paris that fall in a long black cape lined in blue silk and waving a silver-headed cane. Corso had once collaborated with Frank O'Hara at the Poets' Theatre in Cambridge, where his first volume of poetry was published in 1954, thanks to the fund-raising efforts of his then girlfriend, Bunny Lang, at the very time she'd been involved with Mike Goldberg. In Paris, Corso wrote some of his best-known works, like "Bomb," "Hair," and "Marriage," a zany rumination on matrimony. But Joan would never "be mad for the let's howl school—or the too too sneakered poets" whose hipness, raw humor, and diatribes against conformist society were not what she wanted from poetry.

Come December, Joan and Marcelle sped off in Marcelle's Volkswagen for southern France, where they soaked up the sun's rays, slept on dank beaches in moth-eaten sleeping bags, sat in a pine grove to dig Cézanne's Mont Sainte-Victoire, and stayed with André, a "little nice crazy fag" Joan knew who actually lived in Cézanne's old house. By her own cranky account, "little Joanie [was] hard and cynical and very friendly with dogs." Well, "all the world [was] a pile of shit—very tough shit at that."

That January's *ArtNews* listed Joan's March 1957 show as one of the previous year's ten best, and Frank professed that he and "various constituents here look[ed] forward to [her 1958 show] with great woofs and howls of joy: I hope we don't all just leap into [the paintings], like George into Georgica Pond, the first moment they're up!" Eleanor needed the work by February 10, three weeks in advance of the March 3 opening, in order to make the deadlines for the art magazines' March reviews. But Joan hadn't painted for weeks—"something is awfully dead in me," she wrote Mike—and she tensed up under the pressure.

To make matters worse, she was squabbling with Paul over Decrès. Misunderstanding her travel plans—simultaneously blunt and elliptical, Joan was always "[putting] on the table what she was thinking, then later you found out what she was *really* thinking"—Paul had told her he was temporarily renting Decrès to painter Larry Rivers. "Now listen—you old master of indecisions," Joan blasted back,

I cried once in front of you. We had several deals going—and all at once you lit out—now leave me in peace and fuck Larry Rivers. You can always rent the place and in the meantime I'll pay and so will J-P and that's strictly between us and nobody's business. I would like simply that, as we agreed, I can have a couple of weeks chez moi—or even afternoons—to finish this son of a bitch show ... The place is charmingly cold. Since Eleanor sent me a fat check I bought a little electric blower item which keeps my ankles warm only I can't work it with the [electric] blanket because we blow the fuses. I had your place appraised—it is worth between 3 million five and 7 [francs] (just by the way) and I'm still interested.

Thus was Larry kept at bay and Paul put on second notice that Joan was angling to purchase Decrès. Meanwhile, her eleventh-hour attempts to persuade Eleanor to switch her dates with those of painter Fritz Bultman having failed, Joan scrambled to finish the show. She then had the work photographed and airmailed the pictures to New York, but missed the March deadlines. April brought the critical consensus that, notwithstanding their many seductively beautiful passages, the new paintings were as harsh and confrontational as anything she had ever done. One could read therein her insistence upon belonging to the New York School, her love of its brutal rawness, and her scorn for "French-cuisine" painting.

"And honey doll," Joan's letter to Paul turned to the subject of her own return to New York,

somebody's not going to know what hit them—romances have hard angles—and Joanie's coming to town (now—Mother Joan says—relax and keep the aspidistra flying) and merde stop renting your fucking place and screw Jackie a little and trust me a little and find me a stud in N.Y.

Lovingly,
Angel

Having taught for a year at the University of New Mexico, painter Elaine de Kooning had also been far from New York. When she returned after ten months, she "felt like Rip Van Winkle. Greenwich Village was full of coffee shops I hadn't noticed before. The openings and the parties were still going on but the guest lists had burgeoned to a point that made the studios and galleries inhumanly crowded." Not only were the artist-run galleries deluged by the often derivative work of wannabe action painters streaming to Tenth Street from around the country, but also the politics of dealing with proliferating submissions had put an end to the symbolically important Stable Annual. Sheer numbers had defeated the old feeling of us against the world (even though we all disagree with each other), while action painting based in individualistic intuitive truth ceded ground to action painting as established idiom. Was this a new academy? Seasoned artists raised concerns. Some, however, voiced cautious approval of consolidation or argued that New York painting's sine qua non of personal freedom made it academy proof.

The Club too had lost its edge. With older, more successful artists still paying lip service but rarely attending, it had lapsed into "a kind of suburban debating society," griped painter Friedel Dzubas. "It was really a holy bore to go there. You went there and looked around, and you got more and more depressed." Nonetheless, when Irving Sandler brought together Thomas Hess, Harold Rosenberg, and Alfred Barr for a Friday-night panel on the question "Has the Situation Changed?," the polemic was as fierce as any in memory. The trio's inconclusiveness provoked an angry outburst from Mike Goldberg: "You guys are acting like grave diggers—digging your own graves. You are stuck with your original revolution. The revolution is going on, and you can't recognize it." But sculptor Sidney Gordin countered, "The trouble with revolution is that is has become too fashionable, an academy of revolution." When John Canaday became chief art critic at the *New York Times* the following year, the Club would at least again be dignified with a power-

ful enemy: "The Club rises like a pustule, according to its detractors,"
Canaday wrote,

> or like Olympus, according to its devotees, in that section of New
> York where abstract art is lived, breathed and almost literally eaten.
>
> As Olympians, the denizens of The Club recognize Jackson Pol-
> lock as their Cronus, Willem de Kooning as their Zeus, and, let us say,
> Grace Hartigan, Helen Frankenthaler and Joan Mitchell as the god-
> desses who compete for the golden apple—Aphrodite, Athene and
> Hera, although not necessarily respectively.

And while Joan still loved to wash away the unforgiving loneliness
of the studio by squeezing into a booth to drink and gab at the Cedar,
the legendary bar now teemed with newcomers eager to hang out with
"Franz" and "Bill." One night, then–art student Pete Hamill walked
into the Cedar, aware that it supposedly wasn't what it had once been.
"But look: down past the end of the bar, in the first rough booth in the
brightly lit back room: that elegant, beautiful girl is Joan Mitchell. Sitting
with Alfred Leslie. And Philip *Guston*." And the Five Spot was still the
Five Spot. The San Remo too, more or less, only crawling with would-be
Beats.

Nineteen fifty-eight also saw New York School painting packaged
and sent abroad. Curated by the Museum of Modern Art's Dorothy
Miller, The New American Painting brought together work by Pollock,
Newman, Hartigan, Rothko, and thirteen others for a two-year tour
that finally persuaded Europeans that the United States had produced
world-class art. If New York School painting now commanded the full
attention of powerful institutions—and the painters themselves reaped
the benefits of decades of struggle—the new new American art was coming from outside New York School attitudes, indeed, was offering ironic
homages and retorts to New York School art.

That January, for instance, Jasper Johns's encaustic *Target*, a literal but
sensually hand-brushed depiction of a blue and yellow bull's eye topped
with a shelf of plaster half faces, appeared on the cover of *ArtNews*. In
March, at Leo Castelli, Robert Rauschenberg showed "combines" made
of comic strips, paint, rotogravure photographs, reproductions of Old
Master paintings, and objects like Coke bottles and hats, thus accom-
modating, on equal terms, made and found objects as well as commercial
and fine art processes, and redirecting attention from the psyche of the

artist to the multitudinous outside world. And at Hansa, Allan Kaprow was breaking down the barriers between life and art with a cluttered, collaged environment that included random sounds.

Such work provoked puzzlement and tongue wagging. What was happening to the imagination, to the dream? What was this stuff really about? Was it just a palate cleanser after a surfeit of introspective gestural abstraction? Was it neo-Dada? Fraud? Or did it constitute a worthy, if still virtually incomprehensible, visual language?

After Joan borrowed Zog's East Twelfth Street apartment that spring (Paul Jenkins having returned from France), Jean-Paul voiced objections to what he rightly suspected was a decision to delay her return. He fired off daily telegrams delivered between seven and nine a.m., hardly Miss Mitchell's prime time, on top of his many letters ("Joan *chérie* . . ."). One telegram spurred her to dial his home number, then hang up when Françoise answered, upon which Jean-Paul rushed to Decrès, took up paper and pen, and waxed eloquent about his delirious dreams of her and his childish impatience for her presence.

In love though she was, Joan wanted to take full measure of the consequences should she definitively move to Paris. After long hours with Fried, she made her return conditional upon Jean-Paul divorcing Françoise and marrying her. He, however, suffered pangs of doubt about divorce. Once teenage soul mates, he and Françoise had married in defiance of their parents' wishes, and in certain ways she had kept him together. But Joan hung tough. Thus, one Sunday that May Jean-Paul announced to Françoise that he wanted a divorce. Shocked, she reacted with furious, tearful, convulsed arguments. The children too were deeply shaken. The following morning, Jean-Paul wired Joan the news, signing, "SHIT AND LOVE, JEAN PAUL." A stormy sixteen-hour session with Françoise nine days later yielded Françoise's decision to move back to Canada with the children. Divorce proceedings were already underway, Jean-Paul informed Joan, and would take three months. At a Fourth of July party at Zog's place in Springs five weeks later, she told Irving Sandler that she still loved Mike but wanted a man who would carry his share of the responsibility for the children she intended to have, and that man was Riopelle.

Mike was now seriously involved with Patsy Southgate, or, more exactly, Mike, Patsy, and Frank O'Hara had formed a complex romantic and perhaps intimate triangle that Joan found unsettling. A poet and short-story writer and graduate of Smith, Patsy was the daughter of FDR's chief of protocol and the ex-wife of writer and *Paris Review* founder Peter Matthiessen. Women found Patsy too bony to be beautiful, but men stumbled all over themselves in extolling her sky blue eyes, sun-bleached hair, radiant smile, lithe figure, keen intelligence, and saucy wit. William Styron once told Paul Jenkins that Patsy was the one woman he wanted to marry in the next life, and Frank styled her the Grace Kelly of the New York School.

That August, Françoise flew to Montreal and Joan to Paris. No sooner had she arrived than she was overwhelmed by the costs of her choice. She dreamed "ghastly dreams about New York," desperately missed her friends, and wondered what the hell she was doing on this gray edge of the world. Her spirits rose and sank with the arrivals and departures of Barney, Frank, and Saul Steinberg, whose presence so touched her that she choked back tears, and she was surprised and touched to receive an encouraging letter from Grace.

"And the days pass," Joan sighed in a letter to Paul,

> another automobile show—races—[Jean-Paul's mechanic friend] Phillipot from time to time. Spent a crazy evening dancing at Adrien—nights are sometimes drunken at Montparnasse, often with Giacometti . . . But Baby doll maybe everything is tough finally and I suppose one has to see something through as H. James would say. And I can't go home again—or when I go it will be with a different spirit. It's so Sunday afternoon—a little Beethoven and so empty and all my fault.

To make matters worse, Mike married Patsy Southgate that fall. Patsy had two children, so, in what felt like a valedictory dig, Mike became a father, or rather a stepfather, after all. Despite the impossibility between them and her own plans to marry and start a family, Joan felt shocked and betrayed. "Heard all about the wedding bells," she harrumphed to Paul, "some shit. And so another bitter chapter ends . . . The records are spinning and a few tears—Baby—andiamo . . . I hope like hell to get to N.Y. some day—a Goldbergless N.Y.—swing down the street with you and Bluhm." When the newlyweds stopped in Paris on their honeymoon,

Riopelle, unknown woman, Giacometti, Joan, and painter Louis le Brocquy, c. 1960–62

Joan, hoping to raise a little hell, left a note at their hotel inviting them to join her for a drink at the Café de Flore, but they wisely ignored it. In the rawness of the moment, she may also have turned to one of the poems by René Char that Frank had recently typed out for her in French: the gorgeous "To ***," which begins,

> *You've been my love so many years,*
> *My bewilderment at so much waiting,*
> *That not a thing can age or chill;*
> *Even what waited for our death*
> *Or fought against us with patient skill,*
> *Even what's still to us a stranger,*
> *And my eclipses and returns.*

PARIS

Ah Joan!   there
you are
surrounded by paintings
as in another century you would be wearing lipstick
which you wear at night to be old fashioned, of it!
with it!   out!

FRANK O'HARA, "Far From the Porte des Lilas
and the Rue Pergolèse: To Joan Mitchell"

CHAPTER ELEVEN   Seeing Something Through

Joan's social life now revolved around the dimly lit American-style
Bar du Dôme, next door to the Café du Dôme, where, night after
night, Jean-Paul Riopelle's table served as a magnet for artists and
writers including Sam Francis, Kimber and Gaby Smith, Shirley Goldfarb, Samuel Beckett, Bram van Velde, Sam Szafran, Ruth Francken,
Harry Mathews, Pierre Schneider, Shirley Jaffe, Pierre Boudreau, Anne
and Hugo Weber, David Budd, Paquerette Villeneuve, and Alberto
Giacometti. The barman, Jean-Jacques, automatically kept everyone's
stub, and, as the stragglers prepared to leave, Riopelle, always the prof-
ligate Riopelle, would fish out a wad of bills, pay for everything, and
leave a huge tip. On quiet late nights when it was just van Velde, Giacometti, Riopelle, Mitchell, and Beckett, the American painter and the
Irish writer were apt to talk bleakness and gloom, which so irritated
Riopelle that on occasion he bolted. Once, reports Beckett's biographer

Deirdre Bair, Mitchell jumped up and ran after Riopelle and "Beckett followed Mitchell into the door but was too drunk to extricate himself. Round and round he whirled, while Giacometti, like a giant, brooding toad with hooded eyes, sat and watched and said nothing, and while tourists pointed at the poet of nothingness and despair."

For Joan, years at the Dôme could never measure up to one good night at the Cedar, but at least she still qualified for what Frank O'Hara had wittily dubbed the "promiscuous drunks," as opposed to their "reformed type" friends who had started settling down. Jane Freilicher had disappointed Frank by moving into a too-comfortable apartment after she married Joe Hazan, and even Grace had wed and left New York. Yet Joan was also quietly instituting certain reforms, allowing herself no more than a single bottle of wine during evenings alone and, knowing that billiards requires a sharp eye and steady hand, coaching herself into moderate drinking when she went out.

As for Joan's self-presentation, critic Eleanor Munro, writing in *Art-News* that November, pointedly excluded her from "a rather handsomely garbed *monde* of women artists" who had "married and adopted lives of more or less stable rhythm." Munro found Joan "rangy, occasionally awkward in manner and dress." In a letter to the editor, Jane Freilicher leaped to her friend's defense: by setting Joan apart from this *monde*, she wrote, "Miss Munro seems to imply that Miss Mitchell is not as snappy a dresser as she might be (an implication I protest as positively untrue) and that her life ain't got rhythm, which is not a nice thing to say about anybody and constitutes an invasion of privacy as well."

Nonetheless, reading the eyes of Frenchmen acutely aware of women as women and knowing she did often look less than snappy, Joan took pains to fix herself up, wearing lipstick in the evening, patronizing an excellent hairdresser, and purchasing several elegant tailored pantsuits and print dresses. But she still toted the same beat-up handbag, wore baggy unironed shirts, and had a virtual love affair with Paul Jenkins's old corduroy pants, which were falling apart at the seams. Sitting at a café one day with Riopelle and Giacometti, she cast a jaundiced eye upon Yvonne Hagen, who had walked up in a nutria coat. "Why are you wearing that when you should be wearing a torn raincoat?" she scolded the art critic for the Paris edition of the *New York Herald Tribune*, a remark Hagen chalked up to the artist's need for control, especially after Joan herself purchased a $1,500 fur coat from hip New York furrier Jacques Kaplan.

Joan's penchant for masculine dress was not inconsistent with Riopelle's pet name for her: Rosa Bonheur, after the painter of the 1863 *Horse Fair*, which figures among the nineteenth century's most beloved works of art. As radical in her personal life as she was conventional in her painting, Bonheur affected men's waistcoats and trousers, smoked, bluntly spoke her mind, and held her own among members of the opposite sex. "Rosa Bonheur" also suggests rose-colored happiness (*bonheur*). Jean-Paul may have first tossed out the phrase or he may have been responding to comments from Joan triggered by her perception of him as rose pink. Shortly after the two met, back in 1955, she had, without explanation, dropped into a letter to Mike the phrase "*La vie en rose commence*" ("*La vie en rose* begins"), shades of synesthesia and of the soulful signature song of chanteuse Edith Piaf.

The course of the Riopelles' divorce was proving long and tortuous. Prior to 1968, Canada had no federal divorce law, nor did divorce courts or provincial legislation exist in Catholic Quebec, where the Riopelles had wed. In fact, the only way for a Quebecois couple to dissolve a marriage was by private act of the Canadian Parliament. Evidence of adultery (or other grounds for legal separation) had to be submitted to, considered by, and approved by committees of both the Senate and the House of Commons before such an act could be passed. Had these basic facts about the unwieldy Canadian system escaped Jean-Paul's attention when he blithely informed Joan that his divorce would require three months?

That question popped up more than once in letters among Joan, Sally, and Marion. Six months after legal proceedings got underway, Marion encouraged Joan to believe that Jean-Paul had acted in good faith when he urged her to return to Paris pending his divorce. Another six months passed. In one letter to their mother, Sally rattled on:

> I thought that the divorce was being done through London, Canada
> being part of the United Kingdom and therefore the division of the
> church and state—ergo what in hell happened to the London Lawyer.
> However isn't there something in England about proving adultery
> and a six year wait? Seems to me the wife and mother [Jean-Paul's
> mother, a devout Catholic, opposed the divorce] and the Church
> might be hand-in-glove with a money wrench? NO? . . . I don't really
> want to be a kill-joy but I don't see what good a New York boy [Rio-

pelle's new American lawyer] is going to do for a French Canadian who lives in France—but maybe it all could be worked through a bit of a reverse Marshall plan.

Though Sally liked Jean-Paul because he gave Joan "prods of giggles and won't take her seriously," she later added re their mutual *ami*-in-law:

> I think it is just as well that the R.C. church is hanging on forever to their boy because if he stays in the rut of painting-for-money and doesn't expand in the best Mitchelly manner: "his breath, on a canvas, caught" (Balls [Joan] has always chewed her own cakes even though they have been pretty heavy and stale at times) she will hand him back to the church! I think during that last molten expensive telephone chat we came to some charming agreement like: what difference does marriage make at this point? Now Marion, don't get your Victorian dander up and seethe and surge. After all WHAT is the Catholic Church to attempt to tell either of your daughters what they may do!

Canadian politics had compelled further delay: in a 1960 move to force debate over a proposal (opposed by the Catholic Church) to transfer authority for divorce to the courts, members of Canada's New Democratic Party strategically insisted upon detailed study of each petition, thus effectively bringing the process to a standstill.

Jean-Paul and Françoise were finally divorced in France during the summer of 1962, a full four years after the original petition was filed. The cost had mounted so astronomically that Jean-Paul and one of his lawyers joked that the next divorce was being thrown in free of charge. But Jean-Paul had already decided that, crazy as he was about Joan, there would never be a next marriage or divorce, nor would there be a next child.

Joan was to have one or two more abortions. Occasionally she would sigh to some female friend, Well, you have the kids, the husband, the family, I don't. Her childlessness saddened and embittered her: she felt she was missing one of the primal experiences of life. Yet gradually she resigned herself to it, displacing her need to nurture, support, and teach onto Jean-Paul's daughters, young artists, and dogs. She never got over Jean-Paul's perfidy about the marriage, however, pointedly referring to herself as his "mistress," a word she spit out like a bitter seed. Not only had he failed to live up to his bargain with her, but also he had broken his promise to Marion, made during a 1960 visit to Chicago, to marry Joan. For the duration of their life as a couple, Joan taunted him (calling him "Jimmie" after her father): "So, Jimmie, are ya going to marry me tonight? Are ya going to fuck me? Are ya going to marry me? *Huh?*"

Art critic Peter Schjeldahl tells this tale:

At a boozy dinner party that I attended in a New York walkup nearly thirty years ago [around 1973], a woman announced that she was getting married. Joan Mitchell, who was there, exploded. How could anyone even think of doing something so bourgeois? The buzzer sounded. It was Mitchell's longtime lover, the French-Canadian painter Jean-Paul Riopelle. He wanted to speak to her, but he wouldn't come upstairs. From the landing, she told him in scorching terms to leave her alone. Back at the table, she resumed denouncing the insidiousness of marriage as a trap for free souls. The buzzer again. Another cascade of profanity down the stairwell. I was awed.

Back in 1958, however—the divorce papers had just been filed—Joan operated from a sturdy determination to "work out something decent" with Jean-Paul. The right apartment topped her list of priorities. After months of searching, she ferreted out the closest thing to a loft that Paris could offer: an old top-floor warehouse on the light-industrial rue Frémicourt in the plebeian fifteenth arrondissement. For a fifteen-year lease on 3,500 square feet, the owner wanted $2,000 in key money, plus about $300 a month. Extensive renovations were needed, however, and, as giddy with excitement as Joan was over the prospect of Frémicourt, its potential cost staggered her. Like a kid with her heart set on a toy, she coaxed Eleanor Ward:

give me money—please!! and you'll have great pictures! If I get this place I'll never need to sublet and can come and go as I please and I'll be so happy. The whole idea seems like Santa Claus—no more Schnabel—Jenkins—whomever . . . Seriously if you could give me some money—any at all I'd love it—I suppose I'm not being businesslike but hell.

Eleanor eventually coughed up a thousand dollars, but Jimmie bankrolled most of the project, giving each of his daughters a fat check that same year. No doubt Jean-Paul kicked in too, but the territorial Miss

Joan brings Jean-Paul Riopelle to Chicago to meet Jimmie and Marion, c. 1960.

Mitchell brooked no misunderstandings: if she had to live in *his* city, she would do so in *her* apartment: "It makes me pee in my pants when I look at it—and it's *mine*," she crooned.

Polish-born architect and artist Piotr Kowalski was hired to design the living room, kitchen, studio, and bedroom, using angled skylights, gorgeous old wood beams, and hardwood floors, while Jean-Paul's buddy, Greek American artist and Picasso look-alike Alex Costa, super-vised the construction crew, literally a bunch of clowns (Rex, Quito, and Dédé). Hence the zany trapeze in Joan's studio. Or maybe Jean-Paul cooked up the trapeze idea. In any case, he invested demonic energy in designing witty saloon-style swinging doors for Joan's studio, building moveable walls for her paintings, and creating small niches to display sculpture in the living room, which would also have a rustic fireplace. He was all the more enthusiastic since the building's ground floor housed an automobile repair shop where he could keep part of his car collection which, at various times, counted a Ferrari, Alfa Romeo, Duesenberg, Aston Martin, Bristol, Fiat, and Morgan, not to mention his cherished Bugattis.

Only weeks before their planned move into this dream apartment, however, the couple's life blew to smithereens when Joan learned that a young gallery assistant named Yvonne Fravelo was pregnant by Jean-Paul and planned to have the baby. Livid with pain and rage, she reacted like a wounded animal. Coincidentally, she had a plane ticket to New York (for a short visit timed to coincide with Paul Jenkins's to Paris), so she used it: "I am always tying up / and then deciding to depart."

A week or two later, on April 10, Jean-Paul in Paris answered a sour letter from Joan in New York:

> Joan, *Chérie,* I'm at the Falstaff with an old beefsteak and much remorse that I let you leave. This morning I received your letter which is not very encouraging on the subject of your return. I understand that this is probably even more difficult for you, and I hope everything takes a turn for the better . . . The studio is coming along. Poor Alex is having a hell of a time with the floor . . . I really have the impression that you will be able to live in this super-palace very soon. Ten days, two weeks, I invite you, and, if you don't come, I'll smash everything.

Joan didn't budge. Jean-Paul smashed nothing.
More letters flew across the Atlantic:

> Your last letter seems so pessimistic [wrote Jean-Paul]. Regarding the children [his daughters], I've taken no immediate decision, yet, the more I think about it, the more I believe that everything will work out with you, my love, and you have no reason to accuse yourself because without you I can no longer do anything, as you well know, just remember. I want the divorce to happen. When will we be together? You tell me you can be free after May 18th. Wouldn't it be best that you come? So, breathe deeply—as JM always says—because *"tout va très bien, Madame la Marquise."*

At one point, Riopelle proposed they flee the temptations of Paris by going halves with Georges and Marguerite Duthuit on the fifteenth-century Château de Rozay, along the banks of the Cher, but, in the end, he flew to New York, stayed two months, and charmed Joan back to Paris.

Before leaving France, Jean-Paul had arranged to charter the luxury yacht *Fantasia,* captained by an old campaigner from the Queen's Navy, for a Mediterranean cruise *en famille* that would give Joan the perfect opportunity to get acquainted with her "stepdaughters"-to-be. True to pattern, however, the promised "two sailors, two masts, two cabins, two children, two lovers, you and me" multiplied into nine travelers and myriad complications. His mentor, Georges Duthuit, wife Marguerite (née Matisse), and their son Claude accompanied Joan, Jean-Paul, Yseult, and Sylvie on an early-August flight to Athens, from where they sailed to Istanbul, toured the city, then again weighed anchor. The voyage was gorgeous, unreal, and exhausting: not only did the Duthuits have to be entertained but also, Joan felt, Yseult and Sylvie had to be instructed in Greek history and English in the morning (she shopped for textbooks in Athens) and swimming in the afternoon.

As the *Fantasia* approached Mount Athos in the northern Aegean, the travelers' anticipation stirred. A semiautonomous theocracy, Mount Athos, or Hagion Oros, is a center of Eastern Orthodox monasticism comprising twenty monasteries set upon a dusty, splendidly rugged peninsula and housing some of the world's finest Byzantine and post-Byzantine art. Very few outsiders were allowed access to this spiritual center, but Duthuit's status as a specialist in Byzantine art with important connections in Athens had opened its doors. They dropped anchor, dressed for the visit, and eagerly awaited the arrival of the guide who was to take them ashore.

No one had dared tell Joan, however, that, for over nine hundred years, not a single woman had been permitted to set foot upon the Holy Mountain. Even female animals were banned, save chickens, whose eggs are used in the tempera paint needed for icons. The delicate task of announcing these facts fell to their guide. As feared, Joan flew into frenzied, ear-splitting rage over this denial of the opportunity to see great art solely because she was a woman, but, in the end, she had no choice but to cool her heels on the boat with the other females as the males paid their visit.

A black mood then descended upon the *Fantasia*. Joan snapped and snarled, the boat felt cramped, the drinking turned ugly. Before the voyage was out, Riopelle had clashed furiously with Duthuit, and this key player in the French art world had gathered up his wife and son and stalked off at the following port. The break was definitive.

Nonetheless, September found Jean-Paul and Joan once again yachting, now with his New York dealer Pierre Matisse (Marguerite Duthuit's half brother) and wife Patricia. A couple of weeks after the two lovers had settled at last into Frémicourt, Jean-Paul's son, Yann Fravelo-Riopelle,

Joan with her Skye terriers, Isabelle and Bertie, in her Frémicourt studio, c. 1960

was born in Brittany. Joan knew there was no pure joy, except perhaps in painting and looking: that winter, Paris was "lovely with snow — like coconut."

Always up by six or six thirty a.m., Jean-Paul would brew a pot of coffee and gulp down a cup before tearing off to his studio, while Joan slept in, having often painted most of the night. Groggy and silent when she did rise, she would sit reading, sipping from a big cup, and sending curls of cigarette smoke toward the ceiling, then rev up by walking her trio of adored Skye terriers — Idée, Isabelle, and Ibertelle (Bertie), recent gifts from Patricia Matisse.

Virtually every day the couple entertained at lunch, sometimes one or two guests, often a gang. Regulars included Sam Beckett, John Ashbery, reporter Pierre Martory, writer/critics Pierre Schneider and Patrick Waldberg, Riopelle's French dealers Jacques Dubourg and Max Clarac-Sérou, sculptors Marc Berlet and Mario Garcia, painters David Budd, Zao Wou-ki, Zuka Mitelberg, and Anne and Hugo Weber, plus a mix of clowns, musicians, Formula One racers, traveling Canadians and Americans, and assorted strays. The living room, decorated with Riopelle paintings, Jimmie Mitchell drawings, and riotous philodendra, would be buzzing by the time their host popped through the door, raising a ruckus with his robust energy and ebullient laugh. The hairy little Skyes jostled underfoot. Prepared and served by Joan's maid, Paulette, their lunches ran to beef or horse steak, mashed potatoes, and salad, washed down by copious quantities of pastis, wine, and brandy. Jean-Paul would dish up shaggy dog stories, and Joan would prove, by turns, tough and judgmental, flirty and girlish, or bald and provocative. "Eh, Coco," one might make out over the bilingual din, "you know *nothing* about painting!" If Joan found people stupid or sluggish, she'd zing them. If she was bored, she'd make trouble, sometimes with casual cruelty: "So how's your fucking mother and her fucking cancer?" she inquired of one young man who had just flown to Paris to be with his dying parent. Wont to home in on a single guest, Joan would charm out the secrets of his or her childhood, aspirations, or current feud or love affair, as she sipped pastis and reflected genuine caring in her tired brown eyes. When the spirit moved, however, she would turn around and mortify her interlocutor by broadcasting to the entire room these indiscretions from a liquor-loosened tongue. One should be completely honest, Joan insisted, there was *nothing* to be ashamed of!

After her guests departed, Joan might lend a hand to Paulette with the dishes or housework. (She was finicky about keeping ashtrays emptied, dog bowls clean, and food traps immaculate.) Or she might head for her studio to check her colors in daylight. Or sit down to write two or three of her gossipy, stream-of-consciousness letters. In that era, a transatlantic call was still an event and Joan remained cost-conscious, yet, from time to time, she would pick up the phone and natter on to New York, Chicago, or Santa Barbara. She also handled the household bills (Jean-Paul never in his life had a checkbook), plus chores like taking to the dry cleaners the suits her companion wore day in and day out. "You know the only reason I screw Rip [one of her nicknames for Riopelle]," she joked, "is because it's the way I get him to change his clothes. I put his old suit in a bag and make him wear a new one." But hand the man a fresh suit and he'd grunt, "Did you get my boots? Where are my boots!"

Rarely did the couple attend plays, concerts, films, or even art openings, except those of close friends (Riopelle detested schedules and obligations), instead devoting their evenings to the brasseries and watering holes of Montparnasse. These included the new Rosebud, an intimate rue Delambre bar where the style of New York blended with the atmosphere of Paris, a Coltrane record softly spinning as Ionesco or Truffaut sipped kir at a corner table. The Rosebud's famous chili con carne became favorite supper fare, along with the *bifteck* at the Falstaff, the seafood platters at La Coupole, and the lamb curry and omelettes *aux fines herbes* at the Closerie des Lilas. Mostly they drank.

Though the two shunned public displays of affection, their complicity and mutual happiness remained obvious. "Riopelle was very much in love with Joan, wanted her, needed her," reports one of the tribe of artists and writers with whom they partied. Sparring and teasing—as one day when she couldn't shift the gears properly in one of his sports cars—were part of the game. So too were wild, hysterical scenes. Once Joan silenced the Café de Flore by yowling, "Are you going to fuck me tonight, REM-BRANDT?" Another time she stunned the crowd at the Dôme by acting upon her annoyance when Jean-Paul started counting out bills to pay everyone's tab for the thousandth time: lunging for the cash, Joan ripped it up and hurled the bits into the air like confetti.

As time passed, Riopelle's old friend, Suzanne Viau, observed that sometimes

> [Joan] was the mean parent, sometimes [Jean-Paul] was. They lived essentially in fight-and-make-up mode. One could see their brawls as a sort of sexual dance leading up to mating. I remember one dinner. He was harassing her. She was blubbering, the box of Kleenex and everything. Then, all of a sudden, the wind shifted. In the car that was taking us home, I almost felt like one person too many. "Jean-Paul, you're such a baby," she was cooing. They had completely put it behind them.

In truth, Jean-Paul's rampant infidelities and Joan's jealousies had begun corroding their relationship. The virile artist had always had opportunities galore for sex, had always taken advantage of them, and saw no reason to change now. "Riopelle had a huge number of mistresses," remembers Marc Berlet, "really huge!" Painfully aware that there was "nothing in a skirt Riopelle didn't want," Joan appeared to know all about his affairs with other women, whether his casual trysts or his long and vital intimacy with the accomplished, intelligent, and vivacious French sculptor Roseline Granet, eleven years younger than Joan and stiff competition indeed. In her most quarrelsome cigarette-cured voice, Joan would bait Jean-Paul about Roseline until the two were sling-

ing drinks into each other's faces and, liquor fueling their fury, he was
smacking her and she was smacking back.

Other times Riopelle's displeasure about Joan and Sam Beckett pro-
pelled their brawls. His own dalliances notwithstanding, the Canadian
was determined to own Joan one hundred percent: no other man was
going to touch her. Thus all his bristles shot up at the thought of her
intimacy with the famous writer and intellectual.

Not until years later did Joan reveal, and then only to a few friends,
what many had long guessed: that she and Sam, himself an extremely private man, had been lovers. Critic Pierre Schneider puts a fine point on the
writer's feelings, noting that Beckett was "extremely taken by Joan and
petrified by a kind of admiration." (Beckett lived with pianist Suzanne
Deschevaux-Dumesnil, whom he quietly married in 1961 for legal and
financial reasons, but the two led mostly separate lives.)

In the midst of a tribal Montparnasse evening, Joan and Sam would
often disappear for two or three hours. To Joan's glee, "Rip would get
so jealous. Sam and I'd go off and we'd have our little thing, and we'd
go back to the Closerie des Lilas and Riopelle would be so upset." One
night at the Rosebud, Riopelle's verbal brickbats prompted the usually
tolerant Beckett to stand up and change tables and Mitchell to vent her
fury upon her companion. Other nights he publicly took out his anger
on her. Once the same trio had just left the Rosebud, along with John
Ashbery, when Jean-Paul seized Joan by her shirt and started slamming
her into parked cars. At least once he found dark humor in the affair.
Stopping one day to have a word with their concierge, he spotted a coffin
standing upright alongside the trash cans. The concierge's husband had
died, and the coffin had been delivered by the mortuary. The artist continued upstairs. Bounding into their apartment, he shouted, "Joan! Joan!
Beckett is waiting for you at the concierge's," whereupon she rushed
downstairs to discover only the Beckettian mise en scène.

Other incidents too proved worthy of the theater of the absurd. One
late night Beckett was hastening from Frémicourt before Riopelle returned
when, at the bottom of the stairs, he realized that the old-fashioned porte
cochère of the body shop, the only way out, was locked. So he climbed
up its iron bars but fell backward, landing in an oil pit, from which he
emerged looking very much the existentialist character. The next day his
sides ached. It turned out he'd broken a couple of ribs.

In speaking of Joan, Beckett made little distinction between the person and the painting; for Joan too, the art of this literary figure worthy of those she had known as a child played a vital role in their relationship. She had, of course, read much of his oeuvre but most deeply loved his 1959 radio playlet *Embers*.

Set on Killiney Beach on the Irish Sea—Sam's Lake Michigan—near the writer's childhood home, *Embers* weaves present with past, form with formlessness, silence with voice, music, and noise. Its sole character, Henry, conjures hallucinatory dialogues with his drowned father (who may have committed suicide) and his daughter's mother, all the while attempting to override the incessant, radio-static-like clash of the sea. (Scholar Marjorie Perloff labels *Embers* "acoustic art.") Henry also tells himself a story about a man who has summoned his doctor for obscure but hideously troubling reasons. Beckett writes, "not a sound, fire dying, white beam from window, ghastly scene, wishes to God he hadn't come, no good, fire out, bitter cold, great trouble, white world, not a sound, no good. (Pause.) No good. (Pause.)" The writer ventures no further down the road to description, a refusal Joan viewed as parallel to that of a good painter: "If something is green you know it's green, but he doesn't say it's green." The pair conceived of a limited edition of *Embers* that would marry Beckett's words with Mitchell's gouaches. She did about fifty, then decided that *Embers* was perfect without them.

Physically, their relationship was what it was. True to his pattern, the writer had to be prodded into sex. One night after he and Joan had checked into a hotel, Sam consumed his best energies in fumbling around under the bed in search of his misplaced dental bridge. Another time, at the Rosebud, he was overheard to advise her, "Stick to Riopelle, he can fuck and I can't."

As the 1950s waned, Joan's paintings had swung between thinnish-looking, levitating St. Vitus's dances of reds, greens, yellows, blues, and blacks, indebted to Pollock, on one hand, and, on the other, vigorous, fleshy fists of paint: blue blacks, greens, mustard yellows, and opaque whites with becalmed edges, or not. Now she delivered a radiant crayon box of reds, blues, oranges, olives, violets, and yellows, shooting across a distinctly horizontal canvas as if a fierce wind had ripped open one of the slab-built pictures. Then came the splendidly disorienting and panoramic *County Clare*, at once opulent and spare, its light like that preceding

March squalls. Scraps of mossy green, mongrel ochre, and white tatter its edges while tiered zones of white and dried oxblood, one ambushed by gold ochre, brew at near center. Dazzling blue-lined scud throws the eye into spatial confusion. Red skitters through. Brushed, clotted, smeared, and runneled with pigment, *County Clare* strikingly incarnates, as the artist put it, what landscape left her *with*. Her title weaves in after-the-fact associations: the Irish County Clare, the French word "*clair*" (meaning luminous, light in color, transparent, easily understood), the English romantic peasant poet John Clare, author of the melancholy "I Am."

The spring of 1960 found Joan "working like a little beaver" on her first French show for dealer Larry Rubin's Galerie Neufville that April and her first Italian show for the Galleria dell'Ariete in Milan, owned by Rubin's business partner, Beatrice Monti, in May. Once those two were behind her, she would turn her attention to her next show at the Stable, which she wanted to paint in New York. She broached, but Jean-Paul at first resisted, the idea of summering on Long Island. No sooner had he relented than their three-month sojourn ballooned into a vast, unwieldy operation enlisting their young artist friends Marc Berlet and Mario Garcia.

Berlet departed first, aboard the *Liberté*, with Joan's trio of dogs, plus a racing car fresh from Le Mans that Jean-Paul hoped to drive semiprofessionally in the States. Then Riopelle flew to Montreal to collect Yseult and Sylvie before rendezvousing with Joan and Mario in Manhattan, where Frank O'Hara and Joe LeSueur swept them back into the art world with a lavish cocktail soirée. Two or three days later, the Parisians occupied a pair of houses at Hampton Waters, Barney's Three-Mile Harbor real estate venture, where they promptly fell into familiar patterns, Jean-Paul zooming off at dawn in a red Jaguar XK convertible to his studio in Bridgehampton, Joan creeping out late mornings to breakfast on cigarettes and Bloody Marys. Over long talky lunches with Joan's old pals, the two sloshed down bucketsful of negronis. Then it would be Joan's turn to head to her studio, a nearby barn. Or she might drive into town in her borrowed '56 Buick to shop for the dinners she cooked for the kids. An attentive stepmother, she arranged for the girls to take riding and swimming lessons and once organized a day of deep-sea fishing off Montauk with Wilfred Zogbaum and his twelve-year-son Rufus in Zog's boat.

Joan, of course, knew vast numbers of people, many of whom were partying longer and harder than ever that dipsomaniacal summer. The

Zogbaums (Zog had remarried) hosted a boozy brunch, Barney threw a huge lawn party, and Bill de Kooning and his lover Ruth Kligman invited everyone, including the collectors and millionaires the scene now embraced, to a bash at their Southampton rental—only Bill himself vanished before it began. Except with Francophiles like Norm, Frank, and Zog, Jean-Paul seemed out of his element. Once, at Larry Rivers's house, as hordes of guests drunkenly laughed and screamed, he curled up on the living-room floor and fell asleep. When Joan buried herself with Mike in her studio, Jean-Paul acted out: one morning, she showed up with a black eye half concealed behind her dark glasses. Marc considered her "the Billie Holiday of Abstract Expressionist painters": "I love my man though he treats me so bad. That was Joan: masochistic." Goldberg too now drove a Bugatti, but Riopelle snapped his fingers at Mike's car: it was the *wrong kind* of Bugatti. So it went between New York and Paris: in effect, the Americans snubbed Riopelle, who spoke spotty English, did not share their formative history, and incarnated the scorned School of Paris.

Meanwhile, Joan's New York was fast changing. The morning after had dawned upon Abstract Expressionism, revealing frayed friendships and a waning feeling of family. The Cedar ruined by its own popularity, the remnants of the old crowd had migrated to the unassuming Dillon's at Twelfth Street and University Place, but it wasn't the same. Hartigan had ensconced herself in Baltimore, Pollock was dead. For the first time, leaving the city made sense to some. Why not? With the staid Eisenhower administration drawing to a close, the national mood favored new beginnings. Artists were traveling or taking visiting professorships. Bill de Kooning talked restlessly of moving to Springs.

Meanwhile, curators, critics, and art historians had begun considering the fifties retrospectively, collectively borrowing a phrase from the Jewish Museum's 1957 New York School: Second Generation exhibition to label the work of Joan Mitchell, Helen Frankenthaler, Grace Hartigan, Alfred Leslie, Michael Goldberg, Norman Bluhm, Jane Freilicher, Larry Rivers, and others "second generation Abstract Expressionist." Informed by Greenbergian logic, according to which painting has the historical purpose of advancing modernism toward formal purity, the term not only adverts to the American shibboleth of progress but also assumes a homogeneous convention-shattering "first generation."

Not alone in hotly contesting such premises, Joan rejected, first, the concept of a first-generation breakthrough, pointing out that World War II had churned up everything, painting included. Moreover, she insisted that the artists' lived experience had had absolutely nothing to do with generations. Everyone, whether age twenty or sixty, had been painting at the same time. Everyone, whether age twenty or sixty, had been making the same revolution. Besides, the art world inconsistently applied labels "first" and "second," not to mention that "Abstract Expressionism" itself remained a misnomer, New York School painting having to do with attitude and place, not style. Wrong, countered its detractors, it had degenerated into stale imitable manner.

The decline of Abstract Expressionism coincided with the rise of Color Field painting and Pop Art. In 1961, Andy Warhol would paint Campbell's Soup cans, Roy Lichtenstein depict, comic-strip style, a girl holding a beach ball over her head, and Claes Oldenburg rent an East Second Street storefront where he sold crude painted plaster models of consumer goods. The following year, the prestigious Sidney Janis Gallery pushed New York School painting offstage to bring Pop front and center with New Realists, an exhibition that conjoined French Nouveaux Réalistes with new American Pop stars including Lichtenstein, Warhol, Robert Indiana, Wayne Thiebaud, and George Segal. In response, Philip Guston, Robert Motherwell, Mark Rothko, and Adolph Gottlieb severed their affiliations with Janis. Marketed as part of the same consumer culture that was its subject, Pop Art was about to explode into an unprecedented frenzy of collecting, dealing, showing, publishing, and self-promoting.

Joan detested not only isms but also the idea that one kind of art had to wipe out another. (Rather than raze Impressionism, *ArtNews* editor Tom Hess reminded his readers, Cézanne had used it as a point of departure. And Willem de Kooning had long proceeded by reinventing European art.) In truth, Joan could not abide Pop Art—"all money and no cathedral"—because of its passionlessness, superficiality, indifference to paint as such, and glorification of the mass culture she ignored. In contrast, she respected the complex, cerebral work of Jasper Johns: at Bill Berkson's 1961 Christmas party, the two would meet and together dance the twist (while Helen Frankenthaler and her husband, Robert Motherwell, she cattily reported to Mike, sat primly on a sofa).

In the new culture of irony, the emotional sincerity of Joan Mitchell, unreconstructed New York School painter, felt old-fashioned and slightly embarrassing. By continuing to pursue what she called "visual painting," some thought, Joan was trying to stay at the party after the lights had come on. She began spouting the phrase "pop art, op art, slop art, and flop art." She practiced, she said, "slop and flop."

Yet her art remained limber and fresh. Inextricable from her authentic self, "visual painting" was almost a neurobiological need: to work in any other manner would amount to opportunistic dishonesty. While not unaware of her ego involvement in a successful career or of her options for painting saleable work, Joan militantly refused to follow trends in order to get shows. (Luckily she had the financial means to do so.) For this hard-nosed closet Romantic, the visionary energy and unbridled joy that stemmed from truth to oneself and intimacy with nature and paint put to shame the politics of art.

Although Joan sank from view in New York as much because she had moved to Paris as because Pop Art held sway, she started talking of having been kicked out of the art world. By and large, her reviews continued positive, but there were far fewer of them, and far fewer shows. Deprived of institutional and critical support, she undertook a kind of high-wire act without the crowd—continuing to hold herself to the standard of art of the highest intensity, greatest risk, and loftiest ambition.

Though privately bitter, she would rather die than complain. One rose above it, waited it out. The full truth be told, the romantic in her at times enjoyed the role of neglected, misunderstood artist, and the realist got by on the thought that nothing worse could happen to her career. "There'll always be painters around," she once assured John Ashbery, meaning "real painters." "It'll take more than Pop or Op to discourage them—they've never been encouraged anyway. So we're back where we started from."

Back in Manhattan that November following her summer on Long Island, Joan made her first professional foray into printmaking at Tibor Press, which was producing a four-volume boxed-set limited-edition book based in collaborations between New York School poets and painters.

Paired with Ashbery (the others were O'Hara/Goldberg, Schuyler/Hartigan, and Koch/Leslie), she proceeded from the feelings aroused in her by Ashbery's *The Poems,* which shared with her painting a direct absorbing of the world without perspective or logic. Using crayon, she worked directly on silkscreen, then, wanting crisp as well as fuzzy edges,

With poet John Ashbery, 1963

turned to tusche, an inky liquid, for which she fashioned a brush from a broken wooden tongue depressor. She proceeded to apply the tusche to Mylar, from which her imagery was transferred photographically. The collaboration proved fun, the result a modest artistic triumph.

Meanwhile her oils continued to evince Joan's total involvement in the act of painting: complex and alive, they could not be more different from cool, hard-edged Pop. Take that, Pop Art! Joan seems to say. And that! This is what real painting looks like. ("To paint," she once declared, "is to know how to resist paint.") As delectable as they are raw, her paintings court chaos with their sweeps of disrupted syntax, surpassing the viewer's ability to process them in a conscious way. Deep greens, orange reds or persimmons, and cerulean blues—colors she used over and over again—well up into patchy cumuli suspended in thinned whitish washes agitated by wisps, Xs, tattings, and cascading drips of pigment. Everything about these luscious chromatic canvases speaks of the artist's all-consuming lover's quarrel with oils. Paint meets canvas in every conceivable manner: slathered, swiped, dry-brushed, splattered, dribbled, wiped with rags into filminess, smeared with fingers, slapped from a brush, smashed from the tube, affixed like a wad of gum—a glorious visual glossolalia.

The following March, Riopelle took possession of the *Serica* as payment from Pierre Matisse. A forty-seven-foot Bermuda cutter of Sparkman Stephens design, this superbly crafted yacht boasted a wooden hull, teak deck, and mahogany interior. Having berthed it near Cannes, the artist then rented La Bergerie, a villa with servants in a wealthy enclave at Cap d'Antibes where he and Joan

Joan and "Rip"—crazy about each other! c. 1963

spent the summer with Yseult and Sylvie, who arrived from Canada that June. After the girls left, three months later, and summer stretched into autumn and winter, the couple kept the house and continued to spend a great deal of time in the Midi. Joan wrote her mother,

> Everything is closed and the sea quite nice and bleak. When it rains, which it's not supposed to do, I wear a hat, because my studio leaks, and a yellow macintosh. At noon we still eat on the terrace in the winter sun—at night t.v.—and innumerable books on the sea. We're cleaning the hull on the boat—endless job—changing some of the interior which is rather fun—like a jigsaw puzzle—everything has to fit and be useful—J.P.'s idea (vague but real) is to sail across the Atlantic—season for it is Dec. to May . . . would take about 21 days from Gibraltar. Perhaps if we plan it enough we won't really have to do it.

They never crossed the Atlantic, but they did devote weeks and months to plying the Mediterranean and the Adriatic. While Joan had always equated sailing with sunbathing at sea, Jean-Paul loved packing on speed and sweeping along, spinnaker bulging and porpoises chasing behind. Once the pair and their two-man crew fell fortune to three days of weather so heavy they had to don safety harnesses to change the sails, and they expected the mast to snap at any moment. Jean-Paul was in heaven, but Joan panicked and, for once, couldn't get even the cognac down. In truth, she didn't much like sailing. Nerves often sent her below, where she shut herself up and read mysteries. Still, she loved the elasticity of time at sea, the boat's indifference to its passengers, and the sensation of lying open—sun drenched, rain pummeled, storm flailed, moon bathed—to water and sky in their every light, color, and mood.

And, resolved to share her man's passions, she threw herself into sailing, going so far as to take short trips alone with René, the sailor they hired on retainer, in order to hone her skills. (Her determination to make the relationship work also led to crouching behind bales of hay as Jean-Paul whooshed by in his homebuilt racer *Gueule de Bois,* taking skiing lessons in the French Alps, repeatedly enduring the Twenty-four Hours of Le Mans, going duck and pheasant hunting, and once skinning, butchering, and marinating a wild boar her companion had shot.) When the two were happy, as by all appearances they were in Cap d'Antibes, they were intensely happy. But they spoke different languages: she'd say, "Look!" and he'd say, "Let's go!"

In terms of exposure and sales, the very early 1960s were good times for Joan Mitchell's career. Besides her April 1961 show at the Stable, now on East Seventy-third Street, and a cover story in November's *ArtNews* featuring the billowing *Skyes* (the occasion was her ten-year retrospective at the gallery of Southern Illinois University), Joan had her first solo show in Chicago and first solo show on the West Coast. Between July 1, 1960, and December 31, 1962, Eleanor Ward rang up $42,968 in Mitchell sales, of which Joan earned $32,358. But these numbers reflect the catching up of middle-class, corporate, and provincial tastes, as opposed to any growing interest in New York.

In the spring of 1962, the Galerie Dubourg on the Right Bank and the Galerie Lawrence on the Left jointly exhibited Joan's recent paintings. Pierre Schneider wrote a beautiful essay, Jean-Paul worked on the installations, and a crowd of Joan's friends, including Barney, Zuka, Paul, Mike, Beckett, Norm, her sister Sally, and her brother-in-law Newt, turned out for her opening and celebratory dinner. "The gay gigglers sat at one end [of the long table], the egocentric nonsmilers sat at the other, and Joan [pretty in a new blue suit] and Dubourg sat in the middle," Sally

Barney Rosset and Samuel Beckett arrive at one of Joan's shows in Paris, early 1960s.

reported to their mother. Dubourg not only sold out but also laid big plans for future shows. He was old, however, and, in any case, more hail fellow than effective dealer. Nor was the Galerie Dubourg, upstairs in a commercial building, anything spectacular. When his projects came to naught, Joan understood. But when Galerie Lawrence dropped her, she got hopping mad. Its owner, Larry Rubin, had promised to buy $10,000 worth of work annually, an arrangement that lasted one year. Then, as Joan put it, Rubin "kicked me out" on the advice of his new art adviser, critic Clement Greenberg: "Get rid of that gestural horror." Critics were bottom-feeders, in Joan's opinion, and the condescending Greenberg's role in steering galleries and collectors away from her work never ceased to make her blood boil, though she was cagey about when and where she said so. Publicly, she was elliptical or mute; privately, she filleted the still-powerful critic.

Explosive, radiant, and atomized, as delicate and wild as sea spray, the paintings Joan was showing—including *Couscous, Bonhomme de Bois, Frémicourt,* and the panoramic *Grandes Carrières*—shuttled between New York swagger and European pastoralism. Pigment flying upward and outward, the artist had snarled up browns, dark greens, blues, viridians, and, most strikingly, pink corals, roses, and orchids, amid whites helter-skelter with flecks and veiled cascades of drips. Indebted to Bach (whose music she had been playing almost exclusively as she worked) and to memories of feelings stirred by furious tides, inconstant skies, tender meetings of water and light, the paintings recall Rilke's lines in "Bowl of Roses":

> to transform the world
> with its wind and rain and springtime's patience
> and guilt and restlessness and obscure fate
> and the darkness of evening earth and even
> the changing clouds, coming and going,
> even the vague intercession of distant stars,
> into a handful of inner life.

Frenzied and luxuriant filigrees of pinks and greens pulled to the edge of chaos, the paintings of the early 1960s admit a distinctly European color sensibility and sense of beauty also reminiscent of the rapturous late seascapes of British Romantic painter J. M. W. Turner. Critic Holland Cotter sees in them eighteenth-century French Rococo painter Fragonard's "vistas of billowing trees and clouds, and their vignettes of amorous pursuit and encounter [blown by Mitchell]—ecstatically, furiously and repeatedly—to smithereens." And Pierre Schneider evokes "Titian in the way in which [Mitchell's] brush was able to do anything with utter naturalness. The moments when everything falls into place are incredible. Panic, chaos, and anguish overcome. They are sacred moments." In his catalog essay for the painter's 1962 show, Schneider also pronounces a Mitchell canvas "the story of Daphne"—the Greek nymph pursued by Apollo—"a being seized by panic, gasping for breath ... who at the moment her strength fails escapes by transforming herself into a tree."

In Golfe-Juan (where Jean-Paul now berthed the *Serica*) a few days after her opening, Joan received a telegram announcing the death of Franz Kline. Afflicted with a rheumatic heart, Kline had suffered a series of heart attacks, the last one fatal. Deeply shaken by the loss of this exemplary artist and generous spirit who personified *her* New York, Joan arranged for delivery of a big bouquet of black and white tulips for his memorial service. Then the *Serica* weighed anchor for Venice via Corsica and soon hurtled into a squall. Thunder crashed, the boat leaked, Joan was petrified. But she reassured herself: "Well, there's Kline upstairs mixing drinks."

On May 23, the day New York artists gathered to pay tribute to the beloved painter on what would have been his fifty-second birthday, Joan was in Corsica. Later she flew to Venice, joining Riopelle, who had sailed around Italy with friends. He was widely favored to win the top prize for painting at that year's Venice Biennale, and Giacometti, the top prize for sculpture. Surrounded by friends, they had a blast in Venice — where swarms of dealers, collectors, reporters, and artists sipped Bellinis at Harry's Bar and compulsively snapped pictures of each other on gondolas — though Joan responded less to the art than to the watery city with its fabulous colors. Giacometti indeed won the top sculpture prize, but the judges passed over Riopelle for the top painting prize, awarding him instead, along with a Danish painter, the UNESCO Prize, de facto second place. Disappointment briefly clouded the Riopelle camp, yet his (and Giacometti's) dealer, Pierre Matisse, who had joined them in Venice, remained loyal and supportive, and Riopelle himself appeared to shrug off the loss.

With or without the Venice prize, he cut a wide swath. In 1963 he became the youngest artist ever to have a retrospective at the National Gallery in Ottawa (the exhibition then traveled to Montreal, Toronto, and Washington, D.C.), and he won a major commission for Toronto's Pearson Airport. Canada's pride in its international art star helped drive his career, but his market-hardy work also sold briskly to individuals at splashy gallery shows in Montreal, London, Paris, New York, and Lausanne. Joan, on the other hand, did not have a single solo exhibition in 1963. Nor in 1964. She would finish her paintings, let them dry, roll them up, and store them in a little alcove above the kitchen.

After the Biennale, Jean-Paul, Joan, Yseult, Sylvie, and several friends sailed the Yugoslav coast alongside Pierre and Patricia Matisse on their yacht *Old Fox*. A cool eminence in the international art world, Pierre reigned over an elegant Fifty-seventh Street gallery that represented leading European modernists of the highest stature, including Giacometti, Miró, Balthus, Dubuffet, Chagall, Tanguy, and Pierre's father, Henri Matisse. Painter Loren MacIver was one of the few women and few Americans in his stable. Matisse took a long view of his artists, ignoring the vicissitudes of the market as he shaped their careers.

The gallerist was married to the wealthy ex of painter Roberto Matta, Patricia Kane Matisse, a "little monster" who took seriously only what she felt like taking seriously and was forever trading barbed remarks with Joan in what the artist elliptically called "a special relationship." Meanwhile Joan was busy laying siege to Pierre because—stoic as she was about not getting shows, scornful as she was of artists who slavered with ambition, adamant as she was that *never* would she share a dealer with Riopelle—she wanted in the worst way to be represented by Matisse's classy gallery based in art values, not money or trends. She made passes at Pierre, she did (in Marc Berlet's words) "terrible things" to try to persuade him to represent her. But Pierre, who couldn't see the power of her work, was "like a stone."

Joan found herself in the role of artist-wife of a Great Artist, a role not unlike those once played by Lee Krasner vis-à-vis Jackson Pollock or Elaine de Kooning vis-à-vis Willem de Kooning. (People assumed Joan and Jean-Paul were married.) Certainly, she had easy access to all the major players, yet socializing with the powerful rarely translated into professional advantage. For one thing, France was acutely sexist (less than twenty percent of Paris exhibitions presented work by women, and only twelve percent of the work in French national collections was by women), and the international art set, mostly male, automatically put Joan as artist in a backseat to Joan as wife. When renowned Canadian photographer Yousuf Karsh arrived to make a portrait of Riopelle as part of a series of major figures in the arts, he posed Jean-Paul in her studio, but no one brought up the idea of a portrait of Mitchell. Her job was to entertain the photographer and his wife. And, for years, Joan played hostess to "dear old Gimpel"—Peter Gimpel, Jean-Paul's London dealer from Gimpel and Sons—during which time Gimpel purchased a total of five small Mitchells, more or less as a courtesy. (In the end, he did offer Joan a show, which never occurred, probably due to scheduling conflicts.)

If Jean-Paul and Joan competed, they also nurtured each other, helping to plan each other's shows and giving thoughtful advice on materials, contracts, prices, and art politics. Nonetheless, the relationship was asymmetrical: with his career sailing high and hers limping along, it cost him little to help her. At art events where he was hounded by admirers, she would sit smoking, sipping white wine, and chatting. Remembering the Mount Athos episode, she acidulously labeled herself and her own artist friends "just us chickens"—as opposed to "the big rooster," Rip.

Yet she yearned for things to be right between them, and at times, they were. "J.P. is sweetie pie and almost divorced," she cheerfully informed Eleanor Ward that spring, "and sometimes there are whole days when I don't drink at all." Five months later, however, Frank O'Hara and Bill Berkson, visiting Paris, found Joan in a different frame of mind: "I think the happiest days of my life were when I was going to a chiropractor," she told them. "Isn't that the most depressing thing you've ever heard?"

With Jimmie's health failing, Joan had begun traveling to Chicago twice a year. Bound to a wheelchair and oxygen tank in the end, her father died of a heart ailment in January 1963, but not before having praised Joan as "gay, amusing, intelligent, and . . . fully aware of all that is going on worldwide," and thanked her profusely, particularly for all she had done for her aging parents: "you should feel your scapulae each night to detect the first sprouting of wings." He singled out Joan's efforts in 1960, when Marion had been diagnosed with mastoid and brain cancer, and Joan had flown to her side.

From Paris, Joan now mentally followed Marion's medical appointments and treatments, calculating the right times to phone for news. During trips to Chicago, she took the parental role, accompanying her mother to Billings Hospital for her cobalt radiation treatments, comforting her when she wept after they sold her old Chevrolet, and delighting in Marion's girlish pleasure when Joan did Christmas, down to stockings and a tree, as Marion always had when she and Sally were small. (Except for that one long-ago winter with Barney in Paris, Joan had never missed a Christmas in Chicago.) Marion's fragility, isolation, and courage broke Joan's heart, and, because of her open distress, Joan seemed to her Chicago friends more human than before.

The home of her School of the Art Institute classmate, painter Ellen Lanyon, and her husband and fellow painter Roland Ginzel, served as a place to unwind. Joan would show up toting her own bottle of bourbon or Scotch and hang around until her hosts "sort of shoveled her out of the couch" and drove her home. At their New Year's Eve party one year, she drank vast amounts of highly potent punch, as did Dennis Adrian, critic for the *Chicago Daily News* and acid wit of the art community. Artist and critic got into a huge argument, and, to everyone's horrified fascination, Joan "took [Adrian] out . . . absolutely took him out." At another party, at the Lake Shore Drive apartment of Mitchell collectors

With "genius Frank" O'Hara at Frémicourt, c. 1960

Congressman Sidney Yates and his wife Addie, Joan ran into printmaker June Wayne (Addie's cousin), and the two discussed the (never realized) possibility of Joan working at Wayne's Tamarind Lithography Workshop in Los Angeles. Still another time, perhaps in 1963, Joan accompanied dealer Bud Holland, whose Holland-Goldowsky Gallery had shown her in 1961, to the home of collectors Muriel and Albert Newman, she trained as an artist and he (according to what Joan wrote Mike) a businessman who "(supposedly . . . made his millions on rubbers and Negro hair straighteners). Well—Picasso—Leger etc. You couldn't see the forest for the trees and all he talked about was money money money—oh nausee—ick."

That same Christmas, Joan flew from Chicago to Santa Barbara, where she stayed at the beachfront home of Newt and Sally, a voracious reader, accomplished sportswoman, civic activist with a flair for filing and winning lawsuits, and overbearing mother to sixteen-year-old Sally (called Poondie), fourteen-year-old Newt, and twelve-year-old Mitch. Joan took marvelous walks with Sally's dachshunds on Butterfly Beach, and the two sisters, who loved and hated each other, stayed up all hours, smoking, drinking, "shooting the shit," and chewing over the matter of parenting.

Riopelle's daughters, Yseult and Sylvie, had continued to travel to France for each summer vacation, at the approach of which Joan invariably wrestled with mixed feelings. A devoted stepmother, she gave a lot but also demanded a lot. She had grown particularly close to shy fourteen-year-old Sylvie, who played Joan to Yseult's Sally: Sylvie wrote poetry, earned good grades, demonstrated a certain intellectual curiosity, and played a decent game of bridge. Now Yseult, a pretty and very social fifteen-year-old who did her father proud on the *Serica* and ski slopes and asserted her independence by getting into trouble at school, had moved to Paris full-time. At first the teenager had

Joan accompanies her cancer-stricken mother to Billings Hospital in Chicago, c. 1965.

slept in their living room (only steps and a swinging door away from Joan's studio), but eventually they rented for her an apartment downstairs in their building.

Not only Yseult and her friends, but whole armies trooped in and out of Frémicourt, which meant that Joan had precious little privacy in her studio, and, given the vicissitudes of life with Rip, little studio time, period. She had decided not to try to work in the summer, when the household decamped to Golfe-Juan. Back in Paris in September, she would pick up her brushes at last and knock out "very violent and angry paintings."

That summer, and the two that followed, they were joined in Golfe-Juan by fifteen-year-old Rufus Zogbaum, the son of Zog and his ex-wife Betsy, who had been the companion of Franz Kline during the painter's last years. Still grappling with Franz's death, along with the usual problems of adolescence, Rufus found Joan and Jean-Paul, especially Joan, kind and giving in unconventional ways. And he marveled at their talent for beguiling the moment: Jean-Paul tooled around the Côte d'Azur in a magical gold Bugatti with a wooden steering wheel, and the two more or less lived at Chez Margot, a port bistro in Golfe-Juan whose

Joan and Jean-Paul in their living room at Frémicourt, c. 1963

patronne kept their mail and rented them a furnished room near the harbor. They trailed a retinue of children, dogs, domestics, and sailors and their families, plus a bevy of friends—Anglo-Irish painter Anne Madden and her husband painter Louis le Brocquy, May and Zao Wou-ki, composer Earle Brown, mechanic Elie Philippot and his wife Françoise, Pierre and Patricia Matisse—and visitors including Irving and Lucy Sandler, Marion's doctor from Chicago, and the Rolls-driving heir to the Pepperidge Farm fortune. They all schmoozed over drinks *sur la terrasse* at Chez Margot or around the long table aboard the *Serica*, amid a clutter of cameras, playing cards, and packs of Marlboros and Gauloises.

Once they drove up to Vence, where Pierre Matisse gave them a private tour of the exquisite chapel decorated by Henri Matisse with its intensely yellow, green, and blue stained glass windows. Joan was profoundly moved. Another time they rendezvoused at sea with the yacht of millionaire financier and Riopelle collector Joseph Hirshhorn and his bride, Olga. Sometimes they stayed at the Hirshhorns' villa in Cap d'Antibes, where, during long, idyllic days of swimming, eating, and chatting, Joan tutored Olga in French and was "so nice" to her in a dozen other ways. Both Olga and Joe not only grew immensely fond of Joan

The gang at Chez Margot: Joan, Patricia Matisse, Chan May Kan, Jean-Paul, and Zao Wou-ki, c. 1963

but also fell in love with her paintings, of which Joe purchased more than a dozen for the collection that would anchor the Hirshhorn Museum in Washington, D.C. Hirshhorn gave Riopelle the artistic respect he was due, but Mitchell! — "one of the great artists, one of the greatest artists in the world."

VÉTHEUIL

Quis hic locus, quae regio, quae mundi plaga?

T. S. ELIOT's epigraph for "Marina,"
quoting Seneca

CHAPTER TWELVE La Tour

With Yseult away at dance school and Jean-Paul shuttling back and forth to Paris, where he was casting bronzes, Joan, Sylvie, and Rufus held down the camp in Golfe-Juan during the summer of 1965. Joan wrote often to Mike. The two had drifted apart, then grown closer in the aftermath of Mike's latest troubles: he had lifted several drawings from Bill de Kooning's studio, forged the artist's signature, and sold them. After the fraud was discovered, de Kooning took steps to prosecute, but Mike's wife, Patsy, helped deter the older artist by repurchasing the drawings, raising the cash to do so by selling her own Pollock and Kline. After much string pulling and negotiating, Mike wound up at the Psychiatric Institute of the Columbia-Presbyterian Medical Center, where he would remain for eighteen months while psychiatrists attempted to "graft a conscience onto him." Patsy had initiated a divorce. At first furious with Mike, Joan later rallied to his side, reportedly rounding out the amount Patsy had put together to buy back the de Koonings.

Joan's letters to Mike reel off the details of her days. Back in Paris, she and her stepdaughter Sylvie had attended the opening of an exhibition of American sculpture at the Rodin Museum, where New York Museum of Modern Art director René d'Harnoncourt had bought them drinks. Two days later, the pair had flown to Nice with the dogs in crates and Sylvie's pet hamster nibbling lettuce on her tray table. Sylvie was supposed to lose thirty-five pounds before returning to Canada, so Joan had tracked down a Parisian specialist who prescribed appetite suppressants and ordered the weighing of "every pea and radish" the teenager consumed. To help her along, Joan was following the same Spartan diet. Already lean, the artist now looked emaciated.

Of her routine with Sylvie and Rufus, who'd driven down with Jean-Paul, Joan reported,

> My life is strictly them. Not much time to brood. Sometimes I wonder what's it all about—life—that is—the children wax very philosophic—sweet and intelligent—ah youth. So my day—dog walk—provisions for boat—sail—eat at sea—swim—return 8:30ish—wash boat—dog walk—eat—play bridge—sleep. Can't get into much trouble that way. I have developed enormous patience however and I do prefer being alone to seeing lots of devastating people or destructive or time-consuming or boring. (I do like people though.) . . . Rufus and Sylvie intensely ask me advice—O I feel tired . . .
>
> Painting isn't so different either. Well—it takes guts I guess to see "anything through" as H. James would say, even if you don't know what or why you're seeing it through like why put red on or why not . . . I need some time to get at my feelings for painting. My dreams are what all little girls' dreams are made of. My real sadnesses are you and my Mother—I miss you very very very much.

After a two- or three-day sail with Rip and the teenagers, she took up her pen once again:

> I can't go whipping back up [to Paris] . . . much as I would like to do some work. However, in the long run I've learned I'm better not doing it at all than in a half-assed fashion which fills me with anxiety and anger—and I have no place to work. We arrived about 4 am—and

I sat staring at that quay—the light was fabulous—and the black rubber tires under the quay looked like something Motherwell should have seen . . . also there was a mad rock that Rufus took photographs of—little bits of ideas—strange light.

Memories of her feelings about that stony outcropping viewed in dawn light would spawn the hermetic bioluminescent *Rufus' Rock Mistral* and, several months later, *Rufus's Rock.*

From the south of France, Italy, Sardinia, and Corsica, other mental landscapes accumulated. Seduced by Corsica, which they compared to the old, unspoiled Riviera, Joan and Jean-Paul loved to sail, usually with a gang of friends, the stunning and complicated coasts of Cap Corse and the western side of the island, dropping anchor in deep-sheltered inlets where they swam amid shimmying seaweed. Rugged red granite cliffs threw oddly shaped shadows over the water. Beyond the cliffs' edges stretched olive groves and rough, sweet-smelling carpets of maquis (rosemary, myrtle, laurel, butcher's broom) and, beyond that, cypress, beech, and mountain pine forests. As the light softened, the pleasure-seekers would watch the sun set, sip *vin du pays,* and feast on the sea urchins they had gathered or on fresh lobster purchased from peddlers right on the beach. Often the *Serica* weighed anchor in the harbor of the fortress-village of Algajola in Calvi, teeming with legionnaires; or near the splendid, wooded Girolata, "a magical, unviolated spot" inaccessible except by boat or on foot. The paintings of the devouring-eyed Joan were now mostly "[coming] out of trees," as she put it. Perhaps she was picturing one in Corsica when she told John Ashbery, "I'm trying to remember what I felt about a certain cypress tree and I feel if I remember it, it will last me quite a long time."

Joan's paintings of the mid-sixties oppose scruffy, atmospheric whitish areas to hovering clumps of thalo greens, dusty silver greens, mossy greens, and shiny juniper greens, complicated by rusts, cerulean blues, and red violets. Emphatically tactile, they evoke dusk-strangled terrains where light sensuously clings to a green, liquefies a blue, untarnishes a silver. The whole weight of some paintings hangs to one side. Edges are complicated. Here and there heavy bright whites sidle up to greens or blues as if to infringe upon them, yet, for once in Joan's work, the relationship between figure and ground feels unambivalent. On the other hand, whether scabrous or milk thin, her paint never stops metamorphosing from landscape to pigment to landscape again. Large yet less athletic, less expansive, than what came before, the work at times feels elegiac.

What is "the difference between, say, Joan Mitchell's kind of painting and a very loose kind of landscape painting?" Ashbery asks in his 1965 feature story on Joan for *ArtNews*. Depending on the situation, he continues, "one's feelings about nature are at different removes from it": apprehending one's feelings may demand semi-recognizable form or, in contrast, "abstracted impressions." He cites the artist: "I'm trying for something more specific than movies of my everyday life: To define a feeling."

Yet Joan's labeling of works like *Calvi* and *First Cypress* her "black paintings" appears to sanction viewers' tendency to read abstract art in terms of biography. (In fact, there's no black in them, but where thalo green is thickly applied, they look black.) Some people assumed that her dejection over her father's death and her mother's illness explained Joan's use of dark colors. Absolutely not! the artist rejoined. First of all, she strenuously objected to the pathetic fallacy by which black equals sad and yellow equals happy (even though color-emotion synesthesia led her to experience loneliness, for instance, as dark green and to declare, of one work, "It's a yellow painting. There's hope."). Second, believing that to wallow in paint would be unprofessional and self-indulgent, she agreed with Bill de Kooning that, whatever an artist's personal problems, his or her job is to make a good picture. Moreover, she took as an article of faith that one should not timidly try to stay within one's reputation. Pushing herself as a painter, she demonstrated her emotional as well as her formal range.

Some dismissed the "black paintings" as dismal. On the other hand, when *New York Times* critic Stuart Preston reviewed Joan's show at the Stable in April 1965, he swooned a little over the "violent contrasts of dark and light" and "intricate webs of trickling color" that "Mitchell continues to nail . . . to the abstract expressionist mast." Preston wasn't alone. At Joan's opening, landscape painter John Button found himself "covered with goose-flesh—so thrilled and moved that I couldn't participate in the usual 'socializing' . . . those large, scribbled, green-black places are noble and tragic and cool. When an artist uses color that way . . . it is almost too much."

Two years later, Parisian gallerist Jean Fournier would exhibit other "black paintings." Raised in the country, Fournier once responded to a question about Joan's work with the metaphor of a bird building a nest: "A bird works so hard. Bits of hair, cotton threads, and straw are woven into something solid in this work vital to the life and death of birds. The painter too works with what he has at hand, what he has in his heart."

That September Mike heard more from Joan, now back in Paris:

> Well—about me—I'm okay . . . big shows offered in Basel—Zurich and Germany. [None of these materialized.] . . . Hard painting—made a few I like—smallish and thick—harder to make a dark center—don't know where I'm going at all—but have to put in the hours—do love painting still—fuck it—and do love you too, but the painting sometimes bores me and sometimes kills me—and "man"—I guess it has to be "felt" and when I don't feel, it's zero—seems to me "I've sung this song before."
>
> J.P. is being very nice—Well—I'll play it by ear—but life is looking up—and it's a lovely day—the kind to put on my old leather coat—I still have it—and walk to Horatio Street. I never will kick the past, so I might as well indulge in it from time to time.

Joan's measured tone belies the combustibility of life at Frémicourt, where it was not unusual for visitors to find dishes smashed, paintings slashed, tables and chairs overturned, the couple crabby and hung over. There were still sweet moments, yet, night after night, Joan and Jean-Paul would get "so fucking drunk," then bully and beat each other up and turn every scene ugly. Friends got sucked into their dramas. To go out with the pair, one had to be "tough-skinned because it was always, always disaster," remembers Zuka of the midnight rampages through Montparnasse that inevitably ended in four a.m. train wrecks. One early morning, as Zuka's husband Louis dashed from their apartment to buy bread, he nearly tripped over Joan, who was curled up asleep on their doormat. Another time, Joan wildly pounded on the Mitelbergs' door in the dead of night. When Zuka opened, Jean-Paul, in hot pursuit, rushed up, shoved his companion against the doorjamb, and started slamming the door onto her: "They were violent. They were just crazy!"

"Angel child," Joan wrote Mike a few days later, following a brief but dreadful excursion at sea,

I miss you—forgive my silence—my life has been shitty shitty and I haven't felt like writing about it—haven't even written my Mother— "Divorce" or whatever it's called has been imminent—still is I guess—I'm playing it by ear . . . the sailing trip was ghastly—Well—I don't think I'll ever have to do that again. And now there are no children, which is odd, and the maid's on vacation and [the dog] Isabelle is in heat so [the other dog] Berty's in the bathroom crying and I'm trying hopelessly to paint and of course it ain't what I want and I'm certainly in the dark as to what it is I want or feel.

At Calvi one late night, a month or two earlier, a roaring-drunk Riopelle had stormed aboard the *Serica* where Joan awaited, and a memorably nasty battle erupted. The next day she had flown back to Paris with every intention of leaving him and France. But she hadn't. For one thing, she still loved him. For another, he served as psychological ballast: to leap at his throat was at least to exist, to rage at him was to get traction in her art, not that life with Rip left her much time to paint. The thought of finding herself alone terrified Joan. But their sex life reportedly ended.

If Riopelle was (in Marc Berlet's words) "absolutely resentful, couldn't let go of certain things," neither could Joan, who yelled about his mistresses and taunted him about wanting sex with even his daughter Yseult. Joan gave as good as she got: when Rip had a fling with painter Anne Weber, Joan seduced Anne's husband, artist Hugo Weber. (It did not escape her attention that Anne was gorgeous and that she, tired looking and rail thin, was not aging well.) She also slept with eccentric painter, sculptor, filmmaker, and author of erotic novels Norman Rubington, who, using the nom de plume Akbar del Piombo, was doing illustrations for Grove Press. And after her old lover Tim Osato, now a major, moved to Paris to take a position at the prestigious École Supérieure de Guerre, the two resumed their on-again, off-again romance. Once Joan took Tim's daughter, Teru, dress shopping, as if, Teru thought, "compensating for something."

While Joan's loyalty to painting, the fullest expression, she felt, of what it meant to be alive, remained absolute and her self-demand extraordinary, the time and privacy painting demanded continued to elude her. Frustrated and furious over the impossibility of erecting a wall of privacy around her studio, which she'd always thought of as almost sacred space, she lived under siege and considered renting another apartment for herself. Often she phoned Zuka to rant about "how lousy she felt and everything was shit and everything was awful." At times she tried to put aside all but the concrete and the particular, as when she titled one painting *My Plant, My Other Plant*.

The need to stake out her own territory may have played a role too in Joan's acceptance of an invitation to the inauguration of President Lyndon B. Johnson as one of fifty representatives of American arts and letters. In Washington (where she traveled via Chicago and New York) that January, she rubbed elbows with Anne Bancroft, Saul Bellow, Alvin Ailey, Mark Rothko, Edward Albee, George Balanchine, Harper Lee, Jasper Johns, John Updike, and the Mitchells' old family friends, poets Archibald MacLeish, Richard Wilbur, and W. D. Snodgrass. At the inaugural ceremony, she sat next to sixty-year-old New Mexican artist Peter Hurd and was charmed. (Two years later, presidential curator James R. Ketchum hung a Mitchell oil in the Johnson White House.)

Middle age — Joan stood at the threshold of forty — brought a series of losses, a struggle against a sense of narrowing possibilities, and an even more acute awareness of mortality. "I'm trying hard to be *efficace* and some years it's uphill all the way — fuck death," she wrote Mike. First Wilfred Zogbaum, dear old Zog, succumbed to leukemia. Then Giacometti died. Although Joan had not been particularly close to the Swiss artist, she and Riopelle saw him often (Giacometti liked her head, she told friends), and she deeply respected his probity and existential indifference to domestic comfort and material well-being. (In this regard, Giacometti and Riopelle, that lover of expensive toys, were diametrically opposed.) She respected too the fact that Giacometti had set a Sisyphean task for himself: to seek visual truth, to get it down right. At the time of his death, he had been completing *Paris Sans Fin*, a deluxe limited-edition book of 150 lithographs from drawings made in the streets, cafés, studios, and apartments their coterie frequented. Her copy of *Paris Sans Fin* became one of Joan's most cherished possessions.

July 1966 brought devastating news of Frank O'Hara's death. One late night during a weekend at Fire Island, Frank had been riding a jeep beach taxi when the vehicle lost a tire. As passengers awaited a backup, he had wandered off and been struck by another taxi. A day and a half later he died, at age forty, of internal injuries. Everyone had loved Frank: as Larry Rivers famously said at the funeral, "at least sixty people in New York . . . thought Frank O'Hara was their best friend." Yet the ranks of those who, like Joan, cared about Frank's work as intensely as he cared about theirs were much thinner. She undertook a series of paintings titled *July 25*, the day of Frank's death.

Four months earlier, Joan's mother had died. Alone in the bathroom of her Chicago apartment one morning, Marion had been felled by a stroke, but her body was not found for a day or two. After taking the phone call, Joan sped off to Chicago, Yseult in tow. The austere quality of Marion Strobel Mitchell's crowded memorial service at St. Chrysostom's Episcopal Church several days later was "just right," thought her old friend poet John Frederick Nims, "with death getting what he deserves—the coolest possible nod from Marion. Probably the closest the old bastard ever came to being totally ignored."

After friends and relatives, including Yseult and Sally, departed, Joan stayed on in her mother's sadly cluttered apartment, hiring their former maid, "dear darling Nellie," to clean as she herself prepared furniture for shipment to California and other furniture, papers, letters, and books for shipment to France. A few of her mother's thousands of books she set aside as mementos for friends: to George Dillon, she mailed a volume of Robert Frost inscribed to Marion, along with an old postcard that, George later told her, made him hear Marion's laughter. Jimmie's work fared less well at his daughter's hands. Summoned for emotional and practical support, Ellen Lanyon rescued Tiffany lamps, Wedgwood dishes, and medals and trophies from Joan's massive hauls down to the furnace room but was not present when Joan burned two hundred paintings, her own student works plus most of her father's watercolors.

Two years earlier, Joan had painted *Chicago*, in which a rock-solid cerulean indigo presence retraces the familiar curve of Lake Michigan viewed from the Mitchells' apartment, here dissipating into a foggy blue, there rimming a dense white, the forbidding chalky white of depression, that "absolute horror, just horror." Now, acknowledging the irrevocable loss of part of her own past with the death of her second parent, Joan also titled a sixteen-foot-wide triptych-in-progress *Chicago* to honor her mother. So radiantly and deciduously green that one can almost smell the leafy fragrance of summer, yet shaded with sadness, this *Chicago* stirs with three large verdant clusters, stillness in motion, a kind of rondeau (a three-stanza lyrical poem). Joan had come to realize everything she owed Marion, including lessons about feeling and gallantry in the face of solitude, pain, and death.

"Suddenly, from all the green around you, / something—you don't know what—has disappeared: / you feel it creeping closer to the window, / In total silence," begins Rilke's sonnet "Before Summer Rain." Joan knew it, of course, as she knew all of Rilke's work. It ends, "the chill, uncertain sunlight of those long / childhood hours when you were so afraid."

Following Joan's 1965 show at the Stable, her first in New York in four years, the artist's long, warm relationship with Eleanor Ward abruptly curdled. Not only did Ward owe Mitchell a substantial sum, but also, with the Stable teetering toward bankruptcy, the dealer had attempted to raise funds by putting up for auction at Parke-Bernet five paintings whose ownership the two disputed. Infuriated, Joan contacted her bulldog lawyer, who launched a fierce two-year legal battle with Ward. Showing neither sympathy for Eleanor's situation nor sentimentality over their long and important history together, she also threatened to report Ward to the Art Dealers Association. Not long after her work left the walls of the Stable, the painter signed a contract, vetted by her lawyer, with the Martha Jackson Gallery on East Sixty-sixth Street, which also represented Jenkins and Bluhm. She and Jackson's aide Olivier Bernier then talked dates and crating for Joan's first show at Martha Jackson— "no more dark centers alas," promised Joan, "(I sort of miss them) and lots of *color*, saleable, no??"

Meanwhile, the most visible and powerful gallery in Europe had been courting Riopelle. Founded by Aimé Maeght, who had shrewdly and improbably leveraged a modest electrical appliance business in Cannes into an international art empire, the Galerie Maeght exhibited the work of its stable of heavyweights—Braque, Dubuffet, Chagall, Miró, Calder—at corporate-style galleries in Paris, Zurich, Barcelona, and New York. It also operated well-endowed printmaking facilities and published its own tony journal, *Derrière le Miroir,* replete with original prints. Although Joan and Jean-Paul knew Aimé and his wife Guiguite from Golfe-Juan, where the Maeghts too kept their yacht, Jean-Paul had been recruited by the dealer's lieutenant, poet Jacques Dupin.

When she wasn't trying to murder Rip, Joan was giving him her loving support, and now she participated in his long negotiating sessions with Dupin, culminating in a signed contract, champagne toasts, and Riopelle's glittering opening at Maeght's flagship gallery on the rue de Téhéran. Henceforth, Pierre Matisse and Aimé Maeght would divvy up the Canadian's work by the square meter, their sessions—*le partage*—always starting with the flip of a coin. New York would underwrite his art supplies while Paris shelled out a substantial annual advance and played the roles of travel agent, tax accountant, and high-flown factotum.

Riopelle's affiliation with Maeght tipped the couple's social life toward the pretty walled village of Saint-Paul-de-Vence, above Nice, where Aimé and Guiguite lived near the Maeght Foundation, the modern art museum and sculpture garden built to house a portion of their private collection. The foundation doubled as a kind of private club where Jean-Paul and Joan socialized around the pool with other art celebrities whose friendships the dealers cultivated. There, one balmy blue July evening, they fêted painter Joan Miró's seventy-fifth birthday at an al fresco dinner, rubbing elbows with sculptor Alexander Calder, photographer Brassaï, Guggenheim Museum chief Thomas Messer, *Vogue* editorial director Alexander Liberman, and Miró himself. ("What a sweet lovely man he was," Joan told a friend after the Catalan artist died in 1983. "His blue twinkly eyes just reached my tits.")

On another occasion, Jean-Paul piled a gang into his old Citroën DS to drive up to his dealer's château in the Pyrenees. On the last stretch of road, a vast black Rolls heading in the opposite direction popped into view. Jean-Paul crowed, "It's Aimé!" Indeed, Aimé pulled up and stopped, but couldn't manage to roll down his window. Much hilarity ensued. When at last Jean-Paul swung up the driveway of the Maeght estate, he accidentally plowed into a huge, pricy Greek urn. Scolded Aimé's wife, Guiguite, very much the grocer's daughter even in Dior, "Jean-Paul, you naughty boy! We are going to repair this because you are going to make me a large pot." "Yes! And four hundred years from now some idiot will drive into it!" Garboesque behind her dark glasses, Joan smoked and coolly stared at the landscape.

Maeght had offered her nothing. Galleries know that artist-couples, particularly crisis-ridden artist-couples, spell trouble, and, in any case, the glitzy Maeght was not at all what Joan wanted or needed in a gallery. Nonetheless, with Riopelle joining the *monstres sacrés* on Maeght's roster, she once again felt unhappily "under his shadow as an artist." In the long run, however, his move would prove providential.

Beginning in the 1950s, the Galerie Jean Fournier had been including Riopelle's work (and later sometimes Mitchell's) in its group shows. Established as a bookseller in 1952, Fournier had soon begun handling paintings as well. By 1964, the year he moved to a luminous storefront on the rue du Bac, he was more gallerist than bibliopole, though visitors still had to pass among tables and shelves of books, as if following "a humanist initiatory path," in order to stand before the art. As soon as Riopelle aligned himself with Maeght, Fournier invited Mitchell, who had no European gallery, to join, and she accepted.

As low-key and tactful as Maeght was high-powered and brash, Fournier had won respect in the French art world for his rejection of commercial showmanship and his loyal faith in painters including Sam Francis, Shirley Jaffe, and Simon Hantaï. Male and female, young and old, French and American, Fournier's artists—but they were not "his!" he objected—gravitated to abstraction and color. Joan teasingly dubbed this slender, balding, bespectacled shopkeepers' son "Quai d'Orsay" for his discretion and finesse, worthy of a French diplomat. Indeed, he always addressed her using the formal "*vous.*" A "lay monk," as one critic put it, "who never failed to recognize the distance that separated him from the choir," Fournier worshipped Joan and her painting, attempting to meet its authenticity with comprehension at the deepest level and to respond with "my truth." Joan's French dealer for the rest of her life, Jean Fournier worked devotedly and effectively to establish her reputation in Europe. During her first exhibition on the rue du Bac, however, opening in May 1967, the spotlight fell elsewhere and sales were few.

Two summers earlier, Joan and Jean-Paul had underwritten a trip to Paris for their sailor René so that he could undergo back surgery. One of his doctors had been Gabriel Illouz, a rheumatologist and amateur painter married to French American composer Betsy Jolas, the daughter of famed translator Maria Jolas and avant-garde publisher Eugène Jolas. Not long after meeting Gabriel, Joan and Jean-Paul had invited the couple to dinner. "You are a lady composer," Joan pointedly observed to Betsy on that occasion, "and I am a lady painter."

The following summer, Betsy and Gabriel had rented a splendid castle with a crenellated Genoese watchtower on a Corsican promontory high above the sea, installed a piano, and invited a gang of friends including Joan and Jean-Paul, who had sailed over from Golfe-Juan. During their sojourn, these four Corsophiles decided to purchase together a house on the island. In the year that followed, they toured several properties, going so far as to gather estimates for renovations from carpenters, masons, and electricians. Jean-Paul was crazy about the idea of owning a country estate, and the embattled Joan felt this was perhaps just what was needed to "cheer up" their relationship.

Then one day they heard from Betsy, who had stumbled upon an ad in *Le Monde,* of something markedly different: a two-acre property in the village of Vétheuil, about thirty-five miles northwest of Paris, not far from Betsy and Gabriel's country place in Chérence. The property consisted of an imposing stone house called La Tour for its nineteenth-century tower, a scattering of smaller structures including a fourteenth-century portico, a broad sloping lawn, the vestiges of an ancient orchard, and a splendid garden, all perched atop a limestone bluff overlooking the Seine—plus a stucco cottage, once the home of Impressionist Claude Monet, on the road below. The seller was Liliane Schneider, the widow of French steel and armaments king Charles Schneider. Interested parties included future French president Valéry Giscard d'Estaing and his wife Anne-Aymone.

Instantly enamored of Vétheuil, Joan cataloged the reasons to buy. Not only would a country house eliminate the need to dog-walk (she was up to three Skyes and two Brittany spaniels), but also the stone pavilion the Schneiders used as a game room could be turned into a reasonably large and very private studio. Moreover, the fact that the pavilion was one story meant she could remove big paintings without having to roll them up to negotiate a stairwell, as she did at Frémicourt, sometimes causing the paint to crack. They could keep Frémicourt. Joan bargained with Jean-Paul: she would purchase Vétheuil if he paid for remodeling, utilities, and maintenance. She threw in that she never again wanted to hear the name "Roseline Granet." (Jean-Paul and Roseline now owned a foundry together in Meudon, where both made sculpture.) Fine, he replied, you'll never hear it. Almost on a whim, Joan proceeded. She was able to do so because their mother's death had left her and Sally the wealthy income beneficiaries of testamentary trusts from both parents.

So Jean-Paul stood the cost of the carpenters, cabinetmakers, electricians, glaziers, plasterers, and locksmiths hired to repair and improve their *folie à deux* and perhaps also the salaries of Jean and Raymonde Perthuis, the gardener and cook, respectively, who lived in Monet's cottage and "came with" the house. Joan forked out for the installation of heat and skylights in her studio. Ever frugal, she also cut a deal with Louisiana-born artist Ed Clark, whom she had met at La Coupole: Ed and his wife Hettie would house-sit La Tour as a deterrent to the robbers who plague country estates, and he would paint her studio in exchange for its use. Living at Vétheuil for fifteen months, Ed at times felt less like the struggling artist he was than like an aristocrat on the eve of the French Revolution.

In May 1968, after almost a year of shuttling between city and country during the renovations, Joan and Jean-Paul made the full move to Vétheuil just as student protests escalated into street fighting and massive strikes rocked France, threatening at one point to topple President Charles de Gaulle. One might expect two freewheeling artists to enter into the spirit of the street-theater revolution that was extolling the imagination and shutting down creaky institutions, but the apolitical Jean-Paul shrugged and went fishing with Norm Bluhm, while Joan pronounced May '68 "absolutely awful." Egalitarian and left in her politics (she had recently donated a painting to the Black Panthers), she rarely lost an opportunity to egg on radicals and dissidents. Yet, respectful of what merited respect, she scorned May '68 for its collective chaos, romantic naïveté, and indiscriminate trashing of tradition, including painting. She kept a full tank of gas so they could get across the border if necessary, but, other than that, tried to ignore it, attending instead—a harbinger of days to come—to domestic matters, including Prunelle, the stray bird dog they had adopted, who scarfed up rather than retrieved the pheasants Jean-Paul shot, then broke into Yseult's new duck cage and finished off its occupants as well.

Nearly every window at La Tour commanded a dazzling view: between the river and the road below lay a wonderfully unmanicured wet-grass field dotted with locusts, pines, pear trees, willows, ginkgos, and sycamores. Balls of golden mistletoe hung in the trees, their roundness contrasting with the dark rectangularity of a rigorously pruned hedge. Everything moved. Birds twittered and swooped. Wind ruffled the foliage. Church bells rang. Passing blue black and rust barges, laundry flapping on their decks, roiled the Seine, a meandering ribbon of light. Houses clustered on its opposite bank, but Joan mentally ceded that midsection to Monet, focusing instead on the lake beyond, the rolling blue-wooded hills, and the sky, an "immense overturned bowl" often teeming with clouds, swelling or scattershot.

From the time she acquired Vétheuil, its colors and lights pervaded her work. Loose allover quilts of limpid blues, greens, pinks, reds, and yellows, early oils such as *My Landscape I* and *II* fairly burble, their colored lines and shapes registering a painter's fast-moving hands as they rise steeply, floating between inner and outer worlds, to jostle and bank at their tops. In the no less intoxicated *River and Tree* cycle that followed—certain canvases as spare and unfinished looking as late Cézannes—the blue and green spheres of *My Landscape,* now detached, levitate.

A month before moving, Joan had shown the new work, done at Frémicourt but bursting with Vétheuil, at Martha Jackson in New York. She had arranged for her old friend and lover Evans Herman, married with children and living on a farm upstate, to attend her opening. Afterward the two went to a party thrown by their friends Edi and Lucy Franceschini, where Evans's eight-year-old daughter and Joan entertained the crowd by standing on their heads. But as Evans walked Joan home to St. Mark's Place, her mirth ceded to despondency and she expanded upon "the horrors with Riopelle and how drunk she was always and how ugly he was and how violent he was." Evans found her like a restless, unhappy child.

Back in France, she took refuge, as usual, in landscape and painting. Some weeks later (the events of May having disrupted the mail) came a letter from Evans enclosing his poem "A Gift of Violets for Joan Mitchell," and she reciprocated with the small tender drawing "Violets." "Out of your poem I'm [also] painting an enormous violet (cobalt violet)," Joan wrote. Her half-finished reply lay neglected, however, until winter, by which time "the violet pic [had] turned into a sunflower—apologies to Vincent [van Gogh]—and now it's snowing like hell—and beautiful."

The following spring, Joan's gardener, Jean Perthuis, planted beans, tomatoes, pumpkins, carrots, asparagus, basil, squash, and corn. But flowers would always dominate at La Tour: dahlias, tulips, gladioli, hyacinths, bachelor's buttons, poppies, carnations, lilacs, petunias, morning glories, marigolds, jonquils, violets, daisies, roses, zinnias, geraniums, begonias, forget-me-nots, and irises, Joan adored them all. Most afternoons she would climb the thirteen stone steps from her kitchen door up a knoll with ancient cherry trees whose blossoms carpeted the grass each early spring. Before entering the studio to check her colors in daylight, she would pause to cast a loving look at the garden. When Pierre Schneider asked, "Why do you live in France?" she replied, "Because the lilacs are blooming in Vétheuil."

Joan's favorite flowers, sunflowers, were soon blooming too, some varieties eight or ten feet tall. She loved their little bonnets and turning heads, but their colors affected her most. And their dying. She experienced the spent, stooped giants as beautiful and tragic, and she physically felt their demise: "If I see a sunflower drooping, I can droop with it, and draw it, and feel it until its death." Sunflowers were the yellow satin curtains of Vétheuil.

Whether sun spangled and summery or autumnal and bleak, Joan's eidetic feeling-memories of sunflowers had begun infusing her art. In her 1969–70 sunflower paintings, all heightened aliveness, they metamorphose into stirring air, pouring light, and flurries of blazing gold, alizarin crimson, celadon, and blue. Wildly espaliered against radiant matrices of white, these deceptively improvised-looking marks never coalesce into still life or landscape. From a formal point of view, too, the early sunflower paintings are audacious, masterful works in which the artist adroitly juggles emptiness and fullness, balance and unbalance, lightness and weight.

With the move to Vétheuil—a window thrown open—Joan intensified her focus on color and light. She looked with new appreciation at

Joan, her beloved sunflowers, and, just beyond her garden wall, the Église Notre-Dame, often painted by Monet, 1972

Sam Francis's exuberant stained glass–colored paintings built around luminous voids and fell in love all over again with Vermeer's and Matisse's "lights and whites to get luminosity." (She had seen the 1966 Vermeer show at the Orangerie and found it divine.) Above all, she gravitated to the work of van Gogh, especially his sunflower paintings. The graphic strokes of Mitchell's *Sans Pierre,* for instance, evoke those of van Gogh's *Sunflowers* (in the collection of the Metropolitan Museum), and her palette mirrors his, except that Joan added white. (Joan's 1969 *Sunflowers* is today also in the Metropolitan, a gift from Pierre Matisse.) Surely she felt, in van Gogh's words, "the desire to renew myself, and to try to apologize for the fact that my pictures are after all almost a cry of anguish, although in the rustic sunflower they may symbolize gratitude."

One entered La Tour through a bright, spacious living room with a wood-beamed ceiling, white walls, a fireplace, an ocular window overlaid with wrought iron tracery, and a parquet floor. A few fine antiques stood cheek by jowl with a cot, a billiard table, an ordinary cocktail table and chairs, and a rocking chair prone to tipping backward (in which Joan seated selected victims). A flight of stairs led up to everyone's favorite spot, the cozy, dusky octagonal library with its scattered chairs, desk, TV, wall-mounted rifle case, Matisse charcoal nude, and profusion of books. Across the hall beckoned the no less charming dormered and marble-fireplaced bedroom of Joan and Jean-Paul, where a small window framed a particularly lovely view of the Seine. The second-floor vestibule connecting these two rooms also opened onto a spiral staircase mounting to another bedroom, high up in the tower. The tower's ground floor was occupied by the seldom-used formal dining room, its eight angles marked by faux-marble stucco columns. Down the hall were the rather primitive bathroom and kitchen, to the right, and, to the left, another bedroom and the pleasant breakfast room, aka "the little dining room," where books, newspapers, mail, and odds and ends of all kinds accumulated, a bedsheet protected the sofa from dog hair, a phone sat on a ledge above the radiator, and everyone gathered.

For the next twenty-four years, Joan's domestic life would shape itself to the gentle eccentricities of La Tour, which continued to have full play in her art. Off the little dining room, for instance, the small terrace where she liked to linger in the midday sun offered a transfixing panorama she called, referring to Vermeer's masterpiece, "my *View of Delft*" and used in *My Landscape* and many other works. On another side of the house, the living room opened onto a gravel-surfaced terrace crowned by a stately linden tree more than a century old. Thick and airy green in summer, Mondrian stark in winter, it would prove no less useful to Joan's painting than did the garden beyond.

That garden shared a wall with the cemetery (where Monet's wife, Camille, was buried) of the thirteenth-century Gothic Notre-Dame de Vétheuil, whose tower served as scenic backdrop to Joan's flower beds. This little church figures prominently in some of the three hundred paintings Monet did in Vétheuil between 1878 and 1881, as do the river, streets, houses, and fields, including the famous poppy fields, surrounding La Tour.

Like Monet and other Impressionists, Joan adored the rain-washed, cloud-scudding Valley of the Seine for its moody weather and grainy-white light that intensified colors. Everything greened and grew: even the stone walls sprouted climbing roses. The space-feelings were ordered yet open, and the colors—the clear yellows of colza and forsythia, the foamy whites of hawthorn, the tender violets of predawn skies, the grass greens, the evanescent blues of late-spring twilights—deliciously "Frenchie."

The closeness to Jean-Paul that Joan had hoped to gain by her purchase of Vétheuil did not materialize, however. The golden boy was crowding two or three lives into one: meeting important people, having important shows, charging down to Nice. Or into Paris. In his Bristol, he calculated, he could do La Tour–La Coupole in twenty-two minutes flat. He gave Joan a Citroën, but, acknowledging that her drinking made her a menace on the road, she quit driving, managing solo trips into Paris by cab to Mantes-la-Jolie, eight miles south, then the milk-run train to the St.-Lazare station. At night, she usually stayed home. Mute and pitch dark, Vétheuil felt light-years away from the Cedar or even the Rosebud.

But Joan invited easily: artists and poets she'd met here and there, friends and friends of friends from the States, old pals from Paris, everyone mixed at La Tour. Betsy and Gabriel dropped by for a drink almost every afternoon at five; Jacques Dupin, Pierre Schneider, and many others drove out for Sunday lunches or lively dinner parties with superb wines and Raymonde's *cuisine bourgeoise*. Sam Francis's assistant, John Bennett, frequently stayed a few days. Joan had met John one afternoon at the Galerie Jean Fournier, where John was doing an errand for Sam.

"You're George Mitchell," he greeted her. Speaking slowly and wryly, she replied, "George Hartigan [Grace's once pseudonym]. Joan Mitchell." Then she invited him to toddle up the street for a drink at the Pont Royal, where they were joined by Paul Jenkins and Joan proved "very lively and funny."

After her move to Vétheuil, such spontaneous encounters were fewer. Joan once told a friend,

> Abandonment is death also. I mean: somebody leaves and other people also leave. I never say goodbye to people. Somebody comes for dinner and then leaves. I am very nervous. Because the leaving is the worst part. Often in my mind, they have already left before they have come. I guess this is why everyone is reproduced in my imaginary photography album.

"It really looks dreamy—if I may say so," Joan boasted to Sally after hanging her second show at Fournier that May, "just one little pic and all the rest big and spaced." Having recently purchased a pantsuit and three dresses, made to order and expensive, she aimed for a certain chic at the opening, thus palliating, to a degree, the awfulness of "standing in front of one's underwear ie painting and saying Bonjour M. So and So." The following day, she, Jean-Paul, Betsy, and Gabriel flew to Nice, put out from Golfe-Juan, and navigated in marvelous weather to Monte Carlo for the Monaco Grand Prix, the faint rumble of which they picked up from the sea.

But their *Serica* era was fading. Jean-Paul's newfound zeal for hunting and fishing took him elsewhere, and, when he did sail, he usually invited other women. He now called Joan "Rosa Malheur"—Rosa Unhappiness. Their mutual photographer, Jacqueline Hyde, "never saw them do anything but yell. Always stuff about his sleeping around. He was cheating on her, etcetera. It was pathetic." Roseline Granet had the impression of Joan as a little girl, angry, hurt, and longing for unconditional love "beyond what any human being was capable of giving."

During the winter of 1970, tensions spiked: Joan would hammer away at Jean-Paul until he exploded, walloped her, and either stormed out or lapsed into brute silence, in which case she would continue to rub his nose in whatever it was until she set off another fracas. At sober moments, they talked separation. The following April, however, Joan wrote her niece Poondie,

Rip's on his "I love Joan" behavior . . . He's trying out a new Bristol and a Bentley (always raises his spirits) and Tantine [children's French for "little aunt"] bought beautiful—dreamy clothes that even Poo would approve of . . . Poo, I have weathered the winter—there have been worse—and much has been cleared up—I'm not leaving your favorite uncle and he's very much not leaving me . . . Sometimes it pays to put things in question. Certainly it stops stagnation—you know—keep the relationship moving or whatever—God—Rip just arrived (back way—studio) with a mess of things to plant—living and growing. He sends his love to you—and now I guess I'll play togetherness and bend my back.

Riopelle planted a maple tree on the property. One could read: Canada, putting down roots.

But no sooner had the relationship mended than it was once again coming apart at the seams. Visiting from New York, Howard Kanovitz and Mary Rattray witnessed plenty of ugly scenes. On one particularly awful evening, a very soused Riopelle wanted to show them how fast he could drive "this dumb little car, a little Morris Minor that was all fitted up with special engines, special brakes." With the three others as passengers, he was soon flying at over a hundred miles per hour. Mary was getting sick, Joan begging him to take his foot off the gas, Jean-Paul gleefully stomping on the pedal.

Tempers flared anew when Madeleine Arbour, a popular Quebecois television personality, arrived to film a documentary about Riopelle for Radio-Canada and was singled out for a central place in Joan's gallery of mistress-villains. In Arbour's televised portrait of the artist, ironically titled *Strings and Other Games* (also the name of his major 1972 exhibition at the Canadian Cultural Center and Musée d'Art Moderne de la Ville de Paris), La Tour appears in full glory, and Riopelle plays lord of the manor. When Joan's dog Bertie trots down a path, a subtitle flashes: "BERTI." But Joan, who, if nothing else, owned the place, rates nary a mention, even as she pops up in one scene, pseudo-playfully—like a child wanting attention—plucking a beret from the head of her gardener, who stands chatting with Riopelle and Arbour, and depositing it on Arbour's. The journalist whisks it off and keeps right on talking.

Painter Ellen Lanyon's account of the day she spent with Joan in April 1973 attests to the effects of the couple's prodigious drinking. Beginning that morning, when her hostess led Ellen from the train station in Mantes-la-Jolie to the nearest café, Joan never stopped sipping white wine. In her studio that afternoon, she started in on beer from cases stacked in one corner as she pulled out virtually every painting for Ellen's inspection. What did Ellen think of this? What did she think of that? Ellen suddenly perceived Joan as "the most distraught, lonely, agonized person in the world."

After cocktails that evening, Jean-Paul, Joan, and Ellen drove to his huge studio in nearby St.-Cyr, where the Canadian's assistants busied themselves amid acres of perfectly stretched canvases awaiting his touch. There, as if the alcohol had built up and now demanded immediate release, Joan turned scathing and sarcastic, lashing out at Riopelle for what he had and she did not, hurling at him years of accumulated resentment that men wielded all the power. As abruptly as her tirade had begun, it stopped. And the three set off for a country inn.

Toward the end of their rabbit dinner, the liquor still flowing, Joan and Jean-Paul drifted over to the restaurant's bar where they chatted with locals, leaving Ellen to sit and watch as they got even more staggeringly drunk. Soon the two were barking at each other, Jean-Paul socking Joan a few times, Joan once pitching off her bar stool. Several hours elapsed. Around three a.m., a car pulled up outside, and a man entered the restaurant, scooped up Joan, who had passed out, carried her to his car, and motioned to Ellen to follow. "Oh, my God!" she mentally gasped. "What now?" But she went along. They ended up at a pleasant house where the man laid Joan on a bed and gestured to Ellen (who did not speak French) to get some sleep. The next morning, she was fed and driven to the train station. Joan never apologized or explained. As the years went by, Lanyon sometimes compared notes with mutual friends who had recently traveled to France. " 'Did you visit Joan?' They'd say, 'Oh, my God!' "

Lanyon's tale notwithstanding, Joan was rarely a tottering drunk—in other words, she was a true alcoholic. She drank to ward off anxiety and bolster her feelings of self-worth, even though alcohol exacerbated the self-doubts she projected as hypercritical hostility and kept her in depressive cycles. But most fundamentally she drank to get her conscious mind out of the way when she painted. Painting had to rise above the ordinary. Reason had to fall to the wayside. Joan told one friend that if she did not drink she could not paint. "I will use anything that will encourage me or inspire me," she said to another. "Anything at all to feel something. I might read a poem. I might have another Scotch. I might talk to one of my dogs."

In the early 1970s, Joan bestowed upon three major paintings titles that obliquely allude to the irreducibles, birth and death. One was the triptych *Bonjour Julie,* named in honor of Riopelle's first grandchild, recently born to Yseult. (Joan fawned over baby Julie, who lived with her mother on the rue Frémicourt, yet slighted Julie's younger brother, Jim, born the following year, because he was a boy, thus mirroring the behavior of her own father, whose name the child, ironically, shared.) Another, also a triptych, was *Ode to Joy*: its title referred to the chorus of Beethoven's Ninth but also to Frank O'Hara's "Ode to Joy," a paean to erotic love as a means of flouting death. The third was *Mooring,* whose landscape-filtered feelings are congruent (according to Joan) with those stirred by T. S. Eliot's "Marina." Eliot continued to hold a place of honor in the painter's pantheon of poets: characterizing his work as "death warmed over," she responded with all of her being to the sensory language he crafted for "direct communication with the nerves" by means of "a network of tentacular roots reaching down to the deepest terrors and desires."

Derived from a scene in Shakespeare's *Pericles, Prince of Tyre,* "Marina" begins with Pericles' description of a paradisiacal coastal landscape that restores to life his drowned daughter, Marina—"grace dissolved in place"—thus overriding spiritual death and rekindling a feeling of joy. But, he wonders, are his perceptions, "less strong and stronger," truly wakeful or only illusory? Memories of Marina's conception and childhood put his doubts to rest and bring full realization that she is an extension of his own decrepit self/boat. (A boat-like form is decipherable in Joan's painting, recalling John Ashbery's remark that "one's feelings about nature are at different removes from it.") Pericles then senses that the landscape visions with which he is flooded bear directly upon his self/boat, guiding it forward. Worlds mingle. Something lost has been found. Time and death drop away. His soul is renewed.

Like most of Joan's work of the early 1970s, *Mooring,* its misty lavenders and luminous oranges ballasted with black, registers as weather filled. Contrasting scumbled clouds of paint with soft-edged block forms, the cycle of work to which it belongs is more cluttered than those that precede and follow. With their carefully disposed shapes and colors nudging the eye by fits and starts, these paintings bear less resemblance to the fragmented, immediate, and energized work of Willem de Kooning than to the ripe, lyrical, and disorienting work of Pierre Bonnard. Moreover, their highly original syntax takes cues from the formal ideas of Hans Hofmann. Effecting plasticity through color, their resonant orange, green, lavender, blue, and black planes assert themselves as parts yet relate to the whole, luring viewers into the canvas and pushing them back out. The sumptuous *Wet Orange*, for instance, a thesaurus of Hofmannian rectangles—painting as field—is held together by the tensions and harmonies of orange and blue. (Something Joan had seen, perhaps a flower, made her fall in love with tangerine orange, a color she had long disliked. She decided to pair it with the lavender-tinged blue of the Gauloises cigarette pack. The result was *Wet Orange*.)

The painterly intelligence and practiced hand of this veteran artist were not only pulling off unexpected yet felicitous meetings of color—witness the lavenders and oranges of *Mooring*—but also breaking rules of all kinds, sinking yellow behind lavender, for instance, and clumping dark colors at the upper edges of a canvas. Moreover, Mitchell appeared to transubstantiate pigment into light: indeed, light is simultaneously visual sensation and, in the words of curator Marcia Tucker, "part of an expressive tradition that includes radiance as an image of revelation."

From the cobalt blues in *Salut Sally* to the cornflower blues in *Les Bluets* to the inky blues in *Barge Péniche* to the effulgent rain-squall blues in *La Ligne de la Rupture,* blues now came into their own. The paintings hold dear the great French blues of Cézanne, Bonnard, Matisse, and Miró and weave together present and past: the blues of the Seine, the Mediterranean, the Atlantic, and the East River, the ur-blues of Lake Michigan. Water "is the Seine, it's Lake Michigan too . . . it's rather the feeling I have for these things." In her landscape spaces, which are also mental and metaphorical spaces, one blue feeling-memory lapses into another, in enfilade.

In *Blue Territory,* for instance, the artist arranges patches of sensate color, rather like her mental picture gallery, on either side of a central axis to effect a late-winter feeling. This marvel of painterly metamorphosis mobilizes a woolly lavender white, a pale maculated yellow—a spill of light—glazed with green, the brown of a fallow field blurred with frosty lavender (reminiscent of a Monet *Snow Effect*), and, most spectacularly, a purified, star-splashed ultramarine. Mitchell might have had *Blue Ter-*

ritory in mind when she bemoaned to a colleague that art had "lost some of its 'spirituality,'" acknowledging that "spirituality" is "considered a 'hokey' word, but it was what painting had once been about." Not only does *Blue Territory* conjure a book of hours (a devotional book of prayers and meditations specific to various days, months, and seasons) but also shines as Mitchell's *Starry Night.*

On March 25, 1972, an exhibition of forty-nine paintings by Joan Mitchell titled My Five Years in the Country opened at the I. M. Pei–designed Everson Museum of Art in Syracuse, New York. The Everson's director, James Harithas, had originally scheduled Norman Bluhm for that slot, but the timing wasn't working for Bluhm, who suggested Joan in his place. Thus Harithas, long a Mitchell fan, offered the artist her first solo show at a major museum. "Do I have to sleep with you?" she lipped.

Joan attended her opening surrounded by old pals, including Hal Fondren, who came up from New York, and Jean Fournier, who flew over from Paris. (Jean-Paul, on the other hand, did not make it to Syracuse until two weeks later, when he and Joan, livid over some fresh incident involving Roseline Granet, battled their way through the museum's galleries.) On the same weekend as Joan's reception, the Everson hosted a big, lively conference on prison reform (on the heels of the bloody revolt at nearby Attica), which merged with an anti–Vietnam War rally and various art events into a wild, woolly two or three days. At dawn that Sunday, peace activist and poet Reverend Daniel Berrigan, recently freed after eighteen months' incarceration for burning draft records, celebrated his first post-prison Mass in a "garden" of Mitchells.

Yet the only noteworthy critical response to Joan's show came from *New York Times* writer Peter Schjeldahl, who saw the artist's insistence upon "pushing her mastery to the limit, willfully throwing it against 'impossible' problems" and declared that Mitchell deserved recognition "as one of the best American painters not only of the fifties, but of the sixties and seventies as well." Other critics, however, spilled little ink over either the Everson show or the pared-down, two-part version thereof that opened on April 26 at Martha Jackson in New York.

In 1969 Jackson herself had unexpectedly died and her son, David Anderson, had taken the reins of the business. The amiable Anderson found Joan warm, brilliant, and difficult. That summer following the Everson show, in fact, he had to draw upon his every diplomatic skill in

guiding her response to a letter from Marcia Tucker, a curator of painting and sculpture at New York's Whitney Museum. Tucker was offering
a major show at the Whitney in 1974, yet the painter had forwarded her
message to Anderson as "this Whitney bit which of course we cannot
do," ticking off the reasons why. First, the only pictures she would want
to show would be traveling. (Pittsburgh's Carnegie Institute was organizing a three-person show of Mitchell, Sam Francis, and Walasse Ting,
which would go to Toledo, Oklahoma City, and Austin.) Second, she
objected to the Whitney's plan to pair her exhibition with one by painter
Lee Krasner. Not only did Joan feel that her work clashed with Krasner's but she also held her nose at the idea of ghettoization as a woman
artist. Tucker was using her, she ranted, to build her own reputation as
a feminist curator. So Joan would just continue her strategy of staying
underground, meaning showing outside New York City as she waited
out tough times. Besides, she was once again "practically in 'divorce'"
with Jean-Paul and her future was one huge question mark. Anderson
countered that turning the Whitney down flat would be a terrible career
move and argued for asking for more than the museum was offering. He
then requested Joan's permission to meet with Tucker. That past spring
in New York, art critic Phyllis Tuchman had, in fact, brokered a lunch
meeting between Joan and Marcia Tucker, but Tucker had canceled when
she came down with the flu, and Joan then accused the curator of standing her up: "sick—balls."

After Anderson talked with Tucker, she uncoupled Mitchell's show
from Krasner's and again pressed for Joan's commitment in principle.
Anderson urged that she accept.

At this point Joan was producing no more than twenty major paintings annually, albeit some of them mammoth, and this was perhaps
another factor in her foot dragging. David attributed this paucity of
work to her alcoholism, Joan blamed it on the monumental difficulty of
painting. A painting had to be *felt*. Eventually, however, she backed into
the show, writing Anderson,

> Lelong has offered me a show at the Maeght Foundation. [This never
> occurred.] I said in 2 years. I cannot paint 35 pics for a Whitney
> show—or in 2 winters . . . I cannot commit myself to anything—
> I might paint well in the next two years and I might not—disaster. If
> I had the pics I might say yes. Don't want to fall flat on my face on
> half a floor at the Whitney for 2 winters' work that I haven't seen—Of

course I'll paint and do my best—what's the matter with showing at Jackson—do we need the Whitney? Say whatever you want—you know me (I'm just getting underway—have no idea where it's going). I'll take a crack at it.

In her fourteen-by-thirty-foot space on an isolated hill 3,600 miles from Madison Avenue, Joan then put shoulder to the wheel,

wondering [as her young friend, aspiring writer Christian Larson, put it] whether the upper right area of [her] latest canvas needs something or works as is; singing along with rambunctious Verdi who thumbs his nose at the abyss and fills it with music; squeezing innumerable tubes of paint; making squiggly turds of color in pie-tins; and squeezing tubes of cool ointment that ease the itch of Bertie's back; and lifting Bertie up onto the bed from time to time so he can get some rest and a change of perspective; and maybe, if today is a good day, [she'll] lose all track of time.

Plans of the Whitney's fourth floor were tacked to the wall, next to a bulletin board covered with art postcards, snapshots of dogs, and *Peanuts* cartoons clipped from the *International Herald Tribune*. To its right, near the door, a wide plank resting on sawhorses groaned with books, letters, maps, ashtrays, used coffee cups, and bottles of wine, cognac, and Scotch. Pungent odors of turpentine and stale smoke hung in the air. Looking down the long studio toward the painting area, the dogs' daybed stood on the left; completed works leaned against the wall to the right, along with the pre-primed, pre-stretched canvases Joan now used, six or eight deep. Beyond sat her hi-fi and record collection of "painting music": Bach, Beethoven, Liszt, Puccini, Bellini, and Verdi. Italian opera served her well, especially when sung by Montserrat Caballé, Renata Tebaldi, Kiri Te Kanawa, and her beloved Maria Callas. "Music, poems, landscape and dogs make me want to paint," Joan told Tucker. "And painting is what allows me to survive."

In order to paint, the artist established not only auditory and emotional spaces but an optical space as well. Remnants of canvas blacked out all four windows, and, in any case, Joan usually worked at night, which meant that her light was artificial and thus constant. The completed paintings lining the walls faced away. A big piece of plywood covered the fireplace. Thus her setup inscribed the targeting of a single canvas at the far end of her studio. One visitor who watched Joan mix her colors in aluminum loaf and pie tins scattered on the floor among Loyal Dog Food cans stuffed with brushes, then shift her attention to that canvas, likened her gearing up to paint to "a locomotive building up steam."

With the move to Vétheuil, Joan's paintings had grown larger, more expansive, and more often multi-paneled. At Frémicourt she had first become serious about diptychs and triptychs as a way of making large paintings in a small studio. Bigger but never big enough, Vétheuil could accommodate at most two moderately sized adjacent panels, no higher than nine feet two inches, however, because of the ceiling beams. (Joan planned to enlarge the studio, yet, despite Anderson's scolding, never got around to it.) The restrictions on width meant that she could not view large multi-paneled paintings-in-progress in their entirety but, rather, had to put the parts together in her mind.

Joan's favorite multi-panel format was the horizontal triptych composed of vertical modules: she loved the way the cool vertical cuts between the panels undermined the landscape effect and loved too everything she could make happen around those vertical cuts. In the diptychs and triptychs she grappled with likeness and difference, wholeness and parts. Moreover, the panels served as forms to go up against, like stanzas in lyric poetry, which also weds structure to emotional release.

Since moving to Vétheuil, Joan had been painting in cycles ordered around subjects such as the Seine, river and tree, and sunflowers, each cycle opening with two dozen or so small canvases to warm her up to that mode of painting. For the Whitney show, she pursued the field and territory cycle that had already held her attention for over a year.

That cycle points up Joan's lack of a decent sense of direction, which was part and parcel, she felt, of her sometimes frighteningly disoriented self-concept: "For my identity," she claimed, "I need to know where I am, to look at maps." Yet she evinced a keen territoriality. The field and territory paintings functioned as pictorial spaces but also, in a very real way, as physical and emotional sanctuaries, places of psychological protection, and escape from the contingencies of time. She painted them for herself and for her loved ones, human and canine, mapping out each and selecting her colors specifically for the people or dogs she had in mind. *Field for Two*, for instance, she intended as a realm of well-being for her friends Joanne and Philip Von Blon; *Field for Skyes*, for Bertie (who had just died) and her two other dead Skye terriers. The fields and territories also emerged from visual memories far (the cornfields of the Midwest) and near ("You know, those fields near Mantes-la-Jolie").

One afternoon three months before Joan's opening, Whitney curator Marcia Tucker walked through the open door at La Tour, where she planned to spend several days interviewing the artist and finalizing the show. "*Alors*, Madame Whitney has arrived," Joan tossed out, never budging from the living-room chair where she sat chatting with friends. Her cat-and-mouse games had begun. A day or two later, having stalked out of Mitchell's studio after the artist's nth arbitrary attack, Tucker went to get a cup of coffee in the kitchen, where she met Riopelle, who was drunk. After mentally undressing her, he took her hand to kiss it. Just then, the back door burst open: Joan had followed Tucker back to the house. "She's here for *my* work, asshole," she bellowed, in French, "and don't you forget it. I'm a better painter than you'll ever be!" In a flash, his *oeufs au plat* were hurtling toward Joan's head. Tucker too ducked — and fled.

The following morning, as Joan slept, the curator packed and departed, leaving a note asking Joan to meet her for lunch in town at one o'clock. Right after the artist arrived, in big sunglasses and a green scarf, Tucker laid down the law: "I've had enough. I can't work this way, and I won't. If you want the show to happen, then you're going to start behaving, stop insulting me, and get to work. If not, then I'm finished here. I don't need to do this show, and I'm just about at the point where I don't want to." Silence. Then, surprisingly, a mumbled apology from Joan.

No sooner had Tucker left Vétheuil, several days later, than Joan dashed off a letter to Sally: "'Miss Curator Whitney' was here. Joan feels Miss Whitney is using her for Women's Liberation . . . I have a whole floor at the Whitney, lots of footage, am not entirely in accord with the choice of paintings and feel uptight about recent paintings. Please come to the opening and hold my hand."

And when I thought,
"Our love might end"
the sun
went right on shining

JAMES SCHUYLER, "Daylight"

CHAPTER THIRTEEN Vinnie and Thea

Not only Sally but a raft of friends and admirers showed up for
Joan's opening at the Whitney, many of them marveling at her
abiding faith in painting and astounding capacity, even in relative isolation, for art making of the highest caliber. She exhibited ten
single canvases, two diptychs, one quadriptych, and nine immense triptychs (the largest measuring almost nine by twenty-four feet). Among
the latter were *Les Bluets* (*The Cornflowers*), a triple sampler of luscious
blues and whites, and the restive *Clearing,* a slow dance of slabs of radiant jet black with Os of phosphorescent lilac-cloud.

In her catalog essay, Marcia Tucker quoted the artist: the work "comes
from and is about landscape, not about me." Critic Carter Ratcliff would
later respond, "This supports the notion that her painting refers to the
external world. It contradicts the notion that she is an Expressionist.

Understandably, Tucker tries to qualify this seemingly peculiar remark: 'Mitchell continues the romantic tradition of landscape paintings as 'a focus for our own emotions,' but in her case 'emotions are metaphoric rather than personal.'" The boundary between Joan's psyche and the world still easily liquefied: about me, not about me, the two can be nearly the same.

The public warmly received her show at the Whitney. They loved its landscape qualities, its colors, its force. The work reminded Marion's old friend, poet and editor John Frederick Nims, of "a Biblical epic I just saw on television ... The Red Sea opens for the Israelites to pass through, and as they do they look up at these great churning walls of water towering above them on both sides ... All that raw power, but so controlled." But the art world again gave Joan rather short shrift.

In the early 1970s the art market and anti-market were driving an unruly pluralism that included process art, body art, photorealism, earthworks, performance art, and more. Conceptualism gave rise to theory- and language-based, sometimes objectless, art, while the women's movement, war in Vietnam, and Watergate scandal stirred a new social consciousness. Painting, especially painting as romantic calling, felt egocentrically disengaged from both theory and society. "Dropped gradually from avant-garde writing without so much as a sigh of regret," as one critic put it, painting was supposedly dead. Mitchell was passé. Reviews were few and, by and large, tepid.

The art world's indifference rankled. Hungrier than she would admit for what she scorned as "career crap," Joan threw out her chest, proclaimed herself AEOH (Abstract Expressionist Old Hat), and took up cudgels for painting—"real" painting, that is. Art dealer Klaus Kertess, whose first encounter with her two years earlier had been marked by the artist's accusation that he had helped kill painting, now earned a vigorous slap in the face for his less than rhapsodic response to her show.

Meanwhile, feminists like Tucker were disposed to champion Joan's art. Her show took place in the context of the Feminist Art Movement, specifically, several years of pressure on the Whitney from Women Artists in Revolution (WAR), a group fired up by the museum's inclusion of only eight females among the 143 artists in its 1969 annual. In 1972, Women in the Arts (comprised of some four hundred artists, filmmakers, writers, actresses, and dancers) had pulled off a spectacular protest at MoMA, and, the following year, that same organization had stirred up

Joan with Clearing *at her breakthrough 1974 exhibition at New York's Whitney Museum*

the scene with the juried show Women Choose Women (including Joan's *Sunflower V*) at the New York Cultural Center. Now, in a review for *New York* magazine, art historian and reluctant feminist Barbara Rose anticipated the day when brilliant female artists would no longer have to play second fiddle to mediocre males and praised Joan's show as "truly outstanding." Rose led her piece by recalling *Life*'s 1957 article "Women Artists in Ascendance," especially the shots of Joan, Helen Franken-thaler, and Grace Hartigan "with their huge paintings, standing there confidently in paint-splattered jeans when their contemporaries were all wearing tweedy classics in the suburbs, terrorized by the 'feminine mystique.'"

Feminists no doubt expected Joan to rally to their cause: instead they found her cranky and contentious. Although she did beef about discrim-ination against female artists, she refused to differentiate herself from male artists, who, she insisted, had always helped her more than female artists, and, agreeing with Grace that feminist activists were inferior art-ists who organized to cover up their own inferiority, she refused to carry the banner of women's liberation. Joan loved art and artists, as opposed to art by women and women artists, and most definitely did not want

to be considered among the forgotten or neglected, resurrected by feminists. But de facto she was.

At the same time, Joan's lived experience with Riopelle made male
privilege a very sore point. Along with Grace, Helen, Louise Nevelson,
Worden Day, and others, she attended a meeting at the uptown carriage
house studio of artist Ilse Getz to discuss the possibility of organizing a
women-only exhibition in order to open the eyes of museums and galleries. She also showed up at a consciousness-raising meeting at Elaine
de Kooning's studio, where she made nasty cracks about feminism and
growled that *she* was already liberated.

Ironically, in a just-published feature article by Cindy Nemser in the
Feminist Art Journal, based on the writer's 1972 visit to Vétheuil, Joan
had griped about carrying

> the burden of running [Riopelle's] household, taking care of his chil-
> dren and grandchildren and though she's not legally his wife, cook-
> ing and cleaning. "Well," she admitted truculently, "I let things pile
> up, but if the housekeeper doesn't come and it gets too bad, I do it.
> How can I let Riopelle do it, he's not well [well enough, however, to
> go on a hunting expedition that year that took him above the Arctic
> Circle] . . . but of course, I have a bad back myself."

(Joan cited her bad back as the reason she repeatedly interrupted
the interview to take her coffee mug into the bathroom and fill it with
Scotch. She drank for medicinal purposes, she told Nemser.) When the
writer asked whether women artists faced discrimination, Joan put her
own twist on the concept, responding that they did, especially as they
aged, and bemoaning the fact that older women were no longer considered sex objects. " 'Yet,' she asserted adamantly, 'they still have sexual
desires and still want to fuck just like the men—but nobody wants to
fuck with them.' "

Her five weeks in New York gave Joan ample time to catch up with
friends, including Mike Goldberg, Tom Hess, Bill de Kooning, and Harold Rosenberg, who did write a vigorous appreciation of her Whitney
show for the *New Yorker* in which he positioned her as a renewer of the
great tradition of Abstract Expressionism. A figure from a more distant
past, John Frederick Nims met Joan for a drink that stretched into many
drinks. "But it really was great," the poet later enthused. "Not just the

Scotches, but seeing you and talking about the Dear Dead Days and the not so dead ones. You're good to talk to; You Throw Light. As well as warmth."

Less agreeably, Joan had picked a nasty fight with David Anderson on the eve of her opening, after which Anderson received notice from her lawyer that the Martha Jackson Gallery's representation of Mitchell was terminated for cause. Having perceived a tailing off of the gallery's effectiveness in promoting her art and watched dealer Xavier Fourcade work wonders on de Kooning's sagging career, Joan, disdainful though she was of artists who razored their way ahead, had made her decision even before flying to New York. Anderson was issued instructions to transport Joan's paintings to the Fourcade, Droll Gallery on East Seventy-fifth Street.

The son of a wealthy French banker, Xavier Fourcade had begun his art career in 1966 when he took the position of first director of contemporary art at New York's prestigious old-line Knoedler Gallery. A patrician and rather shy man whose shyness was often interpreted as hauteur, Xavier had probably met Joan through his brother, French poet and Matisse specialist Dominique Fourcade. In any case, Xavier had asked Joan for advice about which artists to recruit for Knoedler, and she had suggested de Kooning. The dealer liked the idea, which was seconded by former *ArtNews* editor Tom Hess, who remained close to the Abstract Expressionist. Fourcade then proceeded to secure for de Kooning major exhibitions at the Museum of Modern Art, the Stedelijk, and the Tate. When Fourcade left Knoedler to start his own gallery, de Kooning had followed. Fourcade, Droll (the partnership with dealer Donald Droll would be short-lived) opened its doors in 1970. Besides de Kooning, the new gallery represented Tony Smith, Michael Heizer, Louise Bourgeois, and the Estates of Eva Hesse and Arshile Gorky.

On the day of her Whitney opening, Joan had phoned Xavier, who was in bed with the flu: "You want to be my dealer? Come to my opening." Aware that illness was no excuse in Joan's book, Xavier unsteadily got up, donned a suit and tie, attended the reception, and walked out as her New York representative.

A few days later Joan wandered into the Martha Jackson Gallery and chatted amiably with David, then arranged, as part of their negotiated settlement, to give her major painting *Ode to Joy* to his wife, Becky Anderson, a way of simultaneously thanking the couple and nettling David.

Joan chats with her New York dealer Xavier Fourcade in her studio, 1980s.

.   .   .

Meanwhile, back at the Monet ranch, as Joan's old pal Joe LeSueur liked to say, Iva (pronounced "Eva") awaited. A gift from Guiguite Maeght, Joan's German shepherd puppy had arrived unexpectedly in the arms of Jean-Paul shortly before Bertie's death. Burned out by caring for her elderly Skye terrier, Joan had at first objected to having another dog, yet she swiftly lost her heart to the nervous, scrawny creature she nicknamed "Lily Marlene." Iva had style.

From then on, life at La Tour revolved around Iva, with Joan mothering to an extent some found pathetic and obsessing on every detail of her dog's schedule and care. She trusted Iva's love—deep, wordless, and nonjudgmental, unlike that of humans—and considered the puppy a surrogate for or continuation of herself: "She's a total extension of me, or I am of her." Joan still believed that she herself had "no identity but painting, psychologically," while her training of Iva gave the dog "an identity and a feeling of self-worth," a fix on the selfhood Joan found, except through painting, so elusive.

Notwithstanding Iva's companionship, Joan still experienced intense dramas of merging and separating. At times frighteningly alone, she would lapse into states of agitation. Riopelle came and went. Sylvie (who had recently lost twins at birth) was living at La Tour. Old friends like Shirley Jaffe, Zuka, Jacques Dupin, Pierre Schneider, Nancy Borregaard, and Jean Fournier would drive out for lunch or dinner, sometimes an overnight, and John Bennett still visited every few weeks. Houseguests from the States included art dealer Grace Borgenicht and her husband, painter Warren Brandt, Pierre Matisse, Joe LeSueur, Hal Fondren, Martha Bertolette, Tom Hess's son Philip and his wife Margaret, and Joan's niece Poondie, now in her early twenties. Between times, La Tour could fall eerily silent. "I'm very interested in people," Joan contended. "But for some reason, I remain isolated, no matter how I try."

She worked to her advantage the fact that most guests were at the mercy of taxis and trains. A case in point was the visit of Samuel Beckett's biographer Deirdre Bair, who had been invited to lunch. (Over the years, Joan and Sam had drifted apart, Joan telling one friend she had had to break with the writer because he was so depressed.) Bair had appointments back in Paris that afternoon and evening, yet Joan, drinking heavily, refused to let her leave, and Bair missed train after train. Aware of his biographer's movements, Beckett phoned several times: Joan, you *have* to let her go! But Joan did not.

Joan often "tested" her guests, and the more she'd been drinking, the more outrageous the test. When her old friend, painter Jon Schueler and his wife, art historian Magda Salvesen, lunched with her at La Pierre à Poisson, the local restaurant she had made an extension of her dining room, Joan deliberately misconstrued virtually every remark the two made. Another time, Joan greeted a friend of her sister's by announcing that Sally had had an affair with the woman's husband, then proceeded to needle her guest about the husband's infidelity until at last the Californian fled in tears. In contrast, she lavished kindness upon painter Kimber Smith, who, at her insistence, stayed at Vétheuil while he received radiation treatment in Paris for the cancer he faced with a courage she admired. Kimber had long since passed his test.

Young people too, mostly fledgling painters or writers, visited La Tour, some sent by parents or friends who knew Joan, others having crossed her path in New York or Paris, still others having screwed up the nerve to phone. Those she liked she pulled in fast. Most were intrigued by her realm of music, books, liquor, painting, dogs, landscape, and home-style French cooking, and even more so by their fractious, dry-humored, anxiety-ridden, salty-tongued, self-concept-rattling hostess. One way or another, all got more than they expected, and many felt their relationships with Joan were special.

Typically, she grilled her young guests, which was "horrible," reports Lise Weil, today a writer, "but it came from a place of deep caring. It didn't feel like get-the-guest." (On this point, not everyone agreed.) Endlessly curious about their childhoods, family problems, love lives, and life plans, Joan would rattle on about overcoming one's upbringing, attending to one's feelings, living more on the edge. She made Lise, for one, study pictures of prisoners in Attica in order to feel more intensely. The artist brimmed with disdain for racists, slow wits, bad painters, "silver-spoon people," Californians, academics, and snobs. Nondrinkers got mercilessly ragged, young women from the Seven Sisters were dubbed "Vassar" or "Radcliffe," anyone who used the word "should" was ripped into. As for fledgling painters, they were forbidden to waste time wallowing in self-doubt. Joan geared them up with brisk admonitions: "Be a serious painter!" "Get crackin', man!" "C'mon, let's blow a pic!" Most came away from a stay at La Tour with important new insights about themselves.

Among the young writers who had earlier caught Joan's attention were the then-unknown Lydia Davis and Paul Auster, who had come to Paris in 1971 and were scraping together a living from translations. One evening the couple had been invited to dinner, along with Joan and Jean-Paul, at the home of Christine and Jacques Dupin, whose poetry Paul had translated as a student at Columbia and with whom he had formed a warm friendship. Joan arrived wearing smoky-lensed glasses and looking rail-thin in black. She was already well lit up. Mesmerized by Paul's large, sensual, dark-rimmed eyes, she began taunting him. "She talked *sans cesse* of Paul's eyes," Davis recorded in her journal, " 'does he take drugs, does he wear contact lenses?' How he must be a *phony* with eyes like that, how he must be an egotist to have not gone to her '*vernissage*' in Paris. (Of course he didn't know of it.)" Riopelle dozed on the sofa, and the Dupins, who spoke little English, struggled to follow Mitchell's relentless battering of the flabbergasted Auster: "Who do you think you are, Lord Byron?" But his sangfroid got him through the test, and, the following week, he and Lydia were invited to La Tour, in its May splendor of flowering chestnut and cherry trees, lilacs, and variegated tulips.

Lydia was struck by the household's orderly routine, delicious meals, and devoted attention to dogs. The two spent a pleasant evening and stayed the night. The next morning, Lydia walked up to the studio to find Joan listening to the radio as she worked, friendly, "serious . . . and 'centered'—quite different from the fragmented person who had baited Paul that first evening."

From then on, Lydia and Paul were invited to Frémicourt or Vétheuil every six weeks or so. That July, with Lydia away in Ireland, Paul went out alone, and he and Joan talked for hours. "My stay was marred somewhat," he reported to Lydia, "by one of their typically senseless and brutal arguments after dinner, during which she cried and after which he simply fell asleep with his head on the table . . . I am of the opinion that he treats her like a shit." At first shocking and disturbing, their fights quickly felt boring and sad.

Generous, kind, and approving of Davis's and Auster's strength of purpose as writers, Joan showed genuine interest in their manuscripts, gave Paul a beautiful etching of a sunflower for the cover of the literary magazine he and a friend were starting, and arranged for him to meet Beckett. She earnestly told Lydia that she must have children and would regret it if she did not.

Another young writer friend of Joan's, the beautiful, pale Christian Larson, lived on the Île Saint-Louis and hung on the edges of the *Paris Review* crowd. He stuttered and suffered from severe writer's block. Having prized out the details of his cosseted but troubled New Jersey childhood—an adoring mother, a rejecting father, complex feelings about his sexuality—Joan gave Chris money after his father cut him off and eventually got him writing, leaving him deeply grateful "to Joan, who knows how to bring people out of themselves, who knows how to make people make an effort."

She also introduced him to J. J. Mitchell (no relation), a fabulously handsome creature, once Frank O' Hara's lover and soon Chris's, who lived for several months at La Tour, ostensibly to dog-sit and edit Marion Strobel's poetry for a memorial volume that never saw the light of day. A gregarious charmer with killer blue eyes and perfect white teeth, this alumnus of Harvard courted self-destruction with booze, drugs, and trashy nightlife during his weekly jaunts into Paris. Joan would tuck a big bill or two into his pocket and tell him to have a good time. Back at La Tour, J.J. wrote a friend one four a.m.,

> Here we are—*les brouillards* [the fogs] coming up Monet-like over the torn-up tulips. I'm wavering between petulance and patience, skeptically surveying the only comfortable couch dans la maison

Mitchell . . . I (JJ) hereafter known as boy amanuensis/typist whose fluency and lack of facility matches the finger-painting (yes) and spoken scribblings of girl painter J., currently sprawled in flop/art style in visible attack on unsuspecting canvas(es) . . . enjoying a brief respite (*moi aussi*) from J.P. who fishes in Canada after leaving us hair-raising nightmarish stories of tail-gunning runs on Dresden.

Since 1970 Jean-Paul had been spending two months a year in Canada, fishing in the spring and hunting in the fall. From Montreal, he would dash off to Joan brief, impersonal postcards that closed with the formula, "With great friendship." In the fall of 1974, he had departed earlier and stayed longer than usual. Leaving J.J. to dog-sit, Joan joined him that November in the mountain village of Sainte-Marguerite-du-Lac-Masson, north of Montreal, where, using an inheritance from his mother, who had died two years earlier, he had just built a lovely architect-designed studio-home next to a picture-postcard lake. With his pal, Montreal radiologist, private pilot, and outdoorsman Champlain Charest, he had also purchased the local general store, which the two were transforming into a gourmet restaurant.

In honor of Joan's arrival, Champlain and his wife Réjeanne took pains to prepare a typical Quebecois feast with roast game. In an execrable mood, Joan never touched her dinner, instead drinking, chain-smoking, and finally disgustedly lowering her plate for the dog (recalling the time she served dog food to a group of Canadians whom Riopelle had forced her to entertain). She slept all day every day, and, when she did join the others, spoiled everything by picking petty fights with Jean-Paul. At every turn, she saw him slipping away from her. His new home—number six, counting Vétheuil, Frémicourt, St.-Cyr, the foundry in Meudon, and the *Serica*—belonged to a life she did not share. To Joan, it felt safer to hate than to love: if you love, you have no defense.

Her other defense was the landscape, which she used "for enormous protection from people who were hurting me." In the wake of her trip came the gorgeous *Canada* paintings. The diptych *Canada V* beguiles with its bosky masses, its incantatory lights and darks, its use of white around the cut between its two panels, and its oddly right colors (pale mint, white, claret, and the color of night). The brumal *Returned* pulls taut a tourniquet of white light across the four panels where silent, soft-edged, judiciously placed shapes appear. (Originally, Joan titled the latter *Canada* and gave it to Jean-Paul, but she changed its name after he discarded it. Another painting bears the title *Also Returned.*)

Back in France, life continued unsettled. Learning that their Frémi-court building was to be demolished on March 15, Joan enlisted J.J. to help her sort through the vast piles of rolled canvases and cartons of magazines, catalogs, and books she and Jean-Paul had been storing there, and the past came roaring back. Overwhelmed, she squirreled away doz-ens of paintings in the cistern at Vétheuil and dumped everything else in the living room.

They finished the move only a day or two before Joan's fiftieth birth-day, which she spent home alone with Iva. On that milestone occasion, she had planned to stop drinking, yet she managed only three days without alcohol. Nor had much come of her attempts to cut down on her two-pack-a-day Gauloises habit. Frequently tired, she suffered from chronic hip and back pain—lumbago, she claimed, the upshot of too much skating—yet she remained tough and funny in an ironic, self-deprecating way. In truth, she was battling depression: the ghastly metallic white lurked on all sides.

All that summer and fall, painting eluded her. Having sometimes managed to kick herself by switching mediums when she got stuck, she had J.J. type up some of his own poems, which she cut out, pasted as shapes on sheets of art paper, and "pasteled up." (Other times she used charcoal or Conté crayon.) She planted his blithe stacked poem "Sally Up My Alley" ("You're / my / tanned / and / tantine / Sally / my / Santa / Barbara / family . . ."), for instance, inside a post-and-lintel shape, both diaphanous and vigorous. Chris came out to Vétheuil most week-ends, and they did his poems too, and then, having fun, went on to tackle work by Pierre Schneider, Jacques Dupin, and James Schuyler. Black on white to non-synesthetes, the poets' words, of course, appeared to Joan as multicolored as confetti: the poem-drawings, a secret in plain sight.

They were also a testimony to her capacity for generous friendship. Refusing to sort people out by worldly importance, Joan brought the same intensity to her collaboration with the unknown J. J. Mitchell and Chris Larson as she did to her (indirect) collaboration with her old friend, well-known poet and future Pulitzer Prize winner James Schuy-ler. Pierre Schneider exhibited these little jewels at an alternative gallery in the Marais, after which Joan gave most of them to the poets or other friends.

Her effort notwithstanding, year's end found Joan deeply depressed.

As alarmed that fall by Chris Larson's deteriorating mental state as by her own, she had been prodding him to see a therapist and phoning his family and friends to try to enlist their support. On January 24, 1976, however, he killed himself by slitting his wrists in the bathtub of his Île Saint-Louis apartment. Joan reacted with outsized grief and anger, no doubt all the more intense given her need for self-defense against her own suicidal bent.

Whenever a friend died, Joan painted a tree as both homage and act. Thus *Chris's Dead Tree* made another place for Chris Larson in Joan's imaginary photo album and kept him forever alive and protected. Does it have a real-world counterpart that meant something to Chris? Are its colors—charred green black, lilac, flecks of aqua and white—those of his voice or of his personality? In any case, in the lush, stunted, and splendid *Chris's Dead Tree,* the abyss yawns and spring blooms in Vétheuil.

At the very time Chris lay dying, Iva gave birth to eight puppies, two of which Joan kept. One she named Marion after her mother, and the other Madeleine, after Madeleine Arbour, so that Jean-Paul was forced to use the name of his supposed mistress each time he called the dog. Joan doted upon the "Three Graces," but guests were typically less enchanted. "When they bit," reported one French journalist of the trio of barking, bounding, thumping police dogs, "they were said to prefer the ankles of art dealers, journalists, and other unwelcome visitors whose fear and misfortunes the mistress of the premises, a present-day Hecate, contemplated with delectation." When one of her darlings lunged at Xavier Fourcade, however, Joan scolded, "No! No! Not *him*! He pays our bills!"

By the time the puppies arrived, Riopelle was more often absent than not. Speaking seriously one day, rather than hiding behind his usual humor, the Canadian had lamented to Roseline that Joan "destroyed everything that came near her." Another time, a visiting American friend whom he was driving out to Vétheuil casually inquired why he didn't marry Joan: Jean-Paul stomped on the brake, flung open the passenger door, and ordered the man out of his car. For Riopelle, relationships were all or nothing, and his world had long since stopped revolving around Joan. Yet, never one to address problems directly, he let things drift, claiming that she would commit suicide if he left her. Theirs was now a sailor's "marriage" and a long day's journey into night. His presence at La Tour inevitably brought dreary, alcohol-coarsened battles, with Joan's withering put-downs, sly righteousness, and iron-hard verbal assaults as tiresome as Jean-Paul's storming around and roughing her up.

One winterish afternoon, for instance, as Joan and John Bennett chatted and sipped white wine in the living room, a slam of the door announced Jean-Paul's arrival. Joan snatched a book as if she had been reading.

"I thought I told you to leave the door shut! This is just running the heat!" he greeted her.

"Oh, ah, well, I don't know, I don't know. I'm reading my book."

He stomped across the room, grabbed the book, and ripped it in half. "Here! Maybe this will help you read your book!"

A big macho bear with an easy grin, cigarette dangling from the corner of his mouth, slightly dissolute look, and wild mop of plaster-dust graying hair, Riopelle continued to captivate virtually everyone, from the local butcher to the most distingué art critic, and still found a ready supply of sex partners. Despite a few casual affairs, Joan did not.

Her well-lined face now showed all the signs of hard living, and she wore big, smoky-lensed magnifying glasses behind which those enormous eyes, thought one visitor, "looked like huge eggs swimming in dark liquid." Moreover, her lack of appetite—she craved only cigarettes and booze—had left her spiky and thin, and, while she continued to move like an athlete, she did so less nimbly because of her back and hip pain. She might don an elegant pantsuit to trot off to Paris, but most days she threw on a jogging outfit or a pair of jeans and ratty old sweater.

Having lost her seductive charm, but not her irresistible vitality, Joan saw limited options, and, if she made sporadic efforts to rekindle the old feeling with Rip, it was out of yearning for the comfort and familiarity of a loving relationship. Sometimes she would draw a hot bath for him, but he would stride into the bathroom and pee into the tub. No matter how difficult and repulsive she found Jean-Paul, however, she needed him too: if nothing else, to inflict pain upon him was to forget her own suffering. Worst of all were those times when, the two old warriors too weary to battle it out, an ominous silence hung in the air.

As for Riopelle's art, Joan remained publicly loyal, but, in truth, she could muster little enthusiasm for his return to figuration. The artist's acquisition of a taxidermied owl from a local antique shop in 1969 and encounter with Inuit string games during a 1971 hunting trip to northern Canada had supplied him with new subjects bound up in both empiri-

cal reality and Canadian symbolism. Many critics agreed that the paintings and sculptures of the 1970s were a cut below the classic Riopelles of
the 1950s and 1960s. Moreover, though money still burned a hole in his
pocket, his sales had dropped. He was beginning to look like the hare,
and she the tortoise. The rival in her gloated, but the companion rued
that he wasn't keeping up his end of the bargain. He snapped back: her
canvases were painted by the whiskey, not the artist.

Indeed, Joan's efforts in the studio were still not resolving themselves
into a new painting direction. True, she was by now a crafty old magician
able to shuffle and reshuffle pictorial strategies and pull out what she
needed. That may have happened rather easily in the case of the vigorous *Red Tree,* indebted simultaneously to Mondrian, van Gogh, Mitchell of the fifties, and her winter-naked linden. But for months she had
struggled with the allover diptych *Aires pour Marion,* a glen of electrified
duskiness bisected by the whiteness around its vertical cut, a strategy she
had tried out in *Canada V.*

However, a metamorphosis was shaping up with *Quatuor II for Betsy
Jolas.* While waiting for Jean-Paul one day in his studio, Joan had gazed
out a window upon a copse with marvelous flirting lights between certain
trees. She made a sketch on the spot and soon began painting. The delectable *Quatuor II for Betsy Jolas* lusters with lilac, grass green, fuchsia,
green black, and white. Each of its four panels manifests its own visual
logic and completeness, yet everything relates to everything else—from
the velvety-dark knots on the left to the whoosh of pure white, as explosive as laughter, on the right, to the germinal elements, the tree-inspired
"up and down things," in the center. (As for the work's title, it reprises
that of the recent *Quatuor II* for string trio and soprano by her friend
Betsy Jolas. And could the lilac of Joan's *Quatuor II* be anything but
soprano?)

In *Straw,* which came on the heels of *Quatuor II,* it is as if the viewer
has backed away from the central panels in *Quatuor II,* out of the illuminated stand of trees and into a field so sunny it blazes up. Long, horrent
strokes of ochre, *Straw's* "up and down things" bristle across its lower
edge as strokes of dark thalo green chop up its top right. Like van Gogh,
whose wheat-fields palette *Straw* borrows, Mitchell uses graphic markings to evoke vibrations of wind and light. But her facture is rougher
than his, and she pulls apart the fabric of her painting to reveal its white

ground, thus insisting upon spatial discontinuities. Like Cézanne, she remained fascinated with the way visual relationships shift with every move of one's head and she played with the slippage between two dimensions and three.

That October, Joan's shipper picked up and crated forty-seven paintings—including *Red Tree IV, Aires pour Marion, Quatuor II pour Betsy Jolas,* and *Straw*—which Joan and Jean Fournier accompanied to customs at Roissy airport. Having never procured the *carte de séjour* required for foreigners living in France nor paid French income tax, Joan had put herself in a tricky position when it came to shipping paintings abroad for commercial use. Her strategy was to declare them unfinished sketches, her personal property, and her ploy, that year in any case, to feign mental incompetence so that Fournier, with his marvelous savoir-faire, could handle the paperwork required to ship them to 60 St. Mark's Place, where they were picked up by the Xavier Fourcade Gallery and transported to 36 East Seventy-fifth Street.

Intimate and European in flavor, Fourcade's townhouse gallery, its two floors linked by an elegantly banistered staircase, consisted of several small rooms with hardwood floors, a beautiful mix of natural and artificial light, and only one long uninterrupted wall. Selecting and hanging a Mitchell show for that space was always a challenge. Joan and Xavier would work together on installations, Xavier giving Joan the last word. After she flew to New York that November, they mapped out the placement of twenty-five paintings: *Quatuor II* fit the big wall with only eleven inches to spare.

Even though the new paintings were less readily seductive than those of the early 1970s and the height of the tallest among them surpassed that of the ceilings in most postwar apartments and suburban homes, many (including *Quatuor II,* priced at $35,000) immediately sold. Not only did Fourcade bring a fresh client base, but also he was professional, driven, and highly effective. After fifteen years of scant recognition in New York, Joan saw an abrupt shift in the arc of her career: she had more market success than she had had in a very long time. Eventually Paris would follow. (Fournier and Fourcade had begun alternating Mitchell exhibitions and cycles of paintings, thus setting a tempo for her production.)

Joan's two dealers resembled each other in ways that went beyond their names. Both were French, homosexual, cultured, and publicly reserved yet privately warm (Xavier, unlike Jean, prone to fits of nervous yelling during installations); both deeply believed in her work; and both established close friendships with Joan.

For her New York openings, Xavier would throw wonderful dinner parties, not for wooing collectors but for gathering friends, either at the gallery or at Mortimer's, a ladies-who-lunch bistro at the corner of Lexington and Seventy-fifth. (Refusing to compartmentalize people, Joan put together guest lists that included art world luminaries like art historian Linda Nochlin and artist Malcolm Morley, but also Patricia Malloy, her tenant at St. Mark's Place, and Poondie Perry, her niece.) Xavier also procured for Joan special morning passes to the Museum of Modern Art, escorted her to concerts at Lincoln Center and operas at the Met, and invited her to lively weekend house parties at his second home in Bellport, Long Island, along with Morley, Tony and Jane Smith (he, the sculptor, and she, the actress and opera singer), and others. And each time Joan set eyes upon the Mitchell that graced Xavier's library at Bellport, she insisted she could improve it. That upper left section was wrong—"too Helen Frankenthaler!" But Xavier never let her lay a finger on it.

The first of Joan's seven shows at Xavier Fourcade opened on November 23, the Tuesday before Thanksgiving, a holiday the artist spent in Manhattan with her sister Sally, Sally's children, and the young painter Hollis Jeffcoat.

A year and a half earlier, Joan had received a phone call from a twenty-nine-year-old admirer named Phyllis Hailey, who had wanted Joan to critique her painting. A free spirit from Nashville, Tennessee, with college, a failed marriage, and one year at the New York Studio School behind her, Phyllis was studying at the École des Beaux-Arts in Paris and eking out a living by selling portrait sketches to tourists in Montmartre.

Joan had quickly taken Phyllis under her wing, teaching her to be more visual and more feeling in her work, insisting she unfailingly know what she was doing when her brush hit the canvas, and endlessly talking color. She gave Phyllis tubes of the very best Lefebvre-Foinet oils, but no canvas because, she claimed, Phyllis wasn't yet good enough to paint on canvas. So the younger artist used watercolor blocks for her studies of Joan's garden, the church, the river, and a certain ginkgo tree whose foliage she broke up in a quasi-Impressionist manner. Her work became stronger and freer. In addition to doling out painting advice, Joan loved to "shrink" this rather naive young woman, bolstering her self-confidence and prodding her to live more fully her identity as an artist, even though, Joan stressed, so few people took women artists seriously. Phyllis wrote home that Joan was "truly doing wonders for me painting-wise and person-wise." That went both ways. One of the many notes Joan scribbled for Phyllis reads, "Well if it means anything to you—you got me painting again . . . just being in the studio with you makes me want to work . . . I love you dearly—and it takes a shafted one to recognize another."

One bright June day around noon, after Joan and Phyllis had been acquainted for a year or so, they were sitting on the little terrace overlooking the Seine when Joan's old friend Elaine de Kooning arrived. De Kooning was teaching that summer at the New York Studio School's program at the American Center for Students and Artists on the boulevard Raspail, and she had brought with her the program's administrator, twenty-four-year-old painter Hollis Jeffcoat, a native Floridian and Studio School graduate herself. Tall and willowy at 110 pounds, with blue gray eyes and curly black hair, Hollis was soft-spoken, poised, fetchingly androgynous, and single-minded about painting.

As always, Elaine talked a mile a minute, eventually getting around to the topic of Joan's drinking. With help from a therapist and Alcoholics Anonymous, this once drinker to rival Joan had quit two years before. Wasn't it time Joan did the same? "Oh, come on, Elaine! I stopped for three days, and I didn't see any difference at all. Forget it! I don't know why you want me to stop drinking anyway." It was all very familiar and friendly. After awhile, the four ambled up to Joan's studio to see her newest paintings. Elaine and Phyllis oohed and aahed. Hollis stayed silent.

"Hollis, what do you think of my paintings?"

"Not much."

The others gulped.

"What do you mean?"

Hollis had loved Joan's Whitney show, yet in the recent work she saw an inert materiality and relentless sameness. She felt it didn't go far enough.

Joan had no problem with the arrogance of youth: "Well, tell me more. What would you do to change the paintings?"

Later that evening, after the foursome dined at La Pierre à Poisson, Joan dismissed Elaine and Phyllis and directed Hollis to stay on. The two

With Elaine de Kooning, 1975

talked through the night, mostly about painting, with an intensity Hollis had never known. Years after her Cedar Tavern days, Joan remained ravenous for passionate talk between artists. Before turning in, she gave Hollis charcoal and paper. The next midday she ambled out to the garden, where the younger artist had been drawing all morning. Hollis's work passed the test, and Joan then rustled up canvas and paint.

For the rest of that summer, Hollis lived part-time at Vétheuil, helping with the dogs and reheating the dinners that Joan's cook, Raymonde, prepared before leaving in the late afternoon. She and Joan would sing, listen to opera, loll in the garden, pad around barefoot in the grass. Once or twice Hollis tap-danced in the studio. Sometimes they spent all day in their pajamas. Hollis was Mary ("Ma-ryyy!") and Joan was Rose

("Row-zz!"). Or Hollis was Vinnie (van Gogh) and Joan, Thea (from Theo van Gogh, the painter's helpmeet brother). Every day they painted and batted around ideas about painting. Joan was an additive painter, and Hollis a subtractive painter: what was good and bad about each? And many secrets were divulged. Joan endlessly griped about Riopelle, who was elsewhere that summer: I despise him! I don't want to be with him! But if I leave, he will kill himself. Hollis would reply, But nobody's missing here. I don't feel an absence.

Thus Hollis Jeffcoat delightfully warmed up Joan's life. Her job ended in August, however, and she had to return to New York to teach at the Studio School. There she moved back into the Brooklyn apartment she shared with a gay painter named Carl Plansky.

During Joan's sojourn in New York at the time of her show at Fourcade that November, Hollis and Carl had a fight, his complex feelings over her closeness to the famous painter Joan Mitchell having unbalanced their friendship. Joan used this clash as an argumentative wedge, eventually convincing Hollis to fly back to France with her at semester's end. When Jean-Paul picked the two up at the airport, Hollis was astonished. Tanned and brimming with anecdotes, he was an electric presence, a charmer, rather than the monster she had expected. From then on, Hollis and Joan lived at La Tour, while Jean-Paul shuttled among Vétheuil, Paris, and his studios.

Life settled into routine. Most days Joan would emerge from her bedroom around one thirty to pad down the hall to the little dining room or the terrace, where she would sip from a bowl of steaming café au lait, pick at breakfast (poached eggs or a potato omelette, toast with quince jelly, bacon, and tomato), peruse the mail, pore over the *Herald Tribune*, do the crossword puzzle, read, maybe listen to the early-afternoon "shrink programs" on the radio, and get a start on the day's Ricard. Eventually she would stroll up to the studio, where Hollis had been working since early morning. The two chatted, eyeballed their paintings in daylight, and dog-fed before the light got low, then headed to the library for an apéritif and perhaps some TV. Between seven thirty and nine, the downstairs light would flick on, signaling Jean-Paul's arrival. Then Hollis heated up dinner and set the table where the three often lingered for hours, Joan and Jean-Paul regaling Hollis with tales of the old days at the Cedar, the Hamptons, the Rosebud, and the Dôme. Jean-Paul was nicer to Joan than he had been in a very long time. Finally, he would rise and either go sleep in the library or on the billiard table, or leave for St.-Cyr, while the two women led the dogs back up to the studio, where each took one end of the room. Struggling with the recalcitrant *Posted* that spring, Joan would occasionally call out to Hollis, "What should I do here?" Hollis would walk over and study the canvas. "Well, what it really needs is . . ." "Well, then, bloody well do it."

When Joan was prey to her demons, she would pick up a brush and let fly at a blank canvas—slam! slam! slam!—then creep back the following afternoon to see what damage she had inflicted and figure out what was needed to turn the semi-mess into a painting. Agitated, anxious, sometimes falling-down drunk, she cried almost every night, over the failings of Jean-Paul, even the pointlessness of painting. She, who so vehemently believed that painting was essential and real, would sink into despair: Ah, another Mitchell! Why am I doing this? Just another Mitchell. Could painting still save her? Notwithstanding her recent success, she felt buried in the country at age fifty-one, turning out more pictures she offensively-defensively labeled Old Hat. Moreover, she was stuck in a relationship that was like the old cheese no one would throw out. Life's possibilities had dwindled. Thus she became increasingly possessive of Hollis, a daughter of sorts and surrogate younger self endowed with the confident vitality she herself could no longer necessarily conjure up.

Meanwhile, Joan's relationship with Phyllis Hailey had sputtered along. Spending ten days with his sibling at La Tour, Phyllis's brother John observed the same affectionate rapport Phyllis had described in letters home, but, according to Hollis, Joan had "[thrown] Phyllis over and was abominable. Phyllis was destroyed by it." Phyllis and Hollis had formed a close friendship, going to museums and galleries and running around Paris together—an escape from the pressures of Vétheuil—and, bankrolled by Joan, once traveling to Amsterdam, where they spent a marvelous few days.

That summer Rufus Zogbaum also visited La Tour, where this son of Joan's once lover and late friend, Wilfred Zogbaum, and virtual stepson of Franz Kline began an affair with Hollis. Always an enthusiastic matchmaker, Joan took full credit. Not only were the two practically her children, but also their liaison encapsulated her own past. When Hollis again had to return to New York that fall, she moved in with Rufus. But they didn't last long as a couple: "There was no question about it," Hollis later reflected. "My real passion was with Joan. And hers was with me."

Last known photograph of Phyllis Hailey, 1977

One note survives from that October: "Joanie, You were so sweet on the phone last night. I miss our fun. Did you make your clear blue winter painting? . . . Love you so much."

Meanwhile, having completed and shepherded through customs her second show for Fourcade, Joan spent a delightful day with Jean Lamouroux, a painter friend from Provence, who drove her into Paris to see Paris–New York at the Pompidou and the Courbet retrospective at the Grand Palais. Around the same time, in another of the sagas of intertwined love and pain that inform Joan's life, her Parker School classmate and sporadic lover, Tim Osato, reappeared. Now retired from the military, Osato was a man of (in the words of one of his daughters) "dashed dreams and frustrated everything." The two saw each other a few times, then quarreled by phone. From his hotel in Paris, Tim penned a hurt note. On Christmas Day, several weeks later, he would write again, this time from the Veterans Administration Hospital in Denver, Colorado: "Having nearly broken my word to you those last few days in Paris (sleeping pills, this time), I'm back to square one and there really isn't anything to say except that the memory of the little girl in the light blue coat at the bus stop will never leave her buddy, Tim." Nineteen months later, he shot himself.

All that winter Jean-Paul was hobbling around La Tour in pain, a studio accident having exacerbated an old knee injury to the point where he could not bend his leg more than three inches. "J.P. has been on crutches," Joan reported to Joe LeSueur,

> and he's afraid of an operation—well honey—to get him upstairs and down—etc. etc. Hollis [back from New York] is divine with him and he thinks she's "the end of the world." She has his racing helmet and Moto Solex [motorcycle] and he gives her canvas etc. Her paint-

ing is really good and has changed enormously. What do we do about J.P.'s knee? We live with this—open the back gate—hold him etc. etc. (He goes to his studio or is taken by Philippe [their handyman] and has done some 100 tiny pics seated—beautiful.)

One evening shortly thereafter, Jean-Paul, Joan, and Hollis dined with Jean-Paul's Canadian pal Champlain Charest, after which the foursome drove to St.-Cyr to view those same tiny paintings. Attempting to flatter Riopelle, Joan "shoplifted" one of them, surreptitiously pulling it off the wall and tucking it into her bag as if to say, See! I love your painting so much I have to steal it. Later that night, after she and Hollis had returned to La Tour, Jean-Paul realized what had happened and rushed over in a rage. Bursting into the darkened house shouting and flailing his crutches, he managed to slam the nearest painting from the wall, then, as Joan burst into the room, dove into her, injury or not. Yelling bloody murder, the two tried to kill each other while Hollis did her best to break them up.

That Joan's increasingly erratic behavior accrued in part from a longing for loving domesticity is suggested by her decision that spring to legally adopt Hollis, who was just the right age to be the child she had long desired. (This never happened, however.) Building a different kind of air castle around Hollis, Jean-Paul revealed to the young woman, one evening when Joan was out of town, that he was in love with her. Her jaw dropped. She thought he was a fun, interesting guy, but she did not love him, nor did she desire an affair. Her feelings for Jean-Paul "didn't come close to how I felt about Joan."

It was then decided that, to further her artistic education, Hollis would visit Italy and that Phyllis, who had been to Italy but wanted to return, would accompany her. On Friday, April 7, the two departed for Florence carrying a thousand dollars in traveler's checks, a gift from Joan. They had planned to fly, *Hollis Jeffcoat, 1978*

but Phyllis had met a French couple who happened to be driving to Italy and were willing to take them along for their share of the gas money. Two hours outside Paris, the foursome stopped for coffee in Auxerre. When they returned to the car, the woman, who had only a learner's permit, got behind the wheel. Shortly thereafter, she was pulling out of her lane to pass a semi (chatting and laughing in the backseat, Phyllis and Hollis paid little attention) when a gust of wind walloped the little Renault, and she lost control. The car rolled, lurched backward, struck a tree, burst into flames. Phyllis was ejected, and the car landed on top of her. Hollis jumped out just as it exploded into a ball of flames.

Phyllis's injuries proved grave. The hospital staff led Hollis to believe that her friend faced three months of recuperation, and Hollis so informed Joan, who flew into a frenzy of activity to replace Phyllis's glasses so that she could read during her long hospital stay. But, in truth, Phyllis was brain dead. The day after Jean-Paul and their friend Gabriel Illouz picked up Hollis and the French couple in Auxerre, Phyllis was taken off life support. A doctor phoned Joan, and Joan phoned her parents in Nashville to deliver the news. It was their wedding anniversary.

With this tragedy, terrible grief and confusion descended upon La Tour. How to grasp that Phyllis's life had been snuffed out in an instant? Joan wanted her to be buried in the cemetery next door, but her parents declined, so Joan arranged for the repatriation of her body in a beautiful casket. Working with the U.S. Embassy, she also had Phyllis's paintings shipped home, and, with her handyman Philippe, cleaned Phyllis's apartment in Paris. Two weeks later, Philippe dropped dead of an aneurysm. The sun barely came out that spring. In July, Joan wrote Phyllis's mother, "Do hope we'll have some corn—and I do think it has rained every day because Phyllis isn't painting in the garden. My I do miss her."

Meanwhile, Jean-Paul's knee continued excruciatingly painful, and Hollis had learned that she had sustained a serious back injury in the accident, which doctors said could heal only if she remained flat for long periods. Joan herself continued to suffer from considerable hip pain, but, stoic midwesterner that she was, said little about it. In any case, she was busy waiting on Hollis, sitting for hours in the young woman's bedroom, alternating doses of milk and Scotch, and wavering between mothering and seducing her. Late at night Joan would flirtatiously take off her darkish glasses—"and it was really horrible looking," remembers Hollis—to pour on the charm, and she gave Hollis massages, "concentrating on areas that weren't even injured." The two began a physical relationship that "was not like a typical physical relationship because [Joan] was so much in denial about it. But yes, it was all there . . . So it was always this back-and-forth dance about what was really going on."

Joan's impaired judgment and outrageous behavior that summer flagged her creeping desperation. In June, she, Jean-Paul, and Hollis attended the reception and private dinner for Sam Francis's traveling exhibition opening at the Centre Pompidou. Seated next to Joan at the dinner, artist Ellsworth Kelly had no sooner made an obviously private remark to her than she jumped to her feet and started broadcasting it, so Kelly leapt up and tackled her. Later she laughed so hard that she wet her panties; she dashed to the ladies' room to remove them, then returned to wave them grotesquely in the face of Fournier, who turned green. Seated at a different table, Jean-Paul ignored her, and Sam was furious, afterward telling friends, "I will never speak to her again! I've had it. She ruined my whole dinner." (Later they reconciled.)

Equally tone-deaf was Joan's insistence that Jean-Paul and Hollis spend the rest of the summer together at a clinic in the south of France, he taking physical therapy for his knee, she for her back, and both getting some sun. Perhaps this was the only way to ensure treatment for Riopelle, who feared doctors and neglected his health, yet Joan appeared to be testing Hollis's faithfulness to her while nudging her into unfaithfulness—a way of hanging on to both Hollis and Riopelle and ensuring that she would not be abandoned.

In the south of France, Hollis and Jean-Paul did become lovers. Between the captivating young woman and crazy old Joan, Jean-Paul's choice was easy. But Hollis too blindly plunged ahead, only later examining her conscience: "I've tried so often to understand what I was doing. Jean-Paul is exactly my father's age. How could I have done this to the person I was closest to? Of course, I tried to justify it by saying, 'Well, they're not together, so why not?' " Aware that the famous love affair of Mitchell and Riopelle was vital to their self-narratives, Hollis nonetheless felt it belonged to history, not to everyday reality. Besides, she rationalized, sleeping with Jean-Paul meant little, since her real allegiance lay with Joan. Officially, Joan did not know what had happened, but when the couple returned to Vétheuil that August, "just friends" in Joan's presence, she started pushing the idea that Hollis should have Jean-Paul's baby and the four of them would live together, the perfect little family, at La Tour.

For the time being, however, life on the hill was dismal. In September Joan wrote her niece Poondie,

> Everyone seems to have died here or on crutches (ain't been no way amusing for last 8 mos.) and I have no dog sitter or feeder or garbage taker downer or lawn mower or weeder and I have a show Oct. 15th [at Fournier] which is nowhere (and all "my critics" died too). [That July, Harold Rosenberg had succumbed to a stroke, and two days later Tom Hess had died of a heart attack.]

All that fall, Joan and Jean-Paul—two strong, wild personalities—vied for Hollis, while their own relationship continued to molder. In New York, Joan's pal, soap opera writer Joe LeSueur, who had long toyed with the idea of doing a roman à clef titled *Messy Lives,* raised his eyebrows: "All I can say is, your messy ménage à trois arrangement provides me with a nifty situation for MESSY LIVES PART II."

Then one very early December morning, Joan, having painted all night, stumbled pie-eyed into the house to discover Jean-Paul in Hollis's bedroom. Always up by six or six thirty a.m., he had formed the habit of bringing Hollis coffee in bed and chatting for a few minutes before he shot off to his studio. Nothing else was going on that morning. But the gesture was intimate, symbolic, and familiar from the time when Joan and Jean-Paul had been lovers. Joan howled, flew at the two, and then raged around the house in a long jealous fury, at one point scooping up a pile of Hollis's letters to her and burning them in the fireplace.

In the aftermath, Hollis left them both, traveling to Florida, where she moved in with her mother. Joan called daily. Jean-Paul called daily. Weeks passed. Then one day Jean-Paul announced to Hollis that he had officially left Joan, whatever that meant. Would Hollis come live with him? She accepted. By January, the couple had settled at St.-Cyr.

Immediately, Joan and Hollis were back together, spending their days at La Tour, joined by Jean-Paul for dinner around eight. But afterward he and Hollis would go home to St.-Cyr. Joan was warier, nastier when drunk, and even more taunting with Jean-Paul than before: Hey, Jim, do you want to fuck me tonight? He'd respond, woundingly, *God!* Yet, in one letter to a friend, Joan paints this homey scene of an occasion when Hollis did stay the night: "Hollis and I are trying to push the paint around—5 am—she at one end of studio and me at other—Mozart on machine 'Grand Mass in C Minor' and 3 German shepherds on bed."

As time went on, uneasiness gained upon Joan. Leaving the couple to dog-sit at La Tour, she traveled to New York that February to seek help from Fried. Shortly after her return, Jean-Paul voiced strong objections to Hollis's spending so much time with Joan, and abruptly the couple decamped for good. The minute she realized they were gone, Joan rushed to the phone, frantically dialing friends. One of the first was Mike Goldberg in New York.

"They've run away together!"

"Who are you talking about?"

"Hollis and Riopelle."

Mike was grumpy. "You know, Joan, it's three o'clock in the morning." Then: "Joan, you set it up."

She smashed down the receiver.

Mike's phone rang again.

"HOW CAN YOU BE SO MEAN?!"

"Well, it's the truth. You don't send a young, attractive girl [to the south of France] with a guy like Riopelle."

Abandoned, betrayed, humiliated, and so distraught that she felt she could not cross the street alone, Joan barely functioned. Her childhood traumas were reawakened, her worst fears realized. That she and Riopelle had no longer operated as a couple, that she had been deeply unhappy for years, that she had courted this disaster did nothing to mitigate her despair. She had been pushed off a cliff into the void. For twenty-four years, her relationship with Jean-Paul, however ugly and painful, had at least been *hers*. He was present each time she smelled coffee or gazed upon certain landscapes. The loss of Hollis—her daughter figure, her younger self, the most piquant presence in her life—completed the map of Joan's mental anguish. All of Joan's bitterness about Riopelle's mistresses now upon Hollis.

Rattling around that big house, its emptiness and silence familiar but now terrifying because they stretched out indefinitely, Joan spiraled into depression. For weeks she holed up and drank. In any case, she had no dog-sitter. Rectangles of starkly white wall marked the spots where

Riopelles had hung. Sheets shrouded the unused billiard table piled with suitcases, one always packed for New York, an inadvertent symbol of her profound unbelonging.

The drama into which Joan pulled friends when she called to rant about Jean-Paul's defects and Hollis's treachery was (unlike the byzantine truth) a conventional tale of a sycophantic dog-sitter/assistant who stole a weak-willed man from his rather old-fashioned Anglo-Saxon mate. Joan's later in-person indignant explanation to poet Bill Berkson was typical: "I caught him in bed with my assistant. That was too much!" In Joan's telling, she had kicked Riopelle out. Among the very few letters she wrote during those months of anguish were one or two to Barney: "To realize how nothing one is to someone else is hard," she told him. "Oh God how hard," he replied. "A murderous rage rises up in me . . . my sweet Juana."

Magical childhood land: harmony, refuge, shelter, quietude.
First concerts of insects, frogs, birds, breezes.
Color-territories: water-green meadows, yellows, blues, cobalt violet,
somber ditches, leper-lilies by the thousands. Wind.

Joan intensely felt la Grande Vallée, its presence,
its sweet-passionate vibrations.
She loved it, revisited it, re-entered it.
A shared land transmuted, pure painting, its soul thus affirmed.

The Paintings, each and every one, sublime, ignited into sonorous, luminous,
radiating cathedrals.

GISÈLE BARREAU, "La Grande Vallée"

CHAPTER FOURTEEN **La Grande Vallée**

Joan began her climb out of the wreckage of her twenty-four years
with Jean-Paul Riopelle by scouting around for a dog-sitter—she
found Noël Morel, a sweet, egoless local boy who became her
all-purpose factotum—then flying to New York for a crash-shrink program with Fried, who forced her to face up to the "very creepy" masochistic side of her relationship with Riopelle, "like hitting a kid and it
clings." Back home, she worked with Fried by phone and, for a time,
saw a French analyst too. Probably it was the latter who introduced her
to what became a favorite conceit, that of "little Joan," who stayed home
and painted, and "big Joan," a grown-up version of a child's imaginary
friend, who protected "little Joan" and functioned in the outside world.

Having broadcast that she needed a live-in companion and assistant,
Joan heard from Betsy Jolas about a thirty-one-year-old French com-

poser named Gisèle Barreau. Following a residency at the MacDowell Colony in New Hampshire, Barreau had taken a job prepping desserts at One Fifth (coincidentally Joan's favorite New York restaurant) as she mulled over her next move. At Joan's interview of sorts with the round-eyed, curly-haired young woman, which took place at Barney's West Houston Street home during that same trip to New York, each cheerfully acknowledged that she was ill-natured and each recognized the other's aloneness. "I sleep like butterflies do, here and there," Gisèle once told Joan. "[Life is] often hard—very lonely." It was left "we'll see," but subsequently they agreed to try each other out.

Thus one sultry early-summer evening a few weeks later, Gisèle walked up to La Tour, jet-lagged and craving sleep, to find Joan leading "group therapy" for several young guests. Chiding anyone who did not work hard enough at the exchange, Joan would not hear of the new arrival going to bed. ("Young lady, you have to give and be part of the group!") Later Joan fixed Gisèle a chicken sandwich and crudités to go with her Scotch. Later still—as one of the guests, Hollis Jeffcoat's estranged ex-roommate, painter Carl Plansky, would recall—the very tanked-up mistress of La Tour locked Gisèle out of the house.

Carl too had found himself sucked into a complicated push-pull relationship, too knotty to sum up in a few phrases, with the impossible yet irresistible Joan. It brought haughty declarations ("You're having a problem with me because you're Jewish and I'm sort of an upper-class Wasp"), outrageous acts (because he vaguely resembled Riopelle, she more than once tried to beat him up when she was smashed), and jolting remonstrances (as one night when he walked downstairs in sandals: "You, what's the matter with you? You think you're a little boy! You don't know how to put socks on properly?"). When he wanted to hit the sack at, say, four a.m., he'd get "Aw, you're such a sissy!"

"Well, Joan, you're right. I can't hold my liquor. I'm about to be ungentlemanly."

"Aw, you better go to sleep, ya weak sister!"

Over the next few years Joan would lean heavily on Carl: when he was at La Tour, he cleaned her brushes, took charge of the paint delivered by Lefebvre-Foinet, and moved her big canvases. Much of their relationship was drinking "and having this really creepy *Who's Afraid of Virginia Woolf?* S&M show." But she invited him to use her studio and materials, hounded him about getting active and making an effort, and paid for plane tickets for his several long stays in Vétheuil. (He supported himself as a cook and deli worker.) They shared a passion for opera, and Carl never loved Joan more dearly than when she sat mesmerized by the voice of Maria Callas. (She nursed a grudge against Aristotle Onassis because he had left Callas for Jackie—"That twig!") Carl and Joan saw each other when Joan was in New York, but "the sweetest times" were at Vétheuil. "It was so painful, my relationship with Joan. It hurt so much. But I got so much out of it. It was fantastic."

Among the least prolific painting periods of Joan's career, the months leading up to the debacle of Riopelle and Hollis's departure had seen her *Tilleul* (*Linden Tree*) canvases, which break stride with the rest of her oeuvre in that they resemble literal paint-drawings of the tree outside her house. Though most would disagree, she proclaimed them the best thing she'd ever done. Now, intermittently paralyzed in her studio, she undertook pastels of the same subject, pinning her paper to the wall atop layers of newspaper (for more "give" than the wall alone offered). Unlike most artists, Joan drew vertically, making use of the weight and drag mark of her hand. In the *Tilleul* pastels, as in the paintings, she sets up a central vertical axis and fills much of the rectangle with dense sheaves of dark lightning-stroke lines, here smothered in blue, there torched with yellow orange.

Painting again, if often badly, by November, Joan felt empowered by failure, in the sense that it spurred her to seek new directions in various works-in-progress in which she believed she was relying too heavily upon "'pretty' accidents." She destroyed many. But some worked. Following a rather happy ten-day visit in September to the music-filled home of her painter friend Jean Lamouroux in tiny Sarrians, near Avignon—in the clarifying light of the Midi—Joan's yellow suite had been gestating. (She had recently painted the great yellow-glowing *Salut Tom*, whose title pays homage to her late friend, the urbane writer, critic, and personification of *her* New York, Tom Hess.) In the 1980 diptych *Cypress*, a radiant welter of yellow orange strokes, Joan oddly but effectively placed two lumpy black oblongs—like the backlit dark cypresses of Provence—on either side of the divide at center canvas, as if they were longing to touch. Lest anyone make assumptions about her psychological state from such gloriously sun-filled canvases, however, Joan later told art historian Judith Bernstock that she had painted the yellow suite in the throes of despair.

Continuing to use painting constructively, Joan undertook the monumental half-ironically titled quadriptych *La Vie en Rose* (today in the collection of the Metropolitan Museum of Art). In its four movements, as in a symphony, attenuated blued pinks and bruised yellow grays, tender and bleak, loom over blue blacks and blacks, and brutal stabs of pigment fringe an eloquent emptiness. One might say: fog, wharf, din, breakers, silence. Steeped in the memory-feelings of Rosa Bonheur/Malheur, Joan's tour de force emotional reckoning of her long years with Jean-Paul Riopelle is poignant, elegiac, and haunting.

Six months after her move to La Tour, Gisèle Barreau won the prestigious French Prix de Rome, which required her to live at the Villa Medicis in Rome for the next two and a half years, though she intermittently spent time in Vétheuil. Her departure left Joan to brave by herself the dull, sodden Île de France winter and to rattle around her big house "really hacking it alone," she told a friend, "which is a challenge in this isolation." Her cook and gardener, Raymonde and Jean, were there, of course, as were her "doggies" and Noël. At times it got so cold and drafty that she and Noël shivered as they watched TV wrapped in blankets. Occasionally Joan would throw on her black leather jacket and take a day trip into Paris to go to the bank, see a doctor, visit a friend or two, pop into an exhibition, and/or dine with Fournier at their favorite restaurant, L'Ami Louis. But mostly she holed up, unhappy and distraught, at La Tour.

Come spring, visitors arrived, lifting somewhat the sense of emptiness and loss. Bitter because certain mutual friends had chosen Jean-Paul and Hollis, not her, and because her stepdaughters too, she felt, had abandoned her (later they reconnected), Joan grew more dependent upon the young people with whom she surrounded herself. The number who passed through Vétheuil is astounding: ask among painters of a certain age in any serious art milieu in the United States and you will likely find someone who lunched or dined or spent a few days at La Tour, got drunk on Joan's liquor, maybe painted in the cistern, and has a ready anecdote or two about some test of his or her character, some galvanizing conversation, some hair-raising episode. Carl returned in March 1980. California painter Katy Crowe, then living in Paris, was invited out after she called Joan at the urging of Mike Goldberg, whom she had met at an opening. Bill Scott, also a painter, met Joan at the Galerie Jean Fournier. And Joyce Pensato (who had made Joan's acquaintance when the older artist, tough and glamorous in sunglasses and a fur coat, had dropped by the student studios at the New York Studio School) would begin visiting Vétheuil in 1981. There, many felt, something important lurked in the air. After his sojourn at La Tour, young guitarist Reed Bertolette, the son of Joan's Smith College roommate, told the rowdy near-sixty-year-old: "You have a mind/energy/electricity/feeling that makes me feel like a kindling spark next to a roaring bonfire. But I can feel the oxygen draft surging to your flames."

When it came time for her guests to leave, Joan always sidestepped good-byes, which she considered rehearsals for death. One was supposed to slink out without making a fuss. Even before they departed, some visitors received thank-yous steeped in Joan's appreciation for the precious new memories their stays had afforded her. Preparing to leave for the airport one morning as her hostess slept, Joyce found a note:

> You were lovely company, I wasn't . . . And you'll be glad to get home and work (I hope) and work very well. Your generosity is extravagant. Take some chocolate covered drops for airplane please. We can never eat them all. They are on billiard table. Thank you mostly for coming . . . I think autumn is perhaps exciting in the city and sad in the country. I think we must be quite strong to withstand this place by ourselves . . . *Bon voyage.*

Joan's painting problems had persisted. *Two Sunflowers* had become "'Ludwigs' [meaning heavy and expressionistic à la Beethoven] and I don't really want objects," she confided in Joyce. "What do I want—space?" *No Daisies,* on the other hand, snugged up to the picture plane but achieved little else. The *Petit Matin* group felt unresolved. Her colors verged on the saccharine, and she felt she was repeating herself. "Joan is making a smashing effort," she assured Carl and Joyce, "pics not good but making it alone . . . it's a 'challenge' and if I make it I'll feel really happy [crossed out]—not happy of course but 'somewhere' and not so frightened—panic—not that aloneness or thinking when I paint—what am I doing this for? Etc. When it's the only thing I like to do or that interests me. My painting is bad now—but I've gone through so many periods."

Bad painting—so what else is new? With the sagacity of four decades, she kept her perspective. In New York that March 1980 for the opening of her third show at Fourcade, Joan Mitchell, The Fifties: Important Paintings (so conceived because of the dearth of new work), she brightened somewhat. Xavier threw a festive dinner party in her honor: painter Norman Bluhm and his wife Carey, poet Karen Edwards, writer Eleanor Munro, novelist and later Frank O'Hara biographer Brad Gooch, curator Marcia Tucker, Barney, and pals Joe LeSueur, Hal Fondren, Pierre Boudreau, Carl, Joyce, and Elaine de Kooning, among others, attended. A few days later Joan trekked out to Long Island to visit Bill de Kooning, who had been living in Springs since the early 1960s. Depression, heavy drinking, and the onset of Alzheimer's-like dementia having taken their toll on the master painter, his lawyer had brokered an arrangement with Elaine, still his legal wife despite three decades of separation, whereby she—that "miracle on roller skates," as their mutual friend photographer Denise Browne Hare phrased it—had moved to Springs to supervise the seventy-five-year-old artist's care. On this occasion, Joan lunched with Bill, Elaine, and poet Bill Berkson, who was living in Southampton. Berkson was struck by Joan and Elaine's mutual affection as well as Bill's warm, strong, collegial respect for Joan. De Kooning made her feel that, whatever else happened, *that* war was over. She had won.

Back at Vétheuil, Joan met twenty-five-year-old French painter Michaële-Andréa Schatt, a native of Mantes-la-Jolie who had childhood memories of spotting the famous Abstract Expressionist at her local train station. Their paths had crossed again, without the two actually meeting, when Schatt won a prize at the annual Salon de Montrouge competition thanks to the vote of juror Joan Mitchell. Now, by chance, Michaële had been invited by an American painter friend named Marilyn Riley to accompany her on a visit to La Tour.

Marilyn was beautiful and feminine, a combination that always set Joan to whetting her blades. At the end of their meal, rife with both tension and laughter, Gisèle served a cake, and, responding to some remark from Michaële, the by now very animated and drunk hostess clattered, "Here's what I say about your—" as she slammed a knife into the cake. And clack! Not only did she slice the cake in two but also neatly bisected the ceramic platter. "Shit!" burst out Michaële, convulsed with laughter. "You don't fool around!"

Later that evening, Joan blurted, "Michaële, shall we play tennis? You're Borg, I'm McEnroe. Okay, let's go!" A vociferous tennis fan who followed all the major tournaments on TV and demanded the same concentration, precision, and excellence from athletes as from artists, Joan disliked Jimmy Connors, liked John McEnroe, and adored Björn Borg for "that fixed determination, that calm, that self-containment, that obstinate confidence." She started serving Michaële questions about various painters. Apropos of so-and-so's work: "So what do you think? Do you feel something or what?" Michaële would answer, Joan would counter. The two went back and forth, back and forth, Joan enthusiastically cheering Michaële's glowing yes-reaction to van Gogh: "Okay, you've hit a smash! Excellent, excellent!"

Quickly nicknamed "Françoise Sagan" for her bookishness, mettle, and vague resemblance to the author of *Bonjour Tristesse,* Michaële was for Joan another younger surrogate self. A student of philosopher Gilles Deleuze at the experimental University of Paris 8 in Saint-Denis, she, like Joan, perceived an indispensable link between reading and painting, which is not to say that painting should be literary but rather that both can break the seals on everyday time and space. The two discussed Joan's art in terms of stratification of memory, poetic space, and painting as fabric: while Manet's pictures, for instance, are so tightly woven as to allow virtually no holes, Joan's, like Cézanne's, abound in marvelous slippages, dilations, and discontinuities. Joan sometimes visited Michaële's studio, ordering her protégée to clean it up ("*Quel bazar!* What the hell is all this crap? Get it out of here!"), the better to focus on the work at hand, then delivering the brutally honest critiques.

Michaële conceived of Joan as a sort of pinball wizard:

When she met someone, she would say to herself: "Okay, move over. I'll get this one!" And hup! She pulled the lever and sent out the ball. And she played a game. She played a game of pinball. Ting! Ting! Ting! Ting! . . . When she had in front of her someone who was a player—Joan was *such* a player!—both would play. Superb!

The following February brought another Fourcade exhibition (Joan Mitchell: New Work). After the opening Joan traveled to Washington, D.C., for the 1981 Corcoran Biennial featuring recent art by five veteran Americans: Frank Stella, Agnes Martin, Richard Serra, Richard Diebenkorn, and Joan Mitchell. During its installation, according to *Washington Post* art critic Paul Richard, Joan smoked in the gallery, an absolute no-no, but no one dared speak up. Staffers were scared of her. Mobbed at the reception by friends, fellow artists, and admirers, she responded coyly when a *Post* photographer asked her to pose with Stella: "I'm not sure if I'm famous enough for him." But she did pose, grinning and goofy looking.

As avidly as she sought the company of artists, Joan now kept her distance from the art world as such, which she equated with competition, sycophancy, and tinsel. A few days earlier, in Manhattan, she had conceded to painter Katy Crowe, whom she had once blasted for not moving to New York after graduate school, that Crowe might have been right: "I understand why you didn't come to New York. This is the most backbiting, high-pressure, unsupportive place I can imagine." Joan's own New York scene was long dead, she even seemed a bit lost in New York, yet she had no particular reason to remain in France. Where did that leave her? Mulling over her future, she told her old friends Joanne and Phil Von Blon,

> I wouldn't know where else to go [except Vétheuil] or I'm too lazy to move. I don't think "the Dakota" in N.Y. would suit me or the dogs even if we could afford it—or Southern Italy—good light and cheap real estate—either. Being an outsider anyway i.e. painter and having become even more so, foreigner, in a foreign country, I wonder . . . Yet I feel American whatever that means, perhaps just a label—but no—a feeling—and an objectivity.

After she lost St. Mark's Place to a huge rent increase the following year, Barney urged her to take part of the twenty-three acres he owned in Three-Mile Harbor and build a house. She hesitated but finally said no. Her feeling of unbelonging in New York did not translate into a feeling of belonging in France, however. Though no one would mistake her for a native, her French was very good, and she was savvy about the French system. Still, like many who live abroad, she felt intensely American and detested the word "expatriate." As for Vétheuil, she had never nested there as she had at Frémicourt, and the house had seen better days. It needed a new roof and, Joan still refusing the corruptions of creature comforts, lacked even a single well-cushioned chair. Often passive and despondent, she viewed herself as a prisoner. But the garden remained paradisiacal, the lilacs still bloomed, and, on certain sunny days, she wanted to "drink the landscape."

From Washington, Joan traveled, via New York City, to Bedford in

Joan and master printer Ken Tyler at Tyler Graphics, 1981, photographed by Hans Namuth

Westchester County, where she collaborated with master printmaker and publisher Ken Tyler at Tyler Graphics. Originally from East Chicago, Tyler had graduated from the School of the Art Institute of Chicago a few years after Joan, then founded the Gemini print workshop and Gemini GEL publishing house in Los Angeles before coming east in 1974. He had worked extensively with David Hockney, Robert Motherwell, Helen Frankenthaler, Robert Rauschenberg, Roy Lichtenstein, Frank Stella, and other art stars, and had long since invited Joan to Tyler Graphics, but, reluctant to leave her dogs for more than a week or two, she had taken her time in accepting.

Ken and Joan immediately hit it off. Genial and unflappable, Ken had no problem with Joan's bluntness, cantankerousness, heavy drinking, or need to nose around in everybody's business (including his own six-month-old but already rocky marriage to printer Lindsay Green)—in fact, he found her "a hoot." He admired her quickness to notice and absorb everything, playing her artistic likes and dislikes "like a game of cards," taking lessons even from work she didn't care for—Rauschenberg's, for instance—and then moving on.

That late winter, Joan collaborated with Ken and his staff on four sets of lithographs printed from aluminum plates using up to ten colors each. Officially, no one was allowed in the room when the artist was drawing, yet Ken managed to observe her quick, decisive stroke making: Joan would approach the piece of Mylar pinned to the wall knowing exactly what she intended to do, do it, and then walk away. On to the next color. She had mentally visualized each intricate print before she began. At intervals, she lounged in an old barber chair that stood in the studio, a cigarette in one inky-fingernailed hand, a mug of coffee or glass of Scotch in the other, and scrutinized the results. She and Ken bantered about the Great Abstract Expressionist Mark, and sometimes she jokingly summoned him, "Ken, this might be *it!*" The truth was, says Tyler, there was a rare, magical purity in Joan's drawing, which was "as close as you're going to get to Zen drawing. You think about it, and then you make the stroke. You don't go back on it. You just leave it."

He also observed that, of the hundreds of artists with whom he'd worked, Mitchell had the most complex color sense, based in a lifetime of empirical observation as well as a profound and acutely visual knowledge of art history. She was highly demanding. "*God damn it*, Ken! Can't you make viridian green?" she piped up at one point. And again: "Ken, I want to try a color like the color of dying sunflowers." (So reported art historian Barbara Rose, who visited both Bedford and Vétheuil that spring, for her feature story "The Landscape of Light: Joan Mitchell," photographs by Hans Namuth, which appeared in the June issue of *Vogue*.)

According to Tyler, Joan further distinguished herself by her mental process:

> If she saw the landscape, she recorded it, thought about it. It was like making poetry, right? She probably had fifteen different ways of expressing that in her mind. When she went to paint that or draw that, those fifteen different ways became thirty. By the time she was done, they became ninety. It was that kind of investigative thinking that she was capable of . . . Her painting came from a catalog of visuals that Joan had that no one else had.

That September, Gisèle returned for good from Rome. The two would live together at La Tour until Joan's death eleven years later. As both a convenience and a safety valve, however, Gisèle kept a place on the other side of Paris, near the National Conservatory of Music, where she had once studied and would soon teach. Each woman deeply respected the other's art. "Your paintings are so beautiful," Gisèle once affection-

Joan and Gisèle dining at home, early 1980s

ately encouraged Joan. "I am moved. Go on, Peanut [her nickname for Joan]. *Tu es sur la bonne voie* [You're on the right track]." Having substituted a piano for the table in the formal dining room, which became the music room, Joan loved to listen to Gisèle play. What the composer described as "verbal percussion, sound color, sound/light, subtle vibrations, sympathy, empathy, breath" music lent wings to Joan's painting, and the reverse was true too. Beginning with the 1980 *Aires Pour Marion* for six percussionists and a chorus (its libretto based on the poetry of Saint-John Perse), the feelings of certain Barreau pieces resonate with Mitchell's, as underscored by their mutual titles: *A Small Garden, Two Pianos, A Garden for Audrey, Blue Rain,* and so on.

Born and raised in a small town near Nantes and abused as a child, Gisèle believed that, except for her music, there was nothing special about her. Joan dubbed her companion "Gizée" because not only did she vaguely resemble Joan's late Skye terrier "Izée" (Isabelle) but also she had that same spunky and friendly yet cautious personality. As practical and capable as she was soulful and sensitive, Gisèle knew (and taught Joan) about birds and gardening, keeping her own little plot at La Tour and eventually getting Joan too to scratch around in the dirt and grow plants from cuttings. Joan fussed over her forsythia and raspberry bushes, birthday gifts from Gisèle. Moreover, Gisèle made Joan's appointments, purchased her socks, took her driving in the country, helped her move paintings, set out vitamin C when she was fighting a cold and leftovers when she was dining alone, and scribbled hundreds of notes to her, often upbeat and soothing.

Alternately treated as friend, housekeeper, fellow artist, employee, companion, and dog-sitter, Gisèle frequently bore the brunt of Joan's displeasure with this or that. Warm, thoughtful, and generous one minute, the artist would turn arrogant, hypercritical, and nasty the next. She set up rivalries between Gisèle and others—Noël, for one—and, hawk-eyed defender of Gisèle though she was, at times cruelly walked all over her in front of their friends. More than once the younger woman stalked out of La Tour, steaming mad and intending never to return, but always she did: fundamentally tough, she found that the emotional and artistic rewards of Joan's friendship outstripped the pain. On at least one occasion, after Joan had put her through more hell than usual, Gisèle laid down a blunt ultimatum, thus winning greater respect from Joan, who liked it when people confronted her.

Putting their two lonelinesses together, the pair muddled through everyday life, there for each other when it mattered. "I realize I love you so much, and the puppies, and the house—why is it so painful . . . ," Gisèle once told Joan. "You are not alone—and we have a bet. Remember? Let's be strong for each other." On another occasion a visiting Joe LeSueur intercepted "a rapturous, transfixed expression" on Joan's face "when, during an unguarded moment, she had eyes for no one in the room" but Gisèle. Love with a capital L was emotionally risky, however, and Joan fretted that people would assume she and Gisèle were a couple. "You broke my heart last night," Joan wrote her companion from the studio one dawn, "all the scaffolding [Fried] tried to give me I would gladly give you—more selfishly—I can't bear your sadness—your eyes and the silent dripping. I'll never forget your face—something Romanesque."

Joan had just received news of Edrita Fried's death. Profoundly affected, she wavered between "the awareness that Edrita is no more, and the unwillingness or inability to accept this." Over the years she had continued to see Fried regularly in New York, and she cherished the memory of one "enchanted day" at La Tour with Edrita and her husband

John when, surrounded by dogs, the trio had lingered on Joan's terrace, chatting, teasing, and gazing upon the landscape before moseying up to her studio, a day when "the world [had] felt as if it had no gravity and no grief."

Joan's note to Gisèle continued,

Haven't finished her joint or pad in Paradise yet—it's forming—semi-Viennese and semi-N.Y.—*piscine* [swimming pool]—tons of comfort—2 male cooks—young (she orders them around—they adore her). Females also—very intelligent however and up to the minute. Intellectuals who drop in for tea and cookies—Freud and Anna ... and then someone like Franz Kline who comes in for booze and to pour charm. Eventually she'll put my Mother at ease. She'll flirt with my Father and put him at ease. Flowers—flowers—plants—blue sea—books—and travel. (I haven't developed that part of Paradise—except sea and mountains) ... Well kiddle doo—I have no choice but to take your nice challenge ... Perhaps this pic with a little effort could mix your dying asters garden I loved—kitchen window—in the wind with Edrita and with a bit of courage on my part. What can I complain about? I knew her and I know you and the dogs.

The feeling of those desolate, wind-flung asters outside Joan's kitchen window endures in her four-panel *Edrita Fried,* its bitter oranges battling their way out of tumultuous whitened blues—surely Edrita's colors. For the analyst's daughter, Jaqueline Fried, in any case, the painting's oranges nail her mother's energy and rage, and its blues, her profound sadness. *Edrita Fried* appeared in the 1983 Whitney Biennial, which Jaqui attended. When the museum's elevator doors opened to reveal this twenty-six-foot-wide painting, Jaqui jumped, "because it was as if my mother were standing there ... It was really my mother!"

As Joan was putting the final touches on *Edrita Fried,* her sister Sally, 5,700 miles away, learned she had stomach cancer. A month later, Sally underwent surgery but did not tell Joan. A rift had opened between the two siblings, the major issue for Sally being Joan's "indescribable rudeness." Sally had declared that she never again wanted to hear from or see her younger sister. Even so, Sally's thirty-four-year-old daughter Poondie sensed that Joan *had* to know, so, after much hesitation, she phoned her aunt to break the news. Joan said she'd hop on the next plane.

But Sally objected. So Poondie phoned again, this time putting Joan on strict notice that she would have to be on her very best behavior. And, for three weeks in Santa Barbara, she was.

Though Sally's anger ran deep, the visit was rather like old times: the sisters drank together, gossiped, and criticized everyone. One of their favorite targets was First Lady Nancy Reagan, who had attended Chicago Latin with Sally and briefly dated Sally's ex-husband, Newt. (The Perrys had divorced in 1969.) Newt's society band had played at the debut of the then Nancy Davis, accompanying her when she sang "Oh, You Crazy Moon." Not only did Sally and Joan abhor the Reagans' politics, but also they were adamant that the White House was *lying* about Nancy's age.

After her divorce from Newt, Sally had become a dog trainer, an international authority on the Belgian Malinois, and the author of the definitive handbook on the breed. Among friends and neighbors, stories about Sally's sometimes terrifying guard and attack dogs (so people called them)—Yakie, Pinhead, Lisa, and Studly—are legion. Sharing an adoration of canines, Sally and Joan talked endlessly about their darlings, Joan on the defensive because, unlike Sally's dogs, her Iva, Maddie, and Marion were not trained athletes.

Back in Vétheuil, Joan pressed on with efforts at sisterly closeness. Deeply distraught, sometimes weeping as she wrote, and, judging from her big, scrawled handwriting, often very drunk, she dispatched loving and encouraging letters, rambles through present and past, filled with childhood memories, dog gossip, and news of her upcoming show. After twenty-three years in France, Joan had finally been tapped for her first French museum exhibition, at the Musée d'Art Moderne de la Ville de Paris. She was the first female American artist so honored (she said) by a major French museum since nineteenth-century Impressionist Mary Cassatt.

Joan painted fiercely that spring: "Sal—I'm saying—all I can do is painting and I'm doing it also because you are sick—hard to explain—because it is all I can do." She was especially pleased with *Chez Ma Soeur* and *Pour ses Malinois,* both of which drew upon Santa Barbara memories, alluded to Sally in their titles, and would be included, if she had her way, in what she envisioned as the "Balls to Cancer" section of her show. (She was battling the curators, Béatrice Parent and Suzanne Pagé, over every inch of the installation.) "Anyway I'll try not to embarrass you—as my sister—I'll make it the best I can possibly do (but I sure ain't Van

Joan strolls in her garden at Vétheuil, 1984.

Gogh—that perfection)." Painting, Joan had explained to the curators, is "the opposite of death, it permits one to survive, it also permits one to live. For me, *Chez Ma Soeur,* for example, is profoundly sad . . . it's sadness in full sunlight as there is joy in the rain."

It became obvious that Sally was not going to make it. After she left the hospital that May to die at home, Joan returned to Santa Barbara, taking along a beautiful poem Marion had written shortly before Jimmie died, "When that time comes." Her second visit wasn't ugly, but it wasn't as good as the first. Joan drank heavily and pushed people's buttons until finally Poondie told her it was time to leave. When someone took a last-minute Polaroid of her with one of Sally's friends, Joan looked at it—she was reed thin with tired, parchmenty skin and bags under her reddened eyes—and murmured, "We both look kind of funny, don't we? We both look kind of sad. Well, it's okay to be sad." The silver linings to Sally's cancer, Joan decided, were that she once again considered herself a capable person, that Riopelle had been chased from her mind, and that Sally now understood that Joan loved her.

On June 24, 1982, Joan Mitchell: Selected Paintings, 1970–1982 opened at the Musée d'Art Moderne de la Ville de Paris, accompanied by a handsome catalog. That evening she arrived at the crowded event having traded her usual battered running shoes for red sneakers. When Paul Auster arrived, along with his new wife, writer Siri Hustvedt, Joan rushed to give him a huge hug and later talked nonstop about her sister.

A few days later, young painter Elisabeth Kley visited Vétheuil from New York and was immediately recruited to help with the dogs. Elisabeth found La Tour cluttered and carpeted with dog hair and Joan in a strange paranoid state, "really hooked into tragedy." Yet somehow the atmosphere wasn't gloomy: the phone rang often, and Gisèle, Noël, and others came and went. Elisabeth had never before met anyone so famous, and she certainly never expected someone so famous to be (in certain ways) as open as Joan, who was in the habit of peeing with the bathroom door ajar and yelling at the same time, not to mention that she wrote disarmingly self-revealing notes. One dawn that late July, as Sally was approaching the end, Joan left this message for Elisabeth on the billiard table before heading for bed:

> I called and talked to nurse. Sally couldn't talk . . . 4 AM I am painting. Sally just called and said she loved me etc.—oh God. You are right. This is heavy. This is the first time Sally has called. *Magic Flute ce soir* and tomorrow—*les Noces de Figaro* [*The Marriage of Figaro*].

The next day:

> I did call Calif and I talked only to Beverly (the lovely nurse). Sally is in a state of "withdrawal" (I said you mean terminal? and she said yes). Much less morphine now—"the body takes over its own death" (let's learn). She can't walk of course and barely talks. Seems "very serene" and looks "serene" and Sally said this morning—let's hope it's over now . . . Bev will call me when she dies . . . I too somehow feel serene with the Strauss record [the *Four Last Songs* of Richard Strauss] and the end of such horror and pain for her.

Sally Perry died on July 25, 1982, at age fifty-eight. After arranging by phone for the flowers at her sister's memorial service, Joan once again picked up her pen:

> I'm still listening to Kiri—Strauss—beautiful dawn. Puppies asleep and she's in heaven—my paradise now. Oh fuck how horrible—all of

it—I can't even fight with her anymore—*merde*. Well I'm still having
a hard lousy time. Fuck it—must shake it. Nice though to care about
somebody or love. Really—painful but worth it like painting I guess.

The very day Sally died, art critic Michael Gibson's review of Joan's
exhibition appeared in the *International Herald Tribune*:

> This is obviously painting of the highest quality in a modern idiom.
> But the life the viewer senses in the work comes from an area quite
> beyond the realm of painting. This has always been the case with all
> true painting and it is all the more unusual today because circum-
> stances do not favor the sort of slow maturation that gives an artist
> [such] qualities and scope.

> One senses that painting is something of a religion to Mitchell, at least
> in the sense implied by Alfred North Whitehead when he says that
> "religion is what the individual does with his own solitariness." The
> important word here is "solitariness" and it probably explains why
> there are so few authentic artists—that sort of solitariness is some-
> thing that most people want to avoid at all costs.

Having shared with her *tantine* the heartache of Sally's final months and
having received from her such loving letters, Poondie traveled to Paris
that September believing that Joan's hurtful ways had ended. Instead she
found her aunt "meaner and meaner," her suffering asserted in the pain
she inflicted on others. When she was alone, however, Joan reacted to
little and saw mostly no-color. She did not touch her brushes for a very
long time.

That same year she quit drinking. According to Carl Plansky, Joan
"must have been nauseous a lot. She was hungover a lot." One night in
particular "she looked awful, and she said, 'I don't want to have a drink.'
It was the only time she ever said that. And then around eight she stood
up, and I could see she was shaking, and she said, 'Why don't you put
some beers on?' She really, really needed a drink." Yet, acting on her
own, Joan now managed to quit, and even to paint without liquor. In
December 1983, a year and a half after the loss of her sister, Joan wrote
to Elisabeth Kley, who was back in New York, "It's so nice to paint after

that awful long period of not working. I also stopped drinking entirely for a long time. Now I just drink a bit. Whisky is only for a needed goose in the studio." Within weeks, however, she was drinking full-bore.

Inspired by a story from Gisèle, Joan had plunged into a new cycle of painting. Only three days before Sally's death, Gisèle's twenty-eight-year-old cousin, Jean-Philippe Halgand, had succumbed to cancer. Gisèle's memories of Jean-Philippe centered around la Grande Vallée, a solitary, semi-hidden place, not far from her childhood home, where peasants pastured their cows and where wildflowers, dandelions, birds, and trees abounded. One couldn't see the Loire River, but one felt its presence. There, at age six or seven, Gisèle had begun taking refuge from her troubled home life, arriving by bicycle, sometimes accompanied by her younger cousin, and bringing along pieces of cardboard, a wooden xylophone, and other childish treasures. Years later, as he lay dying, Jean-Philippe had asked Gisèle to take him once more to la Grande Vallée, but that never happened. Enchanted by this story, which she found "very true and very simple" and which her rereading of Proust (for whom "the true paradises are the paradises that we have lost") helped bring into mental focus, Joan decided to paint la Grande Vallée as a place for Sally and Jean-Philippe.

No sooner had she begun, however, than she was blocked, both by practicalities (the studio's heating system died, the house urgently needed reroofing, Christmas had to be organized for her entourage) and by the devastating feeling that painting was "all meaningless again." She fell prey to despair. A few weeks later, she once more set to work.

La Grande Vallée consists of twenty-one paintings (including five diptychs and one triptych), the last five of which Joan conceived for four people who were among her emotional mainstays—Carl Plansky, Jean Fournier, art critic Yves Michaud, and Philippe Le Thomas, a medical student who was taking steps to become a Benedictine monk (his ecclesiastical name was Frère Luc)—plus Iva, her dog. In a sense, these were *Territory* paintings. Each had a strict relationship with its inspirer, and they were not at all interchangeable. Jean Fournier described his as "an emblematic painting: yellow, fog, and blue."

Packed nearly edge to edge, as if with tumbling, overgrown bowers, the *Grande Vallée* paintings—their blues, yellows, reds, pinks, oranges, and greens radiant with inner light—exude the feeling of a teeming, prelapsarian world. Yet shadows lurk and scatterings of black dart "in and out ...," as curator Klaus Kertess once put it, "like an auguring

flock of crows." The artist's color changes are sometimes abrupt, sometimes sustained, and she moves with unfailing grace through a multitude
of painterly situations. Spots of canvas dance like stray sunlight. Built
with compact, bold, multidirectional, often hydrangea-textured strokes,
the paintings are shallow yet spatially complex, further complicated,
in the multi-paneled works, by the effects around the cuts. Their stark
frontality—everything piles up on or near the picture plane—means that
one cannot walk around in *La Grande Vallée*. Like all childhood memories, it leaves one yearning at its edges. At the same time, it reminds viewers that, for Mitchell, "painting is like music—it is beyond life and death.
It is another dimension."

On the occasion of Joan's exhibition at the Musée d'Art Moderne, *People*
magazine had profiled her: "In the Land of Monet, American Painter
Joan Mitchell More Than Pulls Her Weight." (Having never heard of
this publication, Joan at first called it *"People's Magazine."*) Nervously
anticipating the arrival at La Tour of the journalist and photographer,
Joan had told Carl, "Look, when they come, tell them I make a good
ratatouille." Though rarely did she prepare a meal, someone had given
her, and she had mastered, a recipe for ratatouille. So when *People*'s Joyce
Campbell fished for information from Carl, he casually mentioned that
Joan made a good ratatouille. However, when Campbell tried to engage
the artist about her cuisine, "Well, I hear you make a good ratatouille,"
Joan snarled, "I don't cook!"

The feature in *People* also afforded her a choice opportunity to swipe
at Hollis and Jean-Paul. "Three years ago, her lover of 23 years, Riopelle,
left with the 26-year-old woman the artist had hired as a dog-sitter," the
magazine informed its readers. "The betrayal still darkens Mitchell's disposition and, at times, her peppery vocabulary."

Not long thereafter, Joan started running into the "The Twenty-
Four-Year Live-In" on the Paris–Mantes-la-Jolie train. (Still suffering
from knee problems, Riopelle was unable to drive to his studio in St.-
Cyr.) This happened, she told Elisabeth Kley,

twice with her and once alone, at which time we talked at both ends (I
was in first class after all—he in second) oddly enough—and honestly
it didn't bother me at all—he seemed a bit ill at ease however. Well
I deserve champagne, or Fried does (she isn't dead to me). It's only

taken me 4 1/2 years of hard work—but I made it. Whee. He has a show tomorrow—[the] opening [of] which he seemed to want me to see. Unfortunately I can't make the opening—*n'est-ce pas!*—(who is he kidding?). I'm very proud of myself. He looks pitiful too and old and shrunk [Riopelle suffered from osteoporosis] and he's only 60—and I didn't no way feel no compassion.

Not only Fried but also time, painting, and music had played important roles. Over and over, Joan had listened to the cathartic *Dido and Aeneas,* Henry Purcell's opera of love and betrayal, with its powerful lament by the despairing and dying Queen Dido. Joan now spoke of her erstwhile intimates with sadness, bitterness, indifference, and/or pride at having worked through her loss: "That garbage can won't ever be totally rinsed out, but it's in a dark corner." Yet the minute Hollis left Jean-Paul in 1986 and returned to Paris (the couple had been living chiefly in Canada), Joan rang her up: "Will you come back?" Hollis never again set foot in La Tour, but time and again they spoke by phone and saw each other in Paris.

And Joan and Jean-Paul communicated. One winter evening in 1988, he and his new companion, the Quebecoise Huguette Vachon, accompanied Jean Fournier to Vétheuil, where Joan sized up, challenged, and won over Huguette. Following dinner, the artist briefly absented herself to change into her work clothes, then reappeared in black pants and an ancient, oversized, paint-smeared sweater of Jean-Paul's, unraveling so that it hung in clumps under her arms as she flung them up and announced, "My painting outfit!" Huguette found her beautiful like a wild bird.

Several years earlier, the Galerie Jean Fournier had moved from the Left Bank to the Right, near the new Centre Pompidou. With its stunning luminosity, the gallery's rue Quincampoix incarnation, in an ancient building with one slightly crooked wall, proved the perfect setting for the show, which opened on May 28, 1984, of the first sixteen of the *Grande Vallée* paintings.

Joan always pursued her vision until she exhausted it, yet the *Grande Vallée* cycle feels exceptionally unified, both formally and thematically, a feeling enhanced by its installation at Fournier, where it became an environment. The work sold briskly, mostly to Europeans, and never again has it been seen as an ensemble.

For many observers, *La Grande Vallée* clinched the connection between Mitchell and Monet, the vibrant, vegetal lushness of her canvases and the cohesion of the whole bringing to mind his large, semiabstract, multi-panel paintings of water lilies, in which plants, water, air, and sky inextricably mingle. Given Mitchell's enchantment with gardens, love of the pastoral landscape familiar from the Impressionist's scenes, and ownership of the cottage in which Monet had once lived (her address was 12, avenue Claude Monet), on one hand, and the lyricism and radiance of their two oeuvres, on the other, this pairing had long been irresistible to critics. Moreover, as artist Ora Lerman (who worked for a time at Monet's home in nearby Giverny) points out, the moisture-laden atmosphere of the Valley of the Seine "[weaves] all the colors together in a way that allowed Monet and other Impressionists . . . to conceive of form as comprising a whole spectrum of interconnected colors without discrete edges," and Mitchell too had soaked up that soft confluence of color.

Writing in *Artforum,* reviewer John Yau, for one, states that Mitchell's "absorption of Impressionism, particularly late Monet, has played a decisive role in her recent work." A once-tough New York School painter, such comments imply, had succumbed to the temptation of life-is-beautiful Abstract Impressionism.

"The whole linkage is so horrible," objected Joan, who accused "Monette" (as she relished mispronouncing his name) of being a mediocre colorist and of not even tipping the plane forward in his landscapes. Moreover, Monet was concerned with shifting effects of light whereas Mitchell was attempting to capture emotionally charged memories, something fundamentally different. And, unlike Joan, Monet painted directly from nature. Once, after a visit to his home and garden in nearby Giverny, which opened to the public in 1980, she returned to her studio, painted a beautiful Monet water lily, and then, appalled, destroyed it. Yet people assumed that, if administered truth serum, Joan would confess her love of Monet.

She added to this misunderstanding by characteristically seeming to quarrel with her own opinions. If she bothered with Monet at all, as she did, notably in the early 1970s, it was because she felt she had something to learn from him. Following her afternoon in Vétheuil in 1972, writer Cindy Nemser—who saw "the spirit of Monet [hovering] over all of

Mitchell's work"—passed along to her readers that "Joan openly admits her adoration of Monet and urged me repeatedly to visit the Marmottan Museum in Paris where many of his best paintings are to be found." Other visitors at other times noted Joan's mild interest in or cheerful disdain of the Impressionist master.

The matter of Monet leads to the larger issue of the genealogy of Mitchell's art, the distinctly French cast of her later work begging the question of whether or not it merits the label Abstract Expressionist. Certainly, her previsualization had always distinguished her work from that of improvisatory New York action painters, as had her disposition to work in a mode of egolessness. Yet her canvases bristled with Abstract Expressionist energy and love of paint as paint.

As early as 1960, critic Pierre Schneider had argued that Mitchell's New York School connection "helps little to explain the peculiarities of her work, for she is a complex, thoroughly unpredictable, artist." And, in 1974, curator Marcia Tucker had declared Mitchell "no longer an Abstract Expressionist," thereby eliciting strenuous objections from critic Harold Rosenberg. Now, in an essay for the *Grande Vallée* exhibition, French art critic, philosopher, and director of the École des Beaux-Arts Yves Michaud weighed in on the issue. Introduced to Joan by her dealer in 1984, Michaud would champion her work over the several years that followed. A systematic and highly intellectual thinker, he nonetheless understood painting in painting terms, and Joan felt, had the right fix on what she was doing. (Moreover, she liked the brawler in Yves.) "To get right to it," states Michaud,

> the painting of Joan Mitchell is as removed from the visuality of Impressionism as from a kind of Expressionism in which raw subjectivity seeks to go beyond itself. She finds and pursues her path between the two, between nature and subject, between a mental disposition for things and one for interiority.

A decade later, in 1994, Robert Storr, then curator of painting and sculpture at the New York Museum of Modern Art, would argue that

> as time passes, it would seem that [Joan Mitchell's] New York period was more interlude than decisive moment in her career, even if, without it, she would never have reaped the marvels of her last and most fertile decades. Retrospectively, the years in Vétheuil reor-

dered the critical equation that condemned her reputation. Far from being only a precocious talent who joined a movement assured of its triumph—second wave but thus, implicitly, second-rate—Mitchell, despite her early successes, was in many ways a late-blooming painter who, a second wind having given her wings, ended up constituting a one-person group . . .

Rarely did Joan venture into the center of town any longer: not only was she coping with the constant hip pain that made walking difficult but also she had had run-ins with many locals, thus earning a reputation as *sauvage*: "You're supposed to be diplomatic, which I call hypocrisy and lying, really." Direct and tough as she was, however, Joan bruised easily in some respects. She didn't get the toilet in her studio fixed for the longest time because she couldn't bear the thought of the plumber telling everyone that the crazy lady up on the hill had a building full of huge, smeary, childlike paintings. So private was the studio that Joan slept with the key under her pillow. Her studio felt, noted one friend, "like a place that an animal goes to for safety."

When she wasn't painting, Joan would read. Besides poetry (she always had two or three volumes at hand) she devoured art catalogs and monographs, mysteries, the *New Yorker,* French magazines, and the Grove Press books Barney sent by the carton. Favorite novels included V. S. Naipaul's *A Bend in the River,* Alice Walker's *The Color Purple,* and everything by Milan Kundera (whom she had met). Joan was also exceedingly fond of *The Lord Chandos Letter* by Hugo von Hofmannsthal, a gift from Yves Michaud. In von Hofmannsthal's imaginary 1603 communication to philosopher Francis Bacon from Lord Chandos, a man of letters, the latter accounts for his loss of the ability to write. Overwhelmed by a sense of the deadening inadequacy of language in the face of a "watering can, a harrow left standing in a field, a dog in the sun, a run-down churchyard, a cripple, a small farmhouse," he perceives that "any of these can become the vessel for my revelation." "That's it, that's it," amen'd Joan.

Joan also took pleasure in sitting on her terrace, watching the light shift, the barges bevel the Seine, and the titmice dart around and peck at the seeds she put on the table. She phoned friends at any hour, hugged the kitchen radiator as she chatted with Raymonde, made sure her doggies got the choicest cuts of meat, did crossword puzzles, and religiously fol-

lowed tennis, figure skating, and the news on TV. (She was furious about
the rise of French right-winger Jean-Marie Le Pen's National Front Party
and appalled by the Iran-Iraq War.) In warm weather, she puttered in the
garden or soaked up the sun on the stoop of her studio as her dogs milled
around. She also liked organizing little fêtes for friends' birthdays or
openings. When there were no guests, she and Gisèle would linger over
one of Raymonde's simple country dinners: roast chicken with rosemary,
vegetable soup, whatever was fresh from the garden. La Tour had its
moments of ordinary well-being, yet photographer Jacqueline Hyde was
not alone in feeling in "that house and that atmosphere . . . something
tragic."

Come spring and summer, La Tour again stirred with visitors, especially the young artists Joan cultivated and inspired, many of whom considered this unreconstructed painter's painter a hero as well as a friend.
Besides talking, drinking, and hanging out, painting lessons wove themselves into life at La Tour. Joan was wont to bring up with her young
acolytes the vital importance of feeling and seeing, really seeing, color
and light. Once, when a yellow flower in a vase caught the light, she
took Joyce Pensato aside: "*That's* what I mean by color and light." Bill
Scott recalls how Joan would "hold a lemon against a black patch on
the coat of one of her dogs and say that this color juxtaposition, for
her, epitomized Manet. Or at dinner she might challenge anyone to tell
her how they would mix the color of an apple she held, the color of her
drink or the red of her sweater." Guests would paint in the garden or
the cistern. Assuming that everyone was an artist as serious as she, Joan
encouraged both dependence and independence but was open to many
ways of working. Her critical comments were typically brief: "It's not
visual." Or: "Here you're just cleaning your brush." If she felt someone's colors weren't right, she would leave tubes of paint (the finest
Lefebvre-Foinet) on the billiard table. She also purchased her young
friends' art, at prices beyond what most would ever dream of assign-
ing, and hung it in the house, alongside originals by Kline, Matisse, de
Kooning, Francis, Mitchell, and "lady painters" like Shirley Jaffe, Elga
Heizen, and Zuka.

"Let's organize," Joan once admonished her young guests,

> please finish open beer bottles . . . please look for clothes and where
> you have put them—please have them washed . . . I opened some
> portfolios to show paper for fusain [fine charcoal] the other night—no

one seems interested so I'm putting them back on billiard table . . . If someone wants to cry, I have kleenex but I don't like tears in my curry, which was already too salty. If someone wants to talk about their Mothers, I have plenty of tuscany olive oil—or preferably petrol. "Oily Mothers." . . . The "trick" is to care about anything that exists outside of oneself (not what the oilies did to you).

As evening descended, people would gather in the little dining room, liquor would flow, and Joan, dropping the needle on her Ella Fitzgerald and Louis Armstrong album, would inquire, "How was today?" While she operated from the principle that one should never scotch one's true feelings by seeking the approval of others, ironically, she "brought out the sycophant in everybody." Wanting to know people in ways that went beyond the superficial, utterly unimpressed with her own fame or importance, she would ask a million questions. Her ability to sniff out precisely what one did not want publicly exposed was astounding. Flattered by her attention and often half smashed, people would let slip things they had never dreamed of revealing to anyone. Then, typically at the dinner table, the unlucky *victime du jour* (no one, including important curators, collectors, or artists, was automatically exempt) would feel the wind shift, and everything swiftly and very publicly fly back into

Joan and her "doggies" relaxing in front of her studio, 1984

his or her face. That person's insecurities would be "out for dissection so fast that you couldn't believe it." No one dared defend Joan's prey. She considered this "outing" a form of therapeutic honesty that pulled off people's masks and got them to where they might be after, say, six months of psychoanalysis. "It would look so aggressive, and at times it frankly was," reports one observer, "but there was this enormously generous interest inside that was driving it." Yet frequently victims were reduced to tears. Their impulse was to bolt, but that proved difficult and not only for practical reasons.

Artist Robert Harms, for instance, on his first visit to Vétheuil, met with unmerciful criticism for both his Levittown accent and his failure to properly care for the dogs while Joan was out, criticism delivered with such withering authority that it seemed well nigh impossible to contest. Feeling that he had to leave, Harms announced he was going to Paris. Then—following her usual attack, seduce, attack, seduce pattern—Joan "looked at me, and she said, 'What's the matter? You lose your sense of humor?' And I thought, 'Oh, God!' We stayed up that night until six in the morning, drinking Scotch and talking and looking at the paintings. And then she had me."

Following the long, boozy dinner that was the social centerpiece of any day, Joan would begin moving toward the library to watch late-night news or toward her studio to paint. But first, even when she was so drunk she could barely stumble around, she would collect the ashtrays and glasses, carry them to the kitchen, and fastidiously wash every one. Dirty paper napkins and tissues were gathered for use in cleaning her brushes. Nothing should be wasted! If she was painting that night, she would then exit via the back door, toting the box of napkins and tissues, along with her survival bag bulging with a jug of Johnnie Walker, two or three books of poetry, and perhaps a few letters. Along the way she might sing a children's song accompanied by her yowling dogs. Later, the strains of Bach would float from the studio and, much later still, from her bedroom, come a muffled France Culture broadcast, her security sound as she dropped off to sleep.

are all we have. So count them as they pass. They pass too quickly
out of breath: don't dwell on the grave, which yawns for one and all.

JAMES SCHUYLER

CHAPTER FIFTEEN A Few Days

J oan had been having trouble swallowing, and then, in the summer
of 1984, she noticed a lingering sore in her mouth. Overcoming her
fear of anything dental, she consulted Michaële-Andréa Schatt's
mother, a dental surgeon in Mantes-la-Jolie, whose biopsy revealed a
malignancy. Joan was referred to a Paris hospital, where, as she had long
dreaded, she was diagnosed with cancer, advanced cancer of the jaw. She
was told that her jaw had to be surgically removed and replaced with a
prosthesis. In a flash, everything irremediably changed.

Urging a second opinion, Gisèle contacted a cardiologist friend, who
put them in touch with the Curie Institute. One day that October, Joan
walked into her first appointment at Curie white with panic fear and
barely able to get words out of her mouth. But Dr. Bataïni told her that
radiation was an option. She soon began shuttling back and forth to Paris
for every-other-day radiation treatment sessions. Side effects included

enormous sores in her mouth, chronic dry mouth from the destruction of her salivary glands, and a dead jawbone, as fragile as glass. She lived on nutrition drinks and Xylocaine. For the rest of her life she would be limited to purees, soups, and other soft foods, and she had to chew slowly and carefully: she was at risk of breaking and losing her jaw. Moreover, the lower part of her face turned masklike and simian looking. Self-conscious, she would put her index finger on the corner of her mouth or use one hand to half cover her jaw, and often she joked about wearing a chador.

But the treatment succeeded. Declared cancer free by Dr. Bataïni, whom she called "God the Father," Joan celebrated by throwing a small party for Gisèle's thirty-seventh birthday on February 28, 1985. Their guests included Jean Fournier and "lady painters" Zuka, Shirley Jaffe, Elga Heinzen, and Claude Bauret Allard. Joan gave Gisèle an orchid. The day was crisp and cold; the sky was eggshell blue and teeming with birds.

Joan's crisis continued, however, in that her feelings of sadness, solitude, and terror triggered by the cancer knew no bounds. Try as she did, she found it impossible to get beyond a cold, sick, white, metallic numbness. "Write down the despair," urged Gisèle, "or, or, or . . . Write down everything that hurts, *ou t'empêche de peindre* [stops you from painting] . . . The total isolation must be avoided. I am alone and yet I am not . . . Your winter experience has been so painful, so hard—no wonder." Joan probably did not act on Gisèle's advice to write, but heeding Fried's lesson that activeness is essential to mastering depression, she had found a new psychoanalyst, Christiane Rousseaux-Mosettig, whom she had begun seeing that November and had quickly come to love and respect.

A handsome, understated woman with a low, thrilling voice, this classic Freudian originally trained in philosophy fused theory with intuitive understanding, shunned French-style intellectual gamesmanship, and brought literary and artistic references to her practice. (Joan delighted in the fact that Mme. Rousseaux loved the early Kandinsky.) The two set up regular appointments on Tuesday, Wednesday, and Friday afternoons. Simply keeping this schedule was a major commitment for Joan, her commute from Vétheuil to Mme. Rousseaux's office in the eleventh arrondissement, on the opposite side of Paris, entailing long taxi, train, and metro rides. Nonetheless, Joan "never missed, [was] never late, more likely early than late, [came] in every kind of weather, with every kind of flu . . . It was an all-out commitment . . . to work, to work." And from the day she first arrived, in such anguish that the analyst felt she could not be put on the couch because she *had* to have a human face in front of her, Joan made rapid progress. This "doesn't mean that she did not have large gaps, that she was not overwhelmed by depression," explains Mme. Rousseaux, "yes, that happened all the time. But [her depression] did not preclude active interior work." She found Joan "like a child who wants to be loved completely. I believe this was her main problem, [and] she suffered from it acutely." At the same time Joan demonstrated a great deal of rigor vis-à-vis herself and a very intense transference.

Psychic healing also meant painting. When at last she felt able to work, Joan cast about for the right something felt and remembered her "tragic and beautiful sunflowers dying" in autumn against a backdrop of stark clouds and "the fall cool sun—that cold yellow—superb." This memory served as the emotional trigger for her six *Between* paintings as well as *Faded Air I* and *II*.

That thin, brilliant, volatile yellow, in fact, dominates *Faded Air I*, in which Mitchell juxtaposes it à la Manet with lustrous black, along with bluish pink, orangey yam, gray, and cobalt green (an unusual semi-transparent bluish green verging on gray). Both cobalt green and barium yellow were among the hues Joan "used to death" at one time or another, recalls Carl Plansky, who had begun making paint for himself and his friends, including Joan. For the emotion-color synesthete Joan, each fetish color carried its own intense meanings. Cobalt green was extremely unhappy (the metallic chemical element cobalt, used in both paint and cancer treatment—including her mother's, her sister's, and her own—evoking, as it did, "active death and passive death"). As for the white ground that now succeeded the alloverness of much of her earlier work in Vétheuil: "It's death. It's hospitals. It's my horrible nurses. You can add in Melville, *Moby Dick,* a chapter on white. White is absolute horror, just horror. It is the worst."

The lush equanimity of *La Grande Vallée* had vanished. Wild, beautiful, and tremulous, *Faded Air I* skirts chaos, the spiky scrawl of pigment on its left panel pitching diagonally toward the rising tower of scribbles on its right. Its feeling is analogous to that of Joan's musical obsession at the time: Bach's Cantata 78, which she loved for "the way it mounts—fabulous."

As unsettled as *Faded Air,* the *A Few Days (After James Schuyler)* cycle of paintings brought weightless flurries of cobalt teal. The *Before, Again* cycle that followed (its title refers to time relations among medical appointments and procedures) churned with off-hues of yellow, blue, orange, green, pink, and black dashed with red. Joan's upswell of painting then continued with the brutal *Then, Last Time* group—"death warmed over," she said grimly—culminating in *Then, Last Time IV*, a menacing, twofold tidal wave of pigment, cobalt blue, and steely cobalt green.

The first time she consulted Dr. Bataïni he had ordered her to stop smoking and drinking immediately, and she had complied. Joan's old friend, producer Joe Strick, had offered to give her "a clip on the chops if you ever think of going back to smoking," yet, on her own, she made it, learning even to paint without cigarettes. Liquor was something else. The painting imperative to drink outweighed the medical imperative to stop, so she stayed off the hard stuff but took up white wine in a serious way. After drinking up the collection of pricey *grands crus* Riopelle had left behind, she made a deal with Le Hangar, a Parisian restaurant, to store their wine at La Tour and purchase from them, thus, in effect, setting up a twenty-four-hour wine shop only steps from her door.

Joan treated cancer as a test of character and courage. She still wanted to live large, act bawdy, and have fun, but often she was exhausted. She took Speciafoldine for her anemia and Carencyl for her fatigue. Moreover, with cancer literally in her face, forcing her to come to terms with mortality, she continued to battle depression. Cured or not, she figured she didn't have many years left.

Then, just as she geared up to "paint more directly" and not "fuck around anymore," the hip pain from which she had been suffering for years intensified. Joan had osteoarthritis resulting from hip dysplasia, a congenital degenerative condition of the hip joint, which affected both hips severely enough that she had had to move to a bedroom on the ground floor in order to avoid the stairs. It had also taken its toll on her recent work, the thinness of its facture betraying her lack of physical stamina.

Yet she had willed into existence bold eight- or nine-foot-tall paintings, working the tops by clambering up on a metal stool to place a stroke or two or three, then descending and retreating to the back of her studio to study the results before moving in again. Finally Gisèle drove into Mantes-la-Jolie and purchased two ladders, which facilitated Joan's task but which the artist would never have bothered with on her own. From

Joan's point of view, you just got up and did it: "Keep cracking! Don't get discouraged. Just a waste of time."

In December 1985, Joan underwent hip replacement surgery at the Hôpital Cochin in Paris. She had a big emotional investment in this operation; it might have marked a turning point in her mental state. But it proved largely unsuccessful, leaving her in despair and pain, which she self-medicated with Chablis and Sancerre. Friends who visited her at the hospital smuggled in vast quantities of wine under their coats, tokened by the army of empties lined up next to her bed.

Transferred to a clinic in suburban Louveciennes, Joan fell in love with the trees she surveyed from her window. There, during three weeks of recuperation and therapy, she did watercolors for the first time in years. (Artist Malcolm Morley had given her a few tips.) "When I was sick," she later remembered,

> they moved me to a room with a window and suddenly through the window I saw two fir trees in a park, and the grey sky, and the beautiful grey rain, and I was so happy. It had something to do with being alive. I could see the pine trees, and I felt I could paint. If I could see them, I felt I would paint a painting.

Back in Vétheuil, one day several months later, Joan sat outdoors and watched her oils being removed from her studio and loaded into a truck for shipment to New York "and the trees and the garden were beautiful and there was a beautiful light and I saw the painting moving. A big strong man moved them with great ease and I saw all their colors behind the trees moving and it was like a parade and I was happy."

By the mid-1980s, a single-panel Mitchell sold for $30,000 to $40,000 and a multi-panel Mitchell for $50,000 to $100,000. Hanging in Fourcade's foyer during her show that April, the colorful *A Few Days I* and *II (For James Schuyler)* were snapped up, and gallery-goers kept approaching the reception desk to ask if there were more like the two near the door. Virtually everyone saw *A Few Days* as cheery, a viewpoint that amazed Joan: "Only one person got death. So strange." The rest of the show did not sell particularly well, though San Francisco Bay Area collectors Hunk and Moo Anderson bought the powerful *Before, Again IV*, and film critic Gene Siskel and his wife Marlene fell under the spell of a *Then, Last Time* painting. They mulled it over for a long while but finally chose one of the *Grande Vallée* works from Jean Fournier. The two were bitten by the Joan Mitchell bug, remembers Fourcade's assistant, Jill Weinberg, "just completely!"

The show had gotten underway with Xavier's usual convivial dinner party for Joan's friends, but most of the artist's socializing revolved around the suite at the Westbury Hotel, on East Sixty-ninth Street, where she had been staying since losing St. Mark's and where she held court each afternoon. The phone jingled, white wine flowed, old friends and art world emissaries filtered in and out, mingling with the artist's young protégés, who now included Cora Cohen, Billy Sullivan, Rebecca Purdum, Peter Soriano, David Humphrey, and many others. Laughter rang out, friendships were born, jealousies flared. Often the artist swept her entourage off for roving studio and gallery visits. Her hip condition and fatigue cramped her style—she could no longer negotiate steep stairs, nor could she stand for more than twenty minutes, and she needed a cab for even a short distance—yet, leaning on her cane and flanked by young friends, she hobbled into an opening here, a restaurant there. When she ran into Helen Frankenthaler at One Fifth, Joan slyly insulted her by feigning to mistake the artist for her older sister, and once she verbally flogged her niece Poondie, who had flown out from California to be with her, until Poondie stood weeping on the sidewalk. Yet another

Joe LeSueur with his Mitchell at his Second Avenue apartment, c. early 1980s

With her longtime French dealer Jean Fournier, dubbed "Quai d'Orsay," c. 1987

time (notwithstanding fellow guest Hal Fondren's talent for defusing her outbursts with an affectionate "Oh, Joan, shut up!"), she roiled Joe LeSueur's dinner party in her honor with rabbit-punch accusations that "the New York fags" were "ganging up" on her. No, Joan had not mellowed. Indeed, scared by her own decline, she proved more pugnacious than ever.

Back in France that rather lonely summer, big Joan was temporarily retired as little Joan struggled with the psychological and physical difficulties of postoperative painting. She worked small, using an easel for the first time in four decades, with her paints and brushes laid out on rolling tables rather than on the floor. This arrangement hardly afforded the direct registration of bodily movements to which she aspired, but it was the best she could do. Worked less muscularly than usual, her *River* cycle, which evokes consciousness and time, managed nonetheless to effect the surging, scrambling, rampaging paint/water she so loved. As her strength returned, the paintings grew larger.

Despite her joy at once again striving for pictures, the emotional climate at La Tour continued dismal, all the more so because the elderly Iva was failing. Joan's German shepherd—her bedmate, baby, alter ego, companion, and muse—had for thirteen years sat sphinxlike next to her daughters, Marion and Madeleine, on the studio daybed as the artist worked. Sometimes the dogs pissed on her paintings, which Joan found hysterically funny; sometimes she got them to paint with their tails.

Iva died on September 25. Attempting to make positive sense of this fresh heartbreak, Joan wrote to Joanne and Phil Von Blon,

> All all my memories of [Iva] are so full of joy. I feel lucky to have known her or whatever or experienced her or that—let's say—she allowed me to sleep in her bed or live in her house. What a lovely dog. Her "puppies" are confused but I'm trying to be the "lead dog." Who said "only the lead dog sees the landscape"? I dig that statement.

In another tremendous blow, Xavier Fourcade revealed that he had AIDS. Having learned of his condition several months earlier, Joan's New York dealer had grown a beard to cover the sores and kept the illness private as long as possible. Only in the early fall of 1986, as he was leaving for France to pursue an experimental therapy involving blood exchange, had he told his employees and artists. The news forged a closer bond between Joan and the gallery staff, including Jill Weinberg: "We had this shared, deeply, deeply fraught concern. She was just devastated. There was a really horrible, horrible and wonderful, sharing of grief and loss and fear."

Joan and Xavier saw each other often that fall. By December, it was obvious that the French treatment had failed, and Xavier, suffering from chronic respiratory problems and intense pain, was preparing to return to New York. As a way of saying *adieu,* he and Joan traveled to Lille to view a traveling exhibition of works by Matisse from the State Hermitage Museum in Leningrad. En route they stopped at Beauvais to visit the cathedral, the nave of which had collapsed in the thirteenth century when its builders overtaxed the technology in their attempt to create the most resplendent of houses of worship. Each intensely aware of mortality, the two stood shoulder to shoulder in "that crazy late Gothic unfinished superb nutty monument to God."

The other highlight of their excursion was seeing Matisse's 1909–10 *La Danse,* a thirteen-foot-wide oil on canvas commissioned (along with its companion, *La Musique*) by a Russian collector for his Moscow home. This Dionysian painting depicts an edge-to-edge circle of five nude dancers, their dark red bodies pulsing and taut against a sapphire blue sky and emerald green earth. *La Danse* radiates aliveness and joy. One's eyes find no resting place, one's whole physical being is swept into a ceaselessly turning energy.

Joan had first viewed Matisse's masterwork at the artist's 1970 retrospective at the Grand Palais, from which she had emerged weeping with emotion. Later asked which work of art she would choose if she had to live with just one, Joan had replied that she would "take the whole dance-and-music scene of Matisse, those great big murals with the fabulous greens, reds, and blues." Joan's love of *La Danse* had made itself felt in past work, in the buoyant circularity of her enormous 1983 *Grande Vallée* triptych, for instance, and would do so again in the tondos (round paintings) with which she experimented in the late 1980s.

Now, her lyrical *Lille* cycle, created after Xavier's departure, swarmed with knots of intense color, their motion (as the artist put it) "made still, like a fish trapped in ice." Consisting of an activated, edge-brushing core floating on a white ground, the diptych *Lille V* is moving and still, opulent and tough, structured and free—in other words, classic Mitchell. Later that spring, the *Lille* group gave way to the *Chord* paintings—canvases freighted with the knowledge of Xavier Fourcade's death on April 28, 1987, at age sixty—their wheeling, lurching coils of pigment underpinned with black, risking dissolution at any moment, equal parts convulsion and dance.

On June 10, Joan's seventh show opened at the Galerie Jean Fournier, accompanied by a small catalog in which Yves Michaud wrote,

> It is a fact that the last three years of Joan Mitchell's painting cannot be disassociated from a number of serious threats and a great deal of reevaluation: personal physical setbacks, threats upon herself felt as a result of the loss of loved ones, an increase of aggression and distress in reaction to these attacks. To all of this, painting is more than a witness: it is the ground on which the confrontation takes place, on which the crisis is resolved.

The previous winter, in New York, Joan viewed another inspirational exhibition, the Metropolitan Museum's Van Gogh in Saint-Rémy and Auvers. She then went home and painted *No Birds*, a work haunted by the Dutch artist's *Crows over the Wheatfield*, done in Auvers-sur-Oise, only twenty-five miles from Vétheuil. (Her love for *Crows over the Wheat-*

field was hardly new, however. Thirty years earlier, she had written to Mike Goldberg, "Color sends me more than ever and Van Gogh and his crows.") Mythologized as the painter's last work before he shot himself, *Crows over the Wheatfield* depicts three roads fanning out to nowhere in a roiling ocean of golden grain as frightening low-flying crows, a traditional symbol of death, sail out of a claustrophobia-inducing stormy-blue sky. Heavily invested with feeling-memories of *Crows over the Wheatfield*, Mitchell's *No Birds* also adverts to its predecessor's structure, spatial syntax, graphic strokes, and palette (though Mitchell springs the surprise of a tender pink). In her work there are no birds—nor are there, of course, fields or sky—only speeding, slashing ribbons of black that register as ominously and frenziedly as any flock of crows.

Why did Joan single out *Crows over the Wheatfield*, a painting popularly interpreted as a kind of suicide note and bound up in the mythology of van Gogh's suffering, self-destruction, and transcendence? (That year, she titled another diptych *Ready for the River*—meaning suicide, she bluntly informed Robert Harms. Then, making light of her own life-and-death references, she added that for weeks she had heard a birdlike noise in her studio, which turned out to be only a loose tile rattled by wind, hence *No Birds*.) Without a doubt Joan had given serious consideration to ending her life. But if *No Birds* alludes to suicide, this marvel of painterly self-confidence and intelligence also speaks of painting as "the opposite of death," as vibrant, bristling, ripe aliveness. Joan was never one to gloss over emotional dilemmas or fear collisions, on canvas or in life.

No Birds is also, of course, an homage to Vincent van Gogh. For reasons Joan could not begin to articulate, the supremely felt paintings of "Vinnie" had "stayed with" her since the age of six. She responded to their "fanaticism," their spirituality, and their vibrant sense of place, her reaction to Vétheuil having been on the order of his to Arles. Sunflowers, skies, fields, and trees—not least, cypresses—deeply affected both artists, and both projected themselves onto trees. The two felt color intensely and carried myriad colors in their mind's eye. Moreover, both experienced painting as (in the words of one letter from Vincent to his brother Theo) "a way to make life bearable." (Joan owned and treasured a volume of van Gogh's complete letters.) Only painting, as Fried used to say, afforded van Gogh the means to contend with the flood of feelings that threatened to engulf him, which was Joan's case as well. Highly self-critical, she never put herself in the same league as van Gogh, but he, along with Cézanne and Matisse, represented the highest standard of painting, to which she aspired.

The formal lessons Joan learned from van Gogh were myriad. Some had to do with his vigorous dabs, stabs, and swirls bodying forth energy and growth while manifesting paint as paint. Others related to his use of space: the frontal, tipped plane of his *House at Auvers,* for instance, and the color-activated space in the floor in the Musée d'Orsay version of *Bedroom in Arles.* Like van Gogh, Mitchell took full advantage of complementary and near-complementary colors, expressing, as he put it, "the love of two lovers by a wedding of two complementary colors, their mingling and their opposition, the mysterious vibrations of kindred tones." Both artists favored blues and yellows or yellow oranges, working them in crafty ways, Joan, like van Gogh, tucking a few strokes of orange into a corner, perhaps, rather than placing it next to the blue, thus setting up a dynamic pull that made her work sing.

Having revolved around one man, the Xavier Fourcade Gallery was closing, a process which required about a year and entailed the search for appropriate representation for each of its artists. Mitchell ranked fourth or fifth in terms of desirability. Edging toward establishing a gallery of their own, Fourcade's director (and lover) Bernard Lennon and assistant Jill Weinberg were eager to represent her, and the artist was willing, but plans were slow to fall into place and the consensus was that she should not remain too long without a dealer. Thus she visited various galleries, including Robert Miller at Fifty-seventh and Madison, where she loved the light and high ceilings and hit it off well with Miller, who liked her "rugged individualism." They quickly came to an agreement that the Bernard Lennon and Robert Miller Galleries would jointly handle her work. (After Lennon too died of AIDS, on Thanksgiving Day 1990, Mitchell was represented solely by Miller.)

Larger, more assertively stylish, and higher profile than the Xavier Fourcade Gallery, the Robert Miller Gallery focused on painting and photography. Interested in one-of-a-kind artists, undervalued or not, many of whom were women, Miller represented Alice Neel, Lee Krasner, Louise Bourgeois, Bruce Weber, Robert Mapplethorpe, and the Estate of Diane Arbus. Irreverently dubbing it "the fags and females gallery," Joan was delighted to be at Robert Miller and on Fifty-seventh Street, the home of prestigious galleries since her Tenth Street days.

Not long after joining Miller, Joan was asked to pose, as had other gallery artists, for photographer Robert Mapplethorpe. She disliked the idea of having her picture taken, but nonetheless agreed, showing up at the appointed time at Mapplethorpe's Twenty-third Street studio having traded her usual shapeless and unflattering garb for more style-conscious pants, polo shirt, and mannish cardigan. In one of the resulting pictures, the quintessential image of the aging Joan Mitchell, the painter is isolated against a starkly black background. Her left hand rests on her thighs; her right obeys an impulse to hide by pulling together the opening of her shirt. Her fading, well-behaved pageboy, little nose, withered jaw, and sad eyes framed by tinted lenses lend her the air of an elderly child, but the singularity of Mapplethorpe's photograph lies in the artist's expression of grievous concern. Mapplethorpe too had AIDS (he would die the following spring), and the click of his shutter coincided with Joan's full emotional recognition of that shattering fact.

By the time Mitchell joined Robert Miller, preparations were well underway for her first retrospective, guest curated by art historian Judith Bernstock for the Herbert F. Johnson Museum at Cornell University with seed money from the National Endowment for the Arts. Accompanied by a two-hundred-plus-page catalog that comprised a substantial artistic biography focused upon her painting's relation to poetry, it would travel to museums in Washington, D.C.; San Francisco; Buffalo; La Jolla, California; and Ithaca, New York, but not, as she was acutely aware, to more prestigious venues in, say, Los Angeles, Philadelphia, or New York City.

Wasn't Joan pleased about the exhibition? Yes and no. At first she had bridled at the idea of a retrospective, which she viewed as a funeral of sorts, and had sent word via Yves Michaud to Cornell museum director Tom Leavitt that she objected to being "art-historized live." "It's horrible," she harrumphed to one well-wisher. "It's like having nails put in your coffin. But I think if you're offered a show, you do it, no?" Savoring the idea of a big exhibition, on the other hand, she approached the project with characteristic imperiousness and intensity. Jill Weinberg, who shepherded the project from the Lennon Gallery side, had ample occasion to observe artist and curator in action: "Joan really challenged Judith. She yelled at her. She instructed her. She gave her books to read. She disagreed with her. She agreed with her. Joan . . . was reluctant to acknowledge the curator's judgment and prerogative to make a selection

A portrait by Robert Mapplethorpe, who has just told Joan that he has AIDS, 1988

of paintings." Out of this difficult and painful collaboration came the choice of fifty-four paintings, from the 1951 *Cross Section of a Bridge* to the 1987 *Chord VII,* Joan having nixed the usual inclusion of a few examples of student work. Nor did the show comprise drawings or prints.

Joan was equally unwilling to defer to museum staff expertise. No sooner had she hobbled into Washington's Corcoran Gallery of Art one day in late February than she began demanding changes in the installation in progress. Moreover, displeased to find *Sunflower,* on loan from Pierre Matisse, hanging a bit limp on its stretcher (it had been rolled for many years), she ordered a bucket of water and a sponge (wetting the back of a painting tightens the canvas) and would have put former Fourcade staffer Tom Adams to work. But the installers and registrar objected. Artists do not walk in and start improvising treatments to the art. There are procedures. However, Joan put her foot down. In the end, Matisse was called, and she got her way.

Opening events at the Corcoran were marked by Joan's reunions with old friends and admirers, notably a two- or three-hour tête-à-tête with her childhood pal, anthropologist Robert McCormick Adams, now the head of the Smithsonian Institution, and a lavish dinner party at the home of collectors Ann and Gilbert Kinney. Rather formal in manner, the Kinneys (she was an economist, he the head of the Archives of American Art and heir to the Kinney Shoes fortune) owned a very fine mix of art, including Bonnard, O'Keeffe, and Mitchell. Even a whiff of Social Register pretentiousness inevitably brought out the devil in Joan, however, not to mention that she was the worse for innumerable glasses of wine. Thus the sixty-three-year-old guest of honor tottering around with a cane could be observed that evening throwing chicken-in-cream-sauce hors d'oeuvres at someone, chewing out President Carter's former national security advisor, Zbigniew Brzezinski, and asking an African American guest if he was a token black, before turning to her hostess: "What the hell kind of waitress are ya? This place is a dump!" Everyone heard. The room suddenly grew silent. It was painful. Her handlers could not get Joan to leave. She wanted another drink.

Two months later came San Francisco's turn. Housed at that time on two floors of the War Memorial Veterans Building, the San Francisco Museum of Modern Art could not accommodate the entire retrospective, which had to be pared down to thirty-six paintings. When Joan arrived and took in this situation, she went ballistic, giving the curator hell too for a "very messed up installation." For good measure, she railed at the museum for simultaneously showing the work of art star photographers Doug and Mike Starn, which she scorned as trendy and shallow.

Other memorable San Francisco moments came at Harry's Bar, across the street from the museum, where Joan held court with two curators, her niece, and her dealer Robert Miller as *Los Angeles Times* art critic William Wilson attempted an interview that more than once left him "lapsed into defeated silence." At one point, the painter needled the curators "about some minor disagreement between them," writes Wilson. "Apparently the female curator had given in to the handsome male on some aesthetic point. Mitchell told the female curator she was a nice typical girl masochist. As the conversation progressed, the artist promoted her to a Major Masochist and then a Major Mormon Masochist."

Sometime after her second Bloody Mary, Joan fished a letter out of her bag: "Know what this is? This is from the first man who ever fucked me."

No one knew what to say.

" 'Oh. Fascinating. When did you last see him?'

" 'Um. 1950.'

" 'My. How old were you when, you know, it happened?'

" 'Eighteen.'

" 'Good age.'

" 'It wasn't considered proper back then. The kids start even younger these days. You people have kids. They do it?' "

That long-ago lover, painter Dick Bowman, who lived near San Francisco, had been invited to the opening reception and dinner. Spotting Dick soon after he arrived at the museum that evening, Joan limped over, hugged him, and then embarrassed him by grabbing his crotch. Eventually the two found a bench, she lowered herself onto his lap, and they settled in for an affectionate talk.

The following evening, an event billed as an artist's lecture again put Mitchell's cantankerousness at center stage. Joan having, in fact, declined to lecture, her old friend poet Bill Berkson spoke of poetry in relation to her painting, after which the artist fielded questions. As usual, she did not scruple to insult her admirers, responding to the first query with an abrasive "What kind of dumb question is that?" Others got similar treatment. People turned scared. Finally someone brought up Hans Hofmann, and Joan spoke effusively of Hofmann as a great teacher. Afterward, one member of the audience approached Berkson: "My! You certainly had a tiger by the tail!"

Joan's reviews were generally positive, with reservations centering on the prettiness of the early 1980s work and a certain sameness of feeling. Some considered Joan's art in the context of Neo-Expressionism, but she dismissed most Neo-Expressionist work, especially that of David Salle, accusing one friend who owned two cats and a Salle painting of animal abuse. Indeed, the retrospective format of her exhibition illuminated the enormous difference between the slow, organic maturation of what *New York Times* critic John Russell termed Mitchell's "grown-up painting," on one hand, and art created in the context of a market-driven art world, on the other. Joan detested the star system. (Another bête noire was painter Jennifer Bartlett—"Miss Hollywood," in Joan's parlance—whose shows at the Paula Cooper Gallery had dazzled the art world in the 1970s.)

Painters who pursued a focused discipline over the course of a lifetime having grown ever rarer, Joan, the gruff Pasionaria of painting, attempted to rally the young, as during her question-and-answer session at the New York Studio School that spring. There are no more painters, she insisted, only object makers, installation builders, and cartoonists. Nor are there worthy viewers of painting. People just watch TV. But *you*! Be a visual painter, be a serious painter! You have problems, you have people to support—okay, who doesn't? All the same, paint, *paint!*

Despite her insistence that painting was its own reward, Joan had been fretting about whether or not she had made her life a success, which part of her still defined as winning trophies. That year she received the first Distinguished Artist Award for Lifetime Achievement from the College Art Association, was named Commandeur des Arts et Lettres by the French Ministry of Culture, and accepted an Honorary Doctorate of Fine Arts from the School of the Art Institute of Chicago.

Accompanied by Jill Weinberg, Joan traveled to Chicago for the first time since her mother's death, to receive her diploma. She now routinely dismissed Chicago as the "most racist city in the world" yet she had fiercely defended it to one French critic who had not attacked it: "You think that in Chicago there are nothing but savages, but in Chicago is the greatest collection of Rembrandt drawings." This short visit afforded her a kind of emotional reconciliation with her hometown. In the hours preceding the graduation ceremony, she and Jill had settled into an empty bar not far from the Art Institute. Jill recalls that they

> sat in a red leatherette booth beside a dusty plate glass window giving us a view of a perfectly ordinary slice of downtown Chicago. There we sat for hours, and Joan spoke about Chicago and how it felt to be there. She described Chicago as hard and male, a town of testosterone, brutal and beautiful in equal measure. Joan had left there long ago, but

it had not left her. I think Joan found herself unexpectedly excited to be there.

She would never return.

As Joan's artistic reputation grew, her health continued to deteriorate. Facing a second hip replacement, she alternated between crutches and a walker. Arthritic pain was now flying through her hands as well, making it harder to hold her brushes. She joked about having them strapped on as Renoir had in his old age. Because she had no saliva, she had to gargle and rinse constantly. And her glasses got thicker and thicker. She was sick and tired of pain, doctors, medical procedures, hospitals, and the human condition. Yet she demonstrated, in the words of her cook, Raymonde Perthuis, "formidable valor" and "an iron will," and she never complained, though her suffering and fatigue easily triggered aggression.

Quicker than ever to test and judge others, often unfairly, Joan left a trail of hurt feelings behind her. A visit from her old friend artist Marilyn Stark degenerated into an angry tirade from Joan because Marilyn, a widow with two children to support and nothing like Joan's fortune, was not painting full-time. (Having never worked for a paycheck, Joan had little idea of most people's financial realities.) One hard-of-hearing friend was introduced to others as "deaf, as in deaf and dumb." Another, arriving at La Tour, after a hiatus of several years, looking hefty and every bit her age, heard, "*What* happened to you?" The minute she detected a spot of insecurity or guilt, Joan was "putting in the dagger and turning it." Warm and loving one minute, she could turn angry and ugly the next.

What others experienced as grossly insensitive behavior, Joan meant as communicating in an essential way, forcing them to see themselves honestly and fully. Life was precious, and time was short, short: one doesn't have the luxury of coolness and detachment. Yet, even granted what one friend calls the "sweet instinct behind her murderous behavior," it's difficult to square that murderous behavior with Joan's astuteness about people's psychological workings. When they rejected her and she sensed she wasn't loved, says Mme. Rousseaux, Joan acted "like a baby who falls into a rage," and she too suffered intensely from her conflictive relationships.

At the same time she swept those around her into her fierce engagement with living. She made Robert Miller's gallery director John Cheim feel like an elated youth, back in school, adolescent. With her every-thing was interesting. Truly democratic, a conversation with a stranger as drawn out by Joan would turn fascinating—making one realize what a snob one was and how much of life one missed. *Joan missed nothing*. If she was sometimes cruel, at least she was accurate, always bringing to the fore what was kept hidden, examining it, getting on with it.

Witness too Joan's disarmingly unaffected tone in initiating a friend-ship with American artist Sara Holt, who lived in the building where Mme. Rousseaux had her office. One day Sara retrieved a note from her mailbox:

Dear Sara Holt, Our mutual friend Katy Crowe mentioned you to me a long time ago and also Shirley Jaffe and Zuka. . . . Anyway, I'm in your building 3 times a week (see a shrink Mme. Rousseaux) and I thought it would be nice to have coffee . . . If you feel like it, you could call evenings and let it ring or Mon or Thurs afternoons or evenings. Perhaps we could make a date . . . I've heard lots of very nice things about you and your work, and I would love to meet you. Sincerely, Joan (I paint.) Fournier Gallery.

Sara phoned, and, over studio visits and lunches in Paris and dinners and long talks in Vétheuil, a friendship unfolded. With both Sara and her husband, artist Jean-Max Albert, Joan showed herself the soul of open-ness, warmth, and generosity:

Sara—Jean-Max, Wednesday—12:45. Stopped to invite you to new pizza place you talked about. I'll be there if I can find it until 1:45. I should have called. Love, Joan.

Kids . . . I really love your plural work and natch both of you. So nice liking the work and the artists too—it's rather rare I have found . . . I'm very very happy . . . The café was fun. Love, love, J.

Joan purchased Sara's and Jean-Max's art, recommended doctors and dentists, loaded them up with tomatoes from her garden, and urged "anything I can do, please let me know."

And when her friend Jeanne Le Bozec was struggling with cancer,

Joan phoned virtually every day. In fact, Jeanne found Joan kind in every way except to herself. Once, at Vétheuil, the artist casually mentioned to Jeanne and her husband Jean that she had a little package for them, then sent Gisèle to fetch a beautiful diptych. (Joan was in the habit of giving friends paintings, often worth tens of thousands of dollars. Because they could never reciprocate, some hesitated to accept; others, as Joan was well aware, took advantage. Unlike many artists, she kept no records: to this day, important works are scattered or lost.)

On the other hand, friends from the old days who had not seen Joan for a few years were frequently shocked by how she had changed, not for the better. Now in his late thirties, Rufus Zogbaum, who had always considered Joan "a beacon of truth," visited La Tour and found her mean-spirited, grotesque, and humorless. It was Joan against the world. Even the house had an aura of coldness. Sculptor Marc Berlet, also virtually family back in the 1960s, now set foot in Vétheuil for the first time in ages and had a similar reaction. As Joan was showing Marc around her studio one late night, he reached to turn a canvas away from the wall, the gesture of a fellow artist and former studio assistant who had once regularly handled Joan's work, even walked on it, as artists do in their studios. She exploded, "What the fuck do you think you're doing!" Joan herself was casual about taking care of her work—her last painting didn't interest her much, her *next* painting did—yet no one, but no one, touched it without her approval. Berlet was shocked to be treated almost as if he were trying to steal something. He stalked out of La Tour at three a.m., quite certain that Joan was paranoid and that their friendship was dead.

It's true that La Tour's relative isolation had done Joan little good. Barney too, to continue this triage, found her "depressed" and "sinking." Accompanied by his companion, Astrid Myers, and his assistant, Hyehwa Yu, he lunched with Joan in Vétheuil that December. Over the years, the two had remained close, Joan signing her letters to Barney "All my love," and each more or less always coming through for the other. This meeting, however, started off badly. Irritated that the trio had arrived late for lunch, Joan raised her voice in irritated response to some comment by Astrid, thus setting her dogs to yapping. So Barney picked them up by the ears, one by one, and carried them out of the house, at which Joan flew into a rage, especially when Hyehwa laughed at the sight. The bad-tempered mood of this very last time Joan and Barney would ever set eyes upon each other prefigured an ugly episode six months hence.

Nearly four years earlier, in 1985, Barney had sold the financially shaky Grove Press to millionaire entrepreneur Ann Getty and British publisher George Weidenfeld. Later, after the two unexpectedly ousted him, he had founded Blue Moon Books to publish Victorian erotica. In a conversation at the Westbury around that difficult time, Joan had assured Barney that he could count on her, no matter what. Now, in 1989, he took her up on it, asking by phone if he could borrow $50,000. As it happened, Joan had just regularized her situation with the French government, which meant paying a cool million in back taxes. Be that as it may, her refusal was not straightforward but arrogant and accusatory. Thus, at eleven thirty p.m. on August 2, 1989, over a rum-and-Coke at Reilly's Bar at Third Avenue and Twenty-third Street in New York, Barney scrawled a long bitter note to Joan, which nonetheless ended, "But above and beyond all else, Joan, . . . you have meant a—not measurable—force in my life which cannot be belittled and destroyed by the other day. I went to you as a last port. It turned out to be the wrong place. Well, you CAN'T stop me from loving you until I die. So there." Unmoved by his words and by nearly fifty years of unremitting love, Joan, for reasons only she could elucidate, labeled Barney "nuts" and effectively ended their relationship.

Often her ire descended upon men. While she had many male friends—she loved men!—Joan harbored a deep rage over gender politics in the art world. Years of bitter resentment epitomized by Riopelle's past eclipse of her, in terms of collections, exhibitions, prizes, and prices, had convinced her that, in any partnership between a male and a female artist, the male would trample the female. She became, if not a feminist, a gender warrior. Thus when artist Kate Van Houten, staying at La Tour during the summer of 1990, hosted her husband, artist Takesada Matsutani, Joan made no bones about disliking Takesada and wanting him to leave "because [as Kate eventually figured out] he was a man artist [and] she was convinced I was being eaten up by him." Joan also attempted to break up Sara and Jean-Max, for Sara's sake. Her behavior grew erratic, her manner nasty and superior ("Well, I am *Joan Mitchell*"). She had an ax to grind, and she kept grinding it. Eventually, the couple's relationship with her painfully ended.

Increasingly, Joan relied on "lady painters" for emotional sustenance, especially younger "lady painters" like Claude Bauret Allard, Michaële-Andréa Schatt, Monique Frydman, and Mâkhi Xenakis. Although Joan encouraged these protégées' work in every way, at the same time she appeared almost misogynist. Bitter about her own lack of recognition and determined that they should be able to defend themselves, she often attacked, like a demanding trainer putting her novice prizefighters through heavy workouts in the ring. At other times, she was protective, occasionally reaching over to put a hand on someone's arm in a surge of tenderness. With Monique Frydman, she proved unfailingly sweet and solicitous. For Monique, Joan

> truly sought to understand the other person. She had several ways of going about this. She could either do it in an extremely provocative, aggressive, and brutal manner to try to shock the person out of his or her reserve. Or she tried in a much milder and more tender manner, which was my case.

One afternoon, for instance, Joan telephoned Monique: the light in Vétheuil was murky, she complained, which discouraged her from painting.

"And you, Lady Painter, how are things going?"

Frydman normally worked in pastels, a medium she possessed in a manner truly her own; in contrast, she struggled with oils.

"Doubts about my work."

Joan responded: "Come on, Monique, give me your dogs Doubt and Melancholy. I'll take care of them, I'll keep them. But you: Be at ease, paint, work, turn your [old] paintings to the wall, go on to the next one. Paint!"

Over the years, Joan had spoken only rarely and elliptically about her perceptual otherness, once mentioning to Jaqui Fried, for instance, that Gisèle's concert "was very moving—massive sound—marvelous rich colors," once bragging a little to Joanne Von Blon that she was able to "spin back [one of their afternoons together] in my head. It's fun." Questioned about the generative aspects of her art, she asserted that she worked from photographs packed in a mental suitcase, a statement people accepted as valid metaphor. Beyond that, her comments sowed a certain confusion. As curator Jane Livingston puts it,

> She kept insisting that *feeling a place, transforming a memory,* recording something specifically recalled from experience, with all its intense light and joy and perhaps anguish, was what she was doing. She

seemed to assume that everyone would understand what she meant. At the same time, she was aware, disconcertingly so, that her verbal communication left most people at a loss.

During the summer of 1989, however, Joan accorded to Yves Michaud the second of two interviews (the first had taken place in 1986) in which she opened up about not only her painting but also her synesthesia and eideticism (although she did not command those words or concepts). In response to Michaud's "You seem to me to have a strange attitude regarding words and language?" she declared that *sky* is red (*S*), gray blue (*K*), and yellow (*Y*), thus, to her, the sky was a mixture of those colors.

Michaud stopped short: "I'm lost."

"I don't know. That's how it is."

Joan had previously explained to Michaud that she imagined her own identity as "a sort of scaffolding made of painting stretchers around a lot of colored chaos," thus suggesting the centrality of her synesthetic experiences in her self-concept, that is, her art.

Joan also broached the topic of her 1983 visit to the Manet retrospective in Paris, which had included paintings long ago fixed in her mind: "My sister had just died and a friend of mine's cousin had just died and it was terrible, but seeing all those paintings, some from my Chicago childhood, with all that silence and no time involved, no terminations, was wonderful. There was no sadness, no death. It was still." Her words suggest how eidetic remembering, a kind of virtual reality, collapses time and space. No doubt her experience resembled that of synesthete and eidetiker Vladimir Nabokov. For Nabokov, writes historian Kevin Dann,

> the images of his past perennially ready to be recalled for his artistic purposes, never did lose any of their luster. In conjunction with his remarkable linguistic [substitute: "painterly"] gifts, his synaesthesia and eideticism kept him in the green garden of childhood, forever returning to the halcyon days when the world was still largely of his own making.

Freighted with the knowledge that her way of experiencing the world was marvelous yet "wrong" and, in any case, distrusting words and knowing that attempts to explain would meet with deep skepticism, Joan rarely tried. "At some point we [synesthetes] learn that most people do not see what we see and that our perceptions are considered, at best, 'imaginative,' and at worst 'looney' or even suspect," writes Patricia Duffy of synesthetes' lack of validation. "Much of the world does not see what we see and is not convinced that we see it ourselves."

Duffy, of course, writes from the position, unknown to Joan, of one aware that her condition is named, normal, and shared. Many synesthetes experience that discovery as powerful catharsis. Some laugh and cry, many bask in their new knowledge, most feel vindicated. One synesthete has described finding out as akin to the moment when, for the nth time, the blind and deaf child Helen Keller placed one hand under a stream of cool running water while her teacher Anne Sullivan used the manual alphabet to spell "w—a—t—e—r" on the other. All of a sudden, Helen got it! Her face lit up. Everything changed. *This has a name!*

Never to know that experience, Joan sought validation chiefly through art, gravitating to writers and artists like Rilke, von Hofmannsthal, Eliot, Kandinsky, and van Gogh whose work appeared to attest to the soundness of her sensorial perceptions. She adored Beckett's *Embers* in part because of the way in which its character's inner and outer life, present and past, draws breath from colors and sounds. She was fond too of nineteenth-century French poet Arthur Rimbaud's sonnet "Vowels," which begins: "A black, E white, I red, U green, O blue: vowels, / One day I will tell your latent birth." ("I am like Rimbaud," Joan used to tell Michaële-Andréa Schatt.)

Finding common ground with other synesthetes might have stemmed the implacable loneliness that had her lamenting to Jean Fournier, "I am always alone."

The summer of 1989 found a French painter couple, Philippe Richard and Frédérique Lucien, former students at the École des Beaux-Arts, installed at La Tour. Tight with Frédérique, Joan often ragged Philippe about male privilege, yet she engaged him as her studio assistant. That summer she also befriended the young American artists-in-residence at Claude Monet's onetime home in nearby Giverny, inviting them to Vétheuil for a "magical evening" at her local restaurant, La Pierre à Poisson (where she would often insist that the waiters too, now old friends, have a glass of wine). She took a particular shine to photographer Sally Apfelbaum, who created lyrical, layered images of gardens. Suddenly invited to La Tour for lunch or dinner virtually every day, Sally found

Joan disarmingly attentive and exceptionally generous to the young artists in her thrall, introducing them to others, buying their work, and
making sure they got fancy French desserts. Joan proved so lively and
funny, thought Sally, that people didn't realize or forgot, except perhaps
when she cradled her jaw or reached for her walker, that often she was in
atrocious pain.

Trying to ignore her infirmities, Joan felt a new surge of creative
energy, responding positively to an old invitation from an agency of the
Ministry of Culture to create a stained glass window for the Cathedral
of Nevers, in central France (unfortunately, this never happened) and,
painting in the grand Mitchell style, wrapping up her first show for Robert Miller. Maelstroms of blues and greens, her twenty-seven paintings,
many of them multi-paneled works, ranged up to fifteen feet wide. Aware
of her condition, friends gasped: *How* did you manage physically? The
painter would shrug—Joan at her best—"Ah, you gotta hack it." Get up
on "that fucking ladder." So what if you're tired or unwell. Try again.
Something you still haven't gotten quite right? Then get cracking. Painting remained a mystery as well as a joy.

Having watched Joan make the slow, painful trek up to her studio
again and again, Sally observed, "She always climbed that hill."

Whoever you are: in the evening step out
of your room, where you know everything;
yours is the last house before the far-off:
whoever you are.
With your eyes, which in their weariness
barely free themselves from the worn-out threshold,
you lift very slowly one black tree
and place it against the sky: slender, alone.
And you have made the world. And it is huge
and like a word which grows ripe in silence.
And as your will seizes on its meaning,
tenderly your eyes let it go . . .

RAINER MARIA RILKE, "Entrance"

CHAPTER SIXTEEN Ici

The floor plans of the Robert Miller Gallery tacked to her studio wall, Joan was hard at work on her fall show, conceiving of each painting to fit a specific space and aiming for a show that functioned as a whole, which is not to say that she and the staff would not adjust when they saw the canvases in the actual space and light. Among the new works—most bearing elemental titles like *Weather, Hours, Days, Wind,* and *Land*—the vast diptych *Rain* stood out. Simultaneously color and line, its slashing and blurring up-on-the-surface strokes, "motion . . . made still," deliver the feeling of a cold, pelting downpour in a way artist Ora Lerman likens to the "visual-kinetic experience of rain on the windshield of a car, when all background information seems obfuscated." They resonate too with the graphic markings of van Gogh's 1889 *Rain* and with the rhythms of skin instruments and marimbas in Gisèle Barreau's 1988 *Little Rain.*

Another knockout was the thirteen-foot-wide diptych *South.* As deliciously sun soaked as *Rain* is rain slapped, this polychrome homage to Cézanne's paintings of the Mont Sainte-Victoire (and reprise, in a sense, of Mitchell's own long-ago *La Bufa*) knits together often razor-sharp strokes. Her brushes darting around the white canvas, the artist achieves an effect of light so crackling that *South* appears apt to blaze up at any moment.

Joan's crowded opening at Robert Miller that October 25th marked her heady reemergence as an important New York artist. Museums took notice. In 1990, her *River* occupied a prime spot at the Whitney Biennial, the Museum of Modern Art bought *Taillade,* and, through a purchase/ gift, the Metropolitan acquired *La Vie en Rose.* Her prices soared too. The first Mitchell sold by Robert Miller, a quadriptych, went for over $200,000. That same year, the 1956 *King of Spades,* estimated at $180,000 to $250,000, commanded $462,000 at Sotheby's. (This trend continued: in 2004, Christie's sold her *Dégel* for nearly $1.5 million; four years later, *La Ligne de la Rupture* brought over $6 million at Sotheby's in Paris. Meanwhile, a de Kooning had sold for over $24 million and a Rothko for some $80 million.)

Joan's reception at Miller was documented by independent filmmaker Marion Cajori, who had approached the artist two years earlier about doing her cinematic portrait and had met with a lukewarm yet fond "Oh, let's give the poor girl something to do." The daughter of Joan's old Tenth Street pals Abstract Expressionists Charles Cajori and Anne Child (later Weber), Cajori had first known Joan as a nine-year-old living in Paris with her mother and stepfather, painter Hugo Weber, intimates of Joan and Jean-Paul. From the beginning, Joan had touched a chord in young Marion: first by the artist's intense, autonomous, paint-splattered presence under the skylight of her Frémicourt studio in that "classic Parisian light, strong but sad," later by her ability to maintain, in the expat artists' crazy, volatile world, a stern loyalty to her work, later still by the way she had "rescued" Marion with her understanding of adolescent angst.

The filmmaker then sought funding, having to clarify, over and over, that, no, her project had nothing to do with singer Joni Mitchell. After she was turned down by the National Endowment for the Arts and the "American Masters" series on PBS, among others, she got angry, having come to see her problems in securing underwriting as analogous to Mitchell's in achieving recognition of her work: why architect Philip Johnson and painters Jasper Johns and Robert Motherwell on PBS, and not (except for the perennial Georgia O'Keeffe) female-artist *monstres sacrés*? Eventually Cajori and filmmaker Christian Blackwood set up the Art Kaleidoscope Foundation. Twice they requested that Joan donate a painting to help finance the project, and twice they met with her adamant refusal to underwrite her own film. In the end, however, Bob Miller purchased *South* and that money was used as the bulk of the funding for the hourlong documentary that brought to La Tour the camera crew who roiled Joan's life by "traipsing around [for two months] asking rude questions." Intertwining interviews, lyrical city and landscape shots, and stills of Joan's work (accompanied by the music of Charlie Parker, Betsy Jolas, Billie Holiday, and others), Cajori's film reveals a flinty survivor, an artist whose achievement is wed to her rich inner life, a cantankerous grande dame whose tacky-cutesy red teddy bear sweatshirt (a gift from a friend) in one long scene signals her refusal to concede anything to the rules of self-image making.

Scene Two that October evening—never captured on film but impressed in the minds of many—took place at the post-reception dinner in the vast chandeliered and painting-filled dining room of Bob and Betsy Miller's East End Avenue apartment. There Joan started in verbally brutalizing her tablemate Robert Storr, a friend, painter, and important curator who, shortly thereafter, joined MoMA's Department of Painting and Sculpture: Storr was "power-hungry," Joan snarled, and had a "Nazi haircut" besides. In contrast, she had all evening woundingly ignored her old pal Joe LeSueur, who, over the years, had steadfastly loved her and championed her as a great artist. A large Mitchell (a gift from Joan) took place of honor in Joe's little Second Avenue apartment, wall-to-wall with work by Goldberg, Bluhm, Katz, Hartigan, and others. But at another recent dinner party Joan had blasted Joe for selling one of his Mitchells: "This motherfucker sold my painting for a quarter of a million bucks and didn't even ask me!"

Her attention then pivoted, that evening at the Millers', to *New York Times* art critic Michael Brenson, who, the previous spring, had interviewed her at length in Vétheuil and found her "really lovely to be with, open and charming." Brenson had been preparing a feature story about how Paris shaped the working lives of three American artists who had swum against the stream by moving to the French capital in the 1950s. Joan framed her experience in terms of otherness, gender, landscape, light, and dogs: Paris, she observed, was female while New York was male; Paris bridges resembled dachshunds, New York bridges, Great Danes.

Besides Mitchell, Brenson's article (published that June) spotlighted her old friends, painters Shirley Jaffe and Biala. Brenson had seen Joan again only the day before her opening, when he walked into the gallery to review her show and found her in Bob Miller's office, and the three had cordially chatted.

Now, seated across from the critic at a table of eight, the artist, without warning, erupted: "Michael Brenson, you motherfucker! You ghettoized me. You put me with *those* women." "The words '*those* women,'" Brenson reports, "dripped with disgust." A hush fell over the table. The critic remained mute. Joan ranted on. Curator Klaus Kertess, seated nearby, remembers her verbally clubbing Brenson for calling her a "woman artist," something he never did. Joan shortly turned to Klaus: "Maybe I've gone too far." Later, after the tables had broken up, she approached Brenson, who stood examining a painting, hugged him, and made a moist-eyed plea for indulgence: "I only attacked you because I love you so much." Yet no sooner had she coaxed him to sit down with her for a talk than her tone shifted again, to coldly aggressive. Shrugging off the episode as typically Mitchell, Brenson rose and walked out.

Scene Three: The evening having worn on and the crowd dwindling to fifteen or sixteen, Joan drew up close to Jill Weinberg and began reminiscing about Xavier Fourcade and voicing their mutual sadness over his loss. She "started pushing," Jill recalls. "She found this little bruised spot. She just kept pushing until I dissolved in tears." Suddenly everybody was staring at Jill, assuming that Joan was being mean again: "I didn't think of her as being mean . . . It was part of the way she was feeling, about the evening, about the dinner, about who was there and who was not."

"This joint is very vast and lonely and empty empty," Joan lamented in that year's Christmas card to Joanne and Phil Von Blon. Once again she had plunged into Rilke, along with Gerard Manley Hopkins and the metaphysical poets, especially John Donne. (Aware that winter's gloom depressed Joan, Mme. Rousseaux had whet her appetite for Donne by giving her his "A Nocturnal upon St. Lucy's Day Being the Shortest Day.") Musa Mayer's *Night Studio,* a memoir of growing up as the daughter of painter Philip Guston, and V. S. Naipaul's autobiographical novel *The Enigma of Arrival* held Joan equally rapt. A melancholy pastorale, Naipaul's book hangs upon the consciousness in flux of a Trinidadian novelist who has retreated to the English countryside. This writer's uneasy unbelonging and trod-under past filter through the landscape itself—fields, forests, roads, houses, farms—described with precision in changing light, seasons, and weather. Joan adored the novel's marvelous time-warping repetition, as in Monteverdi or a fugue. Little happens in *The Enigma:* for its self-exiled (like Joan) main character "to live and to write are the same thing," she observed, "they are both ways of getting through a certain period of time. Naipaul writes about the fact of living and lives the fact of writing." Neither did Joan separate living and painting: "I take the train to Paris," she told Yves Michaud, "and I see through the window the landscape or the sky or people . . . I am always looking at something—with very bad eyes—but that's what I do. I look and I transcribe all that I see." Indeed, painting was her "means of feeling 'living.'"

The richly evocative *Champs* (*Fields*) paintings, undertaken that winter and spring, exemplify the indistinguishability, for Joan, of living, feeling, and working. The harvest of her many treks to and from the city, into which she no doubt patched sense-memories from the Midwest and elsewhere, they resemble, in feeling and form, tender lyric poems about tilled earth and weather, metaphor for something unsayable. Champs opened at Fournier that early summer with Joan presiding over the vernissage wielding a cane in lieu of a scepter and surrounding herself with a retinue "as if [the gallery]," thought photographer Jacqueline Hyde, "were the court of Louis XIV."

Seven weeks earlier, she had had a second hip replacement, the success of which allowed her to substitute that cane for her walker and made it easier to paint. Yet, despite the several pillows she was constantly pounding and rearranging, Joan could never find a comfortable sleeping position, and her arthritis (though temporarily relieved by the shots she received in her hands, matter-of-factly, as if servicing a car) was getting worse. Moreover, she suffered from osteonecrosis, the deterioration of her dead jawbone. As a result, she had dramatic gum loss, and her teeth were getting loose. In addition, her jaw had become painfully infected, so she was on penicillin, which she disliked because it gave her diarrhea. Worst of all, sharp abdominal pains sent her to the hospital for three days of tests. She was diagnosed with early-stage esophageal cancer, a type of cancer difficult to treat. She told very few people and simply continued living, unblinkered about the future and determined to experience the present in all its fullness. She did not intend to subjugate her painting to lots of medical procedures or health precautions. (Out of sheer fatigue, however, she modified her hours: she now worked in the afternoon, finishing around seven, and turning in at midnight.) "Keep it going, Ada, every syllable is a second gained," Samuel Beckett had written in *Embers.* More than ever, painting sustained her.

She had returned to two of her favorite motifs, memories based in sunflowers and trees. In the new sunflower paintings, crumpled wads of blossoms ride a foaming ocean, tumble through the sky, run riot with bright-shade colors: reds/greens, blues/oranges, reds/blues, lavenders/oranges. Twisting crimson into aqua or throwing a pinkish white veil over a scribble of teal and black, Joan now found in the sunflower singular, saltatory sport. No less variegated, her tree paintings bring to mind rows of poplars or severely pruned plane trees, standing upright and as if backlit with blazing sun, their negative and positive spaces trading places here and there. One cannot help but read these upright forms as metaphors too for human beings, looming and vaguely frightening. When it came time to title this group, Joan phoned Jean to ask, What is the French word for a row of trees along a path or carriage drive on an estate? The word is "*mail,*" but, in the end, mindful of her own battered condition, she chose "*moignons,*" meaning stumps in the sense of the bulbous extremities of severed branches or of amputees. This subtlety did not, however, survive the transatlantic crossing: in the United States they were rebaptized *Trees.*

Joan's summer of 1990 got off to a heartbreaking start. Long vexed with hip dysplasia, the very ailment that plagued the artist, her frail German shepherds, Marion and Madeleine, had to be put down. While her friend Elga Heinzen buried the two in the garden, Joan got very, very drunk in her room. Insisting that animals beat humans, she loved to pepper visitors with stories about her dogs, and she hated the Catholic Church, in part because, she alleged, it forbids dogs and cats in heaven. Yet she had no intention of getting new pets, matter-of-factly pointing out that she would die before they did. So, for the first time in twenty-two years, La Tour was oddly devoid of dogs and dog noises, except the yipping of Fudji, Gisèle's crazy little poodle.

As June slipped into July, Joan took advantage of the glorious weather, idling away long mornings on the terrace over her café au lait, her books, and her crossword puzzles. With Gisèle in Florida and Frédérique and Philippe moving elsewhere (though he would continue as her studio assistant), she was living primarily with young American painter Kate

Van Houten, who had come out from Paris for July and August, and, off
and on, Christopher Campbell (who would also spend the summers of
1991 and 1992 at La Tour).

A PhD candidate in art history at Brown University and a Fulbright
scholar, Campbell had been doing research in Paris for a dissertation on
Cézanne and Pissarro and painting on weekends. When he met Joan at
a party, he had received the inevitable invitation to lunch, "but don't
come if you don't bring your paintings." At Vétheuil the next day, Joan
informed Christopher that his work was "a complete pile of shit" yet
he had talent, so she would be willing to "larn" him painting. Having
refused invitations to teach at the School of the Art Institute of Chicago,
Rhode Island School of Design, and École des Beaux-Arts, among others, she nonetheless wanted to test herself as a teacher, and, from that
point on, Christopher came out every weekend.

Taking a cue from her own training and from Cézanne, Joan had him
draw lemons that first summer during which she repeatedly accused him
of not *seeing*. After he graduated to abstract painting the following year,
she often tore his efforts to shreds, scraping off paint, rotating a canvas-
in-progress ninety degrees as she explained its defects, and stressing the
idea that, if one could get two or three areas going in a Hofmannesque
push-pull, then a painting was beginning to work. She also assigned
Anton Ehrenzweig's *The Hidden Order of Art* so he could better understand how an unconscious involvement with the gestalt of his work
could take him beyond the limits of conscious attention. At one point,
he was perplexed about a Neocolor (water-soluble wax crayon) drawing
that had something, he couldn't figure out what, wrong with it:

> And Joan developed a habit, when she came into the studio [he
> worked in the cistern] of looking at this drawing and saying, "I know
> what's wrong with that." After about the fifth time . . . she pointed
> out that the colors were too aniline, too raw, too ripe, and she must
> have picked five or six grays from this set [of Neocolors] and started
> laying thin bands of gray over certain color masses to consolidate and
> simplify and tone them down, so that the relationships that were there
> had a chance to function, so that there wasn't so much color clattering
> simultaneously. It was an amazing lesson.

But, as much as art per se, Joan talked about feeling.
Only once did he watch her paint. The two had walked up to the stu-

dio to get something one evening after dinner when Joan, glancing at a work-in-progress, suddenly realized what it needed. As Christopher made himself small in a corner, she picked up a brush and dealt with the problem. He was amazed to see her walk, all concentration, the length of that studio, precisely place one mark, then return to the other end and look and look and look. His thoughts flew to Cézanne working at the studio in Les Lauves at the end of his life when "observers just couldn't believe that anybody could wait so long between brush marks. He would mix up the colors, the brush was loaded, it was poised over the canvas, and then, finally, one mark would get made." With Mitchell, "never was the appearance of speed, or, to the unschooled, of haste, more at odds with the deliberation and precision with which marks accumulated on the surface. It was a gorgeous thing to see!"

Teaching, painting, working with Mme. Rousseaux, and hosting visitors still left Joan long hours during that rather quiet summer. She took on a second, very different, student: a local woman hired to clean and run errands at La Tour. This single mother struggling to raise a five- and a seven-year-old was, Joan had been horrified to learn, illiterate. So the artist went to great trouble to track down the right books for her and her children and to teach her to read. Their sessions proved agitated, the two driving each other to exhaustion. Yet Joan maintained with table-thumping assertiveness that the principle was inviolate: You and the children have to be educated! It's the only hope for them! Only if you have knowledge can you defend yourself in the world!

That summer too, Joan attended a concert at the Château de La Roche Guyon, not far from Vétheuil, after which she approached the violinist and almost timidly introduced herself. Jean Mouillère took in this spiky, bulging-eyed sexagenarian so obviously moved by the music: "But I know you, you've been our closest neighbor on the Chérence road [the back entrance to La Tour] for twenty years." Over that period, Jean and his wife Christine had observed that when they came home late, no matter what the hour, a light shone and a Bach cantata, or something of the sort, sounded from the studio. "What!" Joan shot back. "And you never stopped by!" But the Mouillères had been less than eager to encounter Joan's dogs, besides which their owner had a solid reputation for unpleasantness. Joan handed Jean her telephone number, and, the very next day, they saw each other again. From then on, the twosome or threesome frequently lunched or dined together, Joan taking the precaution, when invited, of toting two bottles of wine, usually her favorite

Pouilly-Fumé, La Doucette. When she was impossible, she would phone the next morning: "*Allô,* Coco, I was mad yesterday." One evening over drinks, she inquired of Jean, "How do you do it? Your sound vibrations go all the way to my belly. It's strange." He explained his conception of sound—that the bow is magic and that it effects a geometry involving invisible but constructed lines in space—a conception which so enchanted Joan that she made him come over and spell out the whole thing to Christopher Campbell and, for once, she painted all night.

In 1990, Carnegie Hall in New York commissioned prints from seven eminent artists—Georg Baselitz, Alex Katz, Roy Lichtenstein, Robert Rauschenberg, Larry Rivers, Ed Ruscha, and Joan Mitchell—to be sold to raise funds during its upcoming centennial year. Concerned about the quality of the printing she could obtain locally, Joan hesitated to accept. Then Fournier introduced her to fine art printer and publisher Franck Bordas, whose atelier, in an old-fashioned cobblestoned courtyard off the place de la Bastille, belonged to the contemporary art world yet kept a finger on the métier's past. The grandson of Fernand Mourlot, famed lithographer to Matisse, Braque, Picasso, Miró, and Giacometti, Bordas worked with an immense, twenty-ton vintage flatbed press (among others) once used for the lithographic posters of Toulouse-Lautrec. After meeting Franck and touring his studio, Joan accepted the invitation with alacrity.

She and Bordas got off to a shaky start, however. Everything he and his team did was *dégueulasse!* Lousy! Horrible! They had to start over again and again. Operating by provocation, Joan pushed them and herself—everything she did was *dégueulasse* too—beyond their normal capabilities. The atelier's walls were soon plastered with working proofs. All the while, Joan was taking the measure of her collaborators, testing them, teasing them, dwelling upon their "little acts of cowardice, little acts of demagogy." In truth, she took pleasure in the camaraderie and visually rich studio environment, and, as time went on, they worked in scrappy good humor, laughed, and had fun.

Part of the fierce counterattack Joan was waging against the loss of her powers, the Carnegie Hall project meant commuting to Paris four days a week. On Wednesdays and Thursdays, her regular cabdriver, Jean-Jacques Géry, picked her up around ten thirty and took her to the Bastille; later he would meet the 5:10 from Paris in Mantes-la-Jolie and drive her home. (Often she would nod off to sleep in the cab, then rouse herself and invite him in for a glass of wine.) On Tuesdays and Fridays, Jean-Jacques dropped her instead at Mme. Rousseaux's for what were now twice-a-week double sessions. In either case her day typically included lunch at the old rococo-kitsch brasserie at the place de la Bastille, Les Grandes Marches, where she commanded a regular table with a standing order of two bottles of chilled white wine continually replaced. Creating a congenial, even festive, atmosphere, she would typically convene three or four guests. Not only friends landed at Joan's table but also strangers, who approached her, Bordas observed, "as a sort of living legend, who came to see her as one comes to see an historic monument." She took them in stride, unleashing torrents of questions, inviting those she liked to see her again, and picking up their tabs too, meanwhile consuming vast quantities of wine but eating virtually nothing. Afterward she might detour to a nearby *chocolatier* and return to the atelier with truffles for all.

One day after lunch she nearly stumbled over a man napping on a piece of cardboard spread in the sun outside Bordas's door: "Who's that bum?" The "bum" turned out to be Richard Bellamy, the manager of the Hansa Gallery (an East Twelfth Street artists' cooperative) in the 1950s, and now a private dealer. Bellamy was waiting for sculptor Mark di Suvero, who was also making prints at Bordas. A joyous shout went up, and Dick and Joan fell into each other's arms. They hadn't seen each other for thirty years. In contrast, a certain French painter who taught at the Beaux-Arts once came by to have a word with the artist as she worked in the back. One minute the two were chatting. The next, their voices were rising and she was beating him, hard, with her cane—thwack! thwack! He fled. A low, demonic cackle rolled out of the depths of the atelier.

As agitated as Joan was, Bordas perceived her ability to go to a place of stillness at the core of her being, given that

> a sort of peacefulness came over her as soon as she started working, a kind of silence. I felt in her manner of working something like a soloist beginning a piece by mentally emptying herself. There was something oriental in her touch, in her work. In contradiction with all the violence, the activity, the provocation. There was a grace and a physicality in her gesture, which meant that, at a certain moment, this fragile woman, fairly old, not very stable, who did not walk very well—one often wanted to give her one's arm to help her across the

street—would lift her brush or her crayon and become a force of nature.

When she finished, she might chirp, "Not bad, huh, for a woman?"

Brilliantly layered, Joan's eight-colored Carnegie Hall poster, "a kind of miracle of ink" (in an edition of only sixty-four), proved spectacularly beautiful.

Having fun at Bordas, Joan wanted to continue even though she had little patience for complex printmaking processes. Her real interest lay in doing beautiful drawings. Thus Franck improvised a setup that allowed her to draw vertically and found unconventional methods and materials, like fast-drying inks, that agreed with her way of working: "Ah!" Joan would breathe. "That's better, that's better, that's good! I'm beginning to understand."

Meanwhile, word having gotten out that Joan Mitchell was doing prints at the Atelier Bordas, various dealers and editors popped up, eager to seize the opportunity for what they assumed would be lithographic versions of her paintings. On the basis of handshake agreements, two or three of them ordered editions, which meant that costs could be covered, Bordas could be paid, and Joan could keep going. What these would-be purveyors of Mitchell lithographs did not know was that the artist had further short-circuited the process by limiting her colors to three at most—black, gray, and red—in violent and handsome prints that were almost pure gesture. When Bordas finally offered them previews, he heard but wisely did not pass along to the artist, That's not exactly what we want, get her to add a little more color. He then turned to Fournier, who cared deeply about Joan's happiness: Let her work, do what she wants, the latter responded. We'll take care of things afterward.

In the end, only writer Michel Waldberg of the Éditions de la Différence, who was working on a Mitchell monograph, came through. (The son of sculptor Isabelle Waldberg and writer Patrick Waldberg, whose friendship with Riopelle dated back to the late 1940s, Michel too had known Joan as a youth.) For the others, everything boiled down to money. Joan would continue at the Atelier Bordas almost until she died, albeit less regularly as time went on. Only weeks before the end, she came in to sign her work but tired midway and put the rest aside for later. She was never able to return. Acting with his usual integrity and elegance, Fournier compensated Bordas for everything, including the unsigned and therefore unsaleable prints.

.   .   .

Joan's second show at Robert Miller opened on March 26, 1991. The gallery was mobbed, but she was most thrilled by the presence, at both the reception and the huge party Carl Plansky threw afterward, of the great alto saxophonist and composer Ornette Coleman, whom she had first met at the Five Spot in 1959. Speaking to one of the Termini brothers (the bar's owners) that long-ago year when the Coleman quartet's ten-week gig and maverick album, *The Shape of Jazz to Come,* were rattling the jazz world, Joan had declared the then highly controversial musician (and fellow synesthete?) to be "a genius." In fact, Coleman's eclectic free jazz — weirdly pitched, beautifully dissonant, open-ended in its phrasing, electric, abrupt, layered, and soulful — is analogous to Mitchell's painting, his uncanny timbre not unlike her uncanny color, exemplified by her ability to (as painter Brice Marden once pointed out) "make yellow heavy." Over the years, Joan and Ornette had run into each other here and then, always with pleasure, Ornette feeling a deep kinship with this "just precious" painter — "totally devoted to her creativity" and "free as a bird."

Three days after the opening, a limo picked Joan up at the Westbury and took her to Mount Kisco, where Tyler Graphics was now located and where, living in the artist's apartment above the studio, she devoted the next several weeks to lithographs based on sunflower and tree feelings, including several from the twenty plates she had drawn earlier, many only recently proofed. In the late morning, Joan would clump down the stairs and into the studio, freshly showered and almost giddy from having watched Bob Ross's *The Joy of Painting,* in which the TV artist demonstrates how to create landscapes with "happy little trees" and "pretty little mountains." A long, intense day would follow, yet at midnight Joan would still be going strong. One time she got so drunk that she had to be carried upstairs, then insisted everyone stay for a nightcap. At three a.m. she was typically "yakety-yakety-yak," recalls Tyler. "The conversation was so good, you didn't want to go to sleep, and it got to the point where you couldn't keep up with her. She was too sharp, and you were too foggy. And she'd get grumpy because you weren't playing the same alert game that she was. So she'd start attacking you."

Among Joan's visitors at Tyler that early spring was Nathan Kernan, John Cheim's assistant at the Miller Gallery, who had gotten to know her the previous July when he traveled to France with Bob Miller and spent a night at Vétheuil. On that occasion he had made a point of telling Joan he was a friend of poet James Schuyler, whereupon she had quoted Jimmy: "And when I thought, / 'Our love might end' / the sun / went right on shining." Later that evening it came out that Nathan too wrote poetry, and Joan demanded examples. No sooner had he returned to New York than she was on the phone, pestering him about sending those poems. He mailed off a few, expecting the worst. But Joan liked them, and, from then on, broadcast what he would have kept private: that he was a *poet.*

Nathan's visit to Mount Kisco that April came two days after Schuyler's death following a stroke. Joan had clipped the writer's obituary from the *Times.* Sad (though she hadn't seen Jimmy for years) and solicitous of Nathan's feelings, she peered out the kitchen window of her apartment during their lunch, lifted her eyes to the perfect April-blue sky, and quoted Verlaine: "*Le ciel est, par-dessus le toit / Si bleu, si calme!*" ("The sky, above the roof, / is so blue and still!")

Back in New York in the days that followed, she asked Nathan to escort her to Schuyler's funeral. He came by the Westbury around six that day, and together they took a cab through the light spring rain to the Church of the Incarnation on Madison at Thirty-fifth. The ranks of Joan's old friends were thinning: Elaine de Kooning had died, Pierre Matisse had died, Sam Beckett had died. Publicly stoic, she sat at the back of the church during Jimmy's service, after which she ran into and reconciled with Joe LeSueur.

With other old friends, she had terrible fights. Around this time, Zuka—whose friendship with Joan had survived the vicissitudes of half a century—got to know an American journalist, a delightful woman, albeit a bit of a snob about her Mount Holyoke and family connections. One evening, Joan, Zuka, and Zuka's new friend all attended a dinner party in Paris at which Joan had arrived drunk and determined to get the woman for putting on airs. She gleefully proceeded to do so, until finally Zuka blew up: "Will you *stop* picking on my friend!" With that, Joan trained her guns on Zuka, and the party fell into a shambles. A few days later, both attended a reception at the Orsay Museum where Joan walked up to Zuka and opened with a quick salvo: "You know, the other day, you were absolutely wrong! I mean, she was aggressive with me before I became aggressive with her." Uncharacteristically, Zuka exploded, then turned heel and strode off, and, for weeks, the two did not communicate. Finally

Zuka wrote to suggest they patch things up two minutes at a time. Over the years, Joan had often called her more levelheaded friend in a "truly unhappy, desperate" state and Zuka had prodded her into two minutes of thinking about something else, then two minutes more, and so on, until Joan shed her angst. Zuka now ended her note, "If you think our friendship's worth saving. You decide. I think it is." Joan phoned, but it was never the same after that.

Carl Plansky next felt the lash. Five years earlier, Carl had turned his penchant for paint making into a business, Williamsburg Art Supply, from which Joan now purchased her oils. When a certain blue she had used in quite a few canvases began cracking and falling off, Joan's vituperation knew no bounds. It was aimed at both Carl and (in case the primed canvas was the real culprit) the Montparnasse art store, Adam. A letter of apology from someone at Adam only added fuel to the fire: "as if his letter would make up for the time I lost because of that idiot!" One expert who was consulted reported that the problem was surely Joan's brushes. How often did she wash them? In fact, her brushes, kept in dog food cans on her studio floor, had not been washed in a decade.

Besides the brushes, these cans, one for each color, held turpentine (occasionally topped off), on which floated assorted dead bugs, plus about two inches of pigment that had settled to the bottom. When she wanted to use a particular color, Joan would dash the can with fresh turp and stir it up. "In a sense," Christopher Campbell had realized,

> she got enormous physical complexity out of that situation . . . because you take a brush that's already supercharged with pigment and dripping with turpentine and you charge it with all this fabulous fresh paint and you move it in a big gesture on the canvas and you've got this hypercolored saturated turpentine flying around, you've got the mass of new paint, you've got the old paint, you've got an extremely complicated physics of surface going on.

The result was sometimes an overdiluted layer of paint that did not form a continuous film and thus, when dry, broke apart.

Joan promptly put Christopher to work washing 380 brushes but did not own up to her own role in the blue fiasco or apologize to Carl: "It's a horrible thing to say . . . ," Carl begins—but how to find the words?— "this fabulous art, and anger, anger," Joan's rare, freaky, and chilling rage.

That same episode caused a deep rift in her already tumultuous friendship with Yves Michaud. The artist had given the critic a painting called *Yves,* but when the blue cracked he returned it, a sure way to enrage Joan, who would have destroyed *Yves* had Fournier not stepped in. A painting, after all, was a gift of self.

It mattered not at all that Michaud was an art world luminary. Joan never hesitated to quarrel with an important critic, offend an important collector, pick a fight with an important curator, or slam an important journalist. When cultural critic Deborah Solomon interviewed her that summer for the *New York Times Magazine* (during a four-day stay at La Tour, where Joan had invited her on the condition that she wasn't "some Ivy League type who refuses to do dishes"), the artist, feeling that Solomon didn't "get it," worked herself into a terrible state. "My painting has nothing to do with what's in and what's not," she snapped to Solomon at one point. "I do it. I'm not hurting anyone. I'm not selling Palmolive soap. I'm not asking you to look at my art, and I'm not asking you to buy it. So leave me alone. Let me die in peace. I'm not a story." But she was: Solomon's "In Monet's Light"—again, the Monet connection—appeared that Thanksgiving weekend.

Lunching at the Dôme one day around the same time with John Cheim, Whitney Museum curators Klaus Kertess and Richard Marshall, and the Whitney's director, David Ross, and having gotten out of Ross the story of his health problems, Joan abruptly went after him for supposedly feeling sorry for himself. She blustered on and on. Disgusted with the tirade, Ross stood up to leave, but Joan reached over, yanked him back into his chair, and ordered him to "SIT DOWN!" She hadn't finished yet.

No doubt Joan's physical and mental anguish contributed to her churlishness. It also prompted her to begin settling her moral debts. She purchased (as a loan) a house for Gisèle in Le Pré-Saint-Gervais, near the National Conservatory of Music, and apparently worked out a way for her cook and gardener, Raymonde and Jean Perthuis, to stay in the Monet cottage for the rest of their lives. For Phyllis Hailey, who had died so tragically thirteen years earlier, she painted a tree.

In format, color, and composition, the gloriously wheeling *L'Arbre de Phyllis* (*A Tree for Phyllis*) echoes a certain oil on paper, one of the best of many the young artist had done of her favorite ginkgo tree across the road from La Tour. Joan's calligraphy perfectly captures the ginkgo's ruffled foliage; her shimmering, light-intoxicated yellow conjures its feeling in late October. Simultaneously a means of atonement, parting lesson, and ultimate sanctuary for the young painter, *L'Arbre de Phyllis* once again merges a tree with a person for whom Joan cared deeply, thus embodying her visceral sense of love breaking all boundaries as well as her almost pagan belief that (as she told one visitor), "Phyllis is still painting in these hills."

An unbeliever, Joan had no faith in an afterlife, except that she was always imagining the surroundings of loved ones who had died and always painting havens for their spirits. She felt she had to give them a place. Part of Joan's unspeakable terror of death, after all, had to do with equating the ending of life with blankness. "Blankness to me is absolutely no space, no silence, no sound, no . . . ," she once explained to a friend, segueing from a comment about how she slept with a security sound. "The word blank is what bothers me. It has no image to it. B L A N K. It's nothing . . . That's sort of frightening when one goes blank . . . It's scary."

How did Joan, then, with her consuming fear, come to grips with the gathering darkness? Leading as she did a very considered life, including four hours a week set aside expressly for interior work, she attempted to prepare for death yet found her "morbidity" undented. Burning with fine fury at human mortality—"Do we 'rage rage' ['against the dying of the light'] as Dylan did or quit??"—she strove to die well by continuing to live life to the fullest. She hated the idea of losing self-control as much as that of wasting time on self-pity and felt that the trick was to care deeply about something outside yourself. Poetry and music helped: Rilke, of course ("Let everything happen to you: beauty and terror. / Just keep going. No feeling is final"), and the timelessly beautiful *Four Last Songs* of Richard Strauss, which culminate in serene surrender to the inevitability of death. Joan saw friends, followed tennis and figure skating on TV, fretted over the state of the world, and painted. She may have felt able to salvage from her illness even more intensity than before for her work; on the other hand, she sometimes moped around La Tour, questioning the worth of what she had created: "I feel time is very short, and I've done nothing."

In recent years, tensions had sporadically run high between Gisèle, on one hand, and Frédérique and Philippe on the other, thus aggravating Joan's off-again, on-again feelings of entombment in her big house. La Tour was looking rather shabby: cobwebs trailed from the ceiling, the furniture was battered, the walls needed a fresh coat of paint, stuff had accumulated everywhere. The village too—"*la France profonde,*" as she exaggeratingly called it—depressed Joan, especially in autumn and winter, so rainy, silent, and dull. She considered her living in France to be an accident. With the dogs dead, she had no reason not to move and, at one point, decided to share a place in New York with Valerie Septembre, a painting conservator whose family came from Vétheuil. But then inertia set in. Not just inertia—Joan knew that *her* New York had vanished.

In 1989, Jean Fournier had bled off some of her discontent, however, by renting and fixing up for her a haven in Montparnasse that Joan dubbed her "secret studio" and where she felt free, now that the dogs were gone, to work and spend the night. Situated in a charming old studio building at 23, rue Campagne-Première, a short street where artist Man Ray, photographer Eugène Atget, writers Louis Aragon and Elsa Triolet, and Rilke himself had once lived and where Godard filmed the ending of *Breathless,* Joan's place was high ceilinged, light flooded, and appealingly empty. Among the few friends whom she told of its existence were Mme. Rousseaux, whose new office was only a ten-minute walk, and Michaële-Andréa Schatt, with whom Joan shopped for items she would need in town, all the while expanding upon her dire need for this sanctum for deep rest and intense work, pastels only. Its mezzanine held a bed, a few books, a radio, nothing more. (Serendipitously, one of her neighbors played the piano, rather well, and Joan loved the occasional burst of faint music.) In the main room downstairs stood several canvas chairs, the wooden panels to which she tacked sheets of paper, and the rolling tables on which she arranged her pastels, some jumbo sausage sized, others worn down to nuggets. She used two types, both soft, Sennelier's standard grade and pastels made by a certain little old lady since time immemorial. Laid out in small boxes, they glowed with the éclat of jewels.

As months went on, Joan let more and more people in on the secret. After she told Klaus Kertess, he offered her a pastel show at the Whitney, thus sparking a marathon of drawing, which she did back in her studio in Vétheuil. Wanting to smash all lingering notions of pastel making as a genteel, ladylike pastime, Joan made hundreds of vigorous and sure-handed drawings. Overlaid here and there with plummeting tendrils and gossamer veils, their velvety knots of color, all sensuous after-rain freshness, bristle with sheering spikes and snaggy or sinuous curves. Working on three drawings at a time, Joan devoted herself to this project for several months until finally, one day that fall, she phoned Klaus: "Get your ass over here; I'm tired of the pastel dust on my studio floor. It makes me feel like I'm a 'Lady Artist.'" He promptly arrived, along with John Cheim, to select work for the show, some forty pastels, all untitled, for the museum's Lobby Gallery.

At her opening five months later, the artist, in leather jeans and a turtleneck, greeted visitors surrounded by her "bodyguards" from the Whitney staff. A woman a few years younger than she introduced herself: Sally Turton, the granddaughter of her father's beloved sister Gertrude. Sally and Joan had not set eyes upon each other for decades, but, having read about Joan's upcoming exhibition, Sally had tried to round up as many family members as possible to attend the reception. Other than her daughter, however, not a single one was willing or able. The two had flown out from Chicago. As they chatted, Joan revealed to Sally that she had cancer, adding, "You know who my father was. My father was a cancer specialist. [He wasn't.] But he isn't around to save me. If my father were here, I wouldn't have to die." Fundamentally, Sally thought, cousin Joan hadn't changed a bit: the same hard-edged personality, seemingly indestructible because of her force of character, but also the same fragile little girl longing to be saved by her father. In fact, Joan had recently titled a painting *Gentian Violet,* again (privately, since no one else would get it) fastening upon Jimmie. As the three Mitchell women used to joke, he had treated every scrape and scratch with the antiseptic gentian violet.

Yet Joan knew she was beyond saving. She had made these hundreds of drawings using neither a face mask nor adequate ventilation to protect herself from the fine pastel dust, which is filled, as she was fully aware, with carcinogens and other toxins hazardous to the lungs. She had fatalistically followed the needs of her work, even when it took her into clouds of noxious color.

The summer of 1992 passed. Christopher Campbell again lived at La Tour. Joan painted prodigiously. She continued her psychoanalysis and, though crushingly tired, saw many people. Sometimes she would call her friend, lawyer and writer Guy Bloch-Champfort, and say, "I'm alone, please come," and he would arrive to find her surrounded by people. Wanting in the worst way for her long-ago lover Evans Herman to fly to France and play for her, she pleadingly tried to arrange it through their mutual friend Marilyn Stark, but, for reasons now unclear, it never happened.

All the while, she was feeling intense pain between her ribs but said little about it. Once Gisèle spotted a fleck of blood at the corner of her mouth. Her teeth wobbled, her jaw tormented her. Yet she may have stopped taking the penicillin prescribed for her chronic infection because its side effects annoyed her. Extremely thin, she looked and felt every bit her age. (During the Whitney show, leaving the Westbury with Robert Harms one day, she had paused, stared in the mirror, moved her hair around a bit, and lamented, "God, Harms, it isn't easy, getting old." She was sixty-seven.)

One night Joan had a vivid and deeply troubling dream in which her jaw was missing. That dream occurred as she was preparing to travel to New York, on October 12, to work once again at Tyler Graphics and see the Matisse retrospective at the Museum of Modern Art. She went directly from the airport to Mount Kisco.

Among Joan's projects-in-progress at Tyler were the *Trees, Weeds,* and *Fields* series of prints and the artist's book *Poems.* Having decided several months earlier that she wanted to do an artist's book, she had asked Nathan Kernan to suggest a poet with whom she could collaborate. He had. But, the next thing he knew, it was understood that the two of them were doing a book together, an idea that made him uncomfortable because he felt Joan should work with someone of her own stature. He tried to talk her out of it until finally she said, "Don't worry, let's just make something and have fun." She was, of course, forcing the issue of his being a poet. Now that project awaited final decisions. The result would be dazzling: eight Mitchell lithographs "illuminating" eight Kernan poems, loosely connected by the theme of loss, in a handsome paper folio made of Mitchell's recycled lithographic proofs.

But, ensconced in the artist's apartment at Tyler, Joan uncharacteristically lollygagged in bed, coughing blood from time to time. After three days, Marabeth Cohen-Tyler, Ken's wife, insisted upon taking her to their family physician. Dr. Rummo diagnosed very advanced lung cancer.

Abruptly, the end was upon her. Although she had long expected the worst, Joan was unaware that her cancer had metastasized to her lungs and, like everyone else, was shocked by its severity. Yet she took the news as well as one could, phoning Gisèle: "It's all over. I've got lung cancer." For Fournier, whom she reached at the opening of the Paris FIAC (International Fair for Contemporary Art), she mustered a touch of humor:

"Jean, I'm in really bad shape. I'm returning to Paris. FIACs don't agree with me." (Her cancer of the jaw had been diagnosed on opening day of the FIAC in 1984.)

The very next morning, Joan, in a wheelchair, Ken, Marabeth, Marion Cajori, John Cheim, and Klaus Kertess all met at the Museum of Modern Art to view the mammoth Matisse retrospective. As they rode up in the elevator, Joan broke the hushed silence with a warmly affectionate "Matisse! That motherfuck!" Yet the exhibition itself almost failed to stir her. "You know," she confessed to John, "I really know all these already. As much as I love [this painting], I'm not that interested at this moment. Because I've adored it all, and I know it all." Still, she could not pass up the opportunity to nettle Ken, as he wheeled her through the galleries: "*He* knew how to use blue, Ken! You could learn a lot, Ken. Look at that blue!" Afterward Joan wanted to see the Ellsworth Kelly drawing show at Matthew Marks. Then came lunch at Robert Miller Gallery. Miller was showing the work of seventy-five-year-old Abstract Expressionist Milton Resnick, who also lunched at the gallery that day. Seated next to Milton, Joan started in teasing her old friend, and bursts of laughter kept erupting from their corner of the table. Lunch was followed by visits to the Max Beckmann show at Gagosian, Claes Oldenburg at Pace, contemporary sculpture at Marlborough, Katherine Bowling at Blum Helman, and Ellsworth Kelly prints at Susan Sheehan. Joan beamed.

She seemed in high spirits the next evening too, at a dinner party thrown by Ken and Marabeth for Joan and fifteen friends at Cricket Farm, the original Tyler workshop in Bedford. Though dependent upon friends for material and emotional support, she felt able to give by sharing her deep respect for life and keen enjoyment of aliveness, even at this alarming juncture. Driving that week with the Tylers past fields, horses, and woods in their full October glory, she had never stopped observing, admiring, and pointing out this splendid light, that fabulous color.

Joan's flight had been booked for the following Wednesday, only nine days after her arrival. In the studio, they were still midstream with several etchings, Joan herself "really cooking" with the work. Of course, everyone tiptoed around the fact that she was dying, and there was lots of talk of the future: Ken was going to bring the plates to Vétheuil, and so on. Finally, the artist spoke out: "Let's cut all the bullshit, okay?" she told Ken. "You've got to straighten up and understand a few things about what we're going to do here."

Joan and painter Milton Resnick laugh it up over lunch at the Robert Miller Gallery, a few days after she learned she had advanced lung cancer, 1992.

"I do?"

"Yeah! You're going to finish everything that's up in the press room as fast as you can. I don't have a lot of time. And, second, you're going to promise me that whatever we start out selling these prints for, that's it. You're never going to raise the prices. I don't want these things to go the way the blue-chip guys are going." The normal practice in publishing print editions is to keep increasing the prices, but Joan wanted hers to remain at a level that would not deter young people from buying.

Joan spent her final New York days in Manhattan, seeing friends and completing a panicky rewrite, one of many over the years, of her will. Among its wiser stipulations was the establishment of the Joan Mitchell Foundation, with the mission of demonstrating the vital necessity of painting and sculpture and of helping artists, chiefly through grants and educational programs. Tuesday evening was devoted to a small dinner party at John Cheim's Twentieth Street apartment with Hal Fondren, Robert Harms, and art writers Lisa Liebmann and Brooks Adams. The following morning, as Ken and Marabeth drove her to Kennedy, tears abundantly flowed: Joan was "a wreck when she got on the plane," Ken remembers. "We were wrecks when she left."

Joan lived her final days with courage and grace. Flying on the Concorde, she arrived at Roissy around ten thirty that evening. When Gisèle and their driver, Jean-Jacques, met her, she was unable to swallow. Yet when they got to La Tour, she invited Jean-Jacques to come in as usual for a glass of wine. He knew she was quite ill, nothing more. That night Gisèle's poodle, Fudji, jumped from his mistress's bed and, to Joan's delight, came to sleep with her. One can imagine her feelings the next morning at leaving Vétheuil and arriving at the Curie Institute, which she always found profoundly depressing.

There, Prof. Brugère, whom she called "my gardener" because of the instruments he used, did tests and confirmed that her cancer had spread to the trachea and lungs. It was extremely advanced. She asked for a date. Brugère said fifteen to twenty-one days. There was a high risk of hemorrhage and immediate death.

Eventually Joan was put in a single room, small and banal, with a horizontal window that silhouetted people against the light. Alerted by Gisèle, friends quickly appeared, some refusing to believe that Joan was dying. Among them was Monique Frydman, to whom Joan said good-bye (as it turned out, since Monique had to leave town for several days) with the words "Neither man nor woman. Neither young nor old." She meant painting. "Take care of yourself."

John Cheim, who had crossed the Atlantic close on Joan's heels, also took for granted that she would recover. Though barely able to speak, she remained playful and tough and, when the light showed through her hospital gown, he noticed how beautiful her legs were, like a girl's. Nearly everyone smuggled in white wine. When Zuka arrived, she was amazed to find Joan seated in a chair in the hall amid a coterie of young French painters, sipping Chablis and looking "like a queen holding court." In intense pain and unable even to walk to the toilet, she drank with her friends as long as she could get a glass to her lips.

By Sunday morning she was in terrible pain. Joe Strick and Guy Bloch-Champfort alerted a doctor, who gave her an injection. Hooked up to an IV and heavily sedated, she mostly kept her eyes closed, yet, for a time, stared at the deep blue delphinium someone had placed on the windowsill. Gisèle marveled that Joan remained capable of wonder. She continued to draw upon some primal energy until finally she slipped into a coma. When Christiane Rousseaux visited on Tuesday morning, she found Joan comatose yet showing a glimmer of recognition in her eyes. At her bedside nearly day and night, the devoted Gisèle read her mail to her when it was just the two of them, though surely Joan was beyond comprehension.

On Thursday, a deathwatch began. Gisèle, Frédérique, Philippe, Guy, Hervé Chandès, and Sally Apfelbaum (who couldn't help but think that she represented Joan's ties to her own country) stayed into the night and took turns holding Joan's hands: strong and stubby working hands, Sally realized. She was cradling them that Friday morning, October 30, at 12:50 a.m. when Joan died.

Franck Bordas heard the news from a weeping and devastated Jean Fournier. For Joan's dealer, the artist's final weeks resonated with those of early-eighteenth-century French Rococo painter Antoine Watteau, who, near the end of his short life, had returned to Paris from London, his lungs nearly destroyed by consumption. Watteau's gallerist and friend, Edme Gersaint, cared for the testy, restive, and dying artist, who insisted upon painting a sign for Gersaint's shop "to loosen up his stiff fingers." So ill he could work only in the mornings, Watteau painted in seven days, "no, five days" (as Fournier told this parable of sorts), his enormous oil on canvas, expending much of his remaining life force in the effort. Watteau's painting depicts, as if from the street, minus its façade, the interior of an ideal gallery bustling with activity. A painting about beauty and transience, Watteau's masterwork also attends to the vital role of gallerist as intermediary between artist and art lover and illuminates, in the words of art historian Donald Posner, "the sense and worth of art and the artist's life."

In the months following Joan's death, Fournier advanced preparations for her simultaneous shows at the Musée des Beaux-Arts in Nantes (spanning the period 1951 to 1982) and the Jeu de Paume in Paris (beginning with the *Grande Vallée* suite). This French retrospective had been in the works since 1990, but only shortly before Joan left for New York had its curators, Alfred Pacquement, then director of the Jeu de Paume, and Henry-Claude Cousseau, his counterpart at the museum in Nantes, along with Fournier, spent a "memorable and moving day" at Vétheuil.

After receiving the prestigious Grand Prix des Arts of the City of Paris from French Minister of Culture and Education Jack Lang (center), 1991

Joan had once again resisted the rummaging through the past that a retrospective entails but, at the same time, "violently" (the word is Fournier's) desired the exhibition at the Jeu de Paume. As Jean was driving her to Mme. Rousseaux's one day and speaking of the venerable museum, Joan had gripped his hand: "Jean, I would do *anything* to show there!" Shortly before her death, she had visited the Jeu de Paume to look over the space, and the thought of her paintings in that soft light and on the edge of the Tuileries Gardens had made her supremely happy.

Joan's obituary had made the front page of *Le Monde,* the newspaper of record, and Minister of Culture and Education Jack Lang had issued a statement: "With Joan Mitchell, we lose one of the great women artists of our era." ("Women artists!"—one can hear Joan's harrumph.) The previous December she had received the important Grand Prix des Arts de la Ville de Paris. "I—'Joan Just *Girl*' from Chicago—received the French Grand Prix for painting . . . I couldn't believe it," she wrote the Von Blons.

Around the same time, a Mitchell was hung in the official prime minister's residence, the Hôtel Matignon, where Joan and Jean Fournier lunched with Prime Minister Michel Rocard. A certain French cultural elite appreciated not only her painting, but also her intellectual capabilities, deep knowledge of French culture, excessive personality befitting an artist, even her rather French bent for bristly unpleasantnesses. Her hospitalization at Curie had been an item on French TV news. Yet she was little known to the wider public. Nonetheless, her dual 1994 exhibitions, a popular and critical triumph, drew a record 38,000 visitors to the museum in Nantes and nearly 50,000 to the Jeu de Paume. The latter included her protégée Joyce Pensato, who was taken aback when, as she strolled through one gallery, Cajori's film played in the basement and that familiar voice faintly lashed out.

At the time of her death, Joan had been painting toward a third Robert Miller exhibition. In her studio one morning that August she had carefully arranged her brushes and visually caressed her paints, reassured by the fact that looking at them made her yearn to paint, which meant she *existed.* She could no longer unscrew the caps on her paint tubes, so someone did it for her, and could no longer climb a ladder, so she used extra-long brushes.

One of Joan's last paintings, the consummate *Ici* (*Here*), no doubt completed that summer, brings to mind the day she had arranged to meet her neighbor, Jean Mouillère, in his garden, which had been thrown into more chaos than usual by an early spring heat wave. The first poppies and roses were blooming amid the last tulips and irises. Having hobbled into this horticultural jumble, Joan halted, leaned on her cane, and then, her eyes enormous behind her magnifying-glass lenses, let out a stupefied "*My God!*" before falling intensely silent. Rife with wonder at the raw beauty of the landscape, boisterous with color, movement, and light, *Ici* is Mitchell's "*My God!*" I am alive at this moment in this place!

Completed about the same time, Joan's approximately nine-by-twelve-foot diptych movingly titled *Merci* makes its viewers feel small because of the scale of its strokes, the wallop of its colors, and the vastness of its space. Four powerfully painted calligraphic shapes—five including a scribble of near white on white—hang in the void. Joan's marks are primal, charged, and devoid of convention, cliché, or irony. How anyone frail, arthritic, semi-ambulatory, farsighted, and dying of cancer could make such a swaggeringly bold painting will always be a mystery. Shorthand for Joan's lifelong adoration of painting, *Merci* contains the lake,

Sixty-seven-year-old Joan at her studio in Vétheuil, 1992

the sunflower, and the tree; the blue and the orange; the white; van Gogh, Cézanne, Matisse, and the Great Abstract Expressionist Mark; fear, fury, aloneness, and love.

In Joan's last paintings, all untitled, centered blue or yellow treelike forms, as festive as maypoles, float on white ground. They simultaneously snug the surface and pull away. Here the psyche has very fluid boundaries, dissolving into majestic summer blue or liquid satin-curtain yellow. Trees for herself, as she had painted so many trees for departed friends, they recall Pierre Schneider's long-ago words: "A Joan Mitchell canvas is the story of Daphne, a being seized by panic, gasping for breath . . . who at the moment her strength fails escapes by transforming herself into a tree." And Joan's: "I become the sunflower, the lake, the tree. I no longer exist."

Notes

Minor spelling and punctuation errors in the quotations have been corrected. All translations are mine unless otherwise stated.

PROLOGUE

xix "My sister": Joan Mitchell in a letter to Sarah Mitchell Perry, n.d.

xix "that dark idea": Joan Mitchell in a letter to Michael Goldberg, n.d., Michael Goldberg Papers, Box 1, Archives of American Art/Smithsonian Institution. My description of Joan's painting process is indebted to Irving Sandler's "Mitchell Paints a Picture," *ArtNews* 56:6 (October 1957): 44–47, 69–70.

xx "Ugghrrr": Joan Mitchell, quoted by Michael Goldberg, interview with author, 20 June 2002.

xx "more available": Joan Mitchell, interviewed in Marion Cajori, director, *Joan Mitchell: Portrait of an Abstract Painter* (New York: Art Kaleidoscope Foundation and Christian Blackwood Productions, 1992). Film.

xx "no hands": Joan Mitchell, quoted in Judith E. Bernstock, *Joan Mitchell* (New York: Hudson Hills Press in association with Herbert F. Johnson Museum of Art, 1988), 33.

xxi "I 'stop' ": Mitchell, quoted in Bernstock, 34.

xxi "how to come down": Mitchell to Goldberg, n.d., Michael Goldberg Papers.

xxi "The painting has to": Mitchell, quoted in Sandler, 45.

xxi "All vanitas": Catherine Flohic, "Joan Mitchell," *Ninety* (1993): 4.

INTRODUCTION

4 "will attack": Lytton Strachey, *Eminent Victorians: The Illustrated Edition* (New York: Weidenfeld and Nicolson, 1988), 7.

5 "Everyone is born": Sharon Begley, "Why George Gershwin May Have Called It 'Rhapsody in Blue,' " *Wall Street Journal*, 28 June 2002.

5 "community of feeling": Joan Mitchell in a letter to Michael Goldberg, n.d., Michael Goldberg Papers, Box 1, Archives of American Art/Smithsonian Institution.

6 "love and death": Joan Mitchell, interviewed in Marion Cajori, director, *Joan

Mitchell: Portrait of an Abstract Painter (New York: Art Kaleidoscope Foundation and Christian Blackwood Productions, 1992). Film.

6   "I feel like": Joan Mitchell, quoted in Irving Sandler, "Mitchell Paints a Picture," *ArtNews* 56:6 (October 1957): 45.

6   "an original relation": Ralph Waldo Emerson, "Nature," in Carl Bode, ed., in collaboration with Malcolm Cowley, *The Portable Emerson* (New York: Penguin, 1981), 7.

6   "Of course"; Liz Lufkin, "Triumph for 'Lady Painter,'" *San Francisco Chronicle,* 26 May 1988.

7   "Not bad": Ibid.

CHAPTER ONE: JIMMIE AND MARION

11   "Beams arch high": "Bridges," Marion Strobel, *Lost City* (Boston and New York: Houghton Mifflin, 1928), 40.

12   "could console": Oscar Wilde, *The Picture of Dorian Gray* (Oxford and New York: Oxford University Press, 1988), 110.

12   "glowing, all summer": Joan Mitchell, interviewed by Cora Cohen and Betsy Sussler, "Joan Mitchell," *Bomb* 17 (fall 1986): 24.

12   "touching my own self"; "How strange": "Barbara" [Joan], quoted in Edrita Fried, *On Love and Sexuality: A Guide to Self-Fulfillment* (New York: Grove Press, 1960), 40. In her survey of love and sex as instruments of healthy change, Joan's analyst, Dr. Edrita Fried, addresses the ways in which ego regression refreshes and activates the normal ego yet may provoke anxiety or hostility in someone with a defective ego. She presents a case study of Barbara, a pseudonym for Joan Mitchell (as confirmed by Fried's daughter, psychotherapist Jaqueline Fried). Although the analyst has concealed her patient's identity (making Barbara a musician rather than an artist, for instance), her account of Joan's psychological history and condition, consistent with other sources, appears to be accurate. However, cautions Jaqueline Fried, authors of case studies writing for a popular audience may take liberties with facts in order to make a point.

12   "I feel too much": Mitchell to Goldberg, 20 August 1954, Michael Goldberg Papers, Archives of American Art/Smithsonian Institution.

13   "It comes out": Joan Mitchell, quoted in Carla Hall, "And a Party for the Folks Who Put It Together," *Washington Post,* 19 February 1981.

14   "No one can": Joan Mitchell in a letter to Sarah Mitchell Perry, n.d. [1982]. Collection of Sally Perry.

14   "means of feeling": Mitchell, interviewed by Yves Michaud, "Conversation with Joan Mitchell," in Xavier Fourcade Gallery, *Joan Mitchell: New Paintings* (New York: Xavier Fourcade Gallery, 1986), unpaginated.

14   "If I can't paint": Joan Mitchell, quoted by Sally Perry, interview with author, 14 April 2001.

14   "And it is": Rainer Maria Rilke, *The Notebooks of Malte Laurids Brigge,* trans. Stephen Mitchell (New York: Random House, 1982), 20.

14   "the total influence": Sally Turton, telephone interview with author, 28 December 2001.

15   "You'll never": Joan Mitchell, quoted in Cindy Nemser, "An Afternoon with Joan Mitchell," *Feminist Art Journal* 3:1 (spring 1974): 6.

15   "completely out"; "free [her]": Mitchell, interviewed in Marion Cajori, director, *Joan Mitchell: Portrait of an Abstract Painter* (New York: Art Kaleidoscope Foundation and Christian Blackwood Productions, 1992). Film.

15   "Oh, I'll never": Mitchell to Goldberg, n.d., Michael Goldberg Papers.

15   "a very mixed bag": Joan Mitchell, quoted in Judith E. Bernstock, *Joan Mitchell* (New York: Hudson Hills Press in association with Herbert F. Johnson Museum of Art, 1988), 14.

16   "pioneer stock": Joan Mitchell, quoted in Stephan Westfall, "Then and Now: Six of the New York School Look Back," *Art in America* 73:6 (June 1985): 114.

16   "wife and children": *Democrat Clarion*, 12 June 1874.

17   "Spartan courage": James Herbert Mitchell in a letter to Gertrude Mitchell Sloan, 1 September 1914. Collection of Susan Sloan.

17   "Jim Mitchell hasn't": *Mason County Democrat*, 23 May 1890.

18   "genuine lover": Ibid., 24 April 1891.

18   "He is quite": Sarah Vaughan Mitchell in a letter to Eva Hostman, 6 July 1890. Collection of Sally Perry.

19   "had given": *Mason County Democrat*, 26 September 1890.

19   "parlor tricks": James Herbert Mitchell, quoted in Judith Cass, "Recorded at Random," unknown newspaper, n.d.

20   "Jack of all": Mitchell, interviewed in Cajori.

20   finally managed: Transcript of James Herbert Mitchell, University of Chicago, Office of the University Registrar, Chicago.

20   "you can be": James Herbert Mitchell, quoted by Mitch Waters, telephone interview with author, 30 December 2001. Mitch Waters heard the story from his father, Jeffrey Waters, James Herbert Mitchell's nephew by marriage.

20   "attending to": James Herbert Mitchell to Gertrude Mitchell Sloan, 20 December 1907. Collection of Susan Sloan.

21   "faint voluptuous smell": Marion Strobel, *Ice Before Killing* (New York: Charles Scribner's Sons, 1943), 14. Although her book is fiction, Strobel modeled several characters on family members. Her Archie Soames appears to be based upon James Herbert Mitchell.

21   "It takes a man": Herbert Sloan, quoted in a letter from James Herbert Mitchell to George A. Sloan, 3 October 1914. Collection of Susan Sloan.

21   "Please, please": Marion Strobel in a letter to James Herbert Mitchell, 8 November 1921. Collection of Sally Perry.

22   "Marion Jimmied": Ashton Stevens, "Wits Write Stevens on Names, Drinks," *Chicago Herald-American*, n.d. Collection of Sally Perry.

22   "We are happy": James Herbert Mitchell to Gertrude Mitchell Sloan, 17 December 1922. Collection of Susan Sloan.

22   "Will you go": Marion Strobel to James Herbert Mitchell, 8 November 1921. Collection of Sally Perry.

23   "leaves, and crawling things": Marion Strobel Mitchell in a letter to Morton Zabel, 26 August [1933], Morton Zabel Papers, Newberry Library.

23   "If I had a dandelion": Mitchell to Zabel, n.d., Morton Dauwen Zabel Papers, Box III, Folder 10, University of Chicago Library.

23   Marion's maternal grandparents: Among the children of Daniel Franklin Baxter's great-great-great-great-grandparents was Abigail Baxter, who married Joseph Adams. That couple's great-grandson was President John Adams. Thus

the Chicago Baxters claimed kinship by marriage to both the second president and the sixth president, his son, John Quincy Adams. Joan never touted this connection, yet it added to her sense of herself as an American, which was to be thrown into relief by her living in France. My thanks to Susan Sloan for the information about the Baxter-Adams connection.

23   "a dashing and popular trio": Article from unknown newspaper about the marriage of Charles Louis Strobel and Mary L. Wilkins, n.d. [August 1910]. Collection of Sally Perry.

25   "a structural signature": Thomas J. Misa, *A Nation of Steel: The Making of Modern America, 1865–1925* (Baltimore and London: Johns Hopkins University Press, 1995), 72. My understanding of Strobel's role in the steel industry derives largely from Misa's book as well as Strobel's obituaries.

26   "He never spoke": Joan Mitchell, interviewed by Linda Nochlin, 16 April 1986. Transcript, Archives of American Art, Smithsonian Institution.

26   "beautiful, fabulous": Mitchell, quoted in Bernstock, 22.

27   "Toward Blue": This notebook was among the belongings Joan never claimed after friends moved her out of her apartment at 60 St. Mark's Place.

27   "recollected landscape": Irving Sandler, "Mitchell Paints a Picture," *ArtNews* 56:6 (October 1957): 45.

27   "a visual image": Irving Sandler, "Joan Mitchell," *ArtNews* 56:1 (March 1957): 64.

27   Upend the steel sleeve: Jenney made this comment to the [New York] *Times Herald,* 27 August 1895, William L. B. Jenney and William B. Mundie Papers, Roll 10, Burnham Microfilm Project, Art Institute of Chicago, cited in Misa, 64.

28   he signed contracts: Misa, 74.

28   One of these: Art historian Joseph M. Siry makes this point on page one of his architectural and social history, *The Chicago Auditorium: Adler and Sullivan's Architecture and the City* (Chicago and London: University of Chicago Press, 2002). Amputated in 1952 when Congress Street was widened into Congress Parkway, this rather derelict dowager today occupies a noisy corner of the Loop, its glamour a thing of the past despite the renovation of its glorious theater. The offices and hotel have been turned into classrooms and offices for Roosevelt University.

29   "the ordeal of costumes": "Society," *Chicago Daily Tribune,* 15 January 1905.

29   *"Tapering fingers"*: Marion Strobel, "Hands," *Poetry* 15:6 (March 1920): 315.

30   "In the morning": "Mrs. C. L. Strobel Dies," *Chicago Daily Tribune,* 21 March 1905.

31   "more or less": Sarah Mitchell Perry in a letter to Sally Perry, n.d. Collection of Sally Perry.

32   "To tear down"; "Poetry is": William Carlos Williams, "Notes from a Talk on Poetry," *Poetry* 14:4 (July 1919): 215. My information about Williams's time in Chicago derives from Paul Mariani, *William Carlos Williams: A New World Naked* (New York: McGraw-Hill, 1981); Marion Strobel's 23 April 1919 letter to Williams (William Carlos Williams Papers, University at Buffalo); and William Carlos Williams, *The Autobiography of William Carlos Williams* (New York: Random House, 1951). (Williams's autobiography, however, misdates his visit to Chicago.) Strobel and Williams enjoyed a long but never again close friendship. She got in the last word about the romance. His "A Goodnight"

exhorted, "go to sleep, go to sleep." As if in response, the final stanza of Strobel's poem from the early twenties, "After a Quarrel," reads, "But love / You
told me I might keep / Has gone to sleep / Has gone to sleep."

32   *"Go to sleep"*: William Carlos Williams, "A Goodnight," *Poetry* 9:2 (November 1916): 184.

32   "But in the future": Marion Strobel in a letter to William Carlos Williams, 23
April 1919, William Carlos Williams Papers.

33   "My dear Miss Monroe": Marion Strobel in a letter to Harriet Monroe, 20
December 1918, Poetry Magazine Collection, Gen. 1912–1936, Box 24, Folder
27, University of Chicago Library.

34   "Provided"; "SPIRIT OF '76": William Carlos Williams, *Poetry* 16:3 (June
1920): 173.

34   "that timeless": Marion Strobel, "543 Cass Street," Poetry Magazine Collection, Gen. 1936–1953, Box 68, Folder 28, University of Chicago Library.

34   Yet, as Joan later noted: From September 1942 to April 1946, Strobel coedited
Poetry with Peter de Vries, and, from May 1946 to April 1949, with George
Dillon. The magazine's "official" history is Joseph Parisi's *Poetry* (Chicago:
Modern Poetry Association, 1980).

CHAPTER TWO: SATIN CURTINS REDUX

36   "a momentary vacuum": Vladimir Nabokov, *Speak, Memory* (New York: G. P.
Putnam's Sons, 1966), 139.

36   Thus they were: Joan's birth certificate fixes her date of birth as 12 February
1925. Many reference materials incorrectly state that she was born in 1926.
According to the Mitchell family, this error stems from Joan's fudging her year
of birth in order to compete in a skating event in an age category lower than
her own. At that time, however, eligibility for U.S. Figure Skating Association
events was based on skill level, not age; hence, the event that provoked the date
change must have been a local one. Joan sometimes used 1925 as her birth year;
other times, she used 1926.

36   "I kissed": Marion Strobel, "Two of a Kind," *Lost City* (Boston and New
York: Houghton Mifflin, 1928), 49.

36   As for Jimmie: So Joan told painter Paul Brach. Paul Brach, interview with
author, 27 July 2004.

37   "My father wanted": Joan Mitchell, quoted by Sally Perry, interview with
author, 14 April 2001.

37   "It seemed that": Cindy Nemser, "An Afternoon with Joan Mitchell," *Feminist Art Journal* 3:1 (spring 1974): 6. The interview took place in 1972.

37   Painting, Joan believed: Joan Mitchell in Gisèle Barreau, "Porte Adieu, Joan
Mitchell, souvenirs," in Sandro Parmiggiani, ed., *Joan Mitchell: La pittura dei
Due Mondi/La peinture des Deux Mondes* (Milan: Skira, 2009), 133.

37   Joan's earliest memories: Judith E. Bernstock, *Joan Mitchell* (New York: Hudson Hills Press in association with Herbert F. Johnson Museum of Art, 1988),
15; Zuka Mitelberg, interview with author, 5 January 2002; Joyce Pensato,
interview with author, 14 July 2002. Both Marion and Jimmie spoke German
and may have hired German nannies in an attempt to teach their children the
language.

37 "How do you decide": Christopher Campbell, telephone interview with author, 10 February 2007.

38 "Dress them": John B. Watson, *Psychological Care of Infant and Child* (New York: W. W. Norton, 1928), 81. Watson's behaviorist doctrine was at loggerheads with the theories of Francis Parker, founder of the Francis W. Parker School, which Joan attended. Like his colleague John Dewey, Parker presumed each child's uniqueness and viewed education as a process of enabling the individual to develop from within; Watson believed there was nothing innate to develop. In Watson's view, one molds a child using conditioned responses to various stimuli. Although there is no material evidence that Jimmie was a follower of Watson, the behaviorist's theories were popular, and his appeal to science would have pleased Jimmie, who was unenthusiastic about Parker.

38 "Forced to admit": "Correspondence: Marion Strobel Resigns," *Poetry* 27:1 (October 1925): 54.

38 "the most vital": Marion Strobel Mitchell in a letter to Harriet Monroe, 10 April 1929, Poetry Magazine Collection, Gen. 1912–1936, Box 24, Folder 27, University of Chicago Library.

38 "and if I don't": Mitchell to Monroe, 1 August, n.d., ibid.

38 "flapping around": Mitchell to Monroe, n.d., ibid.

39 "A Cloak for Joan": Strobel, *Lost City,* 57.

39 "Fuck shit": Joan Mitchell to Sarah Mitchell Perry, 22 April 1982. Collection of Sally Perry.

40 A doorman: Baird & Warner Portfolio of Fine Homes, 1928, Chicago Historical Society; 1932 Chicago Social Register.

40 "I remember": Joan Mitchell to Sarah Mitchell Perry, 12 April 1982. Collection of Sally Perry.

41 "nice to have": Ibid.

41 "roosted inside me": Mitchell to Goldberg, 20 July 1954, Michael Goldberg Papers, Archives of American Art/Smithsonian Institution.

41 "Most of the studies": Richard E. Cytowic, *Synesthesia: A Union of the Senses* (Cambridge, MA, and London: MIT Press, 2002), 105. Primary sources on eidetic memory include Akhter Ahsen, "Eidetics: An Overview," *Journal of Mental Imagery* 1 (1977): 5–38, and Ralph Norman Haber, "Twenty Years of Haunting Eidetic Imagery: Where's the Ghost?" *Behavior and Brain Sciences* 2 (1979): 583–629. The most useful secondary sources are Rusiko Bourtchouladze, *Memories Are Made of This: How Memory Works in Humans and Animals* (New York: Columbia University Press, 2002); Kevin T. Dann, *Bright Colors Falsely Seen: Synaesthesia and the Search for Transcendental Knowledge* (New Haven and London: Yale University Press, 1998); and Ulric Neisser, ed. *Memory Observed: Remembering in Natural Contexts* (San Francisco: W. H. Freeman and Company, 1982).

41 "an apparatus": A. R. Luria, *The Mind of a Mnemonist* (New York and London: Basic Books, 1968), 76.

42 "learned clichés"; "very frightening": Mitchell, interviewed by Yves Michaud, "Conversation with Joan Mitchell," in Xavier Fourcade Gallery, *Joan Mitchell: New Paintings* (New York: Xavier Fourcade Gallery, 1986), unpaginated.

42 "She is": Marion Strobel, "Chart," *New Yorker,* 13 July 1940, 24.

42 "describes the rare phenomenon": Daniel Mark Epstein, *What Lips My Lips*

Have Kissed: The Loves and Love Poems of Edna St. Vincent Millay (New York: Henry Holt, 2001), 35.

42   "that robust reality": Vladimir Nabokov, *Speak, Memory* (New York: G. P. Putnam's Sons, 1966), 77.

43   One July afternoon: In 1976, poet Alice Clay Judson Ryerson Hayes founded the Ragdale Foundation, a retreat for writers and artists in Lake Forest, Illinois. My thanks to John Holabird for sharing this photograph.

43   "as wild": Marion Strobel, "Alice Clay and Sally Mitchell," *Lost City*, 53.

44   "wild little brook": Joan Mitchell, "The Snow," *1932 Parker Record*.

44   The school dates: My information about Francis Parker School derives principally from conversations and correspondence with Parker teacher and archivist Andrew Kaplan; the school's archives; Marie Kirchner Stone, *The Progressive Legacy: Chicago's Francis W. Parker School, 1901–2000* (New York: Peter Lang, 2001); Marie Kirchner Stone, ed., *Between Home and Community: Chronicle of the Francis W. Parker School, 1901–1976* (Chicago: Francis W. Parker School, 1976); and conversations with Parkerites Robert McCormick Adams, Jerry Carlin, John Holabird, Ernst Jaffe, Consuelo Joerns, Jean Lyons Keely, and Barney Rosset. Over the decades, Parker has produced many notable contributors to the creative arts, among them architect Edward Barnes, actress Jennifer Beals, artist and writer Edward Gorey, actress Daryl Hannah (whose stepfather, developer Jerry Wexler, was Joan's classmate), actress Anne Heche, architect John Holabird, actress Celeste Holm, writer and director David Mamet, artist Claes Oldenburg, and filmmaker Haskell Wexler.

44   "a catechism": Robert McCormick Adams, "Reflections for Francis W. Parker School Centennial," delivered on 5 October 2001.

45   Often she invited: Pauline Marks in a letter to Joan Mitchell, 1 December 1982. Collection of the Joan Mitchell Foundation.

45   When Connie Joerns's: Consuelo Joerns, telephone interview with author, 4 December 2002.

46   Joan's goldfish: Gisèle Barreau, "Porte Adieu, Joan Mitchell, souvenirs" in Sandro Parmiggiani, ed., *Joan Mitchell: La pittura dei Due Mondi/La peinture des Deux Mondes* (Milan: Skira, 2009), 130.

46   "Joan has": Mitchell to Monroe, 10 April 1929, Poetry Magazine Collection, Gen. 1912–1936, Box 24, Folder 27.

46   Intuiting: Deborah Solomon, "In Monet's Light," *New York Times Magazine*, 24 November 1991, 50.

47   "considered *very*": Katharine Kuh, interviewed in Judy K. Collischan Van Wagner, *Women Shaping Art: Profiles of Power* (New York: Praeger, 1984), 38.

47   "the cornfields": Joan Mitchell, quoted in Bernstock, 119.

48   In the evenings: Catherine Flohic, "Joan Mitchell," *Ninety* (1993): 1.

48   "Dr. Mitchell": John Holabird, interview with author, 25 November 2001.

48   "really beautiful": Mitchell to Zabel, 7 August 1933, Morton Zabel Papers, Arts Club Collection, Newberry Library, Chicago. Painter Herbert Katzman told me about the scar when we talked on 23 July 2001.

49   "I was": Mitchell, interviewed in Marion Cajori, director, *Joan Mitchell: Portrait of an Abstract Painter* (New York: Art Kaleidoscope Foundation and Christian Blackwood Productions, 1992). Film.

49   "Just have": Joan Mitchell, interviewed by Cora Cohen and Betsy Sussler, *Bomb* 17 (fall 1986): 22.

49   "Joan didn't play": Sally Turton, telephone interview with author, 28 December 2001. The daughter of Gertrude Mitchell Sloan's daughter, Sarah Sloan Waters, Sally Turton is actually Joan's first cousin once removed.

51   "the most glamorous place": F. Scott Fitzgerald in Matthew J. Bruccoli, *Some Sort of Epic Grandeur: The Life of F. Scott Fitzgerald* (Columbia, SC: University of South Carolina Press, 2002), 483.

51   Chicago's industrial employment: Allen Weller, "Lorado Taft, the Ferguson Fund, and the Advent of Modernism," in Sue Ann Prince, ed., *The Old Guard and the Avant-Garde: Modernism in Chicago, 1910–1940* (Chicago and London: University of Chicago Press, 1990), 45; Margaret Marshall, "Chicago: Two Exhibits," *Nation*, 28 June 1933, 715–17, in Neil Harris, "The Chicago Setting," in Prince, ed., 18.

52   "I needed": Joan Mitchell to Sarah Mitchell Perry, 12 April 1982. Collection of Sally Perry.

53   To quell her terrors: Irving Sandler, "Conversation with Joan Mitchell on Sunday, Feb. 18, 1957, for *ArtNews* Article," Irving Sandler Papers, Getty Research Institute, Research Library Special Collections and Visual Resources, Los Angeles.

53   vividly colored: Patricia Lynne Duffy, *Blue Cats and Chartreuse Kittens* (New York: Henry Holt, Times Books, 2001), 119–20. Duffy cites a study by neuroscientists Simon Baron-Cohen and John Harrison in which all participating synesthetes reported that they always dream in color. For Joan's synesthesia, see below.

53   "It's not"; "Don't you love"; "Because I was": Joan Mitchell, interviewed by Yves Michaud, "Entretiens," in Musée des Beaux-Arts de Nantes/Galerie Nationale du Jeu de Paume, *Joan Mitchell* (Paris: Éditions du Jeu de Paume, 1994), 31.

54   What she was talking: During Joan Mitchell's lifetime, not only was the general public unfamiliar with synesthesia, but also synesthesia lay outside the concerns of the scientific mainstream. Joan spoke openly about her mode of perception in interviews with Yves Michaud on 12 January 1986 and 7 August 1989.
        The Rosetta Stone of Mitchell's colored letters, a hand-done chart, appears briefly in Marion Cajori's film, along with the painter's note to herself: "This is very unclear and unfair to my letters. Of course in certain words, some letters merge as into water, esp. the greys—metallic—silver—cold blue—I can't get with these crayons. I have ultramarine or cad green or red etc." In describing Joan's letters, I have been as faithful as possible to her color chart, verbal descriptions, and clues as to textures and affect. (Different synesthetes perceive the same letters as different colors with different characteristics. For example, Nabokov describes his *D* as creamy, whereas Mitchell's was metallic blue.)
        Researchers believe (subject to further testing and evaluation) that about ninety percent of synesthetes (so-called associators) see their colors and shapes as if in their minds' eyes; ten percent (so-called projectors) see them as if on a screen floating before them.

54   Pale metallic *O:* This image appears in Marion's poem "Snow," published in the January 1939 issue of *Poetry*. Joan's *O* was silvery white; the notion that Marion got the image from Joan is speculative.

54   "*S* is": Mitchell, interviewed by Michaud, "Entretiens," 31.

54   "Do you associate": Cajori.

55   "Like prolonged echoes": Charles Baudelaire, "Correspondances," in *One Hundred Poems from Les Fleurs du Mal*, trans. C. F. MacIntyre (Berkeley and Los Angeles: University of California Press, 1947), 21.

55   Some investigations suggest: Daphne Maurer and Charles Maurer, *The World of the Newborn* (New York: Basic Books, 1988), 51.

56   "Every time": Jaqueline Fried, interviews with author, 9 January 2003 and 11 January 2006.

56   In addition, Joan: Emotionally mediated synesthesia is the subject of a study at University College, London. See Jamie Ward, "Emotionally Mediated Synaesthesia," *Cognitive Neuroscience* 21:7 (October 2004): 761–72. My descriptions simplify.

56   "dark green and clinging": Joan Mitchell in a letter to Barney Rosset, quoted in Siri Hustvedt, "Joan Mitchell: Remembering in Color," in *Mysteries of the Rectangle: Essays on Painting* (New York: Princeton Architectural Press, 2005), 140.

56   "that white": Mitchell, interviewed by Michaud, "Entretiens," 31.

56   "vague nameless": Herman Melville, *Moby-Dick or The White Whale* (Philadelphia: John C. Winston, 1931), 128.

56   "I need to know": Mitchell, interviewed by Yves Michaud, "Conversation with Joan Mitchell," in Xavier Fourcade Gallery, *Joan Mitchell: New Paintings* (New York: Xavier Fourcade Gallery, 1986), unpaginated.

57   "suddenly felt": Duffy, 3.

57   "chaos perhaps": Mitchell to Goldberg, n.d., Michael Goldberg Papers.

57   "The divide between": Marcia Smilack made this comment to Sean Day's online Synesthesia List on 16 March 2007.

57   Psychiatrist Ernest Hartmann: See Ernest Hartmann, *Boundaries in the Mind: A New Psychology of Personality* (New York: Basic Books, 1991).

57   "involves the whole": Ahsen, 17–18.

58   "visualized now": Vladimir Nabokov, "Torpid Smoke," in *A Russian Beauty and Other Stories* (New York: McGraw-Hill, 1973), 28–29. On Nabokov's eideticism, see Dann, 120–64.

58   "At concerts": Jacques Lusseyran, *And There Was Light* (New York: Parabola Books, 1998), quoted in Duffy, 43.

58   Maybe she: In an article in *Newsweek,* Anne Underwood cites neurogeneticist and synesthete Julian Asher, who as a child attended symphony concerts with his parents and supposed that the lights were dimmed so that the audience could see the colors better. Anne Underwood, "Real Rhapsody in Blue," *Newsweek,* 1 December 2003, 67.

CHAPTER THREE: THE LAKE

59   "Music often takes": Charles Baudelaire, "La Musique," in *One Hundred Poems from Les Fleurs du Mal*, trans. C. F. MacIntyre (Berkeley and Los Angeles: University of California Press), 135.

60   "I'm having": George Dillon in a letter to Harriet Monroe, postmarked 2 May 1932, Poetry Magazine Collection, Gen. 1912–1936, Box 6, Folder 27, University of Chicago Library.

61 "feeble as a rag": Mitchell to Zabel, 10 July 1933, Morton Zabel Papers, Arts Club Collection, Newberry Library, Chicago.

61 "I don't like": Mitchell to Zabel, n.d., ibid.

62 "what kind": Eleanor Munro, *Originals: American Women Artists* (New York: Da Capo, 2000), 239.

62 "Bleakness, through the trees": Joan Mitchell, "Autumn," *Poetry* 48:3 (December 1935): 129.

62 "that eerie line": Paul Richard, "Joan Mitchell's Bleak Horizons: At the Corcoran, A 40-Year Look Back," *Washington Post,* 27 February 1988.

62 "a perfectly normal": Joan Mitchell, quoted in Phyllis Tuchman, "Joan Mitchell Paints Chaos in Color," *New York Newsday,* 13 April 1986.

62 "perilous leaping": Marion Strobel, "Perilous Leaping" [review of *Poems* by T. S. Eliot], *Poetry* 16:3 (June 1920): 157.

62 "weighed and balanced": Marion Strobel, quoted in Dorsey McCarthy, "A Chicago Poet Who Writes Whodunits for Relaxation," *Chicago Sun Book Week,* 26 May 1946.

62 "matted with": Mitchell, "Autumn."

62 "Have you ever": Marion Strobel, *Ice Before Killing* (New York: Charles Scribner's Sons, 1943), 83.

63 "Dear H.M.": Mitchell to Monroe, 22 October 1935, Poetry Magazine Collection. Gen. 1912–1936, Box 24, Folder 27, University of Chicago Library.

63 "Dear Mr. Dillon": Joan Mitchell to George Dillon, 12 December 1935, George Dillon Papers. Folder 3 [Marion Strobel], Special Collections Research Center, Syracuse University Library.

64 "splendid": Eunice Tietjens to the "Poetry Family," 30 September 1936, Harriet Monroe Papers, Box IV, Folder 12, University of Chicago Library. Subsequent winners of the Oscar Blumenthal Prize included Dylan Thomas, Muriel Rukeyser, John Ciardi, James Merrill, Richard Wilbur, and Robert Pinsky.

64 readings by poets: On the subject of the literary lions Joan reportedly met as a child, John Russell's 31 October 1992 *New York Times* obituary is typical. "As a child," writes Russell, "[Mitchell] came to know T. S. Eliot, Ezra Pound, Edna St. Vincent Millay, Thornton Wilder, Dylan Thomas and others as visitors to the family home." Certainly, the family home was filled with writers. However, Joan probably never met Eliot, Pound, or Thomas, at least not as a child. In the fall of 1950, when she was twenty-five and living in New York, Eliot did travel to Chicago, where he did a benefit reading for *Poetry* and made an appearance in the Mitchells' living room. But I found no evidence of any meeting with Joan. As for Pound, he came to the United States in 1939 for the first time in three decades but never ventured beyond the East Coast. He was not to return until 1945, when he was flown from Italy to Washington, D.C., to be indicted on charges of treason and subsequently imprisoned. Any encounter with Thomas also appears highly unlikely. Thomas first traveled to Chicago in March 1950; on his second visit in April 1952 he too read for *Poetry* and was fêted in the Mitchell home. But, again, Joan was in New York. In the fifties and sixties, the Mitchells also entertained Richard Wilbur, W. H. Auden, Nelson Algren, and Oliver St. John Gogarty.

64 hence, he joked: Gilbert A. Harrison, *The Enthusiast: A Life of Thornton Wilder* (New Haven and New York: Ticknor and Fields, 1983), 129.

65   "Now we are having": James Herbert Mitchell, quoted by Alfred Adler, interview with Barney Rosset, 1 April 2000.

65   "Let loneliness": George Dillon, "To Losers," quoted in Alfred Kreymborg, *A History of American Poetry: Our Singing Strength* (New York: Tudor, 1934), 587.

65   "weak, queer": Charles Ellis, quoted in Nancy Milford, *Savage Beauty* (New York: Random House, 2001), 367.

65   "NOTHING is": Marion Strobel Mitchell to George Dillon, "Tuesday" [June 1937], George Dillon Papers, Syracuse University Library.

66   "his full stature": Marion Strobel Mitchell to Adah Dillon, 24 July 1937, ibid.

66   "if I find": Mitchell to Adah Dillon, 1 October 1937, George Dillon Papers.

66   And discipline was: Martha Bertolette, telephone conversation with author, 21 March 2005.

66   "practically jealous": Adler, interview with Rosset, 1 April 2000.

67   "You do": Mitchell, interviewed in Marion Cajori, director, *Joan Mitchell: Portrait of an Abstract Painter* (New York: Art Kaleidoscope Foundation and Christian Blackwood Productions, 1992). Film.

67   "Do you remember": Joan Mitchell to Sarah Mitchell Perry, 25 April 1982. Collection of Sally Perry.

67   "And then": John Gruen, interview with author, 17 July 2002.

68   *"That you take"*: "Bon Voyage," George Dillon Papers, Syracuse University Library.

69   "long and lovely": "To James." Collection of Sally Perry.

69   "best progressive father": Sarah Mitchell Perry in a letter to Marion and James Herbert Mitchell, n.d. Collection of Sally Perry.

69   "The day was": "The Inn" appeared in the 1937 issue of *Parker Prints.*

70   "beet red noses": "Street Scene" was published in 1939, also in *Parker Prints.*

70   "diddle with things": Joan Mitchell, quoted in Joyce Campbell, "In the Land of Monet, American Painter Joan Mitchell More Than Pulls Her Weight," *People Weekly,* 6 December 1982, 83.

70   "no reason": John B. Watson, *Psychological Care of Infant and Child* (New York: W. W. Norton, 1928), 41.

70   "pressure to become": Eleanor Munro, *Originals: American Women Artists* (New York: Da Capo, 2000), 241.

70   "You can't": James Herbert Mitchell, quoted by Joanne Von Blon, telephone interview with author, 22 March 2005.

70   "a solitary arrangement": Mitchell to Goldberg, n.d., Michael Goldberg Papers, Archives of American Art/Smithsonian Institution.

71   "brutal, primitive": Eleanor Jewett, "November Holds First Promise of Art Activities," *Chicago Daily Tribune,* 21 October 1923, quoted in Sue Ann Prince, "'Of the Which and the Why of Daub and Smear': Chicago Critics Take On Modernism," in Sue Ann Prince, ed., *The Old Guard and the Avant-Garde: Modernism in Chicago, 1910–1940* (Chicago and London: University of Chicago Press, 1990), 105.

71   "violent": Mitchell, quoted in Munro, 233.

72   the *Tribune's* Eleanor Jewett: Eleanor Jewett, "An Old Blotter Becomes Art in Miró Exhibition," *Chicago Daily Tribune,* 9 November 1938, in Avis Berman, "The Katharine Kuh Gallery," in Prince, ed., 166.

72   the Ropp School: Underwritten by Arthur and Mary Aldis (the parents of
      Graham Aldis), the Ropp School operated for many years from the third floor
      of the Aldis home at 100 East Chicago Avenue and, in the summer, from the
      family's Lake Forest estate. In 1937 it merged with the School of the Art Insti-
      tute. An artist from Pekin, Illinois, and best boyhood friend of Senator Everett
      Dirksen, Hubert C. Ropp painted murals for Chicago's Palmolive, Montauk,
      and Champlain buildings. See the typescript "The Aldis 'Compound'" in the
      collection of the Lake Forest–Lake Bluff Historical Society.

      Joan once told Michael Goldberg that "The Artist," a short story by Sally
Benson published in the 3 September 1955 issue of the *New Yorker,* reminded
her of the Ropp School. Benson's setting is an old farmhouse in Monroe, Connecticut, the meeting place of a painting class popular with the moneyed summer
people. When an outspoken nine-year-old latches onto the group, his forthright
comments irritate his adult classmates, comfortable in their mediocrity. The boy
then paints a crudely beautiful still life, and the teacher sends him packing.

73   "do for Chicago": Gerald Nordland, "Aaron Bohrod," in Milwaukee Art
      Museum, *Leaders in Wisconsin Art, 1936–1981* (Milwaukee: Milwaukee Art
      Museum, 1982), 25.

73   using casein: Chicago artist Ramon Shiva, working from his factory at 433
      Goethe Street, first marketed casein paints in tubes in 1933.

74   "I loved": John Holabird, interview with author, 25 November 2001.

74   "aggressive, masculine": Consuelo Joerns, telephone interview with author,
      4 December 2002.

74   "Five little sub-debs": *Chicago Herald and Examiner,* n.d. Collection of Sally
      Perry.

74   *"Joan, in a dream"*: Marion Strobel Mitchell, "Joan," *Hygeia* 15:9 (September
      1937): 804.

75   "as well as": Eldon Danhausen, interview with author, 24 November 2001.

75   "close enough": Robert McCormick Adams, telephone interview with author,
      24 January 2005.

75   "I was": Mitchell, quoted in Judith E. Bernstock, *Joan Mitchell* (New York:
      Hudson Hills Press in association with Herbert F. Johnson Museum of Art,
      1988), 15.

76   In that era: John Holabird, interview with author, 25 November 2001.

76   "irritated-at-the-uncoordinated-slob": Sarah Mitchell Perry to Marion and
      James Herbert Mitchell, n.d. Collection of Sally Perry.

77   Having first put: My information about Joan's skating career comes primarily
      from the *Lake Placid News, Skating* magazine, the *Chicago Daily Tribune,*
      and Mitchell family documents. Tim Specht, Mary Lela Wood Bogardus, and
      Helen Davidson Maxson kindly shared their remembrances of Bobby Specht.
      The best source on Gustave Lussi is the Mountain Lake PBS documentary
      Gustave Lussi: The Man Who Changed Skating (Plattsburgh, 1989).

77   "little girls": Unknown Chicago paper, n.d. Collection of Sally Perry.

77   "remote like": Strobel, *Ice,* 32.

78   Joan was: Barney Rosset, interview with author, 18 January 2001.

78   "Chicagoans often": Thalia, "Women Aids of Symphony Celebrate 10th
      Anniversary," *Chicago Daily Tribune,* 11 March 1945.

79   "Do the best": Gustave Lussi, interviewed in *Gustave Lussi.*

79   "courting their nine": Strobel, *Ice,* 4.

79   "who had had tough luck": Ibid., 34.
79   Well aware that: Martha Bertolette, interview with author, 26 July 2004.
82   Decades later: Zuka Mitelberg, interview with author, 5 January 2002.
82   "Damn beautiful city": Joan Mitchell in a letter to Evans Herman, 30 August 1954. Collection of Frances Herman.
82   "looked vast": Mitchell, quoted in Munro, 239.
83   "The Lake": Ibid., 247.

CHAPTER FOUR: WAR AND PEACE

84   "I remember": Mitchell, quoted in Eleanor Munro, *Originals: American Women Artists* (New York: Da Capo, 2000), 233.
85   "bright, poignant": *1942 Parker Record.*
85   "marching to her own": Shirley Petry, telephone interview with author, 20 November 2005.
85   Consider that: Morris L. Ernst and Alan U. Schwartz, *Censorship: The Search for the Obscene* (New York: Macmillan, 1964), 95. Some of the Mitchells' help had to chuckle at Joan's language. Once, kidding around with Sally as the two rode the elevator at 190 East Chestnut alongside their mother, twelve- or thirteen-year-old Joan accidentally whooped, "Oh, balls!," to which Marion blithely responded with some banality about tennis. Charlie, the elevator man, discreetly signaled his amusement, while Joan and Sally practically died laughing. In a letter to Sally dated 4 May (probably 1982), Joan reminisces about this incident.
85   clipping editorials: Anonymous, telephone interview with author, 11 July 2004.
85   "the unusual": Marion Strobel, *A Woman of Fashion* (New York: Farrar and Rinehart, 1931), 179.
85   "a wolf's nose": Marion Strobel, *Ice Before Killing* (New York: Charles Scribner's Sons, 1943), 33.
85   "Isn't it hard": John Holabird, interview with author, 25 November 2001.
86   "a flaw": Zuka Mitelberg, interview with author, 5 January 2002.
86   Joan's new French teacher: My sources on Helen Richard include Paul Richard, telephone interview with author, 16 August 2002; interviews with various Parkerites; and Marie Kirchner Stone, ed., *Between Home and Community: Chronicle of the Francis W. Parker School, 1901–1976* (Chicago: Francis W. Parker School, 1976).
86   Her French "*bleu*": Marion Cajori, director, *Joan Mitchell: Portrait of an Abstract Painter* (New York: Art Kaleidoscope Foundation and Christian Blackwood Productions, 1992). Film. Vladimir Nabokov thus describes the differences between his English and French letters: "The long *a* of the English alphabet ... has for me the tint of weathered wood, but a French *a* evokes polished ebony. This black group also includes hard *g* (vulcanized rubber) and *y* (a sooty rag being ripped). Oatmeal *n*, noodle-limp *l*, and the ivory-backed hand mirror of *o* take care of the whites. I am puzzled by my French *on* which I see as the brimming tension-surface of alcohol in a small glass." See Vladimir Nabokov, *Speak, Memory* (New York: G. P. Putnam's Sons, 1966), 34.
87   "get their goats": Barney Rosset, interview with author, 18 January 2001. Rosset is paraphrasing Joan's psychology teacher, Alfred Adler.

87   "Joanie was": Helen Richard, quoted in Paul Richard, "Joan Mitchell's Bleak Horizons," *Washington Post,* 27 February 1988.

87   "Your mother": Joan Mitchell, quoted by Paul Richard, telephone interview with author, 16 August 2002.

88   "held court": Ernst Jaffe, telephone interview with author, 14 April 2002.

88   "vast visions": Mitchell, quoted in Munro, 242.

88   "Oh, Christ!": Herbert Katzman, interview with author, 23 July 2001.

88   "a cartoon Abstract Expressionist": Paul Richard, telephone interview with author, 16 August 2002.

89   "Wipe that": Ellen Lanyon, interview with author, 27 July 2001.

89   "fact that": Edward Gorey, quoted in Clifford Ross and Karen Wilkin, *The World of Edward Gorey* (New York: Harry N. Abrams, 1996), 33.

89   painting his toenails: Consuelo Jourgensen [Consuelo Joerns] in Amy Benfer, "Edward Gorey," *Salon* 15 (February 2000), www.salon.com.

90   "Ted was": Consuelo Joerns, telephone interview with author, 4 December 2002.

90   "a lot of": Gorey, quoted in Ross and Wilkin, 11.

90   "figure (ah!)": Tim Osato in a letter to Joan Mitchell, 1 September 1939. Collection of the Joan Mitchell Foundation.

90   "just to show": John Holabird, interview with author, 25 November 2001.

90   "Dear Enigma": Osato to Mitchell, 28 June 1943.

90   "I suppose": Osato to Mitchell, n.d.

90   "He was": Barney Rosset, interview with author, 24 July 2001. According to Rosset, Joan's parents disapproved of her friendship with Timmy because he was Japanese American.

92   "verged on the sensational": "Dorothy Goos Wins U.S. Junior Skating Crown," *Chicago Daily Tribune,* 21 February 1942.

92   Her fans' attention: Soon after Bobby Specht won the 1942 U.S. Men's Figure Skating Championship, he joined the Ice Capades as he waited to be drafted. When Joan and her friend Martha Burke (Bertolette) traveled to New Haven that fall to watch him perform, Bobby told Joan that his off-the-charts performance in the Vertigon test (a dizziness test administered to Air Force pilot candidates) had amazed his military testers, and the two old spinning partners had a good laugh. During the war, Bobby flew for the Air Force. He was also named to the 1944 U.S. Olympic team; the games were canceled, however. Later he returned to the Ice Capades as star skater and then director, and he appeared twice on the cover of *Life* magazine. One of the first major athletes to speak openly about his homosexuality, Bobby retired in 1972 and died in 1999.

93   "underlying tension": Susan K. Cahn, *Coming on Strong: Gender and Sexuality in Twentieth-Century Women's Sport* (New York: Free Press, 1994), 4.

93   "BOBBY SPECHT": Howard Barry, "BOBBY SPECHT TAKES FIGURE SKATING CROWN; Joan Mitchell Wins Senior Women's Title," *Chicago Sunday Tribune,* 18 January 1942.

93   "women were": Ellen Lanyon, interview with author, 27 July 2001.

93   "on the inside": Nathalie Sarraute, quoted by Ann Jefferson, "Nathalie Sarraute comme comédie de la critique," *remue.net, collectif littérature,* http://remue.net/article.php3?id_article=187&var_recherche=Sarraute.

94   "whirl in": Robert Goodnough, "Joan Mitchell," *ArtNews* 52:2 (April 1953): 41.

94 "If you use": Mitchell, quoted in Munro, 242.

94 "Painting is": Mitchell, interviewed by Yves Michaud, "Conversation with Joan Mitchell," in Xavier Fourcade Gallery, *Joan Mitchell: New Paintings* (New York: Xavier Fourcade Gallery, 1986), unpaginated.

94 "I don't close"; "meaningful and sensitive": Mitchell, quoted in Irving Sandler, "Conversation with Joan Mitchell on Sunday, Feb. 18, 1957, for *ArtNews* article," Irving Sandler Papers, Getty Research Institute, Research Library Special Collections and Visual Resources, Los Angeles.

94 "I've won": Mitchell, quoted in Joyce Campbell, "In the Land of Monet, American Painter Joan Mitchell More Than Pulls Her Weight," *People Weekly*, 6 December 1982, 84.

95 "*S.R.* [*Social Register*]": Joan Mitchell to Sarah Mitchell Perry, 25 April 1982. Collection of Sally Perry.

95 Of the three: Out of concern for the integrity of secondary education, Parker was taking part in the College Board's experimental Eight-Year Study, which waived entrance exams and guaranteed students from participating schools admission to any college.

95 "death warmed over": Mitchell, interviewed by Linda Nochlin, 16 April 1986. Transcript, Archives of American Art/Smithsonian Institution.

96 "study of liberal arts": "Smith College Class of 1945."

96 "What does": Martha Bertolette, interview with author, 26 July 2004.

96 "wallowing walks": Joanne Von Blon, telephone interview with author, 22 March 2005.

96 "a wonderful friend": Joanne Von Blon, interview by Mary Abbe, "Difficult Beauty," *Minneapolis Star-Tribune*, 12 November 1999.

96 "Can you imagine": Anonymous, interview with author, 12 July 2002.

96 "didn't really": Martha Bertolette, interview with author, 26 July 2004.

97 "Is there anything": Mitchell, interviewed by Nochlin, 16 April 1986.

97 "sense of justice": Joanne Von Blon, telephone interview with author, 22 March 2005.

98 "sexy as hell": Martha Bertolette, interview with author, 26 July 2004.

98 "dirt with a capital D": Sarah Mitchell Perry to Joan Mitchell, 25 June 1943. Other letters cited here are either undated or dated between 25 June and 16 November 1943. Collection of Sally Perry.

99 Back in Chicago: For information about James Bullock Hathaway, I am grateful to his niece Amanda Carver, along with Martha Bertolette and Joanne Von Blon. See also Harvard Class of 1944, Twenty-fifth Anniversary Report.

100 "crazy about Joan": Martha Bertolette, interview with author, 23 July 2002.

100 Founded as: At the time, the Ox-Bow School was loosely associated with the Art Institute of Chicago. Later that affiliation was formalized.

100 "really Frenchy": Mitchell, interviewed by Nochlin, 16 April 1986.

101 "My decision": Mitchell, quoted in Munro, 240.

101 "J-child": Sarah Mitchell Perry to Joan Mitchell, 23 October 1943. Collection of Sally Perry.

101 "I'd always": Mitchell, quoted in Munro, 243.

101 "the first teacher": Margaret Shook, obituary of Helen Randall in the *Smith Alumnae Quarterly* (winter 2000–2001).

101 "lover of Nature": Margaret Drabble, *Wordsworth* (New York: Arco, 1969), 11.

101 "I hate": Mitchell, quoted in Sandler.

102　"the spontaneous overflow": William Wordsworth, "Of the Principles of Poetry and the 'Lyrical Ballads' (1798–1802)," in Rev. Alexander B. Grosart, ed., *The Prose Works of William Wordsworth*, vol. 2 (1876; reprint, New York: AMS Press, 1967), 96.

102　"The surface of": William Wordsworth, *The Prelude*, lines 473–75, in Andrew J. George, ed., *The Complete Poetical Works of William Wordsworth* (Boston and New York: Houghton Mifflin, 1904), 130.

102　"a dull body": Mitchell, quoted in Munro, 240.

102　"not a dead": Drabble, 89.

102　"adult memory": See Ernest G. Schachtel, "On Memory and Childhood Amnesia" in Ulric Neisser, ed. *Memory Observed: Remembering in Natural Contexts* (San Francisco: W. H. Freeman and Company, 1982), 193.

103　"a vision": Ibid.

103　"emotion recollected": Wordsworth, "Of the Principles of Poetry and the 'Lyrical Ballads' (1798–1802)," in Grosart, ed., *Prose Works,* 96. Among the commentators on Mitchell's use of "emotion recollected in tranquillity" are Hayden Herrera, "Reviews and Previews: Joan Mitchell (Whitney Museum of Art)," *ArtNews* 73:6 (summer 1974): 111–12, and Richard Francis, "Mnemotechny," in *Joan Mitchell: Memory Abstracted,* Edward Tyler Nahem Fine Art, 20 June–9 August 2002, 10–11.

103　*"For oft"*: Wordsworth, "The Daffodils," in George, 312.

103　"mental gymnastics": Joan Mitchell to Sarah Mitchell Perry, n.d. [1944]. Collection of Sally Perry.

104　"There is no": Mitchell, quoted in Sandler.

104　Nor, she believed: Bill Scott, interview with author, 31 March 2004.

104　"I don't think": Mitchell, interviewed in Cajori.

104　"This is": Helen Randall note on Joan Mitchell, "Tolstoy's Theory of Art and Its Relation to *War and Peace,*" 15 April 1943. Collection of Sally Perry.

105　Back at Ox-Bow: Author's interviews with Zuka Mitelberg, 5 January 2002 and 24 March 2003.

105　"little dinner with painters": Jane Wilson, interview with author, 17 July 2003.

105　"very Anglo-Saxon": Zuka Mitelberg, interview with author, 5 January 2002.

106　"get good": Richard Bowman in a letter to Joan Mitchell, 27 March 1950. Collection of the Joan Mitchell Foundation.

107　On one wall: Ellen Lanyon, interview with author, 27 July 2001.

107　Four months: "Chicago Marine Honored Posthumously for Heroism," *Chicago Sun,* 14 October 1945; *Harvard Class of 1944: Twenty-fifth Anniversary Report* (Cambridge: Printed for the Class, 1969).

107　"really broken up": Martha Bertolette, conversation with author, 21 March 2005. A year and a half earlier, Stuyvesant Van Buren, the brother of Joan's close friend Joan Van Buren, had been killed at Guadalcanal.

CHAPTER FIVE: TAKING FROM EVERYBODY

108　"I am learning": Rainer Maria Rilke, *The Notebooks of Malte Laurids Brigge,* trans. Stephen Mitchell (New York: Random House, 1982), 5–6.

108　Founded in: Charlotte Moser, "'In the Highest Efficiency': Art Training at the School of the Art Institute of Chicago," in Sue Ann Prince, ed., *The Old*

Guard and the Avant-Garde: Modernism in Chicago, 1910–1940 (Chicago and London: University of Chicago Press, 1990), 193.

110   "Well, unroll them": Leon Goldin, interview with author, 6 January 2003.

110   "Her manner": Ellen Lanyon, interview with author, 27 July 2001.

110   "You deserved": Anonymous interview with author, 11 July 2004.

111   "Oh, poor": Sally Turton, telephone interview with author, 28 December 2001.

111   "Both parents": Joan Mitchell to Sarah Mitchell Perry, n.d. Collection of Sally Perry.

111   "skin and siph": Mitchell, interviewed by Linda Nochlin, 16 April 1986. Transcript, Archives of American Art/Smithsonian Institution.

111   "Man's dearest possession": V. I. Lenin, quoted by Joan Mitchell in a letter to Martha Bertolette, n.d. Collection of the Joan Mitchell Foundation.

112   Picasso had won: Gertje R. Utley, *Pablo Picasso: The Communist Years* (New Haven and London: Yale University Press, 2000), 3.

112   "terribly sick": Joan Mitchell quoted in Irving Sandler, "Conversation with Joan Mitchell at Zog's Studio, July 4, 1958," Irving Sandler Papers, Getty Research Center, Research Library Special Collections and Visual Resources, Los Angeles.

113   she had modeled: Judith Cass, "Ravinia Festival Style Show to Be Next Friday," *Chicago Daily Tribune*, 11 June 1943; Cass, "Most of 1943 Debut Parties Will Be Teas," 24 June 1943; and Cass, "53 Debutantes to Make Bows, Tho War Will Curtail Parties," 13 September 1943.

113   "powerful abstractions": "The Passing Shows," *ArtNews* 49:3 (15–31 March 1945): 25.

114   "unless he was": Richard Bowman, interview with author, 26 August 2001.

114   Marion promised: Consuelo Joerns, telephone interview with author, 4 December 2002.

116   "a lousy": Herbert Katzman, interview with author, 23 July 2001.

117   "Michelangelo had": Zuka Mitelberg, interview with author, 5 January 2002.

118   audaciously bisects: Her Parker classmate Ernst Jaffe remembered that, in the fourth grade, Joan was fascinated with the stereographic photographs (double images that imitate human binocular vision when viewed in a stereoscope) that someone brought to school.

119   "the lost and silver": Marion Strobel, "Joan," *Hygeia* 15:9 (September 1937): 804.

119   "bearing Catholic": Joan Mitchell in a letter to Barney Rosset, 21 March 1947. Collection of Barney Rosset.

120   "it was": Barney Rosset, interview with author, 18 January 2001.

120   "Talented painter": Louis Ritman, transcript of Joan Mitchell, School of the Art Institute of Chicago.

120   "This is": Cindy Nemser, *Art Talk: Conversations with 12 Women Artists* (New York: Charles Scribner's Sons, 1975), 85.

120   "Only the": Ibid., 238.

121   Over coffee: Peggy Bowman, interview with author, 13 October 2001.

121   "Idle hours": "Society Artists," *Chicago Sunday Times*, 14 March 1947.

121   "inscribes art": Ann Bermingham, "The Aesthetics of Ignorance: The Accomplished Woman in the Culture of Connoisseurship," *Oxford Art Journal* 16:2 (1993): 7. Bermingham is discussing eighteenth-century Britain.

121   "What's this?"; "just the Bohemian": Cholly Dearborn, "The Smart Set:

Cholly Dearborn Observes—Hint Joan Mitchell Wed Last Summer in Mexico," *Chicago Herald-American*, 28 May 1947. Joan's denial appears in Judith Cass, "North Avenue Nursery Party Set for June 13," *Chicago Tribune*, 29 May 1947. That Joan did not marry Manuel is confirmed by an official letter from C. Teresa de Jesús Granados Mares, Dirección del Registro Civil, Guanajuato, Mexico, 19 May 2005. She wore this ring, or one like it, more or less all her life. In the fall of 1992, it went with her to New York, where she was diagnosed with advanced lung cancer. By mid-October, when she arrived back in Paris, where she would die on October 30, it had vanished.

122   "*bruja*": Richard Bowman, interview with artist, 26 August 2001.

122   "If anyone": Sarah Mitchell Perry to Marion and James Herbert Mitchell, 5 April 1961. Collection of Sally Perry.

122   "like hell": Mitchell to Rosset, 21 March 1947.

122   She briefly had: Jean Lyons Keely, telephone interview with author, 6 July 2002.

123   "hell I miss you": Mitchell to Rosset, 27 January 1947. The excerpts that follow are from letters dated 29 January, 30 January, 4 February, 11 February, and 24 February 1947.

124   "My darling empathy": Mitchell to Rosset, 18 March 1947.

125   where she scandalized: Kim Bowman, telephone interview with author, 23 July 2003.

125   "taking Ropp": Ellen Lanyon, interview with author, 27 July 2001. Joan told critic Lucy Lippard that she won a second-place fellowship and that "a man who has not been heard of since won the first." See Lucy Lippard, *From the Center: Feminist Essays on Women's Art* (New York: E. P. Dutton, 1976), 182.

126   June brought: See "Youth Wins in the Windy City: The Art Institute's Local Annual," *ArtNews* 46:4 (June 1947): 20. *ArtNews* misidentifies the work, however.

127   "the great": Mitchell to Rosset, 4 June 1948.

127   "like the plague": Mitchell, interviewed by Nochlin, 16 April 1986.

127   What these paintings missed: Mitchell, quoted in Irving Sandler, "Conversation with Joan Mitchell on Sunday, Feb. 18, 1957, for *ArtNews* Article," Irving Sandler Papers, Getty Research Center, Research Library Special Collections and Visual Resources, Los Angeles.

128   "neurotic child": Joan Mitchell in a letter to Joanne Von Blon, 8 February 1949. Collection of Joanne Von Blon.

128   Jackson Pollock's drip paintings: Mitchell, interviewed by Nochlin, 16 April 1986.

128   Back in Chicago she had: "$7,000 Awarded Four Students: Art Institute Foreign Travel Fellowships," News Release from the Art Institute of Chicago, 26 May 1947, Archives of the Art Institute of Chicago.

128   "They were only": Mitchell, quoted in Judith E. Bernstock, *Joan Mitchell* (New York: Hudson Hills Press in association with Herbert F. Johnson Museum of Art, 1988), 17.

130   "squat like"; "charm all over": Mitchell to Von Blon, 8 February 1949.

130   "Christ how I'm missing": Mitchell to Rosset, 9 July 1948.

131   "this view": Mitchell, interviewed by Nochlin, 16 April 1986.

131 "fuck for canvas": Mitchell, quoted by Christopher Campbell, personal communication to author.

131 "Why don't I": Mitchell, quoted in Munro, 244.

131 "and she'd reply": Eldon Danhausen, interview with author, 24 November 2001.

131 "eat enough": Mitchell to Rosset, 16 July 1948.

131 "so much": Mitchell to Rosset, 14 October 1948, in Richard Milazzo, "Barney and Joan: Barney Rosset's Photographs of Joan Mitchell and Joan Mitchell's Letters to Barney Rosset," *Caravaggio on the Beach: Essays on Art in the 1990's* (Tangiers: Éditions d'Afrique du Nord, 2001), 123.

131 "strange how": Mitchell to Rosset, October 1948, in Milazzo, 120–21.

132 "married just so": Mitchell to Rosset, 16 July 1948.

132 "I wait": Mitchell to Rosset, 14 October 1948.

133 "Let's be": Barney Rosset, interview with author, 18 January 2001.

135 Later it was purchased: John Frederick Nims, "Augustine Bowe, Poet," *Chicago Tribune*, 21 May 1967.

135 "He cared": Cynthia Navaretta, interview with author, 25 July 2001.

135 "marriage deal": Mitchell to Rosset, 6 February 1947.

135 "in the deep sense": Marion Strobel Mitchell to Joan Mitchell, 19 July 1948. Marion's letter makes clear that the phrase is a quote from Joan's letter to her. So too is the phrase "maybe I'll close my eyes and do it quickly." Collection of the Joan Mitchell Foundation.

CHAPTER SIX: TENTH STREET

139 "It's so": Franz Kline, quoted in Fred W. McDarrah and Gloria S. McDarrah, *The Artist's World in Pictures: The New York School,* intro. Thomas B. Hess (New York: Shapolsky, 1988), 9.

140 "Well, we don't": John Ferren, "Epitaph for an Avant-Garde," *Arts Magazine* 33:2 (November 1958): 26.

140 "Timid practitioners": Thomas B. Hess, "Reviews and Previews: 'Life's' Young Artists," *ArtNews* 49:2 (April 1950): 42.

140 "What's going on": Milton Resnick, quoted in Mark Stevens and Annalyn Swan, *de Kooning: An American Master* (New York: Alfred A. Knopf, 2004), 292.

141 "The first half": Philip Pavia, quoted in ibid., 292.

141 An old incorruptible: Stevens and Swan, 232.

141 Grace Hartigan: Robert Saltonstall Mattison, *Grace Hartigan: A Painter's World* (New York: Hudson Hills Press, 1990), 18.

141 "You couldn't": Philip Pavia, interview with author, 26 July 2001.

141 "toughness and pressure": Thomas B. Hess, "Seeing the Young New Yorkers," *ArtNews* 49:3 (May 1950): 23.

142 "no manifestoes": Irving Sandler, "The Club," *Artforum* 4:1 (September 1965): 30.

143 "searching itself": Ferren, "Epitaph," *Arts Magazine* 33:2 (November 1958): 25.

143 "It is disastrous": Willem de Kooning, in Robert Goodnough, ed., "Artists' Sessions at Studio 35 (1950)," in Robert Motherwell and Ad Reinhardt, eds., *Modern Artists in America* (New York: Wittenborn, Schultz, 1951), 22.

144   "Gee, Joan": Deborah Solomon, "In Monet's Light," *New York Times Magazine*, 24 November 1991, 50.

144   "ivory tower": Joan Mitchell in a letter to Joanne Von Blon, postmarked 24 March 1950. Collection of Joanne Von Blon.

144   "horrible": Mitchell, quoted in Irving Sandler, "Conversation with Joan Mitchell on Sunday, Feb. 18, 1957, for *ArtNews* Article," Irving Sandler Papers, Getty Research Institute, Research Library Special Collections and Visual Resources, Los Angeles.

145   As she pushed: Eleanor Munro, *Originals: American Women Artists* (New York: Da Capo, 2000), 244. A document in the archives of the St. Paul [Minnesota] Gallery and School of Art establishes 1950 as the year of Mitchell's *Subway, The Bridge, Main Street, Mother and Child, The City, Backyards, Figure and the City,* and *Landscape.* Joan showed in St. Paul that year. Her mother had arranged for a May 1950 exhibition of ten paintings done in Brooklyn and Paris at the Bank Lane Galleries, a tiny Lake Forest venue recently opened by society painter Ruth Meeker Roberts. Still-powerful *Chicago Daily Tribune* critic Eleanor Jewett reviewed the show, calling it "stunning." A modified version then traveled to the St. Paul Gallery and School of Art. In a perceptive article, *St. Paul Dispatch* art critic John H. Harvey judged Joan's work immature and indecisive, yet admirable for its organization of complex form and evocation of feeling and almost sound. See John H. Harvey, "Joan Mitchell's Paintings Displayed at Art Gallery," *St. Paul Dispatch,* 27 October 1950. These shows meant little to Joan.

146   "taking things out": Willem de Kooning, quoted in Aline Louchheim, "Six Abstractionists Defend Their Art," *New York Times Magazine,* 21 January 1951, in Stevens and Swan, 250.

146   he loved: Pete Hamill, "Beyond the Vital Gesture: A Fifties Art Student Turned Journalist Remembers Franz Kline, the Man Behind the Theory," *Art & Antiques* (May 1990): 115.

146   "the most beautiful": Munro, 244.

147   "seedy, exciting": Ibid., 245.

148   "Which reminds me": Franz Kline quoted in Frank O'Hara, "Franz Kline Talking," *Evergreen Review* 2:6 (autumn 1958): 62.

148   "crudeness and accuracy": Irving Sandler, "Conversation with Joan Mitchell (6) on March 21, 1957," Irving Sandler Papers, Getty Research Institute, Research Library Special Collections and Visual Resources, Los Angeles.

148   "about other painters": Joan Mitchell, quoted in a transcript sent by Betsy Zogbaum to Joan Mitchell, 5 July 1972. Kline's companion in later years, Zogbaum was gathering tributes to the recently deceased painter from artists and other friends. Collection of the Joan Mitchell Foundation.

149   "the dream": Franz Kline, quoted in Irving Sandler, "Al Held (1928–2005): A Maverick in the New York Art World," *American Art* 20:1 (2006): 108.

149   "Why doesn't he": Mitchell quoted in Munro, 245.

149   "a glimpse": Willem de Kooning, quoted in David Sylvester, *Interviews with American Artists* (New Haven and London: Yale University Press, 2001), 50.

150   "Do you know": Robert Harms, interview with author, 18 July 2002.

150   "Flesh was": Willem de Kooning, "The Renaissance and Order," a talk delivered at Studio 35, in Stevens and Swan, 325.

150   "the flow of paint": Klaus Kertess, *Joan Mitchell* (New York: Harry N. Abrams, 1997), 23.

150   "this hell of a nice": Mitchell to Goldberg, n.d., Michael Goldberg Papers, Archives of American Art/Smithsonian Institution.

150   "leap of space": Pat Passlof, "1948," *Art Journal* 48:3 (fall 1989): 229.

150   "to get": Mitchell quoted in Sandler, "Conversation with Joan Mitchell (6) on March 21, 1957."

151   "You don't": Ibid.

151   "my father": Lynda Benglis, telephone interview with author, 7 November 2006.

153   Bill and Joan: Barney Rosset, interview with author, 18 January 2001.

153   "visually illiterate": Joan Mitchell quoted in S. E. Gontarski, "Dionysus in Publishing: Barney Rosset, Grove Press, and the Making of a Countercanon," *Review of Contemporary Fiction* 10:3 (fall 1970): 10.

153   "was not": Marilyn Stark, interview with author, 21 July 2004.

153   "I don't know": Cynthia Navaretta, interview with author, 25 July 2001. Goldberg denied that this happened.

154   "a marvelous": Howard Kanovitz, interview with author, 18 July 2002.

154   "a great and charming": Cynthia Navaretta, interview with author, 25 July 2001.

154   "quite crazy"; "Mike used to": Paul Brach, interview with author, 27 July 2004.

154   "Hey! Gimme a pig's foot": Joan uses the phrase "gimme a pig's foot" repeatedly in her letters to Mike.

155   "Painting could"; "vision of what life": Michael Goldberg, interview with author, 13 January 2003.

155   "Darling"; "I know a man": Mitchell to Goldberg, n.d., Michael Goldberg Papers.

155   "I was very": Michael Goldberg, interview with author, 20 June 2002.

155   "dizzy and silent": "Is today's Artist with or against the Past? Part 2, Answers by: David Smith, Frederick Kiesler, Franz Kline, Joan Mitchell," *ArtNews* 57:5 (September 1958): 41.

156   "a highly concentrated": Edward Hirsch, *How to Read a Poem and Fall in Love with Poetry* (New York, San Diego, and London: Center for Documentary Studies in association with Harcourt Brace, 1999), 4. The other characteristics of lyric poetry mentioned here are also set forth by Hirsch.

156   "I confess": Vladimir Nabokov, *Speak, Memory* (New York: G. P. Putnam's Sons, 1966), 139.

156   a lesson learned: Dore Ashton writes of this aspect of Gorky's and de Kooning's work in "A Straggler's View of Gorky," *Arshile Gorky: The Breakthrough Years*, org. Michael Auping (Fort Worth: Modern Art Museum of Fort Worth in association with Rizzoli, 1995), 57.

157   "our function": John Gruen, *The Party's Over Now* (New York: Viking Press, 1972), 41–42. According to Rosset, this never occurred. Yet Gruen and Wilson agree on details down to the green glass bowl from which Joan plucked the tangerine.

158   One day: Barney Rosset, interview with author, 10 January 2003; Michael Goldberg, interviews with author, 20 June 2002 and 13 January 2003; letters from Joan Mitchell to Michael Goldberg, Michael Goldberg Papers.

158   "I have": Mitchell to Goldberg, n.d., ibid.

159   "extremely nice"; "for once"; "someplace without": Mitchell to Goldberg, n.d., ibid.

160   "I've decided": Pat Passlof, interview with author, 18 June 2002.

160   "along fine": Mitchell to Rosset, n.d. Collection of Barney Rosset.

160   "Fucked up": Sandler, "Conversation with Joan Mitchell at Zog's Studio, July 4, 1958," Irving Sandler Papers, Getty Research Institute, Research Library Special Collections and Visual Resources, Los Angeles.

161   "When Barbara": Edrita Fried, *On Love and Sexuality: A Guide to Self-Fulfillment* (New York: Grove Press, 1960), 17.

162   "Mike is in": Paul Brach, interview with author, 19 June 2002.

162   "Michael"; "If I could"; "I'm kissing"; "Someday"; "Darling Michael": Mitchell to Goldberg, n.d., Michael Goldberg Papers.

162   Yet Joan had: Evans Herman, interview with author, 27 March 2004; Zuka Mitelberg, interview with author, 24 March 2003; Mitchell to Goldberg, n.d., Michael Goldberg Papers.

163   "the dark side": Paul Brach, interview with author, 27 July 2004.

163   "He seemed": Mitchell to Goldberg, n.d., Michael Goldberg Papers.

164   By one of several: Celia Stahr, "The Social Relations of Abstract Expressionism: An Alternative History" (PhD diss., University of Iowa, 1997), 140. In a 1994 interview, Resnick told Stahr this version of the exhibition's origins. On the other hand, writer Robert P. Metzger credits Kline and Conrad Marca-Relli with the idea, while gallerist Louis Newman states that Pavia chose the site, handled much of the organizing, and paid some of the bills. (The two write in the catalog of the 2006 exhibition 9th ST.: Nine Artists from the Ninth Street Show, at David Findlay Jr. Fine Art.)

164   So arresting: Max Kozloff, "An Interview with Friedel Dzubas," *Artforum* 4:1 (September 1965): 52.

165   "all said": Munro, 245.

165   "And you": Mitchell interviewed in Marion Cajori, director, *Joan Mitchell: Portrait of an Abstract Painter* (New York: Art Kaleidoscope Foundation and Christian Blackwood Productions, 1992). Film.

CHAPTER SEVEN: SAVAGE DEBUT

166   "Bound by": "Anne Ryan," Charlotte Streifer Rubinstein, *American Women Artists: From Indian Times to the Present* (Boston: G. K. Hall, 1982), 301. Rubinstein's source is Josephine Withers, "Anne Ryan," *Women Artists in Washington Collections* (College Park: University of Maryland and Women's Caucus for Art, 1979), 82.

166   Leaving a party: Joe LeSueur, *Digressions on Some Poems by Frank O'Hara* (New York: Farrar, Straus and Giroux, 2003), 104.

167   "looking like": Pete Hamill, "Vital Gesture," *Art & Antiques* 7 (May 1990): 110.

167   "too blatant": Cynthia Navaretta, interview with author, 25 July 2001.

167   MoMA's curator: Paul Brach, interview with author, 27 July 2004.

167   "most celebrated": "Women Artists in Ascendance," *Life*, 13 May 1957, 75.

167   *"pronunciamentos":* Mitchell to Goldberg, n.d., Michael Goldberg Papers, Archives of American Art/Smithsonian Institution.

167   "make-it-tough-even-ugly": Irving Sandler, *The New York School: The Painters and Sculptors of the Fifties* (New York: Harper and Row, 1978), 71.

167   "tasty French": Mitchell, quoted in Irving Sandler, "Conversation with Joan Mitchell on Sunday, Feb. 18, 1957, for *ArtNews* Article," Irving Sandler Papers, Getty Research Institute, Research Library Special Collections and Visual Resources, Los Angeles.

167   "in a corset": Alfred Leslie, interview with author, 22 June 2002. Hartigan and Frankenthaler shared this opinion.

169   "and all hell": Jon Schueler, *The Sound of Sleat: A Painter's Life* (New York: Picador, 1999), 248.

169   "did not go": Helen Frankenthaler, interview by Barbara Rose, 1969. Helen Frankenthaler Papers, Archives of American Art/Smithsonian Institution.

169   "that Kotex painter": Christopher Campbell, telephone interview with author, 10 February 2007. Joan used this phrase or, as a variant, "that tampon painter," repeatedly. For the latter, see Mark Stevens and Annalyn Swan, *de Kooning: An American Master* (New York: Alfred A. Knopf, 2004), 245.

169   "so what"; "doesn't like": Mitchell to Goldberg, n.d. [spring 1951], Michael Goldberg Papers. German expressionist painter Max Beckmann had died in New York on 27 December 1950. His late work was shown that April at the Buchholz Gallery.

170   "why did"; "millions of": Mitchell to Goldberg, n.d., Michael Goldberg Papers. The term paper resurfaced two years later when Barney took an art history class at Columbia from Meyer Schapiro. Schapiro gave it an A, and was surprised when Barney scored only a D on the final.

170   "tried to take": Mitchell, quoted in "Is Today's Artist with or against the Past? Part 2, Answers by: David Smith, Frederick Kiesler, Franz Kline, Joan Mitchell," *ArtNews* 57:5 (September 1958): 41.

171   "Renaissance look"; "with the help": Mitchell to Goldberg, n.d., Michael Goldberg Papers.

171   "terrified": Mitchell, interviewed by Linda Nochlin, 16 April 1986. Transcript, Archives of American Art/Smithsonian Institution.

171   prevailing attitudes: April Kingsley, *The Turning Point* (New York: Simon & Schuster, 1992), 255.

172   Clem Greenberg had advised: Jane Freilicher, telephone interview with author, 8 January 2003.

172   when veteran painters: *ArtNews* 48:10 (February 1950): 49 and 47 respectively.

172   "because of": Eric Brown, conversation with author, 25 June 2002. Brown got this phrase from Tibor de Nagy, who got it from Joan.

172   "this fat queer": Michael Goldberg, interview with author, 20 June 2002. A review by Lawrence Campbell of Goldberg's show at Tibor de Nagy appeared in the October 1953 issue of *ArtNews*. However, according to Leslie, reviews were based on studio visits preceding the actual shows.

173   "dirty"; "hollow": Mitchell to Goldberg, n.d., Michael Goldberg Papers.

173   "Greta Garbo style": Michael Goldberg, interview with author, 20 June 2002.

173   "stylish, girlish": Roland Pease, personal communication to author, 14 September 2002.

173   "When I go": Grace Hartigan, quoted in John Bernard Myers, *Tracking the Marvelous: A Life in the New York Art World* (New York: Random House, 1983), 127.

173 "was rated": Miriam Schapiro, quoted in Thalia Gouma-Peterson, *Miriam Schapiro: Shaping the Fragments of Art and Life* (New York: Harry N. Abrams in association with Polk Museum of Art, 1999), 25.

174 "community of feeling": Mitchell to Goldberg, n.d., Michael Goldberg Papers.

174 "a strange combination": Cynthia Navaretta, interview with author, 25 July 2001.

174 "like an energy"; "a chop": Jane Wilson, interview with author, 17 July 2002.

174 "something really": John Gruen, interview with author, 17 July 2002.

174 "Ah, no": Alfred Leslie, interview with author, 22 July 2002.

174 "Joan was": Marilyn Stark, interview with author, 21 July 2004.

175 "how to live": Howard Kanovitz, interview with author, 18 July 2002.

175 "very anti-woman"; "a tendency to": Pat Passlof, interview with author, 18 June 2002.

175 "I'm ten": Ross Wetzsteon, *Republic of Dreams: Greenwich Village: The American Bohemia, 1910–1960* (New York: Simon & Schuster, 2002), 551.

175 "gladiatorial": Jane Wilson, interview with author, 17 July 2002.

175 "Go fuck": Walter Kamys, telephone conversation with author, 2 January 2006. I am grateful to Sonja Marck for first telling me this story.

176 Not only: Rose Slivka, interview with author, 19 July 2002.

176 she was drinking: Irving Sandler, telephone interview with author, 23 May 2006.

176 "a lovely girl": Nic Carone, interview with author, 13 January 2003.

176 "very serious girl": Philip Pavia, interview with author, 26 July 2001.

176 "get away with": John Gruen, interview with author, 17 July 2002.

176 Yeah, Joan bragged: Joan Mitchell, interview by Mark Stevens and Annalyn Swan, spring 1991, cited in Klaus Kertess, *Joan Mitchell* (New York: Harry N. Abrams, 1997), 21.

176 "on a decade-long": Elaine de Kooning, quoted in David Lehman, *The Last Avant-Garde: The Making of the New York School of Poets* (New York: Doubleday, 1998), 65.

177 "wonderful person": Edi Franceschini, interview with author, 26 July 2002.

177 "The men": Miriam Schapiro, "Notes from a Conversation on Art, Feminism, and Work," in Sara Ruddick and Pamela Daniels, eds., *Working It Out: 23 Women Writers, Artists, Scientists, and Scholars Talk About Their Lives and Work* (New York: Pantheon Books, 1977), 287.

177 "I have a message"; "phony friends": Evans Herman, interview with author, 27 March 2004.

178 "They loved": John Gruen, interview with author, 17 July 2002.

179 "She never": Evans Herman, interview with author, 27 March 2004.

179 "a pocket": Evans Herman in a letter to Joan Mitchell, 15 July 1968. Collection of Frances Herman.

179 "only ... the moonlight": Mitchell to Goldberg, n.d., Michael Goldberg Papers.

180 "had a big impact": Grace Hartigan, quoted in Jane Livingston, *The Paintings of Joan Mitchell* (New York, Berkeley, Los Angeles, and London: Whitney Museum of American Art in association with University of California Press, 2002), 21.

180 "And I think": Michael Goldberg, interview with author, 13 January 2003.

180 "My heart": Mitchell to Goldberg, n.d. [1957], Michael Goldberg Papers.

180   had "the great": Mitchell to Goldberg, 15 September 1965, ibid.

181   "very French": Jane Freilicher, telephone interview with author, 8 January 2003.

181   "B. Holiday": Mitchell to Goldberg, postmarked 10 June 1954, Michael Goldberg Papers.

181   "wasn't really": Howard Kanovitz, interview with author, 18 July 2002.

181   Two flights: Eugene V. Thaw, telephone interview with author, 10 October 2005. On the mezzanine was Thaw's New Book Shop, which was supposed to turn a profit and support the gallery but never did. Jackson Pollock's visit was the only time Thaw ever set eyes upon the painter. However, Thaw later developed a close friendship with Pollock's widow, artist Lee Krasner, and became the first president of the Pollock-Krasner Foundation.

182   "a fantastic display": Grace Hartigan, *The Journals of Grace Hartigan, 1951–1955*, ed. William T. La Moy and Joseph P. McCaffrey (Syracuse, NY: Syracuse University Press, 2009), 22.

182   "remarkable artist": John Gruen, interview with author, 17 July 2002.

182   "full of talent": Miriam Schapiro, quoted in Gouma-Peterson, 35.

182   "proclaimed ruefully": Thomas B. Hess, "Sensations of Landscape," *New York*, 20 December 1976, 76.

182   "Oh!": Nicolas Calas, untitled essay in *Joan Mitchell* (New York: The New Gallery, 1952).

183   "endlessly interrupted": Ibid.

183   "savage debut": Betty Holliday, "Reviews and Previews: Joan Mitchell," *Art-News* 50:9 (January 1952): 46; Stuart Preston, "Chiefly Abstract," *New York Times,* 20 January 1952.

183   "tense tendons": Paul Brach, "Fifty-seventh Street in Review: Joan Mitchell," *Art Digest,* 15 January 1952, 17–18.

183   Shortly after: Eugene V. Thaw, telephone interview with author, 10 October 2005; letter from William Rubin to Joan Mitchell, postmarked 12 May 1952. Collection of the Joan Mitchell Foundation.

183   "She already knew": Eugene V. Thaw, telephone interview with author, 10 October 2005.

183   "absolutely marvelous": Mitchell to Von Blon, 1–8 December 1952.

184   "airy and perfumed": Marcel Proust, *Swann's Way, In Search of Lost Time,* trans. C. K. Scott-Moncrieff and Terence Kilmartin, rev. by D. J. Enright (New York: Modern Library, 1992), 299.

184   "why it was": Marcel Proust, *Time Regained, In Search of Lost Time,* trans. C. K. Scott-Moncrieff and Terence Kilmartin, rev. by D. J. Enright (New York: Modern Library, 1992), 262.

184   "not motion": Mitchell, interviewed by Yves Michaud, "Conversation with Joan Mitchell," in Xavier Fourcade Gallery, *Joan Mitchell: New Paintings* (New York: Xavier Fourcade Gallery, 1986), unpaginated.

185   "You sat": Rainer Maria Rilke, *The Notebooks of Malte Laurids Brigge,* trans. Stephen Mitchell (New York: Random House, 1982), 26.

186   Rilke wrote: Ibid., 60, 61, 55, 32, and 88, respectively.

186   "neurotics club"; "the most collective": Mitchell to Von Blon, 1–8 December 1952.

186   "Well, I'm sorry": Evans Herman, interview with author, 27 March 2004.

186   "first girl artist": Andy Warhol and Pat Hackett, *POPism: The Warhol Sixties* (New York: Harcourt Brace Jovanovich, 1980), 35.

186   "I imagine": Mitchell to Goldberg, Michael Goldberg Papers.

187   a second chance: My discussion of Joan's analysis derives primarily from my 9 January 2003 interview of Dr. Jaqueline Fried and from Dr. Edrita Fried's book, *On Love and Sexuality* (New York: Grove Press, 1960), which includes Fried's case study of Joan ("Barbara"). I also used *The Drama of the Gifted Child* (first published as *Prisoners of Childhood*), Alice Miller's study of the potentially devastating impact of narcissistic parents upon the lives of talented children. Joan read and loved this book, a gift from her niece Sally Perry.

In the 1950s, Joan's analysis continued to center on the early childhood damage to her ego that impeded normal ego regression. Psychologically healthy people, Fried explained, take pleasure in the self-forgetting that goes hand-in-hand with falling in love, having sex, drinking, listening to music, and so on. But the normally pleasant sensation of the floating away of selfhood easily triggered panic in Joan: spinning out of control, she would lash out at others in order to rebuild a psychological bulwark and thus recover a sense of self. What people saw as indiscriminate antagonism was really the psychological equivalent of the self-protective gesture one makes in the split-second mental registration of an imminent fall. In striking back or distancing themselves, however, people left Joan devastated by feelings of abandonment and tortured by yearning for real intimacy and dependable love.

Notwithstanding her efforts to control Joan's "hostility addiction," Fried stopped short. Respectful of her patient's integrity and artistic achievement, the analyst made allowances and thus failed to tone down behavior that went beyond the impolite and the difficult to the offensive and hurtful. Moreover—a blind spot in the liquor-loving fifties—Fried never addressed the heavy drinking that set off Joan's alarm bells, compromised her judgment, and kept her in cycles of depression.

187   "believing in yourself": Mitchell, quoted in Irving Sandler, "Conversation with Joan Mitchell on Sunday, Feb. 18, 1957, for *ArtNews* article," Irving Sandler Papers, Getty Research Institute, Research Library Special Collections and Visual Resources, Los Angeles.

187   "Just while I": Mitchell to Rosset, n.d., quoted in Robert Miller Gallery, *Joan Mitchell: Paintings 1950 to 1955,* unpaginated.

188   "There was nothing": Barney Rosset, interviewed by Win McCormack, "The Literary Fly Catcher," *Tin House* 2:4 (summer 2001): 7.

CHAPTER EIGHT: THE HURRICANE

189   "White dawns": Stéphane Mallarmé, "Renewal," in Keith Bosley, *Mallarmé: The Poems* (Harmondsworth, England: Penguin, 1977), 77.

190   "a good, kind"; "without any": Divorce Files of the Superior Court, Cook County, no. 52-S 5260, filed 4 April 1952.

190   "he was actively": Patricia Faure, interviewed by Susan Ehrlich, 17, 22, and 24 November 2004. Transcript, Archives of American Art/Smithsonian Institution.

191   "Very bouncy": Mitchell to Von Blon, 1–8 December 1952.

191   "melting staircase": Robert Gottlieb, telephone interview with author, 27 August 2005.

191   "choice young men": Mitchell to Von Blon, 1–8 December 1952.

191   "the real New York": Joan Mitchell, quoted by David Amram, "East Village: An Island Within an Island, August 27, 2004," www.ekayani.com.

192   "one of the most": Linda Nochlin, "Joan Mitchell: A Rage to Paint," in Jane Livingston, *The Paintings of Joan Mitchell* (New York, Berkeley, Los Angeles, and London: Whitney Museum of American Art in association with University of California Press, 2002), 52.

192   historians of neuroscience: See, for example, Amy Ione and Christopher Tyler, "Was Kandinsky a Synesthete?" *Journal of the History of the Neurosciences* 12:2 (2003): 223–26. Organized by Boston's Institute of Contemporary Art, the Kandinsky exhibition was on view at Knoedler from May 12 to 28, 1952.

192   "The violins": Kenneth C. Lindsay and Peter Vergo, ed. and trans., *Kandinsky: Complete Writings on Art*, vol. 1 (Boston: G. K. Hall, 1982), 364.

193   So enamored: Mitchell to Von Blon, 1–8 December 1952.

193   "was in": Written statement by anonymous neighbor, 2005.

193   "an extension": Harold Rosenberg, "The Art World: Artist Against Background," *New Yorker*, 29 April 1974, 72.

193   "music heard so deeply": T. S. Eliot, "The Dry Salvages" ("Four Quartets"), in T. S. Eliot, *The Complete Poems and Plays, 1909–1950* (New York: Harcourt, Brace, Jovanovich, 1971), 136.

193   "I use it": Joan Mitchell, quoted by Gisèle Barreau, interview with author, 29 March 2003.

194   "very tough": Anonymous, telephone interview with author, 4 September 2005.

194   "a great guy": Robert Gottlieb, telephone interview with author, 27 August 2005.

194   "Why don't you": Howard Kanovitz, interview with author, 18 July 2002. Probably Joan learned such skills at Francis Parker, where girls were required to take shop.

194   "could raise walls": Miriam Schapiro in Thalia Gouma-Peterson, *Miriam Schapiro: Shaping the Fragments of Art and Life* (New York: Harry N. Abrams in association with Polk Museum of Art, 1999), 214.

194   "Shit": Mitchell to Michael Goldberg, postmarked 10 June 1954, Michael Goldberg Papers.

194   "family affair": John Ferren, "Stable State of Mind," *ArtNews* 54:3 (May 1955): 23.

195   "bitchy in the grand manner": Jon Schueler, *The Sound of Sleat: A Painter's Life* (New York: Picador, 1999), 96.

195   "six people": Elaine de Kooning in a letter to Bill Brown, n.d. [1955]. My thanks to Celia Stahr for making this letter available to me.

196   "The rain": Mitchell to Goldberg, 10 August 1954, Michael Goldberg Papers.

196   "strikingly vital": Frank O'Hara, "Reviews and Previews: Ernest Briggs, Dugmore, Joan Mitchell," *ArtNews* 54:5 (September 1955): 52. Many have noticed similarities between Joan Mitchell's paintings of this period and those of Philip Guston, but all evidence points to a matter of synchronicity rather than any direct influence.

196   "warmth and ideas": Joan Mitchell in a letter to May and Patia Rosenberg, 18 July 1978. Collection of the Joan Mitchell Foundation.

197   After a rocky start: Paul Jenkins, interview with author, 11 January 2003.

197   "to appear": Harold Rosenberg, "The American Action Painters," *ArtNews* 52:5 (December 1952): 22, 49.

199   "Oh! You're not": Paul Brach, interview with author, 19 June 2002.

199   "to look upon": Edrita Fried, *On Love and Sexuality: A Guide to Self-Fulfillment* (New York: Grove Press, 1960), 40.

200   "even enjoy": Frank O'Hara, "Meditations in an Emergency," in Donald Allen, ed., *The Collected Poems of Frank O'Hara* (New York: Knopf, 1971), 197.

200   Scholar Marjorie Perloff: Marjorie Perloff, *Frank O'Hara: Poet Among Painters* (New York: George Braziller, 1977), 124–39. Perloff quotes art historian Ernst Gombrich's *Art and Illusion: A Study in the Psychology of Pictorial Representation.*

200   "boisterous"; "unexpectedly generous winning": Jane Freilicher, telephone interview with author, 8 January 2003.

200   "I'm serving": Joe LeSueur, *Digressions on Some Poems by Frank O'Hara* (New York: Farrar, Straus and Giroux, 2003), 123.

201   "going on": David Lehman, *The Last Avant-Garde: The Making of the New York School of Poets* (New York: Doubleday, 1998), 111.

201   "a festive quality": John Ashbery, interview with author, 16 May 2006.

201   "embracing a rose bush": John Ashbery, quoted by Jane Freilicher, telephone interview with author, 8 January 2003.

201   "flying circus": May Rosenberg, quoted in Gruen, 175.

201   "by the floods": James Schuyler. My account of the relationship between New York School poetry and painting is indebted to David Lehman's *The Last Avant-Garde* and "Poetry and the Abstract Revolution," in David Acton, *The Stamp of Impulse: Abstract Expressionist Prints* (New York: Hudson Hills Press in association with the Worcester Art Museum, 2001), 27–38.

201   "world about us": Wallace Stevens, *The Necessary Angel: Essays on Reality and the Imagination* (New York: Vintage Books, 1951), 169.

201   "Kisses and falling-downs": Frank O'Hara in a letter to Joan Mitchell, 4 May 1956. Collection of the Joan Mitchell Foundation.

202   "were sitting": John Gruen, *The Party's Over Now* (New York: Viking Press, 1972), 219.

202   "Micha, why aren't": Hofmann, quoted by Mitchell, interviewed in Marion Cajori, director, *Joan Mitchell: Portrait of an Abstract Painter* (New York: Art Kaleidoscope Foundation and Christian Blackwood Productions, 1992). Film.

202   Mike's neighbor: Alvin Novak, telephone conversation with author, 28 June 2004.

202   "really black and blue": Stark, interview with author, 21 July 2004.

202   "as a louche": John Bernard Myers, *The Poets of the New York School* (Graduate School of Fine Arts, University of Pennsylvania, 1969), 14, in Lehman, 22.

202   "violent affair": Alison Lurie, *V. R. Lang: Poems & Plays with a Memoir by Alison Lurie* (New York: Random House, 1975), 8.

203   "You are": V. R. Lang in a letter to Michael Goldberg, "Wednesday 8:30," Michael Goldberg Papers.

203   "ask her old man": Michael Goldberg, interview with author, 20 June 2002.

204   "at a great distance"; "I would like": Mitchell to Goldberg, postmarked 10 June 1954, Michael Goldberg Papers.

204   after a party: Schueler, 248.

204   "Oh, boy!": Hélène de Billy, *Riopelle* (Montreal: Art Global, 1996), 161.

205   "charming and unshaven"; "At least": Mitchell to Goldberg, postmarked 10 June 1954, Michael Goldberg Papers.

206   "Now you're": Eleanor Ward, interviewed by Paul Cummings, 8 February 1972. Transcript, Archives of American Art/Smithsonian Institution.

206   "Why don't": Joan Mitchell, quoted by Paul Brach, interview with author, 19 June 2002.

206   Pavia swung: Thomas B. Hess, quoted in Fred W. McDarrah and Gloria S. McDarrah, *The Artist's World in Pictures: The New York School,* intro. Thomas B. Hess (New York: Shapolsky, 1988), 12.

207   "a bourgeois": Paul Brach, interview with author, 19 June 2002.

207   "What's so sacred": Joan Mitchell, quoted by Carol Braider, telephone interview with author, 30 December 2005.

207   "Seuratish"; "My hand doesn't": Mitchell to Goldberg, 19 August 1954, Michael Goldberg Papers.

208   "one blue": Mitchell to Goldberg, postmarked 10 June 1954, ibid.

208   "I distrust": Mitchell to Goldberg, 13 August 1954, ibid.

208   "a complete synthesis": Irving Sandler, "Conversation with Joan Mitchell (4)," Irving Sandler Papers, Getty Research Institute, Research Library Special Collections and Visual Resources, Los Angeles.

208   By accuracy: Irving Sandler, "Conversation with Joan Mitchell on Wed., Feb. 20, 1957, for *ArtNews* article," Irving Sandler Papers, Getty Research Institute, Research Library Special Collections and Visual Resources, Los Angeles. By 1974, Mitchell had conflated the terms "accuracy" and "intensity." Curator Marcia Tucker writes, "What she seeks is 'accuracy,' by which she means the successful transposition onto the canvas of a feeling about a remembered landscape—or a remembered feeling about a landscape." See Marcia Tucker, "Joan Mitchell" (New York: Whitney Museum of Art, 1974), 8.

208   "that Van Gogh intensity": Mitchell to Goldberg, n.d., Michael Goldberg Papers.

208   "maybe mystically": Mitchell to Goldberg, n.d., ibid.

208   "an absolute": Mitchell to Goldberg, 13 August 1954, ibid.

208   "fucking, emotional": Mitchell to Goldberg, 23 August 1954, ibid.

208   "on the edge": Mitchell to Goldberg, 10 June 1954, ibid.

209   "It was sad": Mitchell to Goldberg, 10 August 1954, ibid.

209   "All through": Lurie, 52–53.

209   "You stopped": Lang to Goldberg, 13 July 1954, Michael Goldberg Papers.

209   "knifing and competition": Mitchell to Goldberg, n.d., ibid.

209   *pronunciamentos*: Mitchell to Goldberg, 10 August 1954, ibid.

210   "Gatsby-like": Gerald Jonas, "The Story of Grove," *New York Times Magazine,* 21 January 1968, 59.

210   "pressure of the summer"; "I feel": Mitchell to Goldberg, 31 July 1954, Michael Goldberg Papers.

210   "pleasant but nightmarish": Elaine de Kooning, quoted in Joseph Liss, "Memories of Bonac Painters," *East Hampton Star,* 18 August 1983.

210   "crappy clothesline": Mitchell to Goldberg, n.d., Michael Goldberg Papers.

210   "the rat race": Mitchell to Goldberg, 13 August 1954, ibid.

210   "How very weak": Mitchell to Goldberg, 10 August 1954, ibid.

211   her adored George: Carol Braider, telephone interview with author, 30 December 2005. Joan claimed she had cured George of distemper, an incurable canine disease.

211   "put all": Mitchell in a letter to Goldberg, 10 August 1954, Michael Goldberg Papers.

211   "Sweetie pie": Mitchell in a letter to Goldberg, 13 August 1954, ibid.

212   "another kind of blue": Mitchell in a letter to Goldberg, 23 August 1954, ibid.

212   "bastard affair": Mitchell to Herman, postmarked 30 August 1954.

212   "We have no": Mitchell to Goldberg, 20 August 1954, Michael Goldberg Papers.

212   "was very beautiful": Michael Goldberg, quoted in Mark Stevens and Annalyn Swan, *de Kooning: An American Master* (New York: Alfred A. Knopf, 2004), 374.

212   "old at last"; "sad about us": Mitchell to Goldberg, 23 August 1954, Michael Goldberg Papers.

212   "I painted": Mitchell to Herman, postmarked 30 August 1954.

213   "levitate about six feet": Paul Brach, interview with author, 27 July 2004.

213   "she [had] had to risk": Written statement by Anonymous, 2005.

213   "It was": Irving Sandler, "Conversation with Joan Mitchell (5), March 14, 1957," Irving Sandler Papers, Getty Research Institute, Research Library Special Collections and Visual Resources, Los Angeles.

213   as Mallarmé: Stéphane Mallarmé, *Correspondance 1862–1871* (Paris: Gallimard, 1959), 103.

CHAPTER NINE: HUDSON RIVER DAY LINE

214   "And in the same": Vladimir Nabokov, "Torpid Smoke," in *A Russian Beauty and Other Stories* (New York: McGraw-Hill, 1973), 28.

214   "I am": V. R. Lang, *I Too Have Lived in Arcadia*, in V. R. Lang, *Poems & Plays with a Memoir by Alison Lurie* (New York: Random House, 1975), 289. Excerpts of *I Too Have Lived in Arcadia* appeared in the April 1955 issue of *Poetry;* that October, *Poetry* awarded it the Vachel Lindsay Prize. Peter Sellars revived Lang's play in 1980 in his New York directorial debut at La Mama. V. R. Lang died of Hodgkin's lymphoma on 29 July 1956.

214   "*Quelle femme*": Lang, 278.

215   "so collapsed"; "Oh Mike": Mitchell to Goldberg, 10 December 1954, Michael Goldberg Papers.

215   "Pose for me": Mitchell to Goldberg, 27 December 1954, ibid.

215   "cross-eyed": Mitchell to Goldberg, 28 December 1954, ibid.

216   "I can see": Mitchell to Goldberg, 27 December 1954, ibid.

216   "the city": Mitchell to Goldberg, 23 August 1954, ibid.

216   "huge sprawling": Al Newbill, *Arts Digest* 29:11 (1 March 1955), 28.

216   "changed much": Mitchell, quoted in Stephen Westfall, "Then and Now: Six of the New York School Look Back," *Art in America* 73:6 (June 1985): 114.

216   "I 'frame'": Mitchell, interviewed by Yves Michaud, "Conversation with Joan Mitchell," in Xavier Fourcade Gallery, *Joan Mitchell: New Paintings* (New York: Xavier Fourcade Gallery, 1986), unpaginated.

217   "secret magic": Patricia Lynne Duffy, conversation with author, 16 June 2005.

217   "I've never": Mitchell, quoted by Jaqueline Fried, interviews with author, 9 January 2003 and 11 January 2006.

217   "waking dream": Marcia Smilack, communication to Sean Day's Synesthesia List, 22 January 2006.

218   "album of photographs": Mitchell, interviewed by Michaud, *Joan Mitchell.*

218   she started prodding: Elaine de Kooning in a letter to Bill Brown, n.d. [1955]. My thanks to Celia Stahr for a copy of this letter.

218   "you do know": Mitchell to Goldberg, 15 September 1965, Michael Goldberg Papers.

219   *"grand dernier"*; "where the barges squat"; "hideous numbness": Mitchell to Goldberg, n.d., ibid.

220   "silent hostility": Ibid.

220   "horizontal propositions": Hélène de Billy, *Riopelle* (Montreal: Art Global, 1996), 117.

220   But she found him: Connie Lembark, telephone interview with author, 18 March 2008. After Joan made the acquaintance, in the 1960s, of art consultant Connie Lembark, who was close to Francis, the two women never got together without Joan launching into a monologue about his deficiencies as a lover.

220   "watered-down Pollock": Mitchell to Goldberg, n.d., Michael Goldberg Papers.

220   "de Kooning's emissary": Mitchell to Barney and Loly Rosset, n.d. Collection of Barney Rosset.

221   "a small town": Mitchell to Goldberg, n.d., Michael Goldberg Papers.

221   "Not much art": Joan Mitchell in a postcard to Harold Rosenberg, 24 April 1959. Harold Rosenberg Papers, Getty Research Institute, Research Library Special Collections and Visual Resources, Los Angeles.

222   "puking in that"; "like a garbage pail": Mitchell to Goldberg, n.d., Michael Goldberg Papers.

222   "fuck you kind": Ibid.

222   "one small child": Joan Mitchell, quoted in letter from Marion Strobel Mitchell to Joan Mitchell, 9 June 1954. Collection of the Joan Mitchell Foundation.

222   "white walls"; "How did I": Mitchell to Goldberg, n.d., Michael Goldberg Papers.

222   "I wonder"; "people who": Ibid.

222   "dished [so much]"; "I want": Ibid.

222   a great deal: Ibid.

223   "Well—fuck": Joan Mitchell in a note to Gisèle Barreau, n.d. Collection of the Joan Mitchell Foundation.

223   "been living"; "What are": David Amram, interview with author, 9 January 2008.

223   "the machinations": David Amram, personal communication to author, 8 December 2007.

224   "great romantic"; "soul connection": David Amram, interview with author, 9 January 2008.

224   "People will": Joan Mitchell, quoted in David Amram, "Seeing the Music, Hearing the Pictures," in David Acton, *The Stamp of Impulse: Abstract Expressionist Prints* (New York: Hudson Hills Press in association with the Worcester Art Museum, 2001), 21.

225   "quit midstream": Mitchell to Goldberg, n.d., Michael Goldberg Papers.

225   "I don't want": Ibid.

225   "[buying] out": Ibid.

225   "paint . . . with": Ibid.

225   "fraught, drunken": Ibid.

226   "The great Riopelle"; "The party": Ibid.

226   "Tonight I will": Jean-Paul Riopelle, quoted by Irving Sandler, telephone interview with author, 23 May 2006. Sandler heard the story from Joan.

226   "I impressed": Mitchell, quoted in Hélène de Billy, *Riopelle* (Montreal: Art Global, 1996), 117.

227   "I go": Jean-Paul Riopelle, quoted by John Bennett, interview with author, 28 June 2002.

227   "seems hardly": Georges Duthuit, "A Painter of Awakening: Jean-Paul Riopelle," trans. Samuel Beckett (New York: Pierre Matisse Gallery, 1954), 1.

227   "the art of": André Breton in Monique Brunet-Weinmann, "Birth of a Signature," in Yseult Riopelle, *Jean-Paul Riopelle: Catalogue raisonné, 1939–1953* (Montreal: Hibou, 1999), 131.

228   he bragged: Elga Heinzen, interview with author, 9 January 2002.

229   "Decisions": Marion Strobel Mitchell to Joan Mitchell, 25 September 1955. Collection of the Joan Mitchell Foundation.

230   "If I stayed": Mitchell to Barney and Loly Rosset, 23 September 1955. Collection of Barney Rosset.

230   "Michael"; "I wanted": Mitchell to Goldberg, n.d., Michael Goldberg Papers.

230   "My memories"; "mess with a sky": Ibid.

231   "little spidery man": David Amram, interview with author, 9 January 2008.

231   "We never"; "Oh, my God!": Joan Mitchell, quoted by Stanley Karnow, telephone interview with author, 6 June 2006.

232   "a charming patent leather": Mitchell to Goldberg, n.d., Michael Goldberg Papers.

233   "Yes—I'm changed": Mitchell to Rosset, 19 September 1955, quoted in Robert Miller Gallery, *Joan Mitchell: Paintings 1950–1955*, unpaginated.

233   "And look, baby doll"; "knifing and competition": Mitchell to Goldberg, n.d., Michael Goldberg Papers.

233   "I think of": Mitchell to Rosset, 19 September 1955.

233   "I will write": Jean-Paul Riopelle in a letter to Joan Mitchell, 29 November 1955. Collection of the Joan Mitchell Foundation.

234   "tell everybody": Mitchell, interviewed by Cora Cohen and Betsy Sussler, *Bomb* 17 (fall 1986): 22.

234   But sales picked up: Laura de Coppet and Alan Jones, *The Art Dealers: The Powers Behind the Scene Tell How the Art World Really Works* (New York: Clarkson Potter, 1984), 39.

234   There were now: Clarence Dean, "Peak Demand for Pictures," *New York Times,* 25 February 1957.

234   As both leader: Mark Stevens and Annalyn Swan, *de Kooning: An American Master* (New York: Alfred A. Knopf, 2004), 387–88.

234   "till they rolled": Philip Pavia in Natalie Edgar, ed., *Club Without Walls: Selections from the Journals of Philip Pavia* (New York: Midmarch Arts Press, 2007), 64.

235   "the transient": Charles Bernstein, "Composing Herself," *Bookforum* (April/ May 2006): 50.

235   "things as they are": David Lehman, *The Last Avant-Garde: The Making of the New York School of Poets* (New York: Doubleday, 1998), 243.

236   "open, lively": Patricia Bailey, "Joan Mitchell in 1950's Remembered Landscapes," *Art/World* 4:7 (19 March–18 April 1980): 4.

236   "bright white": Mitchell to Goldberg, n.d., Michael Goldberg Papers.

236   "crazy about Joan": David Amram, interview with author, 9 January 2008.

236   "all [the old] shit": Mitchell to Goldberg, n.d., Michael Goldberg Papers.

236   Meanwhile, Joan had: Teru Osato Lundsten, telephone interview with author, 27 November 2005.

236   "had a liver": Alfred Leslie, interview with author, 22 July 2002.

236   When Bill was drunk: Stevens and Swan, 505.

237   "I hate it!": Joan Mitchell, quoted by Michael Goldberg, interview with author, 20 June 2002.

237   "a damn good": Michael Goldberg, interview with author, 20 June 2002.

237   "Homely and hasty"; "only loss": Hal Fondren, "Sunday Afternoons with Joan," in Robert Miller Gallery, *Joan Mitchell: Paintings 1950–1955*, unpaginated.

238   "impossible to criticize": EM [Eleanor C. Munro], *ArtNews* 55:4 (June-July-August 1956): 50.

CHAPTER TEN: TO THE HARBORMASTER

239   "To the Harbormaster": Frank O'Hara, *Meditations in an Emergency* (New York: Grove Press, 1957), 1.

239   Spreading a drop cloth: Howard Kanovitz, interview with author, 18 July 2002. Kanovitz saw Mitchell in Paris during this time.

240   Jean-Paul tackled: Robert Bernier, *Jean-Paul Riopelle: Des Visions d'Amérique* (Montreal: Les Éditions de l'Homme, 1997), 94–95.

241   "Such joy": Willem de Kooning, quoted in Mark Stevens and Annalyn Swan, *de Kooning: An American Master* (New York: Alfred A. Knopf, 2004), 244.

241   "the greatness of Jackson Pollock": Joan Mitchell, quoted in "Jackson Pollock: An Artists' Symposium, Part 2," *ArtNews* 66:3 (May 1967): 29.

241   "hazard and decision": Leo Steinberg, "Month in Review," *Arts* 30:4 (January 1956): 46.

241   For a time: According to painter Paul Jenkins, Joan tried this method, invented by Willem de Kooning, at the time she was living and working at Jenkins's studio in Paris.

242   "I don't make": Mitchell, quoted in Irving Sandler, "Conversation with Joan Mitchell on Sunday, Feb. 18, 1957, for *ArtNews* article," Irving Sandler Papers, Getty Research Institute, Research Library Special Collections and Visual Resources, Los Angeles.

242   "little snow cave": Robert Chiarito, interview with author, 21 November 2002.

242   "You make it": Sandler.

242   "dark and blue feeling": "The Vocal Girls," *Time*, 2 May 1960, 74.

242   "Domination of Black": Wallace Stevens, *The Collected Poems of Wallace Stevens* (New York: Knopf, 1955), 8. Notes from critic Irving Sandler's interview of Joan three months later read: "I get images from words. Wallace Stevens's 'Domination of Black.'"

244 "the feeling": Mitchell, quoted in Sandler.

244 "what is being said": Edward Hirsch, *How to Read a Poem and Fall in Love with Poetry* (New York, San Diego, and London: Center for Documentary Studies in Association with Harcourt Brace, 1999), 10.

244 "Sentimentality is": Irving Sandler, "III Feb. 27, 1957," Irving Sandler Papers, Getty Research Institute, Research Library Special Collections and Visual Resources, Los Angeles.

244 "Joan Mitchell continues": Irving Sandler, "Young Moderns and Modern Masters: Joan Mitchell (Stable)," *ArtNews* 56:1 (March 1957): 32.

244 "flatly refused": Stable Gallery Records, Joan Mitchell File, Archives of American Art/Smithsonian Institution.

245 "I urgently": Ibid.

245 "YOU!": Joan Mitchell, quoted by Jane Wilson, interview with author, 17 July 2002.

245 "Best of all": Rudi Blesh, *Modern Art U.S.A.: Men, Rebellion, Conquest, 1900–56* (New York: Alfred A. Knopf, 1956), 291.

246 "Hey, why don't": Michael Goldberg, interview with author, 20 June 2002.

248 "was not always": "'Village' Is Scene of Jazz Concert," *New York Times,* 17 June 1957.

248 "The Day Lady Died": Frank O'Hara, *Lunch Poems* (San Francisco: City Lights, 1978), 27.

249 Knowing that viewers: See Susan Shawver Leonard, "The Influence of Henri Matisse in the Art of Richard Diebenkorn, Ellsworth Kelly, and Joan Mitchell." Master's thesis (School of the Art Institute of Chicago, 1990), 3–7, 26–33, and Judith E. Bernstock, *Joan Mitchell* (New York: Hudson Hills Press in association with Herbert F. Johnson Museum of Art, 1988), 52.

250 "painting as cathedral": Joan Mitchell often used this phrase in writing to Michael Goldberg.

251 "a wonderful airiness": Sandler, "Conversation with Joan Mitchell." Sandler and Mike Goldberg talked Joan out of destroying *Bridge,* which she eventually came to see as a completed work and gave to Sandler, who bequeathed it (keeping a life interest) to the Brooklyn Museum of Art.

251 "her memory": Irving Sandler, *A Sweeper-Up After Artists* (New York: Thames & Hudson, 2003), 218–19. Joan later told art historian Judith Bernstock that the painting may have turned blue because George had died or because his hair had a bluish cast. See Bernstock, 45.

252 "I carry": Mitchell, quoted in Sandler, "Mitchell Paints a Picture," *ArtNews* 56:6 (October 1957), 45.

252 "There are": Sandler, ibid. The photographs that accompany Sandler's article are credited to Swiss-born photographer Rudolph Burckhardt. However, because the artist balked at the prospect of painting in Burckhardt's presence, she was pressed into service. Burckhardt set up a view camera with timer and lights, and Joan took her own pictures. Painting was a private act. See William Corbett, "But Here's a Funny Story . . . ," *Modern Painters* 12:4 (winter 1999): 48–51.

253 "the Impressionist manner": Elaine de Kooning, quoted in Lawrence Alloway, "Some Notes on Abstract Impressionism," catalog of Abstract Impressionism, 11–28 June 1958, unpaginated. In addition to this exhibition (curated by Alloway and Harold Cohen), which traveled throughout Britain, the 1957 show Abstract Impressionism at Mount Holyoke College included Joan's work.

253 Art, O'Hara's great poem suggests: My comments on "To the Harbormaster" are indebted to Jacqueline Gens, "Revisiting Frank O'Hara's 'To the Harbormaster,'" *Poetrymind*, 16 April 2005, http://www.tsetso.blogspot.com.

253 "I'm sure": Joan Mitchell in a letter to Joanne and Philip Von Blon, postmarked 26 January 1982. Collection of Joanne Von Blon.

254 "only a method": Mitchell to Goldberg, n.d. [1957], Michael Goldberg Papers.

254 "One great big": Caroline Lee, interview with author, 23 March 2003.

254 "You know": Caroline Lee in a letter to Joan Mitchell, 23 August 1989. Collection of the Joan Mitchell Foundation.

254 "like having": June Wayne, telephone interview with author, 21 October 2001.

254 the occasion when: Lise Weil, telephone interview with author, 4 December 2005.

254 Buttercup's Chicken Shack: A later letter from Buttercup Powell to Joan and Jean-Paul suggests that the two helped pay for Bud Powell's 1966 funeral.

254 "shockingly the same": Mitchell to Goldberg, n.d., Michael Goldberg Papers.

255 "I'm beginning": Ibid.

255 "were finally": Transcript of letter from Frank O'Hara to Michael Goldberg, 26 August 1957, Allen Collection of Frank O'Hara Letters, Archives and Special Collections at the Thomas J. Dodd Research Center, University of Connecticut Libraries.

256 "Color, all they talked about": Barney Rosset, quoted in Siri Hustvedt, *Mysteries of the Rectangle: Essays on Painting* (New York: Princeton Architectual Press, 2005), 139–40.

257 "large, sprawling canvases": Deirdre Bair, *Samuel Beckett: A Biography* (New York and London: Harcourt Brace Jovanovich, 1978), 488.

257 "oh God": Joan Mitchell in a letter to Paul Jenkins, n.d. Collection of Suzanne and Paul Jenkins.

257 "Your descriptions": Frank O'Hara in a letter to Joan Mitchell, 4 November 1957. Collection of the Joan Mitchell Foundation.

257 One evening: Barney Rosset, interview with author, 24 July 2001; Evans Herman, interview with author, 27 March 2004.

258 "Make no mistake": Catherine Jones, "The Native Genius We've Never Discovered," *Maclean's*, 3 August 1957, 32.

258 "Visibly . . . he was": Mathews, quoted in Hélène de Billy, *Riopelle* (Montreal: Art Global, 1996), 133.

258 "I must be crazy": Riopelle to Mitchell, n.d. Collection of the Joan Mitchell Foundation.

258 "Don't become": Riopelle to Mitchell, 16 March 1958. Collection of the Joan Mitchell Foundation.

258 "When I paint": Riopelle, quoted by Jenkins, interview with author, 15 January 2003.

259 "There is nothing": Mitchell to Goldberg, n.d., Michael Goldberg Papers.

260 Ginsberg's cohort: When Corso's "Marriage" was published in the summer 1959 issue of Barney Rosset's *Evergreen Review*, it was dedicated to "Mr. and Mrs. Mike Goldberg." (Mike had married Patsy Southgate.) Regarding Ginsberg and Corso in Paris, see Barry Miles, *The Beat Hotel: Ginsberg, Burroughs, and Corso in Paris, 1957–1963* (New York: Grove Press, 2000).

260 "be mad for": Mitchell to Goldberg, n.d., Michael Goldberg Papers.

260 "little nice crazy": Ibid.

260   "various constituents": O'Hara to Mitchell, 30 July 1957. Collection of the Joan Mitchell Foundation.

261   "[putting] on the table": Paul Jenkins, interview with author, 11 January 2003.

261   "Now listen": Mitchell to Jenkins, n.d. Collection of Suzanne and Paul Jenkins.

262   "felt like": Elaine de Kooning, quoted in John Gruen, *The Party's Over Now* (New York: Viking Press, 1972), 220.

262   "a kind of suburban": Friedel Dzubas, quoted in Max Kozloff, "An Interview with Friedel Dzubas," *Artforum* 4:1 (September 1965): 51.

262   "You guys"; "The trouble": Michael Goldberg and Sidney Gordin, quoted in Sandler, *Sweeper-Up*, 231.

263   "The Club rises": John Canaday, "In the Gloaming: Twilight Seems to Be Settling Rapidly for Abstract Expressionism," *New York Times*, 11 September 1960.

263   "But look": Hamill, "Vital Gesture," *Art & Antiques* (May 1990): 110.

264   "SHIT AND LOVE": Riopelle to Mitchell, 20 June 1958.

265   "ghastly dreams": Mitchell to Jenkins, n.d.

265   "And the days": Ibid.

265   "Heard all": Mitchell to Jenkins, n.d.

265   When the newlyweds: Robert Harms, interview with author, 18 July 2002. Harms heard the story from his close friend Patsy Southgate.

266   "To ***": *Poems of René Char*, trans. and ann. Mary Ann Caws and Jonathan Griffin (Princeton: Princeton University Press, 1976), 283.

CHAPTER ELEVEN: SEEING SOMETHING THROUGH

269   "Ah Joan!": Frank O'Hara, "Far From the Porte des Lilas and the Rue Pergolèse: To Joan Mitchell," in Donald Allen, ed., *The Collected Poems of Frank O'Hara* (New York: Knopf, 1971), 311.

270   "Beckett followed": Deirdre Bair, *Samuel Beckett: A Biography* (New York and London: Harcourt Brace Jovanovich, 1978), 488.

270   "promiscuous drunks": Frank O'Hara, quoted by Bill Berkson, interview with author, 10 July 2006.

270   "a rather handsomely": Eleanor C. Munro, "The Found Generation," *Art-News* 60:7 (November 1961): 39.

270   "Miss Munro seems": Jane Freilicher, in "Editor's Letters," *ArtNews* 60:8 (December 1961): 6.

270   "Why are you": Yvonne Hagen, interview with author, 19 June 2005.

271   "*La vie en rose*": Mitchell to Goldberg, n.d., Michael Goldberg Papers, Archives of American Art/Smithsonian Institution.

271   "I thought": Sarah Mitchell Perry to Marion Strobel Mitchell, n.d. [stamped "June 1959"]. Collection of Sally Perry.

272   "prods of giggles": Sarah Mitchell Perry to Marion Strobel Mitchell and James Herbert Mitchell, 17 June 1959. Collection of Sally Perry.

272   "I think": Sarah Mitchell Perry to Marion Strobel Mitchell, n.d. [labeled "September 2nd"]. Collection of Sally Perry.

273   "At a boozy": Peter Schjeldahl, "Tough Love," *New Yorker*, 15 July 2002, 88.

273   "work out"; "give me money": Joan Mitchell in letters to Eleanor Ward, n.d. Stable Gallery Records, Joan Mitchell, Archives of American Art/Smithsonian

Institution. When Joan found Kowalski's bill too high, she retaliated by pulling strings through a friend who knew people in the French police and fixing it so that Kowalski's work permit was not renewed. See Yvonne Hagen, *From Art to Life and Back: N.Y.-Berlin-Paris 1925–1962* (Sagaponack, NY: Xlibris, 2006), 209.

274 "It makes me": Ibid.

275 "I am always": Frank O'Hara, "To the Harbormaster." in Donald Allen, ed., *The Collected Poems of Frank O'Hara* (Knopf, 1971), 95.

275 "Joan, *Chérie*": Jean-Paul Riopelle in a letter to Joan Mitchell, 10 April 1959. Collection of the Joan Mitchell Foundation.

275 "Your last letter": Jean-Paul Riopelle in a letter to Joan Mitchell, May 1959. Collection of the Joan Mitchell Foundation.

275 Before leaving: Hélène de Billy, *Riopelle* (Montreal: Art Global, 1996), 145–49.

276 "two sailors": Riopelle to Mitchell, n.d. Collection of the Joan Mitchell Foundation.

277 "lovely with snow": Mitchell to Rosset, n.d. Collection of Barney Rosset.

278 "Eh, Coco": Mitchell, quoted by Schneider, telephone interview with author, 24 September 2006.

278 "So how's your": Mitchell, quoted by Zuka Mitelberg, interview with author, 24 March 2003.

278 "You know": Mitchell, quoted by John Bennett, interview with author, 28 June 2002.

278 "Did you get": Marc Berlet, telephone interview with author, 5 August 2006.

279 "Riopelle was": Ibid.

279 Once Joan silenced: de Billy, 158–59.

279 "[Joan] was": Suzanne Viau, quoted in de Billy, 161.

279 "Riopelle had": Marc Berlet, telephone interview with author, 5 August 2006.

280 Not until: Among those Joan told were artists John Bennett and Elisabeth Kley.

280 "extremely taken": Pierre Schneider, telephone interview with author, 24 September 2006.

280 "Rip would get": Mitchell, quoted by John Bennett, interview with author, 28 June 2002.

280 One night: Anthony Cronin, *Samuel Beckett: The Last Modernist* (New York: HarperCollins, 1997), 433.

280 Once the same trio: John Ashbery, interview with author, 16 May 2006.

280 At least once: Roseline Granet, interview with author, 28 March 2003.

280 One late night: Barney Rosset, interview with author, 10 January 2003.

281 Scholar Marjorie Perloff: Marjorie Perloff, "The Silence That Is Not Silence: Acoustic Art in Samuel Beckett's *Embers*," in Lois Oppenheim, ed., *Samuel Beckett and the Arts: Music, Visual Arts, and Non-Print Media* (New York: Garland Publishing, 1999), 247.

281 "not a sound": Samuel Beckett, *Krapp's Last Tape, and Embers* (London: Faber and Faber, 1959), 35.

281 "If something": Mitchell, quoted in Judith E. Bernstock, *Joan Mitchell* (New York: Hudson Hills Press in association with Herbert F. Johnson Museum of Art, 1988), 106.

281 One night: So Joan told Beckett biographer Deirdre Bair. Author's telephone conversation with Deirdre Bair, 7 June 2006.

281 "Stick to Riopelle": Cronin, 433.

282   Her title: In his essay for Joan Mitchell: Trees and Other Paintings, 1960 to 1990, a 1992 exhibition at Laura Carpenter Fine Art, critic and poet John Yau links the title County Clare to both Ireland and the poet John Clare.

282   "working like": Mitchell to Ward, n.d. Stable Gallery Records, Joan Mitchell, Archives of American Art/Smithsonian Institution

283   Joan rejected: Mitchell, quoted in Stephan Westfall, "Then and Now: Six of the New York School Look Back," Art in America 73:6 (June 1985): 114.

284   Besides, the art world: Sometimes artists are classified by age. Yet Milton Resnick, born in 1917, is usually considered second generation while Philip Guston, born in 1913, achieves first-generation status. Other times the classification is by the period when the artist embraced an avant-garde outlook. However, Grace Hartigan (second generation) did so around the same time as Franz Kline (first generation). Among women, only Lee Krasner, who painted progressively beginning in the 1930s, is categorized as first generation.

284   Rather than: Irving Sandler, The New York School: The Painters and Sculptors of the Fifties (New York: Harper and Row, 1978), 280.

284   at Bill Berkson's: Mitchell to Goldberg, postmarked 4 June 1962, Michael Goldberg Papers.

285   "pop art, op art": Douglas Davis, "The Painters' Painters," Newsweek, 13 May 1974, 108.

285   "There'll always be": Joan Mitchell in John Ashbery, "An Expressionist in Paris," ArtNews 64:2 (April 1965): 64.

285   Using crayon: David Acton, The Stamp of Impulse: Abstract Expressionist Prints (New York: Hudson Hills Press in association with the Worcester Art Museum, 2001), 168.

286   Meanwhile her oils: Many of Joan's paintings from this period are untitled, which was fine with her, but collectors complain about untitled work, and dealers go crazy. Normally she titled her work after it was finished, often during laughter-filled "naming evenings" with friends. At other times (as she told art historian Judith Bernstock) her titles were deeply felt and inextricable from the work. Many refer to music, poetry, places, people, plants, and landscape elements. Quite a few are double entendres. She always knew exactly what had inspired each painting but didn't necessarily reveal it in the title.

286   "To paint": Catherine Flohic, "Joan Mitchell," Ninety (1993): 3.

287   "Everything is closed": Joan Mitchell, quoted in Marion Strobel Mitchell to Sarah Mitchell Perry, n.d. Collection of Sally Perry.

288   Between July 1: Stable Gallery Records, Joan Mitchell File, Archives of American Art/Smithsonian Institution.

288   "The gay gigglers": Sarah Mitchell Perry, quoted in a letter from Marion Strobel Mitchell to Joan Mitchell, 16 May 1962. Collection of Sally Perry.

289   "kicked me"; "Get rid of": Mitchell, interviewed by Linda Nochlin, 16 April 1986. Transcript, Archives of American Art/Smithsonian Institution.

289   Indebted to Bach: Marc Berlet, telephone interview with author, 5 August 2006.

290   "to transform": Rainer Maria Rilke, "The Bowl of Roses," in William H. Gass, Reading Rilke: Reflections on the Problem of Translation (New York: Alfred A. Knopf, 2001), 8.

290   "vistas of billowing": Holland Cotter, "Joan Mitchell," New York Times, 17 June 2005.

290   "Titian in the way": Pierre Schneider, telephone interview with author, 24 September 2006.

290   "the story": Pierre Schneider, essay for Joan Mitchell exhibition at Jacques Dubourg and Galerie Lawrence, 8–26 May 1962.

291   "Well, there's Kline": Joan Mitchell, quoted in a transcript sent by Betsy Zogbaum to Joan Mitchell, 5 July 1972. Collection of the Joan Mitchell Foundation.

292   "little monster": Marc Berlet, telephone interview with author, 5 August 2006.

292   "a special relationship": Hal Fondren in a letter to Joan Mitchell, 28 February 1987. Collection of the Joan Mitchell Foundation.

292   "terrible things": Marc Berlet, telephone interview with author, 5 August 2006.

292   less than twenty: Fabienne Dumont, "Femmes, art et féminisme en France dans les années 1970," *Sisyphe*, 11 April 2005, http://sisyphe.org.

292   "dear old Gimpel": Mitchell to Goldberg, postmarked 5 September 1965, Michael Goldberg Papers.

292   "just us"; "the big rooster": Mitchell, quoted by John Bennett, interview with author, 28 June 2002.

293   "J.P. is sweetie pie": Mitchell to Ward, n.d., Stable Gallery Records, Joan Mitchell File, Archives of American Art/Smithsonian Institution.

293   "I think": Brad Gooch, *City Poet: The Life and Times of Frank O'Hara* (New York: Alfred A. Knopf, 1993), 381.

293   "gay, amusing": James Herbert Mitchell in a letter to Joan Mitchell, 18 November 1960. Collection of the Joan Mitchell Foundation.

293   "sort of shoveled"; "took [Adrian] out": Ellen Lanyon, interview with author, 27 July 2001.

294   "(supposedly ... made": Mitchell to Goldberg, n.d. [Christmas 64]: Michael Goldberg Papers. Mitchell mistakenly refers to Newman as "Mortimer Newman."

294   "shooting the shit": Sally Perry, interview with author, 14 April 2001.

295   "very violent": Mitchell, quoted in Bernstock, 60.

295   Rufus found Joan: Rufus Zogbaum also cites as an example of Joan's kindness her 1970 purchase of a tombstone for his father, Wilfred Zogbaum (who had died in 1965), replacing one she felt unworthy of Zog.

296   "so nice": Olga Hirshhorn in a letter to Joan Mitchell, n.d. Collection of the Joan Mitchell Foundation.

297   "one of the great": Interview with Joseph H. Hirshhorn, conducted by Paul Cummings, New York, 16 December 1976. Archives of American Art/Smithsonian Institution.

CHAPTER TWELVE: LA TOUR

301   "*Quis hic locus*": T. S. Eliot, "Marina," in T. S. Eliot, *Collected Poems, 1909–1962* (New York: Harcourt, Brace & World, 1963), 105–6.

301   "graft a conscience": Brad Gooch, *City Poet: The Life and Times of Frank O'Hara* (New York: Alfred A. Knopf, 1993), 429.

302   reportedly rounding out: Ed Clark, interview with author, 21 June 2002.

302   "every pea and radish"; "My life is": Mitchell to Goldberg, postmarked 8 July 1965, Michael Goldberg Papers, Archives of American Art/Smithsonian Institution.

302   "I can't go": Mitchell to Goldberg, postmarked 27 July 1965, ibid.

303   "a magical, unviolated": Dorothy Carrington, *This Corsica: A Complete Guide* (London: Hammond, Hammond and Company, 1962), 188.

303   "[coming] out": Mitchell to Ward, n.d., Stable Gallery Records, Joan Mitchell, Archives of American Art/Smithsonian Institution.

303   "I'm trying": Mitchell, quoted in John Ashbery, "An Expressionist in Paris," *ArtNews* 64:2 (April 1965): 63.

304   "the difference between": Ibid.

304   she strenuously objected: Yves Michaud, "Entretiens," in Musée des Beaux-Arts de Nantes/Galerie Nationale du Jeu de Paume, *Joan Mitchell* (Paris: Éditions du Jeu de Paume, 1994), 31.

304   "It's a yellow": Mitchell, quoted in Judith E. Bernstock, *Joan Mitchell* (New York: Hudson Hills Press in association with Herbert F. Johnson Museum of Art, 1988), 89. She was speaking of her 1969 *Sunflowers*.

304   agreed with Bill: Mark Stevens and Annalyn Swan, *de Kooning: An American Master* (New York: Alfred A. Knopf, 2004), 232.

304   "violent contrasts": Stuart Preston, "Art and Industry: A New Synthesis," *New York Times,* 25 April 1965, X23.

304   "covered with goose-flesh": John Button in a letter to Joan Mitchell, 21 April 1965. Collection of the Joan Mitchell Foundation.

305   "A bird": Jean Fournier, interview with author, 27 March 2003.

305   "Well—about me": Mitchell to Goldberg, 5 September 1965, Michael Goldberg Papers.

305   "tough-skinned": Zuka Mitelberg, interview with author, 5 January 2002.

305   "Angel child": Mitchell to Goldberg, 15 September 1965, Michael Goldberg Papers.

306   At Calvi: Rufus Zogbaum, interview with author, 10 January 2003.

306   But their sex life: Hollis Jeffcoat, interview with author, 15 January 2002.

306   "absolutely resentful": Marc Berlet, telephone interview with author, 5 August 2006.

306   "compensating for": Teru Osato Lundsten, telephone interview with author, 27 November 2005.

307   Two years later: Olivier Bernier in a letter to Joan Mitchell, 26 January 1967, Martha Jackson Gallery Archives, UB Anderson Gallery, University at Buffalo, Buffalo, New York.

307   "I'm trying": Mitchell to Goldberg, n.d., Michael Goldberg Papers.

307   "at least sixty": Gooch, 10.

308   Alone in the bathroom: Eleanor Wright, interview with author, 13 April 2001.

308   "just right": John Frederick Nims to Joan Mitchell and Sarah Mitchell Perry, n.d. Collection of the Joan Mitchell Foundation.

308   "dear darling Nellie": Joan Mitchell to Sarah Mitchell Perry, n.d.

308   "Suddenly": Rainer Maria Rilke, "Before Summer Rain," in Stephen Mitchell, ed. and trans., *The Selected Poetry of Rainer Maria Rilke* (New York: Random House, 1982), 35.

309   Infuriated: Joan eventually settled for the return of the five paintings, plus a 1954 Franz Kline then valued at $12,000, in lieu of monies owed. See Eleanor Ward's 14 October 1967 letter to Joan Mitchell. Stable Gallery Records, Joan Mitchell File, Archives of American Art/Smithsonian Institution.

309   "no more dark centers": Joan Mitchell in a letter to Olivier Bernier, 29 January 1967, Martha Jackson Gallery Archives.

310   one balmy blue: Paul Waldo Schwartz, "Calder and Miró, Now Past 70, Feted in France," *New York Times,* 23 July 1968.

310   "What a sweet": Joan Mitchell in a letter to Elisabeth Kley, 29 December 1983.

310   On another occasion: John Bennett, interview with author, 28 June 2002.

310   "under his shadow": Elisabeth Kley, telephone interview with author, 7 April 2006.

311   "a humanist initiatory"; "lay monk": Pierre Wat, "Jean Fournier ou la discrétion à l'oeuvre," *Beaux-Arts* (July-August 1994): 42.

311   "my truth": Jean Fournier, interview with author, 27 March 2003.

311   "You are": Joan Mitchell, quoted by Betsy Jolas, interview with author, 26 March 2003.

312   "cheer up": Mitchell, interviewed by Linda Nochlin, 16 April 1986. Transcript, Archives of American Art/Smithsonian Institution.

312   Joan bargained: Yseult Riopelle, telephone interview with author, 17 November 2006.

313   "absolutely awful": Joan Mitchell in a letter to Evans Herman, n.d. Collection of Frances Herman.

313   She kept: Ed Clark, interview with author, 21 June 2002.

313   "immense overturned": Mitchell, quoted in Eleanor Munro, *Originals: American Women Artists* (New York: Da Capo, 2000), 237.

314   "the horrors": Evans Herman, interview with author, 27 March 2004.

314   "Out of your poem": Mitchell to Herman, n.d.

314   "Why do you": Pierre Schneider, "Paris: Literature's Return to Nature," *New York Times,* 10 May 1971.

315   "If I see": Mitchell, quoted in Bernstock, 85.

315   She looked: *Salut Sally,* painted that same year, is among the works that reveal the influence of Sam Francis.

316   "lights and whites": Joan Mitchell in a note to Elisabeth Kley, n.d.

316   "the desire to": Vincent van Gogh in a letter to Wilhelmina J. van Gogh in *Complete Letters of Vincent Van Gogh* (Greenwich, CT: New York Graphic Society, 1958), 468.

317   "my *View of Delft*": Joan Mitchell, quoted in Ora Lerman, "The Elusive Subject: Joan Mitchell's Reflections on van Gogh," *Arts* 65:1 (September 1990): 45.

317   In his Bristol: Hélène de Billy, *Riopelle* (Montreal: Art Global, 1996), 205.

318   "You're George"; "very lively": John Bennett, interview with author, 28 June 2002.

318   "Abandonment is": Mitchell, interviewed by Yves Michaud, "Conversation with Joan Mitchell," in Xavier Fourcade Gallery, *Joan Mitchell: New Paintings* (New York: Xavier Fourcade Gallery, 1986), unpaginated.

318   "It really looks"; "standing in front": Joan Mitchell in a letter to Sarah Mitchell Perry, 15 May 1969. Collection of Sally Perry.

318   But their *Serica* era: One weekend in July 1969 found Joan uncharacteristically entertaining without him at sea. Her guests included sculptor Lynda Benglis, whom she had met through Mike Goldberg. That Sunday the radio brought news of the death of artist Barnett Newman, a non-objective New York School painter and sculptor who had sought to embody pure spirituality in his work.

A friend of Newman's, Benglis was deeply upset. In contrast, Joan (who had once instructed Newman, two decades her senior, to stop using acrylics) bluntly asserted that she felt nothing about Newman's death and even, according to Benglis, more or less cursed the dead painter. Lynda Benglis, telephone interview with author, 7 November 2006.

318   "never saw": Jacqueline Hyde, interview with author, 19 January 2002.

318   "beyond what": Roseline Granet, interview with author, 28 March 2003.

319   "Rip's on his": Joan Mitchell to Sally Perry, n.d. [April 1971]. Collection of Sally Perry.

319   "this dumb little car": Howard Kanovitz, interview with author, 18 July 2002.

319   Tempers flared anew: Madeleine Arbour (interviewer) and Jeannette Tardif (director), *Riopelle: Ficelles et Autres Jeux* (Montreal: Radio-Canada, 1972). Video.

320   "the most distraught": Ellen Lanyon, interview with author, 27 July 2001.

320   Joan told: Elga Heinzen, personal communication to author, 8 May 2002.

320   "I will use": Joan Mitchell, interviewed in Lynn Blumenthal (interviewer) and Kate Horsfield (cameraperson), *Joan Mitchell: An Interview* (Chicago: Video Data Bank [School of the Art Institute of Chicago], 1974). Video.

321   Joan fawned: Yseult Riopelle, telephone interview with author, 17 November 2006.

321   "death warmed over": Mitchell, interviewed by Nochlin, 16 April 1986. Transcript, Archives of American Art/Smithsonian Institution.

321   "direct communication": T. S. Eliot, "Ben Jonson," in *Selected Essays* (London: Faber and Faber, 1963), quoted in Terry Eagleton, *Literary Theory* (Minneapolis: University of Minnesota Press, 1996), 35.

321   "grace dissolved"; "less strong and stronger": Eliot, *Collected Poems*, 105.

321   "one's feelings": Ashbery, "An Expressionist in Paris," *ArtNews* 64:2 (April 1965): 64.

322   Something Joan had seen: Lise Weil, telephone interview with author, 4 December 2005.

322   "part of an expressive": Marcia Tucker, *Joan Mitchell* (New York: Whitney Museum of American Art, 1974), 14.

322   "is the Seine": Joan Mitchell quoted in Musée d'Art Moderne de la Ville de Paris, *Joan Mitchell: Choix de Peintures, 1970–1982* (Paris: ARC, Musée d'Art Moderne de la Ville de Paris, 1982), unpaginated.

323   "lost some": Mitchell, quoted in Lerman, "The Elusive Subject," *Arts* 65:1 (September 1990): 43.

323   "Do I have to": Joan Mitchell, quoted by James Harithas, telephone interview with author, 17 October 2006.

323   "pushing her mastery"; "as one of the best": Peter Schjeldahl, "Joan Mitchell: To Obscurity and Back," *New York Times*, 30 April 1972.

324   "this Whitney bit"; "practically in 'divorce' ": Joan Mitchell in a letter to David Anderson, 2 June 1972. Martha Jackson Gallery Archives.

324   "sick—balls"; "Lelong has offered": Mitchell to Anderson, 24 July 1972, Martha Jackson Gallery Archives.

325   "wondering": Christian Larson in a letter to Joan Mitchell, 12 February 1973. Collection of the Joan Mitchell Foundation.

325   "painting music": Gisèle Barreau, interview with author, 29 March 2003.

325   "Music, poems": Mitchell, quoted in Tucker, 7.

325 In order to: Michaële-Andréa Schatt, interview with author, 19 January 2002.

326 "a locomotive": John Hailey, telephone interview with author, 23 April 2006.

326 "For my identity": Mitchell, interviewed by Michaud, *Joan Mitchell: New Paintings.*

327 "You know": Joan Mitchell, quoted by Rufus Zogbaum, interview with author, 10 January 2003.

327 One afternoon: Marcia Tucker, *A Short Life of Trouble: Forty Years in the New York Art World* (Berkeley, Los Angeles and London: University of California Press, 2008), 105–07.

327 "I've had enough": Tucker, 106.

327 "'Miss Curator Whitney'": Joan Mitchell to Sarah Mitchell Perry, 18 December 1973. Collection of the Joan Mitchell Foundation.

CHAPTER THIRTEEN: VINNIE AND THEA

328 "And when I thought": James Schuyler, "Daylight," in *Collected Poems* (New York: Farrar, Straus & Giroux, 1993), 183.

328 She exhibited: The Whitney exhibition also included twelve paintings done between 1969 and 1972 as a "background" to the 1972 to 1974 work.

328 "comes from": Mitchell, quoted in Marcia Tucker, *Joan Mitchell* (New York: Whitney Museum of American Art, 1974), 8.

328 "This supports": Carter Ratcliff, "Joan Mitchell's Envisonments," *Art in America* 62:4 (July–August 1974): 34.

329 "a Biblical epic": John Frederick Nims in a letter to Joan Mitchell, 11 May 1974. In another Chicago connection, Joan had run into Rue Shaw, the president of the Arts Club of Chicago and an old friend of the Mitchell family, at Pierre Matisse's 1973 St. Patrick's Day party. Afterward, Shaw had conceived of the idea of traveling a portion of the Whitney show to the Arts Club. Joan Mitchell: Recent Paintings opened in Chicago on 23 September 1974. Shaw had coaxed Joan into attending the opening, but, at the eleventh hour, the artist backed out, pleading sciatica and lumbago but later admitting her inability to face the onslaught of Chicago memories. Newberry Library, Arts Club file, Joan Mitchell, Sept. 23–Nov. 9, 1974 (23.9.74 [OMS][C]).

329 "Dropped gradually": Max Kozloff, "Painters Reply," *Artforum* 14:1 (September 1975): 37.

329 "career crap": Mitchell, interviewed in Lynn Blumenthal (interviewer) and Kate Horsfield (cameraperson), *Joan Mitchell: An Interview* (Chicago: Video Data Bank [School of the Art Institute of Chicago], 1974). Video.

329 Art dealer: Klaus Kertess, "Her Passion Was Abstract but No Less Combustible," *New York Times*, 16 June 2002.

330 "truly outstanding"; "with their huge paintings": Barbara Rose, "First-Rate Art by the Second Sex," *New York*, 8 April 1974, 80.

331 Along with Grace: Laurie Lisle, *Louise Nevelson: A Passionate Life* (New York: Summit Books, 1990), 164.

331 She also showed up: Rose Slivka, interview with author, 19 June 2002.

331 "the burden": Cindy Nemser, "An Afternoon with Joan Mitchell," *Feminist Art Journal* 3:1 (spring 1974): 6.

331   "But it really": John Frederick Nims in a letter to Joan Mitchell, 11 May 1974. Collection of the Joan Mitchell Foundation.

332   In any case: Mark Stevens and Annalyn Swan, *de Kooning: An American Master* (New York: Alfred A. Knopf, 2004), 292.

332   "You want": Joan Mitchell, quoted by Jill Weinberg Adams, interview with author, 26 June 2002.

332   A few days: David Anderson, telephone interview with author, 3 July 2005.

333   "She's a total": Mitchell, quoted in Judith E. Bernstock, *Joan Mitchell* (New York: Hudson Hills Press in association with Herbert F. Johnson Museum of Art, 1988), 134.

333   "no identity": Mitchell, interviewed in Blumenthal and Horsfield.

333   "an identity": Harry Gaugh, "Dark Victories," *ArtNews* 87:6 (summer 1988): 157.

334   "I'm very": Mitchell, quoted in Eleanor Munro, *Originals: American Women Artists* (New York: Da Capo, 2000), 235.

334   A case in point: Author's telephone conversation with Deirdre Bair, 7 June 2006.

334   When her old: Jon Schueler, *The Sound of Sleat: A Painter's Life* (New York: Picador, 1999), 249.

334   Another time: Eleanor Wright and Georgia Funsten, interview with author, 13 April 2001.

335   "horrible": Lise Weil, telephone interview with author, 4 December 2005.

335   "silver-spoon people": Joan Mitchell, quoted by Ken Tyler, interview with author, 7 January 2003.

335   One evening: Lydia Davis, telephone interview with author, 7 July 2008.

335   "She talked": Lydia Davis, personal communication to author, July 2008.

335   "Who do you think": Joan Mitchell, quoted in Siri Hustvedt, *Mysteries of the Rectangle: Essays on Painting* (New York: Princeton Architectural Press, 2005), 136.

336   "serious . . . and 'centered'": Lydia Davis, personal communication to author, July 2008.

336   "My stay": Paul Auster in a letter to Lydia Davis, 28 July 1972, personal communication to author; Paul Auster, interview with author, 31 July 2008.

336   the beautiful, pale: Lise Weil, telephone interview with author, 4 December 2005.

336   "to Joan": Christian Larson in a letter to Joan Mitchell, 24 April 1973.

336   Joan would tuck: Robert Harms, interview with author, 18 July 2002. My thanks to Honor Moore for corresponding with me about J. J. Mitchell.

336   "Here we are": J. J. Mitchell to "Harry," n.d. [4 a.m., Pentecost]. Collection of the Joan Mitchell Foundation.

337   Since 1970: Champlain Charest and Réjeanne Charest, interviews with author, 20 July 2001.

337   "With great friendship": The Joan Mitchell Foundation has several such postcards, dating between 1971 and 1977, in its collection.

337   "for enormous protection": Mitchell, quoted in Bernstock, 68.

338   They finished: Mitchell to Goldberg, 10 February 1975. Collection of the Joan Mitchell Foundation.

338   "pasteled up": Mitchell, interviewed by Linda Nochlin, 16 April 1986. Transcript, Archives of American Art/Smithsonian Institution.

338 Her effort notwithstanding: Joe LeSueur in a letter to Joan Mitchell, 4 December 1975. Collection of the Joan Mitchell Foundation.

339 Whenever a friend: Pierre Schneider, telephone interview with author, 24 September 2006.

339 "When they bit": Philippe Dagen, "La Fureur de Joan Mitchell," *Le Monde,* 2–3 August 1992.

339 "No! No!": Joan Mitchell, quoted by Bill Scott, interview with author, 31 March 2004.

339 "destroyed everything": Jean-Paul Riopelle, quoted by Roseline Granet, interview with author, 28 March 2003.

340 "I thought": Jean-Paul Riopelle, quoted by John Bennett, interview with author, 28 June 2002.

340 "looked like huge": Schueler, 249–50.

340 Sometimes she would draw: Paul Auster, interview with author, 31 July 2008.

341 "up and down things": Mitchell, quoted in Bernstock, 143.

342 That October: Joan Mitchell in a letter to Xavier Fourcade, 18 October 1977. Fourcade Gallery Archives.

343 "too Helen Frankenthaler!": Joan Mitchell, quoted by Jill Weinberg Adams, interview with author, 26 June 2002.

344 "truly doing wonders": Phyllis Hailey in a letter to Anne and John Hailey, n.d. [c. June 1976] in The Parthenon, *Phyllis Hailey and Joan Mitchell: The Story of Two Artists in France,* 7.

344 "Well if it means": Joan Mitchell in a note to Phyllis Hailey, n.d., in ibid., 7.

344 "Oh, come on"; "Hollis, what do": Joan Mitchell, quoted by Hollis Jeffcoat, interview with author, 15 January 2002.

347 "What should": Ibid.

347 Ah, another Mitchell!: Carl Plansky, interview with author, 16 January 2001. Hollis Jeffcoat described Joan's feelings in a similar way, as did Mitchell herself in a letter to artist Joyce Pensato.

347 "[thrown] Phyllis over"; "There was": Hollis Jeffcoat, interview with author, 15 January 2002.

348 "Joanie, You were": Hollis Jeffcoat in a letter to Joan Mitchell, 7 October 1977. Collection of the Joan Mitchell Foundation.

348 Joan spent: Joan Mitchell in a letter to Xavier Fourcade, 18 October 1977. Fourcade Gallery Archives.

348 "dashed dreams": Teru Osato Lundsten, telephone interview with author, 27 November 2005.

348 "Having nearly": Tim Osato in a letter to Joan Mitchell, 25 December 1977. Collection of the Joan Mitchell Foundation.

348 "J.P. has been": Joan Mitchell in a letter to Joe LeSueur, 10 March 1978. Collection of Robert Harms.

349 "didn't come close": Hollis Jeffcoat, interview with author, 15 January 2002.

350 "Do hope": Joan Mitchell in a letter to Anne Hailey, 18 July 1978. Collection of Anne Hailey.

350 "and it was": Hollis Jeffcoat, interview with author, 15 January 2002.

351 "concentrating on areas": Ibid.

351 "I will never": Sam Francis, quoted by Hollis Jeffcoat, interview with author, 15 January 2002.

351 "I've tried": Hollis Jeffcoat, interview with author, 15 January 2002.

352   "Everyone seems": Joan Mitchell in a letter to Sally Perry, 1 September 1978. Collection of Sally Perry.

352   "All I can say": Joe LeSueur in a letter to Joan Mitchell, 14 December 1978. Collection of the Joan Mitchell Foundation.

352   "Hollis and I": Joan Mitchell in a letter to Joyce Pensato, n.d. [spring 1979].

353   "They've run away": Joan Mitchell, quoted by Michael Goldberg, interview with author, 20 June 2002.

353   He was present: So Joan told Elisabeth Kley and Gisèle Barreau, respectively.

354   "I caught": Joan Mitchell, quoted by Bill Berkson, interview with author, 10 July 2006.

354   "To realize"; "Oh God": Barney Rosset in a letter to Joan Mitchell, 5 September 1979. Rosset's first sentence quotes Mitchell. Collection of the Joan Mitchell Foundation.

CHAPTER FOURTEEN: LA GRANDE VALLÉE

355   "Magical childhood land": Gisèle Barreau, "La Grande Vallée," 2001.

355   "very creepy": Mitchell, interview by Linda Nochlin, 16 April 1986. Transcript, Archives of American Art/Smithsonian Institution.

355   "like hitting": Mitchell to Von Blon, 12 December 1979.

356   "I sleep": Gisèle Barreau in a note to Joan Mitchell, n.d. Collection of the Joan Mitchell Foundation.

356   "Young lady"; "You're having"; "You, what's the matter"; "Aw, you're such": Joan Mitchell, quoted by Carl Plansky, interview with author, 16 January 2001.

357   "That twig!": Ibid.

357   "It was": Carl Plansky, interview with author, 16 January 2001.

357   atop layers of newspaper: Joyce Pensato, interview with author, 14 July 2002.

357   Unlike most artists: Ken Tyler, interview with author, 7 January 2003.

357   "'pretty' accidents": Joan Mitchell in a letter to Joe LeSueur, n.d. [November 1979]. Collection of the Joan Mitchell Foundation.

357   Lest anyone make assumptions: Judith E. Bernstock, *Joan Mitchell* (New York: Hudson Hills Press in association with Herbert F. Johnson Museum of Art, 1988), 172.

357   Continuing to use: A few days after learning of his longtime companion's death in October 1992, Jean-Paul Riopelle would undertake, in her honor, the monumental *L'Hommage à Rosa Luxemburg,* today on permanent display at the Musée du Québec in Quebec City, Canada. A narrative sequence consisting of thirty canvases totaling approximately 131 feet wide, *L'Hommage à Rosa Luxemburg* is organized as a triptych/environment. Riopelle's title derives, in part, from the fact that German communist Rosa Luxemburg wrote coded letters from her prison cell. The painting's symbology includes a heart pierced by an arrow, a broken watch, a sun caught in a net, a horseshoe, a harness, and a bit.

358   "really hacking": Mitchell to Von Blon, n.d. Collection of Joanne Von Blon.

359   "You have": Reed Bertolette in a letter to Joan Mitchell, 17 April n.d. Collection of the Joan Mitchell Foundation.

359   "You were": Joan Mitchell in a note to Joyce Pensato, n.d. Collection of Joyce Pensato.

359   "'Ludwigs'": Ibid.

359   "Joan is making": Mitchell to Plansky and Pensato, n.d. Collection of Joyce Pensato.

360   "miracle on roller skates": Denise Browne Hare in a letter to Joan Mitchell, 26 May 1984. Collection of the Joan Mitchell Foundation.

360   On this occasion: Bill Berkson, interview with author, 10 July 2006. Art dealer Robert Miller told me about watching Joan stumble upon a particularly fine late de Kooning at the Corcoran Gallery in 1988. She nearly genuflected.

360   "Here's what": Joan Mitchell, quoted by Michaële-Andréa Schatt, interview with author, 19 January 2002.

360   "Shit!": Michaële-Andréa Schatt, interview with author, 19 January 2002.

360   "Michaële, shall we": Joan Mitchell, quoted by Michaële-Andréa Schatt, interview with author, 19 January 2002.

361   "that fixed determination": Joan Mitchell, quoted by Barney Rosset, Rosset to Mitchell, 5 September 1979. Collection of the Joan Mitchell Foundation.

361   "When she": Michaële-Andréa Schatt, interview with author, 19 January 2002.

361   During its installation: Paul Richard, telephone interview with author, 16 August 2002.

362   "I'm not sure": Carla Hall, "Abstract Audacity . . . And a Party for the Folks Who Put It Together," Washington Post, 19 February 1981.

362   "I understand": Katy Crowe, interview with author, 27 October 2001.

362   "I wouldn't know": Mitchell to Von Blon, n.d. Collection of Joanne Von Blon.

362   "drink the landscape": Joan Mitchell to Sarah Mitchell Perry, 14 May 1982. Collection of Sally Perry.

363   "a hoot"; "like a game": Ken Tyler, interview with author, 7 January 2003.

364   "Ken, this might be"; "as close as"; "God damn it": Ibid.

364   "Ken, I want": Joan Mitchell, quoted in Barbara Rose, "The Landscape of Light: Joan Mitchell," Vogue (June 1981): 207.

364   "If she saw": Ken Tyler, interview with author, 7 January 2003.

364   "Your paintings": Barreau to Mitchell, n.d. Collection of the Joan Mitchell Foundation.

365   "verbal percussion": Gisèle Barreau in "Gisèle Barreau: Notes biographiques et catalogue d'oeuvres," Christine Paquelet Édition Arts, Paris.

366   "I realize": Barreau to Mitchell, n.d. Collection of the Joan Mitchell Foundation.

366   "a rapturous": Joe LeSueur, Digressions on Some Poems by Frank O'Hara (New York: Farrar, Straus and Giroux, 2003), 137–38.

366   "You broke": Mitchell to Barreau, n.d. Collection of the Joan Mitchell Foundation.

366   "the awareness that": John Fried in a letter to Joan Mitchell, 16 December 1981. Collection of the Joan Mitchell Foundation.

366   "enchanted day": Ibid.

367   "because it was": Jaqueline Fried, interview with author, 9 January 2003.

367   "indescribable rudeness": Sarah Mitchell Perry to Joan Mitchell, 9 November 1979. Collection of Sally Perry.

368   "Sal—I'm saying": Joan Mitchell to Sarah Mitchell Perry, n.d. Collection of Sally Perry.

369   "the opposite of": Joan Mitchell, quoted in ARC, Musée d'Art Moderne de la Ville de Paris, Joan Mitchell: Choix de Peintures, 1970–1982 (Paris: ARC, Musée d'Art Moderne de la Ville de Paris, 1982), unpaginated.

369   "We both look": Joan Mitchell, quoted by Georgia Funsten and Eleanor Wright, interview with author, 13 April 2001.

370   "really hooked": Elisabeth Kley, telephone interview with author, 7 April 2006.

370   "I called": Joan Mitchell in a note to Elisabeth Kley, n.d. Collection of Elisabeth Kley.

370   "I did call": Ibid.

370   "I'm still listening": Ibid.

371   "This is obviously": Michael Gibson, "Joan Mitchell's Glowing Paintings," *International Herald Tribune*, 24–25 July 1982.

371   "meaner and meaner": Sally Perry, interview with author, 14 April 2001.

371   "must have been": Carl Plansky, interview with author, 16 January 2001.

371   "It's so nice": Mitchell to Kley, n.d. A letter from Joe LeSueur to Joan dated 31 December 1983 in the collection of the Joan Mitchell Foundation confirms that Joan was indeed "on the wagon."

372   "very true": Mitchell, interviewed by Linda Nochlin, 16 April 1986. Transcript, Archives of American Art/Smithsonian Institution.

372   her rereading of Proust: Jean Fournier, interview with author, 27 March 2003. Fournier told me that Joan made an explicit connection between Proust and *La Grande Vallée*. In contrast, Barreau said that Joan made such a connection in terms of her work in general but not specifically *La Grande Vallée*.

372   "the true paradises": Marcel Proust, *Time Regained, In Search of Lost Time*, trans. C. K. Scott-Moncrieff and Terence Kilmartin, rev. by D. J. Enright (New York: Modern Library, 1992), 261.

372   "all meaningless": Mitchell to Kley, 29 December 1983. Collection of Elisabeth Kley.

372   "an emblematic painting": Jean Fournier, interview with author, 27 March 2003.

372   "in and out": Klaus Kertess, *Joan Mitchell* (New York: Harry N. Abrams, 1997), 37. In painting *La Grande Vallée*, Mitchell used a small reducing mirror to defamiliarize her work-in-progress (by reflecting it backward) and help her see it wholly and as if from a greater distance.

373   "painting is like": Gisèle Barreau interviewed by Yvette Y. Lee, in Yvette Y. Lee, "Beyond Life and Death: Joan Mitchell's Grande Vallée Suite," in Jane Livingston, *The Paintings of Joan Mitchell* (New York, Berkeley, Los Angeles, and London: Whitney Museum of American Art in association with University of California Press, 2002), 63. Sarah Mitchell Perry's entrance into and exit from this world both occasioned major artistic achievements, her mother's "Songs for Sally" in the first case and her sister's *La Grande Vallée* in the second.

373   "*People's Magazine*": Joan Mitchell to Sarah Mitchell Perry, 25 April 1982. Collection of Sally Perry.

373   "Look, when they come": Joan Mitchell, quoted by Carl Plansky, interview with author, 16 January 2001.

373   "Three years ago": Joyce Campbell, "In the Land of Monet, American Painter Joan Mitchell More Than Pulls Her Weight," *People Weekly*, 6 December 1982, 84.

373   "The Twenty-Four-Year": Mitchell, interviewed in Marion Cajori, director, *Joan Mitchell: Portrait of an Abstract Painter* (New York: Art Kaleidoscope Foundation and Christian Blackwood Productions, 1992). Film.

373   "twice with her": Joan Mitchell in a letter to Elisabeth Kley, n.d. Collection of Elisabeth Kley.

374   "That garbage can:" Mitchell to Von Blon, n.d. Collection of Joanne Von Blon.

374   "Will you come": Joan Mitchell, quoted by Hollis Jeffcoat, interview with author, 15 January 2002.

374   "My painting outfit!": Joan Mitchell, quoted by Huguette Vachon, interview with author, 19 July 2001.

375   "[weaves] all the colors": Ora Lerman, "The Elusive Subject: Joan Mitchell's Reflections on van Gogh," Arts 65:1 (September 1990): 45.

375   "absorption of Impressionism": John Yau, "Reviews: New York," Artforum 23:9 (May 1985): 105.

375   "The whole linkage": Bernstock, 76.

375   "Monette": Sally Apfelbaum, interview with author, 25 July 2001.

375   Once, after a visit: Bill Scott, interview with author, 31 March 2004.

375   "the spirit": Nemser, 24.

376   "helps little": Pierre Schneider, "Art News from Paris: Left Bank," ArtNews 59:4 (summer 1960): 50.

376   in 1974: Tucker, Joan Mitchell (New York: Whitney Museum of American Art, 1974), 16. Rosenberg responded in "The Art World: Artist Against Background," New Yorker, 29 April 1974, 71–72, 74, 76, 78.

376   "To get right": Yves Michaud, "Couleur," in Joan Mitchell: La Grande Vallée (Paris: Galerie Jean Fournier, 1984), 8–9.

376   "as time passes": Robert Storr, "Joan Mitchell: Pastorale Furieuse," in Musée des Beaux-Arts de Nantes/Galerie Nationale du Jeu de Paume, Joan Mitchell (Paris: Éditions du Jeu de Paume, 1994), 18.

377   "You're supposed": Mitchell, interviewed in Cajori.

377   "like a place": Robert Miller, telephone interview with author, 24 August 2003.

377   "watering can": Hugo von Hofmannsthal, The Lord Chandos Letter, trans. Russell Stockman (Marlboro, VT: Marlboro Press, 1986), 23.

377   "That's it": Mitchell, interviewed by Nochlin, 16 April 1986. Transcript, Archives of American Art/Smithsonian Institution.

378   "that house": Jacqueline Hyde, interview with author, 19 January 2002. Elga Heinzen told me the same thing.

378   "That's what": Joyce Pensato, interview with author, 14 July 2002.

378   "hold a lemon": Bill Scott, "In the Eye of the Tiger," Art in America 83:3 (March 1995): 75–76.

378   "Let's organize": Mitchell to Kley and others ["Now kids"], n.d. Collection of Elisabeth Kley.

379   "brought out": Bill Scott, interview with author, 31 March 2004.

380   "out for dissection"; "It would look": Christopher Campbell, telephone interview with author, 10 February 2007.

380   "looked at me": Robert Harms, interview with author, 18 July 2002.

CHAPTER FIFTEEN: A FEW DAYS

381   "A FEW DAYS": James Schuyler, Selected Poems (New York: Farrar, Straus & Giroux, 1988), 237.

382   "God the Father": Jeanne Le Bozec, interview with author, 25 March 2003.

382   "Write down": Barreau to Mitchell, n.d. Collection of the Joan Mitchell Foundation.

382 "never missed": Christiane Rousseaux, interview with author, 12 January 2002.

383 "tragic and beautiful": Joan Mitchell in a letter to Joyce Pensato, n.d. Collection of Joyce Pensato.

383 "used to death": Carl Plansky, interview with author, 16 January 2001.

383 "active death": Paul Richard, "Joan Mitchell's Bleak Horizons," *Washington Post*, 27 February 1988. Four years earlier, Joan had painted the beautiful and chilling *Cobalt.*

383 "It's death": Mitchell, quoted in Judith E. Bernstock, *Joan Mitchell* (New York: Hudson Hills Press in association with Herbert F. Johnson Museum of Art, 1988), 39.

383 "the way it mounts": Mitchell to Von Blon, postmarked 2 January 1987. Collection of Joanne Von Blon.

384 "death warmed over": Mitchell, interviewed by Linda Nochlin, 16 April 1986. Transcript, Archives of American Art/Smithsonian Institution.

384 "a clip": Joseph Strick in a letter to Joan Mitchell, 16 January 1985. Collection of the Joan Mitchell Foundation.

384 "paint more directly": Mitchell, quoted by Rufus Zogbaum, interview with author, 10 January 2003.

385 "Keep cracking!": Joan Mitchell in a letter to Robert Harms, n.d. [January 1988]. Collection of Robert Harms.

385 "When I was sick": Mitchell, interviewed by Yves Michaud, "Conversation with Joan Mitchell," in Xavier Fourcade Gallery, *Joan Mitchell: New Paintings* (New York: Xavier Fourcade Gallery, 1986), unpaginated.

385 "and the trees": Ibid.

385 By the mid-1980s: Jill Weinberg Adams, interview with author, 9 July 2002; Anne-Elisabeth Moutet, "An American in Paris," *Elle* [February 1988]: 74.

385 "Only one person": Mitchell, quoted in Bernstock, 195.

386 "just completely!": Jill Weinberg Adams, interview with author, 9 July 2002.

387 "the New York fags": Joan Mitchell, quoted by Hal Fondren in a letter to Joan Mitchell, 28 February 1987. Collection of the Joan Mitchell Foundation.

387 using an easel: Mitchell to Von Blon, postmarked 2 January 1987. Collection of Joanne Von Blon.

388 Sometimes the dogs: Paul Auster, interview with artist, 31 July 2008.

388 "All all": Mitchell to Von Blon, postmarked 2 January 1987. Collection of Joanne Von Blon.

388 "We had": Jill Weinberg Adams, interview with author, 26 June 2002.

388 "that crazy": Mitchell to Von Blon, postmarked 2 January 1987. Collection of Joanne Von Blon.

389 Joan had first: Andreas Freund, "Paris Unveils a Grand Matisse Exhibition," *New York Times*, 21 April 1970.

389 "take the whole": Margaret Staats and Lucas Matthiessen, "The Genetics of Art, Part II," *Quest 77* (July–August 1977): 42.

389 "made still": Mitchell, interviewed by Michaud, *Joan Mitchell: New Paintings.*

389 "It is a fact": Yves Michaud, "Accords," in Galerie Jean Fournier, *Joan Mitchell: Peintures 1986 & 1987: River, Lille, Chord* (Paris: Galerie Jean Fournier, 1987), 68.

389 That winter: Ora Lerman, "The Elusive Subject: Joan Mitchell's Reflections on van Gogh," *Arts* 65:1 (September 1990): 44.

390   "Color sends me": Mitchell to Goldberg, n.d., Michael Goldberg Papers, Archives of American Art/Smithsonian Institution.

390   meaning suicide: Robert Harms, interview with artist, 18 July 2002.

390   "the opposite of": ARC, *Joan Mitchell: Choix de Peintures,* unpaginated.

390   "stayed with": Staats and Matthiessen, 42.

390   "fanaticism": Mitchell to Goldberg, 13 August 1954, Michael Goldberg Papers.

390   "a way to make": Vincent van Gogh to Theo van Gogh in *Complete Letters of Vincent Van Gogh* (Greenwich, CT: New York Graphic Society, 1958), 26.

391   Others related: Lerman, 44; Robert Harms, interview with author, 18 July 2002.

391   "the love of": Vincent van Gogh to Theo van Gogh in *Complete Letters,* 26.

391   Both artists favored: In *The Hidden Order of Art: A Study in the Psychology of Artistic Imagination* (Berkeley and Los Angeles: University of California Press), 160, one of Joan's bibles, psychoanalytic and art theorist Anton Ehrenzweig writes that "Van Gogh did not rely on the open clash between complementary or near-complementary colours, like a blue-violet sky against warm yellow fields. He was more concerned to seal them off from each other and so heighten the dramatic tension between them."
        Ehrenzweig also argues that the truly creative thinker can engage with the seeming chaos of the unconscious from which a complex order eventually emerges, characterizes artistic structure as "essentially 'polyphonic,'" and coins the term "poemagogic [from 'hypnagogic'] images" to mean the "tragic images of creativity" including those at the "'oceanic' level where we feel our individual existence lost in mystic union with the universe." His appeal to Joan is evident.

391   "rugged individualism": Robert Miller, telephone interview with author, 24 August 2003.

391   Lennon too: The gallery continues as Lennon, Weinberg.

391   "the fags and females": Joan Mitchell, quoted by Jill Weinberg Adams, interview with author, 9 July 2002.

392   "art-historicized live": Yves Michaud in a letter to Joan Mitchell, 11 February 1987. Collection of the Joan Mitchell Foundation.

392   "It's horrible": Liz Lufkin, "Triumph for 'Lady Painter,'" *San Francisco Chronicle,* 26 May 1988.

392   "Joan really challenged": Jill Weinberg Adams, interview with author, 9 July 2002.

394   Displeased to find: Letter from Rebecca Gregson, Registrar, Corcoran Gallery of Art, to Pierre Matisse, Pierre Matisse Gallery, 7 March 1988. Pierpont Morgan Library. Record Group: Pierre Matisse Gallery. Record Series: Artists. Subseries: Joan Mitchell. Box 24, File 4; Jill Weinberg Adams, interview with author, 9 July 2002.

394   "What the hell": Carl Plansky, interview with author, 16 January 2001; John Cheim, interview with author, 10 July 2002.

394   "very messed up": Dorothy Burkhart, "Joan Mitchell—Nature in Abstraction," *San Jose Mercury News,* 12 June 1988.

394   For good measure: Manny Silverman, interview with author, 26 October 2001.

394   "lapsed into": William Wilson, "Abstracting an Abstract Expressionist," *Los Angeles Times,* 19 June 1988.

395   That long-ago lover: Richard Bowman, interview with author, 26 August 2001; Kim Bowman, telephone interview with author, 23 July 2003; Marvin Vickers, telephone interview with author, 23 July 2003.

395   "What kind": Joan Mitchell, quoted by Bill Berkson, interview with author, 10 July 2006.

395   "My! You certainly": Unknown audience member, quoted by Bill Berkson, interview with author, 10 July 2006.

396   "grown-up painting": John Russell, "Art: Internationalism at La Défense," New York Times, 25 April 1986.

396   her question-and-answer session: Joan refused to cash her $200 lecture fee.

396   "most racist city": A stock phrase of Joan's. Los Angeles art dealer Manny Silverman, for one, told me of lunching with Joan in 1989 at Le Hangar, a little restaurant near the Galerie Jean Fournier. When Fournier arrived with a collector couple from Chicago, Joan greeted them with the remark, "Did you know that Chicago is the most racist city on the face of the earth?" Within twenty minutes she had made "lunch with the artist" so unappealing that, at Fournier's suggestion, the trio departed in mid-meal for the gallery.

396   "You think": Philippe Dagen, "La fureur de Joan Mitchell," Le Monde, 2–3 August 1992.

396   preceding the graduation: Jill Weinberg Adams, Ninety (1993): 35.

397   "formidable valor": Raymonde Perthuis, interview with author, 10 January 2002.

397   A visit: Marilyn Stark, interview with author, 21 July 2004.

397   "deaf, as in"; "What happened": The recipients of these two comments still being alive, I do not divulge their identities.

397   "putting in the dagger": Sara Holt, interview with author, 6 January 2002.

397   "sweet instinct": Christopher Campbell, telephone interview with author, 10 February 2007.

397   "like a baby": Christiane Rousseaux, interview with author, 12 January 2002.

398   "feel like": John Cheim, Ninety (1993): 45.

398   "Dear Sara Holt": Note from Joan Mitchell to Sara Holt. Collection of Sara Holt and Jean-Max Albert.

398   her friend: Jeanne Le Bozec, interview with author, 25 March 2003.

399   "a beacon": Rufus Zogbaum, interview with author, 10 January 2003.

399   "What the fuck": Joan Mitchell, quoted by Marc Berlet, telephone interview with author, 5 August 2006.

399   "depressed": Barney Rosset in a telephone conversation with Richard Milazzo. See Milazzo, "Barney and Joan: Barney Rosset's Photographs of Joan Mitchell and Joan Mitchell's Letters to Barney Rosset," Caravaggio on the Beach: Essays on Art in the 1990's (Tangiers: Éditions d'Afrique du Nord, 2001), 124.

400   "But above and beyond": Rosset to Mitchell, 2 August 1989. Collection of the Joan Mitchell Foundation.

400   "nuts": Mitchell to Von Blon, postmarked 17 December 1990. Collection of Joanne Von Blon.

400   "because . . . he was a man": Kate Van Houten, interview with author, 18 January 2002.

400   "Well, I am": Joan Mitchell, quoted by Jean-Max Albert, interview with author, 6 January 2002.

401   "truly sought": Monique Frydman, interview with author, 16 January 2002.

401   "And you": Monique Frydman, *Ninety* (1993): 26.

401   "was very moving": Mitchell to Jaqueline Fried, postmarked 21 December 1983. Collection of Jaqueline Fried.

401   "spin back": Mitchell to Von Blon, postmarked 21 December 1983. Collection of Joanne Von Blon.

401   "She kept insisting": Jane Livingston, *The Paintings of Joan Mitchell* (New York, Berkeley, Los Angeles, and London: Whitney Museum of American Art in association with University of California Press, 2002), 38.

402   "You seem": Yves Michaud, "Entretiens," in Musée des Beaux-Arts de Nantes/ Galerie Nationale du Jeu de Paume, *Joan Mitchell* (Paris: Éditions du Jeu de Paume, 1994), 30–31.

402   "a sort of": Mitchell, interviewed by Michaud, *Joan Mitchell: New Paintings.* Joan's words recall Proust's account, in the final volume of *In Search of Lost Time,* of his narrator's realization that the euphoria of involuntary memory arises from its transport of the self outside time, beyond the reach of death, and to the hidden essence of things and of one's true being. See Marcel Proust, *Time Regained, In Search of Lost Time,* trans. C. K. Scott-Moncrieff and Terence Kilmartin, rev. by D. J. Enright (New York: Modern Library, 1992), 262–65.

402   "the images of his past": Kevin T. Dann, *Bright Colors Falsely Seen: Synaesthesia and the Search for Transcendental Knowledge* (New Haven and London: Yale University Press, 1998), 159.

402   "At some point": Patricia Lynne Duffy, *Blue Cats and Chartreuse Kittens* (New York: Henry Holt, Times Books, 2001), 57. The other internationally known synesthete artist is painter David Hockney, also a sound-color synesthete. Unlike Mitchell, Hockney does not normally use his synesthesia in making art, with the exception of his stage sets for the Metropolitan Opera. According to Richard Cytowic, who tested Hockney, "David really didn't know that there was anything unusual about his synesthesia until he began painting opera sets, that he began painting paintings to be watched while you listen. For example, he did a series of three French operas at the Met in New York, and the critics said, 'Well this is unlike anything he's ever done, and the colours and the shapes are so strange.' And Hockney said, 'Well I listened to the Ravel music and there's a tree in one part of it, and there's music that accompanies the tree,' and he said, 'When I listened to that music, the tree just painted itself you see.' So for him, it's an additional thing that helps to inform his art, but it's not the driving force of it." See Richard E. Cytowic, interview by Robin Hughes, 8 July 1996, transcript, *The Health Report,* Australian Broadcasting Corporation.

403   "Vowels": Arthur Rimbaud, *Complete Works, Selected Works,* trans. Wallace Fowlie (Chicago and London: University of Chicago Press, 1966), 121.

403   "I am always": Jean Fournier, *Ninety* (1993): 65.

403   "magical evening": Sally Apfelbaum, interview with author, 25 July 2001.

404   "Ah, you gotta": Joan Mitchell, quoted by Kate Van Houten, interview with author, 18 January 2002.

404   "that fucking ladder": Joan Mitchell, quoted by Klaus Kertess, *Joan Mitchell* (New York: Harry N. Abrams), 40.

404   "She always": Sally Apfelbaum, interview with author, 25 July 2001.

CHAPTER SIXTEEN: ICI

405 "Whoever you are": Rainer Maria Rilke, "Entrance" in *The Book of Images*, trans. Edward Snow (San Francisco: North Point Press, 1991), 5. At the time of Joan's last trip to New York, her friend Christian Blackwood, the co-producer of *Joan Mitchell: Portrait of an Abstract Painter*, died of cancer. Wanting someone to read for her a poem by Rilke or Hopkins at Blackwood's funeral, Joan asked Nathan Kernan to suggest some possibilities, which he read to her one day in the back room at Miller. Upon hearing Rilke's "Entrance," she responded, "Save that one for me, you can read that for me." He did, at her memorial service at the Whitney Museum the following April. See Nathan Kernan, "The Presence of Absence: The Paintings of Joan Mitchell," in Cheim & Read Gallery, *Joan Mitchell: Selected Paintings 1956–1992* (New York: Cheim & Read, 2002), unpaginated.

405 "motion . . . made still": Mitchell, interviewed by Yves Michaud, "Conversation with Joan Mitchell," in Xavier Fourcade Gallery, *Joan Mitchell: New Paintings* (New York: Xavier Fourcade Gallery, 1986), unpaginated.

405 "visual-kinetic experience": Ora Lerman, "The Elusive Subject: Joan Mitchell's Reflections on van Gogh," *Arts* 65:1 (September 1990): 44.

406 As deliciously sun soaked: Mitchell once told Bill Scott that one of her favorite dreams was of meeting Cézanne in the woods. Bill Scott, interview with author, 31 March 2004.

406 The first Mitchell: Robert Miller, telephone interview with author, 9 August 2003.

406 "Oh, let's give": Marion Cajori, interview with author, 15 July 2002.

406 "classic Parisian light": Marion Cajori, quoted by Carol Strickland, "Old Friend Films a Portrait of an Artist," *New York Times*, 21 June 1992.

406 "rescued": Marion Cajori, interview with author, 15 July 2002.

407 "traipsing around": Cajori, quoted by Strickland.

407 "power-hungry"; "Nazi haircut": John Cheim, interview with author, 10 July 2002.

407 "This motherfucker": Marc Berlet, telephone interview with the author, 5 August 2006.

407 "really lovely": Michael Brenson, telephone interview with author, 2 February 2007.

408 "Michael Brenson": Ibid.

408 "The words": Michael Brenson, "A Vintage Encounter," letter to the editor, *New York Times*, 30 June 2002.

408 "woman artist"; "Maybe I've gone": Mitchell, quoted by Klaus Kertess, "Her Passion," *New York Times*, 16 June 2002.

408 "I only attacked": Mitchell, quoted by Brenson, telephone interview with author, 2 February 2007.

408 "started pushing": Jill Weinberg Adams, interview with author, 26 June 2002.

408 "This joint": Mitchell to Von Blon, postmarked 17 December 1990. Collection of Joanne Von Blon.

409 "to live"; "I take the train": Mitchell, interviewed by Yves Michaud, "Entretiens," in Musée des Beaux-Arts de Nantes/Galerie Nationale du Jeu de Paume, *Joan Mitchell* (Paris: Éditions du Jeu de Paume, 1994), 30.

409   "means of feeling": Mitchell, interviewed by Michaud, *Joan Mitchell: New Paintings.*

409   "as if": Jacqueline Hyde, interview with author, 19 January 2002.

410   "Keep it going": Samuel Beckett, *Krapp's Last Tape, and Embers* (London: Faber and Faber, 1959), 33.

410   When it came: Jean Fournier, interview with author, 27 March 2003.

411   "but don't come"; "And Joan developed": Christopher Campbell, telephone interview with author, 10 February 2007.

412   "But I know you": Jean Mouillère, personal communication to author, 18 May 2005.

412   "What!": Mitchell, quoted by Jean Mouillère, personal communication to author, 18 May 2005.

413   *"Allo,* Coco": Ibid.

413   "little acts": Franck Bordas, interview with author, 15 January 2002. My thanks to Jack Scharr for the information he provided about the Carnegie Hall project.

414   "as a sort": Ibid.

414   "Who's that bum?": Mitchell, quoted by Bordas, ibid.

414   "a sort of peacefulness": Bordas, interview with author, 15 January 2002.

415   "Not bad": Mitchell, quoted by Bordas, ibid.

415   "a kind of miracle": Bordas, interview with author, 15 January 2002.

415   "Ah!": Mitchell, quoted by Bordas, ibid.

416   "a genius": Joan Mitchell, quoted by David Amram, interview with author, 9 January 2008.

416   "make yellow heavy": Brice Marden, interviewed in Marion Cajori, director, *Joan Mitchell: A Portrait of an Abstract Painter* (New York: Art Kaleidoscope Foundation and Christian Blackwood Productions, 1992). Film.

416   "just precious": Ornette Coleman, telephone interview with author, 19 January 2007.

416   "yakety-yakety-yak": Ken Tyler, interview with author, 7 January 2003.

416   Among Joan's visitors: Nathan Kernan, interview with author, 13 January 2003.

417   "And when I": James Schuyler, "Daylight," in *Hymn to Life: Poems by James Schuyler* (New York: Random House, 1974), 71.

417   "The sky": Paul Verlaine, "Le ciel est, par-dessus le toit . . . ," Paul Verlaine, *Selected Poems,* trans. C. F. MacIntyre (Berkeley and London: University of California Press, 1948), 163.

417   "Will you *stop*": Zuka Mitelberg, interview with author, 5 January 2002.

417   "You know": Mitchell, quoted by Mitelberg, ibid.

418   "truly unhappy": Mitelberg, interview with author, 5 January 2002.

418   "If you think": Mitelberg to Mitchell, 10 February 1991. Collection of the Joan Mitchell Foundation.

418   "as if": Joan Mitchell, quoted in Philippe Dagen, "La fureur de Joan Mitchell," *Le Monde,* 2–3 August 1992.

418   "In a sense": Christopher Campbell, telephone interview with author, 10 February 2007.

418   "It's a horrible": Carl Plansky, interview with author, 16 January 2001.

419   "some Ivy League type": Mitchell, quoted in Solomon, "Light," *New York Times Magazine,* 24 November 1991: 47.

419   "My painting": Ibid.

419   "SIT DOWN!": Mitchell, quoted by John Cheim, interview with author, 10 July 2002.

420   "Phyllis is still": Joan Mitchell, quoted by Cathy Hill in a letter to Joan Mitchell, 6 December 1980. Collection of the Joan Mitchell Foundation. Joan did another painting entitled *Phyllis.*

420   "Blankness to me": Mitchell, interviewed by Cora Cohen and Betsy Sussler, *Bomb* 17 (fall 1986): 20.

420   "The word blank": Ibid., 22.

420   "morbidity": Mitchell to Von Blon, postmarked 17 December 1990. Collection of Joanne Von Blon.

420   "Let everything happen": "Gott spricht zu jedem nur, eh er ihn macht," Rainer Maria Rilke, *Rilke's Book of Hours: Love Poems to God,* trans. Anita Barrows and Joanna Macy (New York: Riverhead Books, 1996), 88.

420   "I feel time": Mitchell, quoted in Solomon, 46.

421   *"la France"*: Mitchell, quoted by Christopher Campbell, telephone interview with author, 10 February 2007.

421   "secret studio": Mitchell, quoted in Kertess, 9.

421   Working on three: Christopher Campbell, telephone interview with author, 10 February 2007.

422   "Get your ass": Mitchell, quoted in Kertess, 9.

422   "You know": Sally Turton, telephone interview with author, 28 December 2001.

422   Joan had recently: She titled another painting *Gentian Violet* in 1961 at the time her father was dying.

422   Sometimes she would: Guy Bloch-Champfort, telephone interview with author, 26 March 2009.

423   "God, Harms": Mitchell, quoted by Robert Harms, interview with author, 18 July 2002.

423   "Don't worry": Mitchell, quoted in Kernan, "The Presence," *Joan Mitchell,* unpaginated.

423   "illuminating": Brochure for *Poems,* Tyler Graphics Ltd.

423   "It's all over": Mitchell, quoted by Gisèle Barreau, interview with author, 29 March 2003.

424   "Jean, I'm in": Mitchell, quoted by Jean Fournier, interview with author, 27 March 2003.

424   "Matisse!": Mitchell, quoted by Ken Tyler, interview with author, 7 January 2003.

424   "You know": Mitchell, quoted by John Cheim, interview with author, 10 July 2002.

424   *"He* knew how": Joan Mitchell, quoted by Tyler, interview with author, 7 January 2003.

424   "really cooking": Tyler, interview with author, 7 January 2003.

424   "Let's cut": Mitchell, quoted by Tyler, ibid.

426   "a wreck": Tyler, interview with author, 7 January 2003.

426   "my gardener": Mitchell, quoted by Gisèle Barreau, interview with author, 29 March 2003.

426   "Neither man": Mitchell, quoted by Monique Frydman, interview with author, 16 January 2002.

426   "like a queen": Zuka Mitelberg, interview with author, 5 January 2002.

427   "to loosen up": Jean Fournier, interview with author, 27 March 2003.

427   "the sense and worth": Donald Posner, *Antoine Watteau* (Ithaca, NY: Cornell University Press, 1984), 277.

427   "memorable and moving": Daniel Abadie and Henry-Clausseau, "Preface," in Musée des Beaux-Arts de Nantes/Galerie Nationale du Jeu de Paume, *Joan Mitchell* (Paris: Éditions du Jeu de Paume, 1994), 8.

428   "Jean, I would": Mitchell, quoted by Jean Fournier, interview with author, 27 March 2003.

428   "With Joan Mitchell": Jack Lang, quoted in "Abstract Painter Joan Mitchell Dies at 66," *Washington Post,* 1 November, 1992, B14.

428   "I—'Joan Just *Girl*' ": Mitchell to Von Blon, postmarked 17 December 1990.

429   Her hospitalization: Guy Bloch-Champfort, telephone interview with author, 26 March 2009.

429   Nonetheless, her dual 1994 exhibitions: Scott, "In the Eye of the Tiger," *Art in America* 83:3 (March 1995): 71.

429   "*My God!*": Mitchell, quoted by Jean Mouillère, personal communication to author, 18 May 2005.

430   "A Joan Mitchell canvas": Pierre Schneider, handwritten essay for Joan Mitchell exhibition at Jacques Dubourg and Galerie Lawrence, 8–26 May 1962.

430   "I become": Mitchell, quoted in Bernstock, 69.

Index

"Before Summer Rain," 308–9
"Bowl of Roses," 290
"Entrance," 405, 484*n*
The Notebooks of Malte Laurids Brigge, 108, 184–5, 219
Rimbaud, Arthur: "Vowels," 403
Riopelle, Françoise, 227, 228, 240, 259, 264, 265
Riopelle, Jean-Paul, 231, 232, 233, *266*, 271–80, *274*, *296*, 307, 334, 335, 356, 357, 384
    arrest of, 258
    background of, 227
    Canadian home and sojourns of, 337–8, 340–1
    daily routine of, 277–9, 282
    divorce of, 264, 271–2, 275
    gallery representation of, 227–8, 309–11
    infidelities of, 274–5, 276–7, 279–80, 306, 312, 318, 323, 339, 340, 349, 351–4
    Jeffcoat's relationship with, 349, 351–4, 357, 373, 374
    Joan's encounters with, after breakup, 373–4
    Joan's infidelities and, 280
    Joan's pregnancies and, 240, 242, 272
    Joan's Quebec rendezvous with (1956), 242
    Joan's relationship with, 226–30, 237, 254, 258, 259, 264, 274–5, 279–80, 283, 292–3, 305–6, 314, 318–20, 327, 331, 336, 337, 339–40, 346–7, 349, 351–4, 356, 358, 369, 373–4
    knee injury of, 348–9, 351, 373
    marriage promise broken by, 272–3
    as painter, 220, 227–8, 239–40, 254, 258–9, 291, 292, 309–11, 340–1, 400, 476*n*
    pet name of, for Joan, 271, 318, 358
    sailing and yachting of, 275–7, *287*, 287–8, 290–1, 303, 318
    social circle of, 269–70, 358
    sporting and athletic pursuits of, 288, 318, 337
    summering in south of France, *287*, 287–8, 290–1, 295–7, *297*, 306, 311
    summering on Long Island, 282, 283
Riopelle, Sylvie, 228, 240, 259, 264, 272, 275, 276, 282, 287, 291, 295, 301, 302, 334, 358
Riopelle, Yseult, 228, 240, 259, 264, 272, 275, 276, 282, 287, 291, 295, 301, 306, 308, 313, 358
    children born to, 321
Ripley, Harry Dwight Dillon, 168
Ritman, Louis, 109, 120, 128
Rive Droite, Galerie (Paris), 220
Rivera, Diego, 116, 117
Rivers, Larry, 168, 183, 198, 199, 200, 206, 209–10, 234, 235, 261, 283, 307, 413
Rocard, Michel, 429
Rockefeller, Nelson, 223–4, 228
Rockland State Hospital, 162, 163, 178, 179, 260
Rodin Museum (Paris), 302
Romantic poetry, 101
Roosevelt, Franklin D., 85
Root, John Wellborn, 28
Ropp, Hubert C., 72, 125–6
Ropp School (Lake Forest, Ill.), 72, 441–2*n*
Rose, Barbara, 169, 330, 364
Rose Cottage (Springs, N.Y.), 198–9, 206
Rosenberg, Harold, 193, 196, 197–8, 205, 206–7, 221, 262, 331, 352, 376
Rosenberg, May Tabak, 196, 201
Ross, Bob, 416
Ross, David, 419
Rosset, Barnet, Jr. ("Barney," husband), 90–1, 119–20, 122–5, *126*, 127–9, 171, 179, 185, 187–8, 210, 230, 233, 265, 282, 283, 288, *289*, 360, 362, 399–400

PERMISSIONS ACKNOWLEDGMENTS

Grateful acknowledgment is made to the following for permission to reprint archived or previously published material.

Alfred A. Knopf: "Domination of Black" from *The Collected Poems of Wallace Stevens* by Wallace Stevens, copyright 1923 and renewed 1951 by Wallace Stevens. Reprinted by permission of Alfred A. Knopf, a division of Random House, Inc.

City Lights Books: Excerpt from "The Day Lady Died" by Frank O'Hara, copyright © 1964 by Frank O'Hara. Reprinted by permission of City Lights Books.

Maureen-Granville-Smith: Quotations of Frank O'Hara, copyright © 2011 by Maureen Granville-Smith. Reprinted by permission of Maureen Granville-Smith.

Grove/Atlantic, Inc.: "To the Harbormaster" from *Meditations in an Emergency* by Frank O'Hara, copyright © 1957 by Frank O'Hara. Reprinted by permission of Grove/Atlantic, Inc.

Joan Mitchell Foundation: "Autumn" and excerpt from "The Inn" by Joan Mitchell, copyright © Estate of Joan Mitchell.

Sally Perry: Excerpt from "Bridges," "A Cloak for Joan," "Bon Voyage," and "Joan," all by Marion Strobel, used by permission of Sally Perry.

Princeton University Press: "To ***," from *Poems of Rene Char* by Rene Char, copyright © 1976 Princeton University Press, 2004 renewed PUP. Reprinted by permission of Princeton University Press.

Random House, Inc.: "Before Summer Rain" from *The Selected Poetry of Rainer Maria Rilke,* translated by Stephen Mitchell, copyright © 1982 by Stephen Mitchell. Reprinted by permission of Random House, Inc., and Stephen Mitchell.

A NOTE ON THE TYPE

This book was set in Garamond, a typeface originally designed by the Parisian type cutter Claude Garamond (ca. 1480–1561). This version of Garamond was modeled on a 1592 specimen sheet from the Egenolff-Berner foundry, which was produced from types thought to have been brought to Frankfurt by Jacques Sabon (d. 1580).

Composed by North Market Street Graphics, Lancaster, Pennsylvania

Printed and bound by Berryville Graphics, Berryville, Virginia

Designed by Maggie Hinders